STREET ATLAS

Cheshire

Ches[ter, Macc]lesfield, North[wich, Wid]nes, Warrington

First published in 1995 by

Philip's, a division of
Octopus Publishing Group Ltd
2-4 Heron Quays, London E14 4JP
An Hachette Livre UK Company

Fourth colour edition 2007
First impression 2007
CHEDA

ISBN-10   0-540-09164-2 (pocket)
ISBN-13   978-0-540-09164-5 (pocket)

© Philip's 2007

OS Ordnance Survey®

This product includes mapping data licensed from
Ordnance Survey® with the permission of the
Controller of Her Majesty's Stationery Office.
© Crown copyright 2007. All rights reserved.
Licence number 100011710.

Data for the speed cameras provided by
PocketGPSWorld.com Ltd.

Ordnance Survey and the OS Symbol are
registered trademarks of Ordnance Survey, the
national mapping agency of Great Britain.

Printed by Toppan, China

Contents

II **List of mobile speed cameras**

III **Key to map symbols**

IV **Key to map pages**

VI **Route planning**

VIII **Administrative and Postcode boundaries**

1 **Street maps** at 2⅔ inches to 1 mile

237 **Street map of Chester city centre**
at 5⅓ inches to 1 mile

238 **Index** of towns, villages, streets, hospitals, industrial
estates, railway stations, schools, shopping centres,
universities and places of interest

Digital Data

The exceptionally high-quality mapping found in this atlas is available as digital data in TIFF
format, which is easily convertible to other bitmapped (raster) image formats.

The index is also available in digital form as a standard database table. It contains all the details
found in the printed index together with the National Grid reference for the map square in which
each entry is named.

For further information and to discuss your requirements, please contact
james.mann@philips-maps.co.uk

Mobile speed cameras

The vast majority of speed cameras used on Britain's roads are operated by safety camera partnerships. These comprise local authorities, the police, Her Majesty's Court Service (HMCS) and the Highways Agency.

This table lists the sites where each safety camera partnership may enforce speed limits through the use of mobile cameras or detectors. These are usually set up on the roadside or a bridge spanning the road and operated by a police or civilian enforcement officer. The speed limit at each site (if available) is shown in red type, followed by the approximate location in black type.

Mike Harrington / Alamy

M6
70 Bradwell, northbound
70 Northwich, northbound
50 Woolston near Warrington, northbound

M62
70 Croft, eastbound and westbound

A50
30 Grappenhall, Knutsford Rd
30 Knutsford, Manchester/Toft Rd
30 Warrington, Long Lane

A54
60&70 Ashton, Kelsall Rd

A56
40 Lymm, Camsley Lane

A57
40 Paddington, New Manchester Rd

A523
30 Poynton, London Rd

A532
30 Crewe, West St

A533
40 Middlewich, Booth Lane

A537
50 Macclesfield, Buxton Rd nr Wildboarclough

A5019
30 Crewe, Mill St

A5032
30 Whitby, Chester Rd

A5034
60 Mere, Mereside Rd

A5104
30 Chester, Hough Green

B5071
30 Crewe, Gresty Rd

B5078
30 Alsager, Sandbach Rd North

B5082
30 Northwich, Middlewich Rd

B5132
30 Ellesmere Port, Overpool Rd

B5153
30 Mill Lane/Hollow Lane (speed indicator sign)

B5463
30 Little Sutton, Station Rd

B5470
30 Macclesfield, Rainow Rd

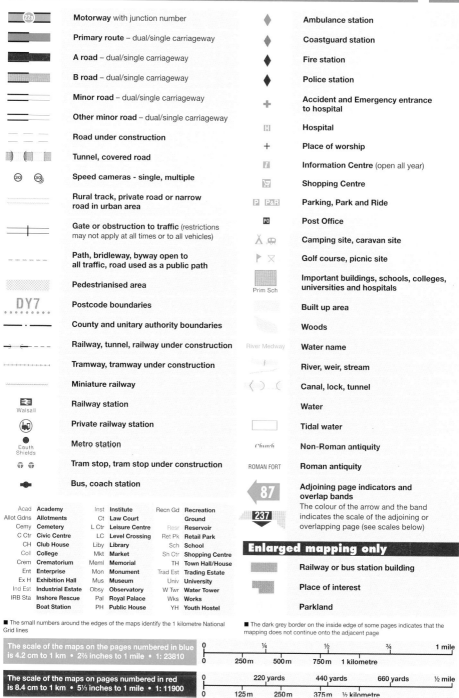

	Motorway with junction number
	Primary route – dual/single carriageway
	A road – dual/single carriageway
	B road – dual/single carriageway
	Minor road – dual/single carriageway
	Other minor road – dual/single carriageway
	Road under construction
	Tunnel, covered road
	Speed cameras - single, multiple
	Rural track, private road or narrow road in urban area
	Gate or obstruction to traffic (restrictions may not apply at all times or to all vehicles)
	Path, bridleway, byway open to all traffic, road used as a public path
	Pedestrianised area
DY7	**Postcode boundaries**
	County and unitary authority boundaries
	Railway, tunnel, railway under construction
	Tramway, tramway under construction
	Miniature railway
Walsall	**Railway station**
	Private railway station
South Shields	**Metro station**
	Tram stop, tram stop under construction
	Bus, coach station

◆	**Ambulance station**
◆	**Coastguard station**
◆	**Fire station**
◆	**Police station**
✚	**Accident and Emergency entrance to hospital**
H	**Hospital**
+	**Place of worship**
ℹ	**Information Centre** (open all year)
	Shopping Centre
P P&R	**Parking, Park and Ride**
PO	**Post Office**
⋏ ⌖	**Camping site, caravan site**
▶ ✕	**Golf course, picnic site**
Prim Sch	**Important buildings, schools, colleges, universities and hospitals**
	Built up area
	Woods
River Medway	**Water name**
	River, weir, stream
⟨ ⟩ ⟨	**Canal, lock, tunnel**
	Water
	Tidal water
Church	**Non-Roman antiquity**
ROMAN FORT	**Roman antiquity**
87	**Adjoining page indicators and overlap bands**
237	The colour of the arrow and the band indicates the scale of the adjoining or overlapping page (see scales below)

Enlarged mapping only

	Railway or bus station building
	Place of interest
	Parkland

Abbr	Full	Abbr	Full	Abbr	Full
Acad	**Academy**	Inst	**Institute**	Recn Gd	**Recreation**
Allot Gdns	**Allotments**	Ct	**Law Court**		**Ground**
Cemy	**Cemetery**	L Ctr	**Leisure Centre**	Resr	**Reservoir**
C Ctr	**Civic Centre**	LC	**Level Crossing**	Ret Pk	**Retail Park**
CH	**Club House**	Liby	**Library**	Sch	**School**
Coll	**College**	Mkt	**Market**	Sh Ctr	**Shopping Centre**
Crem	**Crematorium**	Meml	**Memorial**	TH	**Town Hall/House**
Ent	**Enterprise**	Mon	**Monument**	Trad Est	**Trading Estate**
Ex H	**Exhibition Hall**	Mus	**Museum**	Univ	**University**
Ind Est	**Industrial Estate**	Obsy	**Observatory**	W Twr	**Water Tower**
IRB Sta	**Inshore Rescue**	Pal	**Royal Palace**	Wks	**Works**
	Boat Station	PH	**Public House**	YH	**Youth Hostel**

■ The small numbers around the edges of the maps identify the 1 kilometre National Grid lines

■ The dark grey border on the inside edge of some pages indicates that the mapping does not continue onto the adjacent page

The scale of the maps on the pages numbered in blue is 4.2 cm to 1 km • 2⅔ inches to 1 mile • 1: 23810

0	¼	½	¾	1 mile
0	250 m	500 m	750 m	1 kilometre

The scale of the maps on pages numbered in red is 8.4 cm to 1 km • 5⅓ inches to 1 mile • 1: 11900

0	220 yards	440 yards	660 yards	½ mile
0	125 m	250 m	375 m	½ kilometre

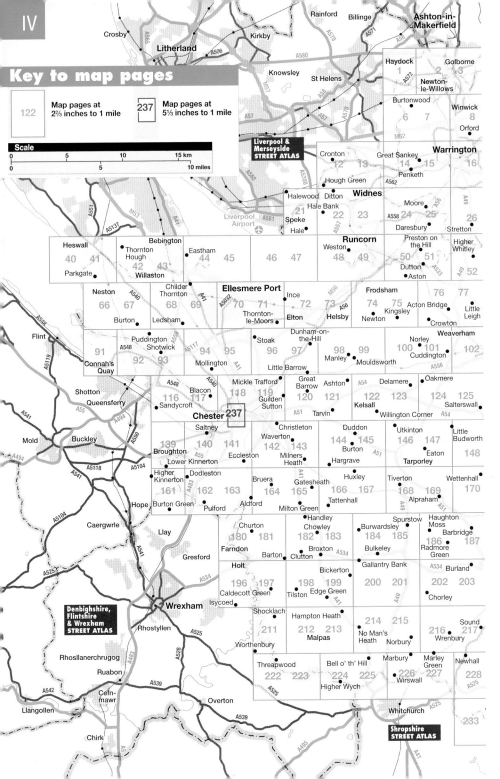

IV

Key to map pages

| 122 | Map pages at 2⅔ inches to 1 mile | 237 | Map pages at 5⅓ inches to 1 mile |

Scale

| 0 | 5 | 10 | 15 km |
| 0 | 5 | | 10 miles |

Crosby
Litherland
Rainford
Billinge
Ashton-in-Makerfield
Kirkby
Knowsley
St Helens
Haydock **1**
Golborne **3**
2
Newton-le-Willows
Burtonwood
6 **7** Winwick **8**
Orford
Cronton **12** **13** Great Sankey **14** **15** Warrington **16**
Penketh
Hough Green
A562
Halewood Ditton **Widnes**
Hale Bank **21** **22** **23** Moore **24** **25** **26**
Speke
Hale
Daresbury Stretton

Liverpool Airport
Heswall **40** **41** Thornton Hough **42** **43** Eastham **44** **45** **46** **47** Weston **48** **49** Runcorn **50** Preston on the Hill **51** Higher Whitley **52**
Parkgate
Willaston
Dutton
Aston

Neston **66** **67** Childer Thornton **68** **69** **70** **71** Ince **72** **73** Frodsham **74** **75** Acton Bridge **76** **77**
Burton Ledsham Thornton-le-Moors Elton Helsby Newton Kingsley Crowton Little Leigh

Flint **91** Puddington Shotwick **92** **93** **94** **95** Stoak **96** Dunham-on-the-Hill **97** **98** **99** **100** Norley **101** **102** Weaverham
Connah's Quay Mollington Little Barrow Manley Mouldsworth Cuddington

Shotton Queensferry **116** **117** Blacon **118** **119** Mickle Trafford Great Barrow **120** Ashton **121** **122** Delamere **123** **124** **125**
Sandycroft Guilden Sutton Kelsall Salterswall
Mold Buckley **Chester** **237** Tarvin Willington Corner

Saltney Christleton Duddon Utkinton Little Budworth
Broughton **139** **140** **141** Waverton **142** **143** **144** **145** **146** **147** **148**
Lower Kinnerton Eccleston Milners Heath Burton Eaton
Dodleston Hargrave Tarporley

Higher Kinnerton **161** **162** **163** Bruera **164** Gatesheath **165** Huxley **166** **167** Tiverton **168** **169** Wettenhall **170**
Hope Burton Green Pulford Aldford Milton Green Tattenhall Alpraham

Caergwrle Handley Spurstow Haughton Moss
Llay Churton **180** **181** Chowley **182** **183** Burwardsley **184** **185** **186** Barbridge **187**
Gresford Farndon Barton Broxton **534** Bulkeley Radmore Green

Holt Bickerton Gallantry Bank Burland
Wrexham **196** **197** **198** **199** **200** **201** **202** **203**
Isycoed Caldecott Green Tilston Edge Green Chorley
Rhostyllen Shocklach Hampton Heath **214** **215** Sound
211 **212** **213** No Man's Heath **216** **217**
Rhoslanerchrugog Worthenbury **Malpas** Norbury Wrenbury

Ruabon Threapwood **222** **223** Bell o' th' Hill **224** **225** Marbury Marley Green Newhall
Cefn-mawr Higher Wych Wirswall **226** **227** **228**
Llangollen Overton Whitchurch
Chirk **233**

Denbighshire, Flintshire & Wrexham STREET ATLAS

Liverpool & Merseyside STREET ATLAS

Shropshire STREET ATLAS

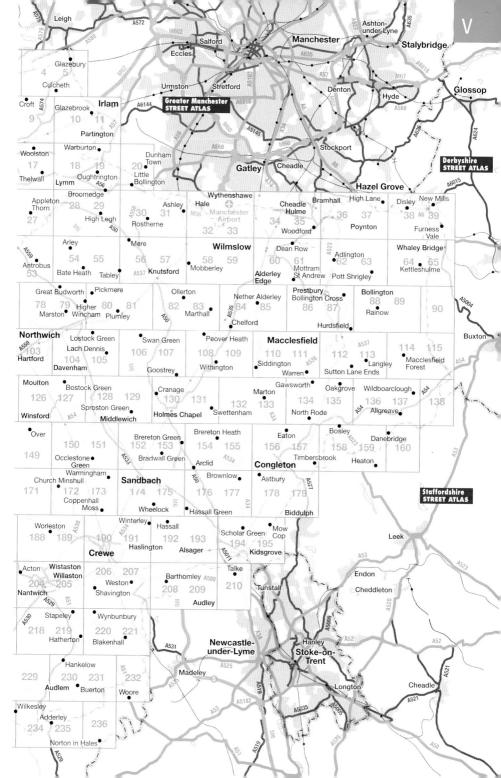

Route Planning

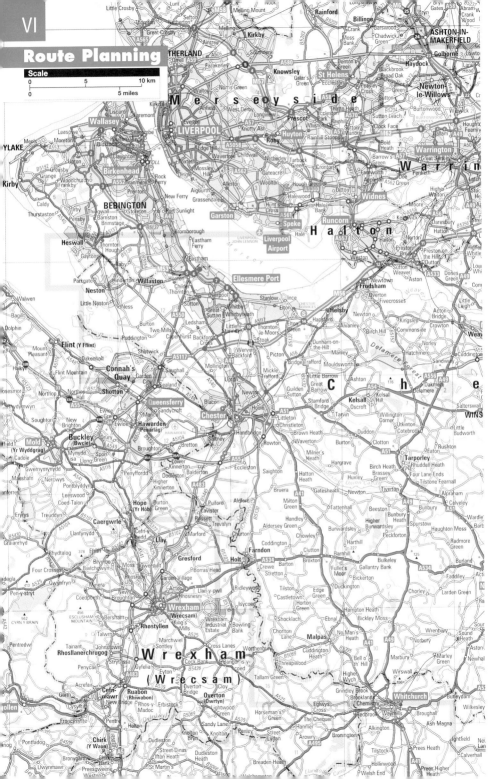

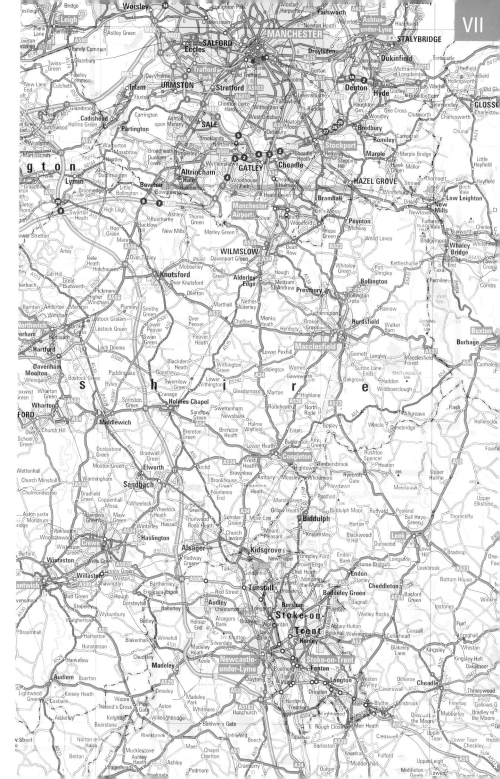

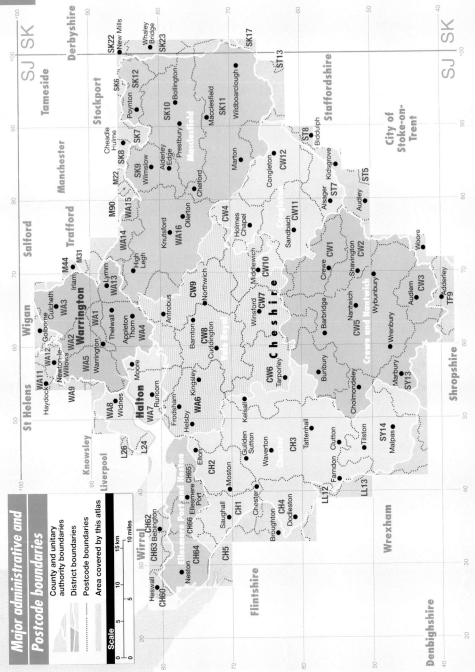

Major administrative and Postcode boundaries

County and unitary authority boundaries
District boundaries
Postcode boundaries
Area covered by this atlas

Scale
0   5   10   15 km
0   5   10 miles

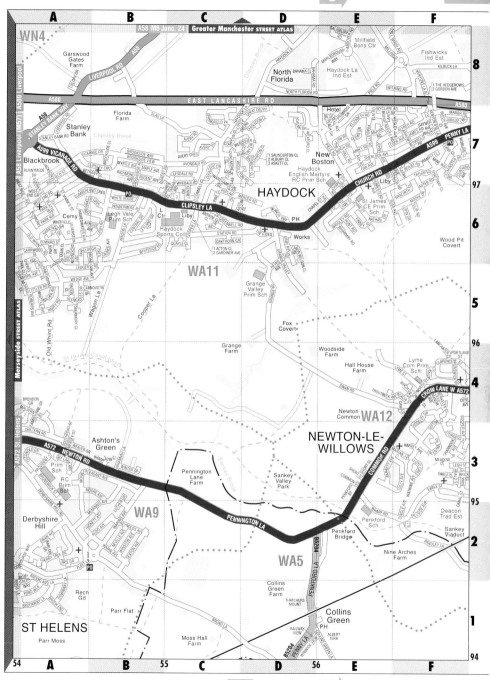

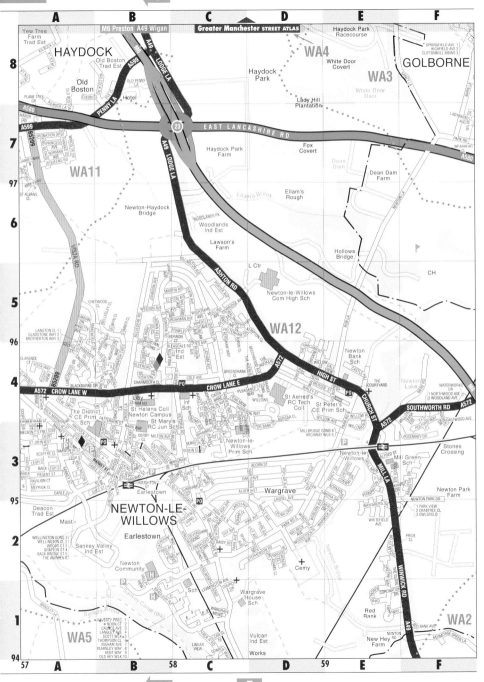

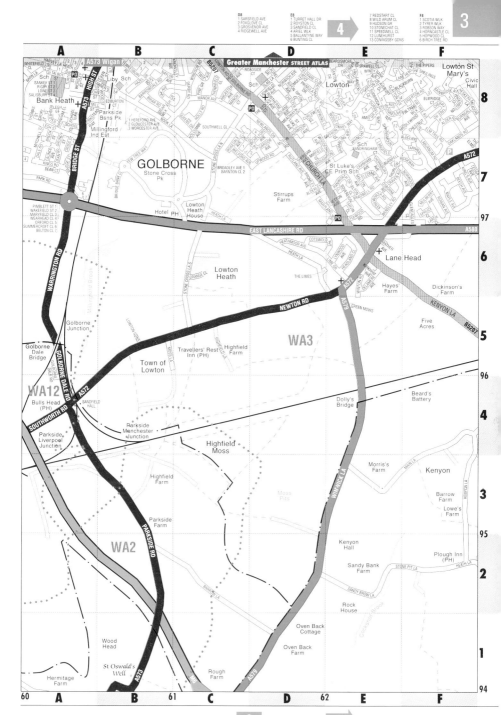

D8
1 SARSFIELD AVE
2 FOXGLOVE CL
3 GROSVENOR AVE
4 RIDGEWELL AVE

E8
1 TURRET HALL DR
2 ROYSTON CL
3 SANDFIELD CL
4 ARIEL WLK
5 BALLANTYNE WAY
6 BUNTING CL

7 REDSTART CL
8 WILD ARUM CL
9 HUDSON GR
10 STONECHAT CL
11 SPEEDWELL CL
12 LUNEHURST
13 CONINGSBY GDNS

F8
1 SCOTIA WLK
2 TYRER WLK
3 ROBSON WAY
4 HORNCASTLE CL
5 HOPWOOD CL
6 BIRCH TREE RD

GOLBORNE

WA3

WA12

WA2

Lowton St Mary's Civic Hall

Lowton

Bank Heath

EAST LANCASHIRE RD

WARRINGTON RD

GOLBORNE DALE RD

PARKSIDE RD

SOUTHWORTH RD

NEWTON RD

WINWICK LA

KENYON LA

Lane Head

Lowton Heath

Town of Lowton

Highfield Moss

Kenyon

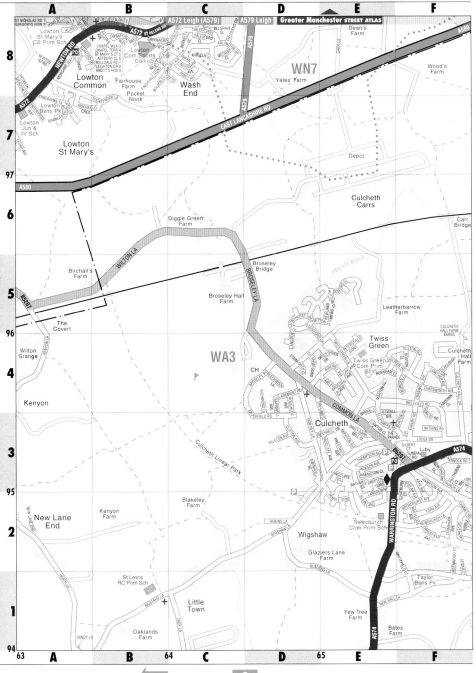

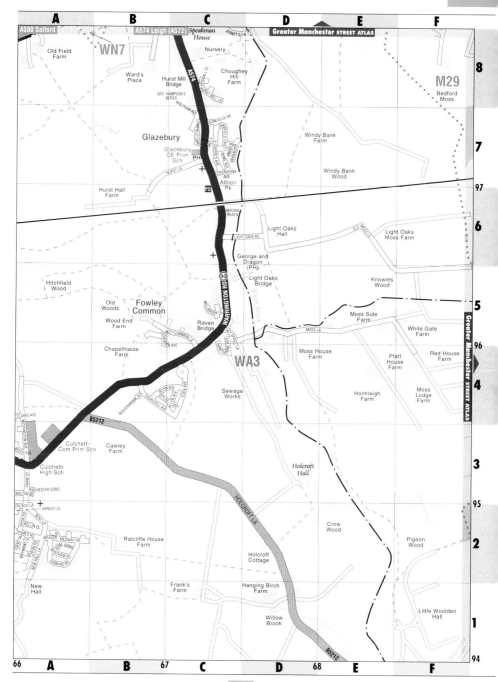

A580 Salford

A574 Leigh (A572)

Speakman House

JENNET'S LA

Greater Manchester STREET ATLAS

WN7

Old Field Farm

Nursery

Ward's Place

Hurst Mill Bridge

GEO. HAMPSON'S BLDGS

SMALL CL.

HURST MILL LA

A574

WALTHAM AVE

Choughey Hill Farm

8

M29

Bedford Moss

Glazebury

ACREVILLE GR

SHIELDS RD

LOWFIELD AV.

DUKE ST

QUEEN'S AVE.

INCARNATION AVE

Windy Bank Farm

7

Glazebury CE Prim Sch

PH

Albion Pk

Windy Bank Wood

Hurst Hall Farm

HURST LA

PO

97

HERONS REACH

Light Oaks Hall

OLD MOSS LA

Light Oaks Moss Farm

6

Hitchfield Wood

LIGHT OAKS RD

George and Dragon (PH)

Light Oaks Bridge

Knowles Wood

Old Woods

Fowley Common

WARRINGTON RD

30

Clarke Brook

Moss Side Farm

White Gate Farm

5

Wood End Farm

Raven Bridge

MILLBROOK LA

OWLEY COMMON LA

GLEN AVE

HEY SHOOT LA

MOSS LA

WA3

LANE

Moss House Farm

Platt House Farm

Red House Farm

96

Chapelhouse Farm

BEAVERBROOK AVE

BRUNT AVE

CHURCHILL AVE

TERN AVE

Sewage Works

Holmleigh Farm

Moss Lodge Farm

4

CLARKE AVE

WITHINGTON AVE

BEECH AVE

B5212

Culcheth Com Prim Sch

Cawley Farm

Holcroft Hall

3

Culcheth High Sch

RIBCHESTER GDNS

WALTON RD

CHURCH LA

SAWLEY CL.

THAMES RD

ROLLIN CL

WEAVER

MEDWAY RD

NEAL GDNS

BENTHAM RD

HOWARD

Ratcliffe House Farm

HOLCROFT LA

Crow Wood

95

Pigeon Wood

2

New Hall

Frank's Farm

Holcroft Cottage

Hanging Birch Farm

Little Woolden Hall

1

Willow Brook

B5212

66

67

68

94

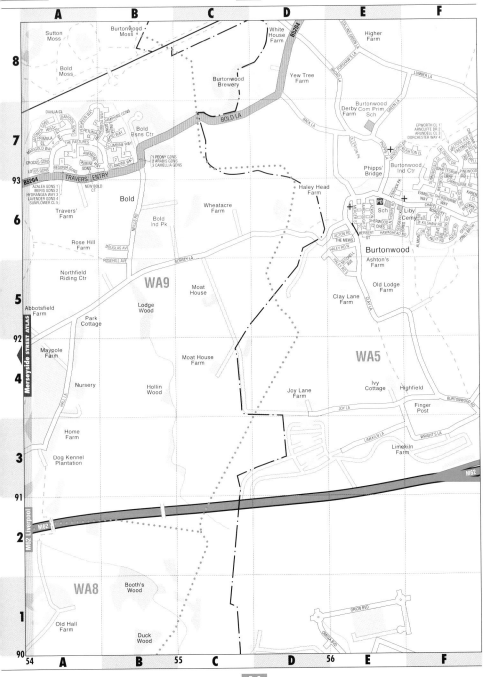

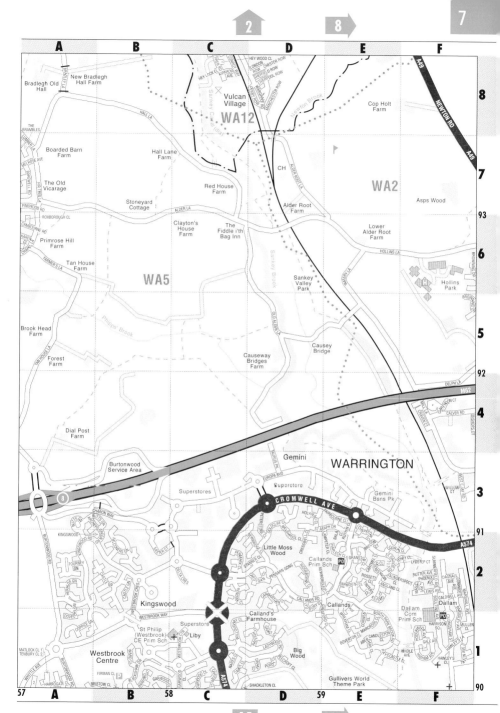

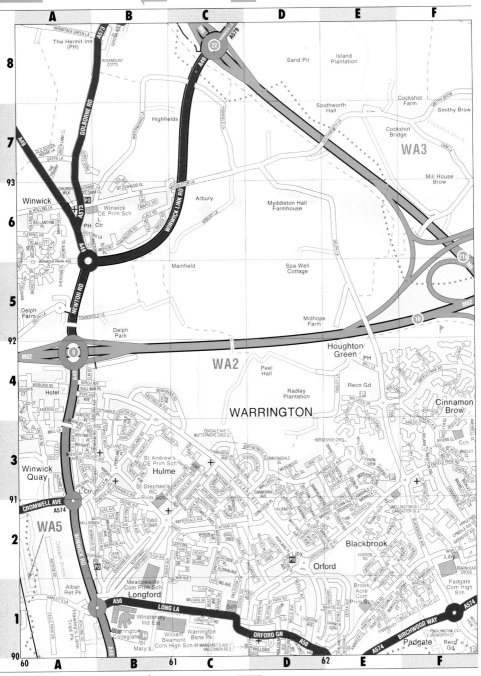

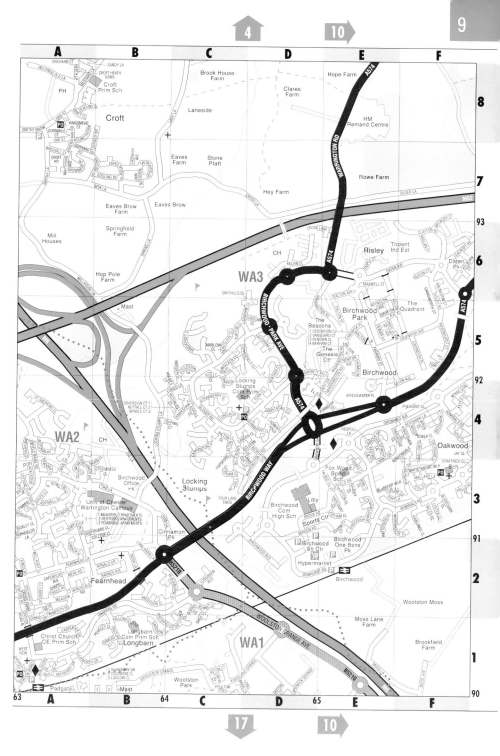

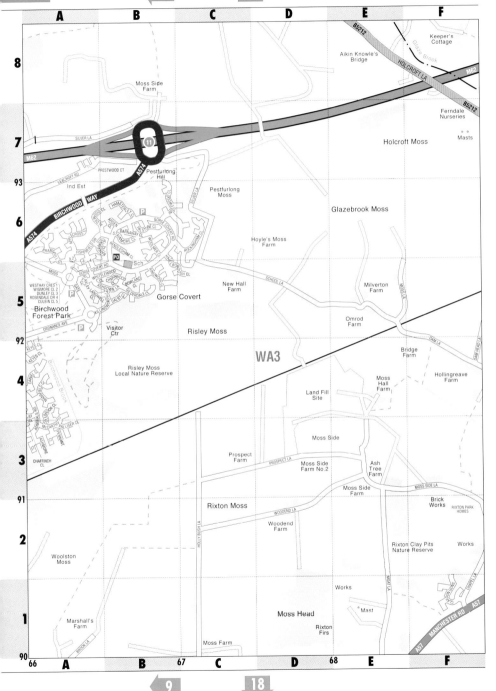

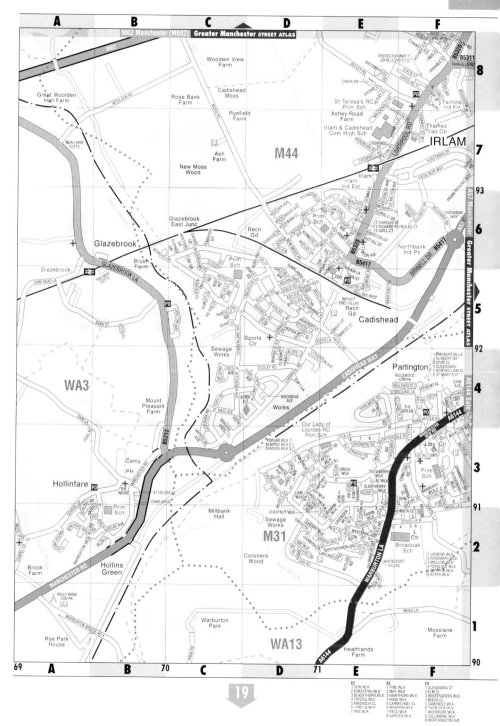

M62 Manchester (M602) **Greater Manchester STREET ATLAS**

Woolden View Farm

Great Woolden Hall Farm

Rose Bank Farm

Cadishead Moss

Ryefield Farm

NEW FARM COTTS

Ash Farm

New Moss Wood

M44

PROTECTOR WAY 1
JOHN LLOYD CT 2

St Teresa's RC Prim Sch
Astley Road Farm
Irlam & Cadishead Com High Sch

Fairhills Ind Est

IRLAM

Thames Trad Ctr

Glazebrook East Junc

Glazebrook

Brush Farm

GLAZEBROOK LA

Glazebrook

DAM HEAD LA

RAILWAY COTTS

BANK ST

VETCH CL

Irlam Ind Est

Prim Sch

Recn Gd

Northbank Ind Pk

Cadishead

Recn Gd

Wright Tree Villas

Prim Sch

Sports Ctr

WA3

Sewage Works

Mount Pleasant Farm

Lincoln

Dudley Rd

Woodbine Ave

Works

CADISHEAD WAY

Partington

Inglewood CVN PK

THE GREEN

Liby Ctr

Our Lady of Lourdes RC Prim Sch

POPLAR WLK 1
ALMOND WLK 2
DAMSON WLK 3

Prim Sch

THE WILLOWS

Prim Sch

Cemy

PH

Hollinfare

THE WEINT

St Helens Rd

DAWLISH CL

Prim Sch

Millbank Hall

Sewage Works

M31

Chestnut Wlk

Broadoak Sch

Ctr

WHITECROFT VILLAS

JASMINE WLK 1
ROSEMARY WLK 2
MALLOW WLK 3
FOXGLOVE WLK 4
SAFFRON WLK 5
ASTER WLK 6

Brook Farm

MANCHESTER RD

Hollins Green

HOLLY BANK CVN PK

WARBURTON BRIDGE RD

Rye Park House

Warburton Park

Coroners Wood

WA13

Heathlands Farm

Mosslane Farm

MOSS LA

E2	E3	F3
1 YEW WLK	1 PINE WLK	1 ALEXANDRA CT
2 FORSYTHIA WLK	2 MAY WLK	2 ELM CL
3 BLACKTHORN WLK	3 HAWTHORN WLK	3 WINTERGREEN WLK
4 THISTLE WLK	4 ROSE WLK	4 BEECH CL
5 MAGNOLIA CL	5 CARMICHAEL CL	5 CAMOMILE WLK
6 LOBELIA WLK	6 MEADOW WLK	6 CHERVIL WLK
7 IRIS WLK	7 FIELD WLK	7 WOODRUFF WLK
	8 GARDEN WLK	8 COLUMBINE WLK
		9 WORTHINGTON AVE

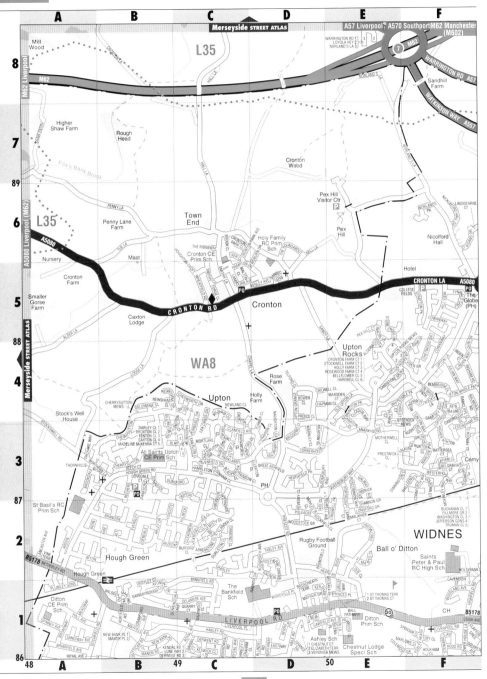

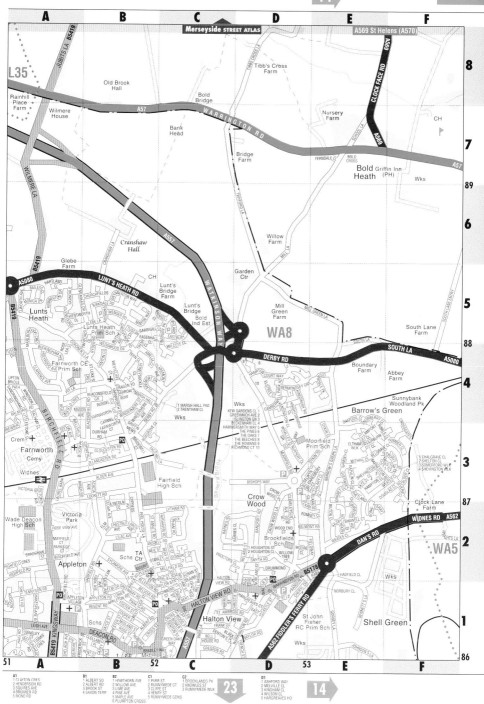

Merseyside STREET ATLAS

A1
1 CLAYTON CRES
2 HENDERSON RD
3 SQUIRES AVE
4 BRUNNER RD
5 MOND RD

B1
1 ALBERT SQ
2 WILLOW AVE
3 BROOK ST
4 SAXON TERR

B2
1 HAWTHORN AVE
2 WILLOW AVE
3 LIME AVE
4 PINE AVE
5 MAPLE AVE
6 PLUMPTON CROSS

C1
1 PARR ST
2 RUNNYMEDE CT
3 CLIFFE ST
4 HENRY ST
5 RUNNYMEDE GDNS

C2
1 BROOKLANDS PK
2 KNOWLES CL
3 RUNNYMEDE WLK

D1
1 ASHFORD WAY
2 MELVILLE CL
3 KINGHAM CL
4 WILSON CL
5 HARGREAVES HO

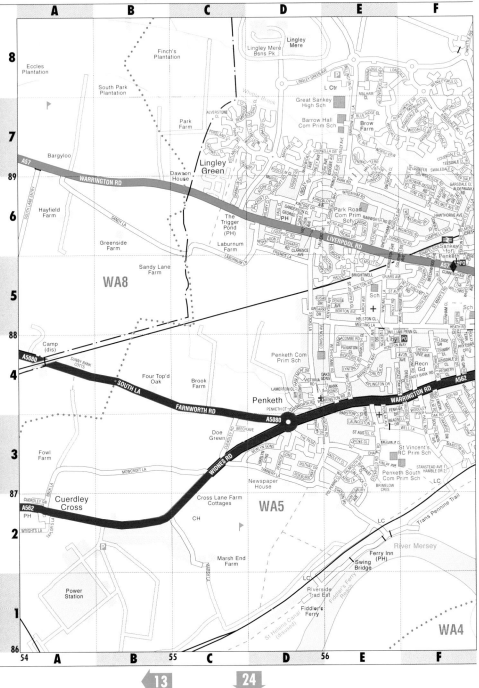

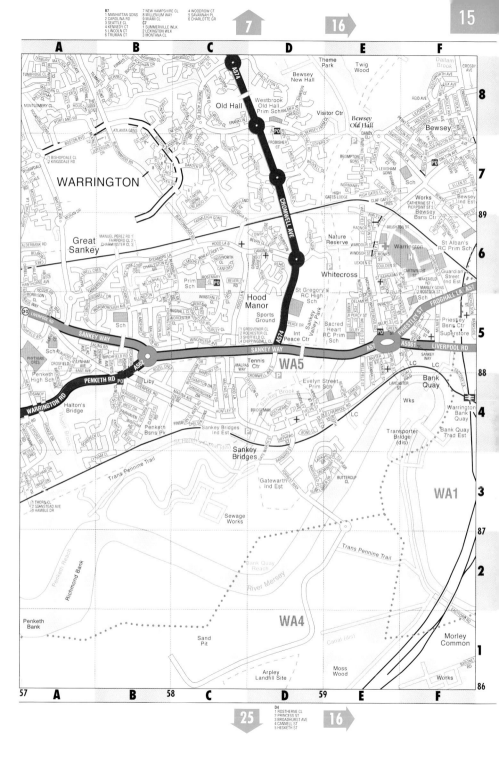

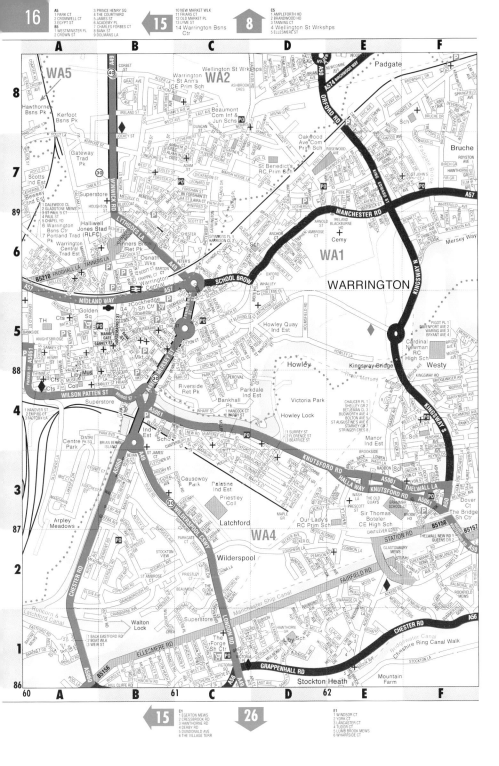

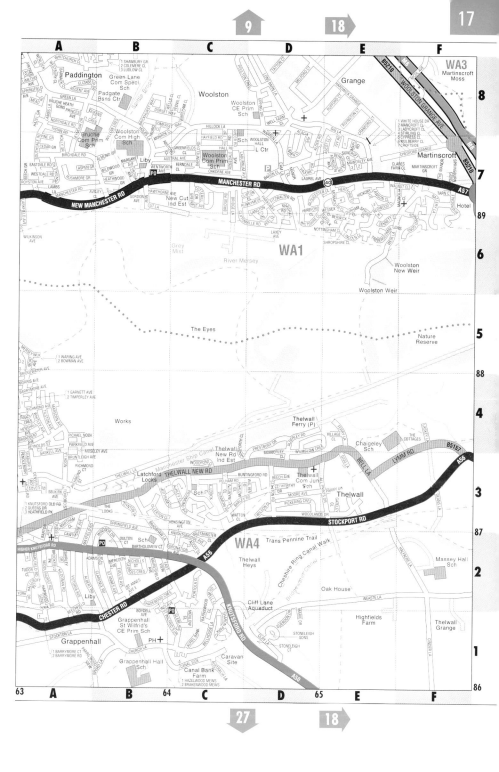

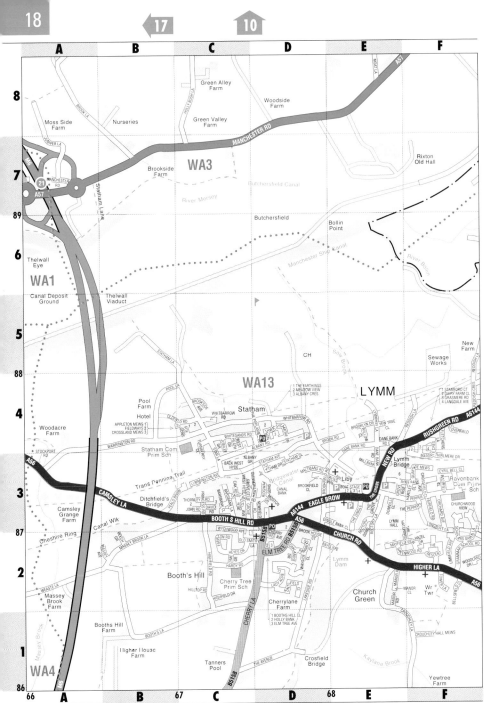

C3
1 THORNLEY CL
2 WATERBRIDGE CT
3 BRIDGEWATER CT

D3
1 THE ANCHORAGE
2 BROOKFIELD COTTS
3 BOOTHS HILL HO

E3
1 LYMM BROOK
2 HENRY ST
3 LEGH ST
4 BRIDGEWATER ST
5 THIRLMERE LODGE
6 THE SQUARE
7 DUKESBRIDGE CT

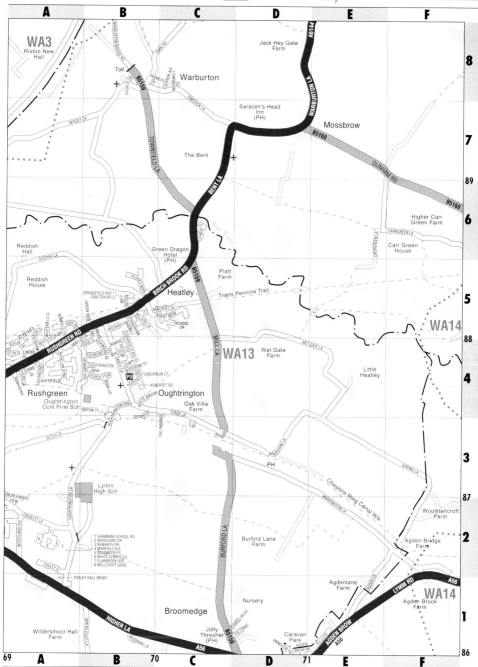

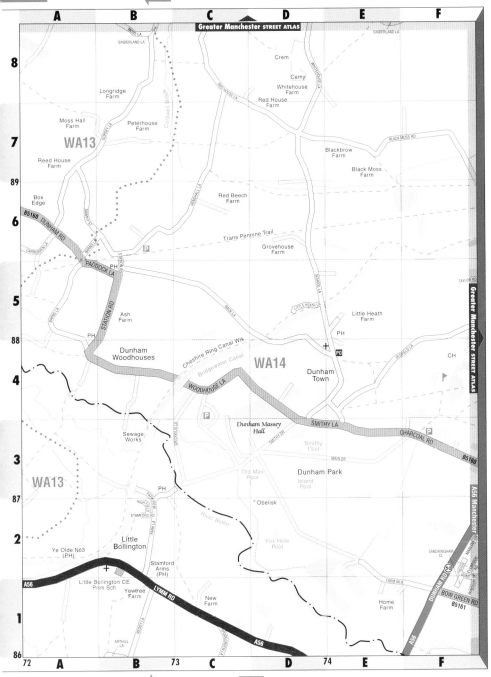

Greater Manchester STREET ATLAS

MOSS LA
SINDERLAND LA
SINDERLAND LA

Crem

Cemy

Whitehouse
Farm

Longridge
Farm

RED HOUSE LA

Red House
Farm

WHITEHOUSE LA

BLACK MOSS RD

Moss Hall
Farm

Peterhouse
Farm

DORSET LA

Blackbrow
Farm

WA13

Black Moss
Farm

Reed House
Farm

89

PENDRILL LA

Red Beech
Farm

Box
Edge

B5160 DUNHAM RD

CARRONESS LA

SANDY LA

BARNS LA

PADDOCK LA

6

Trans Pennine Trail

Grovehouse
Farm

TAYLOR RD

PH

STATION RD

SCHOOL LA

P

BACK LA

LITTLE HEATH LA

Little Heath
Farm

5

BARNS LA

Ash
Farm

CH

PH

88

PH

PO

OLDFIELD LA

Dunham
Woodhouses

Cheshire Ring Canal Wlk

Bridgewater Canal

WA14

Dunham
Town

WOODHOUSE LA

4

Sewage
Works

P

Dunham Massey
Hall

SMITHY LA

CHARCOAL RD

B5160

SMITHY DR

Smithy
Pool

MAIN DR

WA13

PH

Old Man
Pool

Dunham Park

Island
Pool

A56 Manchester

3

87

PARK VIEW

HIGHFIELD

STAMFORD RD

River Bollin

* Obelisk

Fox Hole
Pool

SANDRINGHAM
CL

Ye Olde No3
(PH).

Little
Bollington

Stamford
Arms
(PH)

FARM WLK

50

DUNHAM RD

2

LYMM RD

A56

Little Bollington CE
Prim Sch

Yewtree
Farm

New
Farm

Home
Farm

BOW GREEN RD

B5161

REDDISH LA

LONGRIDGE LA

A56

ARTHILL
LA

A56

1

86

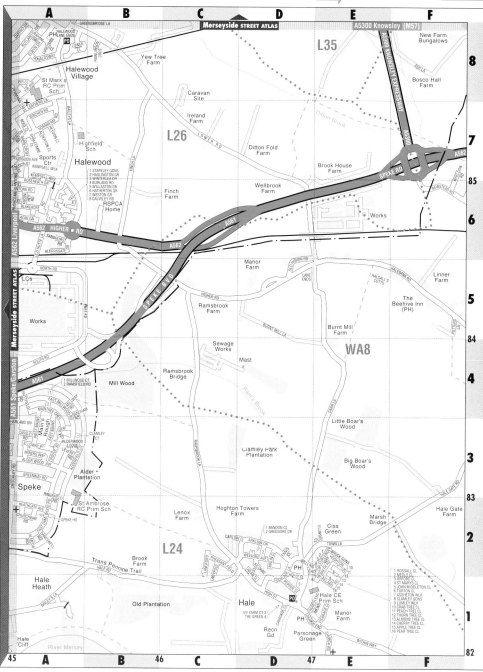

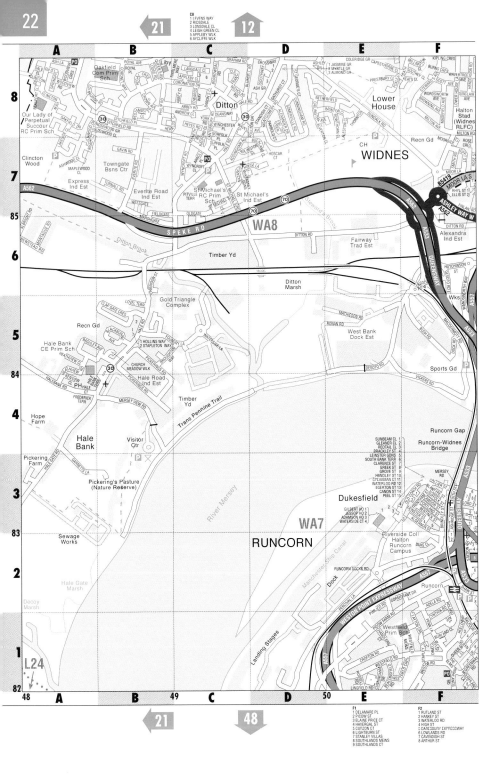

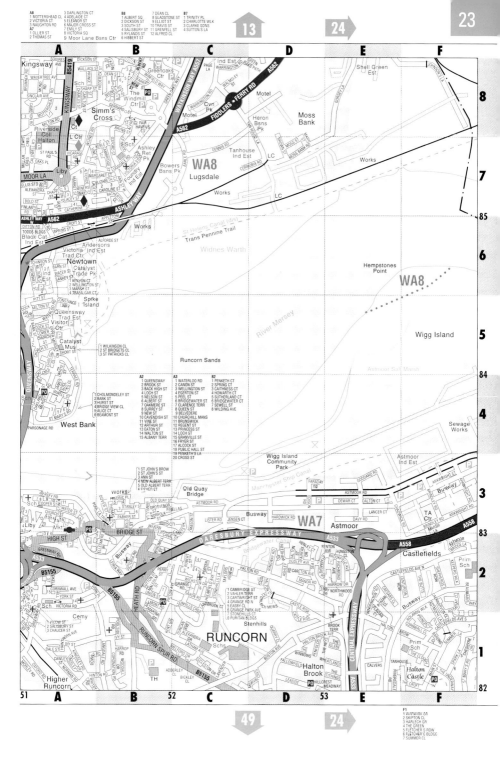

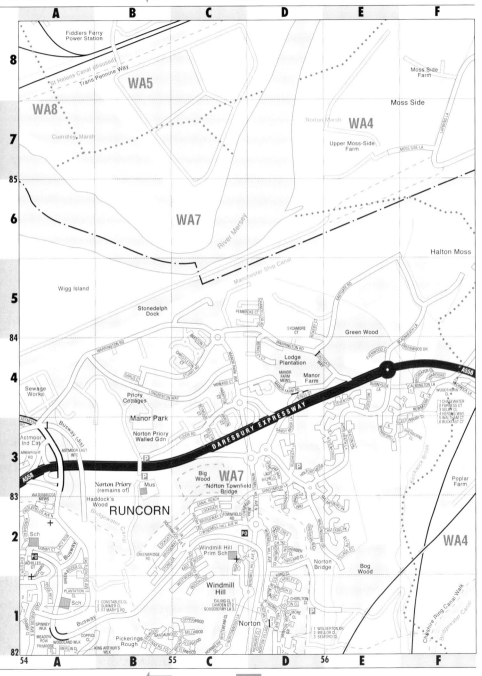

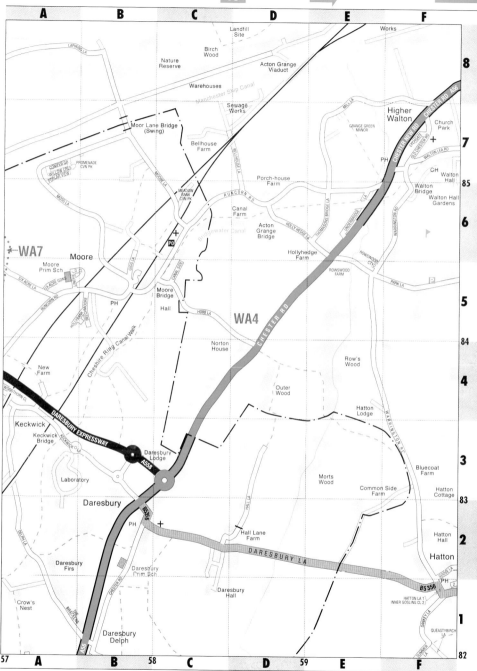

A   B   C   D   E   F

8

Landfill Site

Birch Wood

Nature Reserve

Acton Grange Viaduct

Warehouses

Manchester Ship Canal

Works

Moor Lane Bridge (Swing)

Sewage Works

Higher Walton

CHESTER RD A56

Bellhouse Farm

GRANGE GREEN MANOR

Church Park

7

CONISER GR
WILLOW CRES
POPLAR VIEW
PROMENADE
CVN PK

Porch-house Farm

PH

CHESTER NEW RD

OLD CHESTER RD
WALTON LEA RD

CH   Walton Hall

MOSS LA

MEADOW BANK CVN PK

RUNCORN RD

BELLHOUSE LA

Canal Farm

Acton Grange Bridge

HOLLY HEDGE LA

THOMASONS BRIDGE LA

UNDERBRIDGE LA

Walton Bridge

85

Walton Hall Gardens

6

WA7

Moore

Moore Prim Sch

PO

GIGG LA

Bridgewater Canal

Hollyhedge Farm

WARRINGTON RD

ROWSWOOD CTYD

ROWSWOOD FARM

PARK LA

P

Moore Bridge

PH

CANAL SIDE

Hall

HOBB LA

WA4

Norton House

CHESTER RD

Row's Wood

84

SIX ACRE LA
SIX ACRE GDNS

RUNCORN RD

HOLT LA
BECONSMOORE

Cheshire Ring Canal Walk

Outer Wood

Hatton Lodge

4

New Farm

DARESBURY EXPRESSWAY

KECKWICK LA

WOODTHORN CL

WARRINGTON RD

Keckwick

Keckwick Bridge

A558

Daresbury Lodge

Morts Wood

Common Side Farm

Bluecoat Farm

3

Laboratory

Daresbury

B5356

Hatton Cottage

83

Daresbury

PH

HALL LA

Hatton Hall

Hatton

2

BEEN LA

Daresbury Firs

Daresbury Prim Sch

CHESTER RD

DARESBURY LA

PH

B5356

BIRCH DENE

Daresbury Hall

HATTON LA 1
INNER GOSLING CL 2

SANKEY LA

Crow's Nest

Daresbury Delph

Daresbury Hall

A558

QUEASYBIRCH LA

SUMNER LA

1

82

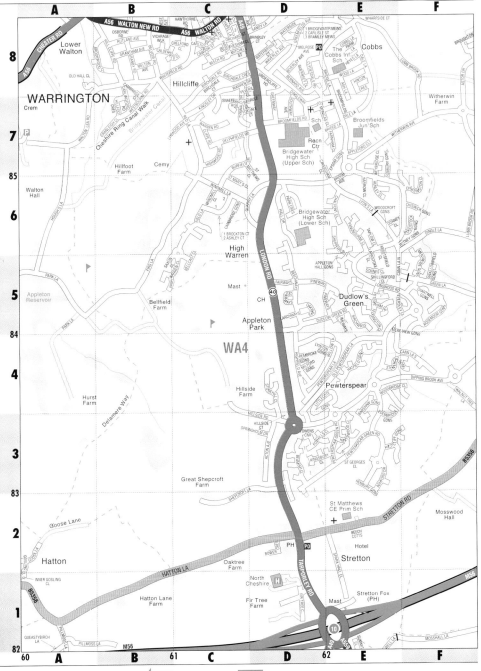

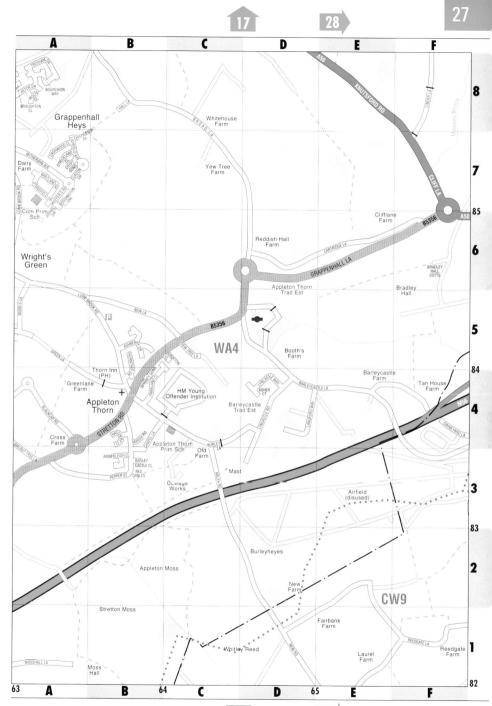

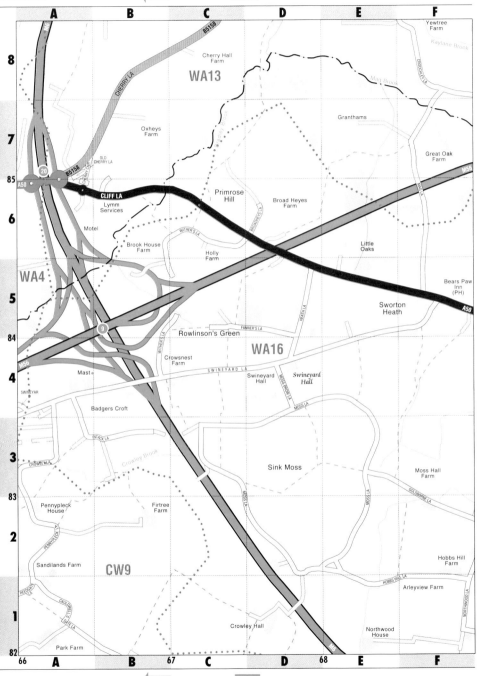

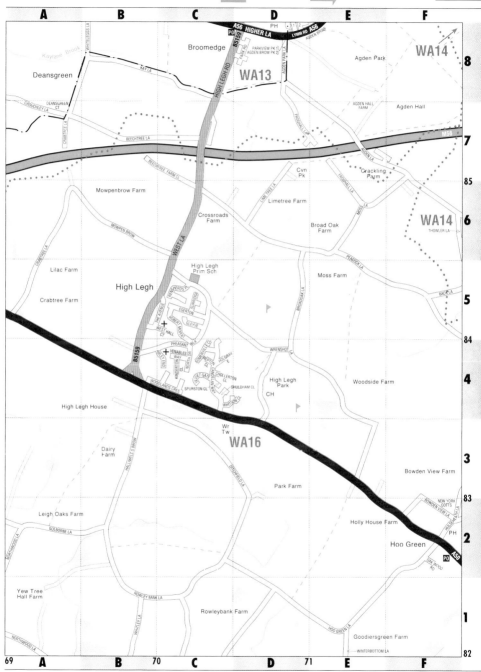

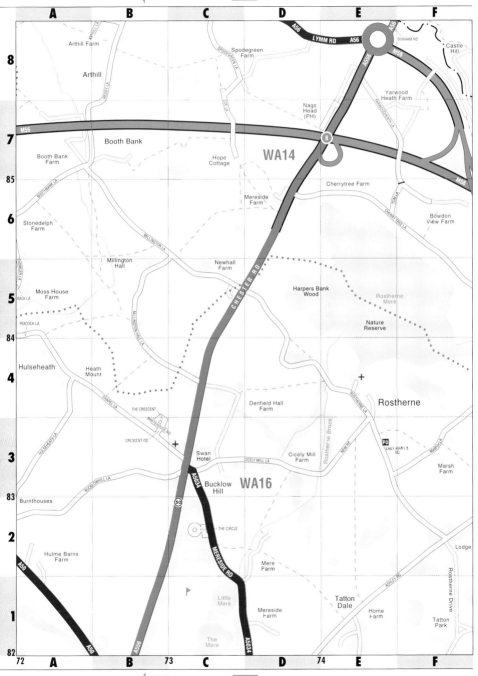

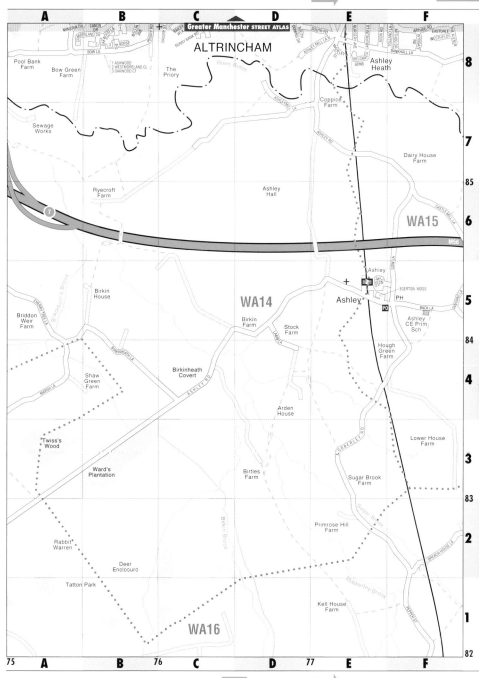

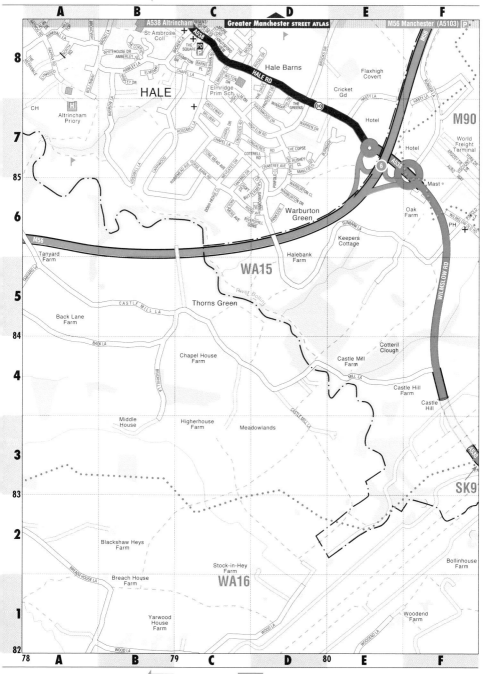

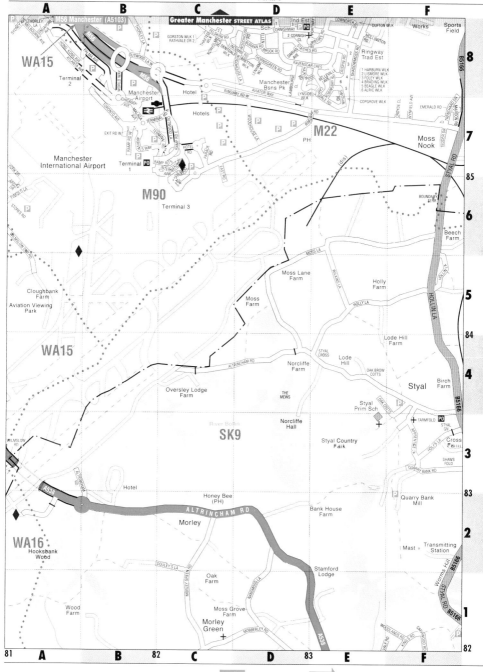

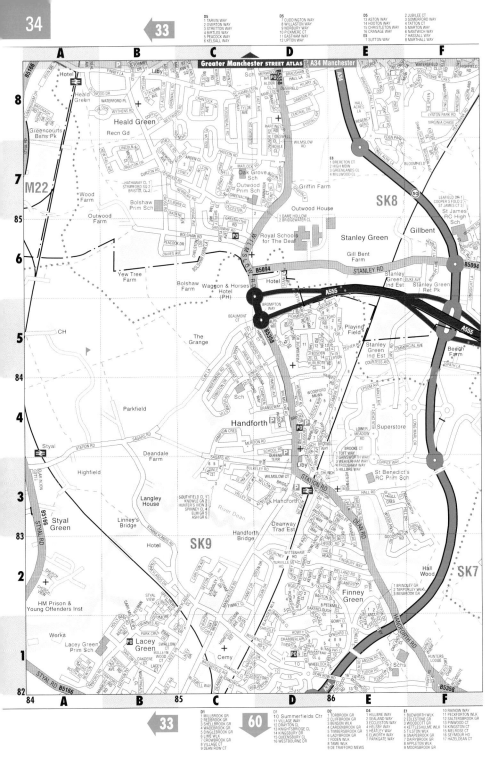

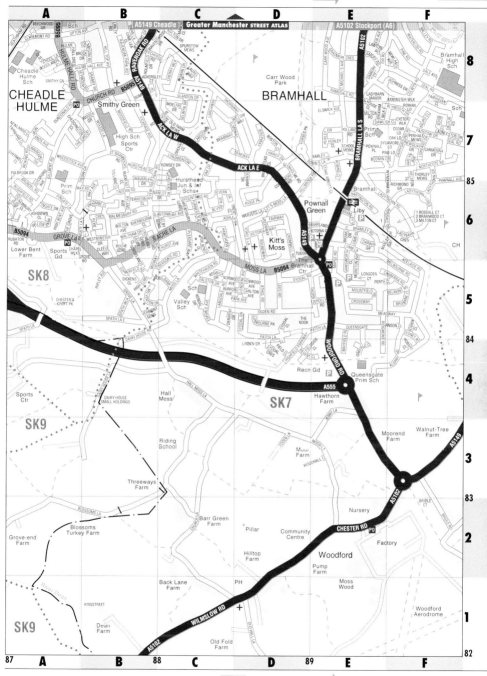

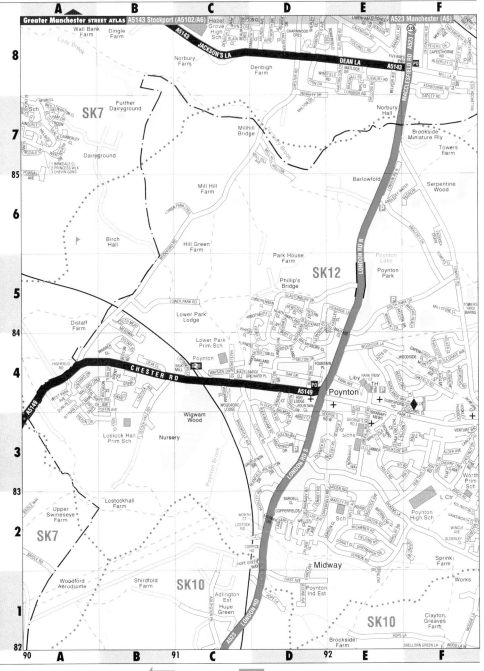

Greater Manchester STREET ATLAS   A5143 Stockport (A5102/A6)   A523 Manchester (A6)

Wall Bank Farm
Dingle Farm
Lady Brook
JACKSON'S LA
A5143
Hazel Grove High Sch
SKIPTON CL
BLAIR
CHARNWOOD CRES
SHEPLEY RD
CAVENHAM
LAVENHAM RD ROWLEY
DEAN LA
A5143
Norbury Farm
Denbigh Farm
WINSFIELD RD
WENSLEY DR
CHESTER RD
MALTON DR
MATLOCK
SUDBURY AVE
LONGNOR RD
BELVOIR AVE
Norbury Hall
FIVEWAYS
PO
CAPESTHORNE RD
ALDERLEY RD
MILL LA
ASHBOURNE RD
DARLEY RD

SK7
Further Dairyground
Millhill Bridge
Brookside Miniature Rly
Towers Farm
Barlowfold
Serpentine Wood

Nevin CL
Sch
WARTON CL
WHAM CL
TROON
CAMBERLEY CL
Dairyground
AINSDALE CL
OGDALE
POWNALL AVE
1 BIRKDALE CL
2 PRINCESS WLK
3 CHEVIN GDNS

Mill Hill Farm
LOWER PARK CRES
Mill Hill
NORBURY BROOK

Birch Hall
Hill Green Farm
Park House Farm
SK12
Poynton Lake
Poynton Park

Distaff Farm
Lower Park Lodge
LOWER PARK RD
Lower Park Prim Sch
GLASTONBURY DR
DUNDRENNAN
ABBOTSBURY CL
Phillip's Bridge
ISCARAGE LA
SOUTH PARK DR
MILLSTONE CL
TOWERS YARD BARNS

HIGHFIELD RD
WARREN
DISTAFF
SOUTH MEAD
MEADOW
DEVA CL
CHESTER RD
A5149
WOODFORD RD
Poynton
SILK MILL
WAYSIDE DR
HAZELBADGE
HAZELBANK CL
ORCHARD PL
OAK GR
P
Liby
PARK VIEW
TH
Poynton
POYNTON PARK
SOMERFORD

Lostock Hall Prim Sch
Wigwam Wood
Nursery
POYNTON BROOK
WOODFORD LODGE
GLOUCESTER
ASH LODGE
BALMORAL
ABBEY CT
FOUNTAIN PL
GEORGE'S
Schs
GRANARY MEWS
PARK LA
SCHOOL CL
VENTURE

Lostockhall Farm
Upper Swineseye Farm
SK7
LOSTOCK RD
WORTH CT
BARDELL CL
COPPERFIELDS
WELLER
Sch
COLUMBER WAY
MICAWBER RD
Poynton High Sch
L Ctr
ADLINGTON RD
GAWSWORTH CL
WINCLE AVE
ALDERLEY

BRIDLE WAY
BRIDLE RD
Woodford Aerodrome
Shirdfold Farm
SK10
COPPICE
HOPE GREEN WAY
Adlington Est Hope Green
FIRST AVE
Midway
Poynton Ind Est
Sprinkl Farm
Works

A523
LONDON RD
HOPE CL
HOPE LA
Brookside Farm
SK10
Clayton Greaves Farm
SKELLORN GREEN LA
WOOD LA W

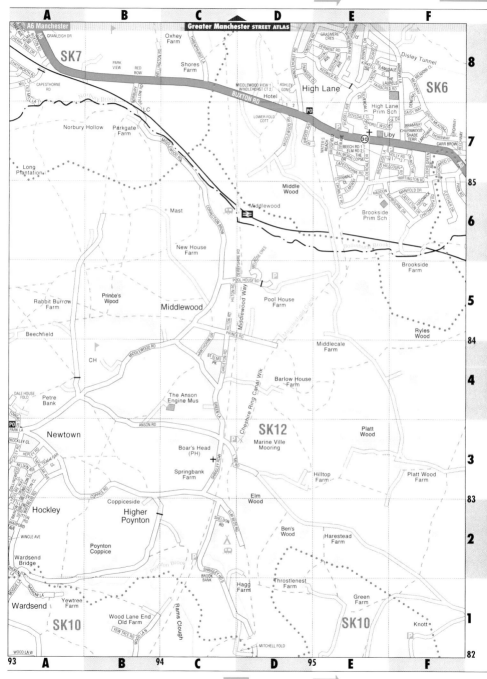

A6 Manchester

Greater Manchester STREET ATLAS

CRANLEIGH DR

SK7

8

CHATSWORTH AV

CHERRY TREE LA

MILL LA

CAPESTHORNE RD

PARK VIEW

RED ROW

OXHEY FARM

SHORES FARM

GRASMERE CRES

DERWENT RD

KESWICK RD

BUXTON RD

MIDDLEWOOD VIEW 1
WINDLEHURST CT 2

ASHLEY GDNS

Hotel

High Lane

THE LAURELS

Disley Tunnel

SK6

Norbury Hollow

Parkgate Farm

LOWER FOLD COTT

PO

High Lane Prim Sch

Liby

7

Long Plantation

MIDDLEWOOD RD

CARR BROW

85

Mast

Middlewood

Middle Wood

Brookside Prim Sch

6

New House Farm

Holborn Brook

Brookside Farm

Rabbit Burrow Farm

Prince's Wood

Middlewood

PERRYSHIRE RD

POOL HOUSE RD

Middlewood Way

Pool House Farm

5

Beechfield

CH

HILTON RD

PRINCES RD

HAMPTON RD

ST EDMO PK

CARLETON RD

Middlecale Farm

Ryles Wood

84

DALE HOUSE FOLD

Petre Bank

Newtown

PO

PARK LA

ANSON RD

GREEN LA

The Anson Engine Mus

Barlow House Farm

Cheshire Ring Canal Wlk

SK12

Platt Wood

4

HOCKLEY CL

NELSON CL

COLLINWOOD CL

OPPICE RD

Boar's Head (PH)

Springbank Farm

Marine Ville Mooring

Hilltop Farm

Platt Wood Farm

3

Hockley

WINCLE AVE

Coppiceside

Higher Poynton

SHELDON RD

Elm Wood

Ben's Wood

Harestead Farm

83

Wardsend Bridge

DIGG LA

MEADOW LA

Poynton Coppice

Holborn Brook

SHRIGLEY CRES

BROOK BANK

Hagg Farm

Throstlenest Farm

Green Farm

2

Wardsend

SK10

Yewtree Farm

Wood Lane End Old Farm

Rams Clough

YEW TREE RD

WOOD LA

MITCHELL FOLD

SK10

Knott

1

WOOD LA W

82

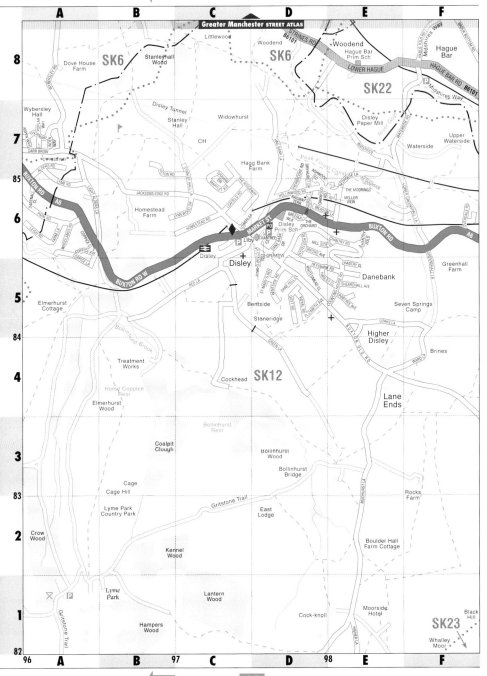

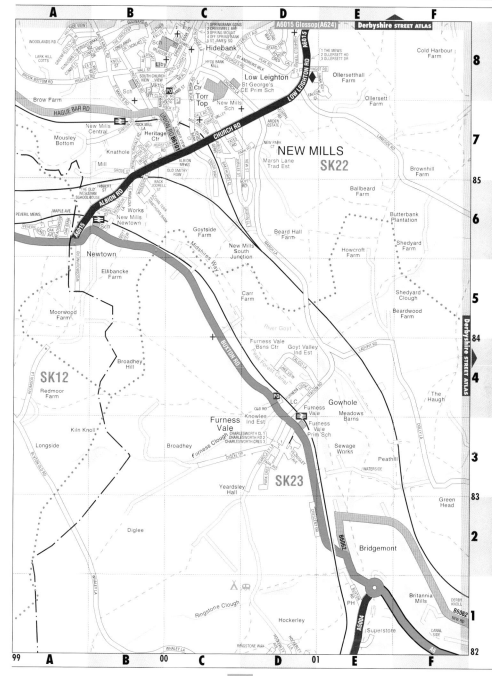

A6015 Glossop(A624)

Derbyshire STREET ATLAS

Hidebank

Low Leighton

St George's
CE Prim Sch

Torr
Top

New Mills
Sch

NEW MILLS

SK22

Ollersetthall
Farm

Ollersett
Farm

Cold Harbour
Farm

New Mills
Central

Heritage
Ctr

Marsh Lane
Trad Est

Brownhill
Farm

Knathole

Mill

Ballbeard
Farm

THE OLD
WESLEYAN
SCHOOLHOUSE

Works
New Mills
Newtown

Butterbank
Plantation

Peveril Mews

Maple Ave

Goytside
Farm

Beard Hall
Farm

Howcroft
Farm

Shedyard
Farm

Newtown

New Mills
South
Junction

Ellibancke
Farm

Midshires Way

Carr
Farm

Shedyard
Clough

Beardwood
Farm

Moorwood
Farm

River Goyt

SK12

Broadhey
Hill

Furness Vale
Bsns Ctr

Goyt Valley
Ind Est

Redmoor
Farm

Peak Forest Canal

The
Haugh

Kiln Knoll

Old Rd

Furness
Vale

Gowhole

Meadows
Barns

Longside

Knowles
Ind Est

Furness
Vale
Prim Sch

Broadhey

Furness Clough

CHARLESWORTH CL 1
CHARLESWORTH RD 2
CHARLESWORTH CRES 3

Sewage
Works

Peathill

Digley Rd

SK23

WATERSIDE

Green
Head

Yeardsley
Hall

Diglee

Bridgemont

Ringstone Clough

Hockerley

Britannia
Mills

DERBY
KNOLL

NEW RD

PH

Superstone

CANAL
SIDE

Ringstone Way

Derbyshire STREET ATLAS

8

85

7

6

84

5

4

3

83

2

1

82

99   A   B   00   C   D   01   E   F

65

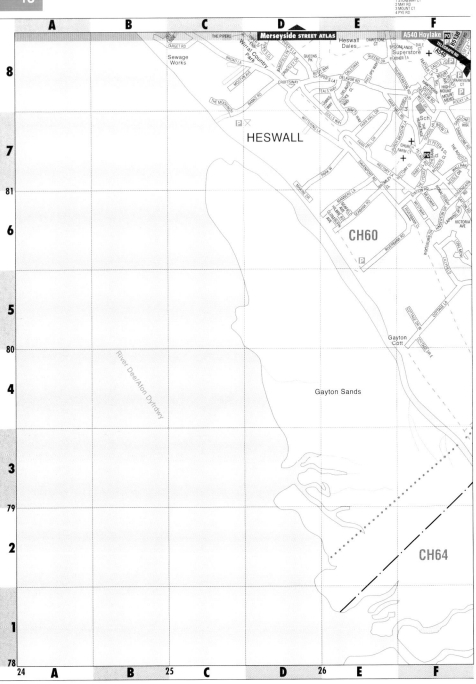

F8
1 STONEWAY CT
2 MAY RD
3 MOUNT CT
4 PYE RD

A540 Hoylake

HESWALL

CH60

CH64

River Dee/Afon Dyfrdwy

Gayton Sands

Gayton Cott

Wirral Country Park

Sewage Works

Heswall Dales

Superstore

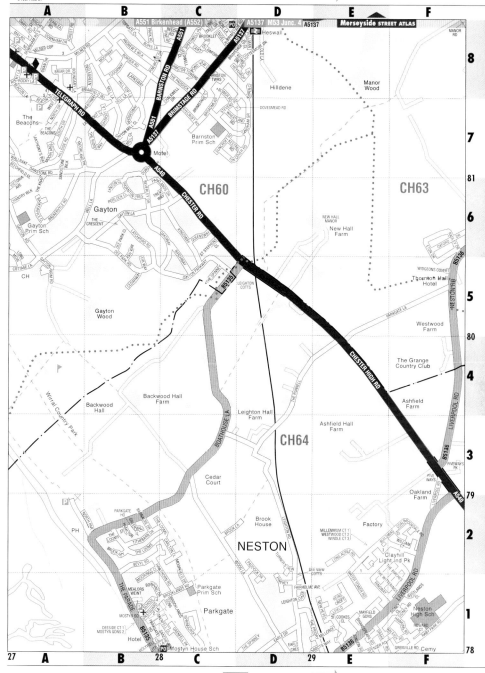

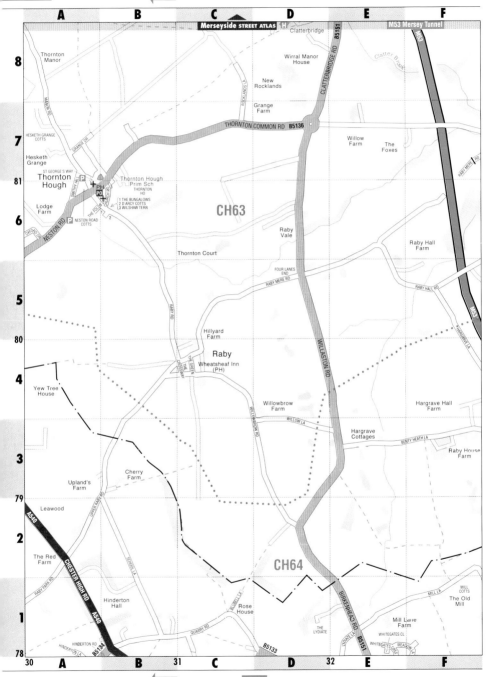

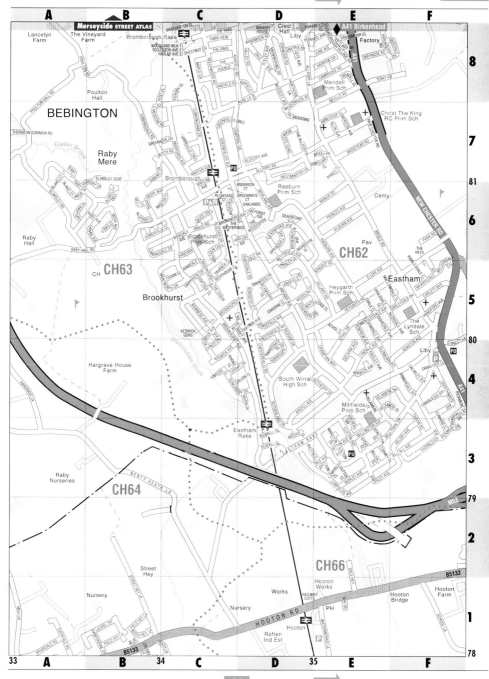

Merseyside STREET ATLAS

River Mersey

8 Eastham Country Park
Visitor Ctr
Eastham Ferry

Eastham Ferry Hotel

The Warrens Farm

7 Wirral Metropolitan Coll

WOOD HEATH WAY

Custom House

Eastham Locks

81 CHAPEL VIEW

CH

Queen Elizabeth II Dock

FERRY RD

6

MAYFIELD DR

SEAVIEW AVE

CH62

ST DAVID RD

Tanks

ST JOHN'S RD

Tanks

5 EASTHAM VILLAGE RD

B5132

Tanks

BANKFIELD DR

Oil Storage Depot

Manchester Ship Canal

Sch

VICARAGE ROW

80 B5132

Tanks

Tanks

HALL FARM
EASTHAM HO

EASTHAM MEWS

Tanks

Tanks

4 B5132

LC

Hooton Park

ERIC FOUNTAIN RD

40

David's Hough

NORTH RD

3

A41

CH65

LC

Booston Wood

79 5

RIVACRE RD

LC

NEW CHESTER RD

6

Kennel Wood

RIDGE WAY

2 REDVERS AVE

VERNON AVE

HOOTON WAY

HOOTON GN

Motor Vehicle Works

CHRISTIE CT

GRANGE COT

ROWNTREE DR

HOOTON RD

Park Farm

B5133

GRANGE CL

HOOTON LA

WOODCLOSE

1 Hooton

A550

WELSH RD

CHESTER RD

CH66

NEW SCHOOL LA

Rivacre Wood

7

M53

A41

B5132

B5132

78 SCHOOL LA

36 **A** B 37 **C** D 38 **E** F

46

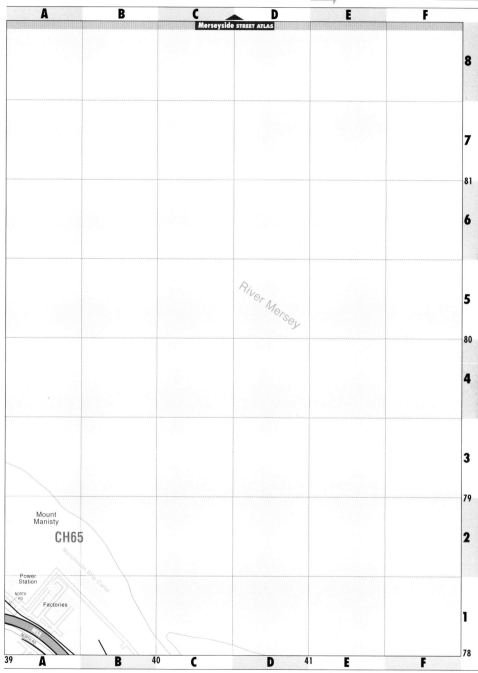

Merseyside STREET ATLAS

River Mersey

Mount
Manisty

CH65

Power
Station

NORTH
RD

Factories

M53

NORTH RD

Manchester Ship Canal

A   B   C   D   E   F

8
7
81
6
5
80
4
3
79
2
1
78

39   40   41

45

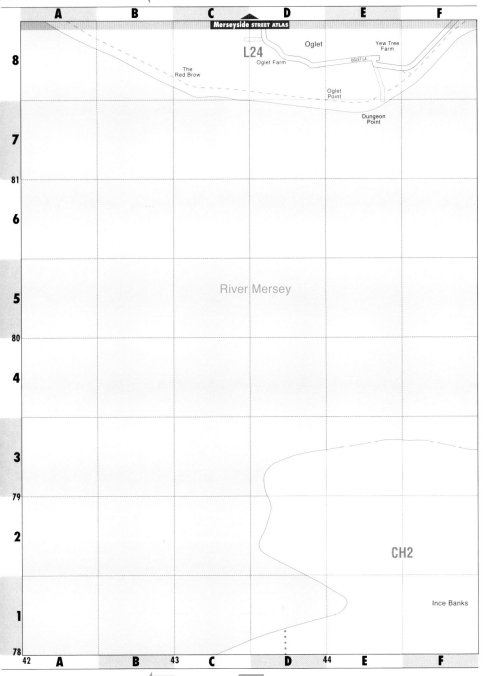

Merseyside STREET ATLAS

L24

Oglet

Yew Tree
Farm

Oglet Farm

OGLET LA

The
Red Brow

Oglet
Point

Dungeon
Point

River Mersey

CH2

Ince Banks

45
71

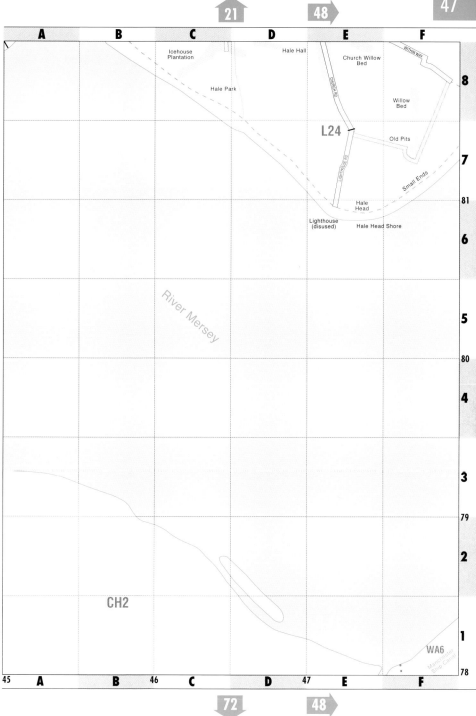

Icehouse
Plantation

Hale Hall

Church Willow
Bed

Hale Park

Willow
Bed

L24

Old Pits

Small Ends

81

Hale
Head

Lighthouse
(disused)

Hale Head Shore

River Mersey

80

79

CH2

78

WA6

Manchester
Ship Canal

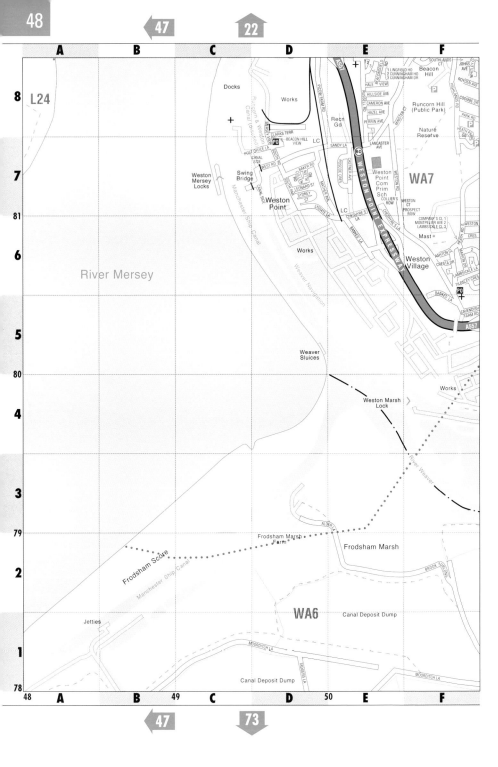

L24

Docks

Works

SOUTHLANDS CT

1 LINGFIELD HO
2 CUNNINGHAM HO
3 CUNNINGHAM DR

Beacon
Hill

JOHN'S
AVE

ROYDEN AVE

HALE RD

HILLSIDE AVE

CAMERON AVE

HAZEL AVE

PERRIN AVE

Recn
Gd

Runcorn Hill
(Public Park)

PARK RD

HEATH RD

Nature
Reserve

COOMBE DR

Weston
Mersey
Locks

Swing
Bridge

CLARK'S TERR

PO

BEACON HILL
VIEW

POST OFFICE LA

CANAL
O/DA

WEST RD

BAKER RD

SOUTH RD

LEONARD ST

MATHER PK

SYDNEY
ST

CANAL SIDE

LYDIATE LA

CHISHOLM

SANDY LA

LC

60

LANCASTER
AVE

WESTON
CT
PROSPECT
ROW

COLLIER'S
ROW

WA7

Weston
Point
Com
Prim
Sch

Weston
Point

Works

RUSSELL RD

ASCROFT AVE

ROSCOE CRES

CHISHOLM LA

BANKS LA

WESTON RD

ROSCOE ST LA

LC

COMPANY'S CL 1
MONTPELIER AVE 2
LAMBSICKLE CL 3

Mast

ASHTON CL

CRESTA DR

LAMBSICKLE LA

WESTON

CRES

Weston
Village

TILDSLEY CRES

PO

River Mersey

Weaver Navigation

Manchester Ship Canal

Runcorn & Weston
Canal (disused)

WESTON POINT EXPRESSWAY

CAVENDISH
FARM RD

A557

Weaver
Sluices

Works

Weston Marsh
Lock

River Weaver

Frodsham Marsh
Farm

ALDER LA

Frodsham Marsh

BROOK FURLONG

Frodsham Score

Manchester Ship Canal

WA6

Canal Deposit Dump

Jetties

MOORDITCH LA

TANYARD'S LA

MOORDITCH LA

Canal Deposit Dump

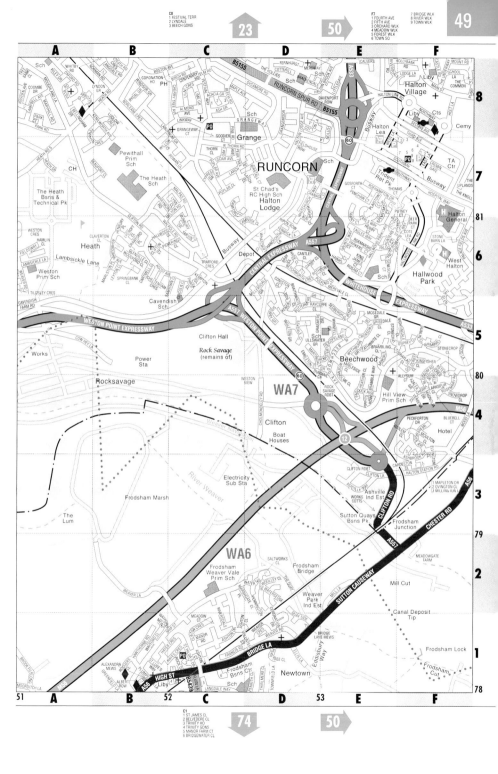

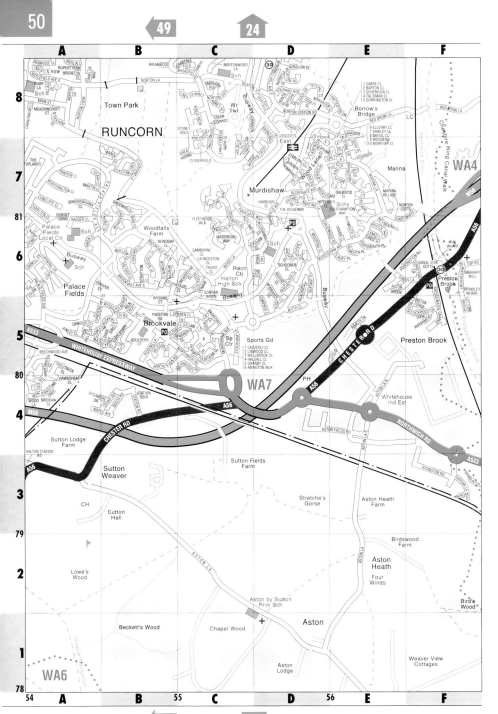

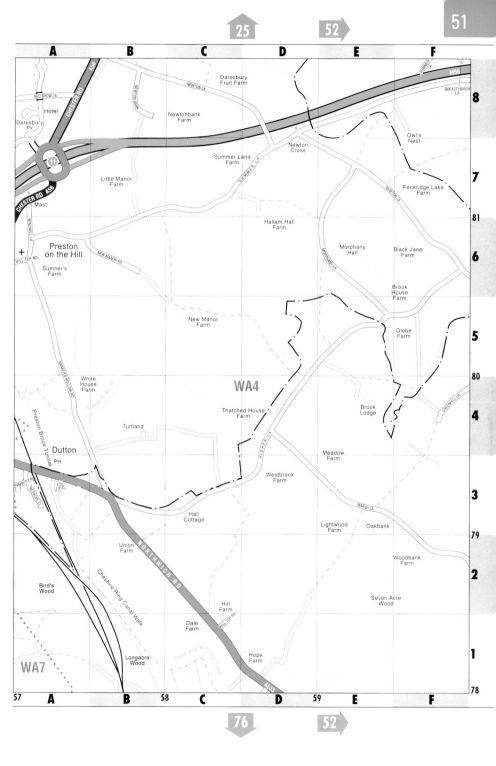

A   B   C   D   E   F

M56

QUEASTYBIRCH LA

8

Daresbury
Fruit Farm

NEWTON LA

RED BROW LA

Hotel

Daresbury
Pk

CHESTER RD A56

Newtonbank
Farm

NEWTON BANK

Owl's
Nest

Newton
Cross

7

Summer Lane
Farm

SUMMER LA

NEWTON LA

Penkridge Lake
Farm

Little Manor
Farm

11

81

CHESTER RD A56

Mast

Hallam Hall
Farm

MORPHANY LA

Morphany
Hall

Black Jane
Farm

6

WINDMILL LA

Preston
on the Hill

NEW MANOR RD

HILL TOP RD

Sumner's
Farm

Brook
House
Farm

New Manor
Farm

Glebe
Farm

5

BANKE'S HOLLOW RD

White
House
Farm

Knowl's Brook

WA4

80

GREENHILL LA

Whitley Brook

Thatched House
Farm

Brook
Lodge

4

Turfland

HIGHER LA

Meadow
Farm

Preston Brook Tunnel

Dutton

PH

Westbrook
Farm

MARSH LA

3

Hall
Cottage

Lightwood
Farm

Oakbank

79

Union
Farm

NORTHWICH RD

Woodbank
Farm

Bird's
Wood

Cheshire Ring Canal Walk

2

HILL TOP RD

Hill
Farm

Seven Acre
Wood

Dale
Farm

Trent and Mersey Canal

Hope
Farm

1

WA7

Longacre
Wood

A533

78

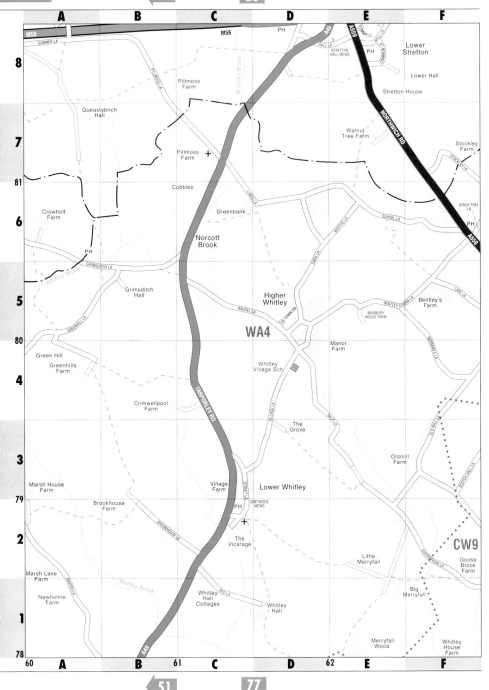

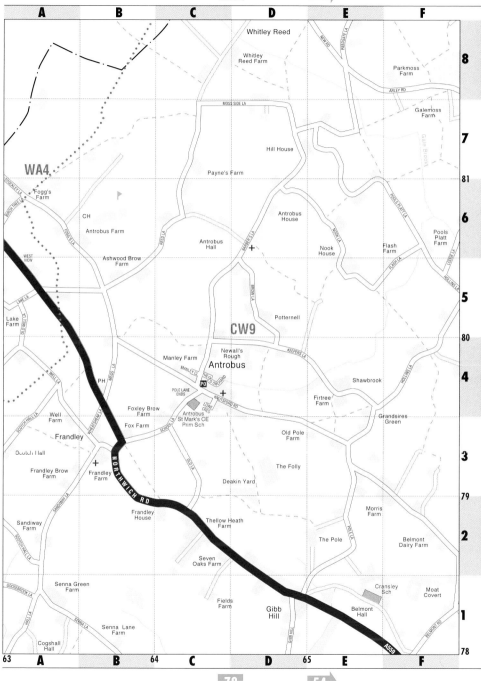

26

27 **54**

A B C D E F

Whitley Reed

8

Whitley
Reed Farm

Parkmoss
Farm

ARLEY RD

Galemoss
Farm

7

NEW RD

REEDGATE LA

MOSS SIDE LA

Hill House

81

Payne's Farm

WA4

Fogg's
Farm

CH

Antrobus Farm

Antrobus
House

6

Antrobus
Hall

Nook
House

Flash
Farm

Pools
Platt
Farm

Ashwood Brow
Farm

STOCKLEY LA

BIRCH TREE LA

FOGGS LA

REED LA

BADGER LA

NOOK LA

FLASH LA

POOLS PLATT LA

LOSSTI LA

HOLLINS LA

Gale Brook

WEST
VIEW

5

Lake
Farm

Potternell

BROW LA

CW9

80

LAKE LA

OLD MILL LA

Keepers LA

Manley Farm

Newall's
Rough

Antrobus

Shawbrook

4

BELL LA

MOSS LA

MANLEY CL

THE CLOSE

CHURCH RD

Firtree
Farm

HOLLINS LA

PH

PO

Pole Lane
Ends

KNUTSFORD RD

Grandsires
Green

Foxley Brow
Farm

Antrobus
St Mark's CE
Prim Sch

LOWE CRES

Well
Farm

Fox Farm

SCHOOL LA

Old Pole
Farm

3

WHEELOCK LA

Frandley

Scotch Hall

The Folly

Frandley Brow
Farm

Frandley
Farm

OLD LA

Deakin Yard

79

SCOTCH HALL LA

NORTHWICH RD

SANDIWAY LA

Morris
Farm

Sandiway
Farm

Frandley
House

Thellow Heath
Farm

The Pole

POLE LA

Belmont
Dairy Farm

2

SCOTCH HALL LA

Seven
Oaks Farm

Senna Green
Farm

Cransley
Sch

Moat
Covert

1

GOOSEBROOK LA

SENNA LA

HALL LA

Senna Lane
Farm

Fields
Farm

Gibb
Hill

GIBB HILL

Belmont
Hall

BELMONT RD

A559

Cogshall
Hall

78

63 A B 64 C D 65 E F

78 **54**

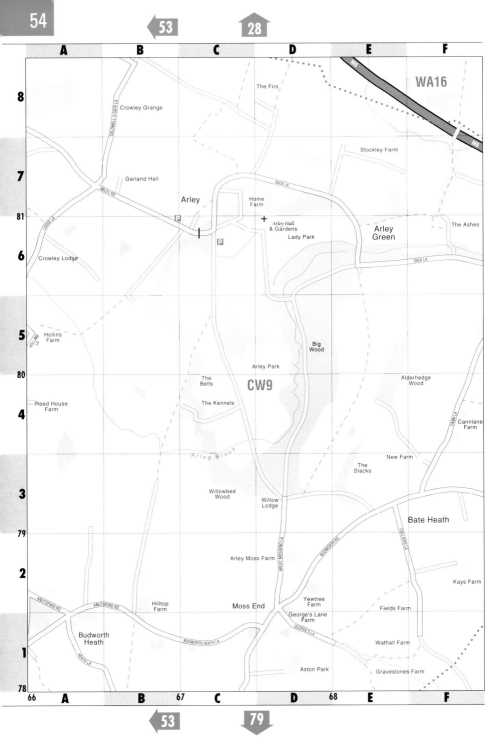

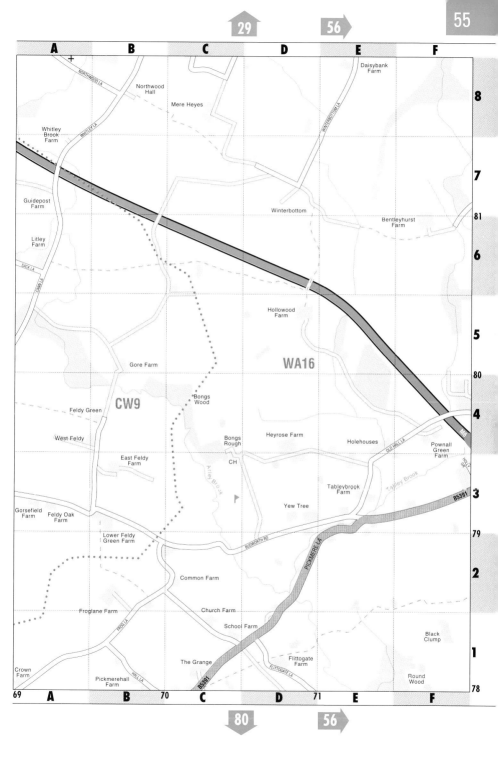

29
56
80
56

Daisybank Farm

Northwood Hall

Mere Heyes

Whitley Brook Farm

NORTHWOOD LA

WHITLEY LA

WINTERBOTTOM LA

Guidepost Farm

Winterbottom

Bentleyhurst Farm

Litley Farm

SACK LA

CANAL LA

Hollowood Farm

Gore Farm

WA16

CW9

Bongs Wood

Feldy Green

West Feldy

Heyrose Farm

Holehouses

OLD HALL LA

Pownall Green Farm

HOLT GATE

M6

Bongs Rough

East Feldy Farm

CH

Arley Brook

Tablevbrook Farm

Tabley Brook

Yew Tree

B5391

Gorsefield Farm

Feldy Oak Farm

Lower Feldy Green Farm

BUDWORTH RD

PICKMERE LA

Common Farm

Froglane Farm

BROOK LA

Church Farm

School Farm

Black Clump

Crown Farm

Pickmerehall Farm

HALL LA

The Grange

B5391

Flittogate Farm

FLITTOGATE LA

Round Wood

69   70   71

78   79   80   81

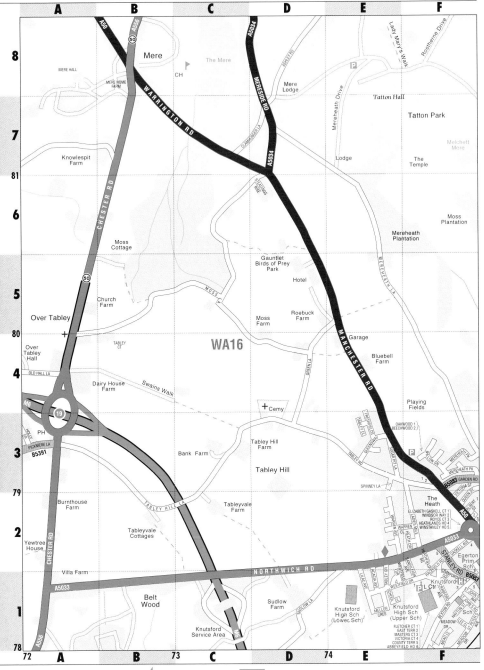

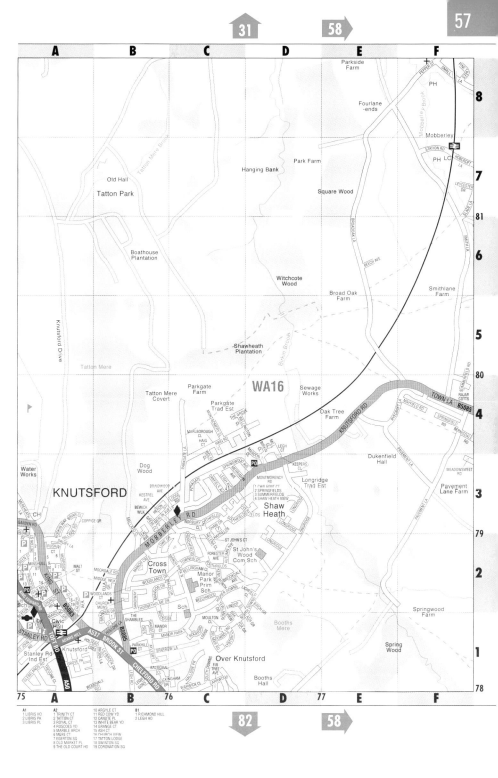

A   B   C   D   E   F

8   Owen House Farm   Oak Farm

Orrell House Farm

Blakeley Farm

The Oaks

7   Sunny Bank Farm

SLADE LA

81   Greenbank

Hazelhurst Farm   Holt GDNS   Holt House   Benkeyhurst Farm

Wee Bridge Farm   DAVENPORT LA   BURLEYHURST LA

6

Wayside Farm

CROFT PK

Valewood Farm   Mobberley CE Prim Sch   Mobberley Hall Farm   Graveyard Farm

5   Dairy Farm   Church Inn (PH)   Park Farm

Works   SPRING GDNS

Sewage Works   Stubbs Farm

80   WA16   STUBBS LA

Mobberley   BARCLAY HALL

B5085   Mobberley Old Hall   Park Farm   Newton Hall   Yewtree Farm

4   GREAT OAK SQ   TOWN LA   HALL LA   Lodge   Bird In Hand (PH)

PO   PH   DAMSON LA   1 TIPPING BROW   Clayhouse Farm

Town Lane Farm   DAM LA   2 HALL BANK N   3 HALL BANK   4 HALL BANK S

1 MEADOWSWEET RD   Dam Head Farm   Knolls Green   KNUTSFORD RD   Clay Lane

2 BERNISDALE RD   3 MALLORY CT   4 MALLORY CL

3   Coppock House   B5085

79   Antrobus Hall   Hillfield Farm

Glevehouse Farm   Antrobus Bridge

2   PH

THE SYCAMORES 1   Warford House

THE LARCHES 2   THE CEDARS 3   THE ELMS 4   THE MAPLES 5   THE OAKS 6   THE PINES 7   CHESTNUT MEWS 8   THE BEECHES 9.   NOONSUN FARM

1   Pedley Brook   Warford Park

78   Mountpleasant Farm   Warford Grange Farm   PEDLEY HOUSE LA   NOAHS ARK LA   Sewage Works

78   A   B   79   C   D   80   E   F

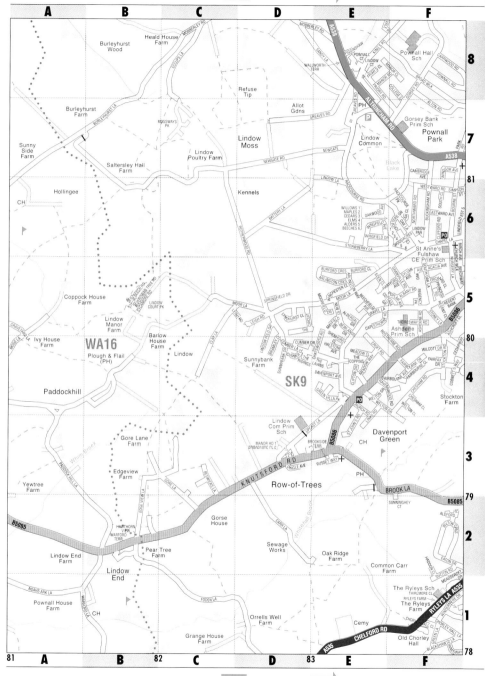

59

34

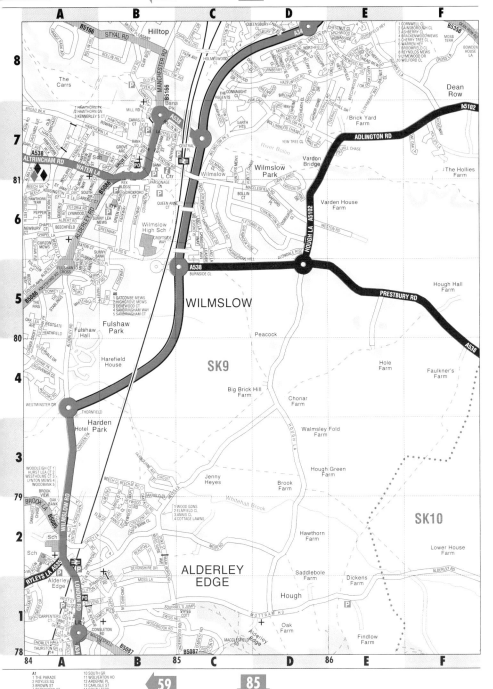

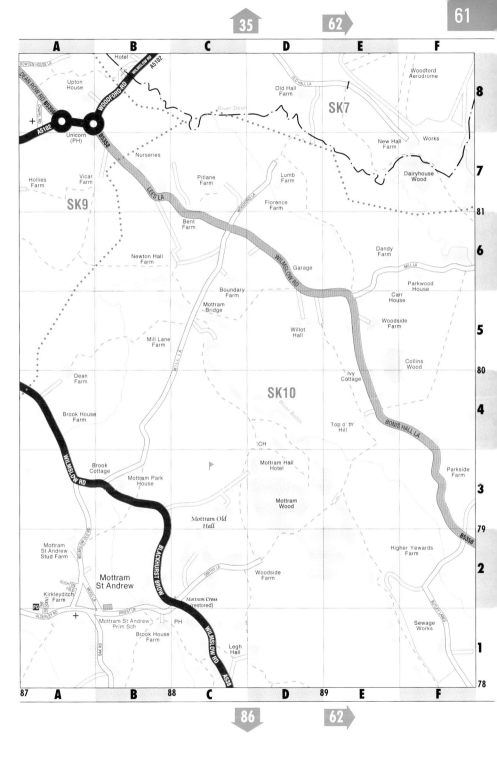

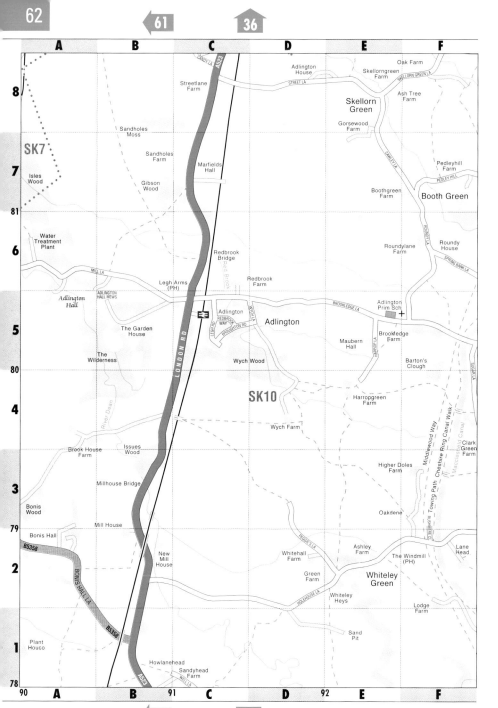

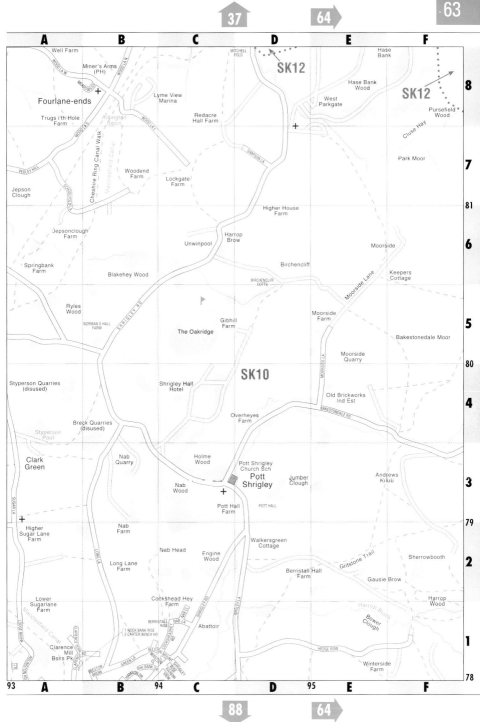

A   B   C   D   E   F

Well Farm

Miner's Arms (PH)

Fourlane-ends

Trugs i'th Hole Farm

Jepson Clough

Springbank Farm

Ryles Wood

Styperson Quarries (disused)

Clark Green

Higher Sugar Lane Farm

Lower Sugarlane Farm

Clarence Mill Bsns Pk

Lyme View Marina

WOOD LA

Addington Basin

Cheshire Ring Canal Walk

Macclesfield Canal

Woodend Farm

Jepsonclough Farm

Blakehey Wood

NORMAN'S HALL FARM

SHRIGLEY RD

Breck Quarries (disused)

Styperson Pool

Nab Quarry

Nab Wood

LONG LA

Nab Farm

Long Lane Farm

Nab Head

Macclesfield Canal

CLARENCE TERRACE

BEESTON BROW

GREEN LA

HAMSON DR

Redacre Hall Farm

Lockgate Farm

Unwinpool

The Oakridge

Shrigley Hall Hotel

Holme Wood

Cockshead Hey Farm

BERRISTALL RISE
1 ROCK BANK RISE
2 CARTER BENCH HO

NAB LA

Abattoir

OAK BANK DR

SHRIGLEY RD

MITCHELL FOLD

SK12

Higher House Farm

Harrop Brow

Gibhill Farm

SIMPSON LA

Birchencliff

BIRCHENCLIFF COTTS

SK10

Overheyes Farm

Pott Shrigley Church Sch

Pott Shrigley

Pott Hall Farm

POTT HALL

Engine Wood

Walkersgreen Cottage

SPITAL LA

Berristall Hall Farm

Hase Bank

Hase Bank Wood

West Parkgate

Cluse Hay

Park Moor

Moorside

Keepers Cottage

Moorside Lane

Moorside Farm

Bakestonedale Moor

Moorside Quarry

MOORSIDE LA

Old Brickworks Ind Est

BAKESTONEDALE RD

Jumber Clough

Andrews Knob

Gritstone Trail

Gausie Brow

Sherrowbooth

Harrop Wood

Harrop Brook

Bower Clough

HEDGE ROW

Winterside Farm

SK12

Pursefield Wood

8

81

7

6

5

80

4

3

79

2

1

78

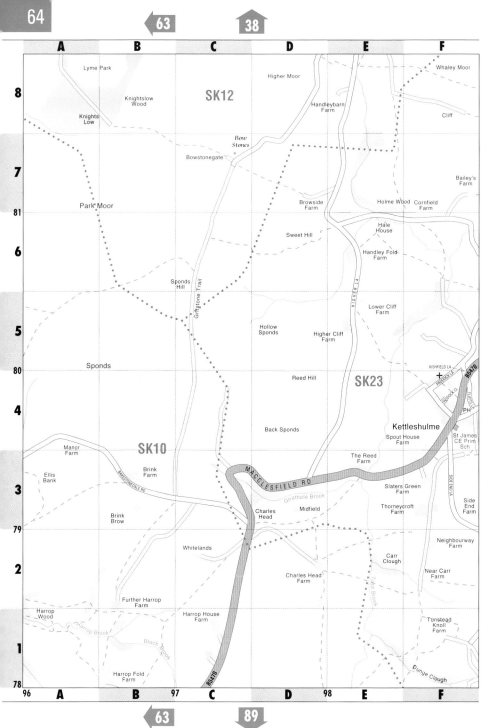

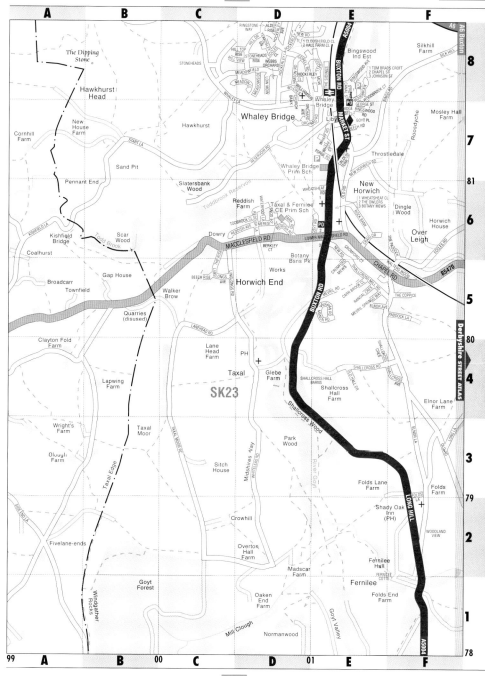

E8
1 MARLOWE RD
2 POPLAR WEINT
3 SCHOLAR'S CT
4 HADDON HO
5 DENWALL HO
6 ASHFIELD HO

7 HARGREAVE HO
8 THE CROSS
9 The Royal Sh Arc
10 ROKLIS GRANGE
F7
1 NORMANO COTTS

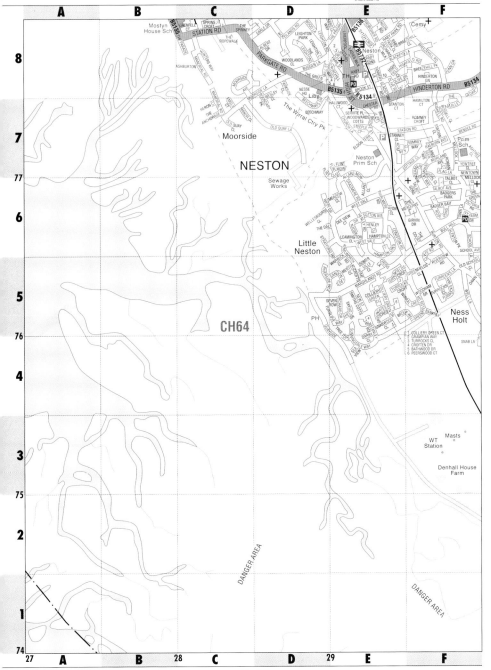

NESTON

Moorside

Little
Neston

CH64

Ness
Holt

Denhall House
Farm

DANGER AREA

DANGER AREA

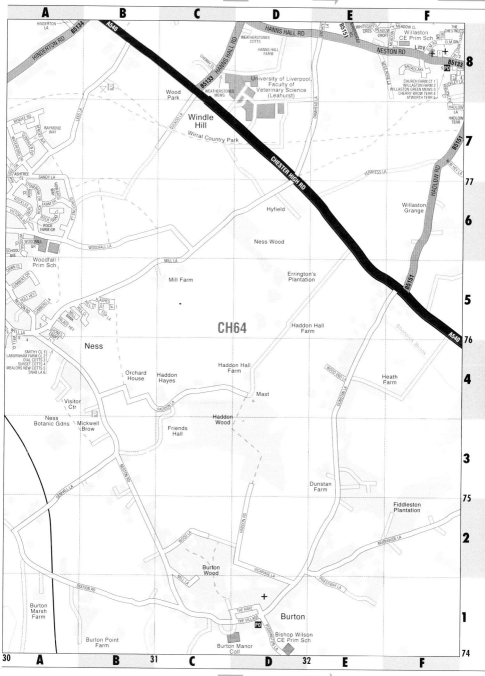

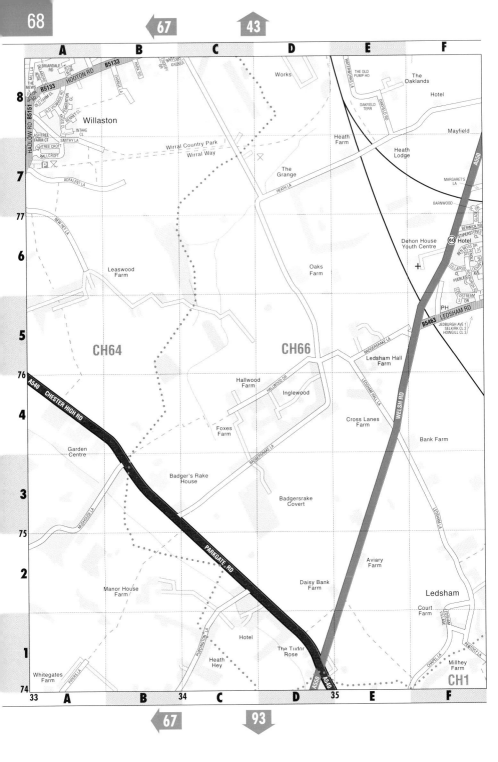

8

Briardale Rd
Old Hall Rd
The Mews
B5133
HOOTON RD
B5133
PARK RD
CHANNEL LA
Works
The Oaklands
Hotel
WATERING LA
THE OLD PUMP HO
OAKFIELD RD

HADLOW RD B5151
OLD VICARAGE RD
EGERTON RD
BENNET CL
BARFORD GRANGE
CROSSLEY RD
OAKFIELD TERR
Mayfield
A540

Willaston
INTAKE CL
ASHTREE
ASHTREE CROFT
SMITHY LA
HALLCROFT
Heath Farm
Heath Lodge

Wirral Country Park
Wirral Way
The Grange
MARGARET'S LA

7
ADFALENT LA
HEATH LA
BARNWOOD

77
NEW LA
BERWICK RD
STIPERSTONES

6
Leaswood Farm
Oaks Farm
Dehon House Youth Centre
60 Hotel
PH NEVIS DR
ULLAPOOL
PEEBLES DR
LOCHEE
OSTREAM DR

PH
B5463
LEDSHAM RD

5
JEDBURGH AVE 1
SELKIRK CL 2
HOWGILL CL 3

CH64
CH66
Ledsham Hall Farm

76
A540
Hallwood Farm
HALLWOOD DR
Inglewood
BADGERSRAKE LA
LEDSHAM HALL LA
WELSH RD

4
CHESTER HIGH RD
Foxes Farm
Cross Lanes Farm
Bank Farm

Garden Centre
Badger's Rake House
BADGERSRAKE LA

3
Badgersrake Covert
LEDSHAM LA

75
MUDHOUSE LA
PARKGATE RD

2
Manor House Farm
Aviary Farm
Daisy Bank Farm
Ledsham
Court Farm
LEDSHAM VILLAGE

1
PINFOLD LA
Hotel
The Tudor Rose
A540
A540
CHAPEL LA
REHOYS LA
Millhey Farm
CH1

Whitegates Farm
PIPERS LA
Heath Hey

74

33   34   35

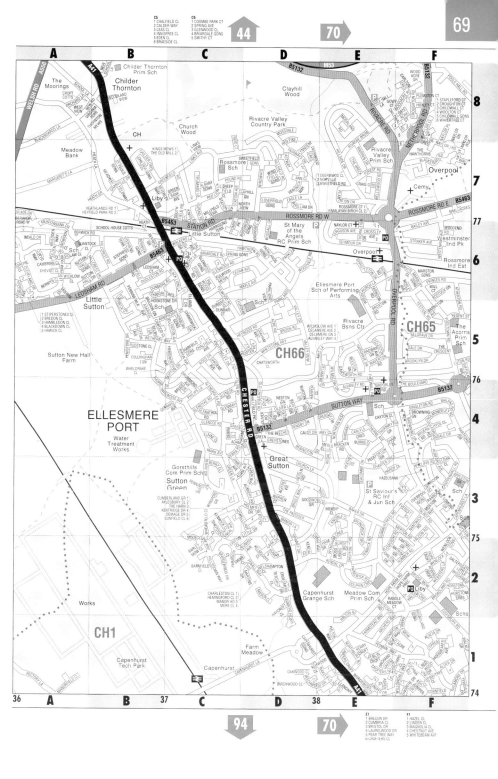

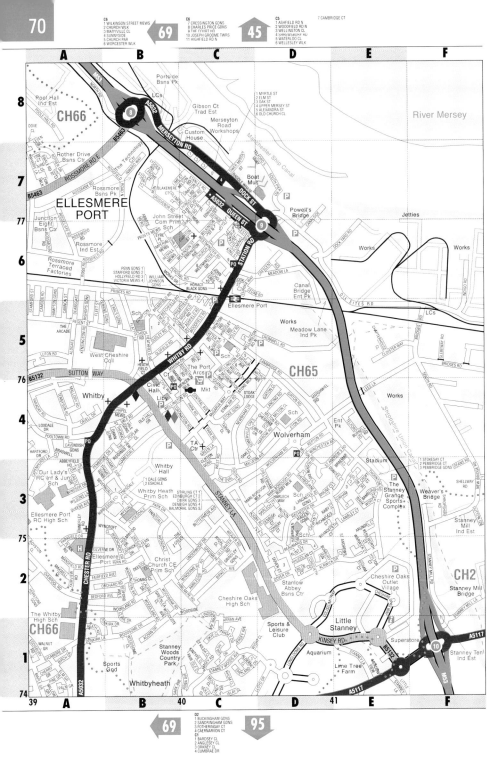

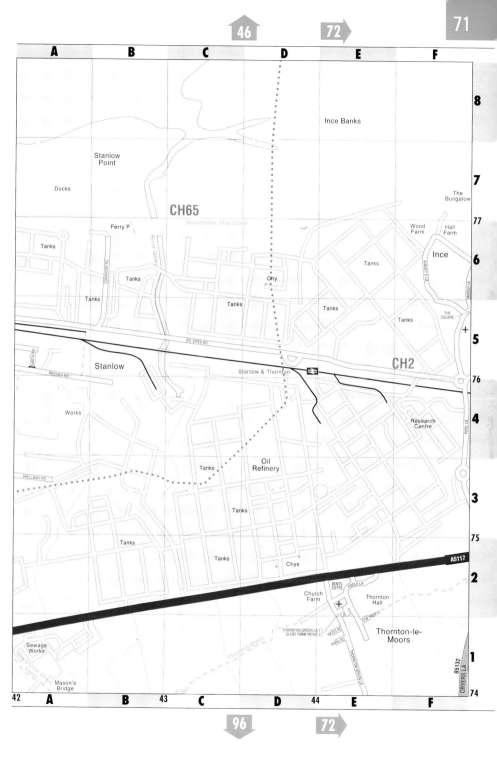

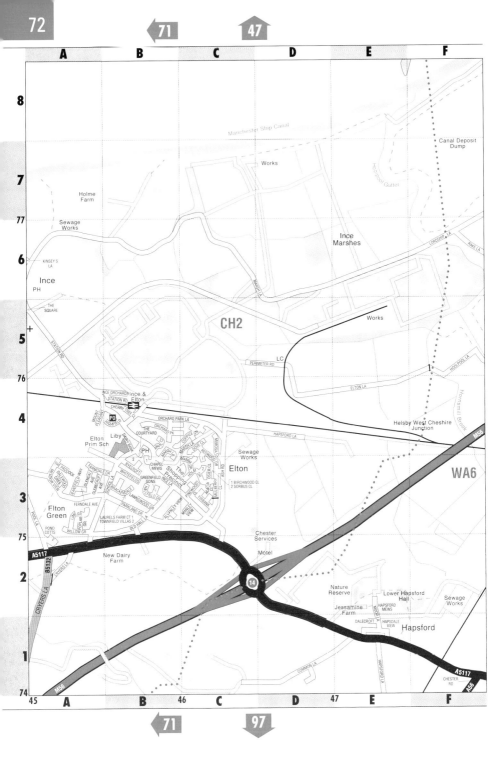

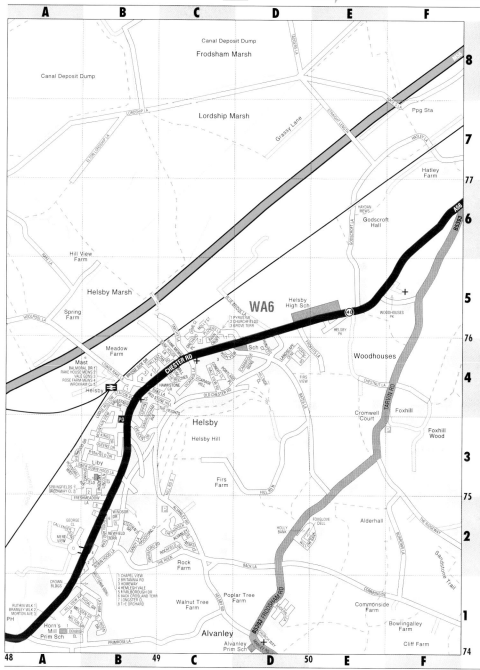

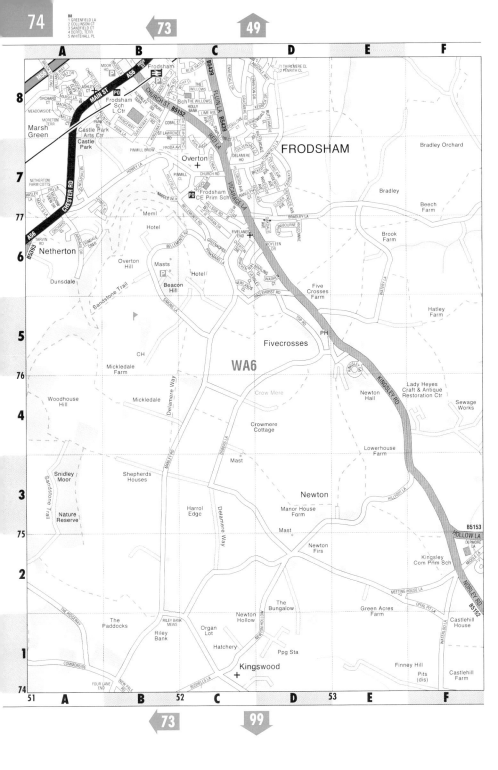

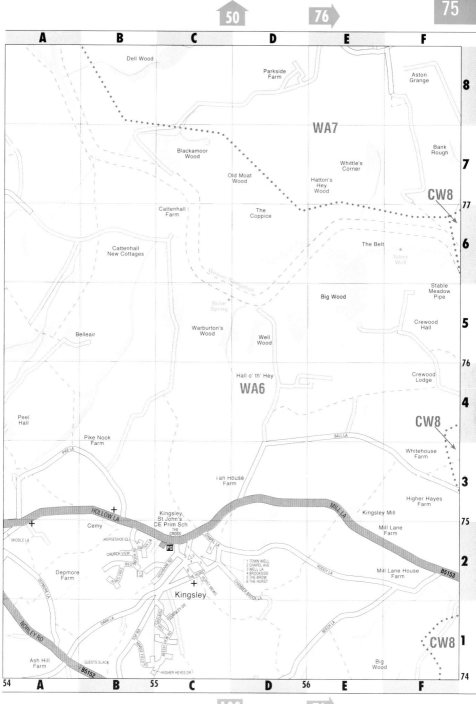

	A	B	C	D	E	F

Dell Wood

Parkside Farm

Aston Grange

8

WA7

Blackamoor Wood

Whittle's Corner

Bank Rough

7

Old Moat Wood

Hatton's Hey Wood

CW8

77

Cattenhall Farm

The Coppice

6

The Belt

Silver Well

Cattenhall New Cottages

Weaver Navigation

Stable Meadow Pipe

Belleair

Brine Spring

Big Wood

Crewood Hall

5

Warburton's Wood

Well Wood

76

Hall o' th' Hey

WA6

Crewood Lodge

4

Peel Hall

BALL LA

CW8

Pike Nook Farm

Whitehouse Farm

PIKE LA

3

Tan House Farm

Higher Hayes Farm

HOLLOW LA

Kingsley St John's CE Prim Sch

MILL LA

Kingsley Mill

75

Cemy

THE CROSS

Mill Lane Farm

MIDDLE LA

HORSESHOE CL

CHAPEL LA

1 TOWN WELL
2 CHAPEL AVE
3 WELL LA
4 BROOKSIDE
5 THE BROW
6 THE HURST

Mill Lane House Farm

B5153

2

CHURCH VIEW

THE CHURCHES

WEST PK

Depmore Farm

HIGHLAND RD

THE HURST

SPINNEY MEWS

CHILBERT BROOK LA

RODOY LA

Kingsley

DARK LA

BECH VIEW RD

DONGSEY DR

BEECH LA

CW8

1

DEPMORE LA

NORLEY RD

Ash Hill Farm

GUESTS SLACK

BARKE FIELD

HIGHER HEYES DR

Big Wood

B5152

74

54	A	B	55	C	D	56	E	F

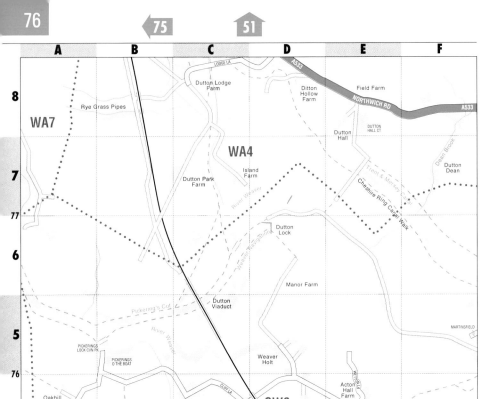

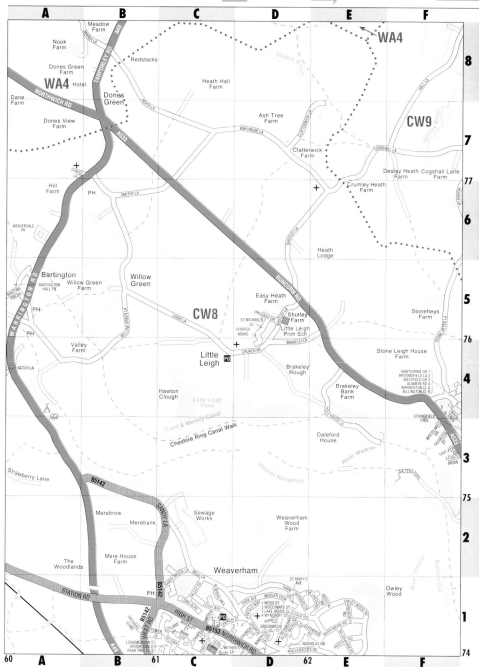

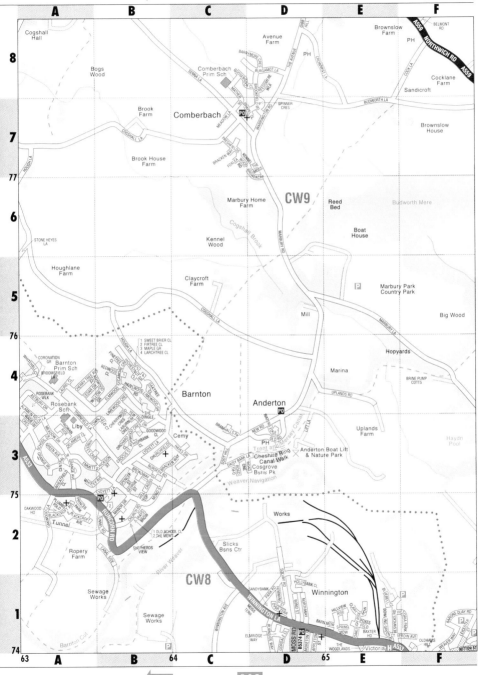

A B C D E F

8

Cogshall
Hall

Bogs
Wood

Brook
Farm

Comberbach

Brook House
Farm

Avenue
Farm

Comberbach
Prim Sch

PH

PO

SPINNER
CRES

BARNYMORE LA
BURJAMOT LA

THE AVENUE

WARBURTON CL

SENNA LA

MEADOW LA

MATHER AVE

Brownslow
Farm

PH

BELMONT
RD

NORTHWICH RD
A559

A559

Cocklane
Farm

Sandicroft

Brownslow
House

BUDWORTH LA

77

CW9

Marbury Home
Farm

Reed
Bed

Budworth Mere

Kennel
Wood

Cogshall Brook

Boat
House

MARBURY RD

STONE HEYES
LA

Houghlane
Farm

Claycroft
Farm

COGSHALL LA

Mill

Marbury Park
Country Park

P

Big Wood

76

CORONATION
GR

Barnton
Prim Sch

BROOMSFIELD

ROSEBANK
WLK

Rosebank
Sch

Liby

1 SWEET BRIER CL
2 FIRTREE CL
3 MAPLE GR
4 LARCHTREE CL

Barnton

Anderton

PO

Marina

Hopyards

BRINE PUMP
COTTS

UPLANDS RD

Uplands
Farm

Haydn
Pool

Cemy

PH

Trient and Mersey Canal

Cheshire Ring
Canal Walk

Cosgrove
Bsns Pk

Anderton Boat Lift
& Nature Park

Weaver Navigation

75

A533

OAKWOOD
HO

Tunnel

PO

RUDHEATH RD

Works

1 OLD SCHOOL CL
2 THE MEWS

SHEPHERDS
VIEW

Slicks
Bsns Ctr

CW8

Ropery
Farm

River Weaver

CANAL SIDE

WINNINGTON LA

SANDYBANK

HOLLYBANK CL

Winnington

Sewage
Works

Sewage
Works

WINNINGTON AVE

MOSS RD

B5374

PO

ELMRIDGE
WAY

HILLVIEW
RISE

BARN MDW

SPRING

THE
WOODLANDS

Victoria H

A533

WOTTON ST

Barnton Cut

74

63 A 64 B C 65 D E F

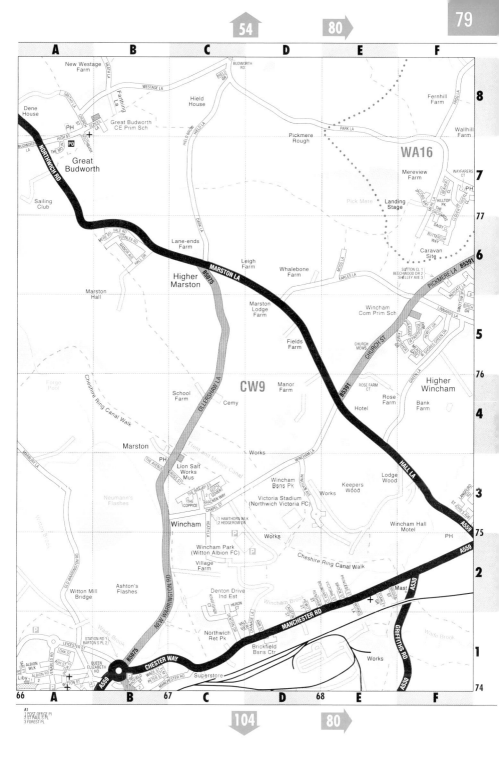

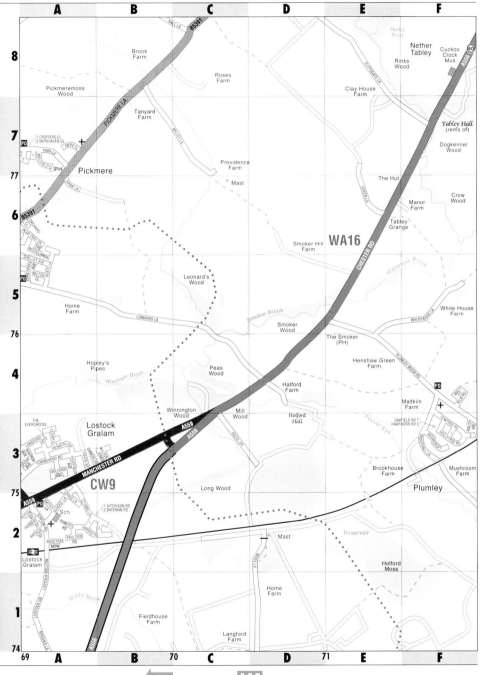

56
82

A   B   C   D   E   F

A556

TABLEY STABLES

Tabley House

Top Willowbed Wood

Blackhill Farm

MEADOW PK
BEXTON RD
GLOUCESTER RD
MALTON RD
ASHWORTH RD
ASHWORTH DR
BLACKHILL LA

8

Parkgate Farm

Bexton Prim Sch

Bexton House

BEXTON LA

Island Wood

Botany Bay Wood

SUDLOW LA

Serpentine Water

Yewtree Farm

7

77

Tabley Mere

Black Clump

Royd Wood

Parkside Farm

Bexton Hall

Bexton Wood

6

Parkside Cottage

Diamond Farm

Ullardhall Farm

Ash Wood

5

Nursery **WA16**

76

Wash Farm

Wood's Tenement

PINFOLD LA

Bucklow Farm

Hucknall Farm

Victoria Wood

4

Plumley

Beech House Farm

PH

Pinfold Farm

Holly Tree Farm

The Grange

Plumleylane Farm

3

75

PLUMLEY MOOR RD

Beech Farm

Merry Farm

Smithy Green

Heesom Green Farm

B5081

MIDDLEWICH RD

BROOK LA

2

TROUTHALL LA

Plumley Moor

Lower Peover Hall

CHEADLE LA

Moss Farm

CH

Fields Farm

Peover Eye

Brookfield House

FREE GREEN LA

East Brook

SOUTH PARK DR
BROOK

The Fields Farm

Lower Peover

PH
THE COBBLES

1

B5081

CROWN LA

Lower Peover CE Prim Sch

M6

74

72 A   B 73 C   D 74 E   F

106
82

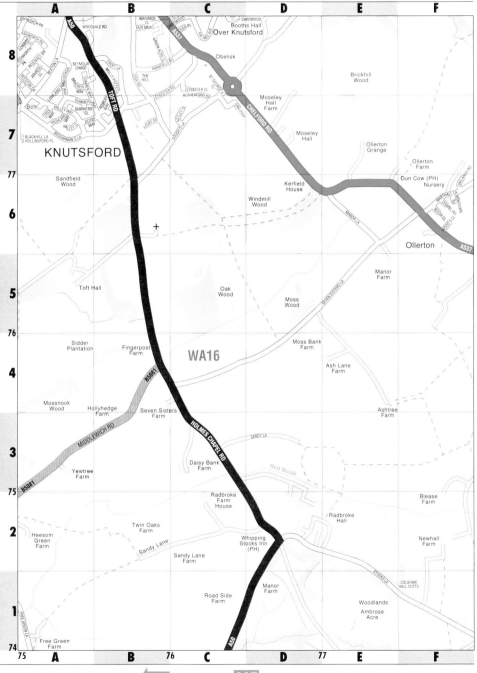

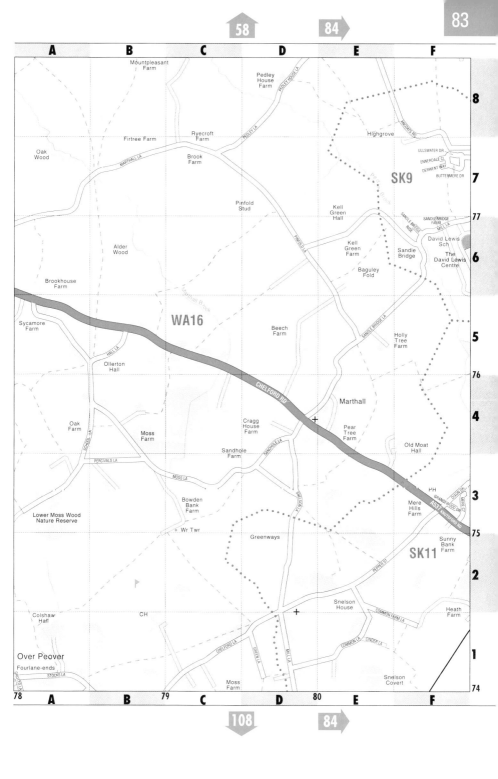

A B C D E F

8

WA16

Tanyard
Farm

Oswald
Farm

Little Moss
Farm

ABBERLEY
HALL

Field's
Farm

7

Heathgate
Farm

Sandpit Farm

SK9

GREEN LA

Manor
Farm

IVY HO

CHELFORD RD

PH

MILL LA

WARFORD CRES

Warford Hall
Farm

Dane Villa

Walton Farm

ORCHARD
CRES

77

David Lewis
Sch

David Lewis
Centre

Warford Hall

Grogram
Cottage

SOSSMOSS LA

6

Soss Moss
(Mary Dendy Unit)

H

WELSH ROW

Stelfoxes

Dean Green

Gatley Green
Farm

SAND LA

Dog Hole
Wood

Sossmoss Wood

Peckmill
Bottoms

Wyche's
Farm

NURSERY LA

5

Lomas's Bottom

76

Peck Mill
Farm

Corbishley
Bridge

Sossmoss
Hall

SK10

Heawood Hall
Farm

Firtree Farm

CARTER LA

Corbishley

Heawood
Hall

4

Callwood's
Moss

Line
Pits

Roadside
Farm

Sandle Heath

Chandler's
Farm

WOODLAND
END

MILL BANK

ALDERLEY RD

Yarwoods

3

Sch

ELMSTEAD RD

SK11

BOLLINGTON LA

ROBIN CL

ASTLE CT

Mere Farm

Bollington Pits

75

A537

KNUTSFORD RD

Chelford

DIXON
CT

2

Chelford

Yewtree
Cottages

Bloor's Pits

George's Wood

HOLMES CHAPEL RD

CHELFORD RDBT

PO

A535

Willow Gaff

Knowsley
Farm

CHELFORD RD

Fallows Hall
Farm

Dumville's
Farm

A537

1

74

81 A B 82 C D 83 E F

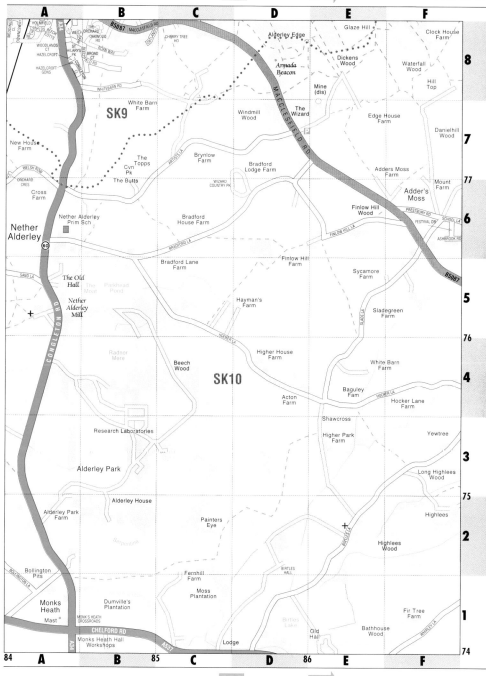

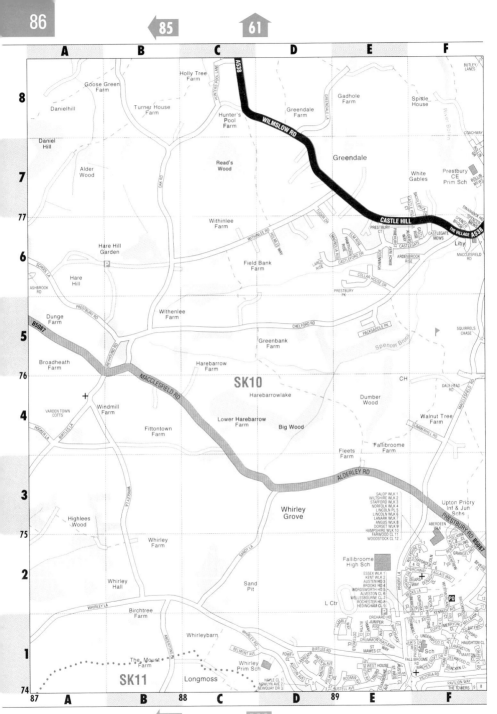

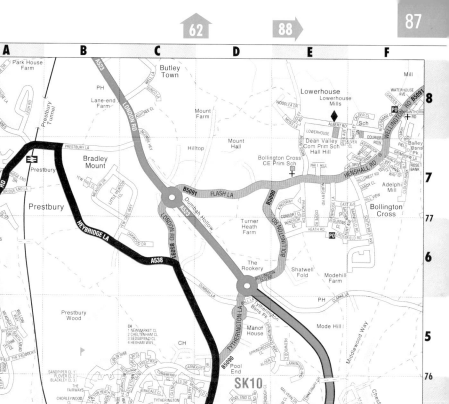

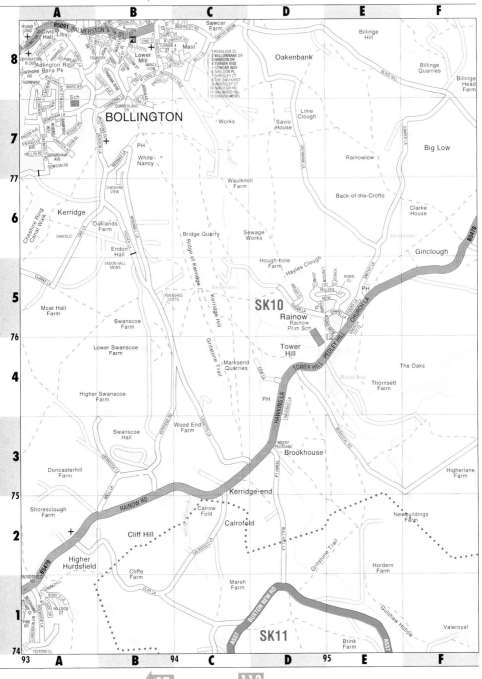

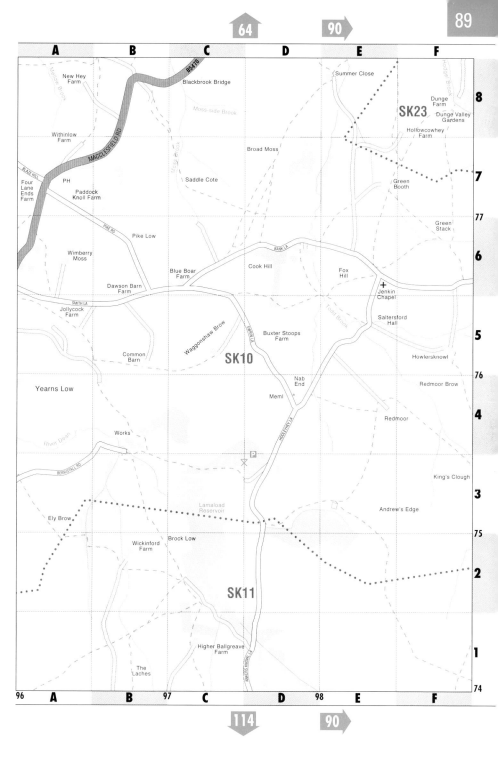

A B C D E F

8

SK23

New Hey
Farm

Blackbrook Bridge

Summer Close

Dunge
Farm

Dunge Valley
Gardens

Moss-side Brook

Withinlow
Farm

Hollowcowhey
Farm

Broad Moss

MACCLESFIELD RD

B5470

7

BLACK HILL

Four
Lane
Ends
Farm

PH

Paddock
Knoll Farm

Saddle Cote

Green
Booth

77

PIKE RD

Pike Low

Green
Stack

6

Wimberry
Moss

Blue Boar
Farm

BANK LA

Cook Hill

Fox
Hill

Jenkin
Chapel

Dawson Barn
Farm

Saltersford
Hall

SMITH LA

Jollycock
Farm

Waggonshaw Brow

SK10

Buxter Stoops
Farm

Todd Brook

5

Howlersknowl

Common
Barn

Nab
End

76

Yearns Low

Meml

Redmoor Brow

River Dean

Works

Redmoor

4

BERRISTALL RD

P

King's Clough

3

Lamaload
Reservoir

Andrew's Edge

Ely Brow

75

Wickinford
Farm

Brock Low

2

SK11

Higher Ballgreave
Farm

1

The
Laches

74

96 A B 97 C D 98 E F

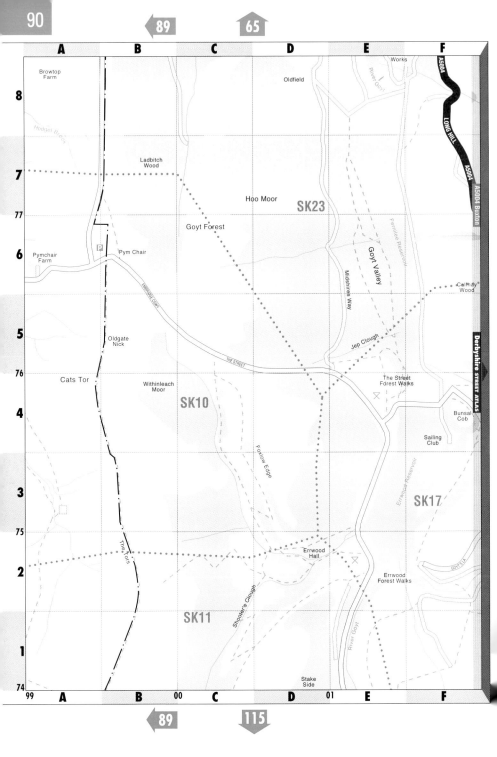

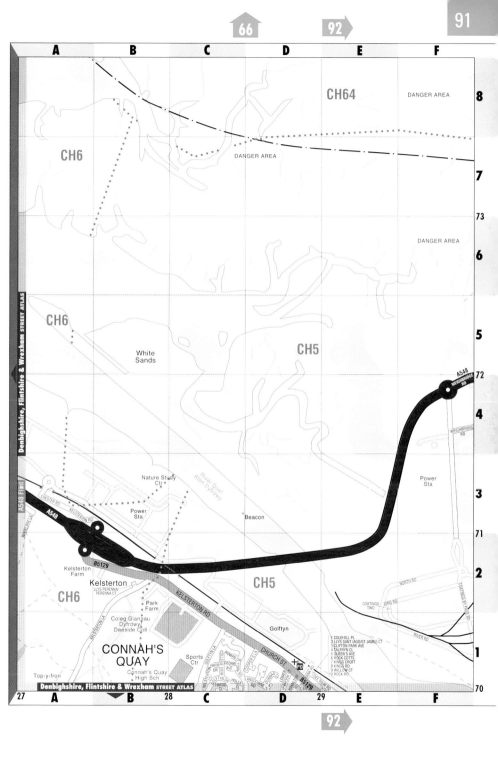

| | A | B | C | D | E | F |

8 CH64 · DANGER AREA

CH6 · DANGER AREA

7

73

DANGER AREA

6

CH6 · CH5

White Sands

5

A548 WEIGHBRIDGE RD **72**

4 WEIGHBRIDGE RD

Nature Study Ctr · River Dee Afon Cyfrdwy · Power Sta

3

CHESTER RD · KELSTERTON RD · Power Sta · Beacon

A548 · A548 Flint

B5129 · **71**

Kelsterton Farm · **2**

Kelsterton · LLYS PERENNA PERENNA CT

CH6 · Park Farm · KELSTERTON RD · CH5

Golftyn

NORTH RD

COATINGS TWO · KING RD · COATINGS BYPASS RD

RIVER RD

Coleg Glannau Dyfrdwy Deeside Coll

CONNAH'S QUAY · Sports Ctr · CHURCH ST

1 COLEHILL PL
2 LLYS SANT IAGO/ST JAMES CT
3 CLIFTON PARK AVE
4 TALFRYN CL
5 QUEEN'S AVE
6 ROCK COTTS
7 KINGS CROFT
8 KINGS
9 WILLOW CT
10 ROCK RD

PO · B5129

Top-y-fron · Connah's Quay High Sch · **1**

27 A | B **28** C | D **29** E | F **70**

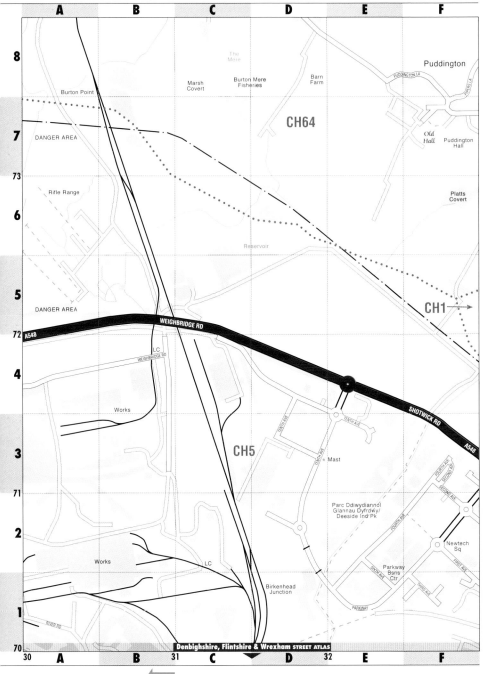

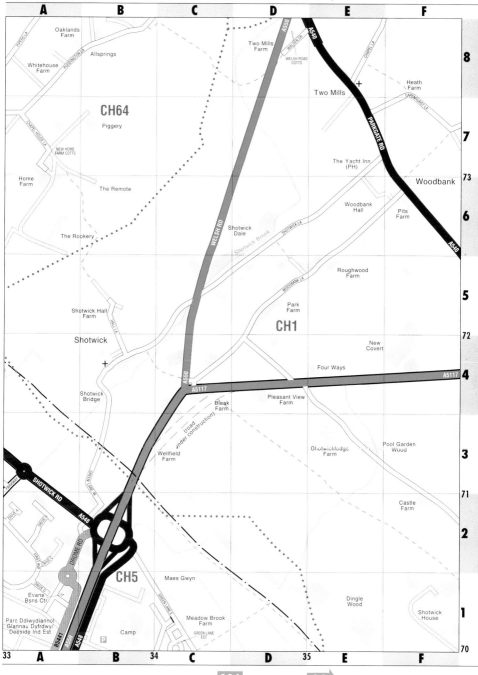

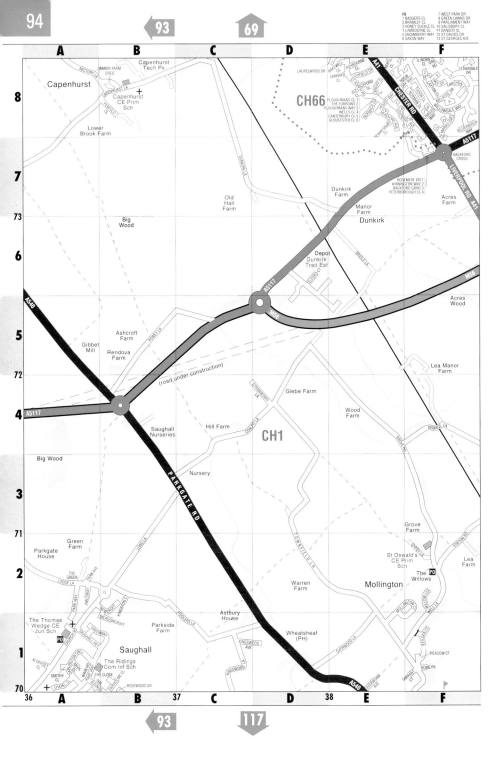

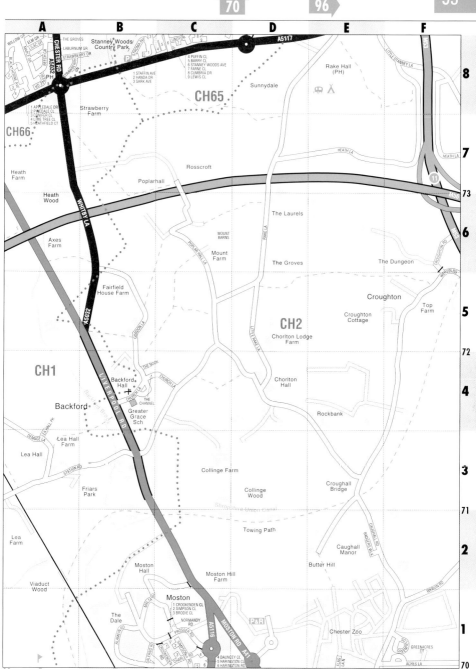

A   **B**   **C**   **D**   **E**   **F**

WILLOW GR
ELM GR
CHESTER RD A5032
BLACKHORSE LA
THE GROVES
ABURNUM GR
STRAWBERRY DR
Stanney Woods
Country Park

8

PH

1 STAFFIN AVE
2 HANDA DR
3 SARK AVE

4 PUFFIN CL
5 BARRY CL
6 STANNEY WOODS AVE
7 FARNE CL
8 CUMBRIA DR
9 LEWIS CL

LUNDY DR

A5117

Rake Hall
(PH)

Sunnydale

CH65

1 APPLEDALE DR
2 PINEDALE CL
3 CONIFER CL
4 LIME TREE CL
5 HEATHFIELD CT

Strawberry
Farm

CH66

7

Heath
Farm

HEATH LA

WHITBY LA

Heath
Wood

Rosscroft

Poplarhall

73

6

Axes
Farm

MOUNT
BARNS

The Laurels

RAKE LA

The Dungeon

CROUGHTON RD

POPLAR HALL LA

Mount
Farm

The Groves

Fairfield
House Farm

A5032

GORDON LA

Croughton

Croughton
Cottage

WEAVEN RD

Top
Farm

5

CH2

LITTLE RAKE LA

Chorlton Lodge
Farm

72

CH1

THE NOOK

LIVERPOOL RD

Backford
Hall

Backford

CHURCH LA

THE
CHANNEL

Greater
Grace
Sch

Chorlton
Hall

Rockbank

4

Barrow Bk Ns

DEMAGE LA

LEA HALL PK

Lea Hall

Lea Hall
Farm

STATION RD

Collinge Farm

Collinge
Wood

Croughall
Bridge

3

Friars
Park

Shropshire Union Canal

71

Lea
Farm

Towing Path

Caughall
Manor

CAUGHALL RD

BADGERS RAKE LA

2

Viaduct
Wood

Moston
Hall

Moston Hill
Farm

Butter Hill

WEAVEN RD

The
Dale

ALLANSON RD

Moston

MAIN RD

1 CROOKENDEN CL
2 SIMPSON CL
3 BRODIE CL

NORMANDY
RD

A5116

MOSTON RD A41

P&R

Chester Zoo

SOUTH GREEN RD

GREENACRES
CT

1

PROSSER RD

SHEPPEY RD

CHARLES RD

4 DAUNCEY CL
5 HARINGTON CL
6 HARINGTON RD

FLAG
LA

ACHES LA

70

39   **A**   **B**   **40**   **C**   **D**   **41**   **E**   **F**

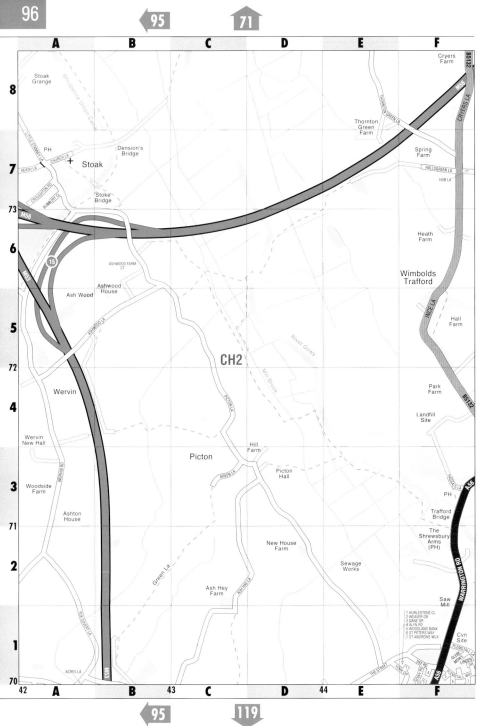

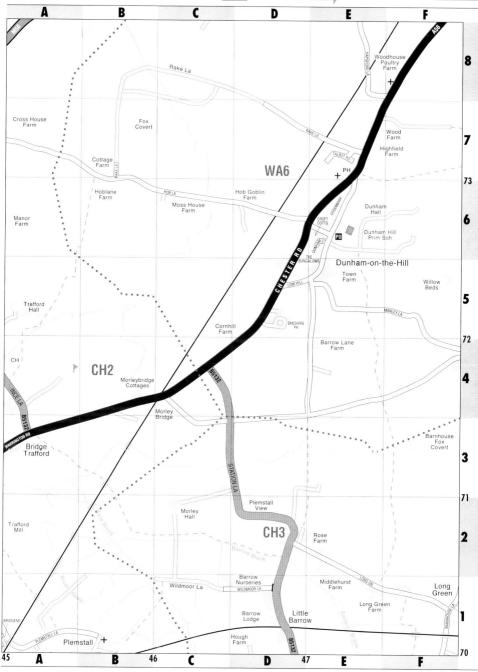

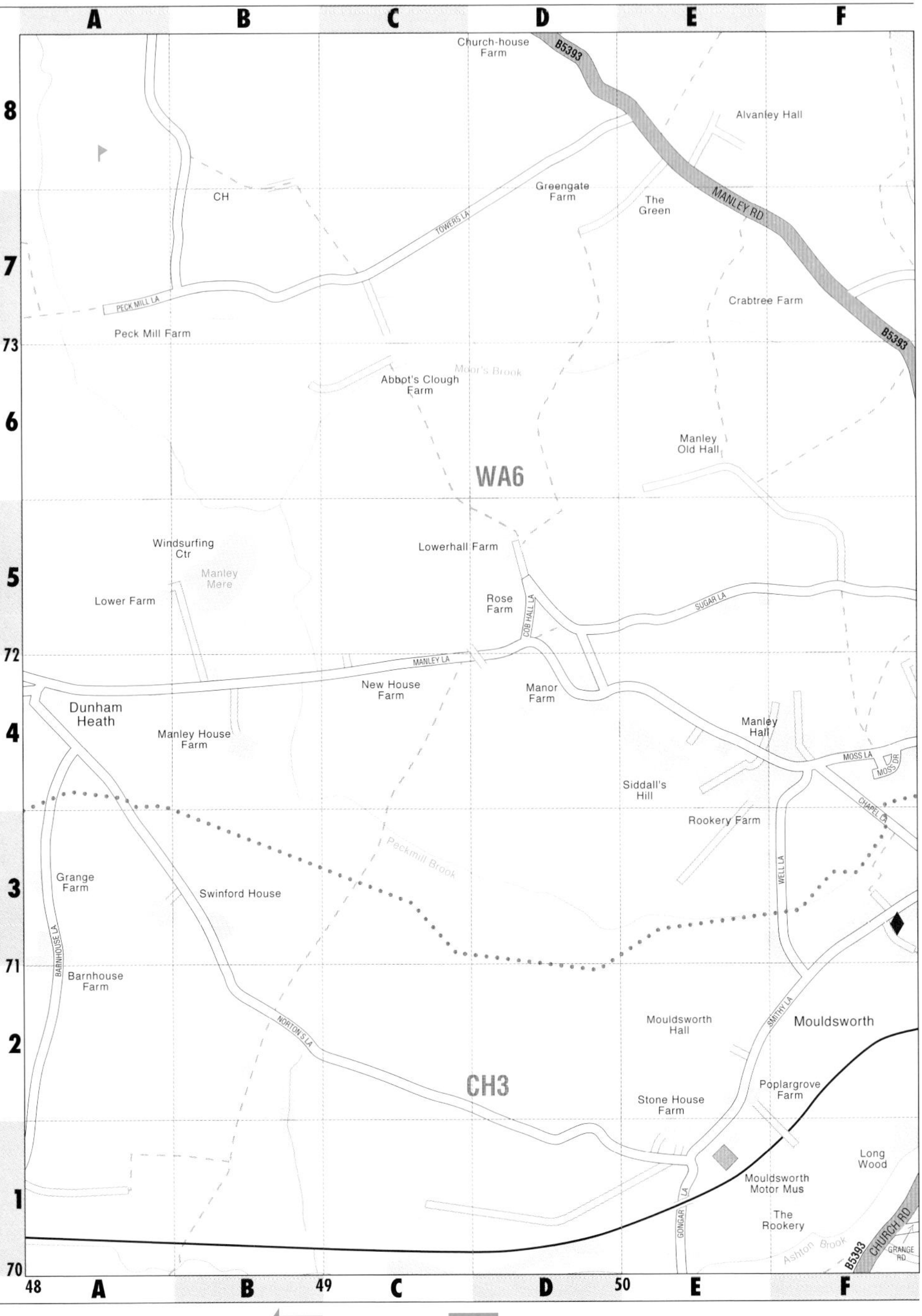
A
B
C
D
E
F
8
7
73
6
5
72
4
3
71
2
1
70
48
49
50
Church-house Farm
B5393
Alvanley Hall
CH
Greengate Farm
The Green
MANLEY RD
TOWERS LA
PECK MILL LA
Crabtree Farm
Peck Mill Farm
B5393
Moor's Brook
Abbot's Clough Farm
Manley Old Hall
WA6
Windsurfing Ctr
Lowerhall Farm
Manley Mere
Lower Farm
Rose Farm
SUGAR LA
COB HALL LA
MANLEY LA
New House Farm
Manor Farm
Dunham Heath
Manley Hall
Manley House Farm
MOSS LA
MOSS DR
Siddall's Hill
CHAPEL LA
Rookery Farm
Peckmill Brook
Grange Farm
WELL LA
Swinford House
BARNHOUSE LA
Barnhouse Farm
SMITHY LA
Mouldsworth Hall
Mouldsworth
NORTON'S LA
CH3
Poplargrove Farm
Stone House Farm
Long Wood
Mouldsworth Motor Mus
The Rookery
GONGAR LA
Ashton Brook
B5393
CHURCH RD
GRANGE RD

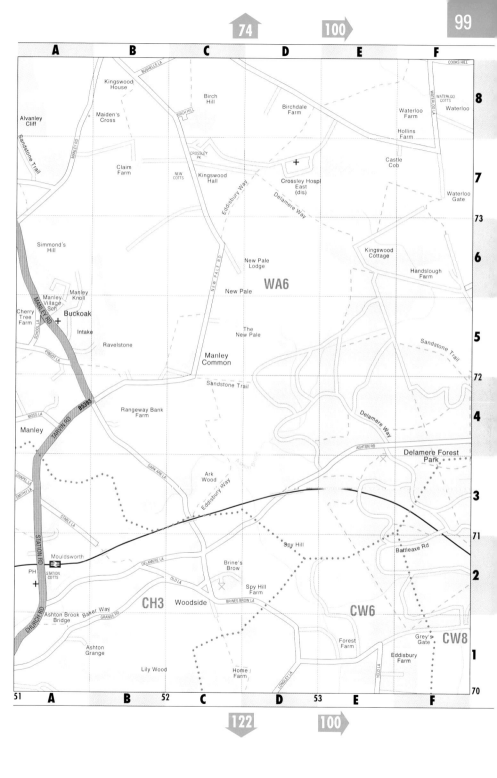

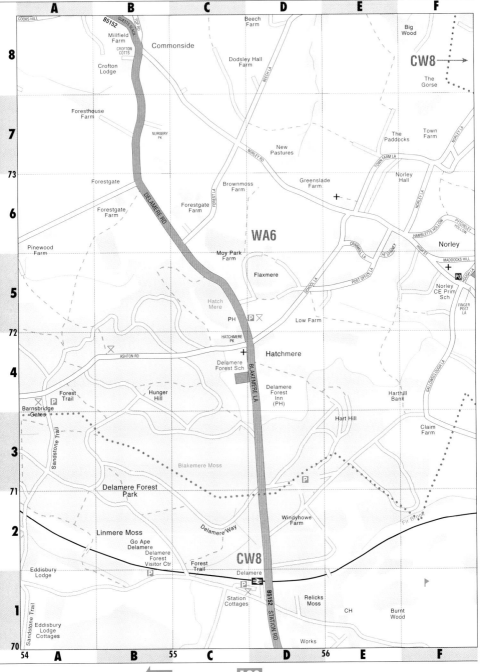

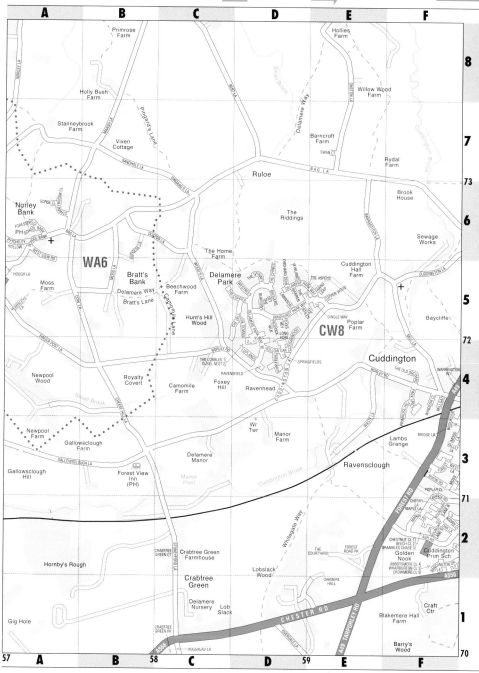

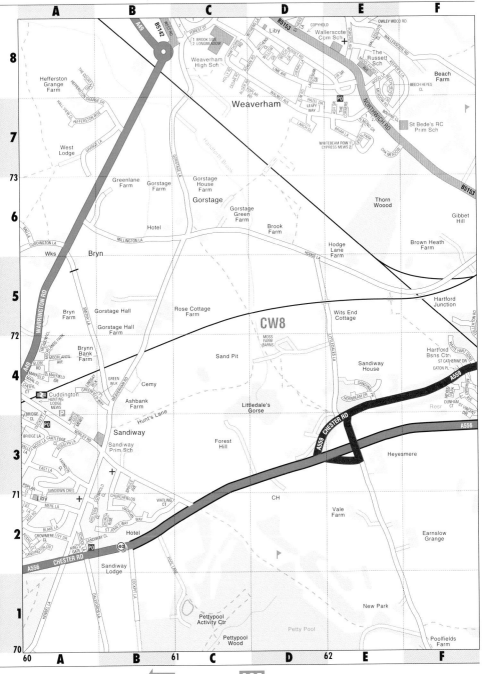

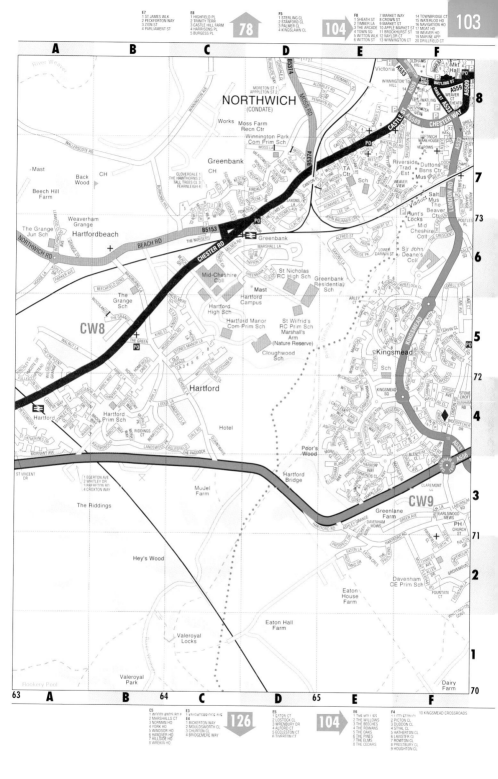

A8
1 JOHN ST
2 CRUM HILL
3 MEADOW ST
4 WESLEY PL
5 ST HELEN S RD

B8
1 ALVINGHAM CL
2 KELSTERN CL
3 BIRKDALE CT
4 MANCHESTER RD
5 SLADE ST
6 WILLIAM ST

7 SIDDALL ST
8 SALKELD ST

103

79

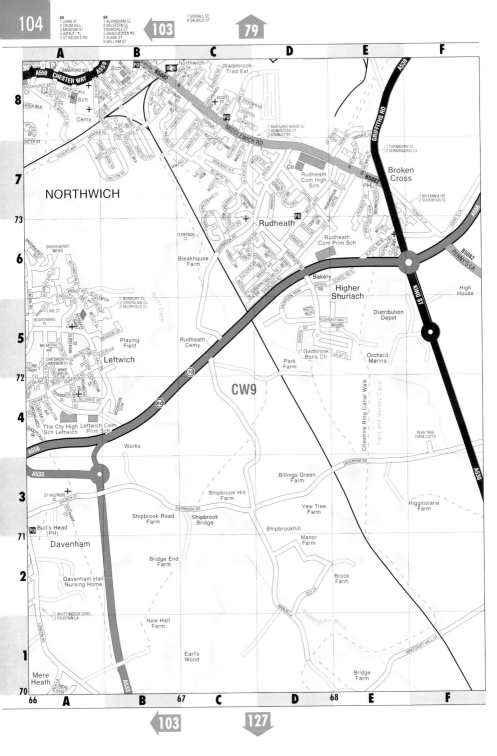

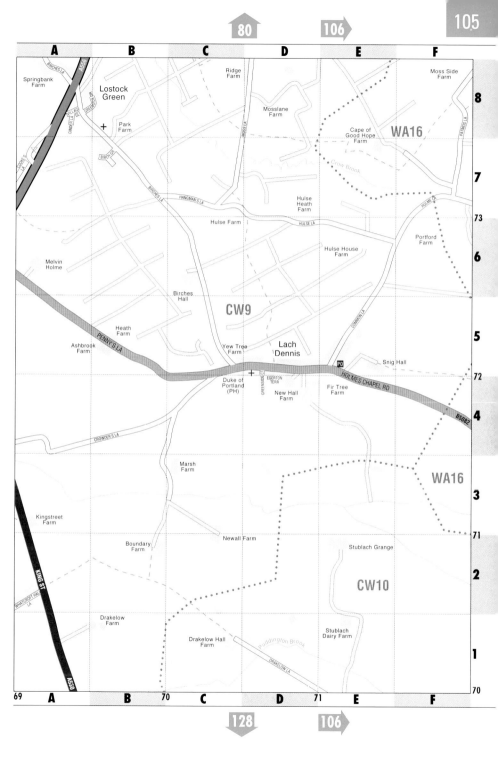

Map Grid Labels

A B C D E F

8

Cheadle Farm
Crown Lane Farm
CROWN LA
B5081
Parkside Farm
Mill Bank Farm
Foxcovers

New Farm
CHEADLE LA
BACK LA
Back Lanes Farm
Crown Inn (PH)
Swan Green
Yewtree Farm

Daniel Eye

7

Backlane Farm
Mast
BIRCHENDOD DR
CHERRY WALK
HOLLY TREE DRI
FOXCOVERT LA
Heath Farm

Millgate Farm
HULME LA
Birch Farm
Springfield
HEATH LA
SANDY LA

73

Hulme Covert
BAKER'S LA
Bradstone Brook
Springbank Farm
Bradshaw House
Heath Farm

6

CW9
Hulme Hall
Graybrook Farm
TOWNFIELD LA

Bradshawbrook Farm
Old Mill Farm
Townfield Farm

5

WA16
Chapel Farm
MIDDLEWICH RD
+

72

HULME HALL LA
Washlone Farm
DAMS LA

4

B5082
Hole House
Hole House Wood
Motel
A50

Highfield House
Allostock Hall
HOLE LA
Axon's Smithy Farm
CHAPEL LA
Allostock
Brookhouse Farm
BROOK VIEW

3

HOLMES CHAPEL RD
Three Greyhounds (PH)
Shakerley Mere
WEST LA
Chapel House Farm
PRINCESS RD
LONDON RD
Widow's Home Farm

Sculshaw Green Farm
B5081

71

Sandhole Farm

2

Chestnut House Farm
The Croft
Woodlands Farm
WOODLANDS CVN PK
Rudheath Woods
Newplatt Wood

CW10
Stublach Farm
KING'S LA
King's Lane Farm
NORTHWICH RD
SANDY LA
NEW PLATT LA
CW4

1

Works

Earnshaw House Farm
B5081
KNUTSFORD RD
A50
B5082
Warrington Common

70

72 A B 73 C D 74 E F

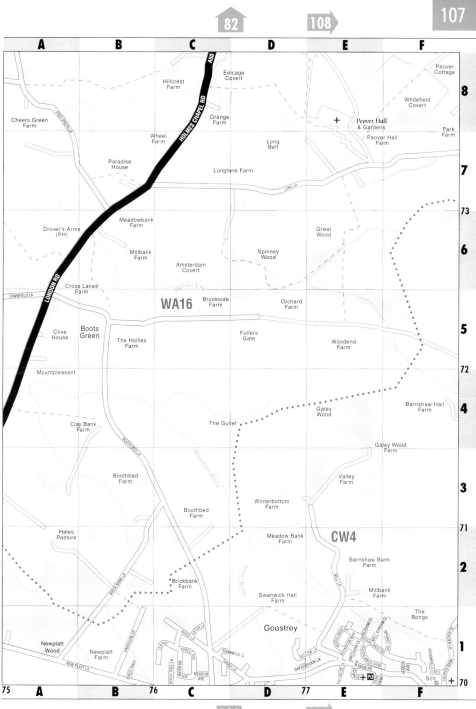

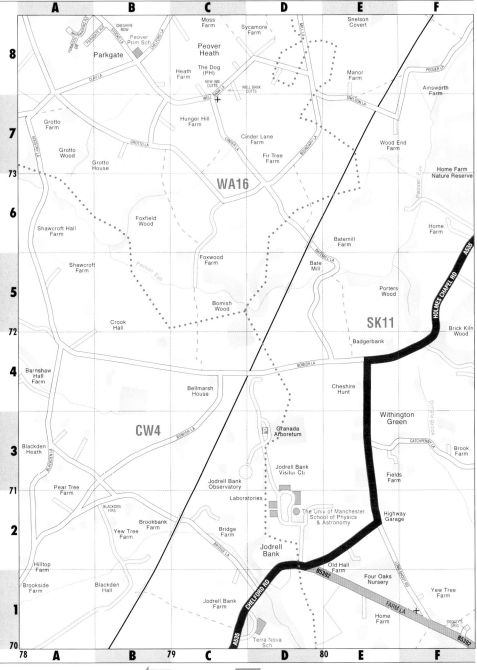

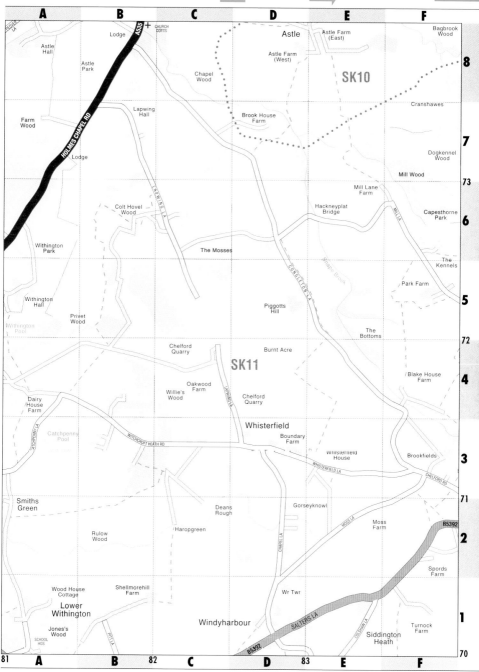

A B C D E F

8

Bagbrook Wood
Bridge Wood
A34
Bagbrook Bridge
Birtles Hill Farm
Birtles Bridge
CHELFORD RD
WHIRLEY LA
A537
Pale Farm
Pale Lodge
Bagbrook Farm
SK10

Home Farm
North Lodge
Cranshawes
7
Big Wood

Park Plantation
Ley Plantation
Henbury Hall

73
Capesthorne Park
Marlheath Farm
The Cave

6
Capesthorne Hall
East Lodge
Smithy Wood
Henbury Smithy
SCHOOL LA

CONGLETON RD
Lingards Farm
Huntley Wood
BEARHURST LA

Lodge Farm
Sandbach Wood

5
MILL LA
Boathouse Covert
SK11
Henbury Moss
Bearhurst Farm

72
Fanshawe
Sycamore Farm
FANSHAWE LA
Henbury Moss Farm

4
Redes Mere
Fanshawe Brook

Redesmere Farm
REDESMERE LA
Hills Green Farm
Hazelwall Wood
Hazelwall
B5392

NURSERY LA
P
Thornycroft Farm

3
Siddington
PEXHILL RD
Thornycroft Hall

71
CHELFORD RD
PO
B5392
Simon's Wood
Simonswood
HENSHAW LA
Keepers Cottages
Thorneycroft Pools

B5392
Buck's Hill
Pyethorne Wood

2
Meadow Bank
Siddington Hall Farm
Henshaw Hall Farm
Walkersheath

Snape Brook

1
Ettily Wood
Heskey Wood
Hammerpool Wood
Ranker's Ford

A34
Horse Wood
Moss Woo
MARTIN LA

70

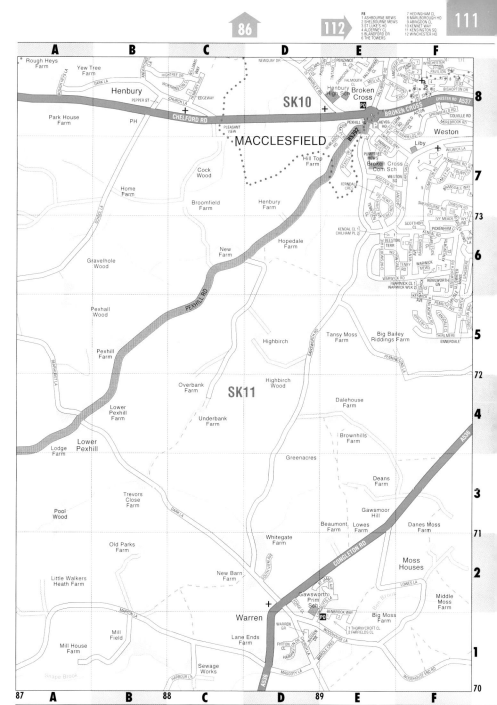

F8
1 ASHBOURNE MEWS
2 SHELBOURNE MEWS
3 ST LUKE'S HO
4 ALDERNEY CL
5 BLANDFORD DR
6 THE TOWERS

7 HEDINGHAM CL
8 MARLBOROUGH HO
9 ABINGDON CL
10 KENNET WAY
11 KENSINGTON SQ
12 WINCHESTER HO

A B C D E F

8

Rough Heys Farm
Yew Tree Farm
Henbury
Park House Farm
PH
PEPPER ST
CHELFORD RD
CHURCH LA
EDGEWAY
PLEASANT VIEW
WILLIAMS WAY
HIGHTREE DR
WORTHINGTON
TENBY RISE
KNIGHT FIELDS

NEWQUAY DR
SCHOLARS
WHITLEY RD
PENZANCE
TINTAGEL CL
FALMOUTH CL
MEG LA

SK10
Henbury High Sch
Broken Cross
PO
BISHOPTON DR
CHESTER RD A537
COLVILLE RD
BREBROOK RD
Weston
WILWICK LA
WINCHESTER PAVILION

MACCLESSFIELD
A537
PEXHILL RD

Cock Wood
Hill Top Farm
Broomfield Farm
Henbury Farm
Hopedale Farm
New Farm
Home Farm

Broken Cross Com Sch
WESTON
FERNDALE CRES
PUMPTREE MEWS
PARKETT
PRINCES WAY
HEYES HO
BOSTOCK RD
KENDAL CL 1
CHILHAM PL 2
BEESTON TERR
PICKENHAM
SCOTTHOPE CL
Liby
PEMBROKE RD
WANSDALE WAY
SHERBOURNE RD
DAWSON RD
IVY MEADE
WARWICK MEWS
KENILWORTH GN
CRANMERE
WARWICK RD
WARWICK CL 1
WARWICK WLK 2
KESWICK AVE
PENRITH
ENNERDALE
THIRLMERE

7

73

6

Gravelhole Wood
Pexhall Wood
Pexhill Farm
SCHOOL LA
BEARHURST LA
PEXHILL RD

Highbirch
LONGWORTH RD

Tansy Moss Farm
Big Bailey Riddings Farm

5

72

Overbank Farm
SK11
Highbirch Wood
Underbank Farm
Lower Pexhill Farm
Lodge Farm
Lower Pexhill
DARK LA

Dalehouse Farm
Brownhills Farm
Greenacres
Deans Farm
A536

4

3

71

Pool Wood
Trevors Close Farm
Old Parks Farm
Beaumont Farm
Lowes Farm
Gawsmoor Hill
Danes Moss Farm
Moss Houses

Little Walkers Heath Farm
New Barn Farm
SOUTH VIEW AVE
Gawsworth Prim Sch
Big Moss Farm
1 THORNYCROFT CL
2 FARFIELDS CL
LOWES LA
Middle Moss Farm

2

Mill House Farm
Mill Field
MARTON LA
Warren
Lane Ends Farm
WARREN GR
PYTTON LA
HARRI
CHURCH LA
WOODHOUSE LA
BENBROOK WAY
PO
WADDLE CRES
MAGGOTY LA
HARBOUR LA
Sewage Works
A536
WOODHOUSE END RD
CONGLETON RD

1

Snape Brook

70

F7
1 VICARAGE WAY
2 DUDLEY WLK
3 PEVERIL WLK
4 PORTLAND WLK
5 SOMERTON CL
6 WARDOUR CL

7 COUNTESS CL
8 WAKEHAM CHASE
9 HILTON CL
10 IVY MEADE CL
11 DAWSON CL

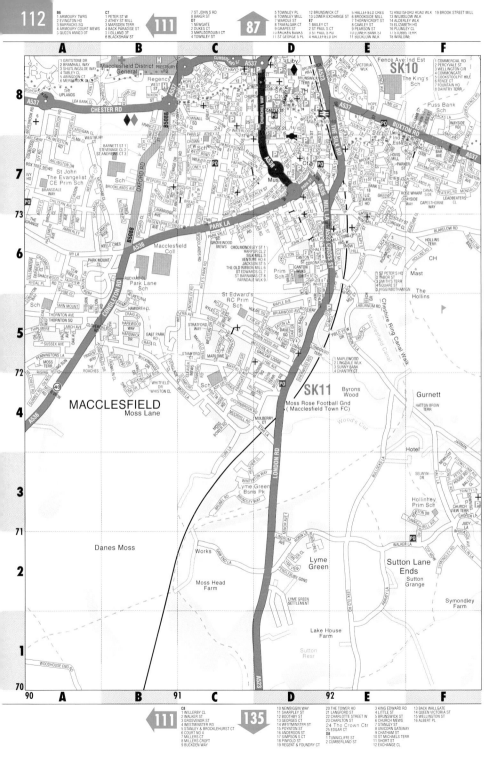

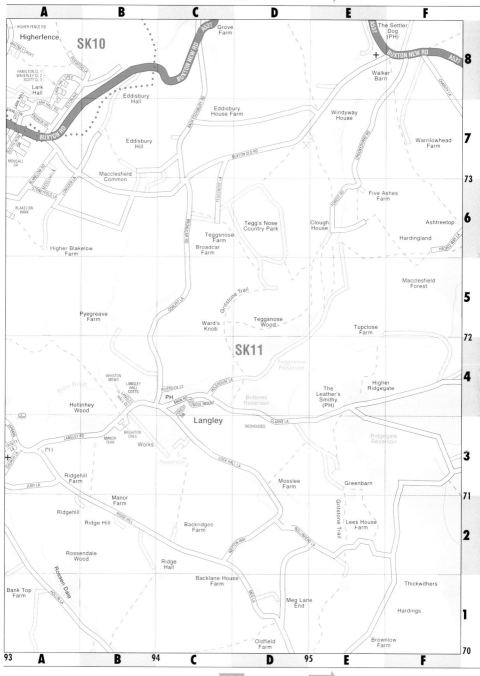

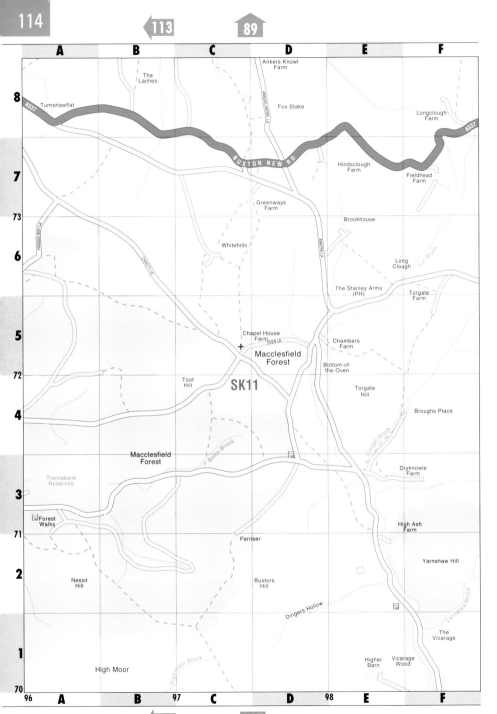

113

89

A B C D E F

Ankers Knowl
Farm

The
Laches

8 Turnshawflat A537 Fox Stake

ANKERS KNOWL LA

Longclough
Farm

A537

BUXTON NEW RD

7 Hindsclough
Farm

Fieldhead
Farm

73 Greenways
Farm

Brookhouse

HACKED WAY LA

ANKERS LA

6 Whitehills

Long
Clough

Fur Brook

The Stanley Arms
(PH)

Torgate
Farm

Chapel House
Farm

OVEN LA

Chambers
Farm

5 + Macclesfield
Forest

Bottom-of-
the-Oven

72 Toot
Hill

SK11

Torgate
Hill

Broughs Place

4

Clough Brook

Macclesfield
Forest

Bollin Brook

P Dryknowle
Farm

Trentabank
Reservoir

3

P Forest
Walks

High Ash
Farm

71 Ferriser

Yarnshaw Hill

Lowerhead Brook

2 Nessit
Hill

Buxtors
Hill

P

Dingers Hollow

The
Vicarage

1 Vicarage
Wood

Higher
Barn

High Moor

Highmoor Brook

70

96 A B 97 C D 98 E F

113

137

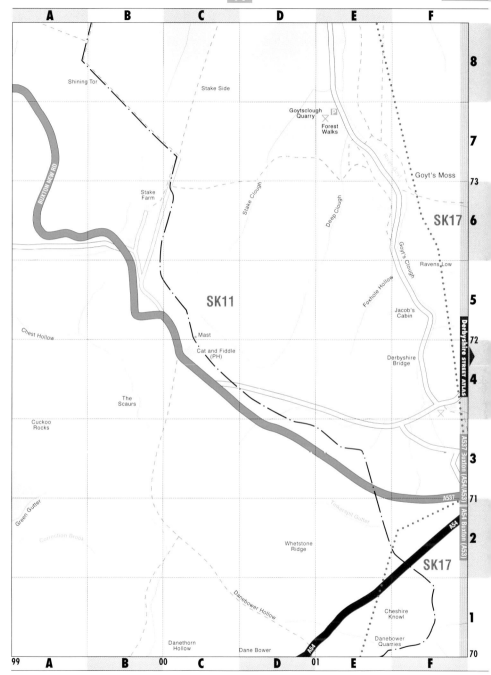

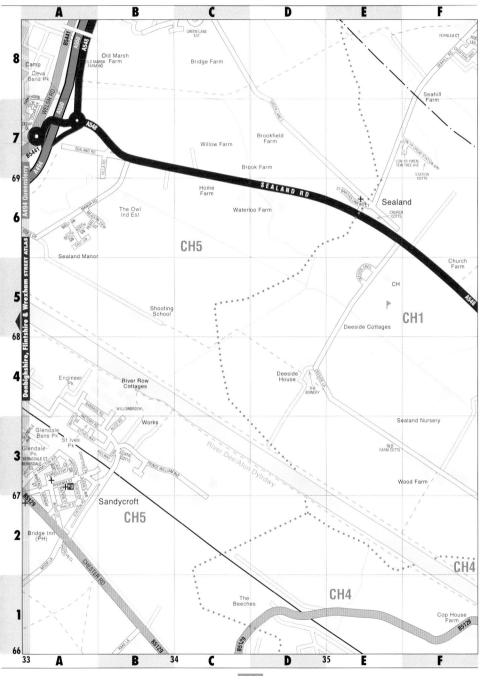

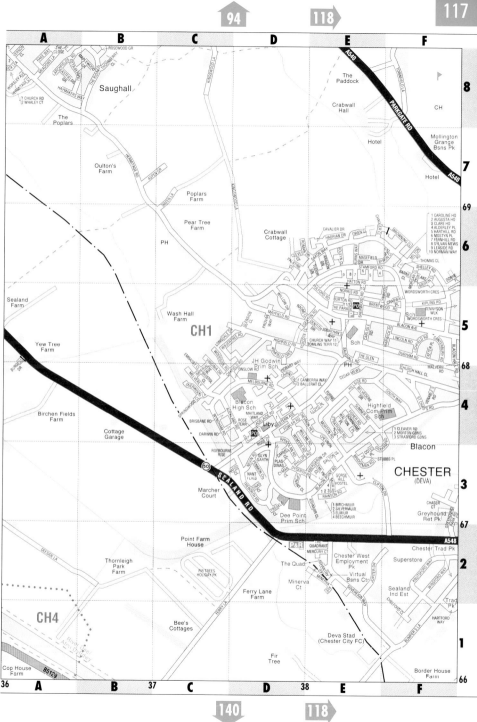

94
118
140
118

Saughall

The Poplars

Oulton's Farm

Poplars Farm

Pear Tree Farm

Crabwall Cottage

The Paddock

Crabwall Hall

Hotel

Mollington Grange Bsns Pk

Hotel

Sealand Farm

Yew Tree Farm

Wash Hall Farm

CH1

Birchen Fields Farm

Cottage Garage

Blacon High Sch

JH Godwin Prim Sch

Highfield Com Prim Sch

Blacon

CHESTER (DEVA)

Chaser Ct

Greyhound Ret Pk

Marcher Court

Dee Point Prim Sch

Thornleigh Park Farm

Point Farm House

Ferry Lane Farm

The Quadrant
Mercury Ct

The Quad

Minerva Ct

Chester West Employment Pk

Virtual Bsns Ctr

Chester Trad Pk

Superstore

Sealand Ind Est

Trad Pk

Hartford Way

CH4

Bee's Cottages

Fir Tree

Deva Stad (Chester City FC)

Cop House Farm

Border House Farm

1 CAROLINE HO
2 AUGUSTA HO
3 CLARE HO
4 ALDERLEY PL
5 MARTHILL RD
6 MOSTYN PL
7 FERNHILL RD
8 SYLVAN MEWS
9 LEASIDE RD
10 NORMAN WAY

1 CLEAVER RD
2 MORTON GDNS
3 STRATFORD GDNS

1 BIRCHMUIR
2 SILVERMUIR
3 ELMUIR
4 BEECHMUIR

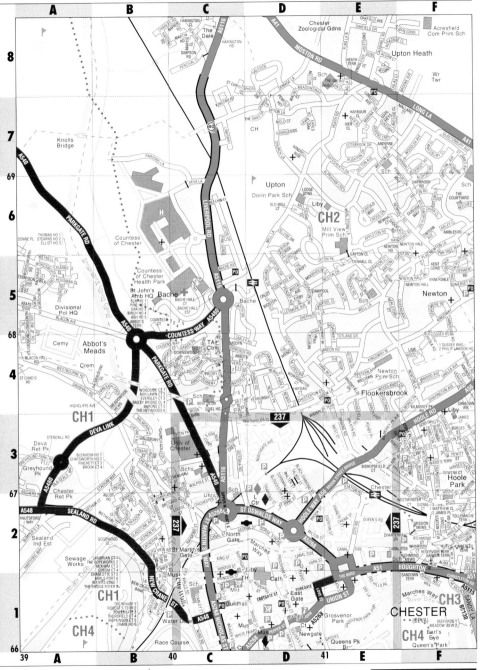

For full street detail of the
highlighted area see page
237.

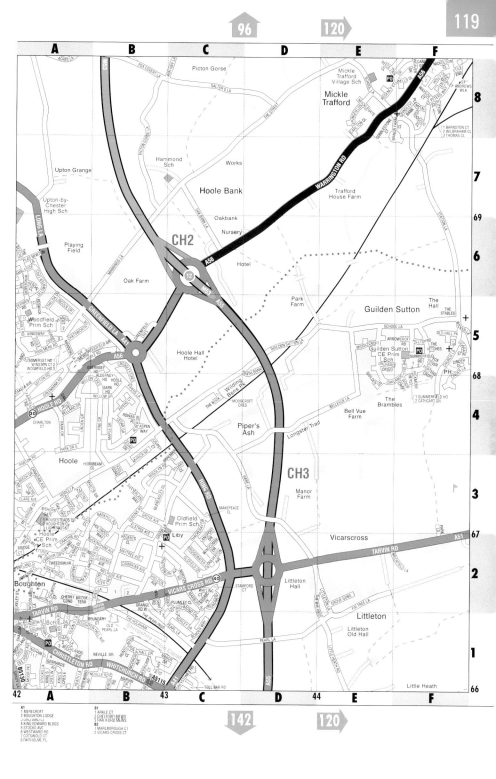

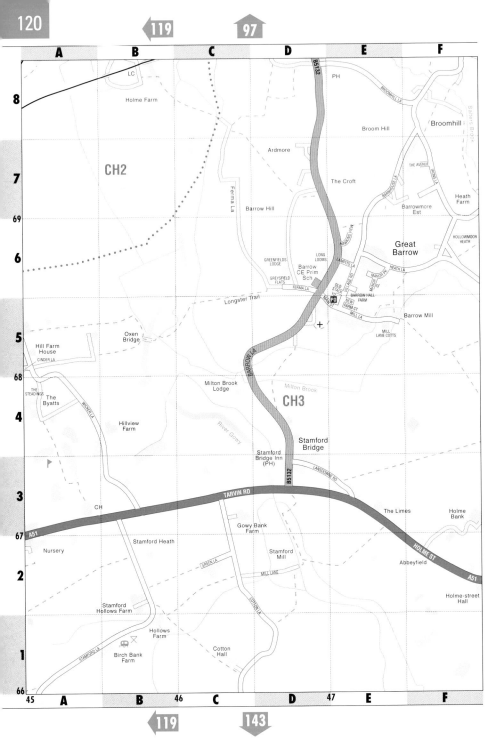

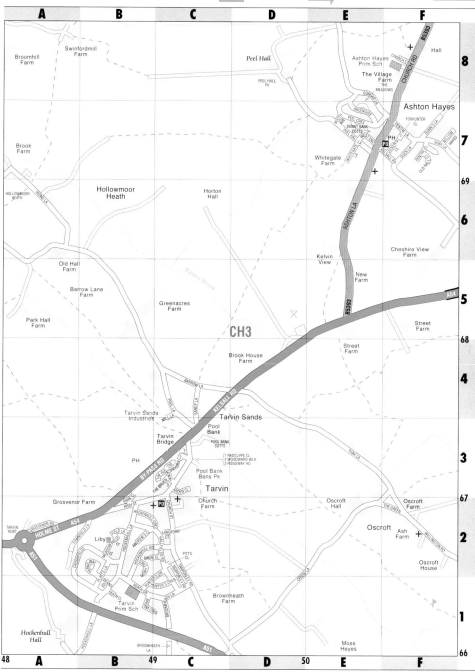

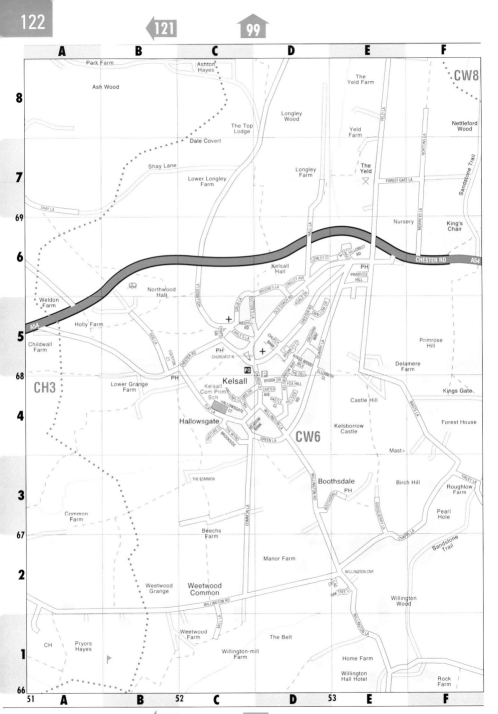

CW8

Park Farm

Ash Wood

Ashton Hayes

The Top Lodge

Dale Covert

Shay Lane

Lower Longley Farm

Longley Wood

Longley Farm

The Yeld Farm

Yeld Farm

The Yeld

Nettleford Wood

YELD LA

FOREST GATE LA

MORRIS LA

NORTH LA

Sandstone Trail

SHAY LA

Nursery

King's Chair

CHESTER RD

A54

Kelsall Hall

Weldon Farm

Northwood Hall

HOLLANDS LA

DUTTON'S LA

HALL LA

EMLEY CT

HILLCREST

PH

PRIMROSE HILL

BROOM S LA

LONGLEY AVE

FIDALE RD

OLD COACH RD

CHESTER RD

OAKS CL

ASH GR

A54

Holly Farm

Childwall Farm

DICK LA

EGERTON CT

CHAPEL LA

GRUB LA

GR

REDHILL RD

EAGLES LA

CHURCH BANK

BEAMLEY CT

KINGS WOOD WLK

THE DELL

ORCHARD WAY

QUARRY LA

ELIZABETH CL

Primrose Hill

Delamere Farm

Kings Gate

CH3

Lower Grange Farm

PH

PH

CHESTER RD

CROFTS RD

Kelsall Com Prim Sch

PO

P

Kelsall

BROOKSIDE

CARTER AVE

CASTLE CL

FOX HILL

WILLINGTON RD

Castle Hill

Kelsborrow Castle

Forest House

Hallowsgate

HALLOWSGATE CT

FLAT LA

PASTURES

THE WYND

MEADOW BANK

GREEN LA

CW6

Boothsdale

PH

Birch Hill

Roughlow Farm

Mast

TIRLEY LA

THE COMMON

COMMON LA

Beechs Farm

Manor Farm

WILLINGTON RD

BOOTHSDALE

GOOSEBERRY LA

CHEES LA

Pearl Hole

Sandstone Trail

Common Farm

Willington Wood

Weetwood Grange

Weetwood Common

WILLINGTON RD

WILLINGTON CNR

OAK TREE

Willington Wood

CH

Pryors Hayes

Weetwood Farm

MILL LA

Willington-mill Farm

The Belt

Home Farm

WILLINGTON LA

Willington Hall Hotel

Rock Farm

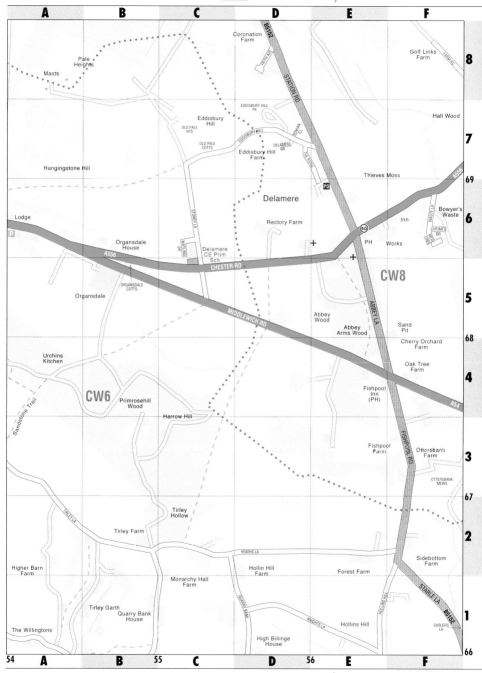

123
101

	A	B	C	D	E	F

8

Crown Farm

A556
CHESTER RD

CRABTREE
GREEN PK

Masseys
Lodge

CW8

Whitegate Way

Cheshire
Kennels

OVERDALE LA
A49

FARM RD

OAKMERE
BARNS
Delamere
Lodge

CROWN
COTTS

Oakmere

7

A556

MOSSHALL LA

Sand Pit

Nunsmere

KENNEL LA

Reeking
Hole

69

Fourways
Sand Quarry

Hogshead
Wood

Shemmy
Moss

6

Waste
Farm

Nunsmere
Hall
Hotel

Abbotsmoss
Wood

Folly
Farm

Horse Training Ground

Abbotsmoss
Hall

5

Keeper's
Cottage

TARPORLEY RD

Abbots Moss

CW7

68

Oak Mere

Polo Ground

SHAY'S LA

4

Corner
Farm

Greenlands

Spring
Farm

Shaw's
Farm

Shay's
Farm

A54

Cabbage Hall
(PH)

Shay's Lane Brook

3

Sandymere
Plantation

Sandybrow

Stonehouse
Farm

CW6

LONGSTONE LA

CW7

Sandymere
House

Common Side

67

Shrewsbury Arms
(PH)

Butts
Farm

A54

Moss Hall
Farm

2

Rosebank
Farm

Heathfield

BEECH RD

Oaktree
Farm

WHITEHILL LA

SHOP LA

Burslem Cottage
Farm

RACECOURSE LA

COACH RD

Sunnybank
Farm

SPONGE BLACK

PICKS RD

1

Sandiford
Lodge

Polo
Ground

A49

White
hall

Poolhead
Farm

SADLERS LA

BS152
STARE LA

66

57	A	**58**	B	C	**58**	D	**59**	E	F

123
147

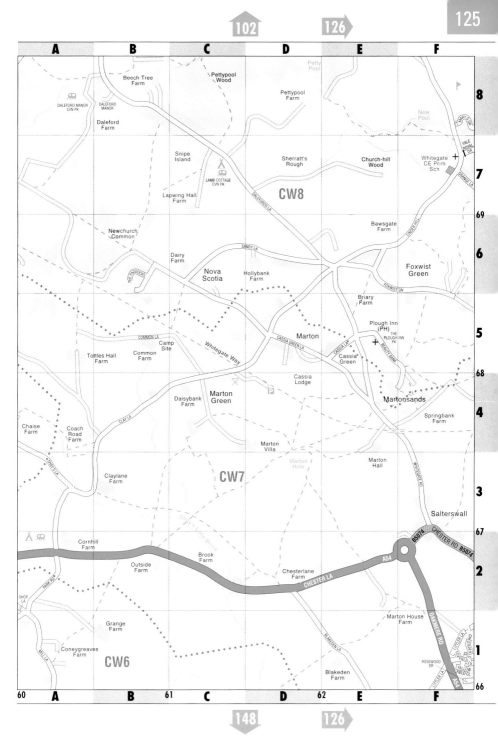

A · B · C · D · E · F

8

7

69

6

5

68

4

3

67

2

66

Beech Tree Farm

Pettypool Wood

Pettypool Pool

Pettypool Farm

New Pool

DALEFORD MANOR CVN PK

DALEFORD MANOR

Daleford Farm

Daleford Manor

Snipe Island

Sherratt's Rough

Church-hill Wood

Whitegate CE Prim Sch

GLASTY LA

VALE ROYAL DR

GRANGE LA

LAMB COTTAGE CVN PK

Lapwing Hall Farm

DALEFORD LA

CW8

Newchurch Common

Bawsgate Farm

CINDER HILL

Dairy Farm

SANDY LA

Foxwist Green

THE PADDOCKS

Nova Scotia

Hollybank Farm

FOXWIST GN

Briary Farm

Plough Inn (PH)

THE PLOUGH INN PK

COMMON LA

Camp Site

Whitegate Way

CASSIA GREEN LA

Marton

CASSIA LA

Cassia Green

BEAUTY BANK

Tottles Hall Farm

Common Farm

Cassia Lodge

Martonsands

Chaise Farm

Coach Road Farm

CLAY LA

Daisybank Farm

Marton Green

Springbank Farm

Marton Villa

Marton Hole

Marton Hall

WHITEGATE RD

Claylane Farm

CW7

Saltgreen LA

Cornhill Farm

Brook Farm

Saltenswall

B5074

CHESTER RD

B5074

A54

Outside Farm

Chesterlane Farm

CHESTER LA

OAKMERE RD

PARK AVE

SHOP LA

Grange Farm

Marton House Farm

ROSEWOOD DR

TITTLER LA

CHESTNUT CL

TALLOW FIELD CL

Coneygreaves Farm

MILL LA

CW6

Blakeden Farm

BLAKEDEN LA

A54

TITTLER LA

60 · 61 · 62

A · B · C · D · E · F

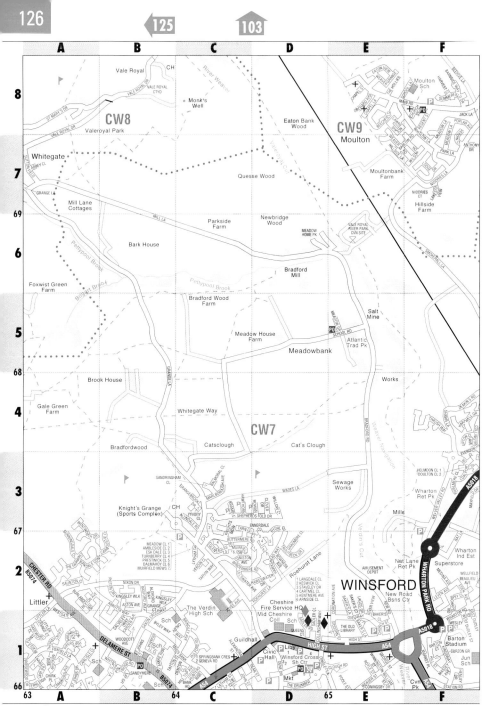

8

CH
Vale Royal
VALE ROYAL
VALE ROYAL CTYD

Monk's
Well

Eaton Bank
Wood

ST MARY'S DR

CW8
Valeroyal Park

CW9
Moulton

Moulton
Sch

PO

VALE ROYAL DR

Whitegate

ABBEY CL

7

GRANGE LA

Mill Lane
Cottages

Quesse Wood

Moultonbank
Farm

NIDDRIES
CT

Hillside
Farm

69

MILL LA

Parkside
Farm

Newbridge
Wood

MEADOW
HOME PK

VALE ROYAL
RIVER PARK
CVN SITE

Pettypool Brook

6

Bark House

Bradford
Mill

Foxwist Green
Farm

Bogart Brook

Pettypool Brook

Bradford Wood
Farm

Salt
Mine

5

Meadow House
Farm

PO
SCHOOL RD

Atlantic
Trad Pk

Meadowbank

68

GRANGE LA

Brook House

Works

4

Gale Green
Farm

Whitegate Way

CW7

Bradfordwood

Catsclough

Cat's Clough

WEAVER RD

BRADFORD RD

3

SANDRINGHAM
CL

GRANGE BRCH

BELMORAL AVE

MARLBOROUGH AVE

WADES LA

WILLOW CL

Sewage
Works

HELMDON CL 1
DOULTON CL 2

Wharton
Ret Pk

A5018

MAYFAIR

Knight's Grange
(Sports Complex)

CH

PRIORY
CL

SHEPHERDS FOLD DR

ENNERDALE

Verdin's Cut

Mills

67

PO

MEADOW CL 1
AMBLESIDE CL 2
ESK DALE CL 3
TURNBERRY CL 4
PRESTWICK CL 5
DALMAHOY CL 6
MUIRFIELD MEWS 7

TARN CL

BUTTERMERE RD

CONISTON
AVE

Roehurst Lane

Amusement
Depot

Nat Lane
Ret Pk

Wharton
Ind Est
Superstore

WELLFIELD

BEAULIEU
AVE

2

CHESTER RD

B5074

Littler

NIXON DR

KINGSLEY WLK

ASTON AVE

GRANGE
CT

Cheshire
Fire Service HQ
Mid Cheshire
Coll

Sch

QUEENS

WINSFORD

New Road
Bsns Ctr

WHARTON PARK RD

A5018

P

Barton
Stadium

Jun
Sch

1

DELAMERE ST

WOODCOTT
AVE

BYLEY WAY

The Verdin
High Sch

Guildhall

Civic
Hall

Lidl

1 SPRINGBANK CRES
2 GENEVA RD

HIGH ST

Winsford Cross
Sh Ctr

PO

The Old
Library

HIGH ST

BAKER'S

A54

River Weaver

Cvn
Pk

A54

66

CHIRK
PL

Sch

PO
SANDYMERE

B5074

A54

Mkt

The DRUMBER

CONINGSBY DR

STATION RD

63 | **A** | **B** | **64** | **C** | **D** | **65** | **E** | **F**

A1
1 BADGERS CL
2 OTTERS BANK
3 REDSTONE DR
4 BECKENHAM GR
5 FINSBURY WLK

D1
1 QUEEN'S PAR
2 FOUNTAIN CT
3 THE ROW
4 DINGLE WLK
5 JUBILEE WAY

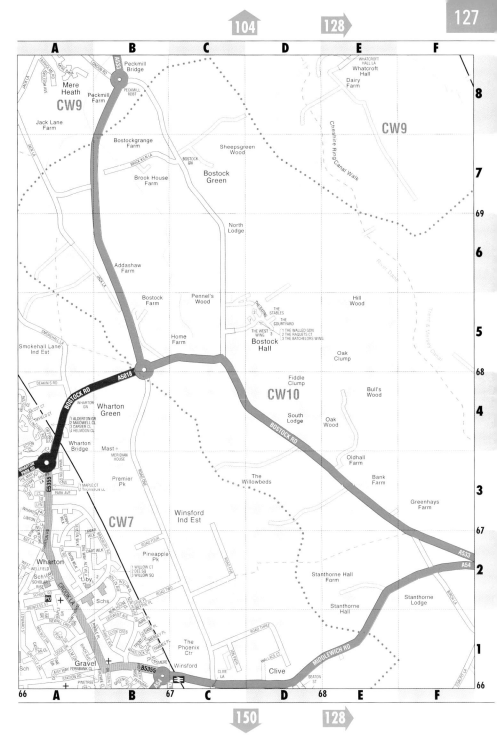

104
128
150
128

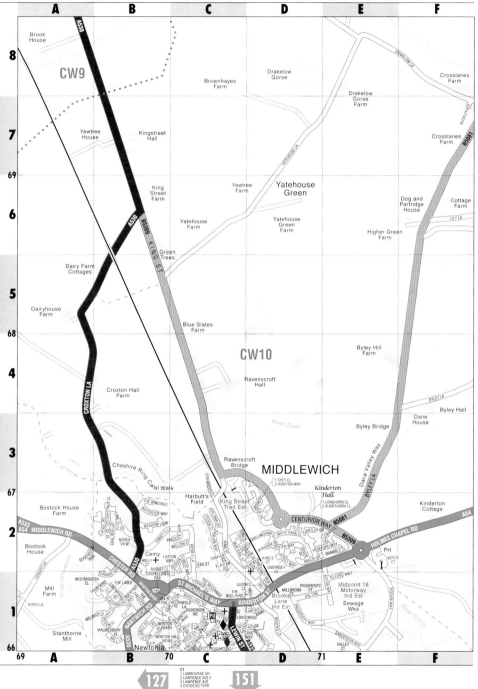

CW9

Brook House

A530

Yewtree House

Kingstreet Hall

Brownhayes Farm

Drakelow Gorse

Drakelow Gorse Farm

Crosslanes Farm

Crosslanes Farm

B5081

DRAKELOW LA

BUCKLEY AVE

King Street Farm

A530

B5309 KING ST

Yewtree Farm

Yatehouse Green

Yatehouse Farm

Yatehouse Green Farm

Dog and Partridge House

Cottage Farm

LILY LA

Green Trees

Higher Green Farm

YATEHOUSE LA

Dairy Farm Cottages

Dairyhouse Farm

Blue Slates Farm

CW10

Byley Hill Farm

Croxton Hall Farm

CROXTON LA

Ravenscroft Hall

BYLEY LA

Byley LA

Byley Hall

River Dane

Dane House

Byley Bridge

Dane Valley Way

Cheshire Ring Canal Walk

Ravenscroft Bridge

MIDDLEWICH

1 SPEY CL
2 HONITON WAY

Kinderton Hall

1 LONGHORN CL
2 SHORTHORN CL

Kinderton Cottage

A54

Bostock House Farm

THE WINDINGS

Harbutt's Field

King Street Trad Est

CENTURION WAY

B5081

HOLMES CHAPEL RD

WATERSIDE WAY

MEADOW VIEW

CHILLINGHAM L

WHITE PARK CL

HARTLEY GR

RECORD WAY

B5309

PH

VERITY CT

A533 A54 MIDDLEWICH RD

Bostock House

CHESTER RD

A530

Cemy

HOLLY CL

WILLOW CL

DEAN ST

AYRSHIRE CL

DEXTER WAY

GUERNSEY CL

ANGUS GR

BRAMBLE CL

TELFORD WAY

Midpoint 18 Motorway Ind Est

PROSPERITY CT

DALTON

Sewage Wks

River Croco

Mill Farm

BIRCH LA

WESTMINSTER CL

FOUNTAINS

THE LIMES

RUSSET CL
ODDFELLOWS PAS

ST MICHAEL'S WAY

KINDERTON ST

THE BULL RING

QUEEN'S CT

Brooks Lane Ind Est

MILLBROOK

ASTON WAY

ALSTON WAY

POCHIN WAY

Stanthorne Mill

MALMESBURY CL

A530

NANTWICH RD

NEWTON HEATH

NEWTON HALL MEWS

DICKENSON HO

LONGCROSS

LEWIN ST A533

Lib

PO

Civic Hall

SANDERSON WAY

VALLEY CT

Sch

Newtonia

C1
1 LAMBOURNE GR
2 LAWRENCE AVE E
3 LAWRENCE AVE
4 DIERDENS TERR

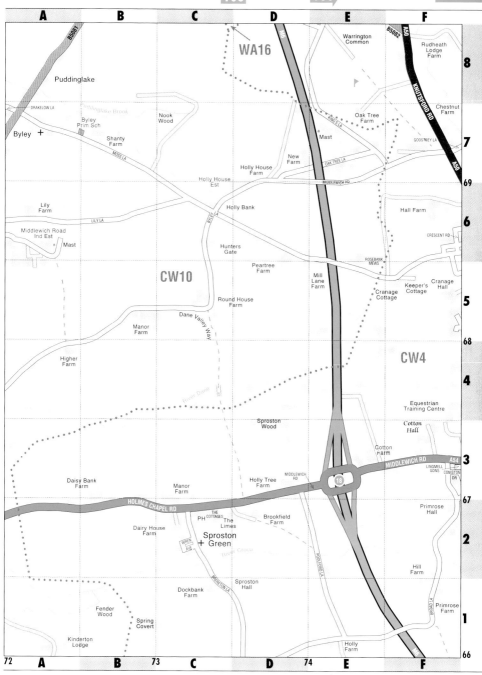

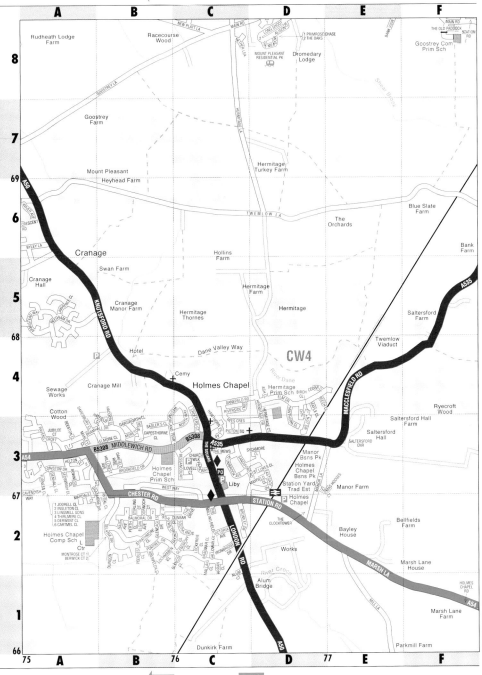

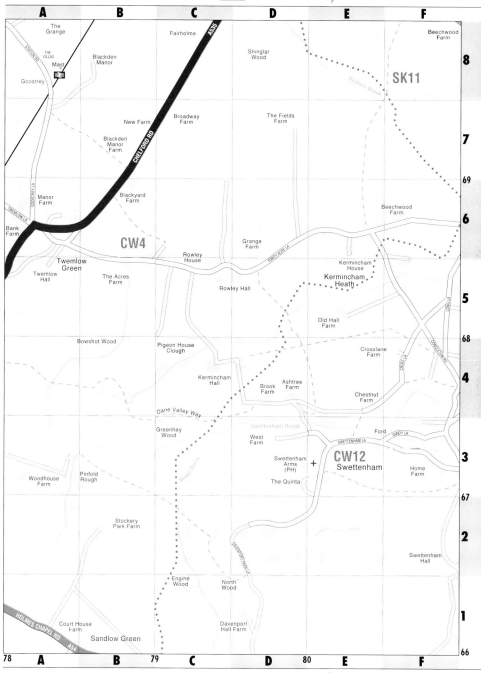

A   B   C   D   E   F

The Grange

THE VILLAS
SATES RD
Mast
Goostrey

Blackden Manor

Fairholme

A535

Shinglar Wood

Beechwood Farm

SK11

8

Redlion Brook

New Farm

Broadway Farm

The Fields Farm

7

Blackden Manor Farm

CHELFORD RD

69

TWEMLOW LA

Manor Farm

Blackyard Farm

Beechwood Farm

6

Bank Farm

CW4

Twemlow Green

Rowley House

Grange Farm

FORTY ACRE LA

Kermincham House

Kermincham Heath

Twemlow Hall

The Acres Farm

Rowley Hall

LONG LA

5

Old Hall Farm

CONGLETON RD

68

Bowshot Wood

Pigeon House Clough

Crosslane Farm

CROSS LA

Kermincham Hall

Brook Farm

Ashtree Farm

Chestnut Farm

4

Dane Valley Way

Swettenham Brook

Ford

SANDY LA

Greenhey Wood

West Farm

SWETTENHAM LA

CW12
Swettenham

3

River Dane

Swettenham Arms (PH)

Home Farm

Woodhouse Farm

Pinfold Rough

The Quinta

67

Stockery Park Farm

DAVENPORT PARK LA

2

Swettenham Hall

Engine Wood

North Wood

1

HOLMES CHAPEL RD
A54

Court House Farm

Sandlow Green

Davenport Hall Farm

66

78   A   B   79   C   D   80   E   F

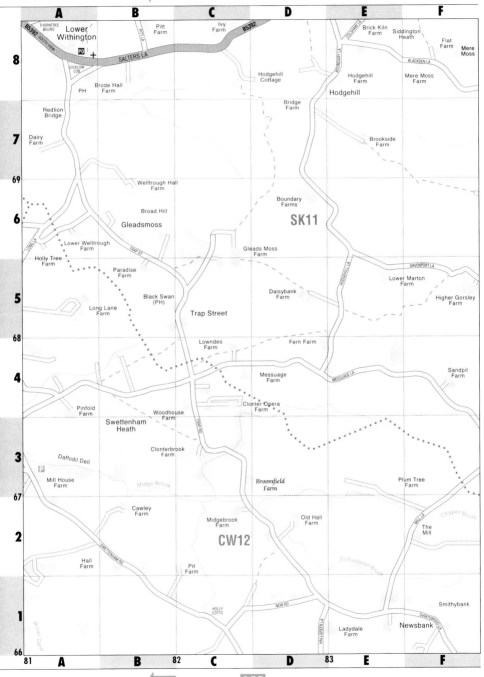

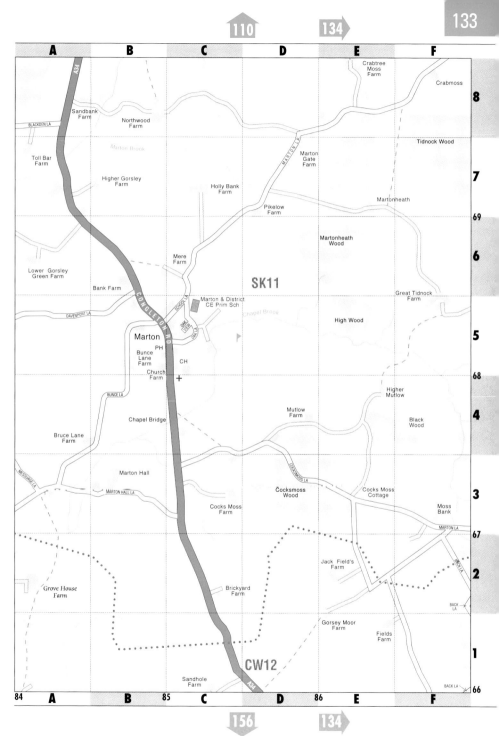

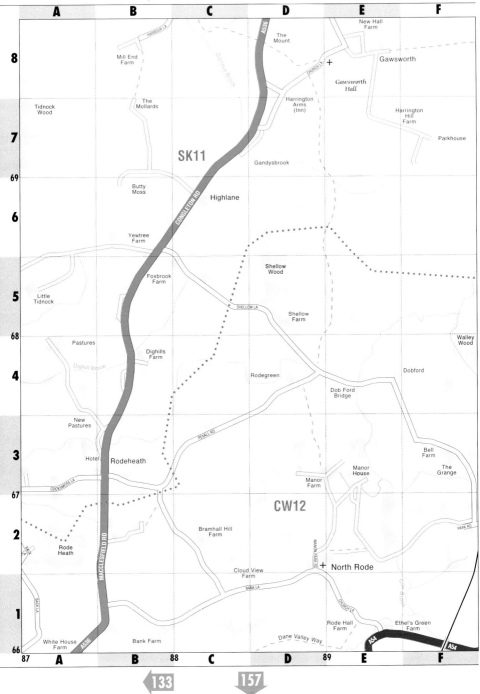

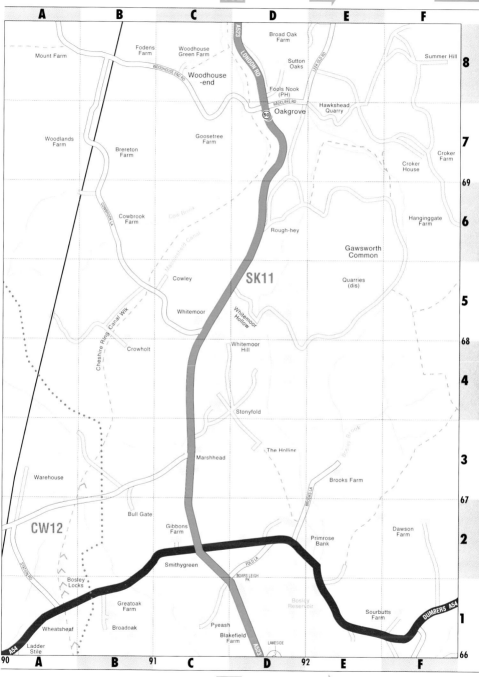

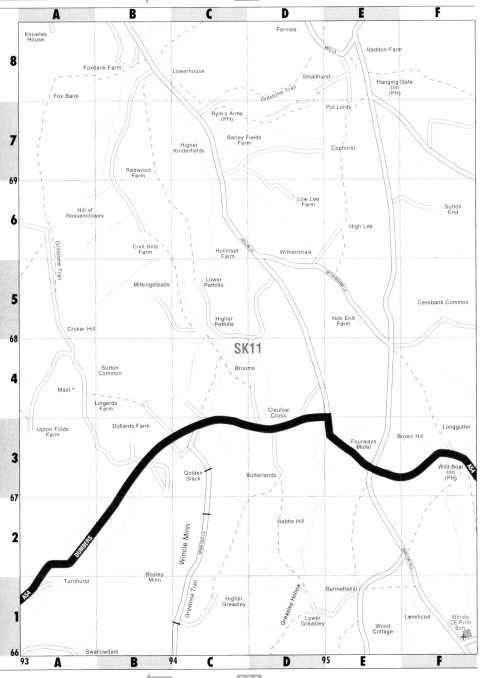

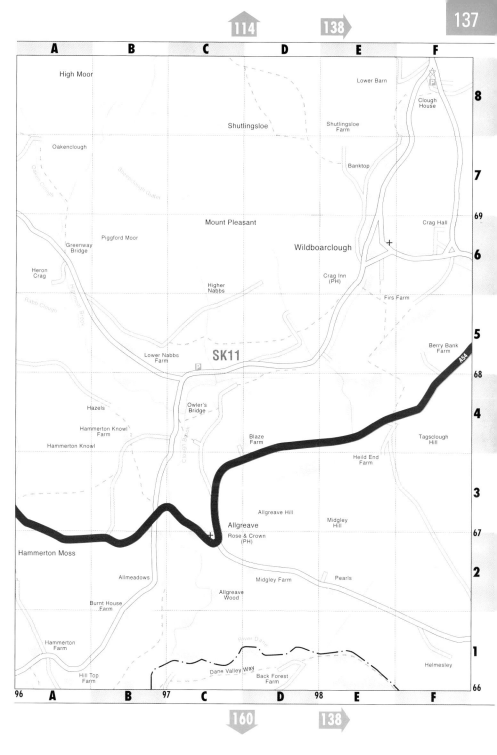

114
138

High Moor

Oakenclough

Shutlingsloe

Lower Barn

Clough House

8

Shutlingsloe Farm

Banktop

7

Mount Pleasant

Piggford Moor

Greenway Bridge

Wildboarclough

Crag Hall

69

6

Heron Crag

Higher Nabbs

Crag Inn (PH)

Firs Farm

Rabb Clough

Lower Nabbs Farm

SK11

Berry Bank Farm

A54

5

68

Hazels

Owler's Bridge

Blaze Farm

Heild End Farm

Tagsclough Hill

4

Hammerton Knowl Farm

Hammerton Knowl

3

Allgreave Hill

Midgley Hill

Hammerton Moss

Allgreave

Rose & Crown (PH)

67

Allmeadows

Midgley Farm

Pearls

2

Burnt House Farm

Allgreave Wood

Hammerton Farm

River Dane

Dane Valley Way

Back Forest Farm

Helmesley

1

Hill Top Farm

66

160
138

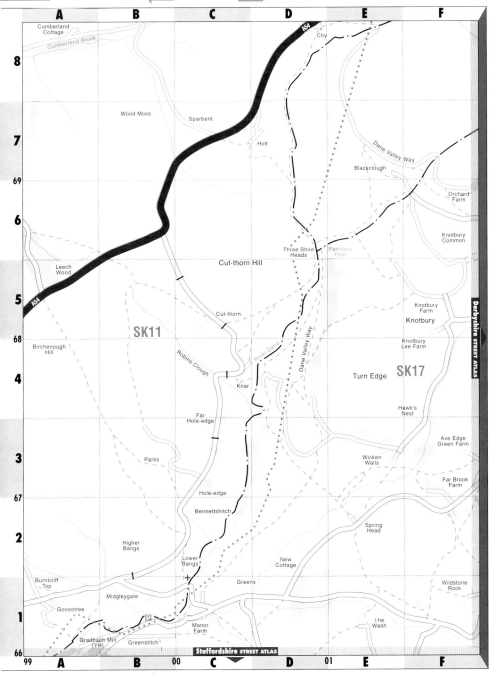

Cumberland
Cottage

Cumberland Brook

A54

Chy

Wood Moss

Sparbent

Dane Valley Way

Holt

Blackclough

Orchard
Farm

Three Shire
Heads

Panniers
Pool

Knotbury
Common

Cut-thorn Hill

Leech
Wood

A54

Cut-thorn

Robins Clough

River Dane

Knotbury
Farm

Knotbury

SK11

Birchenough
Hill

Dane Valley Way

Knotbury
Lee Farm

Knar

Turn Edge

SK17

Far
Hole-edge

Hawk's
Nest

Parks

Axe Edge
Green Farm

Wicken
Walls

Hole-edge

Far Brook
Farm

Bennettshitch

Spring
Head

Higher
Bangs

Lower
Bangs

New
Cottage

Greens

Wildstone
Rock

Burntcliff
Top

Midleygate

P

Goosetree

Manor
Farm

The
Wash

Gradbach Mill
(YH)

Greenstitch

Derbyshire STREET ATLAS

Staffordshire STREET ATLAS

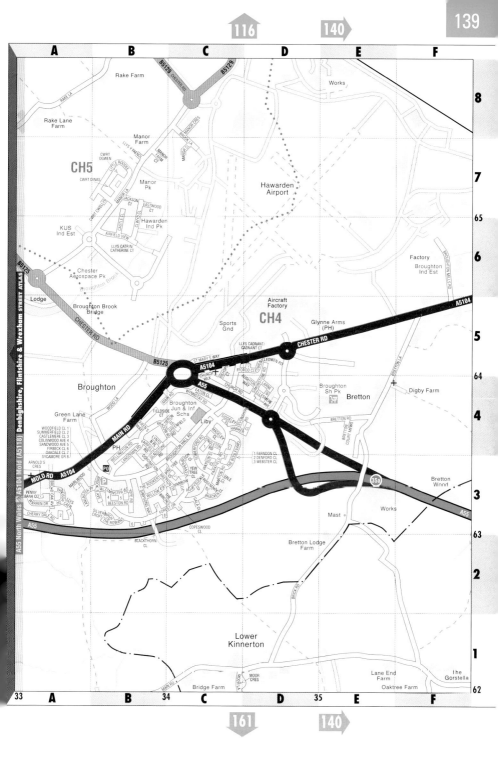

A B C D E F

8

7

65

6

5

64

4

3

63

2

1

62

Rake Farm

B5129 CHESTER RD

B5129

Works

Rake Lane Farm

RAKE LA

Manor Farm

LLYS Y HAFEL

MANOR DRIVE

BROOK LA

MANOR LA

Manor Farm Cft

CH5

CWRT OGWEN

LITTLE ROODEE

LLYS JACKSON CT

EASTWOOD CT

Manor Pk

Hawarden Airport

CWRT DINAS

CWRT CWELTON

MANOR RD

CASTLE CT

CLWYD ST

CH4

KUS Ind Est

AIRFIELD VIEW

Hawarden Ind Pk

LLYS CATRIN / CATHERINE CT

Factory

B5125

Broughton Ind Est

BROUGHTON MILL RD

Chester Aerospace Pk

Broughton Brook

Lodge

CHESTER RD

Broughton Brook Bridge

Aircraft Factory

CH4

Glynne Arms (PH)

A5104

Sports Gnd

CHESTER RD

BRETTON LA

B5125

ST MARY'S WAY

A5104

LLYS CADNANT / CADNANT CT

YGLEDWEN RD

FFORDD DEL

Broughton Sh Pk

Bretton

Digby Farm

Broughton

WOOD LA

CHURCH LA

EATON CL

CHURCH RD

CHURCH WLK

MARSH RD

WYNNSTAY RD

Broughton Jun & Inf Schs

Libry

CHAPEL CT

Green Lane Farm

FIELDSIDE CT

BRETTON RD

WOODFIELD CL 1
SUMMERFIELD CL 2
CASTLEMERE CL 3
COLINWOOD AVE 4
SANDWOOD AVE 5
FIRBECK CL 6
OAKDALE CL 7
SYCAMORE GR 8

PH

BRETTON COURT MEWS

MAIN RD

WELLINGTON RD

LANSDOWNE RD

COPPICE CL

THE MEADOWS

MOSSLEY RD

HAWKER

YEW TREE CL

1 FARNDON CL
2 DENFORD CL
3 WEBSTER CL

ARNOLD'S CRES

MOLD RD

A5104

MARLWOOD

PO

WESTMINSTER RD

THE ROOKERY

YARROW

PARK VIEW

HIGHWAY CL

VALE

BEESTON RD

WILLOW CL

DALE

BRACKEN CL

BRETTON Wood

PENNY BANK CL

WARREN DR

LLWYN

LARK

SILVERBIRCH CROFT

THE BOWERY

CURLEW DR

A55

Mast

Works

A55

CHERRY DALE RD

A55

BLACKTHORN CL

COPESWOOD CL

Bretton Lodge Farm

BRICK RD

Lower Kinnerton

MAIN RD

MOOR CRES

Bridge Farm

Lane End Farm

The Gorstella

Oaktree Farm

35a

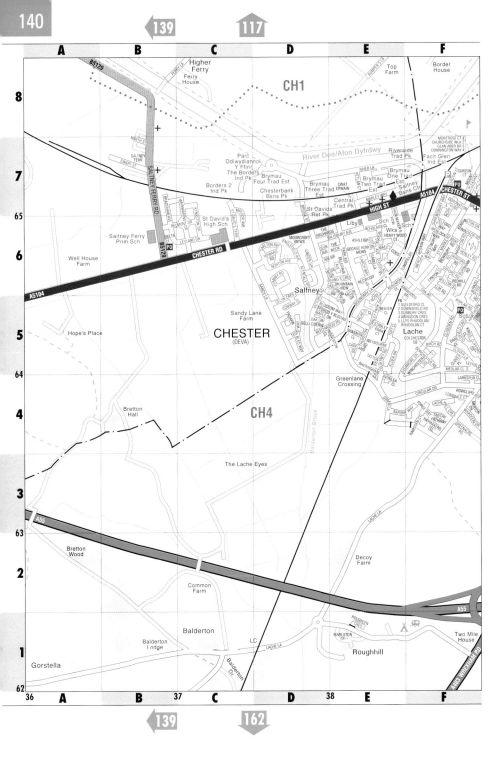

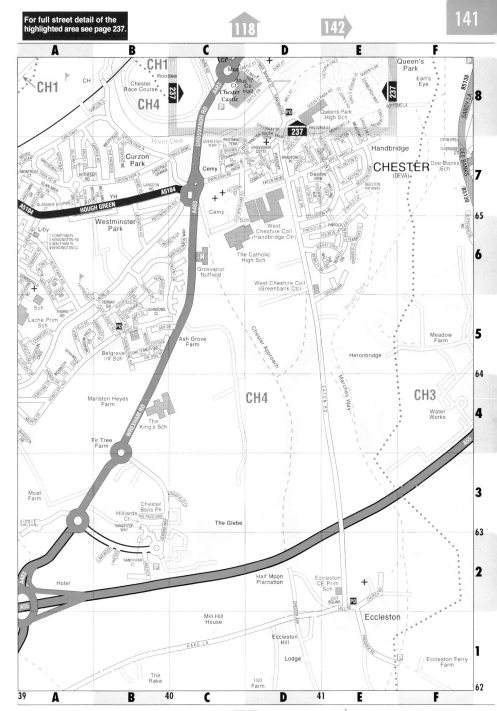

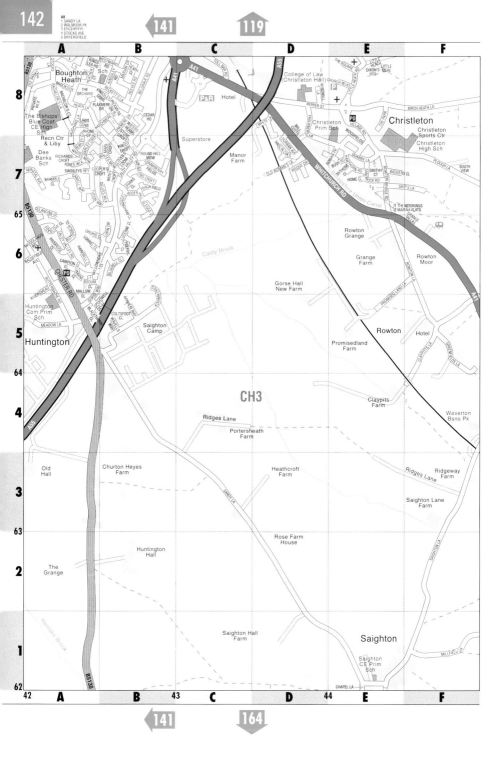

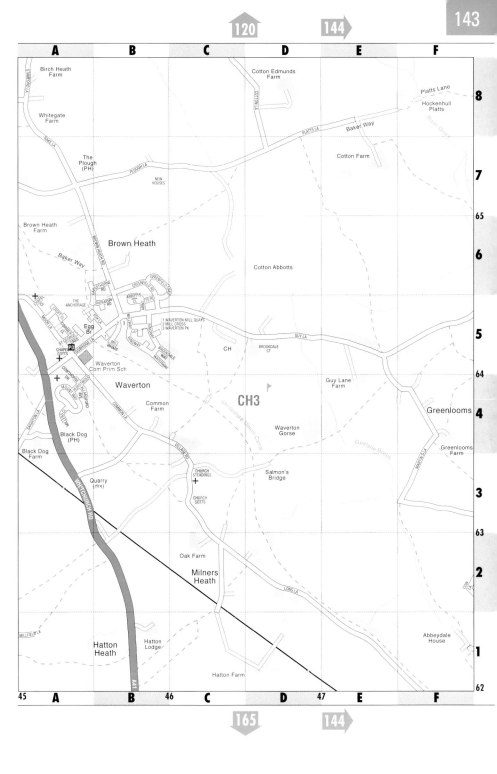

120 144

A B C D E F

Birch Heath Farm

Cotton Edmunds Farm

COTTON LA

Platts Lane

Hockenhull Platts

8

Whitegate Farm

River Gowy

PLATTS LA

Baker Way

RAKE LA

The Plough (PH)

PLOUGH LA

Cotton Farm

7

NEW HOUSES

65

Brown Heath Farm

Brown Heath

Cotton Abbotts

6

BROWN HEATH RD

Baker Way

HAWTHORNE RD

GREENFIELD PK

THE ANCHORAGE

SHERATON RD

ABBOTTS DR

GUY LA

5

ST GEORGES CRES

Egg Br

MILL LA

RINGWAY

1 WAVERTON MILL QUAYS
2 MILL CROSS
3 WAVERTON PK

CH

EGGBRIDGE LA

MILL WHARF

BROOKDALE WAY

BROOKDALE CT

CHAPEL COTTS

PO

Waverton Com Prim Sch

64

COMMONHALL DN

Waverton

CH3

Guy Lane Farm

Greenlooms

4

SAIGHTON LA

Common Farm

COMMON LA

Waverton Gorse

Greenlooms Farm

MARTIN'S LA

Black Dog (PH)

VILLAGE RD

Shropshire Union Canal

Guylane Brook

Black Dog Farm

Quarry (dis)

CHURCH STEADINGS

Salmon's Bridge

3

WHITCHURCH RD

A41

CHURCH COTTS

63

Oak Farm

Milners Heath

LONG LA

2

MILLFIELD LA

Hatton Heath

Hatton Lodge

Abbeydale House

1

Hatton Farm

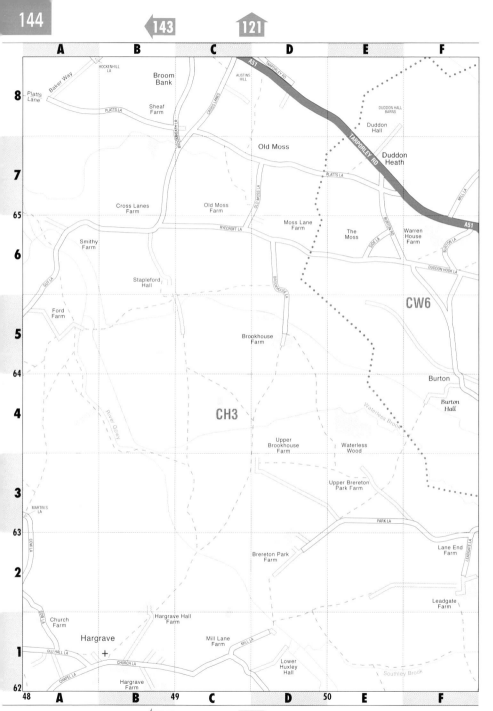

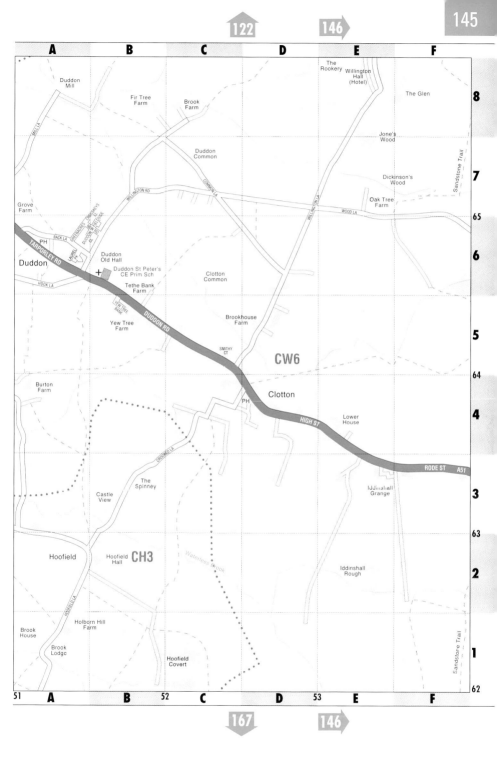

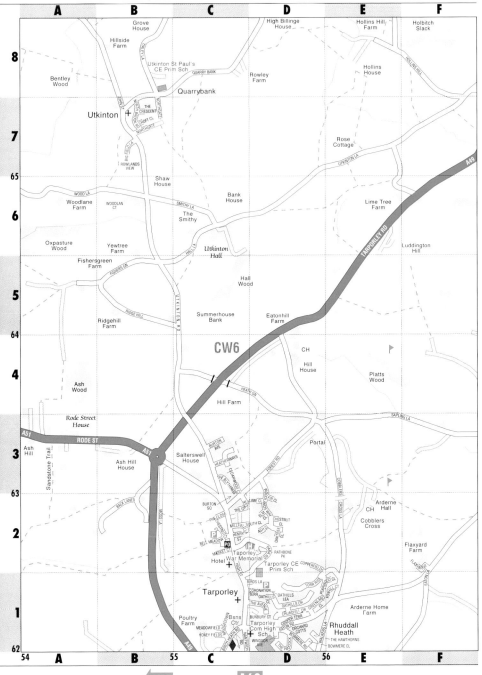

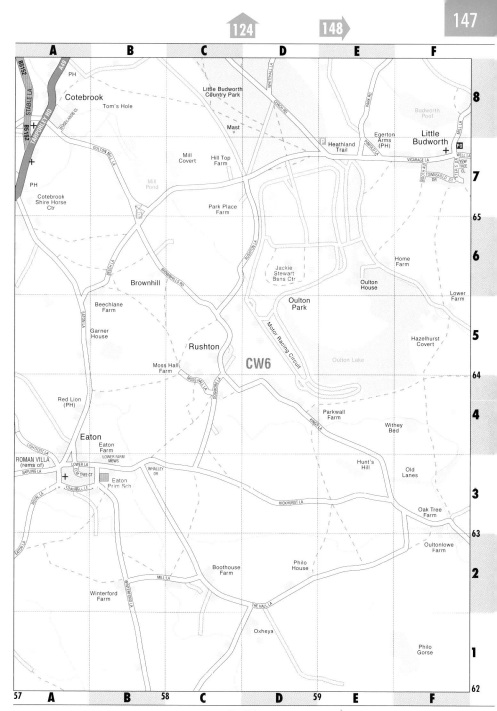

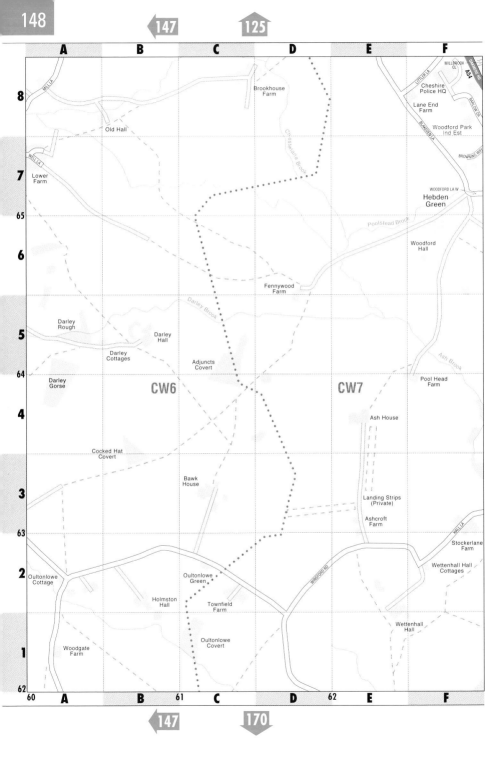

147

125

A **B** **C** **D** **E** **F**

8

Brookhouse
Farm

LITTLER LA

MILLBROOK
CL

A54

DARLING RD

Cheshire
Police HQ

Lane End
Farm

Woodford Park
Ind Est

Old Hall

BLACKERS LA

BROWNING WAY

WELL LA

7

Lower
Farm

WOODFORD LA W

Hebden
Green

Crossleyne Brook

Poolstead Brook

65

Woodford
Hall

6

Fennywood
Farm

Darley Brook

Darley
Rough

Darley
Hall

Ash Brook

5

Darley
Cottages

Adjuncts
Covert

Pool Head
Farm

64

Darley
Gorse

CW6

CW7

4

Ash House

Cocked Hat
Covert

Bawk
House

3

Landing Strips
(Private)

Ashcroft
Farm

WELL LA

Stockerlane
Farm

63

Oultonlowe
Cottage

WINSFORD RD

Wettenhall Hall
Cottages

2

Oultonlowe
Green

Holmston
Hall

Townfield
Farm

Wettenhall
Hall

1

Woodgate
Farm

Oultonlowe
Covert

62

60 **A** **B** 61 **C** **D** 62 **E** **F**

147

170

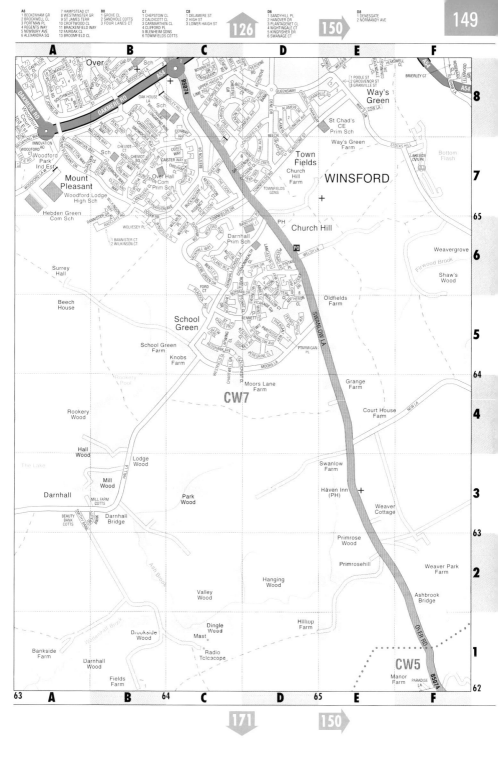

A6
1 BECKENHAM GR
2 BROCKWELL CL
3 PORTMAN PL
4 REGENTS WAY
5 NEWBURY AVE
6 ALEXANDRA SQ

7 HAMPSTEAD CT
8 WESTMINSTER CL
9 ST JAMES TERR
10 CROFTWOOD CL
11 BRACKENFIELD WAY
12 FAIROAK CL
13 BROOMFIELD CL

B8
1 GROVE CL
2 SANDHOLE COTTS
3 FOUR LANES CT

C7
1 CHEPSTOW CL
2 CALDICOTT CL
3 CARMARTHEN CL
4 CLIFFORD PL
5 BLENHEIM GDNS
6 TOWNFIELDS COTTS

C8
1 DELAMERE ST
2 HIGH ST
3 LOWER HAIGH ST

D6
1 SANDYHILL PL
2 HANOVER DR
3 PLANTAGENET CL
4 NIGHTINGALE CL
5 KINGFISHER DR
6 SWANAGE CT

D8
1 DENESGATE
2 NORMANDY AVE

126   150

Over   Sch

Way's Green

St Chad's CE Prim Sch

Town Fields

WINSFORD

Church Hill Farm

Church Hill

Weavergrove

Firwood Brook

Mount Pleasant

Woodford Park Ind Est

Innovation

Woodford Lodge High Sch

Hebden Green Com Sch

Darnhall Prim Sch

Shaw's Wood

Surrey Hall

Oldfields Farm

Beech House

School Green

School Green Farm

Knobs Farm

Moors Lane Farm

CW7

Grange Farm

Rookery Wood

Court House Farm

Hall Wood

Swanlow Farm

The Lake

Lodge Wood

Mill Wood

Mill Farm Cotts

Darnhall

Park Wood

Haven Inn (PH)

Weaver Cottage

Beauty Bank Cotts

Darnhall Bridge

Primrose Wood

Primrosehill

Weaver Park Farm

Hanging Wood

Valley Wood

Ashbrook Bridge

Bankside Farm

Brookside Wood

Mast

Dingle Wood

Radio Telescope

Hilltop Farm

Darnhall Wood

Fields Farm

CW5

Manor Farm

171   150

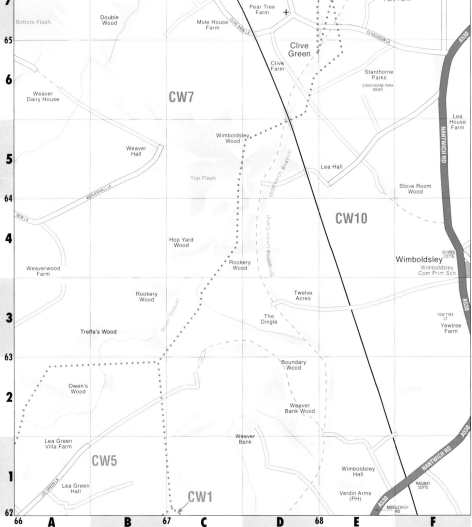

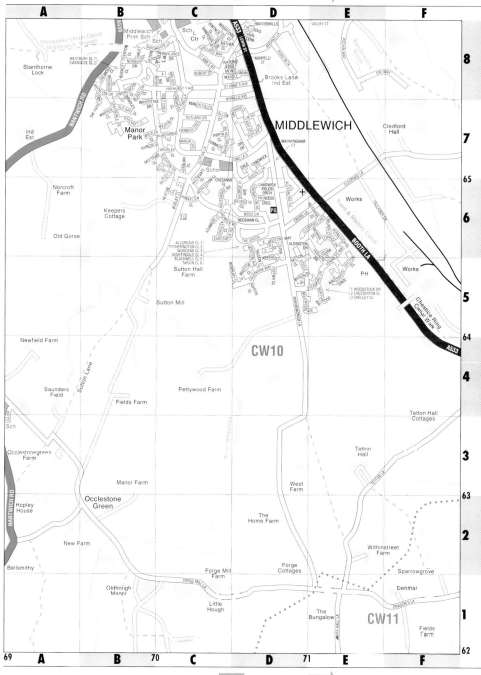

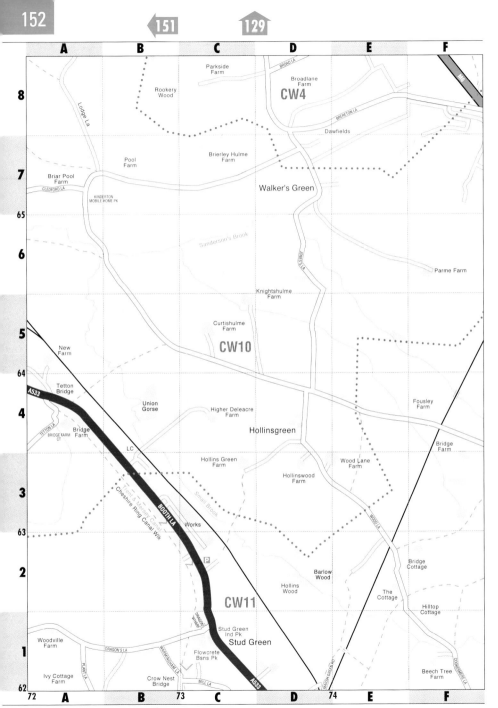

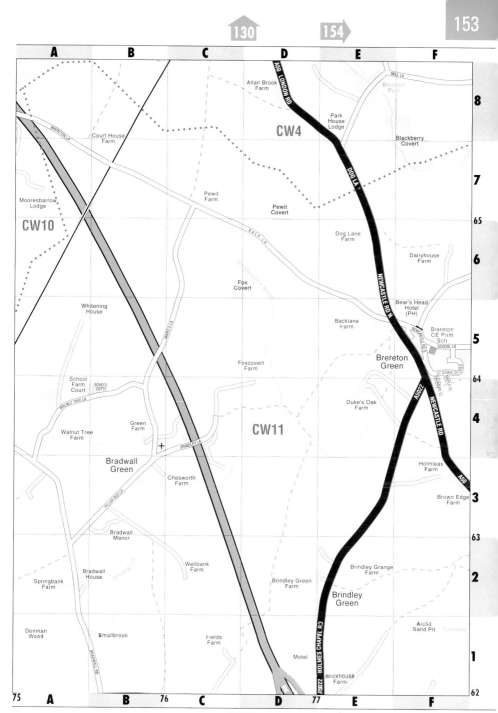

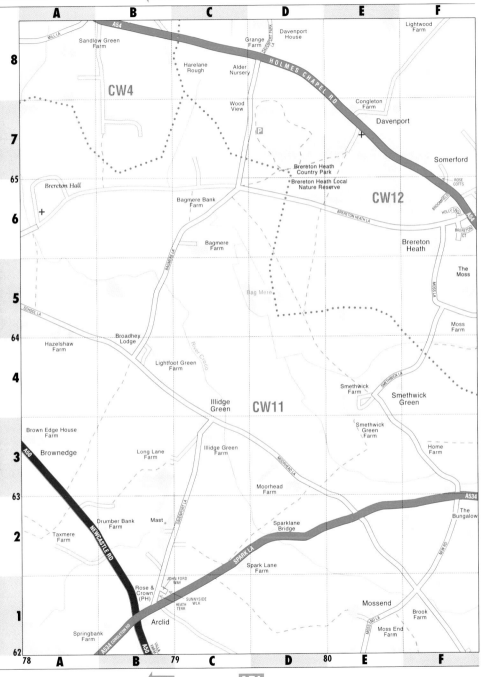

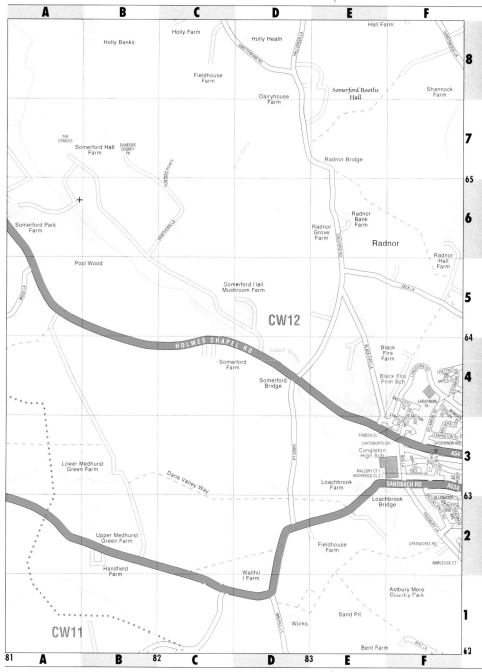

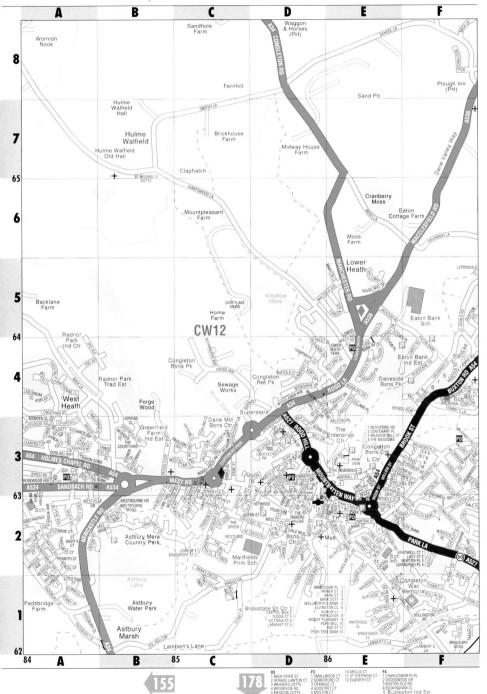

D3
1 BACK RIVER ST
2 HORACE LAWTON CT
3 WEAVERS COTTS
4 BROOKSIDE RD
5 MEADOW COTTS
6 STONEHOUSE GN

F3
1 SMALLWOOD CT
2 SOMERFORD CT
3 CRANAGE CT
4 GOOSTREY CT
5 MOSTON CT
6 BETCHTON CT
7 RODE CT
8 TETTON CT
9 NEWBOLD CT

10 ARCLID CT
11 ST STEPHENS CT
12 ELWORTH CT

F4
1 CHARLESWORTH PL
2 DODDSWOOD DR
3 BUXTON OLD RD
4 BUCKINGHAM RD
5 Buglawton Ind Est
6 Havannah Bsns Ctr
7 COUNCIL HOS

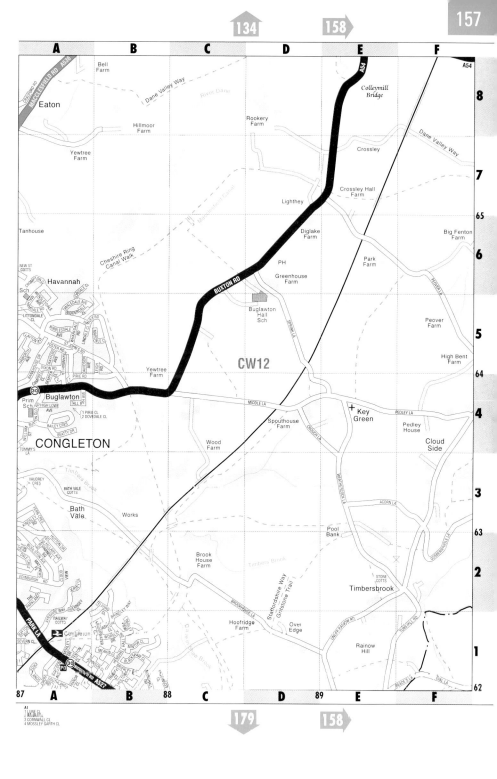

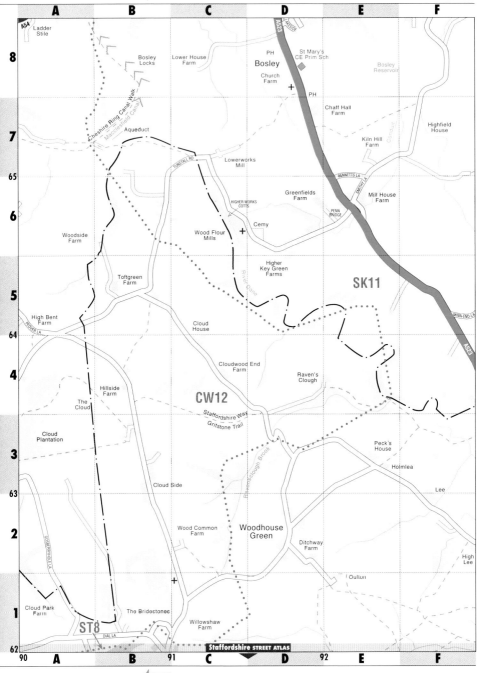

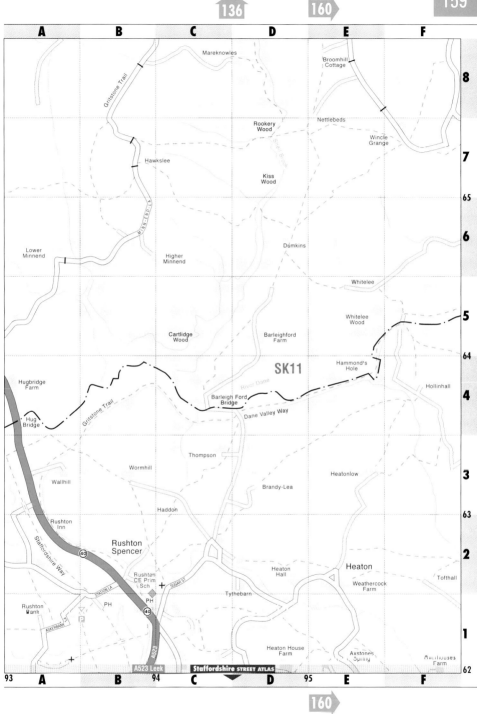

Mareknowles

Broomhill
Cottage

8

Gritstone Trail

Rookery
Wood

Nettlebeds

Wincle
Grange

7

Hawkslee

65

Kiss
Wood

6

Lower
Minnend

Higher
Minnend

Dumkins

Whitelee

Whitelee
Wood

5

Cartlidge
Wood

Barleighford
Farm

64

SK11

Hammond's
Hole

Hollinhall

Hugbridge
Farm

Gritstone Trail

River Dane

4

Barleigh Ford
Bridge

Dane Valley Way

Hug
Bridge

Thompson

Wormhill

Brandy-Lea

Heatonlow

3

Wallhill

Haddon

63

Rushton
Inn

Rushton
Spencer

Staffordshire Way

40

Heaton
Hall

Heaton

2

Rushton
CE Prim
Sch

SUGAR ST

Tofthall

Weathercock
Farm

PH

Tythebarn

STATION LA

Rushton
Bank

PH

40

Heaton House
Farm

Axstones
Spring

1

ASHERBANK

P

A523

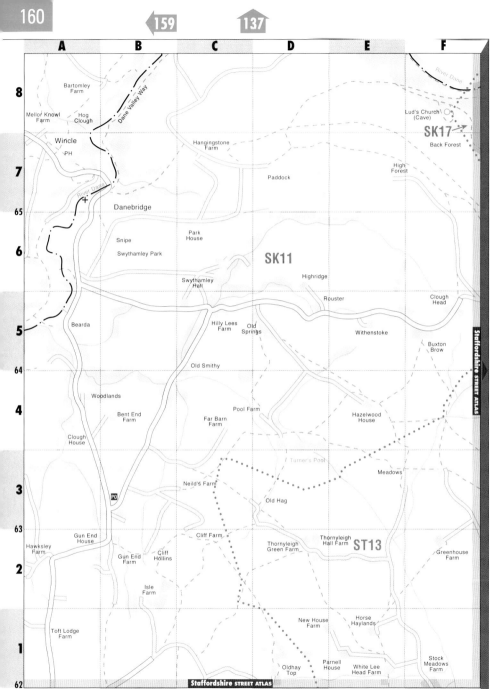

A B C D E F

8

Bartomley
Farm

Mellor Knowl
Farm

Hog
Clough

Wincle

PH

Dane Valley Way

River Dane

Lud's Church
(Cave)

SK17

Back Forest

Hangingstone
Farm

High
Forest

Paddock

7

River Dane

Danebridge

65

Park
House

Snipe

Swythamley Park

SK11

Highridge

6

Swythamley
Hall

Rouster

Clough
Head

Bearda

5

Hilly Lees
Farm

Old
Springs

Withenstoke

Buxton
Brow

Old Smithy

64

Woodlands

Bent End
Farm

Far Barn
Farm

Pool Farm

Hazelwood
House

4

Clough
House

Turner's Pool

Meadows

Neild's Farm

3

Old Hag

63

Gun End
House

Cliff Farm

Thornyleigh
Hall Farm

ST13

Hawksley
Farm

PO

Gun End
Farm

Cliff
Hollins

Thornyleigh
Green Farm

Greenhouse
Farm

2

Isle
Farm

New House
Farm

Horse
Haylands

1

Toft Lodge
Farm

Oldhay
Top

Parnell
House

White Lee
Head Farm

Stock
Meadows
Farm

62

96 A B 97 C D 98 E F

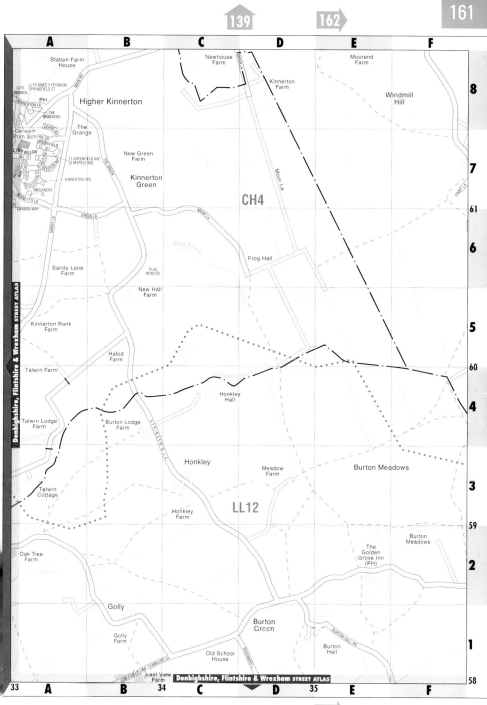

Station Farm House

Newhouse Farm

Moorend Farm

Kinnerton Farm

Windmill Hill

LLYS MAES Y FFYNNON/ SPRINGFIELD CT

LLYS DERWEN

PH

KINNERTON LA

THE BRACKENS

Higher Kinnerton

MAIN RD

DEANS WAY

Derwen Prim Sch

OAK DR

SPRINGFIELD CL

WILLOW

LIB

The Grange

New Green Farm

FAULKNERS CL

KINNERTON HTS

1 GREENFIELD AVE

2 MYRTLE AVE

Kinnerton Green

THE GREEN

CH4

BENNETT'S LA

CANNON WAY

SANDY LA

GREEN LA

MOOR LA

Moor La

Brad Brook

Frog Hall

61

Sandy Lane Farm

PLAS NEWYDD

New Hall Farm

Kinnerton Bank Farm

Hafod Farm

Talwrn Farm

Honkley Hall

5

60

4

Talwrn Lodge Farm

Burton Lodge Farm

STRINGER'S LA

Honkley

Meadow Farm

Burton Meadows

Talwrn Cottage

LL12

Honkley Farm

59

Oak Tree Farm

The Golden Grove Inn (PH)

Burton Meadows

2

Golly

Golly Farm

Burton Green

BURTON HALL RD

Burton Hall

ROSEMARY

1

East View Farm

CIBBLES LA

Old School House

58

33

34

35

A B C D E F

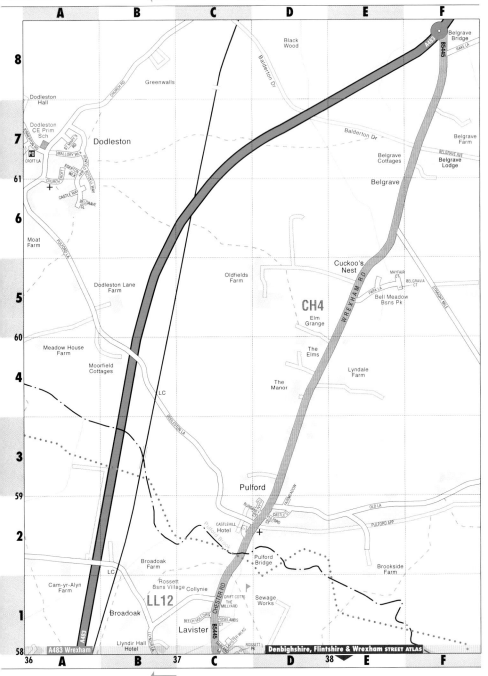

8

7

61

6

5

60

4

3

59

2

1

58

Dodleston Hall

Dodleston CE Prim Sch

PO

CROFT LA

Dodleston

MALLORY WY

CHURCH RD

KINBERLEY RD

EGGERTON ST WLK

CASTLE WAY

BELGRAVE CL

CHURCH

Moat Farm

PULFORD LA

Greenwalls

CHURCH RD

Dodleston Lane Farm

Meadow House Farm

Moorfield Cottages

LC

DODLESTON LA

LC

Cam-yr-Alyn Farm

Broadoak

LL12

Broadoak Farm

Rossett Bsns Village

Collynie

BEECH HOLLOW

LLYNDIR

Llyndir Hall Hotel

Lavister

CHESTER RD

B5445

Pulford Brook

Black Wood

Balderton Dr

Balderton Dr

Belgrave Cottages

Belgrave

Oldfields Farm

CH4

Elm Grange

The Elms

The Manor

Pulford

BURGAGE CT

CASTLE CT

COMMEADOW

PULFORD

CASTLEHILL Hotel

Pulford Brook

DRIFT COTTS

THE MILLYARD

ROSELANDS CT

DUNGATE WLKS

ROSSETT PK

Sewage Works

Pulford Bridge

Belgrave Farm

BELGRAVE AVE

Belgrave Lodge

RAKE LA

Belgrave Bridge

A483

B5445

Cuckoo's Nest

WREXHAM RD

PARK LA

MAYFAIR CT

BELGRAVIA CT

Bell Meadow Bsns Pk

Lyndale Farm

STRAIGHT MILE

OLD LA

PULFORD APP

Brookside Farm

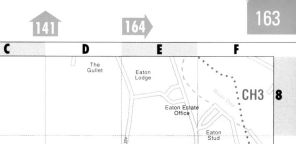
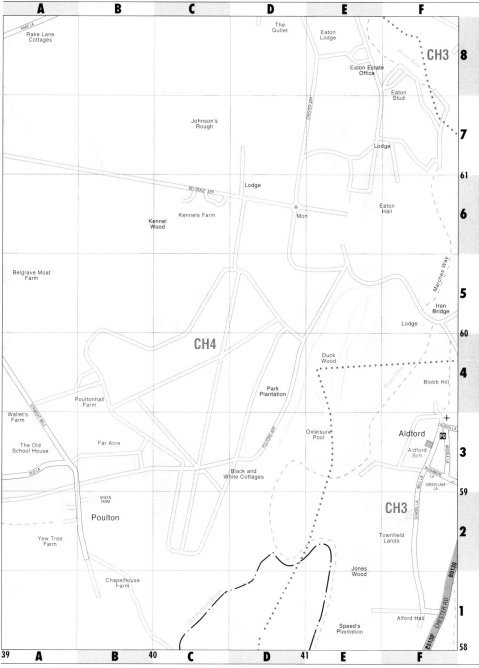

163
142

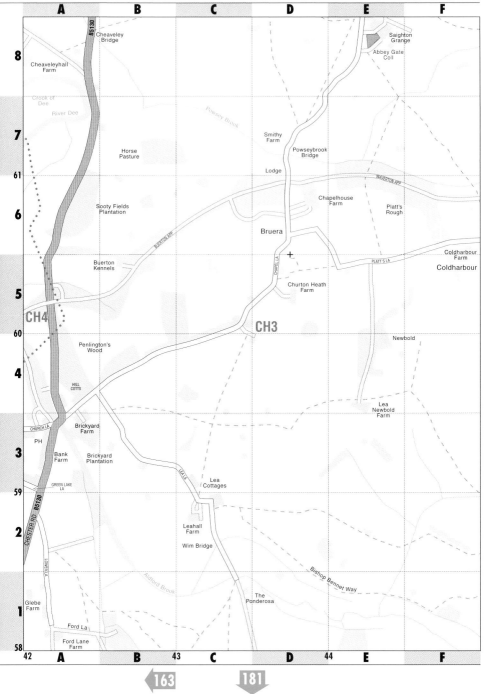

163
181

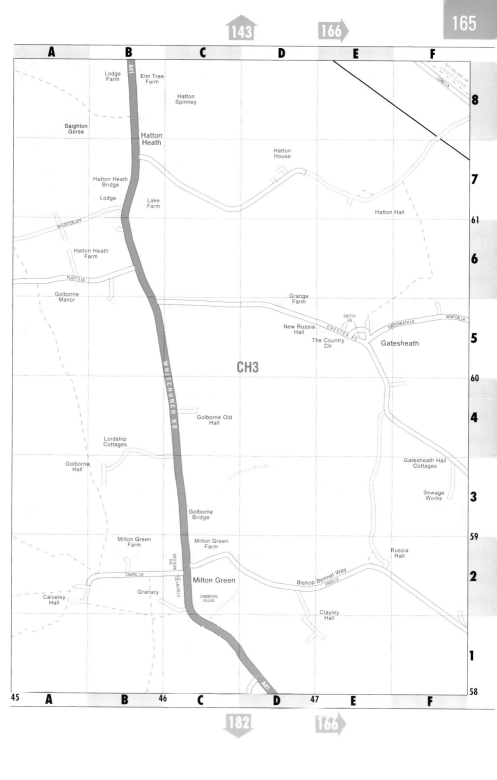

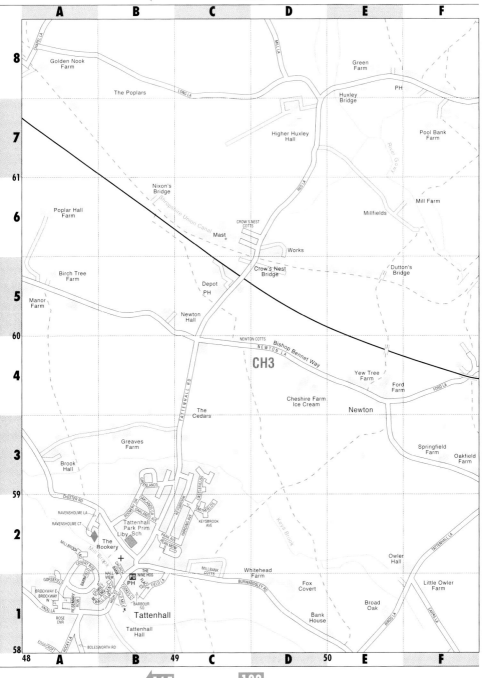

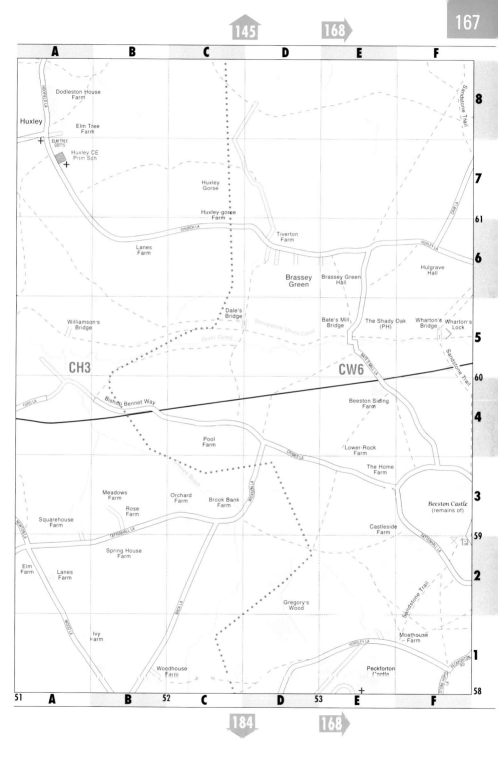

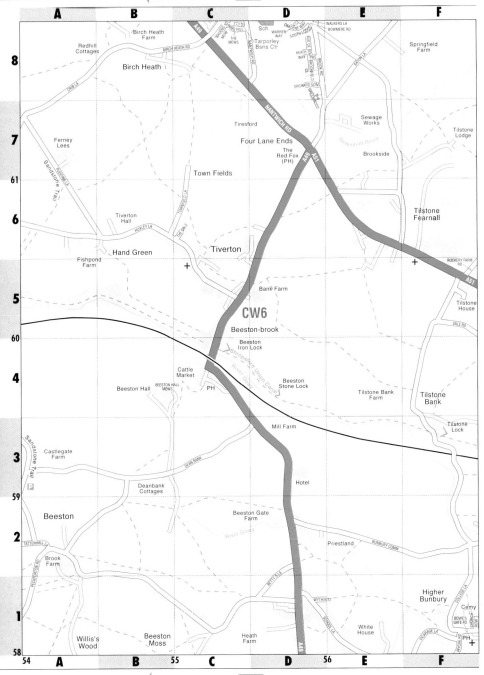

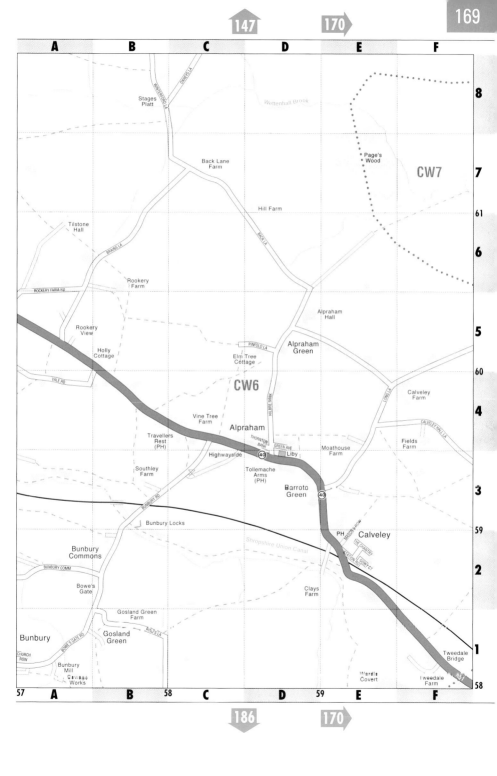

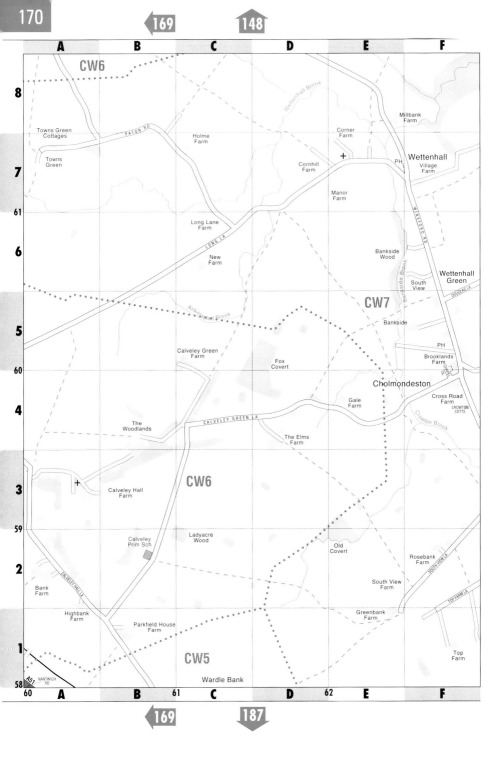

CW6

Towns Green Cottages

EATON RD

Holme Farm

Millbank Farm

Corner Farm

Towns Green

Cornhill Farm

PH

Wettenhall Village Farm

Wettenhall

Manor Farm

Long Lane Farm

New Farm

Bankside Wood

South View

Wettenhall Green

Ankerwatt Brook

CW7

Bankside

Calveley Green Farm

Fox Covert

Bankside Brook

PH

Brooklands Farm

WINSFORD RD

DOUGLAN LA

The Woodlands

CALVELEY GREEN LA

Gale Farm

Cholmondeston

Cross Road Farm

CROWTON COTTS

Croxton Brook

CW6

The Elms Farm

Calveley Hall Farm

Calveley Prim Sch

Ladyacre Wood

Old Covert

Rosebank Farm

SOUTH VIEW LA

Bank Farm

CALVELEY HALL LA

South View Farm

TOP FARM LA

Highbank Farm

Parkfield House Farm

Greenbank Farm

Top Farm

CW5

Wardle Bank

NANTWICH RD

A51

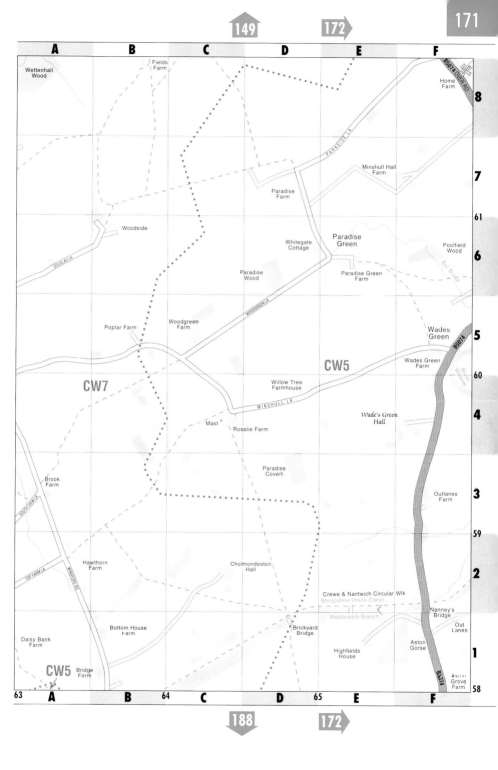

Wettenhall Wood

Fields Farm

Home Farm

8

PARADISE LA

Minshull Hall Farm

7

Paradise Farm

61

Woodside

Whitegate Cottage

Paradise Green

Poolfield Wood

6

DOUGLAS LA

Paradise Wood

Paradise Green Farm

Eel Brook

WOODGREEN LA

Wades Green

5

Poplar Farm

Woodgreen Farm

B5074

Wades Green Farm

CW5

60

CW7

Willow Tree Farmhouse

MINSHULL LA

4

Mast

Rosalie Farm

Wade's Green Hall

River Weaver

Brook Farm

Paradise Covert

Outlanes Farm

3

SOUTH VIEW LA

59

Hawthorn Farm

Cholmondeston Hall

2

TOP FARM LA

WINSFORD RD

Crewe & Nantwich Circular Wlk
Shropshire Union Canal
Middlewich Branch

Nanney's Bridge

Bottom House Farm

Brickyard Bridge

Out Lanes

Daisy Bank Farm

Highfields House

Aston Gorse

1

CW5

Bridge Farm

B5074

Aston Grove Farm

58

171
150

8

HOME FARM PK
LEA GREEN LA

Lea Green

Sandicroft Wood

River Weaver

B5074

Newfield

Newfield Hall Farm

CW10

Walley's Green

Weaver Wood Rookery

7

Lower Elms

Higher Elms

Woodside Farm

Mast

Brook House Farm

BROOKHOUSE LA

Ivy Cottage

The Woodlands

61

OVER RD

WEAVER LDN

Weir

Worsley Covert

Moat House Farm

Church Minshull

6

PH

Cross La

Minshullhill

Cross Lane

Eardswick Wood

Shropshire Union Canal
Middlewich Branch

Minshull Vernon

Dairy Farm Cottage

5

B5074

HURLESTON
MILL IN ROW

VILLAGE FARM

Eardswick Hall Bridge

Eardswick Hall

EARDSWICK LA

Dairy Farm

MIDDLEWICH RD

Crewe & Nantwich Circular Wlk

60

Old Hoolgrave

CW5

River Weaver

High Farm

CW1

4

Crewe & Nantwich Circular Wlk

3

Prescott's Bridge

Church Farm

59

Hoolgrave Manor

Bradfield Green

PH

OVER SL CRES

MOSS LA

2

Bradfield Green Farm

B5076

FLOWERS LA

Red Hall Wood

Red Hall

Leighton Lodge

1

Leighton

B5076

The South Cheshire Private

A530

H H

SMITHY LA

58

66 A **B** **67** C **D** **68** E **F**

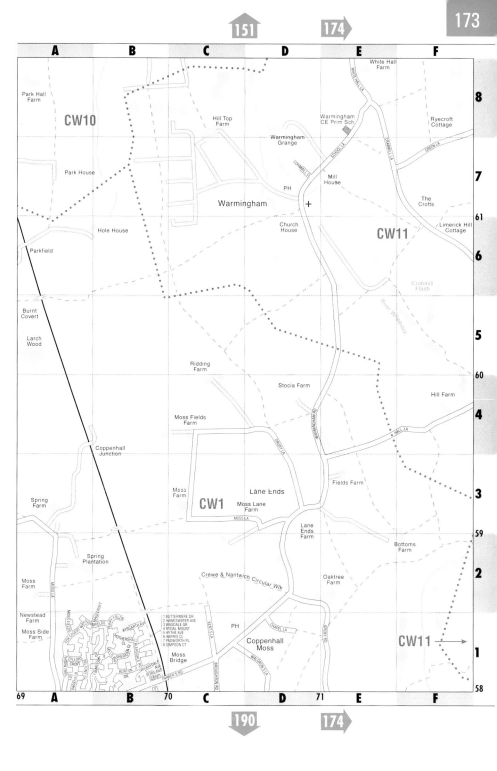

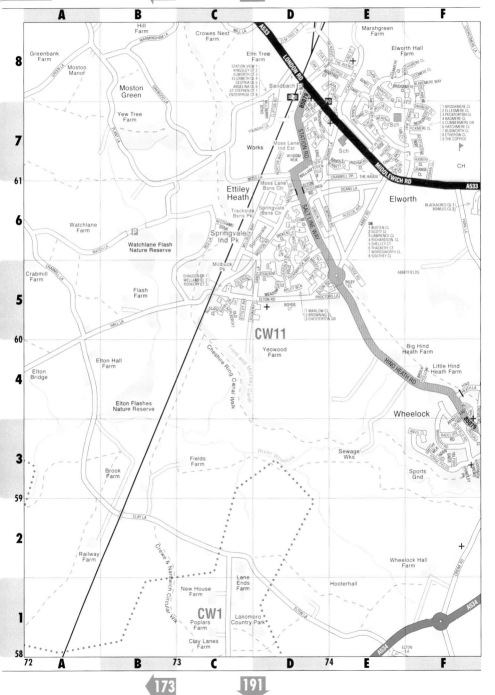

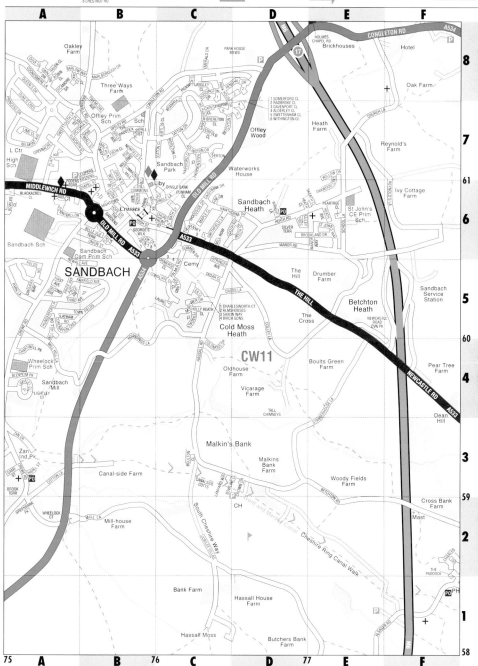

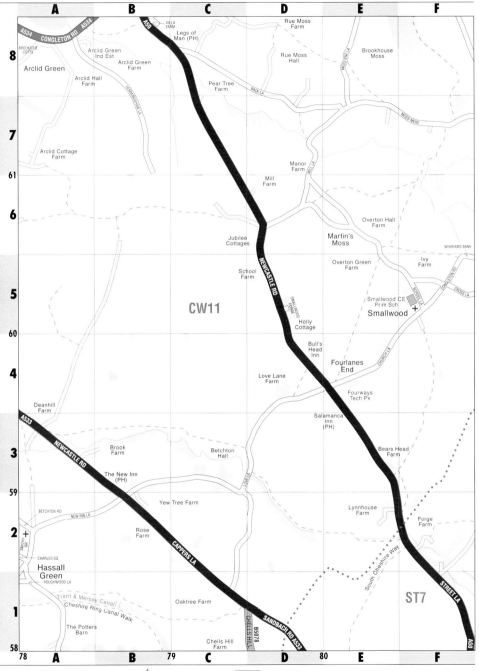

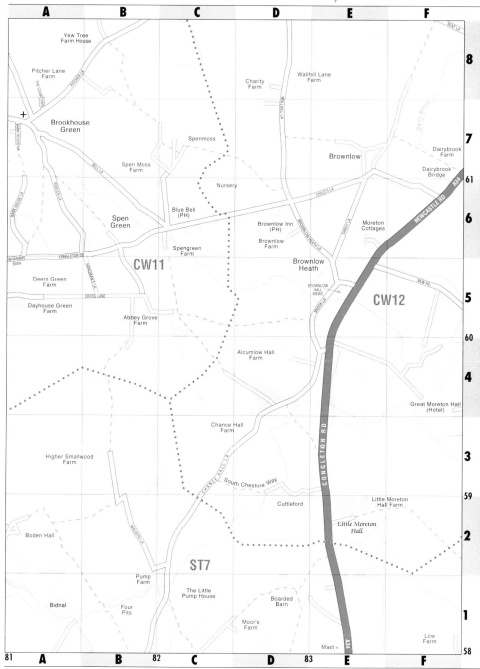

A	B	C	D	E	F

8

Yew Tree Farm House

Pitcher Lane Farm

PITCHER LA

THE COURTYARD

Charity Farm

WALLHILL LA

Wallhill Lane Farm

BENTL LA

DAIRY BROOK

Brookhouse Green

+

BANK HOUSE LA

7

Spenmoss

Brownlow

Dairybrook Farm

Spen Moss Farm

Nursery

Dairybrook Bridge

NEWCASTLE RD

A34

61

BELL LA

PIDGLE LA

Blue Bell (PH)

CHILD'S LA

Brownlow Inn (PH)

BROWNLOW INCH LA

Moreton Cottages

6

Spen Green

Spengreen Farm

Brownlow Farm

SANDY LA

CW11

Brownlow Heath

NEW RD

WHARAMS BANK

CONGLETON RD

Deers Green Farm

HACKNEYS LA

CROSS LANE

Brownlow Hall Mews

BROOK LA

CW12

5

Dayhouse Green Farm

Abbey Grove Farm

60

Alcumlow Hall Farm

4

Great Moreton Hall (Hotel)

Higher Smallwood Farm

Chance Hall Farm

3

CHANCE HALL LA

South Cheshire Way

CONGLETON RD

Little Moreton Hall Farm

59

WALKERS LA

Cuttleford

Little Moreton Hall

2

Boden Hall

ST7

Pump Farm

The Little Pump House

Boarded Barn

Bidnal

Four Pits

Moor's Farm

1

Mast

A34

Low Farm

58

81	A	B	82	C	D	83	E	F

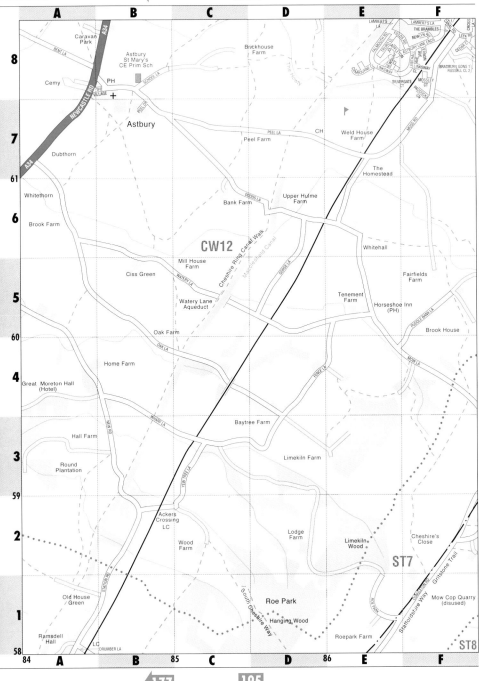

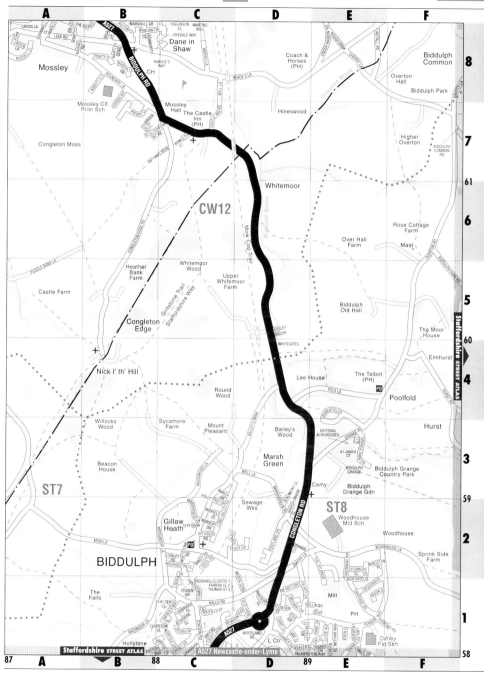

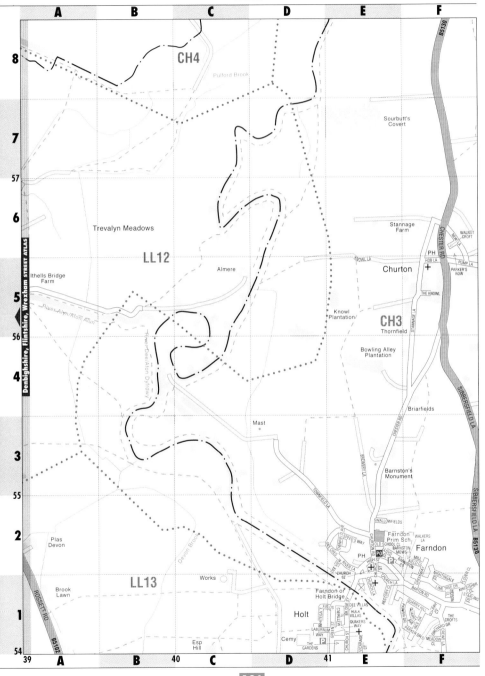

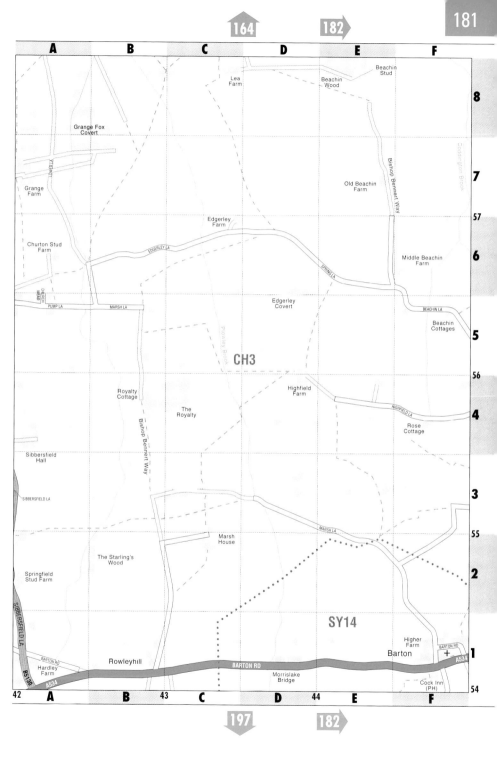

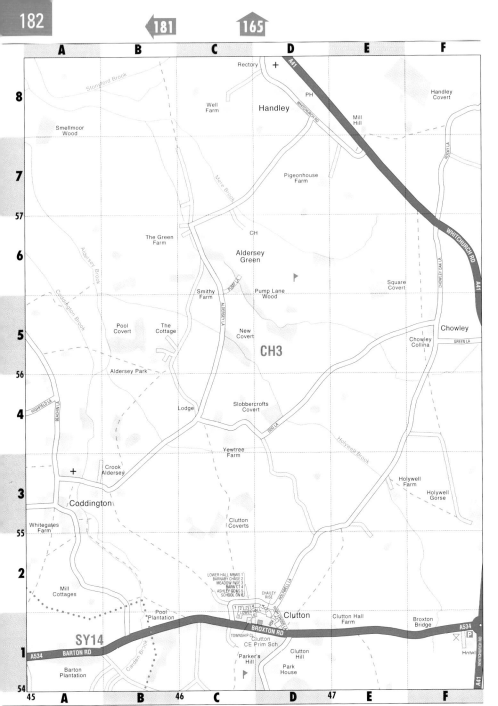

181

165

	A	B	C	D	E	F

8

Rectory

Smellmoor Wood

Well Farm

Handley

PH

Mill Hill

Handley Covert

Stonyford Brook

WHITCHURCH RD

A41

7

Pigeonhouse Farm

Mere Brook

ROCKY LA

57

The Green Farm

CH

WHITCHURCH RD

6

Aldersey Green

Square Covert

Aldersey Brook

Coddington Brook

PUMP LA

Smithy Farm

Pump Lane Wood

ALDERSEY LA

CHOWLEY OAK LA

A41

5

Pool Covert

The Cottage

New Covert

CH3

Chowley Collins

Chowley

GREEN LA

56

Aldersey Park

HIGHFIELD LA

BEACHIN LA

4

Lodge

Slobbercrofts Covert

DOE LA

Holywell Brook

3

Crook Aldersey

Yewtree Farm

Holywell Farm

Holywell Gorse

Coddington

55

Whitegates Farm

Clutton Coverts

HOLYWELL LA

2

Mill Cottages

LOWER HALL MEWS 1
BARNABY CHASE 2
MEADOW RISE 3
BARN CT 4
ASHLEY GDNS 5
SCHOOL GN 6

CHAILEY RISE

Clutton Hall Farm

Broxton Bridge

A534

1

Pool Plantation

SY14

A534 BARTON RD

Carden Brook

LOWER HALL

BROXTON RD

Clutton

TOWNSHIP CL

Clutton CE Prim Sch

Clutton Hill

Park House

Clutton

Hotel

P

WHITCHURCH RD

A41

54

Barton Plantation

Parker's Hill

45	A		B	46	C		D	47	E		F

181

198

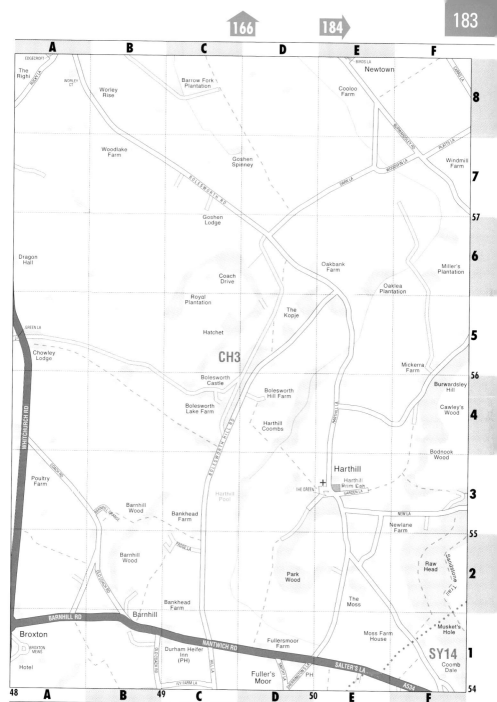

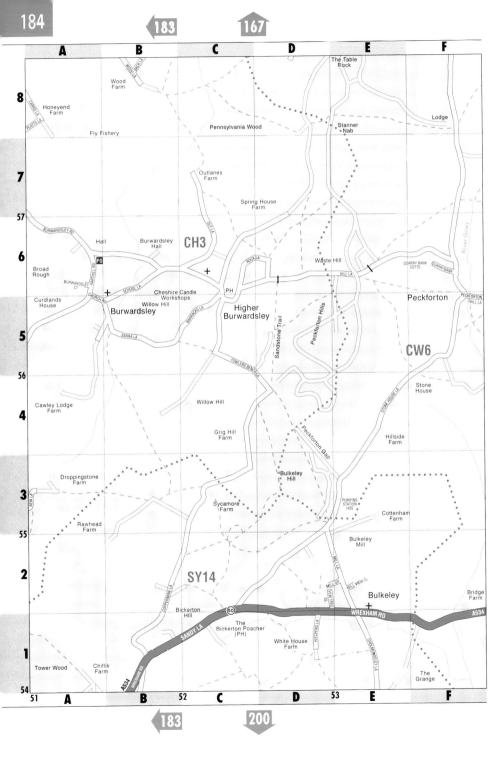

A B C D E F

8

The Table Rock

Honeyend Farm

Wood Farm

Fly Fishery

Pennsylvania Wood

Stanner Nab

Lodge

7

Outlanes Farm

Spring House Farm

57

BURWARDSLEY RD

Hall

Burwardsley Hall

CH3

River Gowy

6

Broad Rough

PO

Waste Hill

HILL LA

QUARRY BANK COTTS

QUARRY BANK

Curdlands House

BURWARDSLEY CT

Cheshire Candle Workshops

PH

Peckforton

PECKFORTON HALL LA

SCHOOL LA

Willow Hill

Burwardsley

Higher Burwardsley

Peckforton Hills

CW6

BARRACKS LA

Sandstone Trail

SARRA LA

5

56

ROCK LA

BULL LA

FOWLERS BENCH LA

Stone House

Cawley Lodge Farm

Willow Hill

4

Grig Hill Farm

Peckforton Gap

Hillside Farm

STONE HOUSE LA

Droppingstone Farm

Bulkeley Hill

3

NEW LA

Sycamore Farm

PUMPING STATION HOS

Cottenham Farm

Rawhead Farm

55

Bulkeley Mill

2

SY14

Bridge Farm

COPPERMINE LA

MILL LA

MILL VIEW CL

Bulkeley

MILL LN

NEW TREES

Bickerton Hill

50

The Bickerton Poacher (PH)

WREXHAM RD

A534

1

SANDY LA

HITCHENS LA

White House Farm

CROS MANLEY LA

Tower Wood

Chiflik Farm

A534

The Grange

54

51 A 52 C 53 E F
B D

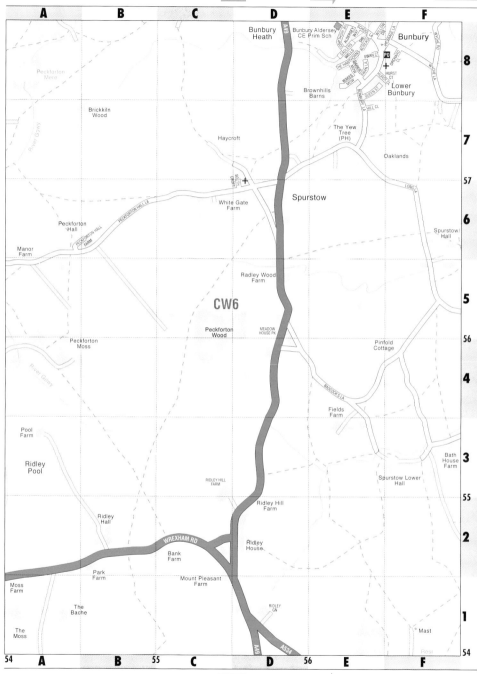

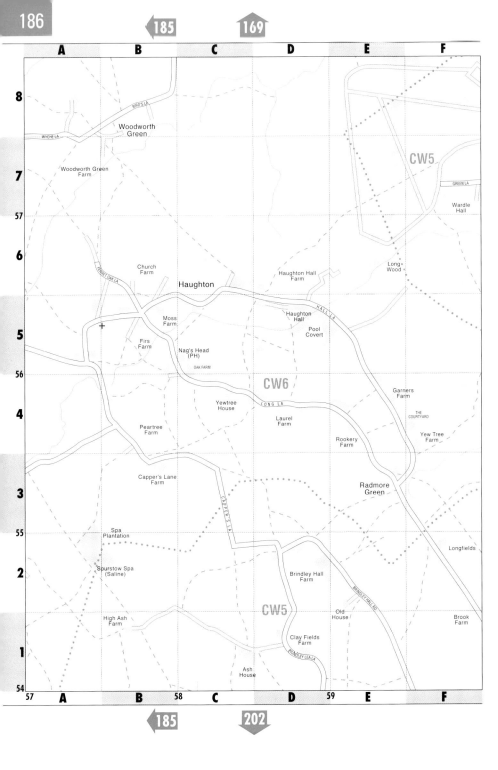

185
169

A B C D E F

8

BIRD'S LA

Woodworth
Green

WYCHE LA

Woodworth Green
Farm

7

CW5

GREEN LA

57

Wardle
Hall

6

TENNET OAK LA

Church
Farm

Haughton

Haughton Hall
Farm

Long
Wood

Moss
Farm

Haughton
Hall

HALL LA

5

Firs
Farm

Nag's Head
(PH)

Pool
Covert

OAK FARM

56

CW6

Garners
Farm

4

Yewtree
House

LONG LA

Laurel
Farm

THE
COURTYARD

Peartree
Farm

Rookery
Farm

Yew Tree
Farm

3

Capper's Lane
Farm

CAPPER'S LA

Radmore
Green

55

Spa
Plantation

Longfields

2

Spurstow Spa
(Saline)

Brindley Hall
Farm

BRINDLEY HALL RD

CW5

Old
House

Brook
Farm

High Ash
Farm

Clay Fields
Farm

1

BRINDLEY LEA LA

Ash
House

54

57 A B 58 C D 59 E F

185
202

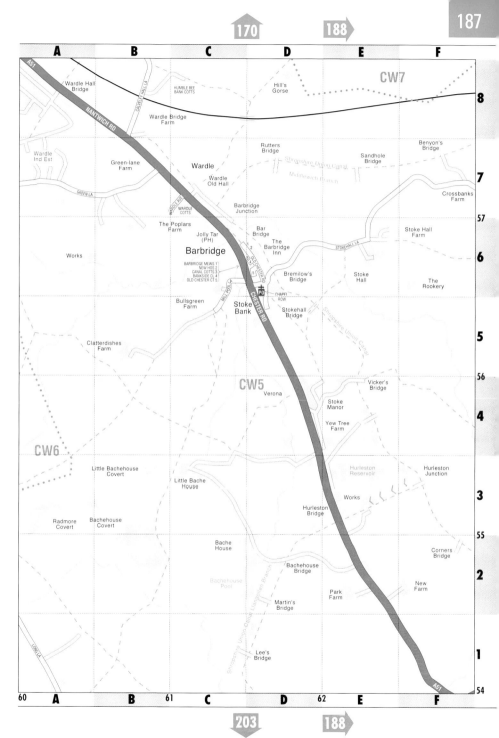

A · B · C · D · E · F

CW7

Wardle Hall
Bridge

NANTWICH RD

Hill's
Gorse

8

Humble Bee
Bank Cotts

Wardle Bridge
Farm

Wardle
Ind Est

Green-lane
Farm

Rutters
Bridge

Shropshire Union Canal

Sandhole
Bridge

Benyon's
Bridge

Wardle
Ind Est

Wardle

Wardle
Old Hall

Middlewich Branch

7

GREEN LA

WARDSE AVE
WARDLE
COTTS

Barbridge
Junction

Crossbanks
Farm

57

The Poplars
Farm

Jolly Tar
(PH)

Bar
Bridge

Stoke Hall
Farm

Works

Barbridge

BARBRIDGE MEWS 1
NEW HOS 2
CANAL COTTS 3
BANKSIDE CL 4
OLD CHESTER CT 5

The
Barbridge
Inn

STOKEHALL LA

6

Bremilow's
Bridge

Stoke
Hall

The
Rookery

Bullsgreen
Farm

MILL POOL LA

CHESTER RD

Stoke
Bank

PO

CHAPEL
ROW

Stokehall
Bridge

Shropshire Union Canal

5

Clatterdishes
Farm

56

CW5

Verona

Vicker's
Bridge

Stoke
Manor

4

Yew Tree
Farm

CW6

Little Bachehouse
Covert

Little Bache
House

Hurleston
Reservoir

Hurleston
Junction

Works

3

Radmore
Covert

Bachehouse
Covert

Hurleston
Bridge

55

Bache
House

Bachehouse
Bridge

Corners
Bridge

Shropshire Union Canal Llangollen Branch

Bachehouse
Pool

New
Farm

2

Martin's
Bridge

Park
Farm

LONG LA

Lee's
Bridge

A51

1

54

60 · A · B · 61 · C · D · 62 · E · F

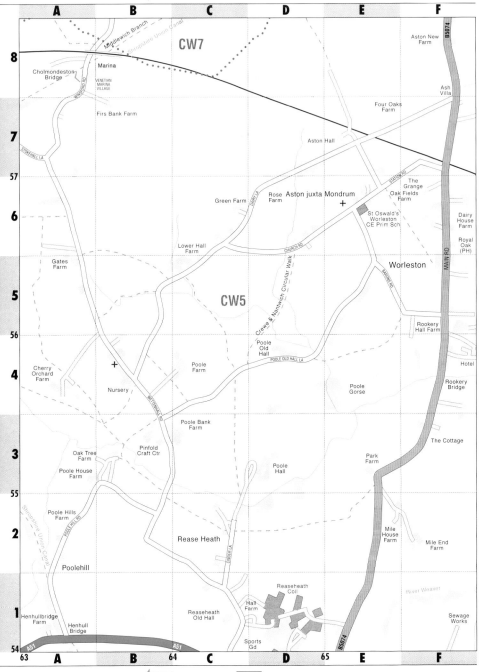

CW7

CW5

Middlewich Branch
Shropshire Union Canal

Cholmondeston
Bridge

Marina

VENETIAN
MARINA
VILLAGE

Firs Bank Farm

WINSFORD RD

Aston New
Farm

B5074

Ash
Villa

Four Oaks
Farm

Aston Hall

STOKEHALL LA

Green Farm

DAIRY LA

Rose
Farm

Aston juxta Mondrum

Oak Fields
Farm

St Oswald's
Worleston
CE Prim Sch

The
Grange

STATION RD

Dairy
House
Farm

Royal
Oak
(PH)

MAIN RD

Lower Hall
Farm

CHURCH RD

Worleston

Gates
Farm

Crewe & Nantwich Circular Walk

NARINE RD

Rookery
Hall Farm

Poole
Old
Hall

Hotel

Cherry
Orchard
Farm

Poole
Farm

POOLE OLD HALL LA

Poole
Gorse

Rookery
Bridge

Nursery

WETTENHALL RD

Poole Bank
Farm

Park
Farm

The Cottage

Oak Tree
Farm

Pinfold
Craft Ctr

Poole
Hall

Poole House
Farm

Poole Hills
Farm

POOLE HILL RD

Shropshire Union Canal

Rease Heath

CINDER LA

Mile
House
Farm

Mile End
Farm

Poolehill

Reaseheath
Coll

River Weaver

Henhullbridge
Farm

Henhull
Bridge

A51

Reaseheath
Old Hall

Hall
Farm

Sewage
Works

A51

Sports
Gd

B5074

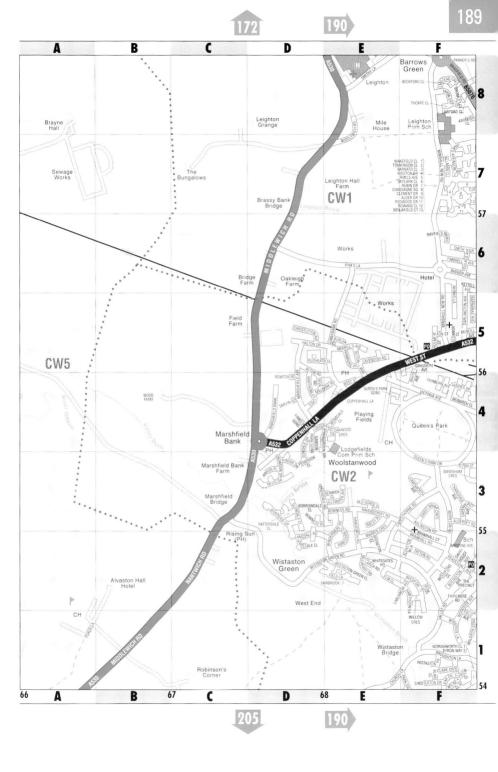

CREWE

CW1

CW2

Coppenhall

Maw Green

Sydney Bridge

Crewe Mill Bridge

MMU Cheshire (Crewe Campus)

The Valley

Tipkinder Park

Loco Works

Kings Grove Sch

Gainsborough Prim Sch

St Thomas More RC High Sch

South Cheshire Coll

Ruskin Sports Coll & Com High Sch

Victoria Com Tech Sch

Grand Junction Ret Pk

Macon Ind Est

Valley Brook Bsns Ctr

The Railway Age Mus

Cheshire Acad

Crewe Gates Farm Ind Est

Crewe Bsns Pk

The Weston Ctr

Gresty Road Football Gd (Crewe Alexandra FC)

Holly Tree Farm

Race Farm

Groby Farm

Stoneley Farm

Monks Coppenhall Prim Sch

Cumberland Sports Ctr

Brierley Bsns Ctr

Playing Field

Underwood Bsns Pk

Superstore

Wistaston Road Bsns Ctr

Imperial Mews

Ex Ctr

Works

BRADFIELD RD · NORTH ST · WEST ST · DUNWOODY WAY · EARLE ST · VERNON · MACON WAY · CREWE RD · NANTWICH RD · WESTON RD · EDLESTON RD · MILL ST · MIDDLEWICH ST · OAK ST

A532 · A5078 · A534 · B5076 · B5071 · GRESTY RD

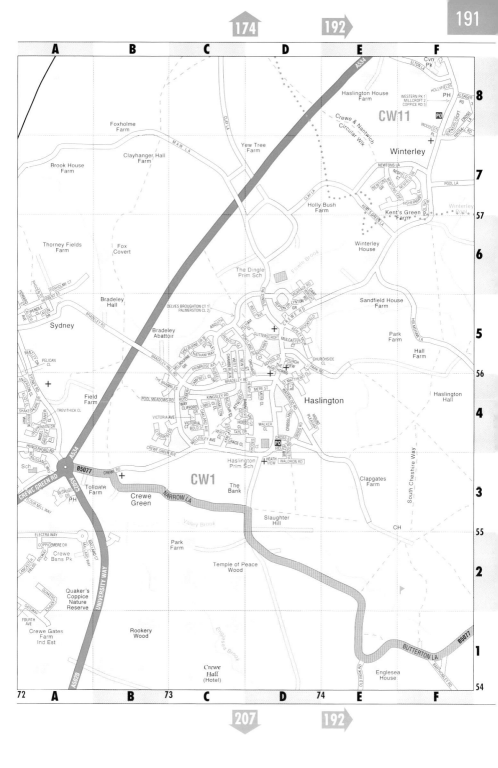

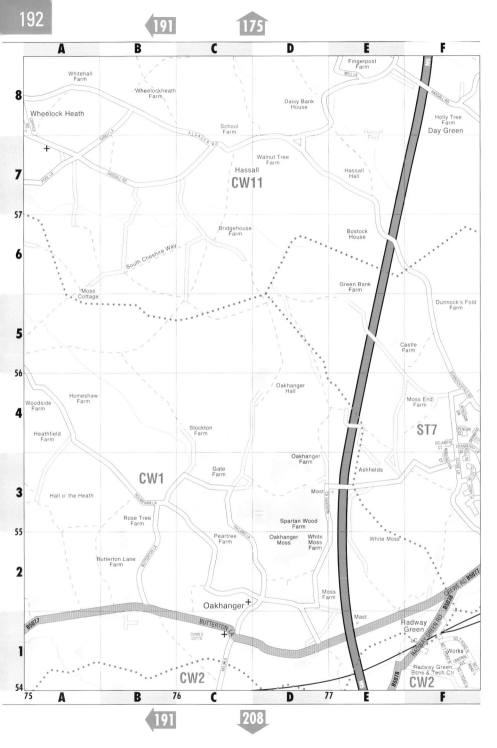

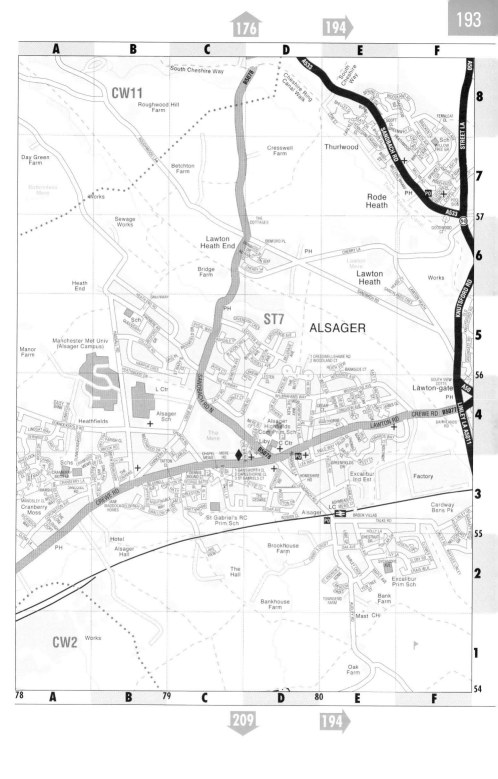

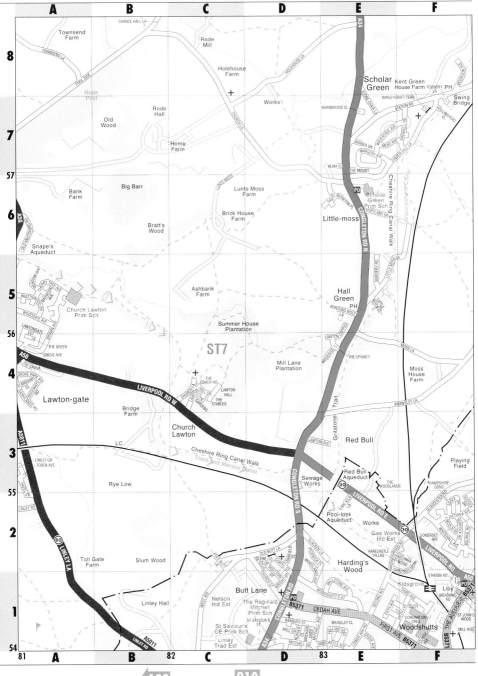

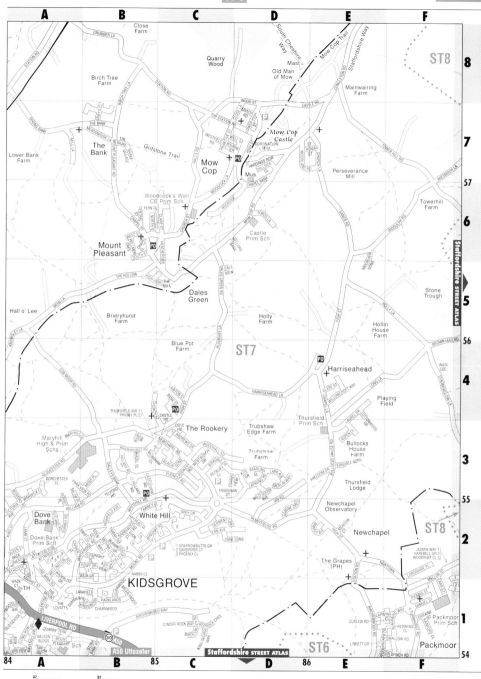

A2
1 KINNERSLEY ST
2 GILBERT CL
3 NAPIER GDNS
4 PEEL CT
5 BANK CT
6 HIGHERLAND CT
7 WESLEY GDNS
8 VICTORIA CT

B2
1 SWALLOW CL
2 WHEELOCK WAY
3 DIAMOND AVE
4 MOSSFIELD CRES
5 LITTLE ROW
6 BRIGHTO AVE
7 BIRCHES WAY
8 SILVERMINE CL
9 MAGPIE CRES

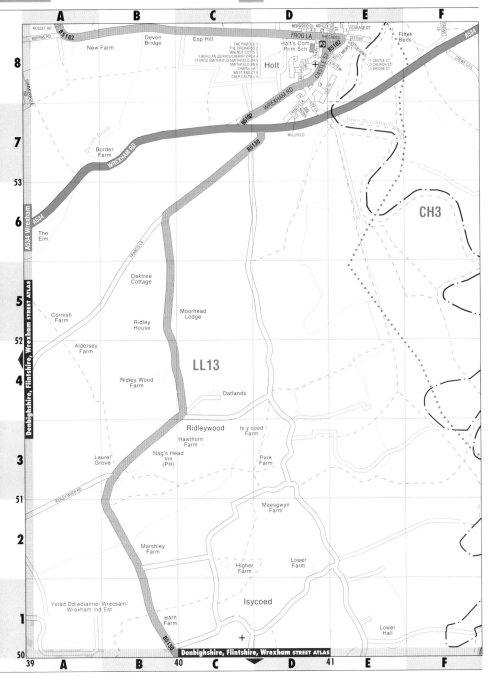

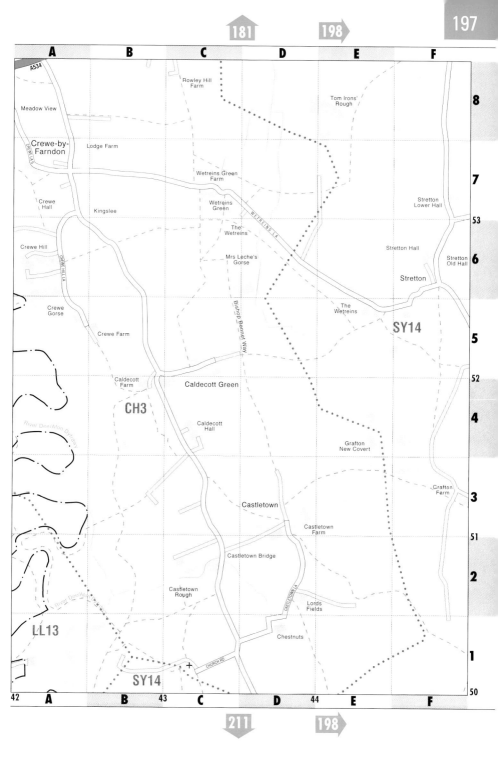

197
182

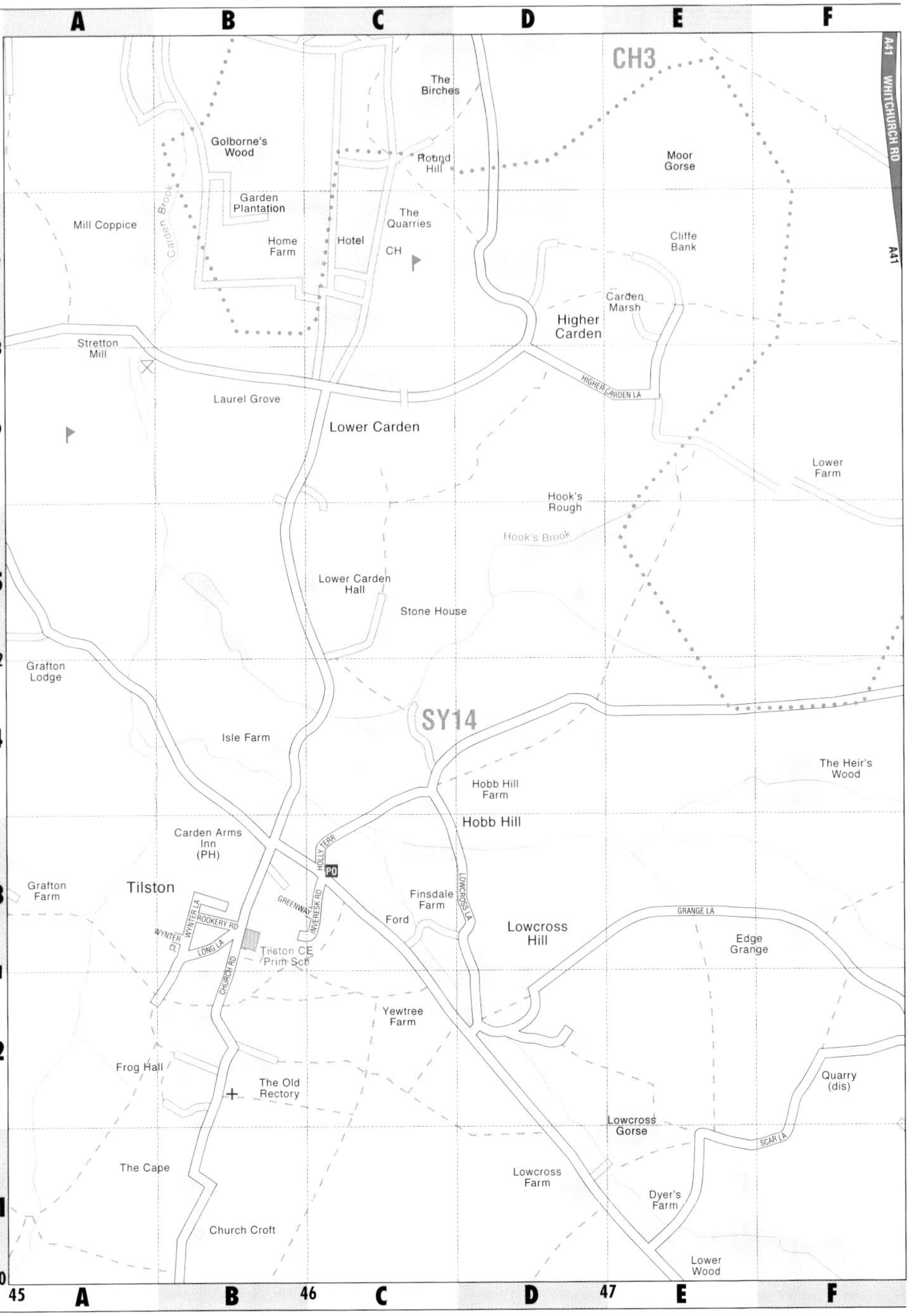

A B C D E F

CH3

The Birches

Golborne's Wood

Garden Plantation

Round Hill

Moor Gorse

Mill Coppice

Carden Brook

Home Farm

Hotel

The Quarries

CH

Cliffe Bank

Carden Marsh

Higher Carden

A41
WHITCHURCH RD
A41

Stretton Mill

Laurel Grove

Lower Carden

HIGHER CARDEN LA

Lower Farm

Hook's Rough

Hook's Brook

Lower Carden Hall

Stone House

SY14

Grafton Lodge

Isle Farm

The Heir's Wood

Hobb Hill Farm

Hobb Hill

Carden Arms Inn (PH)

HOLLY TERR

PO

Tilston

Grafton Farm

WYNTER CL
TILSTON LA
ROOKERY RD
GREENWAY
INNER LA RD
CHURCH RD

Tilston CE Prim Sch

Finsdale Farm

Ford

LONGMEAD LA

Lowcross Hill

GRANGE LA

Edge Grange

Yewtree Farm

Frog Hall

The Old Rectory

Quarry (dis)

Lowcross Gorse

SCAR LA

The Cape

Lowcross Farm

Dyer's Farm

Church Croft

Lower Wood

45 A B 46 C D 47 E F
50 51 52 53 8 7 6 5 4 3 2 1

197
212

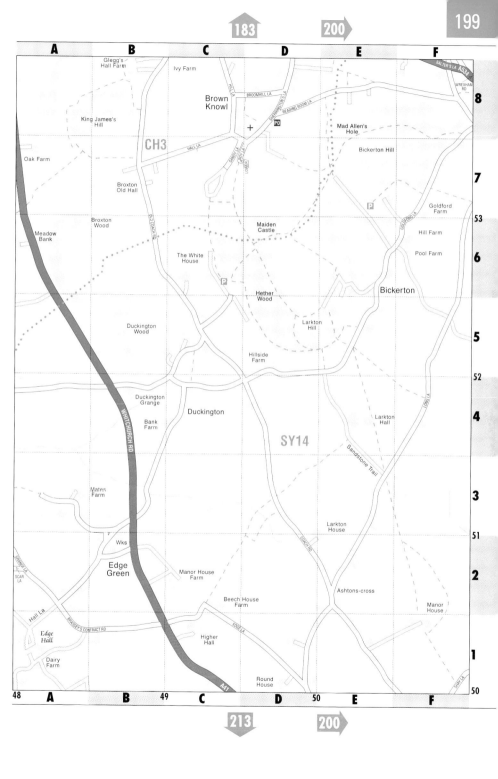

A B C D E F

SALTER'S LA A534

WREXHAM RD

8

Glegg's Hall Farm

Ivy Farm

BROOMHILL LA

CHORRINGTON ST LA

READING ROOM LA

Brown Knowl

King James's Hill

PO

Mad Allen's Hole

CH3

HALL LA

SANDY LA

HILL LA

LOWER

Bickerton Hill

Oak Farm

7

Broxton Old Hall

Broxton Wood

OLD COACH RD

P

GOLDFORD LA

Goldford Farm

53

Meadow Bank

Maiden Castle

Hill Farm

Pool Farm

The White House

6

P

Bickerton

Hether Wood

Duckington Wood

Larkton Hill

5

Hillside Farm

52

Duckington Grange

LONG LA

4

Duckington

Bank Farm

SY14

Larkton Hall

Sandstone Trail

3

Mates Farm

Larkton House

51

Wks

COACH RD

Edge Green

Manor House Farm

2

GRANGE LA

SCAR LA

Beech House Farm

Ashtons-cross

Manor House

Hall La

BRASSEY'S CONTRACT RD

EDGE LA

Edge Hall

Higher Hall

1

Dairy Farm

A41

Round House

SCAR LA

50

48 A B 49 C D 50 E F

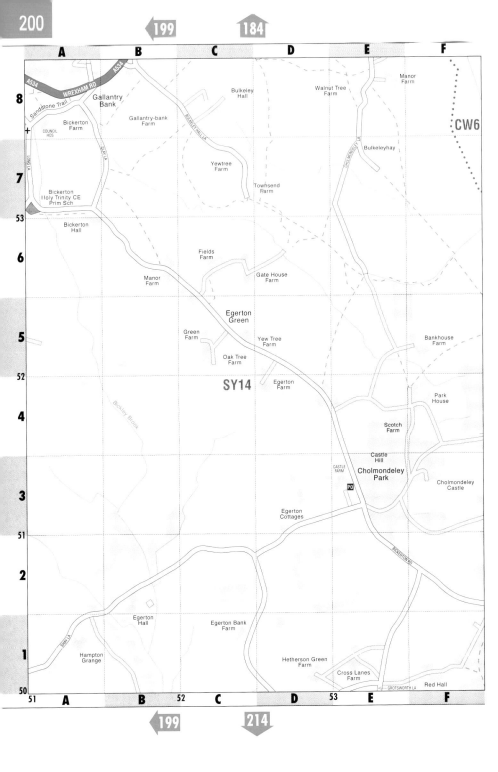

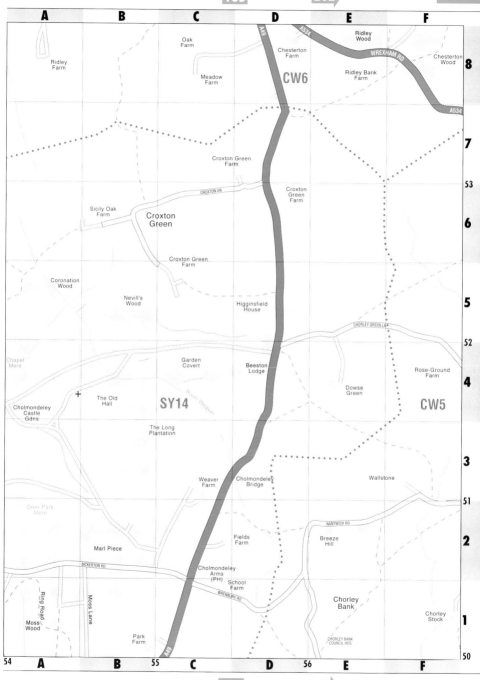

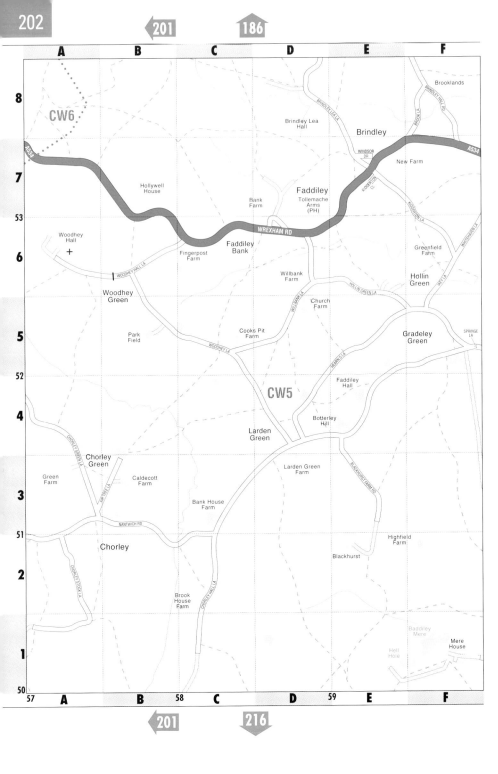

CW6

Brooklands

8

Brindley Lea
Hall

Brindley

WINDSOR
DR

New Farm

A534

7

Hollywell
House

Bank
Farm

Faddiley

Tollemache
Arms
(PH)

53

Woodhey
Hall

WREXHAM RD

Greenfield
Farm

Fingerpost
Farm

Faddiley
Bank

Hollin
Green

6

WOODHEY HALL LA

Willbank
Farm

Woodhey
Green

Church
Farm

Park
Field

Cooks Pit
Farm

Gradeley
Green

SPRINGE
LA

5

WOODHEY LA

WILLBANK LA

HOLLIN GREEN LA

52

CW5

Faddiley
Hall

Larden
Green

Botterley
Hill

4

Chorley
Green

Larden Green
Farm

BLACKHURST FARM RD

Green
Farm

Caldecott
Farm

3

Bank House
Farm

Highfield
Farm

NANTWICH RD

51

Chorley

Blackhurst

2

Brook
House
Farm

CHORLEY HALL LA

Baddiley
Mere

Mere
House

1

Hell
Hole

50

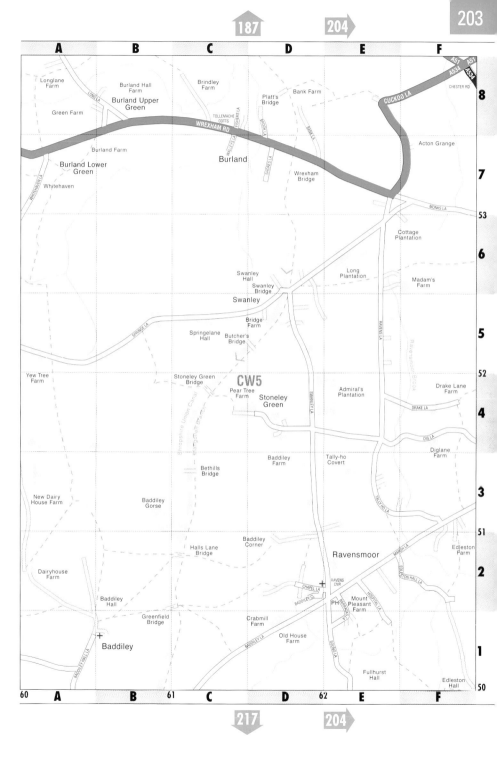

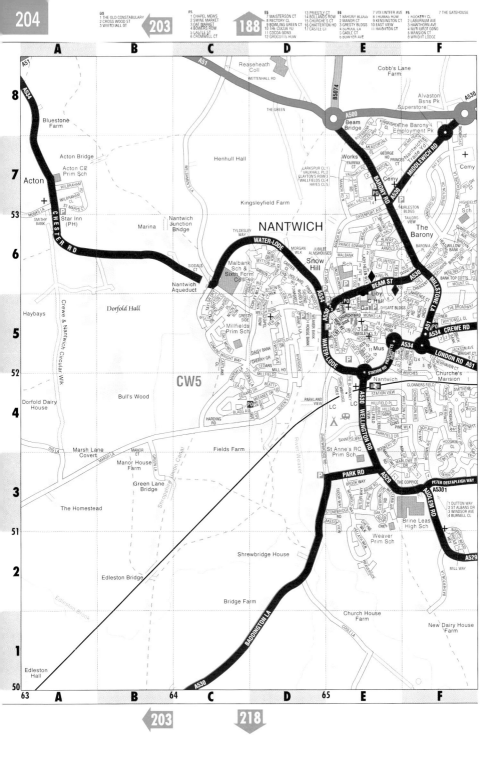

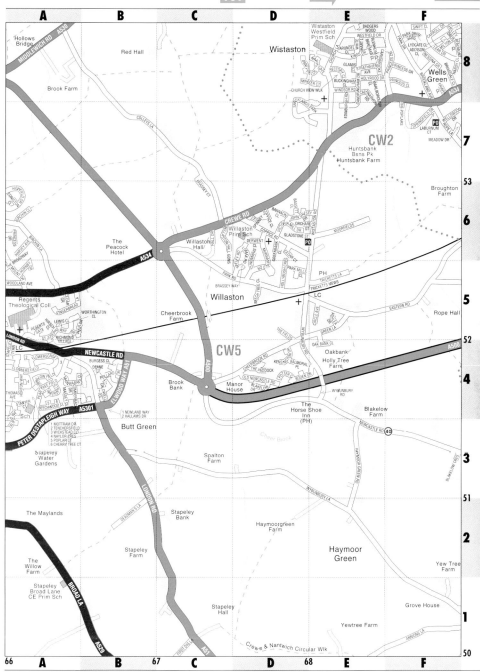

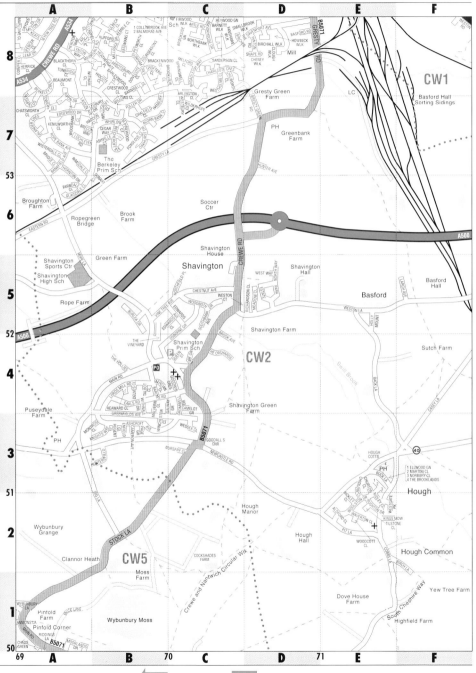

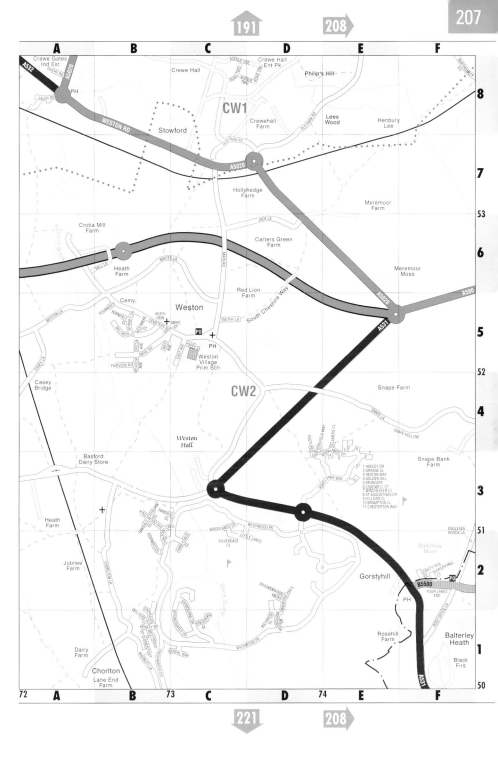

A   B   C   D   E   F

8
7
53
6
5
52
4
3
51
2
1
50

Crewe Gates
Ind Est
PH
Savoy Rd
WESTON RD
Stowford
Crewe Hall
AVENUE ONE
AVENUE TWO
Crewe Hall
Ent Pk
Philip's Hill
CW1
Crewehall
Farm
Lees
Wood
Henbury
Lee
A5020
Hollyhedge
Farm
Meremoor
Farm
JACK LA
Crotia Mill
Farm
Carters Green
Farm
MILL LA
WHITE LA
Heath
Farm
MAIN RD
Red Lion
Farm
Meremoor
Moss
A5020
A500
Cemy
Weston
South Cheshire Way
SMITHY LA
A531
FERNDALE
MILL BROK
MERE
CT
HEATH
VIEW
CEMETERY RD
PO
PH
FAIRVIEW AVE
MEADOW
AVE
POPPY CL
Weston
Village
Prim Sch
WESTON LA
CASEY LA
FOURNAIS
CROTIA
AVE
EAST AVE
Casey
Bridge
Snape Farm
CW2
SNAPE LA
Snape Hollow
Weston
Hall
PETERSFIELD WAY
MERE CL
LAMERE DR
Snape Bank
Farm
Basford
Dairy Store
1 HADLEY DR
2 GRANGE CL
3 HEATON WAY
4 GOLDEN HILL
5 DEANGATE
6 GRANDWELL CT
7 MANCHESTER CT
8 ST AUGUSTINES DR
9 HILLSIDE CL
10 BRAMPTON CL
11 CHESTERTON WAY
JUBILEE PARK WAY
Heath
Farm
HAVERHILL
KINGSWOOD
CRES
WOODLANDS DR
WYCHWOOD PK
ENGLESEA
BROOK LA
Balterley
Mere
CHORLTON LA
SILVERDALE
CL
LITTLE LAKES
Gorstyhill
GORSTY HILL
GORSTY HILL
PO
B5500
FOUR LANES
END
Jubilee
Farm
BRACKENWOOD DRES
MEADOWSIDE CL
RICHWOOD
CL
PH
POST OFFICE LA
Balterley
Heath
Heath
Farm
ASHBOURNE DR
SPRINGWATER CRES
KINGSWOOD
HENLEY RD
ST CUTHBERTS
GHILLESPIE CL
Rosehill
Farm
Black
Firs
Dairy
Farm
KENDAL WAY
Chorlton
Lane End
Farm
A531

A532
A5020
A5020

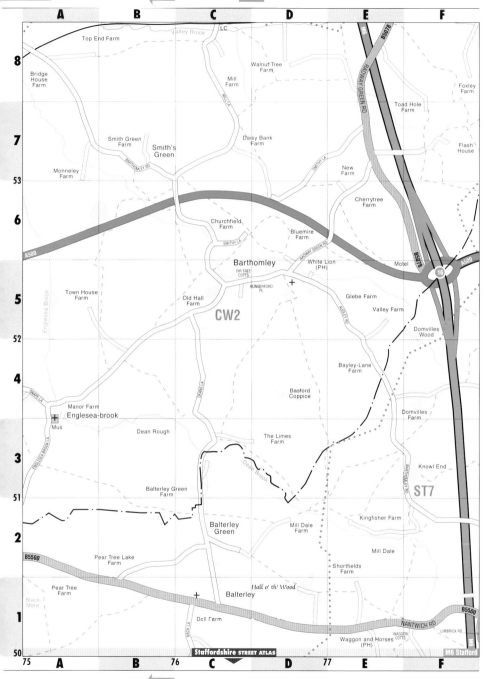

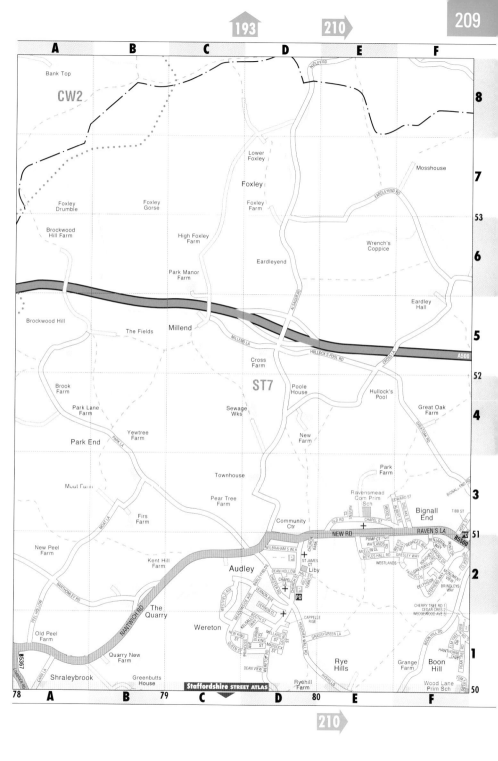

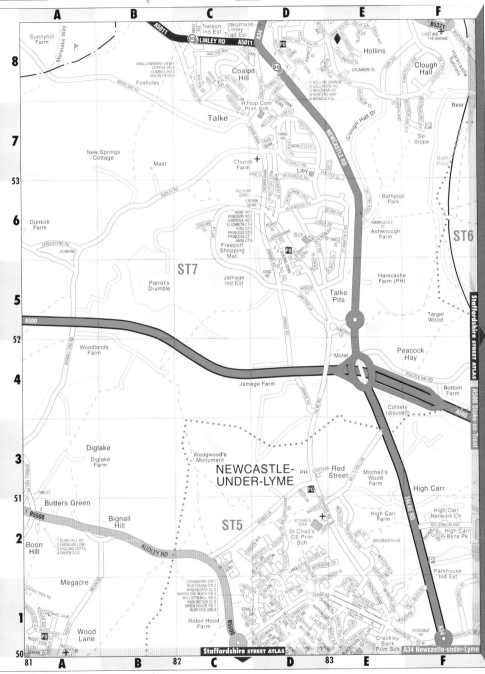

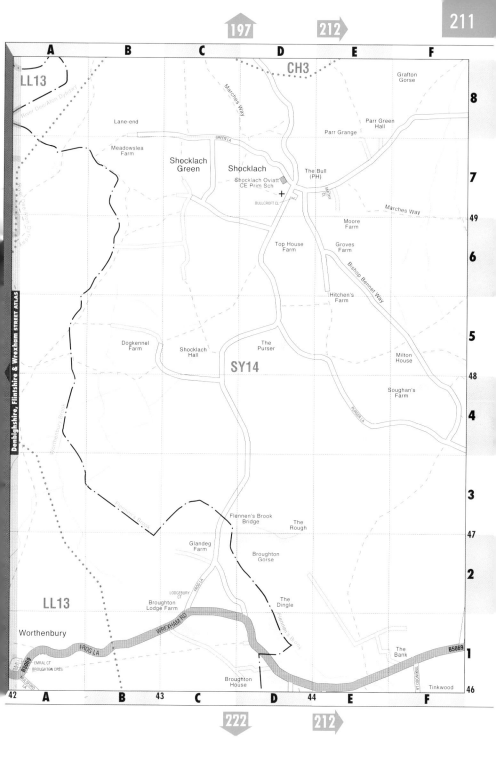

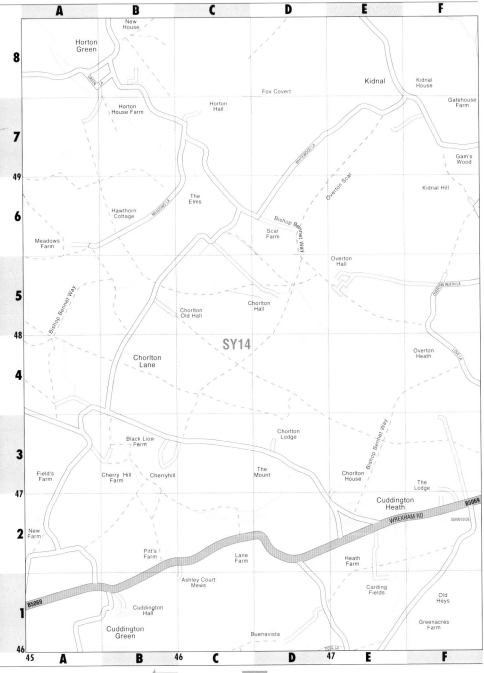

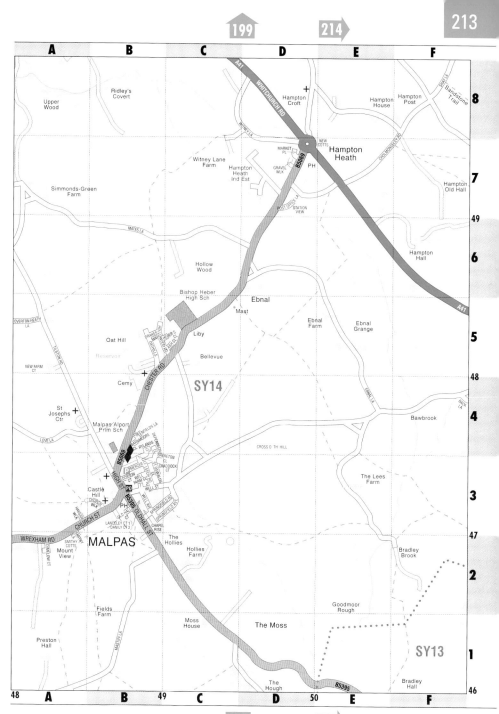

213
200

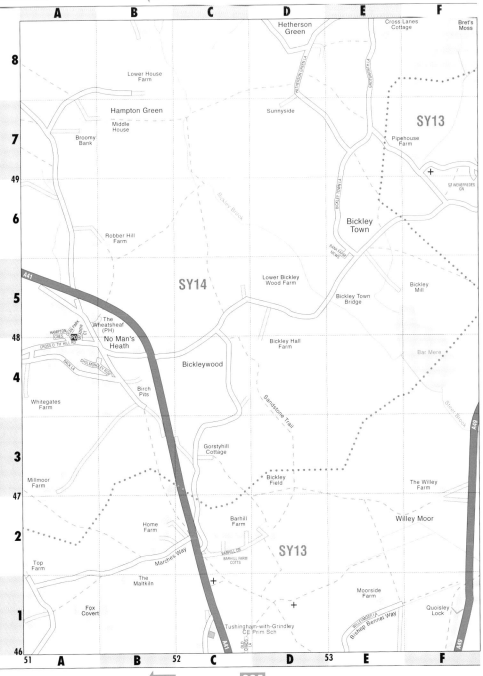

213
225

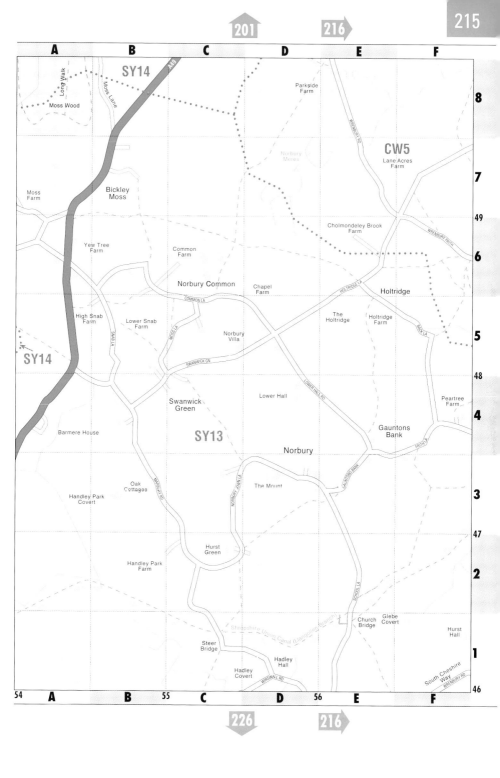

SY14

Long Walk

Moss Lane

A49

Parkside
Farm

Moss Wood

8

Norbury
Meres

CW5

Lane Acres
Farm

7

Moss
Farm

Bickley
Moss

WRENBURY RD

49

Cholmondeley Brook
Farm

WRENBURY FRITH

Yew Tree
Farm

Common
Farm

6

High Snab
Farm

Norbury Common

Chapel
Farm

HOLTRIDGE LA

Holtridge

COMMON LA

The
Holtridge

Holtridge
Farm

Lower Snab
Farm

SNAB LA

MOSS LA

Norbury
Villa

BAG LA

SY14

5

SWANWICK GN

48

LOWER HALL RD

Lower Hall

Peartree
Farm

Swanwick
Green

SY13

Barmere House

Norbury

Gauntons
Bank

FRITH LA

4

Oak
Cottagee

NORBURY RD

The Mount

NORBURY LA

GAUNTONS BANK

3

Handley Park
Covert

47

Hurst
Green

2

Handley Park
Farm

FRITH LA

Shropshire Union Canal (Llangollen Branch)

Church
Bridge

Glebe
Covert

Hurst
Hall

Steer
Bridge

Hadley
Hall

1

Hadley
Covert

WIRSWALL RD

South Cheshire Way

WRENBURY RD

215
202

A **B** **C** **D** **E** **F**

8

Chorley Hall

Baddiley Resr

7

Frith Green Farm

Wrenbury Wood

Frith Farm

New Covert

WRENBURY FRITH

49

Wrenbury Wood

Sprostonwood Farm

6

Bank Farm

COUNCIL HOUSES

The Heald

Heald Covert

CW5

Sprostonwood House

Wrenbury Hall

Ivy House Farm

Wrenbury Frith

Sproston Hill Farm

5

CHOLMONDELEY RD

Porter's Hill

Wrenbury Bridge

Wrenbury Church Bridge

Starkey's Bridge

48

HALTMORE LA

Cotton Arms (PH)

Wrenbury House

Wrenbury

4

Wrenbury Frith Bridge (Draw-bridge)

FRITH LA

HALTMORE COTTS

CROUCH FARM

PO

OAK VILLAS 1 OAK COTTS 2

Wrenbury Prim Sch

Frith-hall Farm

Thomason's Bridge

Shropshire Union Canal (Llangollen Branch)

NANTWICH RD

Sandfield House

3

Ryebank

Marbury Brook

River Weaver

Hill Farm

47

Canal Covert

South Cheshire Way

Smeaton Hall

NEW RD

2

SY13

Marbury Heyes

Pinsley Green Rd

Pinsley Green Rd

SMEATON WOOD

1

Hurst Hall

Townley Farm

Pinsley Green

Smeaton Wood Farm

Hewitt's Moss

46

WRENBURY RD

MARLEY GN

HOLLYHURST RD

Townley Cottage

Yew Tree Farm

57 **A** **B** **58** **C** **D** **59** **E** **F**

215
227

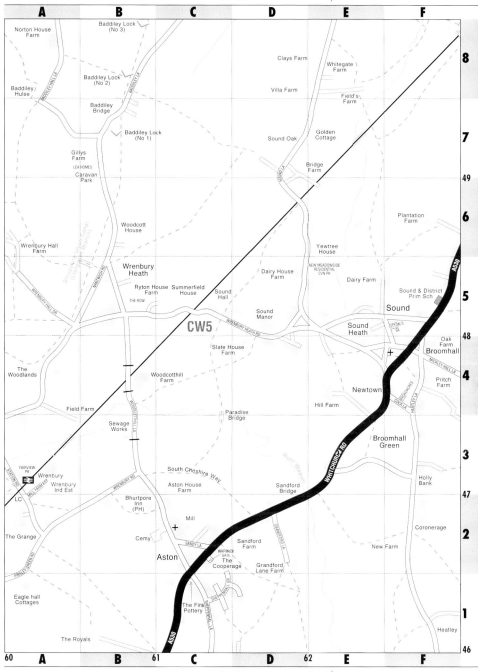

203
218

A   **B**   **C**   **D**   **E**   **F**

Norton House Farm

Baddiley Lock (No 3)

Clays Farm

8

Whitegate Farm

Baddiley Hulse

Baddiley Lock (No 2)

Villa Farm

Field's Farm

Baddiley Bridge

BADDILEY HALL DR

BADDILEY LA

Golden Cottage

7

Baddiley Lock (No 1)

Sound Oak

Gillys Farm

LEA HOMES Caravan Park

LONGHILL

Bridge Farm

49

A530

Wrenbury Hall Farm

Woodcott House

6

Plantation Farm

Yewtree House

MAYWOOD RD

Wrenbury Heath

Dairy House Farm

NEW MEADOWSIDE RESIDENTIAL CVN PK

Dairy Farm

Sound & District Prim Sch

5

Ryton House Farm

Summerfield House

Sound Hall

Sound

SELWYN'S LN (Llangollen Branch)

THE ROW

WRENBURY HALL DR

Sound Manor

Sound Heath

FITTON'S CL

CW5

WRENBURY HEATH RD

Slate House Farm

48

Oak Farm

Broomhall

The Woodlands

Woodcotthill Farm

Newtown

MICKLEY HALL LA

Pritch Farm

4

WOODCOTTHILL LA

Field Farm

Paradise Bridge

Hill Farm

BROADOAKS

COCK LA

HEATLEY LA

Sewage Works

River Weaver

Broomhall Green

3

FAIRVIEW PK

Wrenbury

South Cheshire Way

WHITCHURCH RD

Holly Bank

47

STATION RD

Wrenbury Ind Est

WRENBURY RD

Aston House Farm

Sandford Bridge

MILL FARM EST

LC

Bhurtpore Inn (PH)

Mill

Coronerage

2

The Grange

Cemy

SANDY LA

Sandford Farm

GRANDFORD LA

New Farm

PINSLEY GREEN RD

Aston

WARWICK GATE

The Cooperage

Grandford Lane Farm

Eagle hall Cottages

A530

The Firs Pottery

SHEPPENHALL LA

1

Heatley

The Royals

46

60   **A**   **B**   61   **C**   **D**   62   **E**   **F**

228
218

217

204

	A	**B**	**C**	**D**	**E**	**F**

8

Batherton Hall

Crewe and Nantwich Circular Walk

The Brooklands

Baddington Lane Bridge

Baddington Bank Farm

BADDINGTON LA

A530

ATCHERLEY CL

CRISHAM AVE

7

Old Hall Austerson

WHITCHURCH RD

The Grange

Baddington Farm

49

A530

6

Broomhall Gorse

Baddington Farm

Hack House Farm

Hackgreen Locks

Poplars Farm

Hack Green

Gorse Covert

Hackgreen Bridge

FRENCH LANE END

5

Burrow's Bridge

New Farm

FRENCH LA

Hack Farm

CW5

New Houses

Austerson Farm

48

Hack House

Mast

Hack Green Secret Nuclear Bunker

Seven Oaks Farm

4

MICKLEY HALL LA

Shropshire Union Canal

COOL LA

Austerson Hall

3

Mickley Hall

+

47

Mickley Bridge

Old Hall

South View Farm

2

South Cheshire Way

Devil's Nest

Westview Cottages

BRINE PITS LA

Finnaker Brook

1

Top of the Town

Heatley

Austin's Bridge

Top House Farm

Cool Lane Bridge

CW3

46

63	**A**	**B**	**64**	**C**	**D**	**65**	**E**	**F**

217

229

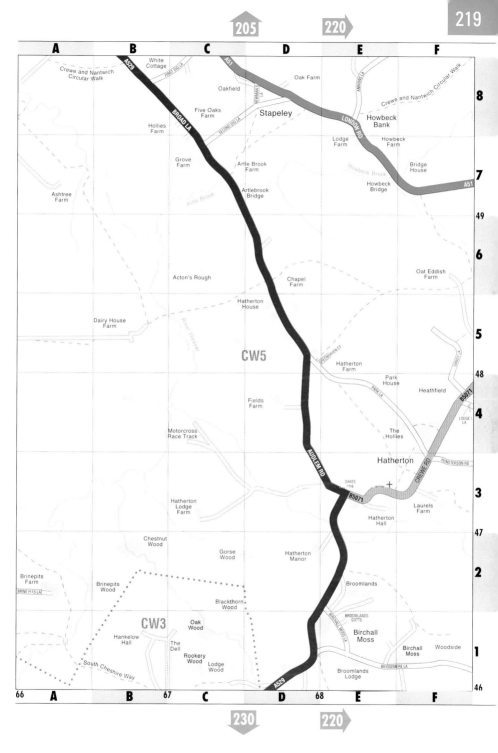

205
220

| | A | B | C | D | E | F |

8

White Cottage

Crewe and Nantwich Circular Walk

A529

FIRST DIG LA

Oakfield

NEWMAN'S LA

Five Oaks Farm

SECOND DIG LA

Stapeley

Oak Farm

London Rd

ANNUN LA

Howbeck Bank

Crewe and Nantwich Circular Walk

Hollies Farm

BROAD LA

Lodge Farm

Howbeck Farm

Bridge House

7

Grove Farm

Artle Brook Farm

Artlebrook Bridge

Artle Brook

Hosbeck Brook

Howbeck Bridge

A51

49

Ashtree Farm

6

Acton's Rough

Chapel Farm

Oat Eddish Farm

Hatherton House

Dairy House Farm

River Weaver

5

CW5

GREENHAVEN CT

Hatherton Farm

Park House

Heathfield

SANDY LA

48

Fields Farm

PARK LA

B5071

4

Motorcross Race Track

The Hollies

LODGE LA

AUDLEM RD

CREWE RD

HUNSTERSON RD

Hatherton

3

Hatherton Lodge Farm

OAKES CNR

B5071

+

Laurels Farm

Chestnut Wood

Hatherton Hall

47

Gorse Wood

Hatherton Manor

Brinepits Farm

BRINE PITS LA

Brinepits Wood

Broomlands

2

Blackthorn Wood

BIRCHALL MOSS LA

BROOMLANDS COTTS

CW3

Oak Wood

Hankelow Hall

The Dell

Rookery Wood

Lodge Wood

Birchall Moss

Birchall Moss

Woodside

1

South Cheshire Way

A529

Broomlands Lodge

BRIDGEMERE LA

46

| 66 | A | B | 67 | C | D | 68 | E | F |

230
220

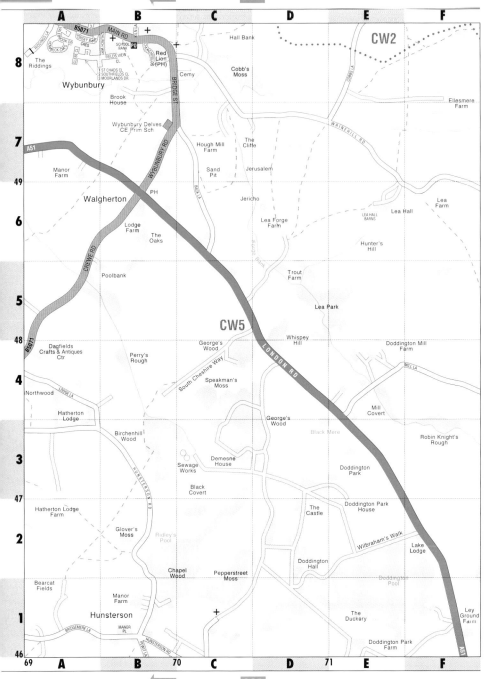

Map labels

CW2

The Riddings

Wybunbury

B5071
MAIN RD
PO
SCHOOL BANK
Red Lion (PH)
Cemy
FIELDS VIEW CL
1 ST CHADS CL
2 SOUTHFIELDS CL
3 MOORLANDS DR
COSSEY BANK
CRES
CHURCH WAY
BRIDGE ST
HOUGH CL

Hall Bank

Cobb's Moss

Ellesmere Farm

Brook House

Wybunbury Delves CE Prim Sch

WYBUNBURY RD

A51

Manor Farm

Walgherton

PH

CREWE RD

Lodge Farm

The Oaks

Poolbank

Hough Mill Farm

The Cliffe

Sand Pit

Jerusalem

Jericho

BACK LA

Lea Forge Farm

LEA HALL BARNS

Lea Hall

Lea Farm

Hunter's Hill

WRINEHILL RD

Trout Farm

Lea Park

CW5

George's Wood

Perry's Rough

South Cheshire Way

Speakman's Moss

LONDON RD

Whispey Hill

Doddington Mill Farm

MILL LA

B5071

Dagfields Crafts & Antiques Ctr

Northwood

LODGE LA

Hatherton Lodge

Birchenhill Wood

HUNSTERSON RD

George's Wood

Black Mere

Mill Covert

Robin Knight's Rough

Sewage Works

Demesne House

Black Covert

Doddington Park

Hatherton Lodge Farm

Glover's Moss

Ridley's Pool

The Castle

Doddington Park House

Wilbraham's Walk

Lake Lodge

Bearcat Fields

Manor Farm

Hunsterson

MANOR PL

BRIDGEMERE LA

Chapel Wood

Pepperstreet Moss

Doddington Hall

Doddington Pool

HUNSTERSON RD

The Duckery

Doddington Park Farm

Ley Ground Farm

A51

69   70   71

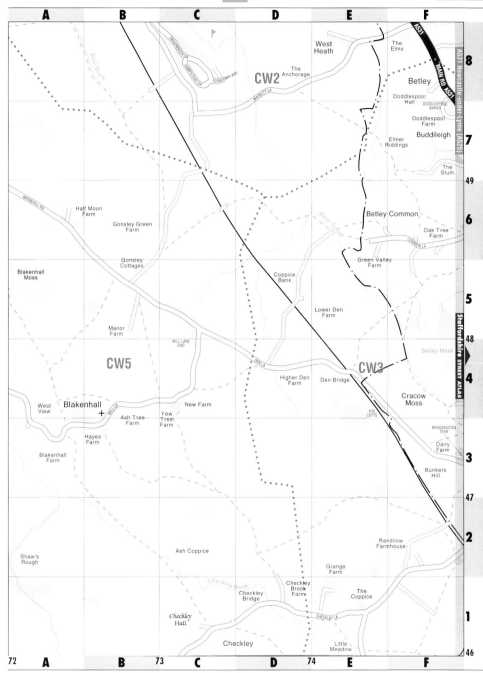

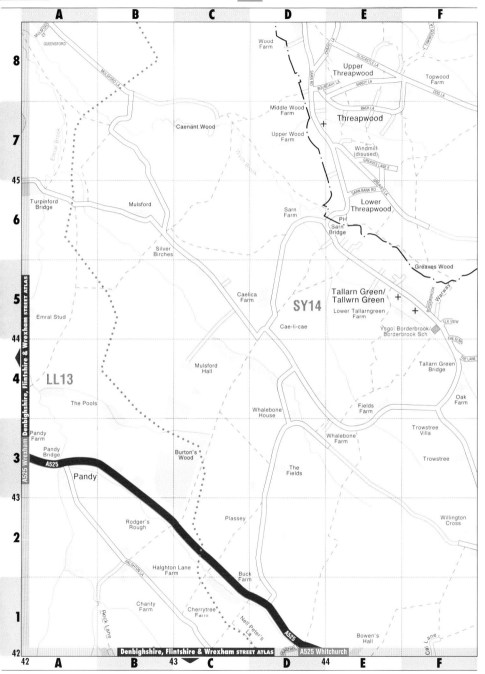

8

7

45

6

5

44

4

3

43

2

1

42

A   **B**   **C**   **D**   **E**   **F**

MULSFORD
CT
Queensford

MILSFORD LA

Emral Brook

Caenant Wood

Wych Brook

Turpinford
Bridge

Mulsford

Silver
Birches

Emral Stud

Caelica
Farm

Cae-li-cae

SY14

LL13

The Pools

Mulsford
Hall

Pandy
Farm

Pandy
Bridge

A525

Pandy

Burton's
Wood

Rodger's
Rough

HALGHTON LA

Halghton Lane
Farm

ROCK LANE

Charity
Farm

Cherrytree
Farm

Neil Peter's
La

Plassey

The
Fields

Buck
Farm

Whalebone
House

Whalebone
Farm

Fields
Farm

A525

CHERRYTREE LA

Wood
Farm

CHAPEL LA

SARN RD

OLDCASTLE LA

BOUNDARY LA

Upper
Threapwood

SANDY LA

Topwood
Farm

DOG LA

TINWOOD LA

Middle Wood
Farm

Upper Wood
Farm

BACK LA

Threapwood

Windmill
(disused)

GREAVES LANE E

GREAVES LA

SARN BANK RD

Sarn
Farm

PH
Sarn
Bridge

Lower
Threapwood

Greaves Wood

BORDERBROOK

Warway

Tallarn Green/
Tallwrn Green

Lower Tallarngreen
Farm

Ysgol Borderbrook/
Borderbrook Sch

ELK VIEW

THE ELMS

THE LANE

Tallarn Green
Bridge

Oak
Farm

Trowstree
Villa

Trowstree

The
Fields

Willington
Cross

Bowen's
Hall

Cal Lane

A525 Whitchurch

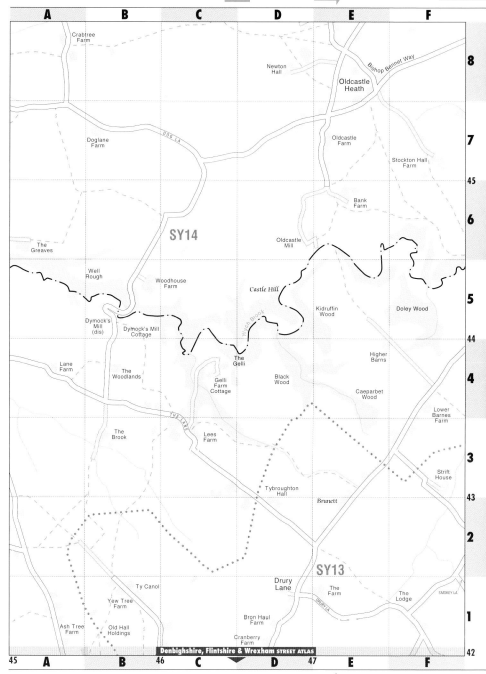

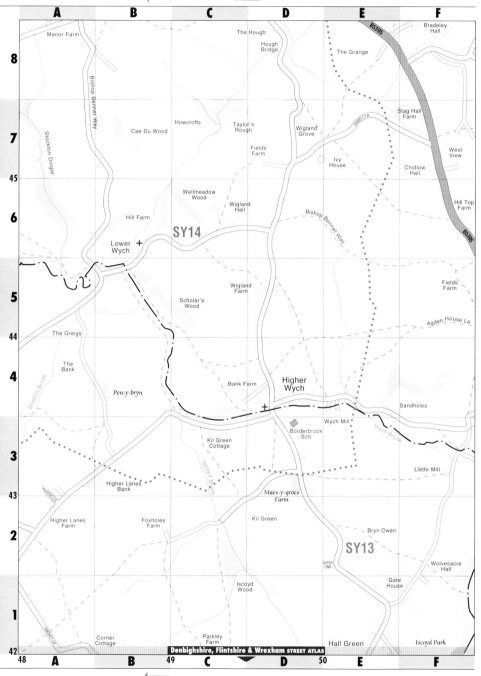

A B C D E F

8

7

45

6

5

44

4

3

43

2

1

42

Manor Farm

Bishop Bennet Way

Stockton Dingle

Cae Du Wood

Howcrofts

Taylor's Rough

The Hough

Hough Bridge

B5395

The Grange

Bradeley Hall

Stag Hall Farm

DODD'S LA

Wigland Grove

Fields Farm

Ivy House

West View

Chidlow Hall

Hill Top Farm

B5395

Wellmeadow Wood

Hill Farm

Lower Wych

SY14

Wigland Hall

Bishop Bennet Way

Scholar's Wood

Wigland Farm

Fields Farm

Agden House La

The Greigs

The Bank

Pen-y-bryn

Shothill Brook

Bank Farm

Higher Wych

Sandholes

Wych Brook

Borderbrook Sch

Wych Mill

Llethr Mill

Kil Green Cottage

Iscoyd Brook

Higher Lanes Bank

HIGHER LA

Higher Lanes Farm

Foxholes Farm

Maes-y-groes Farm

Kil Green

Bryn Owen

SY13

Wolvesacre Hall

Iscoyd Wood

GIPSY CNR

Gate House

SMART LA

Corner Cottage

Parkley Farm

Hall Green

Iscoyd Park

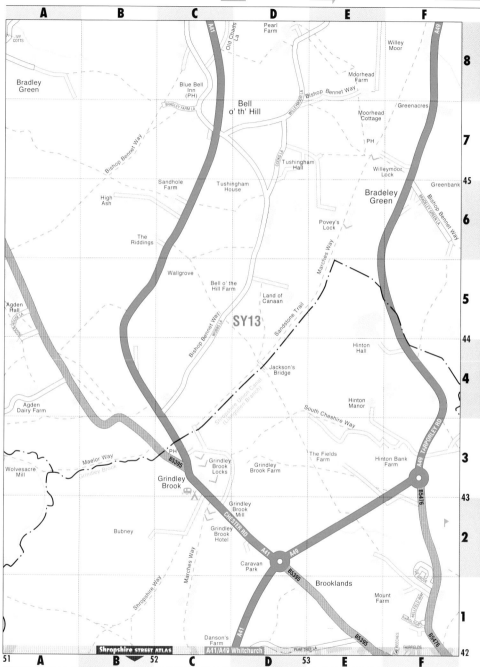

	A	B	C	D	E	F

8

IVY COTTS

Bradley Green

Blue Bell Inn (PH)

BRADLEY FARM LA

Pearl Farm

Bell o' th' Hill

Willey Moor

Moorhead Farm

Bishop Bennet Way

Greenacres

7

Bishop Bennet Way

Old Chads La

WILLEYMOOR LA

Moorhead Cottage

Tushingham Hall

PH

CROSS LA

Willeymoor Lock

45

Sandhole Farm

Tushingham House

Bradeley Green

Greenbank

BRADELEY GREEN LA

Bishop Bennet Way

6

High Ash

The Riddings

Povey's Lock

Wallgrove

Bell o' the Hill Farm

Land of Canaan

Marches Way

5

Agden Hall

WROMS LA

Bishop Bennet Way

SY13

Sandstone Trail

44

Hinton Hall

4

Agden Dairy Farm

Jackson's Bridge

Shropshire Union Canal (Llangollen Branch)

Hinton Manor

South Cheshire Way

A49 TARPORLEY RD

3

Wolvesacre Mill

Maelor Way

Grindley Brook

PH

B5395

Grindley Brook Locks

Grindley Brook Farm

The Fields Farm

Hinton Bank Farm

43

Grindley Brook

Grindley Brook Mill

B5476

2

Bubney

CHESTER RD

Grindley Brook Hotel

A41

Caravan Park

A49

B5395

Brooklands

Mount Farm

WILLIELD WAY

FAIRFIELDS

Marches Way

Shropshire Way

1

Danson's Farm

A41

PEAR TREE LA

B5395

B5476

42

	A	B	C	D	E	F

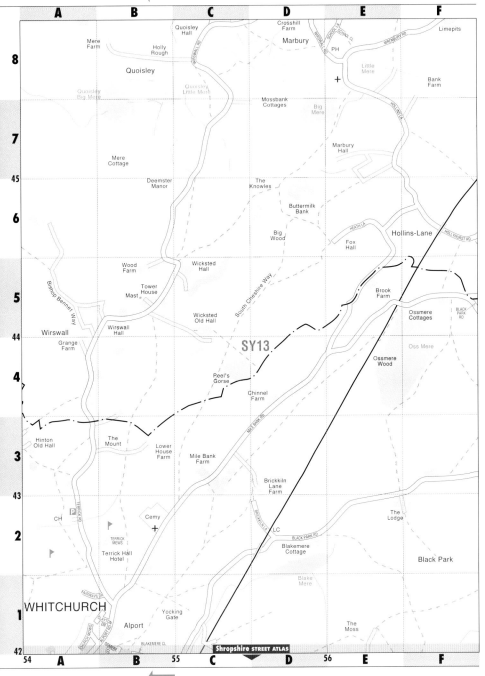

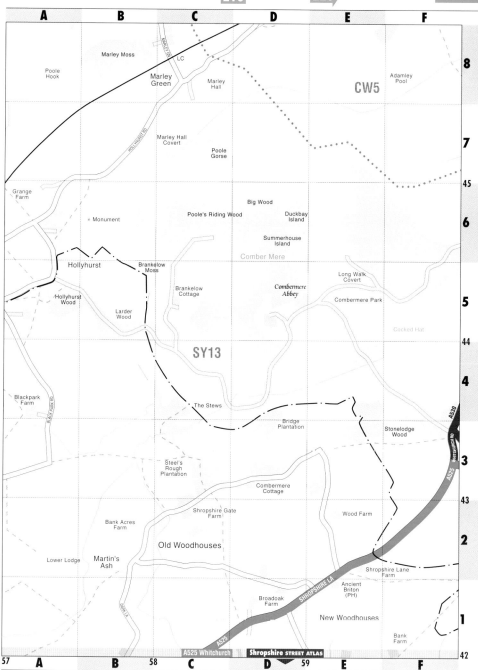

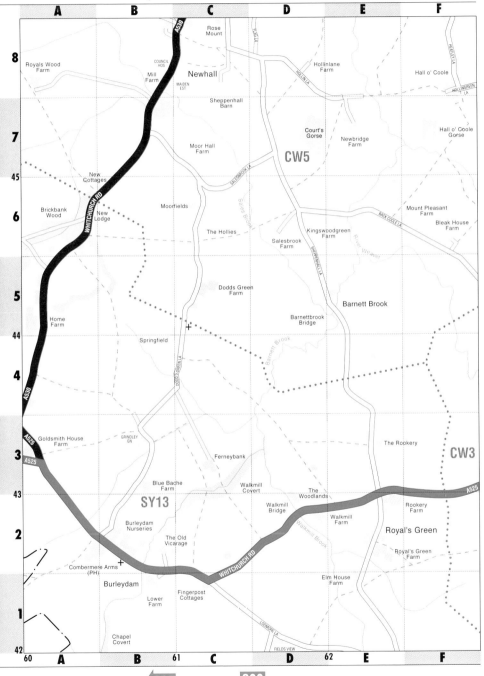

227

217

A **B** **C** **D** **E** **F**

8

Royals Wood
Farm

COUNCIL
HOS

Mill
Farm

MAIDEN
EST

Newhall

Rose
Mount

Holtinlane
Farm

Hall o' Coole

HEATLEY LA

HOLLINGREEN LA

Sheppenhall
Barn

Court's
Gorse

Newbridge
Farm

Hall o' Coole
Gorse

7

CW5

Moor Hall
Farm

SALESBROOK LA

45

New
Cottages

Brickbank
Wood

New
Lodge

Moorfields

The Hollies

Salesbrook
Farm

Kingswoodgreen
Farm

Mount Pleasant
Farm

BACK COOLE LA

Bleak House
Farm

6

River Weaver

SHEPPENHALL LA

Sares Brook

5

Dodds Green
Farm

Barnett Brook

Home
Farm

Barnettbrook
Bridge

44

Springfield

Barnett Brook

4

A530

DODDS GREEN LA

Goldsmith House
Farm

GRINDLEY
GN

The Rookery

CW3

3

A525

Ferneybank

A525

43

Blue Bache
Farm

Walkmill
Covert

The
Woodlands

Rookery
Farm

SY13

Walkmill
Bridge

Walkmill
Farm

Royal's Green

2

Burleydam
Nurseries

The Old
Vicarage

Walkmill Brook

Royal's Green
Farm

Combermere Arms
(PH)

WHITCHURCH RD

Elm House
Farm

Burleydam

Lower
Farm

Fingerpost
Cottages

1

LOGMORE LA

Chapel
Covert

FIELDS VIEW

42

60 **A** **B** 61 **C** **D** 62 **E** **F**

WHITCHURCH RD

A530

227

233

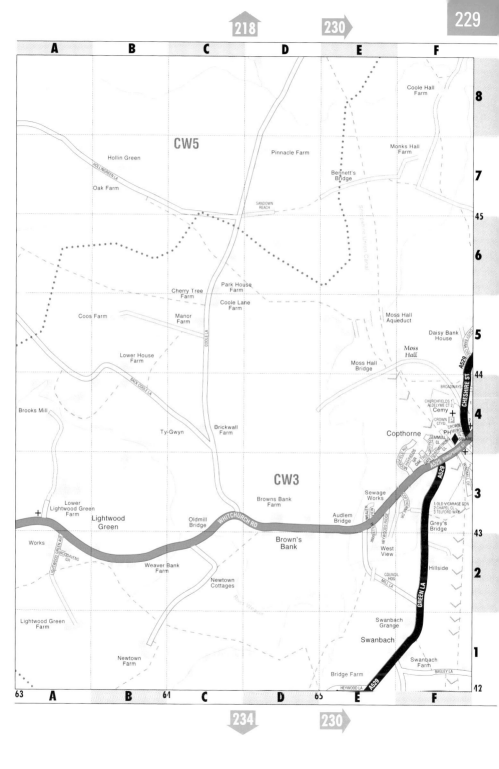

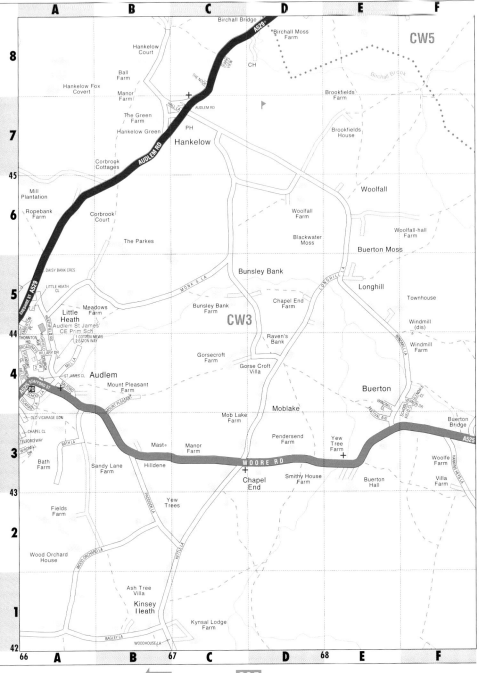

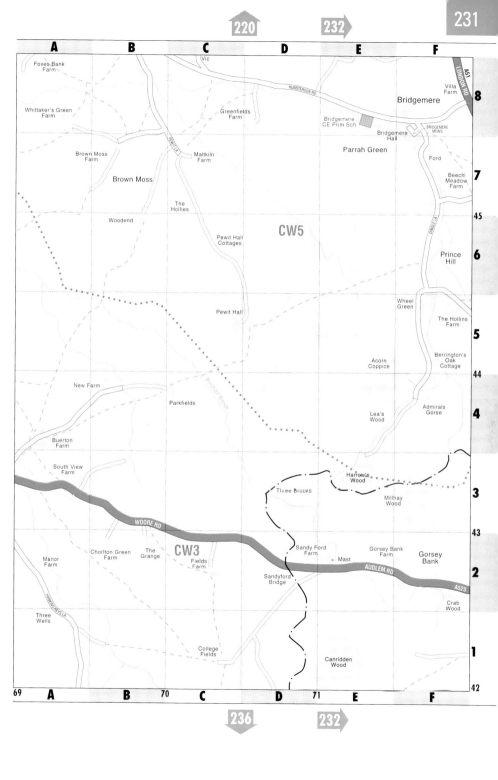

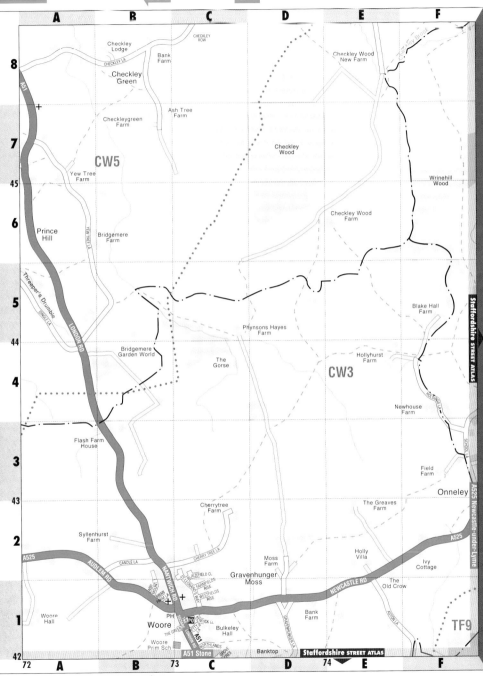

Staffordshire STREET ATLAS

A51

Checkley Lodge

Checkley Row

Bank Farm

CHECKLEY LA

Checkley Green

Checkley Wood New Farm

Checkleygreen Farm

Ash Tree Farm

CW5

Checkley Wood

Yew Tree Farm

Wrinehill Wood

Prince Hill

Bridgemere Farm

Checkley Wood Farm

YEW TREE LA

Threapper's Drumble

DINGLE LA

LONDON RD

Blake Hall Farm

Phynsons Hayes Farm

Bridgemere Garden World

The Gorse

Hollyhurst Farm

CW3

Newhouse Farm

Flash Farm House

Field Farm

Onneley

A525 Newcastle-under-Lyme

Cherrytree Farm

The Greaves Farm

Syllenhurst Farm

CHERRY TREE LA

A525

Holly Villa

Ivy Cottage

A525

CANDLE LA

Moss Farm

Gravenhunger Moss

AUDLEM RD

NANTWICH RD

ALTZEFIELD CL

FARMFIELDS RISE

WESTFIELDS RISE

NEWCASTLE RD

The Old Crow

Woore Hall

PH

Woore

A51

Bank Farm

TF9

Bulkeley Hall

Woore Prim Sch

NORTHLANDS

BRACKENHEDGE LA

ASTON LA

A51 Stone

Banktop

Staffordshire STREET ATLAS

72   A   B   73   C   D   74   E   F

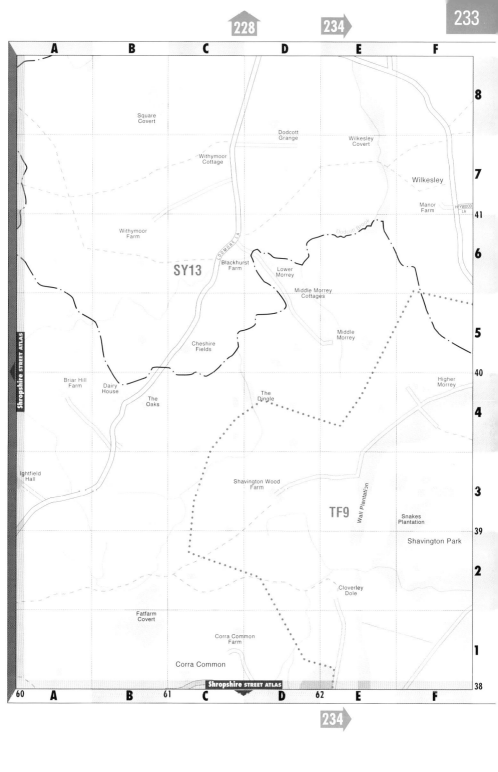

A   B   C   D   E   F

8

Square
Covert

Dodcott
Grange

Wilkesley
Covert

7

Withymoor
Cottage

Wilkesley

Manor
Farm

HEYWOOD
LA

41

Withymoor
Farm

Dodcott Brook

SY13

Blackhurst
Farm

Lower
Morrey

6

Middle Morrey
Cottages

Middle
Morrey

Cheshire
Fields

5

40

Briar Hill
Farm

Dairy
House

The
Oaks

The
Dingle

Higher
Morrey

4

Lightfield
Hall

Shavington Wood
Farm

Wall Plantation

TF9

3

Snakes
Plantation

39

Shavington Park

Cloverley
Dole

2

Fatfarm
Covert

Corra Common
Farm

1

Corra Common

38

60   A   B   61   C   D   62   E   F

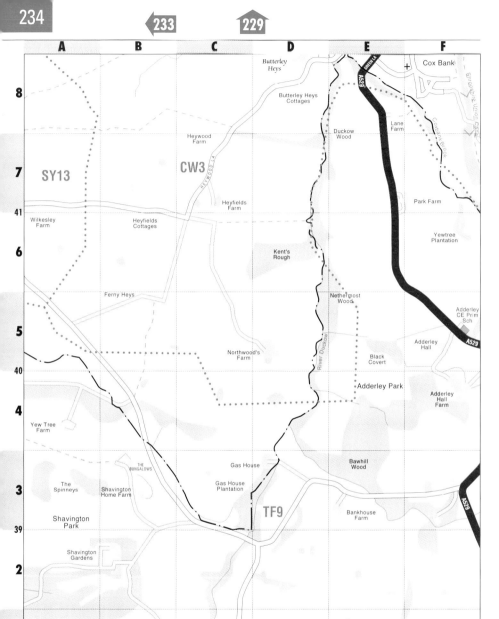

8

Butterley
Heys

Butterley Heys
Cottages

Duckow
Wood

Lane
Farm

Cox Bank

7

SY13

CW3

Heywood
Farm

Park Farm

41

Wilkesley
Farm

Heyfields
Cottages

Heyfields
Farm

Yewtree
Plantation

6

Kent's
Rough

Ferny Heys

Nethermost
Wood

Adderley
CE Prim
Sch

5

Northwood's
Farm

River Duckow

Black
Covert

Adderley
Hall

40

Adderley Park

Adderley
Hall
Farm

4

Yew Tree
Farm

Gas House

Bawhill
Wood

3

The
Spinneys

Shavington
Home Farm

THE
BUNGALOWS

Gas House
Plantation

TF9

Bankhouse
Farm

39

Shavington
Park

2

Shavington
Gardens

1

Big Wood

Big Pool

Tittenley
Pool

Adderley
Lodge

38

GREEN LA

A529

Coxbank Brook

Shropshire Union Canal

A529

A529

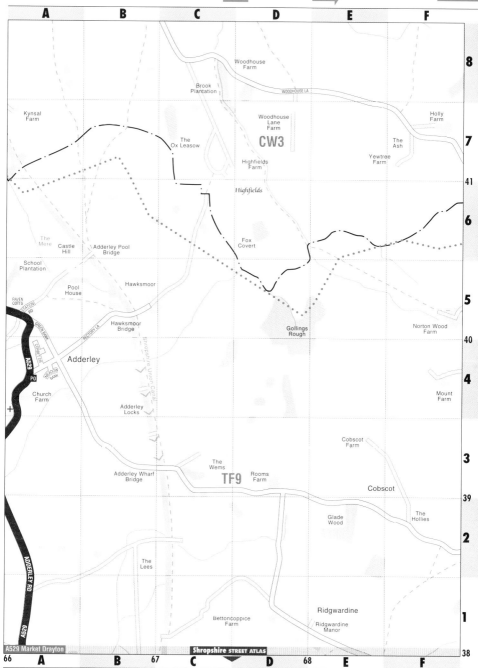

Woodhouse Farm

Brook Plantation

WOODHOUSE LA

Kynsal Farm

Holly Farm

The Ox Leasow

Woodhouse Lane Farm

CW3

The Ash

Yewtree Farm

Highfields Farm

Highfields

The Mere

Castle Hill

Adderley Pool Bridge

Fox Covert

School Plantation

Pool House

Hawksmoor

Norton Wood Farm

RAVEN COTTS

STATION RD

Hawksmoor Bridge

RECTORY LA

Shropshire Union Canal

Gollings Rough

GREEN BANK

A529

LOUDRE TERR

Adderley

MEADOW BANK

PO

Mount Farm

Church Farm

Adderley Locks

Cobscot Farm

Adderley Wharf Bridge

The Wems

Rooms Farm

TF9

Cobscot

Glade Wood

The Hollies

The Lees

Ridgwardine

ADDERLEY RD

A529

Bettoncoppice Farm

Ridgwardine Manor

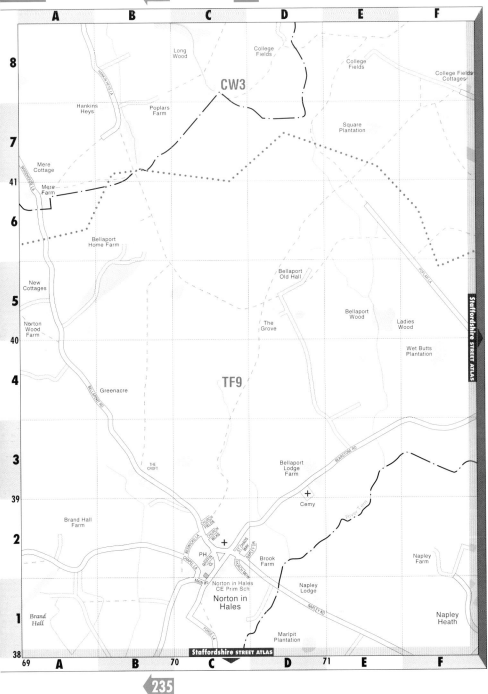

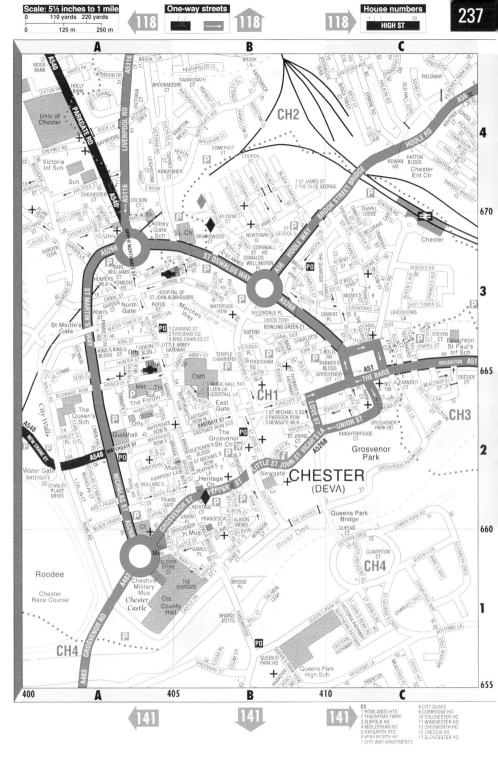

Index

Place name May be abbreviated on the map

Location number Present when a number indicates the place's position in a crowded area of mapping

Locality, town or village Shown when more than one place has the same name

Postcode district District for the indexed place

Page and grid square Page number and grid reference for the standard mapping

Church Rd **6** Beckenham BR2.........**53** C6

Cities, towns and villages are listed in CAPITAL LETTERS   Public and commercial buildings are highlighted in magenta
Places of interest are highlighted in blue with a star ★

Abbreviations used in the index

Acad	**Academy**	Comm	**Common**	Gd	**Ground**	L	**Leisure**	Prom	**Promenade**
App	**Approach**	Cott	**Cottage**	Gdn	**Garden**	La	**Lane**	Rd	**Road**
Arc	**Arcade**	Cres	**Crescent**	Gn	**Green**	Liby	**Library**	Recn	**Recreation**
Ave	**Avenue**	Cswy	**Causeway**	Gr	**Grove**	Mdw	**Meadow**	Ret	**Retail**
Bglw	**Bungalow**	Ct	**Court**	H	**Hall**	Meml	**Memorial**	Sh	**Shopping**
Bldg	**Building**	Ctr	**Centre**	Ho	**House**	Mkt	**Market**	Sq	**Square**
Bsns, Bus	**Business**	Ctry	**Country**	Hospl	**Hospital**	Mus	**Museum**	St	**Street**
Bvd	**Boulevard**	Cty	**County**	HQ	**Headquarters**	Orch	**Orchard**	Sta	**Station**
Cath	**Cathedral**	Dr	**Drive**	Hts	**Heights**	Pal	**Palace**	Terr	**Terrace**
Cir	**Circus**	Dro	**Drove**	Ind	**Industrial**	Par	**Parade**	TH	**Town Hall**
Cl	**Close**	Ed	**Education**	Inst	**Institute**	Pas	**Passage**	Univ	**University**
Cnr	**Corner**	Emb	**Embankment**	Int	**International**	Pk	**Park**	Wk, Wlk	**Walk**
Coll	**College**	Est	**Estate**	Intc	**Interchange**	Pl	**Place**	Wr	**Water**
Com	**Community**	Ex	**Exhibition**	Junc	**Junction**	Prec	**Precinct**	Yd	**Yard**

Index of towns, villages, streets, hospitals, industrial estates, railway stations, schools, shopping centres, universities and places of interest

2nd–Alb

2nd Ave CW12 . . . . 156 A4
3rd Ave CW12 . . . . 156 A4
1875 Bakers Ct CH1,
CH3 . . . . 237 C3

A

Aarons Dr ST7. . . . . 209 F2
Abberley Hall SK9 . . . . 84 D7
Abbey Cl
Croft WA3 . . . . .9 A8
Whitegate CW8 . . . . 126 A7
Widnes WA8 . . . . 22 C8
Winsford CW7 . . . . 149 D5
Abbey Ct SK12 . . . . 36 D3
Abbeydale Cl CW2 . . . . . . 207 C2
Abbeyfield Ho
2 Crewe CW2 . . . . 190 D2
Ellesmere Port CH65 . . . . . 70 A3
Knutsford WA16 . . . . 56 F1
Abbeyfields CW11 . . . . . . 174 F5
Abbey Fields CW2 . . . . . . 205 E8
Abbey Gate Coll CH3 . . . . 164 E8
Abbey Gate Sch CH2. . . . . 237 A3
Abbey Gn CH1. . . . . 237 A3
Abbey Hey WA7 . . . . 50 C8
Abbey La
Delamere CW8 . . . . 123 E5
Hartford CW8 . . . . 103 B4
Abbey Mill SK10 . . . . 87 A6
Abbey Park Way CW2 . . . . 207 E3
Abbey Pl CW1 . . . . 190 D6
Abbey Rd
Golborne WA3 . . . . 4 C8
Haydock WA11. . . . . 1 E7
Macclesfield SK10 . . . . 87 B2
Sandbach CW11 . . . . 174 E6
Widnes WA8 . . . . 22 C8
Abbey Sq CH1 . . . . 237 B3
Abbey St CH1 . . . . 237 B3
Abbey Way CW8 . . . . 103 B4
Abbeyway N WA11 . . . . 2 A7
Abbeyway S WA11 . . . . 2 A7
Abbotsbury Cl
Poynton SK12 . . . . 36 D5
Wistaston CW2 . . . . 206 B8
Abbots Cl SK10 . . . . 87 B2
Abbots Ct CH2 . . . . 118 C4
Abbot's Dr CH2. . . . . 118 C4

Abbotsfield Cl WA4 . . . . 26 E6
Abbot's Grange CH2 . . . . . 237 A4
Abbots Knoll CH2. . . . . . . 118 C4
ABBOT'S MEADS 118 A4
Abbotsmere Cl CW8 . . . . . 101 F2
Abbots Mews CH65 . . . . . . 70 B6
Abbot's Nook CH2 . . . . . . 237 A4
Abbots Pk
Chester CH2 . . . . 118 C4
Runcorn WA7 . . . . 50 C5
Abbot's Terr CH1 . . . . 118 B5
Abbots Way
Hartford CW8 . . . . 103 B4
Neston CH64 . . . . 41 E1
Abbotts Cl
Runcorn WA7 . . . . 49 A8
Waverton CH3 . . . . 143 B5
Abbott's Cl CW12 . . . . 179 B8
Abbotts Cl CH3 . . . . 143 B5
Abbotts Way CW7 . . . . . . 126 B2
Aberdare Cl WA5 . . . . 7 E1
Aberdeen Dr CH1 . . . . 117 E3
Aberdeen Wlk SK10. . . . . . 86 F3
Aberfeldy Cl WA4 . . . . 130 B2
Abingdon Ave WA1 . . . . . . 17 E7
Abingdon **9** SK11. . . . . . 111 F8
Abingdon Cres **4**
CH4 . . . . 140 F6
Abington Cl CW1 . . . . 190 B6
Abington Wlk WA7 . . . . 50 C5
Abstone Cl WA1 . . . . 17 B7
Acacia Ave
Knutsford WA16 . . . . 56 E1
Warrington WA4 . . . . 17 D7
Widnes WA8 . . . . 13 B3
Wilmslow SK9 . . . . 59 F5
Acacia Cl CH2 . . . . 72 C3
Acacia Cres CW1 . . . . 190 E6
Acacia Dr
Ellesmere Port CH66. . . . . . 69 F1
Sandbach CW11 . . . . 174 E7
Acacia Gdns ST7 . . . . 195 C3
Acacia Gr WA7 . . . . 49 C8
Acacia St WA12 . . . . 1 F4
Academy Pl **6** WA1 . . . . . . 16 B5
Academy St WA1 . . . . 16 B5
Academy Way WA1 . . . . . . 16 B5
Acer Ave CW7 . . . . 190 E7
Achilles Ave WA2. . . . . 8 B2
Achilles Ct WA7 . . . . 24 A2
Ackerley Cl WA2 . . . . 8 F3
Ackers La WA4 . . . . 26 E1

Ackersley Ct SK8 . . . . 35 B8
Ackers Rd WA4 . . . . 16 E1
Ack La E SK7 . . . . 35 D7
Ack La W SK8 . . . . 35 C7
Acorn Bank Cl CW2. . . . . . 206 B7
Acorn Cl
Cuddington CW8 . . . . 101 F2
Winsford CW7 . . . . 150 A8
Acorn Ct CH2. . . . . 118 E8
Acorn Dr CH65 . . . . 70 B1
Acorn La CW12 . . . . 157 E3
Acorns Prim Sch The
CH65 . . . . 69 F5
Acorn St WA12 . . . . 2 D3
Acorns The CH2 . . . . 118 E8
Acorn Terr SK22 . . . . 39 B6
Acreage The
Bunbury CW6 . . . . 185 E8
Goostrey CW4 . . . . 107 E1
Acrefield Rd WA8. . . . . 12 B1
Acre Gn L26 . . . . 21 A6
Acre La
Bebington CH62. . . . . 43 D8
Cheadle SK8 . . . . 35 C6
Heswall CH60 . . . . 41 B8
Acre Rd CH66 . . . . 69 D5
Acres Cres WA6 . . . . 75 B2
Acresfield Com Prim Sch
CH2 . . . . 118 F8
Acres La CH2. . . . . 119 A8
Acreville Gr WA3 . . . . 5 C7
ACTON 204 A7
Acton Ave WA4 . . . . 26 D3
ACTON BRIDGE 76 E3
Acton Bridge Sta CW8 . . . . 76 F1
Acton CE Prim Sch
CW5. . . . . 204 A7
Acton Cl WA11 . . . . 1 C6
Acton La CW8 . . . . 76 F4
Acton Pl SK11 . . . . 111 F8
Acton Rd
Burtonwood WA5. . . . . 6 E6
Crewe CW2 . . . . 189 D4
Acton Way ST7 . . . . 193 D6
Adam Ave
Ellesmere Port CH66. . . . . . 69 D3
Ellesmere Port, Great Sutton
CH66. . . . . 69 C4
Adams Cl
Newton-le-W WA12. . . . . 2 D2
Poynton SK12 . . . . 36 E2
Adams Hill WA16. . . . . 57 A1

Adamson Ct WA4 . . . . 17 B2
Adamson Ho WA7 . . . . 22 E3
Adamson St WA4 . . . . 16 B3
Adam St WA2 . . . . 16 C7
Adaston Ave CH62 . . . . 43 F4
Adder Hill CH3 . . . . 142 B7
ADDERLEY 235 A4
Adderley CE Prim Sch
TF9 . . . . 234 F5
Adderley Cl WA7 . . . . 23 C1
Adderley Rd TF9. . . . . 235 A2
ADDER'S MOSS 85 F6
Addingham Ave WA8 . . . . . 22 C7
Addison Cl CW2 . . . . 205 F8
Addison Sq WA8. . . . . 13 A1
Adelaide Ct **4** WA8. . . . . . 23 A7
Adelaide Rd
Blacon CH1 . . . . 117 D4
Bramhall SK7. . . . . 35 F5
Adelaide Sch CW1 . . . . . . 190 C5
Adelaide St
Crewe CW1 . . . . 190 C5
Macclesfield SK10 . . . . 87 E1
Adey Rd WA13. . . . . 19 A5
Adfalent La CH64 . . . . 68 A7
Adlam Cres CH66 . . . . 69 C6
ADLINGTON 62 D5
Adlington Cl SK12 . . . . 36 F2
Adlington Ct WA3 . . . . 9 F6
Adlington Dr
Northwich CW9 . . . . 104 A5
Sandbach CW11 . . . . 175 C7
Adlington Est SK10 . . . . . . 36 C1
Adlington Hall Mews
SK10. . . . . 62 B5
Adlington Pk SK10. . . . . . . 36 C1
Adlington Prim Sch
SK10. . . . . 62 E5
Adlington Rd
Bollington SK10 . . . . 63 A1
Crewe CW2 . . . . 189 F3
Runcorn WA7. . . . . 24 D2
Wilmslow SK9 . . . . 60 E7
Adlington Road Bsns Pk
SK10. . . . . 88 A8
Adlington St SK10 . . . . . . 112 C8
Adlington St SK10 . . . . 62 C5
Admirals Rd WA3 . . . . 9 F3
Adshead Ct SK10 . . . . 88 B7
Adwell Cl WA3 . . . . 4 A8
Afton CH66 . . . . 12 A2
Agden Brow WA13. . . . . . . 19 E1

Agden Brow Pk
Broomedge WA13 . . . . 19 D1
Lymm WA13. . . . . 29 D8
Agden Hall Farm
WA13. . . . . 29 E7
Agden House La
SY13. . . . . 225 A5
Agden La
Broomedge WA13 . . . . 19 E1
Little Bollington WA13. . . . . 29 E7
Agden Park La WA13 . . . . . 29 D8
Agecroft Rd CW9 . . . . 104 C7
Ainley Cl WA7 . . . . 50 A5
Ainscough Rd WA3 . . . . 9 E3
Ainsdale Cl
Bebington CH63. . . . . 43 C5
Bramhall SK7. . . . . 36 A7
Warrington WA5 . . . . 14 F4
Ainsworth La CW8 . . . . 76 B3
Ainsworth Rd CW8. . . . . . . 77 E1
Aintree Gr CH66 . . . . 69 D3
Airdrie Cl CH62. . . . . 43 D3
Aire WA8. . . . . 12 B2
Aire Cl CH65 . . . . 70 A7
Airedale Cl WA5 . . . . 14 F7
Aire Pl CW7 . . . . 127 B1
Airfield View CH5 . . . . 139 B6
Aitchison Rd CW9 . . . . 80 A2
Ajax Ave WA2 . . . . 8 B2
Akesmoor La
Biddulph ST8 . . . . 179 B1
Mow Cop ST7. . . . . 195 F7
Alamein Cres WA2. . . . . . . 16 C7
Alamein Dr CW7. . . . . 149 D8
Alamein Rd
Barnton CW8 . . . . 78 A4
Chester CH2 . . . . 95 B1
Alan Dr WA15 . . . . 32 A8
Alan St CW9. . . . . 104 B8
Alban Ret Pk WA2 . . . . 8 A1
Alban St CW1 . . . . 190 C5
Albany Cres WA13 . . . . 18 D4
Albany Gdns CH66 . . . . 69 C7
Albany Gr WA13 . . . . 18 C4
Albany Rd
Bramhall SK7. . . . . 35 F4
Lymm WA13. . . . . 18 D4
Wilmslow SK9 . . . . 59 F5
Albany Terr **15** WA7 . . . . . 23 A2
Albert Dr
Neston CH64 . . . . 66 D8
Warrington WA5 . . . . 14 D6

Albert Pl
Congleton CW12 156 E2
16 Macclesfield SK11 112 D8
Northwich CW9 104 B8
Albert Rd
Bollington SK10 87 E8
Warrington WA4 17 A2
2 Widnes WA8 13 B1
Wilmslow SK9 60 A6
Albert Row WA6 49 B1
Albert Sq 1 WA8 23 B8
Albert St
Audley ST7 209 F3
Chester CH1 237 C3
Crewe CW1 190 C5
Irlam M44 11 E6
Knutsford WA16 56 F2
Macclesfield SK11 112 C8
Nantwich CW5 204 E6
6 Runcorn WA7 23 A2
Albert Terr WA5 1 E1
Albion Ct CW12 156 E2
Albion Mews
Chester CH1 237 B2
New Mills SK22 39 C7
Albion Pk WA3 5 C7
Albion Pl CH1 237 B1
Albion Rd
New Mills SK22 39 B6
Northwich CW9 79 A1
Albion St
Chester CH1 237 B2
Crewe CW2 190 A3
Albion Wlk CW9 79 A1
Albright Rd WA8 22 A6
Albury Cl WA11 1 D7
Alcock St 17 WA7 23 A3
Alconbury Cl WA5 15 B6
Alcott Pl WA2 8 A6
Aldcliffe WA3 3 F8
Aldelyme Ct CW3 229 F4
Alder Ave
Poynton SK12 36 F3
Widnes WA8 13 B3
Alderbank Rd WA5 15 A6
Alder Cl SK8 34 D8
Alder Cres WA2 16 C8
Alder Ct SK10 87 E5
Alderdale Dr SK6 37 E7
Alderdale Gr SK9 59 E5
Alder Dr
Crewe CW1 189 F7
Ellesmere Port CH66 69 F1
Alderfield Dr L24 21 A3
Alder Gr CH2 119 B4
Alderhay La ST7 195 C4
Alder La
Burtonwood WA2, WA5 7 C7
Cronton WA8, L35 12 A5
Frodsham WA6, WA7 48 D3
Warrington WA2 16 B8
Alderley Ave WA3 3 D7
Alderley Cl
Hazel Grove SK7 36 F8
Poynton SK12 36 F2
Sandbach CW11 175 D7
ALDERLEY EDGE 60 C2
Alderley Edge* SK9, SK10 85 D8
Alderley Edge Prim Sch SK9 60 A2
Alderley Edge Sch for Girls SK9 60 A2
Alderley Edge Sta SK9 60 A2
Alderley Lo SK9 60 A5
Alderley Pl CH1 117 F6
Alderley Rd
Alderley Edge SK10, SK9 60 F2
Chelford SK10 84 C3
Northwich CW8 103 E8
Prestbury SK10 86 E3
Warrington WA4 17 D4
Wilmslow SK9 60 A6
Alderley Wlk 14 SK11 112 E7
Alderman Bolton Com Prim Sch WA4 16 F3
Alderney Cl
Ellesmere Port CH65 70 C1
4 Macclesfield SK11 111 F8
Alderney Ho CH2 119 B4
Alder Rd
Golborne WA3 3 F8
Warrington WA1 17 D7
Weaverham CW8 102 D8
Alder Rise SK23 65 D8
Alder Root La WA2 7 D7
Alders SK9 59 F6
Aldersey Cl
Runcorn WA7 24 D1
Saughall CH1 94 A1
ALDERSEY GREEN 182 C6
Aldersey La CH3 182 C5
Aldersey Rd CW2 190 A2
Aldersey Way CW6 185 E8
Aldersgate SK22 39 B8
Aldersgate Ave WA7 50 D7
Aldersgate Dr L26 21 A6
Aldersgate Rd SK8 35 C5
Alders Green Ave SK6 37 F7
Alders Rd SK12 38 A7
Alder St WA12 2 C3
Alders Way SK10 86 F6
Alderton Cl L26 21 A7
Alderton Gr CW7 127 A4
Alder Wood Ave L24 21 A3
Alderwood Ct WA8 12 E4
Alderwood Lo L24 21 A3
Aldewood Cl WA3 10 A6
ALDFORD 163 F3
Aldford Cl
Bebington CH63 43 B6
Hough CW2 206 E2
Aldford Pl SK9 59 F2
Aldford Rd CH2 118 F6
Aldford Sch CH3 163 F3
Aldford Way CW7 126 B2
Aldgate CH65 70 A5
Aldington Dr CW10 151 D5
Aldridge Dr WA5 6 F7
Aled Way CH4 140 D5
Alexander Ct CH3 237 C2
Alexander Dr WA8 22 D8
Alexandra Ct 1 M31 11 F3
Alexandra Gr
Irlam M44 11 F8
Runcorn WA7 23 C1
Alexandra Ind Est WA8 22 F7
Alexandra Mews WA6 49 B1
Alexandra Pl CW1 190 B5
Alexandra Rd
Middlewich CW10 151 D6
Warrington, Stockton Heath WA4 16 D1
Warrington WA4 16 F2
Alexandra Sq 6 CW7 149 A8
Alexandra St
Ellesmere Port CH65 70 C7
Warrington WA1 16 E7
Widnes WA8 23 A7
Winsford CW7 126 C1
Alexandria Way CW12 156 C4
Alford Ct 4 CW9 103 E5
Alforde St WA8 23 A7
Alfred Cl 12 WA8 23 B8
Alfred Rd
Golborne WA3 4 A8
Haydock WA11 1 F7
Alfred St
Irlam M44 11 E6
Newton-le-W WA12 2 E3
Northwich CW9 103 E6
Widnes WA8 23 B8
Algernon St
Runcorn WA7 22 F3
Warrington, Stockton Heath WA4 16 C1
Warrington WA1 16 D6
Alice Ct WA8 23 A4
Alison Dr
Goostrey CW4 130 D8
Macclesfield SK10 87 F1
Alistair Dr CH63 43 C6
Allans Cl CH64 66 E6
Allansford Ave CH3 143 A4
Allans Mdw CH64 66 E7
Allcard St WA5 15 F7
Allen Ave WA3 5 C4
Allenby Rd M44 11 D4
Allendale WA7 50 B6
Allen Dr CW9 103 F2
Allen Pl CW1 190 B5
Allen Rd WA7 48 D7
Allen St
Bollington SK10 88 B8
Macclesfield SK11 112 E7
Warrington WA2 16 A6
Allerby Way WA3 3 E8
Allerton Rd WA8 13 B1
ALLGREAVE 137 C3
Allgreave Cl CW10 151 C6
All Hallows RC High Sch SK11 112 B7
Allington Pl CH4 141 E7
Allman Cl CW1 189 F7
ALLOSTOCK 106 E3
Allotment Rd M44 11 D6
Allport La CH62 43 D8
Allport Rd CH62, CH63 43 D7
Allports The CH62 43 D7
All Saints Dr WA4 17 E3
All Saints RC Prim Sch WA3 3 B8
All Saints Upton CE Prim Sch WA8 12 B3
Allysum Ct WA7 49 F4
Alma Ave CW1 190 C6
Alma Cl
Macclesfield SK11 112 A7
Scholar Green ST7 194 E7
Alma La SK9 60 A7
Alma Rd SK7 37 A8
Alma St
Chester CH2 118 F2
Newton-le-W WA12 2 B3
Almeda Rd L24 21 A2
Almer Dr WA5 15 C5
Almond Ave
Crewe CW1 190 D6
Runcorn WA7 49 C8
Almond Dr WA5 6 F6
Almond Gr
Warrington WA1 17 B7
Weaverham CW8 102 E7
Widnes WA8 22 D8
Almond Pl ST5 210 E1
Almond Tree Cl L24 21 E1
Almond Wlk M31 11 D3
Almshouses CW11 175 C6
Alnwick Dr CH65 70 D2
Alpass Ave WA5 16 A8
Alpine St WA12 2 A3
ALPORT 226 B1
Alport Rd SY13 226 B1
ALPRAHAM 169 D4
Alpraham Cres CH2 118 E6
Alpraham Gn CW6 169 E5
ALPRAHAM GREEN 169 D5
Alric Wlk M22 33 E8
ALSAGER 193 E5
Alsager Highfields Com Prim Sch ST7 193 D4
Alsager Rd
Audley ST7 209 D5
Haslington CW11 192 C7
Sandbach CW11 175 E1
Alsager Sch ST7 193 B4
Alsager Sta ST7 193 E3
Alsfeld Way SK22 39 A8
Alt WA8 12 B2
Alton Dr SK10 87 F1
Alton Rd SK9 59 F7
Alton St CW2 190 B3
ALTRINCHAM 31 C8
Altrincham Priory Hospl WA15 32 A7
Altrincham Rd
Styal SK9 33 D4
Wilmslow SK9 33 C2
Alt Wlk CW7 127 A2
Alumbrook Ave CW4 130 C3
Alum Ct CW4 130 C2
Alun Cres CH4 141 A6
Alundale Rd CW7 126 C3
ALVANLEY 73 C1
Alvanley Dr WA6 73 C2
Alvanley Prim Sch WA6 73 D1
Alvanley Rd
Ellesmere Port CH66 69 E4
Helsby WA6 73 C2
Alvanley Rise CW9 104 A6
Alvanley Terr WA6 74 B8
Alvanley View CH2 72 B3
Alvanley Way CH66 69 E4
Alvaston Bsns Pk CW5 204 F8
Alvaston Rd CW5 204 F5
Alvaston Wlk CW2 189 F2
Alverstone Cl WA5 14 C7
Alverton Cl WA8 22 D8
Alveston Cl SK10 86 F1
Alveston Dr SK9 60 C8
Alvingham Ct 1 CW9 104 B8
Alvis Rd CH5 116 B3
Alwyn Gdns CH2 118 F8
Alyndale Rd CH4 140 D6
Alyn Rd CH2 96 F1
Amberleigh Cl WA4 27 B3
Amberley Dr WA15 32 B8
Amberley Rd SK11 112 A6
Ambleside CH2 119 A6
Ambleside Cl
Bebington CH62 43 E7
Crewe CW2 189 E2
Macclesfield SK11 111 F6
Runcorn WA7 49 E5
Winsford CW7 126 C3
Ambleside Cres WA2 8 C3
Ambleside Ct CW12 156 A2
Ambleside Rd CH65 70 C2
Ambrose Ct WA1 16 D6
Ambuscade Cl CW1 190 E5
Amelia Cl WA8 13 B4
Amelia St WA2 16 C7
Amersham Cl SK10 87 C3
Amis Gr WA3 3 E8
Ampleforth Ho 1 WA1 16 C5
Amusement Depot CW7 126 E2
Amy St CW2 190 C3
Anchorage The
1 Lymm WA13 18 D3
Neston CH64 66 C7
Waverton CH3 143 A5
Anchor Cl WA7 50 D6
Anchor Ct WA1 16 D6
Ancoats Rd WA16, SK9 83 F8
Anderson Cl
Crewe CW1 191 A4
Warrington WA2 9 B2
Anderson Ct CH62 43 D6
Andersons Ind Est WA8 23 A6
Anderson St 16 SK10 112 C8
ANDERTON 78 D4
Anderton Boat Lift & Nature Pk* CW9 78 D3
Anderton Grange CW9 103 F7
Andertons La SK10, SK11 86 B1
Anderton Way SK9 34 D3
Andover Cl WA2 8 E1
Andover Rd WA11 1 E8
Andrew Cl WA8 22 C8
Andrew Cres CH4 237 C1
Andrew Gr SK10 113 A7
Andrew La SK6 37 F8
Andrew's Cl CH3 121 B2
Andrew's Wlk CH60 41 B8
Andromeda Way WA9 6 B7
Anemone Way WA9 6 A7
Angelina Cl CW11 174 D7
Anglers Rest M44 11 E5
Anglesey Cl 2 CH65 70 C1
Anglesey Dr SK12 36 F6
Anglesey Water SK12 36 E6
Angus Gr CW10 128 D2
Angus Rd CH63 43 C6
Angus Wlk SK10 86 F2
Ankers Knowl La SK11 114 D8
Ankers La SK11 114 D6
Annable Rd M44 11 F8
Annan Cl 2 CW12 157 A1
Ann Cl CH66 69 D7
Anne Ct ST7 210 D6
Anne's Way CH4 237 C1
Annette Ave WA12 2 A5
Annie St WA2 16 C6
Annions La CW5 205 F1
Annis Cl SK9 60 B2
Annis Rd SK9 60 B2
Ann St W WA8 23 B7
Ann St
Northwich CW9 79 D1
Runcorn WA7 23 B3
Ansdell Rd WA8 13 C2
Anson Cl SK7 35 F5
Anson Engine Mus The* SK12 37 C4
Anson Rd
Handforth SK9 34 E1
Poynton SK12 37 B3
Anthony Dr CW9 126 F7
Anthony's Way CH60 41 A7
Antons Ct L26 21 A6
Antons Rd L26 21 A6
Antony Rd WA4 16 B1
Antrim Cl WA11 1 C6
Antrim Dr CH66 69 F2
Antrim Rd WA2 8 A2
ANTROBUS 53 C4
Antrobus St CW12 156 D3
Anvil Cl
Elton CH2 72 B4
Haslington CW11 174 F3
Saughall CH1 94 A1
Appleby Cl
Macclesfield SK11 111 F5
Widnes WA8 22 C8
Appleby Cres WA16 58 A4
Appleby Gr CH62 43 D6
Appleby Rd WA2 8 C3
Appleby Wlk 5 WA8 22 C8
Applecroft ST5 210 E1
Applecross Cl WA3 10 A6
Appledale Dr CH66 95 A8
Applefield CW8 103 D7
Appleford Cl WA4 26 E7
Apple Market St 10 CW9 103 F8
APPLETON 13 A2
Appleton Cl CW12 178 E8
Appleton Dr CH65 69 F3
Appleton Hall Gdns WA4 26 E5
Appleton Mews WA13 18 C4
APPLETON PARK 26 D5
Appleton Rd
Chester CH2 118 E6
Widnes WA8 13 B1
Appleton St
Widnes WA8 23 B7
Winnington CW8 78 D1
APPLETON THORN 27 B4
Appleton Thorn Prim Sch WA4 27 C4
Appleton Thorn Trad Est WA4 27 D5
Appleton Village WA8 13 B1
Appleton Wlk 8 SK9 34 E1
Apple Tree Cl L24 21 E1
Appletree Gr WA2 8 F2
Apple Tree Gr CH66 94 F8
Appleyards La CH4 141 E7
Apprentice La SK9 33 F3
April Rise SK10 87 A1
Arabis Gdns WA9 6 B7
Aragon Ct WA7 24 C3
Aragon Gn CH1 117 E6
Aran Cl L24 21 D1
Arbour Cl
Macclesfield SK10 87 D3
Northwich CW9 104 C8
Arbour Cres SK10 87 D3
Arbourhay St SK10 87 E1
Arbour Mews SK10 87 D3
Arbour St ST7 210 D5
Arbury La WA2 8 C6
Arcade The
Ellesmere Port CH65 70 A5
3 Northwich CW9 103 F8
Archer Ave WA4 16 F2
Archer Cl SK10 87 E7
Archers Gn CH62 43 E3
Archers Green Rd WA5 7 B3
Archers Way
Blacon CH1 118 A2
Ellesmere Port CH66 69 E1
Arches Com Prim Sch The CH1 117 E5
Archway Wlk WA12 2 E3
ARCLID 154 B1
Arclid Cl SK9 34 E1
Arclid Ct 10 CW12 156 F3
ARCLID GREEN 176 A8
Arclid Green Ind Est CW11 176 B8
Arden WA8 12 A2
Ardenbrook Rise SK10 86 F6
Arden Cl
Gatley SK8 34 C7
Tarvin CH3 121 C3
Warrington WA3 10 B6
Arden Ct CW12 179 B7
Arden Dr CH64 66 E6
Arden Est SK22 39 D7
Ardens Mdw CW6 168 C8
Arden St SK22 39 C7
Arderne Ave CW2 190 A2
Arderne Ho CH2 118 F7
Arderne Pl 12 SK9 60 A1
Ardern Lea WA6 73 D1
Ardleigh Cl CW1 189 F8
Arena Gdns WA2 16 D8
Argosy Dr M90 32 F7
Argyle Ct 10 WA16 57 A2
Argyll Ave
Bebington CH62 43 D4
Chester CH4 141 A7
Argyll Cl SK10 87 A1
Ariel Gdns WA3 5 A2
Ariel Wlk 4 WA3 3 E8
Arizona Cres WA5 15 B7
Arkenshaw Rd WA3 9 A7
Arkenstone Cl WA8 12 C2
Arkle Ave SK8, SK9 34 E4
Arkle Ct 1 CH3 119 B1
Arklow Dr L24 21 D2
Arkwright Cl CW7 149 A8
Arkwright Ct WA7 23 F3
Arkwright Rd WA7 23 F3
ARLEY 54 C7
Arley Ave WA4 26 D8
Arley Cl
Alsager ST7 193 C3
Chester CH2 118 F6
Macclesfield SK11 112 A7
Arley Ct CW9 103 E5
Arley Dr WA8 12 B2
Arley End WA16 29 C4
ARLEY GREEN 54 E6
Arley Hall & Gdns* CW9 54 D6
Arley Mossend La CW9 54 D2
Arley Pl CW2 206 A8
Arley Rd
Antrobus CW9 54 B7
Appleton Thorn WA4 27 C3
Northwich CW9 104 C8
Arley Wlk CW11 174 D5
Arlington Cl CW2 206 C8
Arlington Cres SK9 59 E5
Arlington Dr
Golborne WN7 4 C8
Macclesfield SK11 112 A7
Poynton SK12 36 D3
Warrington WA5 14 E4
Arlington Way SK9 59 E5
Armistead Way CW4 130 A5
Armitstead Rd CW11 174 F4
Armitt St SK11 112 C7
Armour Ave WA2 8 B1
Armoury Court Mews 4 SK11 112 B6
Armoury Twrs 1 SK11 112 B6
Armstrong Cl
Audlem CW3 229 F4
Warrington WA3 9 D4
Armthorpe Dr CH66 69 C5
Arncliffe Dr WA5 6 F6
Arndale WA7 49 E5
Arnhem Cres WA2 16 C7
Arnhem Way CH3 142 B5
Arnold Pl WA8 22 C7
Arnold's Cres CH4 139 A3
Arnold St
Nantwich CW5 204 E6
Warrington WA1 16 D6
Arnside Ave
Congleton CW12 156 A2
Haydock WA11 1 B6
Arnside Cl
High Lane SK6 37 E8
Winsford CW7 126 D2
Arnside Gr WA4 16 B2
Arpley Rd WA1 16 B4
Arpley St WA1 16 A4
Arradon Ct CH2 118 E5
Arran Ave CH65 70 C1
Arran Cl
Holmes Chapel CW4 130 C2
Warrington WA2 9 A2
Arran Dr WA6 74 C6
Arrivals Way M90 33 B7
Arron Pl CW2 189 D3
Arrowcroft Rd CH3 119 F5
Arrowsmith Dr ST7 193 B3
Arrowsmith Rd WA11 1 F7
ARTHILL 30 B8
Arthill La
Little Bollington WA14 20 B1
Rostherne WA14 30 B8
Arthog Dr WA15 31 F8
Arthog Rd
Altrincham WA15 31 F8
Altrincham WA15 32 A8
Arthur Ave CH65 70 C5
Arthur St
Chester CH1 118 A2
3 Crewe CW2 190 D2
Lostock Gralam CW9 80 A2
12 Runcorn WA7 23 A2
Warrington WA2 16 A6
Artists La SK10 85 C7
Artle Rd CW2 206 C8
Arundel Ave SK7 36 D8
Arundel Cl
Knutsford WA16 82 A8
Macclesfield SK10 87 F2
Wistaston CW2 205 E8
Arundel Ct CH65 70 E3

Arundell Cl WA5 . . . 6 F6
Arundel Rd SK8 . . . 35 A6
Ascol Dr WA16 . . . 80 C3
Ascot Ave WA7 . . . 49 B6
Ascot Cl
Congleton CW12 . . . 156 D4
Macclesfield SK10 . . . 87 C3
Warrington, Martinscroft WA1 . . . 17 E7
Warrington WA4 . . . 17 C2
Ascot Ct CW9 . . . 104 C8
Ascot Dr CH66 . . . 69 E3
Ascot Ho CH1 . . . 118 B2
Ash Ave
Irlam M44 . . . 11 D5
Newton-le-W WA12 . . . 2 C2
Ashbank CW9 . . . 104 D7
Ashberry Cl SK9 . . . 60 D8
Ashberry Dr WA4 . . . 27 B5
Ashbourne Ave WA7 . . . 49 B6
Ashbourne Cl CH66 . . . 94 E8
Ashbourne Dr
Chorlton CW2 . . . 207 C1
High Lane SK6 . . . 37 F6
Ashbourne Mews [1] SK10 . . . 111 F8
Ashbourne Rd
Hazel Grove SK7 . . . 36 F8
Warrington WA5 . . . 15 B5
Ashbrook Ave WA7 . . . 49 F3
Ashbrook Cres WA2 . . . 16 D8
Ashbrook Dr SK10 . . . 87 A6
Ashbrook Rd
Bollington SK10 . . . 87 F7
Nether Alderley SK10 . . . 85 F6
Ashburton CH64 . . . 66 C8
Ashbury Cl WA7 . . . 24 D2
Ashbury Dr WA11 . . . 1 D7
Ashby Dr CW11 . . . 174 C5
Ashby Pl CH2 . . . 237 C4
Ash Cl
Ellesmere Port CH66 . . . 69 F1
Holmes Chapel CW4 . . . 130 D4
Malpas SY14 . . . 213 C5
Tarporley CW6 . . . 146 D2
Ashcroft Ave CW2 . . . 206 B3
Ashcroft Cl SK9 . . . 59 F5
Ashcroft Ct M44 . . . 11 D5
Ashcroft Rd WA13 . . . 19 B4
Ash Ct [15] WA16 . . . 57 A2
Ashdale Cl ST7 . . . 193 C5
Ashdene Prim Sch SK9 . . . 59 F5
Ashdene Rd SK9 . . . 59 F5
Ashdown Cl SK8 . . . 35 A6
Ashdown La WA3 . . . 10 B5
Ashdown Rd WA16 . . . 82 F6
Ashenhurst Rd ST7 . . . 193 F3
Ashenough Rd ST7 . . . 210 D6
Asher Ct WA4 . . . 27 D4
Ashfield Cl WA13 . . . 19 B4
Ashfield Cres
Bebington CH62 . . . 43 D8
Blacon CH1 . . . 117 D5
Ashfield Dr SK10 . . . 87 A2
Ashfield Gdns WA4 . . . 16 F3
Ashfield Gr M44 . . . 11 E6
Ashfield Ho [6] CH64 . . . 66 E8
Ashfield Rd
Bebington CH62 . . . 43 C8
Ellesmere Port CH65 . . . 70 C5
Ashfield Rd N [1] CH65 . . . 70 C5
Ashfield St CW10 . . . 151 D8
Ashford Cl SK9 . . . 34 C4
Ashford Dr WA4 . . . 26 E3
Ashford Rd SK9 . . . 60 A4
Ashford Way [1] WA8 . . . 13 D1
Ashgate La CW9 . . . 79 F6
Ash Gr
Chester CH4 . . . 141 B5
Congleton CW12 . . . 156 A3
Ellesmere Port CH66 . . . 69 C6
Gatley SK8 . . . 34 B8
Golborne WA3 . . . 3 B8
Handforth SK9 . . . 34 C3
Knutsford WA16 . . . 57 D1
Macclesfield SK11 . . . 112 C4
Middlewich CW10 . . . 151 D7
Nantwich CW5 . . . 204 F3
Rode Heath ST7 . . . 193 F7
Runcorn WA7 . . . 49 C8
Warrington WA4 . . . 16 D3
Weaverham CW8 . . . 102 E7
Widnes WA8 . . . 22 D8
Ashgrove CW7 . . . 149 D8
Ash Grove Prim Sch SK11 . . . 112 C4
Ash Hay La
Hoole Bank CH2 . . . 119 C8
Picton CH2 . . . 96 C2
Ash Ho
Chester CH2 . . . 118 C5
[8] Sandbach CW11 . . . 175 B6
Ash House La CW8 . . . 77 D7
Ash La
Warrington WA4 . . . 26 E8
Widnes WA8 . . . 22 A8
Ashlands WA6 . . . 74 C7
Ash Lawn Ct CH2 . . . 118 C4
Ashlea Dr CW5 . . . 205 E5
Ashleigh Cl CH4 . . . 140 E6
ASHLEY . . . 31 E5
Ashley CE Prim Sch WA15 . . . 31 F5
Ashley Cl WA4 . . . 17 C3
Ashley Ct
Frodsham WA6 . . . 74 A8
Holt LL13 . . . 196 D8
Warrington WA4 . . . 26 C6
Ashley Dr
Bramhall SK7 . . . 35 C6
Hartford CW8 . . . 103 A6
Ashley Gdns
Clutton CH3 . . . 182 C1
High Lane SK6 . . . 37 D8
Ashley Gn WA8 . . . 22 D8
Ashley Grange CW9 . . . 103 E3
ASHLEY HEATH . . . 31 E8
Ashley Mdw CW1 . . . 191 D5
Ashleymill La WA14 . . . 31 D7
Ashley Mill La N WA14 . . . 31 E8
Ashley Rd
Ashley, Ashley Heath WA14, WA15 . . . 31 E7
Ashley WA14, WA15, WA16 . . . 31 C4
Handforth SK9 . . . 34 B1
Mere WA16 . . . 56 D8
Runcorn WA7 . . . 23 D2
Ashley Ret Pk WA8 . . . 23 B7
Ashley Sch WA8 . . . 12 D1
Ashley Sta WA15 . . . 31 E5
Ashley Way WA8 . . . 23 B7
Ashley Way W WA8 . . . 22 F7
Ash Lo SK12 . . . 36 D4
Ashmead Cl ST7 . . . 193 E3
Ashmead Mews ST7 . . . 193 E3
Ashmore Cl
Middlewich CW10 . . . 151 C6
Warrington WA3 . . . 10 A3
Ashmore's La ST7 . . . 193 D3
Ash Mount CW3 . . . 232 B1
Ashmuir Cl
Blacon CH1 . . . 117 E3
Crewe CW1 . . . 190 B6
Ashness Dr SK7 . . . 35 E8
Ash Priors WA8 . . . 12 D3
Ash Rd
Crewe CW1 . . . 190 D6
Cuddington CW8 . . . 101 F2
Elton CH2 . . . 72 C3
Haydock WA11 . . . 1 E7
Hollinfare WA3 . . . 11 A2
Lymm WA13 . . . 18 C3
Partington M31 . . . 11 D3
Poynton SK12 . . . 36 F3
Warrington WA5 . . . 14 F4
Winwick WA2 . . . 8 B6
Ashridge St WA7 . . . 22 F3
Ash St CW9 . . . 79 A1
Ash Terr SK11 . . . 112 C4
Ashton Ave SK10 . . . 86 D1
Ashton Cl
Bebington CH62 . . . 43 E3
Congleton CW12 . . . 157 B1
Frodsham WA6 . . . 49 C1
Middlewich CW10 . . . 151 D5
Northwich CW9 . . . 103 E4
Runcorn WA7 . . . 48 F6
Ashton Ct WA6 . . . 49 C1
Ashton Dr WA6 . . . 49 C1
ASHTON HAYES . . . 121 F7
Ashton Hayes Prim Sch CH3 . . . 121 F8
Ashton La CH3 . . . 121 E6
Ashton Rd
Manley WA6 . . . 99 E4
Newton-le-W WA12 . . . 2 C5
Norley WA6 . . . 100 B4
ASHTON'S GREEN . . . 1 B3
Ashton St WA2 . . . 16 B6
Ashtree Cl
Neston CH64 . . . 67 A7
Prestbury SK10 . . . 87 C8
Ashtree Croft CH64 . . . 68 A7
Ashtree Ct CH2 . . . 237 C4
Ashtree Dr CH64 . . . 67 A7
Ashtree Farm Ct CH64 . . . 68 A7
Ash View ST7 . . . 195 B2
Ashville Ct CW2 . . . 206 B7
Ashville Ind Est WA7 . . . 49 E3
Ashville Way WA7 . . . 49 E3
Ash Way CH60 . . . 41 B6
Ashwood WA14 . . . 31 B8
Ashwood Ave
Golborne WA3 . . . 3 D8
Warrington WA1 . . . 16 E7
Ashwood Cl
Barnton CW8 . . . 78 B4
Ellesmere Port CH66 . . . 69 D1
Widnes WA8 . . . 22 A7
Ashwood Cres CW8 . . . 78 B3
Ashwood Ct CH2 . . . 119 A3
Ashwood Farm Ct CH2 . . . 96 B6
Ashwood La CH2 . . . 96 B5
Ashwood Rd SK12 . . . 38 D6
Ashworth Pk WA16 . . . 81 F8
Asiatic Cotts CH5 . . . 116 B3
Askerbank La SK11 . . . 159 A1
Askett Cl WA11 . . . 1 C7
Askrigg Ave CH66 . . . 69 B5
Aspen Cl
Ellesmere Port CH66 . . . 69 E1
Harriseahead ST7 . . . 195 E3
Heswall CH60 . . . 41 D8
Aspen Gr
Saughall CH1 . . . 117 B7
Warrington WA1 . . . 17 A7
Aspens The CW8 . . . 101 E5
Aspen Way
Chester CH2 . . . 119 B4
High Lane SK6 . . . 38 A7
Aspinall Cl WA2 . . . 9 A3
Aspull Cl WA3 . . . 9 C4
Asquith Cl CW1 . . . 191 C5
Assheton Cl WA12 . . . 2 B4
Assheton Wlk L24 . . . 21 E2
ASTBURY . . . 178 B7
Astbury Cl
Crewe CW1 . . . 190 A7
Golborne WA3 . . . 4 B8
Kidsgrove ST7 . . . 195 C3
Astbury Dr CW8 . . . 78 A4
Astbury Lane Ends CW12 . . . 178 F8
ASTBURY MARSH . . . 156 B1
Astbury Mere Ctry Pk* CW12 . . . 156 B2
Astbury St Mary's CE Prim Sch CW12 . . . 178 B8
Astbury St CW12 . . . 156 C2
Aster Cres WA7 . . . 49 F5
Aster Rd WA11 . . . 1 F7
Aster Wlk M31 . . . 11 F2
ASTLE . . . 109 D8
Astle Cl CW10 . . . 151 C7
Astle Ct SK11 . . . 84 A3
Astle La SK10 . . . 84 E1
Astley Cl
Knutsford WA16 . . . 82 C7
Warrington WA4 . . . 16 B3
Widnes WA8 . . . 12 C3
Astley Ct M44 . . . 11 E8
Astley Rd M44 . . . 11 E8
ASTMOOR . . . 23 E3
Astmoor Bridge La WA7 . . . 23 F2
Astmoor East Intc WA7 . . . 24 A3
Astmoor Ind Est WA7 . . . 23 F3
Astmoor La WA7 . . . 23 F1
Astmoor Prim Sch WA7 . . . 23 F2
Astmoor Rd
Runcorn, Astmoor WA7 . . . 23 E3
Runcorn WA7 . . . 23 C3
ASTON
Nantwich . . . 217 C2
Runcorn . . . 50 D1
Aston Ave
Warrington WA3 . . . 9 F4
Winsford CW7 . . . 126 B2
Aston by Sutton Prim Sch WA7 . . . 50 C2
Aston Ct WA1 . . . 9 C1
Aston Fields Rd WA7 . . . 50 E4
Aston Forge WA7 . . . 50 F5
Aston Gn WA7 . . . 50 E6
ASTON HEATH . . . 50 E2
ASTON JUXTA MONDRUM . . . 188 D6
Aston La
Aston WA7 . . . 50 C2
Runcorn WA7 . . . 50 F5
Woore CW3 . . . 232 E1
Aston La N WA7 . . . 50 E4
Aston La S WA7 . . . 50 E3
Aston Rd ST5 . . . 210 D1
Aston Way
[13] Handforth SK9 . . . 34 D5
Middlewich CW10 . . . 128 E1
Astor Dr WA4 . . . 26 F8
Atcherley Cl CW5 . . . 218 E8
Athelbrae Cl CW8 . . . 103 F7
Atherton La M44 . . . 11 E5
Atherton Rd CH65 . . . 69 F6
Athey St Mill [2] SK11 . . . 112 C7
Athey St SK11 . . . 112 C8
Athlone Rd WA2 . . . 8 A1
Athol Cl
Bebington CH62 . . . 43 E5
Newton-le-W WA12 . . . 1 F4
Athol Dr CH62 . . . 43 E5
Atholl Ave CW2 . . . 190 C1
Atholl Cl SK10 . . . 87 A1
Athol Rd SK7 . . . 35 D5
Atkin Cl CW12 . . . 156 A3
Atlanta Ave M90 . . . 33 A8
Atlanta Gdns WA5 . . . 15 B8
Atlantic Trad Pk CW7 . . . 126 E5
Atlas Way CH66 . . . 69 F7
Atterbury Cl WA8 . . . 12 C2
Attlee Ave WA3 . . . 5 C4
Attwood Cl CW1 . . . 191 C4
Attwood Rise ST7 . . . 195 A2
Attwood St ST7 . . . 195 A2
Atworth Terr CH64 . . . 67 F8
Aubourn Cl WA8 . . . 12 C3
Auckery Ave CH66 . . . 69 D3
Auckland Rd CH1 . . . 117 D4
AUDLEM . . . 230 B4
Audlem Cl WA7 . . . 49 F4
Audlem Dr CW9 . . . 104 A6
Audlem Rd
Hankelow CW3 . . . 230 C7
Hatherton CW5 . . . 219 D3
Nantwich CW5 . . . 204 F3
Audlem St James' CE Prim Sch CW3 . . . 230 A5
AUDLEY . . . 209 C2
Audley Cres CH4 . . . 141 E6
Audley Rd
Alsager ST7 . . . 193 E1
Barthomley CW2 . . . 208 E5
Newcastle-u-Lyme ST7, ST5 . . . 210 B2
Talke ST7 . . . 210 B6
Audley St W CW1 . . . 190 D5
Audley St CW1 . . . 190 D5
Audre Cl WA5 . . . 14 D6
Aughton Way CH4 . . . 139 D4
Augusta Dr SK10 . . . 87 B4
Augusta Ho CH1 . . . 117 F6
Austell Rd [3] M22 . . . 33 D8
Austen Cl [1] CW11 . . . 174 D6
Austen Dr WA2 . . . 8 A6
Austen Ho SK10 . . . 86 F1
Austin Cl CW7 . . . 149 C6
Austins Hill CH3 . . . 144 C8
Austin St CW9 . . . 79 D1
Austral Ave WA1 . . . 17 C7
Australia La WA4 . . . 17 C1
Autumn Ave WA16 . . . 57 C2
Avebury Cl
Golborne WA3 . . . 3 E8
Widnes WA8 . . . 13 F3
Aveley Cl WA1 . . . 17 B7
Avens Rd M31 . . . 11 F3
Avenue One CW1 . . . 207 C8
Avenue The
Alderley Edge SK9 . . . 60 A1
Alsager ST7 . . . 193 D4
Altrincham WA15 . . . 31 F8
Bebington CH62 . . . 43 C8
Comberbach CW9 . . . 78 D8
Great Barrow CH3 . . . 120 F7
High Legh WA16 . . . 29 C5
Kidsgrove ST7 . . . 194 F1
Lymm WA13 . . . 18 D1
Marston CW9 . . . 79 B3
Newton-le-W WA12 . . . 2 D4
Sandbach CW11 . . . 174 E8
Tarporley CW6 . . . 146 D1
Avenue Two CW1 . . . 207 C8
Avery Cl WA2 . . . 8 E2
Avery Cres WA11 . . . 1 C7
Avery Rd WA11 . . . 1 C7
Avery Sq WA11 . . . 1 C7
Aviemore Dr WA2 . . . 9 A3
Avocet Cl
Newton-le-W WA12 . . . 2 C4
Warrington WA2 . . . 8 D3
Avocet Dr CW7 . . . 149 D6
Avon WA8 . . . 12 A2
Avon Ave WA5 . . . 14 F4
Avon Cl
Kidsgrove ST7 . . . 195 B2
Macclesfield SK10 . . . 87 A2
Neston CH64 . . . 66 E6
Avon Ct ST7 . . . 193 C5
Avondale CH65 . . . 70 B2
Avondale Ave CH62 . . . 43 F5
Avondale Dr WA8 . . . 12 B1
Avondale Rd WA11 . . . 1 C7
Avondale Rise SK9 . . . 60 D6
Avon Dr
Congleton CW12 . . . 156 F1
Crewe CW1 . . . 191 A5
Avonlea Cl CH4 . . . 140 E4
Avon Rd
Altrincham WA15 . . . 31 E8
Culcheth WA3 . . . 5 A2
Gatley SK8 . . . 34 C7
Avonside Way SK11 . . . 112 C5
Avon Wlk CW7 . . . 127 A2
Avro Way M90 . . . 32 F7
Axminster Wlk SK7 . . . 35 E7
Aycliffe Wlk [6] WA8 . . . 22 C8
Aylesbury Cl
Ellesmere Port CH66 . . . 69 C3
Macclesfield SK10 . . . 87 D3
Aylesby Cl WA16 . . . 57 B1
Aylsham Cl WA8 . . . 12 C4
Ayrshire Cl CW10 . . . 128 D2
Ayrshire Way CW12 . . . 157 A1
Aysgarth Ave CW1 . . . 173 B1
Azalea Gdns WA9 . . . 6 A7
Azalea Gr WA7 . . . 49 F4

B

Babbacombe Rd WA5 . . . 14 E4
Babbage Rd CH5 . . . 116 A4
BACHE . . . 118 B5
Bache Ave CH2 . . . 118 C5
Bache Dr CH2 . . . 118 D5
Bachefield Ave CH3 . . . 142 A6
Bache Hall Ct CH2 . . . 118 C5
Bache Hall Est CH2 . . . 118 C5
Bachelor's Ct CH3 . . . 142 A8
Bachelor's La CH3 . . . 142 A8
Bache Sta CH2 . . . 118 D5
Back Bridge St WA12 . . . 2 B3
Back Brook Pl WA4 . . . 16 E3
Back Coole La CW3 . . . 229 B4
Back Crosland Terr WA6 . . . 73 B2
Back Cross La
Congleton CW12 . . . 179 A8
Newton-le-W WA12 . . . 2 B4
Back Eastford Rd WA4 . . . 16 A1
Back Eddisbury Rd SK11 . . . 113 C7
BACKFORD . . . 95 A4
Backford Cl WA7 . . . 50 C5
Backford Cross CH66 . . . 94 F7
Backford Gdns CH1 . . . 94 F7
Back Forshaw St WA2 . . . 16 C7
Back Heathcote St ST7 . . . 195 A2
Back High St [3] WA7 . . . 23 A2
Back Jodrell St SK22 . . . 39 B7
Back La
Alpraham CW6 . . . 169 D6
Altrincham WA15 . . . 32 B4
Bate Heath CW9 . . . 54 D7
Betley CW2 . . . 208 C1
Brereton Green CW11 . . . 153 D6
Back La *continued*
Burtonwood WA5 . . . 6 D7
Congleton CW12 . . . 156 A4
Duddon CW6 . . . 145 A6
Helsby WA6 . . . 73 D2
Higher Whitley WA4 . . . 52 E4
High Legh WA14 . . . 29 F5
Marton CW12, SK11 . . . 133 F2
No Man's Heath SY14 . . . 214 A4
Norbury SY13 . . . 215 F5
Partington WA14 . . . 20 C5
Plumley WA16 . . . 81 B1
Shavington CW2 . . . 206 E4
Smallwood CW11 . . . 176 D8
Swan Green WA16 . . . 106 B8
Tattenhall CH3 . . . 167 C2
Threapwood SY14 . . . 222 E7
Warrington WA5 . . . 14 A3
Wybunbury CW5 . . . 220 C6
Backlands CW1 . . . 190 C6
Back Lanes CW6 . . . 146 B2
Back Legh St WA12 . . . 2 A3
Back Market St WA12 . . . 2 A3
Back Paradise St [4] SK11 . . . 112 C7
Back Park St CW12 . . . 156 E2
Back Queen St CH1 . . . 237 B3
Back River St [1] CW12 . . . 156 D3
Back Union Rd [3] SK22 . . . 39 C7
Back Wallgate [13] SK11 . . . 112 D8
Badbury Cl WA11 . . . 1 D7
Badcock's La CW6 . . . 185 E4
BADDILEY . . . 203 B1
Baddiley Cl CW5 . . . 203 D2
Baddiley Hall La CW5 . . . 217 A8
Baddiley La CW5 . . . 203 D1
Baddington La CW5 . . . 204 C1
Badger Ave CW1 . . . 190 B5
Badger Bait CH64 . . . 66 F6
Badger Cl WA7 . . . 50 A6
Badger Ho SK10 . . . 87 D2
Badger Rd
Macclesfield SK10 . . . 87 D2
Prestbury SK10 . . . 87 A7
Badgers Cl
Christleton CH3 . . . 142 E7
[1] Ellesmere Port CH66 . . . 94 F8
[1] Winsford CW7 . . . 126 A1
Badgers Croft ST5 . . . 210 E1
Badgers Pk CH64 . . . 66 F6
Badgersrake La CH66 . . . 68 D3
Badgers Set CW8 . . . 101 D5
Badgers Wlk CH2 . . . 95 E2
Badgers Wood CW2 . . . 205 E8
Bag La
Cuddington CW8, WA6 . . . 101 E7
Norley WA6 . . . 101 A6
Bagley La CW3 . . . 230 B1
Bagmere Cl
Brereton Green CW11 . . . 153 F4
Sandbach CW11 . . . 174 F7
Bagmere La CW11 . . . 154 B5
Bagnall Cl WA5 . . . 15 C5
Bagot Ave WA5 . . . 15 F8
Bagstock Ave SK12 . . . 36 E2
Baguley Ave WA8 . . . 22 A5
Bahama Cl WA11 . . . 1 D8
Bahama Rd WA11 . . . 1 D8
Baildon Gn CH66 . . . 69 B5
Bailey Ave CH65 . . . 69 F6
Bailey Bridge Cl CH2 . . . 118 D4
Bailey Bsns Pk SK10 . . . 87 F7
Bailey Cl CW1 . . . 190 C7
Bailey Cres
Congleton CW12 . . . 157 A4
Sandbach CW11 . . . 175 D6
Bailey Ct
Alsager ST7 . . . 193 E3
[1] Macclesfield SK10 . . . 112 E7
Bailey La M31 . . . 11 F3
Bailey's Bank ST8 . . . 179 D3
Baileys Cl WA8 . . . 13 A5
Baileys La L26 . . . 21 A7
Bailey's La L24 . . . 21 A1
Bailey Wlk WA14 . . . 31 C8
Bainbridge Ave WA3 . . . 3 F8
Bainbridge Cres WA5 . . . 14 E8
Baines Ave M44 . . . 11 F8
Bakehurst Cl SK22 . . . 39 C7
Baker Cl CW2 . . . 190 A2
Baker Dr CH66 . . . 69 E3
Baker Rd WA7 . . . 48 D7
Baker's Cl CW7 . . . 126 E1
Baker's Ct CW7 . . . 126 E1
Baker's La
Swan Green WA16 . . . 106 D6
Winsford CW7 . . . 126 E1
Bakers Pl WA2 . . . 16 B7
Baker St [8] SK11 . . . 112 C7
Bakers Villas The CW12 . . . 156 D2
Bakestonedale Rd SK10 . . . 63 E4
Bakewell Cl CH66 . . . 94 E8
Bakewell Rd
Burtonwood WA5 . . . 7 A7
Hazel Grove SK7 . . . 36 E8
Bala Cl WA5 . . . 7 E2
BALDERTON . . . 140 C1
Baldock Cl WA4 . . . 17 C3
Balfour Cl CW1 . . . 191 C4
Balfour St WA7 . . . 22 F1
Balham Cl WA8 . . . 13 A4

Balharry Ave WA11 . . . . 1 E7
Ballantyne Pl WA2 . . . . 8 A6
Ballantyne Way **5** WA3 . . . 3 E8
Ballater Cres WA3 . . . . . . 119 B2
Ballater Dr WA2 . . . . 8 E4
Ballerat Cl CH1 . . . . 117 D4
Balliol Cl SK11 . . . . 112 F3
Ball La
  Bollington SK10 . . . . 87 D5
  Kingsley WA6 . . . . 75 E4
BALL O' DITTON 12 E2
Ball Pathway WA8 . . . . 12 E1
Balmoral Ave
  Crewe CW2 . . . . 190 B1
  Northwich CW9 . . . . 104 A5
Balmoral Cl
  Knutsford WA16 . . . . 57 B1
  Winsford CW7 . . . . 126 C3
Balmoral Cres SK10 . . . . . . 87 F2
Balmoral Dr
  Helsby WA6 . . . . 73 B4
  High Lane SK6 . . . . 37 E7
  Holmes Chapel CW4 . . . 130 B2
  Poynton SK12 . . . . 36 D3
Balmoral Gdns
  Congleton CW12 . . . . . . 156 F4
  Ellesmere Port CH65 . . . . 70 D3
Balmoral Pk CH1 . . . . 118 B3
Balmoral Pl CW5 . . . . 205 D4
Balmoral Rd
  Warrington WA4 . . . . 16 F2
  Widnes WA8 . . . . 13 A4
Balmoral Way SK9 . . . . 60 A6
BALTERLEY 208 C1
BALTERLEY GREEN 208 C2
BALTERLEY HEATH 207 F1
Baltimore Gdns WA5 . . . . . 15 C7
Bamburgh Ct CH65 . . . . . . 70 E3
Bamford Cl
  Bollington SK10 . . . . 88 A7
  Gatley SK8 . . . . 34 D8
  Runcorn WA7 . . . . 49 C7
Bamford St SK10 . . . . 87 E1
Banastre Dr WA12 . . . . 2 F3
Banbury Cl SK10 . . . . 87 E2
Banbury Dr WA5 . . . . 15 C5
Banbury St ST7 . . . . 194 D1
Bancroft CW8 . . . . 76 F4
Bancroft Rd WA8 . . . . 13 D2
Bandon Cl L24 . . . . 21 D2
Banff Ave CH63 . . . . 43 D5
Bangor Cl **1** CH66 . . . . . 94 F8
Bank Cl
  Chester CH2 . . . . 118 E5
  Macclesfield SK11 . . . . . 112 E7
  Neston CH64 . . . . 67 A6
Bank Cott CW12 . . . . 156 E2
Bank Ct **5** ST7 . . . . 195 A2
Bankes' La
  Runcorn, Weston Point
    WA7 . . . . 48 E6
  Runcorn, Weston WA7 . . . 48 F5
Bank Farm Mews
  SY14 . . . . 214 E6
Bankfield Ave
  Irlam M44 . . . . 11 D5
  Wistaston CW2 . . . . 206 A7
Bankfield Rd WA8 . . . . 12 C1
Bankfield Sch The
  WA8 . . . . 12 D1
Bankfields Dr CH62 . . . . . . 44 B5
Bank Gdns WA5 . . . . 14 E4
Bankhall La WA14,
  WA15 . . . . 31 F8
Bankhall Pk WA1 . . . . 16 C4
BANK HEATH 3 A8
Bankhey CH64 . . . . 66 F5
Bank Ho CW7 . . . . 126 C1
Bankhouse Dr CW12 . . . . . 157 A5
Bank House La
  Helsby WA6 . . . . 73 C4
  Smallwood CW11 . . . . . . 177 A6
Bank La
  Burland CW5 . . . . 203 D8
  Congleton CW12 . . . . . . 134 C2
  Rainow SK10 . . . . 89 D6
Banklands Cl M44 . . . . 11 D5
Bank Mews WA6 . . . . 73 C4
Bank Pl SK9 . . . . 60 B7
BANK QUAY 15 F4
Bank Quay Trad Est
  WA1 . . . . 15 F4
Bank Rd CH5 . . . . 91 D1
Banks Cl CW12 . . . . 156 C3
Banks Cres WA4 . . . . 16 F4
Bankside
  Altrincham WA15 . . . . 32 D6
  Runcorn WA7 . . . . 50 E7
  Warrington WA1 . . . . 16 A5
Bank Side CW8 . . . . 77 C1
Bankside Cl
  Barbridge CW5 . . . . 187 D6
  Handforth SK9 . . . . 34 D1
Bankside Ct ST7 . . . . 173 C5
Bank Sq SK9 . . . . 60 B7
Banks Rd CH60 . . . . 40 D8
Bank St
  Congleton CW12 . . . . . . 156 E2
  Hollinfare WA3 . . . . 11 B5
  Kidsgrove ST7 . . . . 195 C4
  Macclesfield SK11 . . . . . 112 E7
  Newton-le-W WA12 . . . . . 1 F3
  8 Warrington WA1 . . . . . 16 B5
  Widnes WA8 . . . . 23 A4
Bank The ST7 . . . . 195 B7
Bank Top Cotts CW5 . . . . . 204 F6
Bank View WA4 . . . . 107 E1
Banky Fields CW12 . . . . . . 156 C2

Banky Fields Cres
  CW12 . . . . 156 C1
Bannacks Cl CW5 . . . . 205 D6
Bannister Ct CW7 . . . . 149 B7
Bannister Gr CW7 . . . . 149 B6
Barbauld St WA1 . . . . 16 B5
Barber Dr ST7 . . . . 194 E7
Barbery Wlk M31 . . . . 11 F3
Barber's La
  Antrobus CW9 . . . . 53 D6
  Northwich CW8 . . . . 103 E8
Barber St SK11 . . . . 112 E6
Barbondale Cl WA5 . . . . . . 14 F7
Barbour Sq CH3 . . . . 166 B1
BARBRIDGE 187 C6
Barbridge Mews
  CW5 . . . . 187 D6
Barbridge Rd ST5 . . . . 210 D2
Barclay Hall WA16 . . . . 58 D4
Barclay Rd SK12 . . . . 36 E2
Bardell Cl SK12 . . . . 36 D2
Bardsey Cl **1** CH65 . . . . . 70 C1
Bardsley Ave WA5 . . . . 7 F1
Barford Cl WA5 . . . . 7 B1
Barford Dr
  Golborne WA3 . . . . 4 A8
  Handforth SK9 . . . . 34 C1
Barford Grange CH64 . . . . . 68 B8
Barham Ct WA3 . . . . 9 D4
Barhill Dr SY13 . . . . 214 C2
Barhill Farm Cotts
  SY13 . . . . 214 C2
Barington Dr WA7 . . . . 50 E7
Baristow Cl CH2 . . . . 237 B4
Barker's Hollow Rd
  WA4 . . . . 51 A5
Barker St
  Crewe CW2 . . . . 190 D1
  Nantwich CW5 . . . . 204 E5
Barkhill Rd CH3 . . . . 119 B3
Bark St CW12 . . . . 156 E2
Barley Castle Cl WA4 . . . . . 27 B3
Barleycastle La WA4 . . . . . 27 D4
Barleycastle Trad Est
  WA4 . . . . 27 D4
Barley Croft
  Alsager ST7 . . . . 193 E2
  Chester CH3 . . . . 142 A7
Barleycroft Terr ST7 . . . . . 194 F7
Barley Dr SK7 . . . . 35 E7
Barleyfields ST7 . . . . 209 D2
Barley Mow Cl CW9 . . . . . . 69 C2
Barley Rd WA4 . . . . 17 C3
Barleywood Cl CW2 . . . . . 206 B8
Barlow Dr CW7 . . . . 148 F8
Barlow Gr WA9 . . . . 1 A2
Barlow Hill SK11 . . . . 136 F2
Barlow Rd
  Handforth SK9 . . . . 34 B1
  Moulton CW9 . . . . 126 F7
Barlow Way CW11 . . . . 175 A8
Barmouth Cl WA5 . . . . 7 E2
Barnabas Ave CW1 . . . . . . 189 F5
Barnaby Chase CH3 . . . . . 182 C2
Barnaby Rd SK12 . . . . 36 D2
Barnack Cl WA1 . . . . 17 A8
Barnacre Dr CH64 . . . . 41 B2
Barnard Cl SK11 . . . . 111 F6
Barnard St WA5 . . . . 15 D3
Barnato Cl CW1 . . . . 189 F7
Barnbridge Cl WA7 . . . . . . 194 E7
Barncroft WA7 . . . . 50 D7
Barn Croft WA6 . . . . 73 C4
Barncroft Cl SK11 . . . . 84 A3
Barn Croft Rd L26 . . . . 21 A7
Barnes Ave WA3 . . . . 182 C2
Barnes Cl WA2 . . . . 9 B2
Barnes Cl
  Blacon CH1 . . . . 117 F6
  Haslington CW1 . . . . 191 C4
  Warrington WA5 . . . . 15 A5
  Widnes WA8 . . . . 13 D2
Barnes Rd WA8 . . . . 13 C3
Barneston Rd WA8 . . . . . . 13 E3
Barnett Ave WA12 . . . . 2 B3
BARNETT BROOK 228 E5
Barnett Gr CW12 . . . . 156 A3
Barnett St SK11 . . . . 112 B7
Barnett Wlk CW2 . . . . 206 C8
Barnfield CH3 . . . . 166 A2
Barnfield Ave WA7 . . . . 50 D7
Barnfield Cl CH66 . . . . 69 C2
Barnfield Rd
  Bollington SK10 . . . . 87 F6
  Warrington WA1 . . . . 17 C7
Barnham Cl WA3 . . . . 3 A8
BARNHILL 183 B1
Barnhill Grange CH3 . . . . . 183 B3
Barnhill Rd CH3 . . . . 183 B1
Barnhouse La
  Great Barrow CH3 . . . . . . 120 E7
  Mouldsworth CH3 . . . . . . 98 A3
Barn La WA3 . . . . 2 F0
Barn Mdw CW5 . . . . 78 E1
Barnmoore Cl SY14 . . . . . . 213 B4
Barn Rd CW12 . . . . 156 D4
Barnside Way
  Macclesfield SK10 . . . . . . 87 C3
  Moulton CW9 . . . . 126 F8
Barns La
  Partington WA14 . . . . 20 A5
  Partington WA14 . . . . 20 A6
Barns Pl WA15 . . . . 32 C8
Barn St WA8 . . . . 23 A6
Barnstaple Way WA5 . . . . . 14 E4
Barns The CW10 . . . . 127 D5
Barnston Ave CH65 . . . . . . 69 F5

Barnston Ct
  Farndon CH3 . . . . 180 E2
  Mickle Trafford CH2 . . . . 119 F8
Barnston Mews CH3 . . . . . 180 E2
Barnston Prim Sch
  CH60 . . . . 41 C7
Barnston Rd CH60 . . . . 41 C8
Barnston Towers Cl
  CH60 . . . . 41 C8
Barnston Twrs CH60 . . . . . 41 C8
Barnswood Cl WA3 . . . . . . 17 C1
BARNTON 78 C4
Barnton Cl WA3 . . . . 3 D7
Barnton Prim Sch
  CW8 . . . . 78 A4
Barnwell Ave WA3 . . . . 2 B3
Barnwell Ave WA2 . . . . 4 D4
Barnwell Cl CW2 . . . . 206 B8
Barnwood CH66 . . . . 68 F7
Baron Cl WA1 . . . . 17 D7
Baronet Mews WA4 . . . . . . 16 A1
Baronet Rd WA4 . . . . 16 A1
Baron Gn SK8 . . . . 34 D7
Baronia Pl CW5 . . . . 204 F6
Baron's Ct WA4 . . . . 23 F1
Baron's Cl WA8 . . . . 22 C8
Barons Ct CH2 . . . . 118 C4
Barons Quay Rd CW9 . . . . 78 F1
Barons Rd
  Shavington CW2 . . . . 206 B4
  Worleston CW5 . . . . 188 C5
Barony Bldgs **1** CW5 . . . . 204 E7
Barony Ct CW5 . . . . 204 E7
Barony Employment Pk
  The CW5 . . . . 204 F8
Barony Rd CW5 . . . . 204 F8
Barony Terr CW5 . . . . 204 E6
Barony Way CH4 . . . . 140 E4
Barracks La
  Burwardsley CH3 . . . . . . 184 C5
  Macclesfield SK10 . . . . . 112 F8
  Ravensmoor CW5 . . . . . . 203 E2
Barracks Sq **3** SK11 . . . . 112 B6
Barrastitch La CW9 . . . . . . 101 E6
Barratt Rd ST7 . . . . 193 F3
Barrel Well Hill CH2 . . . . . 118 F1
BARRETS GREEN 169 D3
Barrie Gdns ST7 . . . . 210 C8
Barrie Gr CW1 . . . . 190 E4
Barrington Dr CW10 . . . . . 151 C2
Barrow Ave WA2 . . . . 8 E2
Barrow CE Prim Sch
  CH3 . . . . 120 D6
Barrowdale Rd WA3 . . . . . . 3 B8
Barrow Hall Com Prim Sch
  WA5 . . . . 14 E7
Barrow Hall Farm
  CH3 . . . . 120 E5
Barrow Hall La WA5 . . . . . 14 E7
Barrow La
  Altrincham WA15 . . . . 32 B7
  Golborne WA2 . . . . 3 C2
  Great Barrow CH3 . . . . . . 120 C5
  Tarvin CH3 . . . . 121 C4
Barrow Mdw SK8 . . . . 34 E8
Barrowmore Est CH3 . . . . . 120 F7
Barrow's Brow WA16 . . . . . 81 E1
Barrow's Cl WA1 . . . . 190 A8
BARROWS GREEN 189 F8
BARROW'S GREEN 13 E4
Barrow's Green La
  WA8 . . . . 13 E3
Barrow's Row WA8 . . . . . . 13 B4
Barrule Cl WA4 . . . . 26 D7
Barry Cl CH65 . . . . 95 C8
Barrymore Ave WA4 . . . . . 16 F4
Barrymore Cres CW9 . . . . 78 D8
Barrymore Ct WA4 . . . . . . 17 A1
Barrymore Rd
  Runcorn WA7 . . . . 49 B7
  Warrington WA4 . . . . 17 A1
  Weaverham CW8 . . . . . . 77 E1
Barrymore Way CH63 . . . . 43 B6
Barry St WA4 . . . . 16 C4
Barsbank Cl WA13 . . . . . . 18 C3
Barsbank La WA13 . . . . . . 18 C3
Barshaw Gdns WA4 . . . . . 26 E4
Bars The CH1, CH3 . . . . . . 237 C2
Bartholomew Ct WA4 . . . . 17 B2
Bartholomew Way
  CH4 . . . . 141 C6
BARTHOMLEY 208 C5
Barthomley Cres
  CW2 . . . . 189 D4
Barthomley Rd
  Barthomley CW2 . . . . 208 B7
  Betley ST7 . . . . 208 F3
BARTINGTON 77 A5
Bartington Hall Pk
  CW8 . . . . 77 A4
Bartlegate WA7 . . . . 50 B5
BARTON 181 F1
Barton Ave WA4 . . . . 17 A2
Barton Cl
  Handforth SK9 . . . . 34 C5
  Runcorn WA7 . . . . 50 D7
Barton Ct
  Warrington WA2 . . . . 16 B6
  Winsford CW7 . . . . 149 A8
Barton Rd
  Barton CH3, SY14 . . . . . . 181 D1
  Barton SY14 . . . . 181 D1
  Congleton CW12 . . . . . . 156 F3
  Farndon CH3 . . . . 180 D1
Barton's Pl CW9 . . . . 79 B1
Barton St SK11 . . . . 112 C2
Barton Stad CW7 . . . . 126 F1
Barwood Ave ST7 . . . . 194 A5

Barwoods Dr CH4 . . . . 140 F6
BASFORD 206 E5
Basford Rd CW2 . . . . 206 D8
Basford Way CW7 . . . . 126 B2
Baskervyle Cl CH60 . . . . . . 41 A6
Baskervyle Rd CH60 . . . . . 41 A6
Baslow Dr
  Gatley SK8 . . . . 34 C8
  Hazel Grove SK7 . . . . 36 F8
Bassett Cl CW5 . . . . 205 D6
Batchelors Wing The
  CW10 . . . . 127 D5
BATE HEATH 54 F3
Bateman Almshouses
  ST8 . . . . 179 E3
Bateman Cl CW1 . . . . 190 B4
Bateman Rd CW9 . . . . 80 B2
Batemans Ct CW2 . . . . . . 206 B8
Batemill Cl SK10 . . . . 86 F1
Batemill La WA16,
  SK11 . . . . 108 E5
Bates La WA6 . . . . 73 D4
Bates Mill La CW6 . . . . . . 167 E5
Bath Cres SK8 . . . . 35 B6
Bath Ho WA16 . . . . 157 A5
Bath La CW3 . . . . 230 A3
Bath St
  Chester CH1 . . . . 237 C2
  Sandbach CW11 . . . . . . 175 C6
  Warrington WA1 . . . . 16 A5
BATH VALE 157 A3
Bath Vale Cotts
  CW12 . . . . 157 A3
Bathwood Dr CH64 . . . . . . 66 E5
Batterbee Ct CW1 . . . . 191 D5
Battersby La WA2 . . . . 16 C6
Battersea Ct WA8 . . . . 12 F3
Battery La
  Warrington WA1 . . . . 17 F7
  Wilmslow SK9 . . . . 59 D6
Bawtry Ct WA2 . . . . 8 E1
Baxter Cl WA7 . . . . 50 D7
Baxter Ho CW8 . . . . 78 E1
Baxter St WA5 . . . . 15 E5
Baycliffe WA13 . . . . 18 D2
Bayley Rd CW5 . . . . 205 D6
Bayswater Cl WA7 . . . . 24 F4
Baytree Cl CW8 . . . . 69 F1
Bayvil Cl WA7 . . . . 50 E7
Beach Ct CW8 . . . . 103 E6
Beachin La CH3 . . . . 182 A4
Beach Rd CW8 . . . . 103 B6
Beacon Cl **4** CH60 . . . . . . 41 A8
Beacon Hill View WA7 . . . . 48 D7
Beacon La CH60 . . . . 41 A7
Beaconsfield Cres
  WA8 . . . . 13 A4
Beaconsfield Gr WA8 . . . . . 13 B4
Beaconsfield Rd
  Runcorn WA7 . . . . 22 E1
  Widnes WA8 . . . . 13 B4
Beaconsfield St CH3 . . . . . 237 C2
Beacons The CH60 . . . . . . 41 A7
Beacons The WA3 . . . . 9 D5
Beadnell Dr WA5 . . . . 14 F3
Beagle Point CW7 . . . . 126 A1
Beagle Wlk M22 . . . . 33 E8
Beames Ho CW1 . . . . 190 B4
Beam Heath Way
  CW5 . . . . 204 F7
Beamish Cl WA4 . . . . 26 D3
Beamont St WA8 . . . . 23 A4
Bean St CW5 . . . . 204 E6
Beard Cres SK22 . . . . 39 D8
Beardsmore Dr WA3 . . . . . 3 E8
Bearhurst La SK11 . . . . . . 111 A5
Bearstone Rd TF9 . . . . 236 E3
Beasley Cl CH66 . . . . 69 D3
Beata Rd ST5 . . . . 210 F1
Beatrice St WA4 . . . . 16 D3
Beatty Ave WA2 . . . . 8 C1
Beatty Dr CW12 . . . . 157 A4
Beatty Rd CW5 . . . . 204 D4
Beaufort Chase SK9 . . . . . 34 F1
Beaufort Cl
  Alderley Edge SK9 . . . . . 60 B2
  Runcorn WA7 . . . . 49 B7
  Warrington WA5 . . . . 15 A5
  Widnes WA8 . . . . 22 A8
Beaufort St WA5 . . . . 15 E4
Beaumaris Cres SK7 . . . . . 36 C8
Beaumaris Dr CH65 . . . . . . 70 D2
Beaumaris Way WA7 . . . . . 23 F2
Beaumont Cl
  Biddulph ST8 . . . . 179 D3
  Chester CH4 . . . . 140 E6
  Wistaston CW2 . . . . 205 F8
Beaumont Com Inf & Jun
  Schs WA2 . . . . 16 C7
Beaumont Ct
  Handforth SK9 . . . . 34 C5
  Warrington WA2 . . . . 16 B6
Beauty Bank
  Whitegate CW7 . . . . 125 E5
  Winsford CW7 . . . . 149 B3
Beauty Bank Cotts
  CW7 . . . . 149 A3
Beaverbrook Ave WA3 . . . . 5 B4
Beaver Cl
  Chester CH4 . . . . 140 E5
  Pickmere WA16 . . . . 79 F7
Beaver Ctr The CW9 . . . . . 103 F7
BEBINGTON 43 A7
Bebington Rd CH66 . . . . . . 69 D4
Becconsall Cl CW1 . . . . . . 190 A8
Becconsall Dr CW1 . . . . . . 190 A8

Bechers WA8 . . . . 12 B3
Beckenham Cl WA8 . . . . . . 13 D4
Beckenham Gr **4**
  CW7 . . . . 126 A1
Beckett Ave CW7 . . . . 150 D8
Beckett Dr
  Lymm WA13 . . . . 19 B8
  Winwick WA2 . . . . 8 A5
Beckett's La CH3 . . . . 142 B8
Beckford Ct CW1 . . . . 189 F8
Becks La SK10 . . . . 86 F2
Bedells La SK9 . . . . 60 A6
Bedford Ave CH65 . . . . 70 A2
Bedford Ave E CH65 . . . . . 70 B2
Bedford Ct CW2 . . . . 190 D1
Bedford Gdns CW2 . . . . . . 190 C1
Bedford Gn M44 . . . . 11 B6
Bedford Gr ST7 . . . . 193 B5
Bedford Pl CW2 . . . . 190 C1
Bedford Rd
  Kidsgrove ST7 . . . . 195 A3
  Macclesfield SK11 . . . . . 112 B7
Bedford Rise CW7 . . . . 149 C6
Bedford St
  Crewe CW2 . . . . 190 C1
  Warrington WA4 . . . . 26 C8
Bedward Row CH1 . . . . 237 A2
Beech Ave
  Culcheth WA3 . . . . 5 A3
  Frodsham WA6 . . . . 74 C8
  Golborne WA3 . . . . 3 F7
  Haydock WA11 . . . . 1 A7
  Mobberley WA16 . . . . 57 E6
  Rode Heath ST7 . . . . 193 F8
  Warrington, Thelwall
    WA4 . . . . 17 D3
  Warrington WA5 . . . . 14 C3
Beech Bank SK10 . . . . 87 D1
Beech Cl
  Alderley Edge SK9 . . . . . 60 B3
  Congleton CW12 . . . . . . 156 A4
  Cuddington CW8 . . . . . . 101 F2
  Holmes Chapel CW4 . . . 130 D4
  Newton-le-W WA12 . . . . . 2 C2
  Ollerton WA16 . . . . 82 F6
  4 Partington M31 . . . . . 11 F3
Beech Cotts
  Alderley Edge SK9 . . . . . 85 A8
  Widnes WA8 . . . . 26 E1
Beech Cres SK12 . . . . 36 E4
Beechcroft Ave CW2 . . . . . 206 B7
Beechcroft Dr CH65 . . . . . . 70 B2
Beech Ct WA8 . . . . 12 B3
Beech Dr
  Crewe CW2 . . . . 189 F2
  Knutsford WA16 . . . . 57 C2
  Talke ST7 . . . . 210 E8
Beeches The
  Chester CH2 . . . . 119 A6
  Ellesmere Port CH66 . . . . 69 D4
  Helsby WA6 . . . . 73 C4
  Mobberley WA16 . . . . 58 E1
  Nantwich CW5 . . . . 204 F5
  3 Northwich WA6 . . . . . 103 E6
  Whitchurch SY13 . . . . . . 225 F1
  Widnes WA8 . . . . 13 D4
Beech Farm Dr SK10 . . . . . 87 D2
Beechfield
  Moulton CW9 . . . . 126 E8
  Wilmslow SK9 . . . . 60 A6
Beechfield Ave SK9 . . . . . . 59 E5
Beechfield Cl CH60 . . . . . . 41 A7
Beechfield Dr CW10 . . . . . 128 B2
Beechfield Gdns CW8 . . . . 103 B6
Beechfield Rd
  Alderley Edge SK9 . . . . . 85 B8
  Cheadle SK8 . . . . 35 B8
  Ellesmere Port CH65 . . . . 70 B5
  Warrington WA4 . . . . 17 A2
Beechfields CW7 . . . . 150 B8
Beech Gdns **3** WA7 . . . . . 49 C8
Beech Gr
  Chester CH2 . . . . 119 A3
  Crewe CW1 . . . . 190 E5
  Ellesmere Port CH66 . . . . 95 A8
  Lymm WA13 . . . . 18 B2
  Macclesfield SK11 . . . . . 112 C5
  Sandbach CW11 . . . . . . 175 D6
  Warrington, Latchford
    WA4 . . . . 16 D3
  Warrington WA1 . . . . 17 A7
  Weaverham CW8 . . . . . . 102 D8
  Wilmslow SK9 . . . . 60 A6
  Winsford CW7 . . . . 149 D8
Beech Hall Dr SK10 . . . . . . 87 C2
Beech Hall Sch SK10 . . . . . 87 C2
Beech Heyes Cl CW8 . . . . . 102 E8
Beech Heyes Dr CW8 . . . . 102 E8
Beech Hey La CH64 . . . . . . 43 B1
Beech Hollows LL12 . . . . . 162 C1
Beech La
  Barnton CH3 . . . . 78 A3
  Cotebrook CW6 . . . . 147 B6
  Macclesfield SK10 . . . . . . 87 D1
  Norley WA6 . . . . 75 E1
  Wilmslow SK9 . . . . 60 A6
Beechlands Ave CH3 . . . . . 119 A1
Beechmill Dr WA3 . . . . 4 E5
Beechmoore WA4 . . . . 25 B5
Beechmuir CH1 . . . . 117 E3
Beech Rd
  Alderley Edge SK9 . . . . . 60 B3
  Aston WA7 . . . . 50 B4
  Heswall CH60 . . . . 41 C8

BEECH RD continued
High Lane SK6 . . . . .37 F7
Little Budworth CW8 . . . . . .124 D2
Paddockhill WA16 . . . . .59 B5
Runcorn WA7 . . . . .49 C8
Warrington WA4 . . . . .26 C8
Whaley Bridge SK23 . . . . . . .65 E7
Beech Rise
Crowton CW8 . . . . .76 B2
Horwich End SK23 . . . . .65 C5
Beech St W CW1 . . . . . . .190 L4
Beech St CW10 . . . . .128 C1
Beech Tree Cl CW5 . . . . .205 D5
Beechtree Farm Cl
WA16 . . . . .29 C7
Beechtree La WA3 . . . . . .29 B7
Beech View Rd WA6 . . . . .75 C1
Beechway
Bollington SK10 . . . . .88 A7
Chester CH2 . . . . .118 C6
High Lane SK6 . . . . .37 F7
Neston CH64 . . . . .66 D7
Warrington WA9 . . . . .59 F5
Beechways WA4 . . . . .26 D5
Beechways Dr CH64 . . . . .66 D7
BEECHWOOD 49 E5
Beechwood
Knutsford, Cross Town
WA16 . . . . .57 C2
Knutsford WA16 . . . . .56 F3
Beechwood Ave
Hartford CW8 . . . . .103 A6
Newton-le-W WA12 . . . . .2 D4
Runcorn WA7 . . . . .49 E5
Warrington, Padgate
WA1 . . . . .16 F7
Warrington WA5 . . . . .14 F5
Beechwood Cl CW5 . . . . .205 A4
Beechwood Dr
Alsager ST7 . . . . .193 B4
Eaton (nr Congleton)
CW12 . . . . .156 F8
Ellesmere Port CH66 . . . . . . .69 D1
Higher Wincham CW9 . . . . . .79 F6
Wilmslow SK9 . . . . .60 E8
Beechwood Gr SK8 . . . . .35 A8
Beechwood La WA3 . . . . . .4 D4
Beechwood Mews
SK10. . . . . .87 C2
Beechwood Prim Sch
WA7 . . . . .49 E5
Beechwood Rd
Bebington CH62 . . . . .43 C8
Saltney CH4 . . . . .140 E5
Beechwood Sch CW1 . . .190 C5
Beecroft Cl WA5 . . . . .7 D1
Beehive La CW9 . . . . .126 F8
BEESTON 168 A2
BEESTON–BROOK 168 C5
Beeston Brow SK10 . . . . . .88 B8
Beeston Castle*
CW6. . . . . .167 F3
Beeston Cl
Bollington SK10 . . . . .63 C1
Holmes Chapel CW4 . . . . . .130 A3
Middlewich CW10 . . . . .151 D5
Warrington WA3 . . . . .9 D4
Beeston Ct WA7 . . . . .24 C4
Beeston Dr
Alsager ST7 . . . . .193 C3
Knutsford WA16 . . . . .82 A8
Winsford CW7 . . . . .149 C7
Beeston Gn CH66 . . . . .69 E5
Beeston Hall Mews
CW6. . . . . .168 B4
Beeston Mount SK10 . . . . .63 C1
Beeston Pathway
CH4 . . . . .141 E7
Beeston Rd
Broughton CH4 . . . . .139 B3
Handforth SK9 . . . . .34 D5
Higher Kinnerton CH4 . . . . .161 A7
Beeston St CW8 . . . . .103 E7
Beeston Terr WA16 . . . . . .111 E6
Beeston View CH4 . . . . . .141 E7
Beggarman's La WA16 . . .82 A7
Begonia Gdns WA9 . . . . . . .6 A7
Beilby Rd WA11 . . . . .1 E7
Belfry Cl SK9 . . . . .60 D8
Belfry Dr SK10 . . . . .87 C4
BELGRAVE 162 E6
Belgrave App CH3 . . . . . .163 C6
Belgrave Ave
Alsager ST7 . . . . .193 D5
Congleton CW12 . . . . .156 D3
Eccleston CH4 . . . . .162 E7
Saltney CH4 . . . . .140 E6
Warrington WA1 . . . . .16 F6
Belgrave Cl
Dodleston CH4 . . . . .162 A6
Golborne WN7 . . . . .4 C8
Widnes WA8 . . . . .13 E3
Belgrave Dr CH65 . . . . .69 F5
Belgrave Inf Sch CH4 . . . .141 B5
Belgrave Rd
Chester CH3 . . . . .142 B8
Crewe CW2 . . . . .190 B2
Irlam M44 . . . . .11 D5
Macclesfield SK11 . . . . .112 C4
Northwich CW9 . . . . .104 A4
Belgrave St CH1 . . . . .237 C3
Belgravia Ct
Pulford CH4 . . . . .162 E5
Widnes WA8 . . . . .12 F3

Belgravia Gdns WA15 . . . .31 E8
Bellaport Rd TF9 . . . . .236 A4
Bellard Dr CH2 . . . . .119 A4
Bell Ave SK11 . . . . .112 F3
Bellcast Cl WA4 . . . . .26 C5
Bellemonte Rd WA6 . . . . . .74 C4
Belleville Ave WA2 . . . . . . .33 E8
Bellevue La CH3 . . . . .119 E4
Belle Vue Terr CW11 . . . . .175 B6
Bell Farm Ct SK10 . . . . . . .87 C3
Bellflower Cl WA8 . . . . . . .12 E4
Bellhouse La
Higher Walton WA4 . . . . .25 D7
Warrington WA4 . . . . .17 C1
Bell House Rd WA8 . . . . . .13 C1
Bellingham Cl WA4 . . . . . .57 C2
Bellingham Dr WA7 . . . . . .49 A8
Bell La
Smallwood CW11 . . . . .177 B7
Warrington WA4 . . . . .17 E3
Bell Meadow Bsns Pk
CH4 . . . . .162 E5
Bell Meadow Ct CW6 . . . .146 C2
BELL O' TH' HILL 225 D7
Bellsfield Cl WA3 . . . . .18 F2
Bell's Hollow ST5 . . . . . . .210 E3
Belmont Ave
Macclesfield SK10 . . . . .86 C1
Sandbach CW11 . . . . .175 A7
Warrington WA4 . . . . .16 F3
Belmont Cres WA5 . . . . . . .15 A6
Belmont Dr CH4 . . . . .140 C6
Belmont Rd
Bramhall SK7. . . . . .35 F5
Great Budworth CW9 . . . . . .53 F1
Northwich CW9 . . . . .104 C7
Widnes WA8 . . . . .13 E2
Belton Cl WA3. . . . . .3 A7
Beltony Dr CW1 . . . . .173 A1
Belvedere SK10 . . . . .23 A3
Belvedere Cl WA6. . . . . . . .49 C1
Belvedere Dr CH1 . . . . . . .117 E4
Belvedere Rd WA12 . . . . . . .2 B5
Belvedere Terr ST7 . . . . . .193 F7
Belvoir Ave SK10 . . . . .36 E8
Belvoir Rd
Warrington WA4 . . . . .26 B8
Widnes WA8 . . . . .13 B1
Bembridge Cl
Warrington WA5 . . . . .14 C7
Widnes WA8 . . . . .12 F4
Bembridge Ct CW10 . . . . .151 C8
Bembridge Dr CW10 . . . . .151 C8
Benbrook Gr SK9 . . . . .34 E2
Benbrook Way SK11 . . . . .111 E1
Bendee Ave CH64 . . . . .67 A7
Bendee Rd CH64 . . . . .67 A7
Benjafield Ct CW1 . . . . . . .189 F7
Benjamins Way ST7 . . . . .209 F2
Bennet Cl CH64 . . . . .68 A8
Bennet Rd CW9 . . . . .104 D6
Bennett Ave WA1 . . . . .16 F6
Bennett Cl CW1 . . . . .190 E4
Bennett St CW7 . . . . .149 D5
Bennetts La SK11 . . . . . . .158 E7
Bennett's La
Higher Kinnerton CH4 . . . . .161 A7
Widnes WA8 . . . . .13 E1
Bennett St WA1 . . . . .16 B5
Ben Nevis Dr CH66 . . . . . . .68 F6
Benson Rd WA3 . . . . .9 D3
Benson Wlk SK9 . . . . .34 D2
Bentham Ave WA2 . . . . .8 F3
Bentham Rd WA3. . . . . .5 A2
Bentinck St WA7 . . . . .22 F3
Bent La
Astbury CW12 . . . . .178 A8
Culcheth WA3 . . . . .5 A2
Lymm WA13. . . . . .19 C6
Norley CW8 . . . . .101 C8
Bentley Dr CW1 . . . . .191 A5
Bentley Gr CW7 . . . . .149 C6
Bentley's Farm La WA4 . . .52 E5
Benton Dr CH2 . . . . .118 C4
Bentside Rd SK12 . . . . .38 D5
Benty Heath La CH64,
CH66 . . . . .43 B3
Beresford Ct SK9 . . . . .60 A1
Beresford St WA1 . . . . .16 E7
Berisford Ho CW12 . . . . . .156 E3
Berkeley Ave ST7 . . . . . . .193 D5
Berkeley Cl WN7 . . . . .4 C8
Berkeley Cres CW2 . . . . . .206 A8
Berkeley Ct
Newton-le-W WA12. . . . . .1 F4
Runcorn WA7 . . . . .24 D4
Berkeley Prim Sch The
CW2. . . . . .206 B7
Berkeley Rise CW7 . . . . . .149 A8
Berkley St SK23 . . . . .65 D6
Berkley Dr CH4 . . . . .141 D6
Berkshire Dr
Congleton CW12 . . . . .156 D4
Irlam M44 . . . . .11 C5
Warrington WA1 . . . . .17 D6
Bermondsey Gr WA8 . . . . .13 D4
Bernard Ave WA4 . . . . .26 D8
Bernisdale Rd WA16 . . . . . .57 F4
Bernsdale Cl CH5 . . . . . . .116 A3
Bernsdale Ct/Llys
Bernsdale CH5 . . . . .116 A3
Berristall Rise SK10 . . . . . .63 C1
Berristal Rd SK10 . . . . .88 E3
Berry Cl
Ellesmere Port CH66 . . . . . . .69 C3
Wilmslow SK9 . . . . .60 A5

Berry Dr CH66 . . . . .69 C3
Berry Rd WA8 . . . . .12 D1
Berrystead LW8 . . . . .103 B4
Bertram St WA12 . . . . .2 A4
Berwick Ave CH62 . . . . .43 E4
Berwick Cl
Macclesfield SK10 . . . . .86 F2
Warrington WA1 . . . . .17 E6
Berwick Ct CW4 . . . . .130 B2
Berwick Gdns CH66 . . . . . .69 B6
Berwick Gr CH66 . . . . .69 B6
Berwick Rd CH66 . . . . .69 A6
Berwick Road W CH66 . . . .69 A6
Berwyn Cl LH66 . . . . .69 A6
Beswick Dr CW1 . . . . .191 A3
Beswicks La
Norton in Hales TF9 . . . . . .236 C2
Row-of-Trees SK9 . . . . .59 C3
Beswick Rd CW8 . . . . .78 E1
Beswick St SK11 . . . . .112 B7
Betchton Cl CW11 . . . . . . .175 C7
Betchton Ct CW12 . . . . . . .156 F3
BETCHTON HEATH 175 C6
Betchton Rd CW11 . . . . . . .175 E3
Betchworth Cres WA7 . . . .49 D6
Betchworth Way SK10 . . . .87 C4
Bethany Cl WA4 . . . . .16 F4
Betjeman Cl WA4 . . . . .16 F4
Betjeman Way CW1. . . . . .190 F5
BETLEY 221 F8
Betley Cl CW9 . . . . .104 A5
Betley St CW1 . . . . .190 C4
Betsyfield Dr WA3 . . . . .9 A7
Bettisfield Ave CH62 . . . . .43 D6
Betty's La
Beeston CW6 . . . . .168 D1
Woore CW3 . . . . .232 C1
Bevan Ave ST7 . . . . .210 E6
Bevan Cl WA5 . . . . .15 D6
Bevan Ct WA4 . . . . .15 F7
Bevan View WA5 . . . . .15 F7
Beverley Ave WA4 . . . . .26 D8
Beverley Dr CH60 . . . . .41 B6
Beverley Rd WA5 . . . . .15 C6
Beverley Way
Ellesmere Port CH66 . . . . . . .69 B7
Macclesfield SK10 . . . . .87 C4
Bevin Ave WA3 . . . . .5 B4
Bevyl Rd CH64 . . . . .41 B2
Bewick Wlk WA16 . . . . .57 B3
Bewley Ct CW4 . . . . .142 A7
BEWSEY 15 F8
Bewsey Bsns Ctr WA5 . . . .15 F6
Bewsey Farm Cl WA5 . . . . .15 D8
Bewsey Ind Est WA5 . . . . .16 A7
Bewsey Lodge Prim Sch
WA5 . . . . .15 F7
Bewsey Park Cl WA5 . . . . .15 F7
Bewsey Rd WA2, WA5 . . . . .16 A6
Bexhill Ave WA2 . . . . .8 B4
Bexington Dr CW1 . . . . . . .190 B8
Bexton Ave CW7 . . . . .126 A2
Bexton La WA16 . . . . .82 A8
Bexton Prim Sch WA16 . . .81 F7
Bexton Rd WA16 . . . . .56 F1
Bibby Ave WA1 . . . . .16 E6
Bibby's La SK10 . . . . .88 A1
Bibby St ST7 . . . . .193 E7
BICKERTON 199 E6
Bickerton Ave WA6 . . . . . . .74 D7
Bickerton Cl WA3 . . . . .9 D4
Bickerton Holy Trinity CE
Prim Sch SY14 . . . . .200 A7
Bickerton Rd SY14 . . . . . . .201 B2
Bickerton Way
CW9 . . . . .103 E4
Bickley Cl
Hough CW2 . . . . .206 E2
Northwich CW9 . . . . .103 E5
Runcorn WA7 . . . . .23 C1
Warrington WA2 . . . . .8 F3
BICKLEY MOSS 215 B7
BICKLEY TOWN 214 E6
Bickley Town La SY14 . . . .214 E6
BICKLEYWOOD 214 C4
Bicknell Cl WA5 . . . . .15 B8
Bida La CW12 . . . . .179 B8
BIDDULPH 179 B2
Biddulph Common Rd
ST8. . . . . .179 F7
Biddulph Grange Ctry Pk*
ST8. . . . . .179 F3
Biddulph Grange Gdn*
ST8. . . . . .179 E3
Biddulph Park Rd
ST8. . . . . .179 F5
Biddulph Rd
Congleton CW12 . . . . .179 B8
Harriseahead ST7 . . . . .195 F6
Biddulph St CW12 . . . . . . .179 C7
Bideford Rd WA5 . . . . .14 E4
Bidston Cl CH2 . . . . .118 D5
Bidston Dr SK9 . . . . .34 E2
Bidston Gn CH66 . . . . .69 D4
Bidvale Way CW1. . . . . . . .190 D7
Big Field La CW6 . . . . .146 B7
Biggin Ct WA2. . . . . .8 E1
Biggs Way CW12 . . . . .156 E5
BIGNALL END 209 F3
Bignall End Rd
Audley ST7 . . . . .210 A3
Newcastle-u-Lyme ST7 . . . .210 A4
Billington Ave WA12 . . . . . . .2 C5
Billington Cl
Barnton CW8 . . . . .77 F4

Billington Cl continued
Crewe CW2 . . . . .190 A2
Warrington WA5 . . . . .14 E8
Billington Rd WA5 . . . . . . .12 B3
Bilton Cl WA8 . . . . .13 E2
Bilton Way CW7 . . . . .126 F1
Bings Rd SK23 . . . . .65 F8
Bingswood Ave SK23. . . . . .65 E8
Bingswood Ind Est
SK23. . . . . .65 E8
Bingswood Rd SK23 . . . . . .65 E7
Binney Rd CW9 . . . . .104 B8
Binyon Way CW1 . . . . .191 A4
Birchall Ave WA3 . . . . .4 E4
BIRCHALL MOSS 219 E1
Birchall Moss La
CW5 . . . . .219 E1
Birchall St WA3 . . . . .9 A7
Birchall Wlk CW2 . . . . .206 D8
Birch Ave
Alsager ST7 . . . . .193 E2
Crewe CW1 . . . . .190 F5
Irlam M44 . . . . .11 D5
Macclesfield SK10 . . . . .87 B1
Widnes WA8 . . . . .13 E3
Wilmslow SK9 . . . . .59 F6
Winsford CW7 . . . . .127 A1
Birch Brook Rd WA13 . . . . .19 C5
Birch Cl
Crewe CW1 . . . . .190 F5
Holmes Chapel CW4 . . . . . .130 D3
Birch Cres WA12. . . . . .1 F4
Birch Ct CW12 . . . . .155 F3
**Birches Green CW4 . . . . . . .26 C8
Birchdale Ct CW4 . . . . .26 C8
Birchdale Rd
Warrington, Paddington
WA1 . . . . .17 A7
Warrington WA4 . . . . .26 C8
Birkdale Rd
Warrington WA5 . . . . .14 F4
Widnes WA8 . . . . .13 B5
Birkenhead Rd CH64 . . . . . .42 E1
Birkenhead St CW9 . . . . . .104 C8
Birkett Ave CH65 . . . . .70 C2
Birkin Cl WA16 . . . . .57 D4
Birkinheath La WA14 . . . . . .31 B4
Birley St WA12 . . . . .2 D4
Birstall Ct WA7 . . . . .49 D7
Birtles Cl CW11. . . . . .175 C7
Birtles Hall SK10 . . . . .85 D2
Birtles La SK10 . . . . .85 E2
Birtles Rd
Macclesfield SK10 . . . . .86 D1
Warrington WA2 . . . . .8 D1
Birtles Way SK9. . . . . .34 D5
Birtley Ct WA8. . . . . .12 B1
Birtwistle Rd CW9 . . . . . . .104 D6
Bisham Pk WA7 . . . . .24 D2
Bishopdale Cl WA5 . . . . . . .14 F7
Bishopgates Dr CW9 . . . . .103 E4
Bishop Heber High Sch
SY14 . . . . .213 C5
Bishop Rd SK10 . . . . .88 A7
Bishop Reeves Rd WA11 . . .1 E7
Bishops' Blue Coat CE
High Sch The CH3 . . . . .142 A8
Bishop's Cl ST7. . . . . .210 D8
Bishops Ct
Broughton CH4 . . . . .139 C4
Warrington WA2 . . . . .8 A4
Bishopsfield Ct CH2 . . . . .118 F3
Bishops Gate CH2 . . . . . . .119 A3
Bishops Gdns CH65 . . . . . . .70 A5
Bishop St CH2. . . . . .118 F3
Bishops Way WA8 . . . . .13 D3
Bishops Wood CW5 . . . . . .204 F2
Bishopton Dr SK11. . . . . . .111 F8
Bishop Wilson CE Prim
Sch CH64 . . . . .67 D1
Bispham Rd WA5 . . . . .15 B4
Bittern Cl
Poynton SK12 . . . . .36 A4
Runcorn WA7 . . . . .50 D8
Warrington WA2 . . . . .8 D3
Bittern Gr SK10 . . . . .87 A1
Blackacres Cl CW11 . . . . .174 F6
Blackbird Way ST7 . . . . . . .195 F1
Blackboards La CH66 . . . . .69 A8
BLACKBROOK
Haydock 1 A7
Warrington 8 E2
Blackbrook Ave WA2. . . . . . .8 F2
Blackbrook Cl WA8 . . . . . . .12 C3
Blackburn Cl WA3 . . . . .3 E8
Blackburne Ave WA8 . . . . .22 B5
Blackburne Cl WA12 . . . . . . .2 A2
Blackburne Dr WA12. . . . . . .2 A4
Blackcap Rd WA4 . . . . .27 A4
Blackcap Wlk WA3 . . . . .9 E3
Black Cat Ind Est WA8 . . . .23 A6
Blackcroft Ave CW8 . . . . . . .78 A2
Blackden Firs CW4 . . . . . . .108 B2
Blackden La
Goostrey CW4 . . . . .108 A3
Siddington SK11 . . . . .132 F8
Black Denton's Pl WA8 . . . .13 C1
Blackden Wlk SK9 . . . . .34 D1
Black Diamond St
CH1 . . . . .237 B4
Blackdown Cl CH66 . . . . . . .69 A5
Blackeys La CH64 . . . . .66 E8
Black Firs La CW12 . . . . . .155 E4
Black Firs Prim Sch
CW12 . . . . .155 F4
Black Friars CH1 . . . . .237 A2
Blackheath La WA7 . . . . . . .24 F4
Blackhill La WA16 . . . . .81 F8
Blackhurst Brow SK10 . . . .61 B2
Blackhurst Farm Rd
CW5 . . . . .202 E3

Blackhurst St WA1........16 B5
Black La SK10...........87 E1
Blackledge Cl WA2.......9 A3
Blackley Cl
  Macclesfield SK10.......87 B4
  Warrington WA4.........16 D3
Black Lion La CH66.......69 C6
Black Moss Rd WA14......20 F7
BLACK PARK............226 F2
Black Park Rd SY13......226 D2
Black Rd SK11..........112 F7
Blackshaw Cl CW12......157 B1
Blackshaw Dr WA5........7 B1
Blackshaw La SK9........59 F1
Blackshaw St 🔢
  SK11................112 C7
Blackstairs Rd CH66......69 F7
Blackthorn Cl
  Broughton CH4.........139 B3
  Huntington CH3........142 A5
  Wistaston CW2........206 B8
Blackthorne Ave CH66.....95 A8
Blackthorn Pl ST5.......210 E1
Blackthorn Wlk 🔢
  M31................11 E2
Blackwell Cl CW10.......151 D6
BLACON...............117 F3
Blacon Ave CH1.........118 A5
Blacon Hall Rd CH1......117 F5
Blacon High Sch CH1.....117 D4
Blacon Point Rd CH1.....117 E3
Bladon Cres ST7........193 C5
Blagg Ave CW5..........204 C4
Blair Cl SK7............36 C8
Blair Dr WA8...........12 C3
Blairgowrie Dr SK10......87 B4
Blaizefield Cl CW3......232 C2
Blakeacre Rd L26........21 A6
Blake Cl
  Blacon CH1...........117 F6
  Crewe CW2...........189 F1
Blakeden La CW7........148 F8
Blake La CW8...........102 A2
Blakeley Brow CH63......43 A6
Blakeley Ct CH63........43 A7
Blakeley Dell CH63......43 B6
Blakeley Dene CH63......43 B7
Blakeley La WA16........58 F8
Blakeley Rd CH63........43 A6
Blakelow Bank SK11......112 F6
Blakelow Cl CW10.......151 B8
Blakelow Cres CW5......205 F3
Blakelow Dr CW5........205 D4
Blakelow Rd SK11.......112 F6
Blakemere Cl SY13......226 B1
Blakemere Ct CH65.......70 C7
Blakemere Dr CW9.......103 E5
Blakemere La WA6.......100 D4
Blakemere Way CW11.....174 F8
BLAKENHALL...........221 A4
Blake St CW12..........156 C3
Blandford Dr
  🔢 Macclesfield SK11.....111 F8
  Northwich CW9........103 D7
Blandford Rd WA5........15 B5
Blankney The CW5.......204 E4
Blantern Rd CH4........161 A7
Blantyre St WA7.........22 F3
Blaze Hill SK10.........88 E8
Bleadale Cl SK9.........34 D1
Bleasdale Rd
  Crewe CW1...........173 B1
  Newton-le-W WA12......2 C4
Bleeding Wolf La ST7...194 E5
Blenheim Cl
  Macclesfield SK10......87 A1
  Northwich CW9.........103 F4
  Poynton SK12..........36 F4
  Warrington WA2........8 F2
  Wilmslow SK9..........60 D7
  Wistaston CW2........205 E8
Blenheim Ct ST7........193 D5
Blenheim Gdns 🔢
  CW7................149 C7
Blenheim Ho CH1........118 B3
Blenheim Pk CW5........175 A4
Bloomfield Cl SK8.......34 E7
Bloomsbury Way WA8.....12 D3
Blossom Hts CW8........103 D7
Blossom Rd M31.........11 E2
Blossoms La SK7........35 A3
Blossom Way/Ffordd Y
  Blodau CH4...........140 D5
Blount Cl CW1..........190 B4
Blubell La CH64.........42 C1
Bluebell Ave WA11.......1 E7
Bluebell Cl
  Huntington CH3........142 B6
  Macclesfield SK10......87 D3
  Winnington CW8........78 E1
Bluebell Ct WA7.........49 F4
Bluebell La SK10........87 C3
Bluebell Mews 🔢
  SK10................87 D3
Bluebell Way
  Alsager ST7..........193 B3
  Handforth SK9.........34 C1
Blue Bridge La WA6......73 C5
Bluecoat St WA2.........16 B7
Blue Hatch WA6.........74 C8
Blue Planet Aquarium *
  CH65................70 D1
Blue Ridge Cl WA5......14 E7
Blundell Rd WA8........22 D8
Blunstone Cl CW2.......190 A2
Blyth Cl
  Macclesfield SK10.......86 C1
  Runcorn WA7...........50 D5

Blythe Ave
  Bramhall SK7..........35 C6
  Congleton CW12........156 A2
  Widnes WA8...........13 B5
Blythe Pl CW7..........127 B2
Blythings The WA6.......146 C3
Blyth Rd CH63...........43 C7
Boardmans Pl CW9.......104 A5
Boars Leigh Pk SK11....135 D1
Boathorse Rd ST7.......210 F8
Boathouse La CH64.......41 C3
Boat Mus The* CH65......70 C7
Boat Stage WA13........18 B3
Boat Wlk WA4...........16 A1
Bob's La WA4...........11 D4
Boddington Dr WA4.......27 A7
Boden Dr CW5..........205 D4
Boden St SK11..........112 D8
Bodiam Ct CH65.........70 E2
Bodmin Ave SK10........86 E1
Bodmin Cl WA7..........50 B6
Bodmin Dr SK7..........35 E7
Bodnant Cl CW1.........190 A8
BOLD.................6 B6
Bold Bsns Ctr WA9.......6 B7
Bold Cross WA8.........13 E7
BOLD HEATH...........13 C5
Bold Ind Est WA8........13 C5
Bold Ind Park WA9.......6 B6
Bold La WA5, WA9........6 C7
Boldt Pl CH1...........237 B3
Bold Sq CW1...........237 C3
Bold St
  Haslington CW1........191 C4
  Runcorn WA7..........23 B3
  Sandbach CW11........175 B6
  Warrington WA1........16 A5
  Widnes WA8...........23 A7
Bolesworth Hill Rd
  CH3................183 C4
Bolesworth Rd
  Chester CH2..........118 F6
  Tattenhall CH3........183 C7
Boleyn Cl CH1..........117 E6
Boleyn Dr WA7..........24 C3
Bolland's Cl CH4........5 D8
Bollands Row 🔢 CW5....204 E5
Bollin Wood Ct SK9......34 B1
Bollin Ave
  Altrincham WA14.......31 B8
  Winsford CW7.........127 B2
Bollinbarn SK10.........87 B2
Bollinbarn Dr SK10.......87 A2
Bollinbrook CE Prim Sch
  SK10................87 B2
Bollinbrook Rd SK10......87 B2
Bollin Cl
  Alsager ST7..........192 F3
  Culcheth WA3..........5 A2
  Lymm WA13...........19 A4
  Sandbach CW11........174 E7
  Winsford CW7.........127 B2
Bollin Ct SK9...........60 C6
Bollin Dr
  Congleton CW12.......156 F1
  Lymm WA13...........19 A4
Bollin Gr
  Biddulph ST8..........179 E1
  Prestbury SK10.........87 A7
BOLLINGTON..........88 B7
Bollington Ave CW4......104 A5
BOLLINGTON CROSS.....87 F7
Bollington Cross CE Prim
  Sch SK10.............87 F7
Bollington Ho CW12.....156 F1
Bollington La SK10.......84 E2
Bollington Old Rd
  SK10................87 D6
Bollington Rd SK10......87 E6
Bollinhead La SK11......113 D2
Bollin Hill
  Prestbury SK10........87 A5
  Wilmslow SK9..........60 B8
Bollin Mews SK10.......86 F7
Bollinway WA15.........32 A8
Bollin Way SK10.........87 A6
Bollin Wlk SK9..........60 C7
Bollinwood Chase SK9....60 D7
Bolshaw Cl WA3.........5 D8
Bolshaw Farm La SK8.....34 C6
Bolshaw Prim Sch SK8....34 B7
Bolshaw Rd SK8.........34 C6
Bolton Ave
  Cheadle SK8..........35 B6
  Warrington WA4........16 F4
Bolton Cl
  Golborne WA3..........4 B8
  Poynton SK12..........36 D4
Bomish La CW4, SK11....108 C3
Bond Cl WA5...........15 D4
Bond St
  Macclesfield SK11......112 C7
  Warrington WA8........78 D1
Bonis Hall La SK10.......61 F4
BOON HILL............210 A2
Boon Hill Rd ST7.......209 F1
Booth Ave
  Ashton Hayes CH3.....121 E7
  Little Budworth CW6...147 F7
  Sandbach CW11........175 C6
BOOTH BANK...........30 B7
Boothbank La WA14......30 A6
Booth Bed La WA16,
  CW4................107 B4
Boothby St 🔢 SK10.....112 C8
Boothfields WA16........57 C2
DOOTH GREEN..........62 F7

Booth La
  Middlewich CW10......151 E6
  Middlewich, Stud Green CW10,
  CW11................152 B3
Booth Rd
  Handforth SK9.........34 A1
  Hartford CW8..........103 A4
Boothsdale CW6........122 D3
Boothsdale CW6........122 D3
BOOTH'S HILL..........18 C2
Booths Hill Cl WA13......18 C2
Booths Hill Ho 🔢
  WA13................18 D3
Booth's Hill Rd WA13....18 C3
Booths La WA4.........18 D3
Booth's La WA13........18 B3
Boothsmere Cl CW11....174 F8
Booth St
  Audley ST7...........209 D1
  Congleton CW12.......156 C2
  Warrington WA5........15 E4
BOOTS GREEN.........107 B5
Borderbrook Sch
  Higher Wych SY14.....224 D3
  Tallarn Green/Tallwrn Green
  SY14................222 F5
Border Rd CH60.........52 E6
Borders 2nd Pk CH4.....140 C7
Borders Ind Pk The/Parc
  Didwydiannol Y Ffin
  CH4................140 C7
Border Way CH3........119 C1
Borough Rd CW12......156 F3
Borras Rd LL13........196 A8
Borron Cl WA12.........2 B4
Borron Rd WA12.........2 B5
Borron Road Ind Est
  WA12................2 C4
Borrowdale Ave WA2......8 C3
Borrowdale Cl
  Crewe CW2...........189 E3
  Frodsham WA6.........74 D8
Borrowdale Rd WA8......22 C8
Bosden Cl SK9...........34 D5
BOSLEY..............158 D8
Bosley Brook CW12.....179 D5
Bosley Cl
  Handforth SK9.........34 D2
  Middlewich CW10......151 C6
Bosley Dr SK12..........37 A3
Bosley View CW12.......157 B1
Bostock Gn
  Bostock Green CW9....127 C2
  Ellesmere Port CH65....69 F6
BOSTOCK GREEN.......127 C2
BOSTOCK HALL.........127 D5
Bostock Rd
  Macclesfield SK11......111 E7
  Winsford CW7.........127 A4
Bostock St WA5.........15 E6
Boston Ave WA7........23 D1
Boston Cl
  Bramhall SK7.........35 D7
  Culcheth WA3..........4 F4
Boswell Ave WA4........16 B2
Botany Bsns Pk SK23....65 D6
Botany Mews SK23......65 E6
Boteler Ave WA5.........15 F7
Bottoms La CH4.........141 F8
Boughey Rd ST7.......209 F2
Boughton CW1..........119 A2
Boughton Cl CH3.......118 F2
BOUGHTON............119 A1
Boughton Hall Ave
  CH3................119 A1
Boughton Hall Dr
  CH3................119 B1
BOUGHTON HEATH.....142 A8
Boughton Heath Prim Sch
  CH3................142 B8
Boughton Lo 🔢 CH3....119 A1
Boughton St Paul's Inf Sch
  CH3................237 C3
Boulevard The
  Broughton CH4........139 C3
  Ellesmere Port CH65....69 F4
Boulting Ave WA5.........7 F1
Boulton Cl CW11.......175 C3
Boundary Ct CH3.......119 B1
Boundary La
  Chester CH4..........140 E5
  Congleton CW12.......179 B8
  Heswall CH60..........41 A8
  Over Peover WA16,
  SK11................108 D7
  Siddington SK11......132 E8
  Threapwood SY14.....222 E8
Boundary Lane N
  CW8................101 F2
Boundary Lane S
  CW8................101 F2
Boundary Pk CH64.......66 D7
Boundary St
  Northwich CW9........79 E2
  Warrington WA1........16 E7
Bourchier Way WA4.....27 A8
Bourne Ave WA3.........3 D8
Bourne Cl CW6.........102 E7
Bournemouth Cl WA7....50 D6
Bourne Rd ST7.........194 F2
Bourne St
  Mow Cop ST7.........195 C7
  Wilmslow SK9..........59 F0
Bouverie St CH1.......237 A4

Boverton Cl WA5........7 E1
Bowden Cl
  Congleton CW12.......156 A3
  Culcheth WA3..........4 F4
Bowden Cres SK22......39 D8
Bowden Dr CW9.......104 C8
Bowden House La SK9....61 A8
Bowden View La WA16....29 F2
Bowdon Cl WA1.........16 F8
Bowen Cl
  Bramhall SK7.........35 F5
  Widnes WA8...........12 D4
Bowen Cooke Ave
  CW1................190 A5
Bowen St CW2.........190 A3
Bower Cres WA4........26 D2
Bowerfield Ave SK7......36 D8
Bowerfield Cres SK7.....36 E8
Bower Rd CH60.........41 C8
Bowers Bsns Pk WA8....23 B7
Bowers Row 🔢 CW5....204 E5
Bower St WA8...........34 F6
Bowery Cl CW3........116 D4
Bowe's Gate Rd CW6....169 A1
Bowfell Cl CH62.........43 D3
Bowfell Dr SK6..........37 E8
Bow Green Rd WA14.....20 F1
Bowkers Croft CW11....191 F8
Bow La WA14...........31 B8
Bowland Cl
  Runcorn WA7..........49 E5
  Warrington WA3........10 B5
Bowland Croft CW1.....173 B1
Bowland Rise CW7......149 B7
Bowles Cl CW11.......175 A6
Bowline Cl CW11.......175 D3
Bowling Green Ct
  Chester CH1..........237 B3
  🔢 Nantwich CW5.....204 E5
  Winnington CW8........78 E1
Bowman Ave WA4.......17 A5
Bowmans The SK10......87 B1
Bowmere Cl
  Biddulph ST8.........179 C1
  Tarporley CW6........146 D1
Bowmere Dr CW7.......149 C8
Bowmere Rd CW6.......146 D1
Bowness Ave
  Bebington CH63........43 C5
  Irlam M44...........11 D4
  Warrington WA2........8 C2
  Winsford CW7.........126 D2
Bowness Cl CW4.......130 A3
Bowness Ct CW12.....156 A1
Bowness Rd CW2......189 E3
Bowood Ct WA2.........8 A4
Bowring Dr CH64........41 B1
Bowyer Ave 🔢 CW6....204 E6
Boxgrove Cl WA8........13 B3
Box La CW12..........155 F3
Boxmoor Cl CH4.......141 A5
Box Tree Mews SK11....112 A7
Box Wlk M31...........11 E3
Boydell Ave
  Warrington WA4........16 F4
  Warrington, Westy WA4...16 F4
Boydell Way CH4.......162 A6
Boyle Ave WA2...........8 E1
Boyles Hall Rd ST7.....209 E2
Bracken Cl
  Broughton CH4........139 C3
  Macclesfield SK10......86 F1
  Rode Heath ST7......193 E8
  Warrington WA3........9 A3
Brackendale
  Elton LW/............72 B3
  Runcorn WA7..........49 D8
Brackenfield Way 🔢
  CW7................127 A4
Bracken Rd CH66........69 E4
Brackens The
  Daresbury WA4........25 A1
  Higher Kinnerton CH4...161 A8
Bracken Way
  Barnton CW8..........78 B3
  Comberbach CW9......78 C7
  Frodsham WA6.........74 C6
  Knutsford WA16........82 A8
  Wincham CW9..........79 C3
Brackenwood Cl CW2...206 B8
Brackenwood Dr WA8....22 A8
Brackenwood Mews
  Chorlton CW2.........207 D2
  Wilmslow SK9..........60 E8
Brackley Ave M44.......11 D6
Brackley St
  Runcorn WA7..........22 F3
  Warrington WA4........16 C3
Bradburn Rd M44........11 E7
Bradburns La CW8......103 B6
Bradbury Gdns CW12...156 F1
Bradbury Rd CW7......127 B2
Braddon Cl CW9.......103 F4
BRADELEY GREEN......225 C6
Bradeley Green La
  SY13................225 B6
Bradeley Hall Rd
  CW1................191 B5
Bradeley Terr SK11.....191 C4
BRADFIELD GREEN.....172 E3
Bradfield Rd CW1......190 B7
Bradford La SK10.......85 C6
Bradford Pl CH4........141 D7
Bradford Rd LW/.......126 E4
Bradgate Cl CW9........34 D8
Bradgate Cl WA5........15 F6

Brading Wlk M22........33 E8
Bradlegh Rd WA12........2 B1
Bradley Cl CW10.......151 B7
Bradley Farm La
  SY13................225 C7
BRADLEY GREEN.......225 A8
Bradley Hall Cotts
  WA4................27 F6
Bradley La
  Frodsham WA6.........74 D7
  Newton-le-W WA5, WA12...2 A1
BRADLEY MOUNT.......87 B7
Bradley St SK11........112 E6
Bradley Way WA8........13 B1
Bradmoor Rd CH62......43 D8
Bradshaw Ave CH4......140 B7
Bradshaw Com Prim Sch
  WA4................17 B2
Bradshaw La
  Cheadle SK8..........34 E8
  Gatley SK8...........34 D8
Bradshaw La
  Lymm WA13...........19 D3
  Warrington WA4........17 B3
Bradshaw Pl CW12......156 E2
Bradshaw St WA8........13 A2
BRADWALL GREEN.....153 B3
Bradwall Rd CW11......175 B7
Bradwall St CW11......175 B7
Bradwell Cl CH65........70 A4
Bradwell Ct CW12......156 F2
Bradwell Dr SK8........34 C7
Bradwell Gr CW12......156 F2
Bradwell Rd
  Golborne WA3..........3 E7
  Hazel Grove SK7.......36 E8
Braemar Ave CW9......104 C7
Braemar Cl
  Chester CH3..........119 C3
  Holmes Chapel CW4....130 C2
  Warrington WA3........9 A3
  Wistaston CW2.........205 E8
Braemar Ct CH65........70 E3
Braeside Cl
  🔢 Ellesmere Port
  CH66................69 C5
  Macclesfield SK11......112 F6
Braidwood Ave WA16....57 C3
Brains La CW6..........169 B6
Braintree Rd M22.......33 E8
Braithwaite Cl WA7.....49 D5
Braithwaite Rd WA3......3 A8
Brakeley La CW8.........77 D4
Brakenwood Mews
  WA4................17 C1
Brake The ST7..........195 B7
Brake Village CW7......195 B7
Bramall Cl CW11.......175 C7
Bramble Cl
  Chester CH3..........142 A7
  Macclesfield SK10......87 B2
  Middlewich CW10......128 E2
  Warrington WA3........14 E3
  Winsford CW7.........126 C3
Brambles Chase CW8....101 F2
Brambles The
  Burtonwood WA5........7 A7
  Congleton CW12.......178 F8
  Haslington CW1........191 B4
  Wincham CW9..........79 C3
Bramble Way WA7.......49 E4
Brambling Cl WA7.......49 F5
Brambling Way WA3......9 A4
BRAMHALL............35 E6
Bramhall Cl CW2.......126 B1
Bramhall Ct CW2.......189 F2
Bramhall Ct The SK7.....35 E6
Bramhall Dr
  Bebington CH62........43 F4
  Holmes Chapel CW4....130 A3
Bramhall High Sch
  SK7................35 F8
Bramhall La S SK7......35 E7
Bramhall Rd CW2......189 F2
Bramhalls Pk CW9.......78 C3
Bramhall St WA5.........15 F6
Bramhall Sta SK7.......35 E6
Bramhall Way SK10.....112 A8
Bramley Cl
  🔢 Ellesmere Port CH66...94 F8
  Wilmslow SK9..........59 D4
Bramley Ct CW6.......122 D5
Bramley Dr SK7.........35 E6
Bramley Mews WA4.....26 C8
Bramley Rd SK7.........35 E6
Bramley Wlk WA6.......73 A1
Brampton Ave SK10......87 A2
Brampton Ct CW2.......207 E3
Brampton Ct WA9.........1 B3
Bramshill Cl WA3........10 A6
Bramway
  Bramhall SK7.........35 C7
  High Lane SK6........37 F7
Bramwood Ct SK7.......35 E6
Brancaster Dr WA3.......4 A7
Branceph Ct CH65.......70 E3
Branch Way WA11........1 E6
Brancote Gdns CH62.....43 C7
Branden Dr WA16........57 B1
Brandon WA8...........12 F3
Brandon Cl SK9.........34 D2
Brandon Gr WA2.........8 B2
Brandwood Ho 🔢
  WA1................16 C5

Bramhall La WA7 . . . . 14 F1
Bransdale Way SK11 . . . . . 111 F7
Brontfield Ct WA2 . . . . 8 E2
Brassey Ct CW5 . . . . 205 C6
BRASSEY GREEN 167 D6
Brassey's Contract Rd
SY14 . . . . 199 A1
Brassey St CH3 . . . . 118 F1
Brassey Way CW5 . . . . . . 205 D5
Brassington Terr
CW3 . . . . 221 F3
Brathay Cl WA2 . . . . 8 C3
BRATT'S BANK 101 B5
Brattswood Dr ST7 . . . 194 A5
Bray Cl
Crewe CW1 . . . . 190 E5
Runcorn WA7 . . . . 49 D6
Bray Rd CH4 . . . . 140 F6
Breach House La
WA16 . . . . 32 A1
Bread St SK11 . . . . 112 C2
Breck Rd WA8 . . . . 13 B1
Breck The CH66 . . . . 69 E7
Brecon Cl SK12 . . . . 36 F4
Brecon Ct WA5 . . . . 7 E2
Brecon Dr [1] CH66 . . . . . . 69 E1
Breconway CW7 . . . . 149 B8
Brecon Way CW2 . . . . . . 206 A4
Bredon Cl CH66 . . . . 69 A6
Breen Cl CH3 . . . . 166 B3
Breezehill Cl CH64 . . . . . . 66 F8
Breezehill Pk CH64 . . . . . . 66 F8
Breezehill Rd CH64 . . . . . . 66 F8
Brendon Ave WA2 . . . . . . 8 A3
Brendon Gr WA9 . . . . 1 A4
Brennus Pl CH1 . . . . 237 A3
Brent Cl SK12 . . . . 36 B4
Brentfield WA8 . . . . 12 D2
Brentnall Cl WA5 . . . . 15 C5
Brentwood Ave M44 . . . . . 11 D6
Brentwood Rd CH1 . . . . . 117 E5
Brereton CE Prim Sch
CW11 . . . . 153 F5
Brereton Cl
Crewe CW2 . . . . 189 E2
Malpas SY14 . . . . 213 B3
Runcorn WA7 . . . . 50 A8
Sandbach CW11 . . . . . . 175 C7
Brereton Green
Brereton Green
[1] Cheadle SK8 . . . . . . 34 E8
Brereton Dr CW5 . . . . . . 204 F7
Brereton Gr M44 . . . . 11 E6
BRERETON GREEN 153 E5
BRERETON HEATH 154 F6
Brereton Heath Ctry Pk*
CW12 . . . . 154 D7
Brereton Heath La CW11.
CW12 . . . . 154 E6
Brereton Heath Local
Nature Reserve*
CW12 . . . . 154 D6
Brereton La CW4 . . . . . . 152 E8
Brereton Rd
Handforth SK9 . . . . 34 E3
Hartford CW8 . . . . 103 A4
Bretland Dr WA4 . . . . 27 A7
Breton Cl CH2 . . . . 118 E5
BRETTON 139 E4
Bretton Court Mews
CH4 . . . . 139 E4
Bretton Dr CH4 . . . . 139 B3
Bretton La CH4 . . . . 139 E5
Bretton Rd CH4 . . . . 139 E4
Bretton Wlk M22 . . . . 33 D8
Brewery La CH3 . . . . 180 E3
Brian Ave
Warrington, Stockton Heath
WA4 . . . . 16 E1
Warrington WA2 . . . . . . 16 D8
Brian Bevan Island
WA1 . . . . 16 B4
Briar Ave WA3 . . . . 11 B2
Briar Cl WA16 . . . . 57 A3
Briardale Cl CW2 . . . . . . 205 F8
Briardale Gdns [4]
CH66 . . . . 69 C6
Briardale Rd
Ellesmere Port CH66 . . . 69 C6
Willaston CH64 . . . . 43 A1
Briar Dr CH60 . . . . 41 A8
Briarfield Ave WA8 . . . . . 12 A1
Briarfield Rd
Ellesmere Port CH65 . . . 70 B5
Heswall CH60 . . . . 41 B8
Briar La CW8 . . . . 102 E7
Briarlands Cl SK7 . . . . . . 35 D6
Briar Rd WA3 . . . . 3 B8
Briarstead Cl SK7 . . . . . . 35 D7
Briarswood
Biddulph ST8 . . . . 179 D1
Kidsgrove ST7 . . . . 195 B1
Briarswood Ct CH1 . . . . 237 B3
Briar Wlk WA3 . . . . 3 B8
Briarwood
Runcorn WA7 . . . . 50 B8
Wilmslow SK9 . . . . 60 C7
Briarwood Ave
Macclesfield SK11 . . . . 112 D5
Warrington WA1 . . . . . . 16 E7
Briarwood Ct CW7 . . . . . 149 C8
Brick Bank CW5 . . . . . . 204 F5
Brick Bank La WA16,
CW4 . . . . 107 B2

Brickfield Bsns Ctr
CW9 . . . . 79 D1
Brickfield La CH3 . . . . . . 119 F2
Brickhill Ct WA1 . . . . 31 B4
Brickhurst Way WA1 . . . . 17 B8
Brickkiln La
Little Bollington WA14 . . 20 C3
Whitchurch SY13 . . . . . 226 D2
Brick Kiln La CW10 . . . . 127 B7
Brickley Ct CW8 . . . . 77 C1
Brick Rd CH4 . . . . 139 D2
Brick St
Newton-le-W WA12 . . . . . 1 F3
Warrington WA1 . . . . . . 16 C5
Bridestone Sh Ctr
CW12 . . . . 156 D2
Bridewell Ct WA8 . . . . . . 13 B3
Bridge Ave WA4 . . . . 16 F4
Bridge Ave E WA4 . . . . . . 16 F5
Bridge Bank Cl WA3 . . . . 3 B7
Bridge Cl
Audley ST7 . . . . 209 F2
Cuddington CW8 . . . . . 102 A3
Lymm WA13 . . . . 19 B4
Wistaston CW2 . . . . . . 206 A7
Bridge Cotts CH4 . . . . . 237 B1
Bridge Ct
Chester CH2 . . . . 119 A2
Holt LL13 . . . . 196 E8
Neston CH64 . . . . 66 E1
Bridgedown CW6 . . . . . 146 C1
Bridge Dr
Christleton CH3 . . . . . . 142 D7
Handforth SK9 . . . . 34 D3
Bridge End Dr SK10 . . . . 87 A7
Bridge End La SK10 . . . . 87 A7
Bridge Farm Ct CW10 . . 152 A4
Bridgefield Ave SK9 . . . . 34 C1
Bridgefoot Ind Est
WA4 . . . . 16 B4
Bridge Foyer The
CH1 . . . . 118 B2
Bridge Gn SK10 . . . . 87 A7
Bridge La
Cuddington CW8 . . . . . 101 F3
Frodsham WA6 . . . . 49 D1
Goostrey CW4 . . . . 108 C2
Warrington WA4 . . . . . . 26 E7
Warrington WA4 . . . . . . 26 E8
Warrington, Woolston
WA1 . . . . 17 C7
Bridge Lane Mews
WA6 . . . . 49 D1
Bridgeman Rd CH1 . . . . 117 E3
Bridgeman St WA5 . . . . . 15 D4
Bridge Mdw CH66 . . . . . . 69 F2
BRIDGEMERE 231 F8
Bridgemere CE Prim Sch
CW5 . . . . 231 E8
Bridgemere Cl CH11 . . . 174 F8
Bridgemere Garden
World* CW5 . . . . 232 B4
Bridgemere La CW5 . . . 219 E1
Bridgemere Mews
CW5 . . . . 231 F8
Bridgemere Way [4]
CW9 . . . . 103 E4
BRIDGEMONT 39 E2
Bridgend CH2 . . . . 97 A1
Bridgend Cl WA8 . . . . . . 12 D3
Bridge Pl CH1 . . . . 237 B1
Bridge Rd WA1 . . . . 17 C7
Bridge Row CW12 . . . . . 156 F4
Bridge St Row E CH1 . . . 237 B2
Bridge St Row W CH1 . . 237 B2
Bridge Sh Ctr The
WA4 . . . . 16 F3
Bridge Side Dr WA6 . . . . 73 B4
Bridges Rd CH65 . . . . . . 70 F5
Bridge St
Chester CH1 . . . . 237 B2
Congleton CW12 . . . . . 156 D2
Golborne WA3 . . . . 3 A7
Holt LL13 . . . . 196 D8
Macclesfield SK11 . . . . 112 C7
Neston CH64 . . . . 66 E7
Newton-le-W WA12 . . . . . 2 B3
Northwich CW9 . . . . 79 E2
Runcorn WA7 . . . . 23 B2
Saltney CH4 . . . . 140 D7
Warrington WA1 . . . . . . 16 B4
Warrington WA1 . . . . . . 16 B4
Whaley Bridge SK23 . . . 65 E7
Wybunbury CW5 . . . . . 220 B8
Bridge Terr CH3 . . . . . . 119 B2
BRIDGE TRAFFORD 97 A3
Bridge View Cl WA8 . . . . 23 A4
Bridgewater Ave WA4 . . . 16 F4
Bridgewater Cl
Congleton CW12 . . . . . 157 B1
[6] Frodsham WA6 . . . . 49 C1
Gatley SK8 . . . . 34 D7
Bridgewater Ct
[3] Lymm WA13 . . . . . . 18 C3
[6] Runcorn WA7 . . . . . 23 B2
Bridgewater Dr CH3 . . . 119 C2
Bridgewater Grange
WA7 . . . . 50 F5
Bridgewater High Sch
(Lower Sch) WA4 . . . . 26 D6
Bridgewater High Sch
(Upper Sch) WA4 . . . . 26 D7
Bridgewater Mews
WA4 . . . . 26 C8
Bridgewater Pl WA3 . . . . 9 E4
Bridgewater St
[4] Lymm WA13 . . . . . . 18 E3
[6] Runcorn WA7 . . . . . 23 A3

Bridgeway E WA7 . . . . . . 24 C2
Bridgeway W WA7 . . . . . 24 C2
Bridge Wlk [7] WA7 . . . . 49 F7
Bridgewood CH1 . . . . 117 E3
Bridgfield Cl SK6 . . . . . . 37 E7
Bridgnorth Gr ST5 . . . . . 210 E2
Bridle Cl CH62 . . . . 43 E7
Bridle Ct
Bramhall SK7 . . . . 35 F2
Crewe CW2 . . . . 190 B4
Bridle Hey CW5 . . . . 204 F2
Bridle La CH1 . . . . 94 E6
Bridlemere Ct WA1 . . . . . 16 E8
Bridle Pk CH62 . . . . 43 E7
Bridle Rd
Bebington CH62 . . . . . . 43 E6
Crewe CW2 . . . . 190 B4
Woodford SK7 . . . . 35 F2
Bridle Way
Ellesmere Port CH66 . . . 69 D3
Woodford SK7 . . . . 36 A2
Briedden Way CH66 . . . . 69 A6
Brierley Bsns Ctr
CW1 . . . . 190 D4
Brierley Ct CW7 . . . . 149 F8
Brierley Prim Sch
CW1 . . . . 190 D4
Brierley Rd CW12 . . . . . 157 B1
Brierley St CW1 . . . . 190 D4
Briers Cl WA2 . . . . 8 F3
Brieryhurst Rd ST7 . . . . 195 B3
Briggs Ave CW2 . . . . . . 190 D1
Brighton Cres SK11 . . . . 113 B3
Brighton St WA8 . . . . 15 E6
Brights Ave [6] ST7 . . . 195 B2
Bright St CW1 . . . . 190 B5
Brightwell Cl WA5 . . . . . 14 E5
Brimelow Cres WA5 . . . . 14 E3
Brimstage Cl CH60 . . . . . 41 C8
Brimstage Gn CH60 . . . . 41 D8
Brimstage Rd CH60 . . . . 41 C7
BRINDLEY 186 E8
Brindley Ave
Warrington WA4 . . . . . . 16 F4
Winsford CW7 . . . . 126 C1
Brindley Cl
Kidsgrove ST7 . . . . 194 E1
Talke ST7 . . . . 210 E8
Brindley Ct WA4 . . . . 26 D8
Brindley Gr SK9 . . . . 34 E2
BRINDLEY GREEN 153 E2
Brindley Hall Rd CW5 . . 186 E2
Brindley La CW11 . . . . . 153 C4
Brindley Lea La CW5 . . . 186 D1
Brindley Pk CW11 . . . . . 174 F3
Brindley Rd WA7 . . . . . . 23 F3
Brindley St WA7 . . . . 22 F3
Brindleys Way ST7 . . . . 209 F2
Brindley Way
Congleton CW12 . . . . . 157 B1
Macclesfield SK11 . . . . 112 C3
Brindley Wharf WA4 . . . . 50 F6
Brine Leas High Sch
CW5 . . . . 204 F3
Brinell Dr M44 . . . . 11 F6
Brine Pits La CW5 . . . . . 218 F2
Brine Pump Cotts CW9 . . 78 F4
Brine Rd CW5 . . . . 204 E3
Brines Brow La CH3 . . . . 99 C2
Brinley Cl CH62 . . . . 43 D5
Brinton Cl WA8 . . . . 22 E8
Brisbane Cl SK7 . . . . 35 F5
Brisbane Rd CH1 . . . . . . 117 C4
Bristol Ave WA7 . . . . 50 E6
Bristol Cl
Blacon CH1 . . . . 117 C4
Gatley SK8 . . . . 34 C7
Bristol Dr [3] CH66 . . . . 69 E1
Bristow Cl WA5 . . . . 15 B8
Britannia Dr CW9 . . . . . 104 E7
Britannia Rd WA6 . . . . . . 73 B2
Brittania Gdns WA6 . . . . 73 B1
Brixham Ave SK8 . . . . . . 34 F7
Brixham Wlk SK7 . . . . . . 35 E7
Broadacre CW5 . . . . 78 D6
Broadacre Pl SK9 . . . . . . 59 D3
Broadacres CW5 . . . . . . 217 F4
Broadbent Ave WA4 . . . . 16 F4
Broadcar Rd SK11 . . . . . 113 C6
Broad Cl SK9 . . . . 85 B8
Broadfields WA7 . . . . 50 C8
Broadheath Terr WA8 . . . 12 D1
Broadheys La WA16 . . . . 28 D6
Broadhurst Ave
Culcheth WA3 . . . . 4 F2
[3] Warrington WA5 . . . 15 D4
Broadhurst La CW12 . . . 156 C3
Broad La
Altrincham WA15 . . . . . 32 B8
Appleton Thorn WA4 . . . 27 C8
Burtonwood WA5 . . . . . . 6 E8
Haydock WA5, WA9 . . . . 1 C1
Heswall CH60 . . . . 40 C8
Holmes Chapel CW4 . . 129 F1
Stapeley CW5 . . . . 205 A1
Broadlake CH64 . . . . 67 F8
Broadland Gdns CH66 . . 69 F2
Broadland Rd CH66 . . . . 69 F2
Broadleigh Way CW2 . . 206 C8
Broadley Ave WA3 . . . . . 3 C7
Broadmead
Chester CH3 . . . . 142 B8
Heswall CH60 . . . . 41 C7
BROADOAK 162 B1
Broad Oak Ave
Broughton CH4 . . . . . . 139 A3
Haydock WA11 . . . . 1 A6
Warrington WA5 . . . . . . 14 E4

Broad Oak Com Prim Sch
WA9 . . . . 1 A3
Broadoak La
High Legh WA16 . . . . . . 29 D3
Mobberley WA16 . . . . . . 57 E6
Broadoak Sch M31 . . . . . 11 F2
Broad St CW1 . . . . 190 C6
Broadwalk SK10 . . . . 87 A5
Broadway
Altrincham WA15 . . . . . 32 A8
Barnton CW8 . . . . 78 B3
Widnes WA8 . . . . 12 A1
Wilmslow SK9 . . . . 60 B6
Broadway E CH2 . . . . . . 118 E5
Broadways CW3 . . . . . . 230 A4
Broadway The CW5 . . . . 204 F5
Broadway W CH2 . . . . . 118 D5
Broad Wlk SK9 . . . . 59 F8
Broadwood Cl SK6 . . . . . 37 F7
Broady Ct [5] CW2 . . . . 190 D2
Brock Dr SK8 . . . . 35 B8
Brock Gdns L24 . . . . 21 E2
Brock Hollow CW11 . . . . 174 F4
Brockhurst Mews
WA9 . . . . 104 A6
Brockhurst St CW9 . . . . 104 A8
Brockhurst Way CW9 . . 104 A6
Brocklebank Dr CW8 . . . 103 E7
Brocklehurst Ave SK10 . . 87 F2
Brocklehurst Ct [2]
SK10 . . . . 87 D3
Brocklehurst Dr SK10 . . 87 A7
Brocklehurst Manor
SK10 . . . . 87 E1
Brocklehurst Mews [3]
SK10 . . . . 87 D3
Brocklehurst Way
SK10 . . . . 87 D3
Brock Rd WA3 . . . . 9 D3
Brocks Croft Gdns
ST8 . . . . 179 C1
Brock St
Macclesfield SK10 . . . . 87 D1
Macclesfield SK10 . . . . 112 D8
Brockton Ct WA4 . . . . . . 26 C6
Brockway E CH3 . . . . . . 166 A1
Brockway W CH3 . . . . . 166 A1
Brockwell Cl [2] CW7 . . 149 A8
Brodie Cl CH2 . . . . 95 C1
Brogden Ave WA3 . . . . . . 4 E4
Broken Banks [10]
SK11 . . . . 112 D7
BROKEN CROSS 111 E8
BROKEN CROSS 111 F8
BROKEN CROSS 104 E7
Broken Cross Com Sch
SK11 . . . . 111 E7
Brompton Gdns WA5 . . . 15 E7
Brompton Way
Ellesmere Port CH66 . . . 69 E1
Handforth SK9 . . . . 34 C5
Bronington Ave CH62 . . . 43 D6
Bronte Cl WA2 . . . . 8 A6
Brook Acre Com Prim Sch
WA2 . . . . 8 E1
Brookash Rd M22 . . . . . . 34 A8
Brook Ave
Handforth SK9 . . . . 34 D4
Shavington CW2 . . . . . 206 C5
Warrington, Stockton Heath
WA4 . . . . 16 E1
Warrington, Westy WA4 . . 16 F5
Brook Bank SK12 . . . . . . 37 C2
Brook Bottom Rd SK22 . . 39 A8
Brook Cl
Crewe CW1 . . . . 190 F4
Cronton WA8 . . . . 12 C6
Brook Ct
Chester CH1 . . . . 118 B3
Sandbach CW11 . . . . . 175 B6
Brookdale WA8 . . . . 12 A3
Brookdale Ave CH66 . . . . 57 C2
Brookdale Ct CH3 . . . . . 143 D5
Brookdale Pk CW2 . . . . . 190 A3
Brookdale Pl CH1 . . . . . 237 B3
Brookdale Way CH3 . . . . 143 B5
Brook Dr
Kelsall CW6 . . . . 122 D4
Warrington WA5 . . . . . . 15 A5
Brook End CW5 . . . . 204 E5
Brooke Ave CH2 . . . . 118 F4
Brooke Ct SK9 . . . . 34 E4
Brooke Dr SK9 . . . . 34 D4
Brook End WA8 . . . . 13 C6
Brook Ho WA3 . . . . 4 E1
Brookes Ave CH4 . . . . . 139 B3
Brooke Way SK9 . . . . 34 E4
Brook Farm Cl M31 . . . . 11 E2
Brookfield CW7 . . . . 191 D1
Brookfield Ave
Poynton SK12 . . . . 36 F3
Runcorn WA7 . . . . 23 E2

Brookfield Cl
Lymm WA13 . . . . 18 D3
Tarporley CW6 . . . . . . 168 D8
Brookfield Cotts [8]
WA13 . . . . 18 D3
Brookfield Cres CW4 . . . 107 F1
Brookfield Ct CW11 . . . . 190 B5
Brookfield Dr
Alsager ST7 . . . . 193 C5
Chester CH2 . . . . 118 E4
Holmes Chapel CW4 . . 130 B3
Brookfield La SK11 . . . . 112 F7
Brookfield Pk WA4 . . . . . 17 A2
Brookfield Rd
Comberbach CW9 . . . . . 78 D8
Culcheth WA3 . . . . 4 D3
Lymm WA13 . . . . 18 D3
Brookfields Sch WA8 . . . 13 D2
Brookfield St WA12 . . . . . 2 B3
Brook Furlong WA6 . . . . . 48 F2
Brook Gdns ST8 . . . . . . 179 D1
Brook Hey CH64 . . . . 41 B2
Brook Ho WA4 . . . . 16 F3
BROOKHOUSE 88 D3
Brookhouse Cl SK10 . . . 86 F1
Brook House Ct WA13 . . 18 D3
Brookhouse Dr CW2 . . . 206 C8
BROOKHOUSE GREEN
. . . . 177 A7
Brookhouse La
Church Minshull CW1,
CW10 . . . . 172 D7
Congleton CW12 . . . . . 157 C2
Duddon CH3 . . . . 144 D6
Lower Whitley WA4 . . . . 52 B2
Brookhouse Rd
Alsager ST7 . . . . 193 D3
[5] Sandbach CW11 . . 175 B6
BROOKHURST 43 C5
Brookhurst Ave CH63 . . . 43 C5
Brookhurst Cl CH63 . . . . 43 C5
Brookhurst Prim Sch
CH63 . . . . 43 C6
Brookhurst Rd CH63 . . . 43 C5
Brook La
Alderley Edge SK9 . . . . 59 F3
Astbury CW12 . . . . 177 E5
Broughton CH5 . . . . . . 139 C7
Burland CW5 . . . . 203 D8
Chester CH2 . . . . 118 E4
Faddiley CW5. . . . . 202 F8
Knutsford WA16 . . . . . . 57 B1
Neston CH64 . . . . 41 C2
Northwich CW9 . . . . . . 104 D7
Warrington WA3 . . . . . . 18 A8
Brookland Ave CW2 . . . 205 F8
Brookland Dr CW11 . . . . 175 E6
Brookland La WA9 . . . . . . 1 A1
BROOKLANDS 225 E1
Brooklands Ave SK11 . . 112 B7
Brooklands Dr
Goostrey CW4 . . . . 107 F1
Northwich CW9 . . . . . . 104 A4
Brooklands Gdns CH64 . . 41 C1
Brooklands Gr CW1 . . . 190 A6
Brooklands Pk [1] WA8 . . 13 C2
Brooklands Rd
Congleton CW12 . . . . . 155 F2
Neston CH64 . . . . 41 C1
Brookland St WA1 . . . . . 16 E7
Brooklands The CW2 . . 206 E3
Brookledge La SK10 . . . . 62 E5
Brooklet Rd CH60 . . . . . . 41 C8
Brooklyn Dr
Ellesmere Port CH65 . . . 69 F5
Lymm WA13 . . . . 18 E4
Brooklyn St CW2 . . . . . 190 C2
Brookmere Cl CW11 . . . 174 E8
Brookmills Cotts ST8 . . . 179 C1
Brookmoore Ct CH2 . . . 237 A4
Brook Pl
Chester CH1 . . . . 237 B3
Warrington WA4 . . . . . . 16 E3
Brook Rd
Ellesmere Port CH66 . . . 69 D5
Lymm WA13 . . . . 18 E4
Tarporley CW6 . . . . . . 168 D8
Brooks Dr WA15 . . . . 32 D8
Brookside
Ashton Hayes CH3 . . . 121 E7
Chester CH3 . . . . 142 A8
Cuddington CW8 . . . . . 101 F3
Kelsall CW6 . . . . 122 C4
Kingsley WA6 . . . . 75 C2
Warrington WA4 . . . . . . 16 E3
Brook Side CW8 . . . . . . 102 C8
Brookside Ave
Lymm WA13 . . . . 18 C4
Poynton SK12 . . . . 36 E3
Sutton Lane Ends SK11 . 112 D2
Warrington, Stockton Heath
WA4 . . . . 16 D1
Warrington WA5 . . . . . . 15 A4
Brookside Cl WA11 . . . . . 1 B7
Brookside Cotts
CW11 . . . . 176 A8
Brookside Ct SK10 . . . . . 87 A1
Brookside Gn CW2 . . . . 206 C8
Brookside La SK6 . . . . . . 37 E7
Brookside Mill [6]
SK11 . . . . 112 C7
Brookside Miniature Rly*
SK12 . . . . 36 F7
Brookside Prim Sch
Ellesmere Port CH66 . . . 69 E4
High Lane SK6 . . . . 37 E6
Brookside Rd
[4] Congleton CW12 . . 156 D3

Brookside Rd continued
Frodsham WA6 . . . . .74 A8
Brookside Terr
Chester CH2 . . . . .237 C4
Wilmslow SK9 . . . . .59 E3
Brookside View WA11 . . . . .1 B7
Brookside Way WA11 . . . . .1 B7
Brooks La
Bosley SK11 . . . . .135 E2
Middlewich CW10 . . . . . . .128 D1
Brook Slack CW6 . . . . . . .124 D1
Brooks Lane Ind Est
Middlewich CW10 . . . . . . .128 D1
Middlewich CW10 . . . . . . .151 D8
Brook St
Chester CH1 . . . . .237 B3
Congleton CW12 . . . . .156 F3
Crewe CW2 . . . . .190 D3
Golborne, Bank Heath
WA3 . . . . .3 A8
Knutsford WA16 . . . . .57 B1
Macclesfield SK11 . . . . . . .112 E7
Neston CH64 . . . . .66 E8
Northwich CW9 . . . . .79 A1
Northwich, Lostock Gralam
CW9 . . . . .79 E2
2 Runcorn WA7 . . . . .23 A2
15 Widnes WA8 . . . . .13 B1
Brook Street Bridge CH1,
CH2 . . . . .237 C4
Brook Street Mill 19
SK11 . . . . .112 E7
Brook Terr
Runcorn WA7 . . . . .23 E1
Sandbach CW11 . . . . .175 A3
BROOKVALE 50 B5
Brookvale Ave N WA7 . . . .50 B6
Brookvale Ave S WA7 . . . .50 B6
Brookvale Cl WA5 . . . . .6 F6
Brookvale Prim Sch
WA7 . . . . .50 B5
Brook View
Alderley Edge SK9 . . . . . . .60 A3
Allostock WA16 . . . . .106 F3
Northwich CL CW2 . . . . . . .206 C8
Brook Villas ST7 . . . . . . .193 E3
Brook Way
Hartford CW8 . . . . .103 B4
Nantwich CW5 . . . . .204 E3
Warrington WA5 . . . . .15 A5
Brookway La WA9 . . . . .1 A1
Brook Well CH64 . . . . .66 F5
Brookwood Cl WA4 . . . . . .26 B8
Broom Ave WA4 . . . . .26 E6
BROOM BANK 144 B8
Broom Cres CW11 . . . . . . .121 B1
Broome Ct WA7 . . . . .50 B5
BROOMEDGE 29 C8
Broomehouse Ave
M44 . . . . .11 E8
Broomfield CW12 . . . . . . .154 F6
Broomfield Cl
Chelford SK11 . . . . .84 A3
Wilmslow SK9 . . . . .60 E8
13 Winsford CW7 . . . . . .149 A8
Broomfields WA4 . . . . . . .26 E7
Broomfields Jun Sch
WA4 . . . . .26 E7
Broomfields La CW8 . . . . .77 F4
Broomfields Rd WA4 . . . . .26 D7
BROOMHALL 217 F4
BROOMHALL GREEN 217 F3
Broomheath La
Tarvin, Broom Bank
CH3 . . . . .144 C7
Tarvin CH3 . . . . .121 C1
Broomhill La
Brown Knowl CH3 . . . . . . .199 D8
Great Barrow CH3 . . . . . . .120 E8
Broom La WA16 . . . . .81 F2
Broomlands Cotts
CW5 . . . . .219 E1
Broom Rd M31 . . . . .11 F2
Broomsfield La CW8 . . . . .78 A4
Broom's La CW6 . . . . .122 D6
Broom St CW1 . . . . .190 A6
Broseley Ave WA3 . . . . .4 D4
Broseley La WA3 . . . . .4 D5
Brotherton Cl CH62 . . . . . .43 C8
Brotherton Way WA12 . . . . .2 B4
Brough St W SK11 . . . . . .112 C7
BROUGHTON 139 A4
Broughton Ave WA3 . . . . . .3 D7
Broughton Cl WA4 . . . . . . .26 F8
Broughton Cres SY14 . . . .211 A1
Broughton Hall Rd
CH4 . . . . .139 C4
Broughton Ind Est
CH4 . . . . .139 F6
Broughton Inf Sch
CH4 . . . . .139 C4
Broughton Jun Sch
CH4 . . . . .139 C4
Broughton La CW2 . . . . . .189 F1
Broughton Mills Rd
CH4 . . . . .139 F6
Broughton Rd
Adlington SK10 . . . . .62 C5
Crewe CW1 . . . . .190 C8
Broughton Sh Pk CH4 . . . .139 E4
Broughton Way WA8 . . . . . .22 B5
Brow Com Prim Sch The
WA7 . . . . .23 F1
Brow La
Antrobus CW9 . . . . .53 D5
Heswall CH60 . . . . .40 F7
Browmere Dr WA3 . . . . .9 A7

Brown Ave
Lawton-gate ST7 . . . . .194 A5
Nantwich CW5 . . . . .204 F4
BROWNEDGE 154 A3
BROWN HEATH 143 B6
Brown Heath Rd CH3 . . . .143 B6
BROWNHILL 147 B6
Brownhill Dr WA1 . . . . . . .16 F8
Brownhills Rd CW6 . . . . . .147 C6
Browning Ave WA8 . . . . . .22 F8
Browning Cl
Blacon CH1 . . . . .117 F6
Sandbach CW11 . . . . .174 D5
Browning Dr
Ellesmere Port CH65 . . . . . .69 F4
Winwick WA2 . . . . .8 A6
Browning Gn CH65 . . . . . . .69 F4
Browning Gr ST7 . . . . . . .210 C8
Browning St CW1 . . . . . . .190 C4
Browning Way CW7 . . . . . .149 A7
BROWN KNOWL 199 C8
Brown Lees Cl CW1 . . . . .190 B1
Brown Lees Rd ST7 . . . . .195 F4
BROWNLOW 177 E7
Brownlow Cl SK12 . . . . . . .36 E2
Brownlow Hall Mews
CW12 . . . . .177 E5
BROWNLOW HEATH 177 D5
Brownlow Heath
CW12 . . . . .177 E5
Brownlow Heath La
CW12 . . . . .177 D6
BROWN MOSS 231 B7
BROWN'S BANK 229 D2
Brown's La
Chester CH4 . . . . .141 C7
Wilmslow SK9 . . . . .60 E8
Brown St
3 Alderley Edge SK9 . . . . .60 A1
Congleton CW12 . . . . .156 E3
Macclesfield SK11 . . . . . . .112 C7
Widnes WA8 . . . . .23 D7
Brow The WA6 . . . . .75 C2
BROXTON 183 A1
Broxton Ave CW10 . . . . . .151 D6
Broxton Cl WA8 . . . . .12 C3
Broxton Mews CH3 . . . . . .183 A1
Broxton Rd
Clutton CH3 . . . . .182 D1
Ellesmere Port CH66 . . . . . .69 E5
Bruce Ave WA2 . . . . .8 D1
Bruce Cres CH43 . . . . .43 C6
Bruce Dr CH66 . . . . .69 C4
BRUCHE 16 F7
Bruche Ave WA1 . . . . .16 F8
Bruche Com Prim Sch
WA1 . . . . .17 A7
Bruche Dr WA1 . . . . .17 A8
Bruche Heath Gdns
WA1 . . . . .17 A8
Bruen The CH3 . . . . .121 C3
BRUERA 164 D6
Bruera Rd CH65 . . . . .69 F4
Brunel Cl CW9 . . . . .104 E5
Brunel Rd SK11 . . . . .112 C3
Brunner Gr CW5 . . . . .205 A5
Brunner Rd WA8 . . . . .23 A8
Brunsborough Cl CH62 . . . .43 C6
Brunswick 11 WA7 . . . . . . .23 A3
Brunswick Cres CH66 . . . . .69 E3
Brunswick Ct 12
SK11 . . . . .112 D7
Brunswick Hill SK10 . . . . .112 D8
Brunswick Rd WA12 . . . . . .1 F4
Brunswick St
Congleton CW12 . . . . .156 F3
5 Macclesfield SK10 . . . .112 D8
St Helens WA9 . . . . .1 A3
Brunswick Terr SK10 . . . . .112 D8
Bruntleigh Ave WA4 . . . . . .17 A3
Bryant Ave WA4 . . . . .16 F5
Brymau Four Trad Est
CH4 . . . . .140 D7
Brymau One Trad Est
CH4 . . . . .140 E7
Brymau Three Trad Est
CH4 . . . . .140 D7
Brymau Two Trad Est
CH4 . . . . .140 E7
BRYN 102 A6
Brynlow Dr CW10 . . . . . . .151 B8
Brynmore Dr SK11 . . . . . .112 F7
Brynn St WA8 . . . . .23 B8
Brynton Cl SK10 . . . . .87 C1
Brynton Rd SK10 . . . . .87 C1
Buchanan Cl WA8 . . . . .12 F3
Buchan Cl WA5 . . . . .15 B8
Buchan Gr CW2 . . . . .190 B3
Buckbean Way CW4 . . . . .107 E1
Buckden Way 9
SK10 . . . . .112 C8
Buckfast Ave WA11 . . . . . . .2 A7
Buckfast Cl
Cheadle SK8 . . . . .35 B6
Macclesfield SK10 . . . . . . .87 C2
Warrington WA5 . . . . .36 D5
Buckfast Ct WA7 . . . . .24 E3
Buckfast Way CW10 . . . . .128 B1
Buckingham Ave
Chester CH3 . . . . .119 B2
Widnes WA8 . . . . .13 A1
Buckingham Cl
4 Congleton CW12 . . . . .156 F4
Wistaston CW2 . . . . .205 E8
Buckingham Dr
Knutsford WA16 . . . . .57 B2
Macclesfield SK11 . . . . . . .112 B5

Buckingham Dr continued
Northwich CW9 . . . . .103 E4
Warrington WA5 . . . . .15 C4
Winsford CW7 . . . . .149 C7
Buckingham Gdns 1
CH65 . . . . .70 D2
Buckingham Rd
Irlam M44 . . . . .11 C6
Poynton SK12 . . . . .36 D3
Wilmslow SK9 . . . . .59 F6
Buckingham Rise
SK11 . . . . .112 B4
Buck La CW2 . . . . .206 E3
Buckland Cl WA8 . . . . .22 D7
Buckley Ave CW10 . . . . . .128 F7
Buckley Cl CW10 . . . . .151 B8
Buckley Ct CH64 . . . . .67 F8
Buckley St
Macclesfield SK11 . . . . . . .112 D7
Warrington WA2 . . . . .16 B6
Bucklow Ave
Mobberley WA16 . . . . .58 A4
Partington M31 . . . . .11 F3
Bucklow Gdns WA13 . . . . . .19 A4
BUCKLOW HILL 30 C3
Bucklowhill La WA16 . . . . . .30 B3
Bucklow Wlk 11 SK11 . . . . .112 E7
BUCKOAK 99 A5
Buckton St WA1 . . . . .16 D7
BUDDILEIGH 221 F7
Bude Cl
Alsager ST7 . . . . .193 B3
Bramhall SK7 . . . . .35 F7
Crewe CW1 . . . . .190 B8
Bude Rd WA8 . . . . .12 E2
Budworth Ave
Warrington WA4 . . . . .16 F4
Widnes WA8 . . . . .12 D2
Budworth Cl
Runcorn WA7 . . . . .49 D7
Sandbach CW11 . . . . .174 F7
BUDWORTH HEATH 54 A1
Budworth Heath La
CW9 . . . . .54 C1
Budworth La CW9 . . . . .78 E7
Budworth Rd
Bate Heath CW9 . . . . .54 E2
Ellesmere Port CH66 . . . . . .69 E2
Over Tabley WA16 . . . . .55 C2
Budworth Wlk 11 SK9 . . . .34 E1
BUERTON 230 E4
Buerton App CH3 . . . . . . .164 B6
BUERTON MOSS 230 E6
Buffs La CH60 . . . . .41 B8
Buggen La CH64 . . . . .66 D8
BUGLAWTON 157 A4
Buglawton Hall Sch
CW12 . . . . .157 D5
Buglawton Ind Est 5
CW12 . . . . .156 F4
Buglawton Prim Sch
CW12 . . . . .157 A4
Buildwas Rd CH64 . . . . . . .41 F2
BULKELEY 184 E2
Bulkeley Hall La SY14 . . . .200 C8
Bulkeley Rd
Handforth SK9 . . . . .34 D3
Poynton SK12 . . . . .36 E3
Bulkeley St
Chester CH3 . . . . .119 A1
Crewe CW1 . . . . .190 E3
Bullcroft Cl SY14 . . . . . . .211 D7
Bull Hall CH64 . . . . .66 F6
Bull-Hill-La SK10, SK11 . . .88 D2
Bullocks House Rd
ST7 . . . . .195 F3
Bullocks La SK11 . . . . . . .112 E3
Bull Ring CW9 . . . . .103 F8
Bull Ring The CW10 . . . . .128 C1
Bumper's La CH1 . . . . . . .117 F1
BUNBURY 185 F8
Bunbury Aldersey CE Prim
Sch CW6 . . . . .185 E8
Bunbury Cl
Middlewich CW10 . . . . . . .151 D5
Northwich CW9 . . . . .104 A5
Stoak CH2 . . . . .96 A7
Bunbury Comm CW6 . . . . .168 E2
BUNBURY COMMONS 169 A2
Bunbury Ct CW6 . . . . .146 D1
Bunbury Dr WA7 . . . . .49 C6
Bunbury Gn CH65 . . . . .70 D2
BUNBURY HEATH 185 D8
Bunbury La CW6 . . . . .185 E8
Bunbury Mill CW6 . . . . . . .169 A1
Bunce La SK11 . . . . .133 B4
Bunce St CH1 . . . . .237 A1
Bungalow Rd WA12 . . . . . . .2 E1
Bungalows The
Adderley TF9 . . . . .234 B3
Dunham-on-t-H WA6 . . . . . .97 E6
Thornton Hough CH63 . . . . .42 B6
BUNSLEY BANK 230 D5
Bunting Cl 6 WA3 . . . . .3 E8
Buntingford Rd WA4 . . . . . .17 C2
Bunts La CW12 . . . . .156 E1
Burdett Rd CH64 . . . . .66 F7
Burfield Dr WA4 . . . . .26 D7
Burford Ave
Bramhall SK7 . . . . .35 D5
Newcastle-u-Lyme ST5 . . . .210 D1
Burford Cl SK9 . . . . .59 E5
Burford Cres SK9 . . . . .59 E5
Burford La WA13 . . . . .19 D2
Burgamot La CW9 . . . . .78 D8
Burganey Ct CH4 . . . . .126 D2

Burgess Ave WA4 . . . . .16 B2
Burgess Cl CW5 . . . . .205 B4
Burgess Dr CH1 . . . . .117 A5
Burgess La WA6 . . . . .100 B6
Burgess Pl 5 CW8 . . . . . .103 E8
Burgess St SK10 . . . . .112 F8
Burges St CH3 . . . . .118 F3
Burjen Way CW1 . . . . .190 B6
Burkhardt Dr WA12 . . . . . . .2 E3
BURLAND 203 C7
Burland Cl WA7 . . . . .22 F1
Burland Gr CW7 . . . . .126 A2
BURLAND LOWER GREEN
. . . . .203 A7
Burland Rd
Halewood L26 . . . . .21 A6
Newcastle-u-Lyme ST5 . . . .210 D2
BURLAND UPPER GREEN
. . . . .203 B8
Burlea Cl CW2 . . . . .189 E5
Burlea Dr CW2 . . . . .206 B5
BURLEYDAM 228 B1
Burleyhurst La SK9,
WA16 . . . . .59 B7
Burley La WA4 . . . . .27 C4
Burnell Cl CW5 . . . . .204 F3
Burnell Rd CH65 . . . . .70 E4
Burnet Cl WA2 . . . . .9 C2
Burnell WA3 . . . . .3 E7
Burnham Cl
Culcheth WA3 . . . . .4 E4
Warrington WA5 . . . . .14 F5
Widnes WA8 . . . . .12 C3
Burnham Rd CH4 . . . . .140 F6
Burnsall Ave WA3 . . . . .3 F8
Burnsall Dr WA8 . . . . .12 C3
Burns Cl
Ellesmere Port CH66 . . . . . .69 E4
Rode Heath ST7 . . . . .193 E8
Burns Cres WA8 . . . . .22 F8
Burns Dr CW1 . . . . .190 F4
Burns Gr WA2 . . . . .8 C2
Burnside WA15 . . . . .32 D7
Burnside Cl WA4 . . . . .16 D1
Burnside Cl SK9 . . . . .60 C6
Burnside Way
Northwich CW8 . . . . .103 D8
Winnington CW8 . . . . .78 D1
Burns Rd CW12 . . . . .157 A2
Burns Way CH1 . . . . .117 E6
Burnt Acre SK11 . . . . .84 B3
Burnt Mill La WA8 . . . . . . .21 D5
Burnwood Gr ST7 . . . . . . .195 B2
Burran Rd M22 . . . . .33 D8
Burrough Cl WA3 . . . . .9 F3
Burrows Hill CW8 . . . . . . .103 B7
Burrows La WA6 . . . . .73 F2
Burrows St WA11 . . . . .1 A6
Burrows The CW8 . . . . . . .101 D5
Bursar Cl WA12 . . . . .2 D4
Burslam St CW12 . . . . . . .156 E2
BURTON
Duddon 144 F4
Neston 67 D1
Burton Ave CW6 . . . . .146 C3
Burton Cl
Culcheth WA3 . . . . .4 F3
Widnes WA8 . . . . .12 F3
Burton Dr SK12 . . . . .36 D4
Burton Gn CH66 . . . . .69 D4
Burton Gr CW1 . . . . .173 B1
BURTON GREEN 161 D1
Burton Hall Rd LL12 . . . . .161 E1
Burton La CW6 . . . . .144 F6
Burton Manor Coll
CH64 . . . . .67 D1
Burton Rd
Blacon CH1 . . . . .117 E5
Duddon CW6 . . . . .144 E6
Neston CH64 . . . . .66 F6
Warrington WA2 . . . . .8 D1
Burton Sq CW6 . . . . .146 C2
BURTONWOOD 6 E6
Burtonwood Com Prim
Sch WA5 . . . . .6 E7
Burtonwood Ind Ctr
WA5 . . . . .6 E7
Burtonwood Rd
Warrington, Great Sankey
WA5 . . . . .15 C6
Warrington, Kingswood
WA5 . . . . .7 A2
BURWARDSLEY 184 B5
Burwardsley Ct CH3 . . . . .184 A6
Burwardsley Rd CH3 . . . . .166 D1
Burwardsley Way
CW9 . . . . .103 E4
Bushell Cl CH64 . . . . .66 F7
Bushell Rd CH64 . . . . .66 F7
Bushells La WA6 . . . . .99 B8
Bush Rd
Christleton CH3 . . . . .142 E7
Widnes WA8 . . . . .22 F5
Bush Way CH60 . . . . .40 D8
Butler Way CW5 . . . . .204 E3
Butley Cl
Macclesfield SK10 . . . . . . .87 D3
Middlewich CW10 . . . . . . .151 C7
Butley Hall SK10 . . . . .87 A7
Butley Lanes SK10 . . . . . . .61 F1
BUTLEY TOWN 87 C8
Butterbache Rd CH3 . . . . .142 A6
Butterbur Cl CH3 . . . . . . .142 A6
Buttercup Cl WA5 . . . . .15 E3
Buttercup Way WA16 . . . . .79 F6
Buttermarket St WA1 . . . .16 B5
Buttermere Ave
Ellesmere Port CH65 . . . . . .70 C3

Buttermere Ave continued
Warrington WA2 . . . . .8 C3
Buttermere Cl WA6 . . . . . . .74 D8
Buttermere Cres WA2 . . . . .8 C3
Buttermere Ct CW12 . . . . .156 A2
Buttermere Dr
Alderley Edge SK9 . . . . . . .83 F7
Altrincham WA15 . . . . .32 D6
Crewe CW1 . . . . .173 B1
Buttermere Gr WA7 . . . . . . .49 D5
Buttermere Rd
Partington M31 . . . . .11 E3
Winsford CW7 . . . . .126 C2
BUTTERS GREEN 210 A2
Butterton La
Oakhanger CW1 . . . . .192 B2
Oakhanger CW1 . . . . .192 C1
BUTT GREEN 205 B3
BUTT LANE 194 D1
Butts Gn WA5 . . . . .7 A3
Butts The
Alsager ST7 . . . . .193 D4
Runcorn WA7 . . . . .23 F2
Buxton Ave CW1 . . . . .190 E4
Buxton Cl WA5 . . . . .15 A8
Buxton New Rd
Macclesfield SK11 . . . . . . .115 A6
Macclesfield Forest
SK11 . . . . .114 D7
Macclesfield SK11 . . . . . . .88 E1
Buxton Old Rd
Congleton CW12 . . . . .157 A4
Disley SK12 . . . . .38 E4
Macclesfield SK11 . . . . . . .113 D7
Buxton Rd
Congleton CW12 . . . . .157 C6
High Lane SK6, SK7,
SK12 . . . . .37 D8
Horwich End, New Horwich
SK23 . . . . .65 E6
Macclesfield SK10,
SK11 . . . . .88 E1
New Mills SK22, SK23 . . . .39 C4
Whaley Bridge SK23 . . . . . .39 E1
Buxton Rd W SK12 . . . . . . .38 B5
Bye Pass The CH3 . . . . . . .119 E2
Byland Ave SK8 . . . . .35 B6
Byland Cl WA8 . . . . .13 C5
Bylands Cl SK12 . . . . .36 D4
BYLEY 129 A7
Byley La
Cranage CW4, CW10 . . . . .129 C6
Middlewich CW10 . . . . . . .128 E3
Byley Prim Sch CW10 . . . .129 B7
Byley Way CW7 . . . . .126 B1
Byng Ave M44 . . . . .11 F7
By-Pass Rd CH3 . . . . .121 B3
Byron Cl
Blacon CH1 . . . . .117 F6
Crewe CW1 . . . . .190 F4
Middlewich CW10 . . . . . . .151 D5
Rode Heath ST7 . . . . .193 E7
Sandbach CW11 . . . . .174 D6
Byron Ct WA2 . . . . .8 C2
Byron's La SK11 . . . . .112 E5
Byrons St SK11 . . . . .112 D6
Byron St WA7 . . . . .23 A1
Byron Way CW2 . . . . .190 A1
Byron Wlk CW5 . . . . .204 D6
Bythom Cl CH3 . . . . .142 E7

C

Cabot Cl WA5 . . . . .7 C1
Cabul Cl WA2 . . . . .16 E5
CADISHEAD
Cadishead Prim Sch
M44 . . . . .11 E6
Cadishead Way M44 . . . . . .11 F6
Cadnant Cl CH1 . . . . .117 D3
Cadnant Ct/Llys Cadnant
CH4 . . . . .139 D5
Cadshaw Cl WA3 . . . . .9 D5
Caer Castell LL13 . . . . . . .196 D8
Caerleon Cl CW7 . . . . .149 A8
Caerllew LL13 . . . . .196 E1
Caernarvon Ave CW7 . . . . .149 B7
Caernarvon Cl WA7 . . . . . .23 E2
Caernarvon Ct 4
CH65 . . . . .70 D2
Caernarvon Rd CW2 . . . . .205 E8
Caesars Cl WA7 . . . . .23 E2
Cairn Brae WA12 . . . . .2 C4
Cairns Cres CH1 . . . . .117 D4
Caira St WA1 . . . . .16 B5
Caister Way CW7 . . . . .149 C7
Caithness Ct 3 WA7 . . . . .23 B2
Calamine St SK11 . . . . . . .112 E6
Calday Gr WA11 . . . . .1 A8
Caldbeck Ave WA2 . . . . .8 D2
CALDECOTT GREEN 197 C4
Caldene Terr SK23 . . . . . . .65 E7
Calder Ave CW1 . . . . .191 A5
Calder Cl
Bollington SK10 . . . . .87 F8
Poynton SK12 . . . . .36 D3
Widnes WA8 . . . . .13 E3
Calderfield Cl WA4 . . . . . . .26 B8
Calder Way 2 CH66 . . . . . .69 C5
Caldicott Ave CH62 . . . . . . .43 D7
Caldicott Cl 2 CW7 . . . . .149 C7
Caldwell Ave WA5 . . . . .7 F2
Caldwell Cl CW5 . . . . .205 B4
Caldwell Rd WA8 . . . . .23 A7

Caldwell's Gate La
CW9 . . . . 54 B8
Caldy Cl CH2 . . . . 118 D5
Caldy Dr CH66 . . . . 69 D4
Caldy Rd
Alsager ST7 . . . . 193 D4
Handforth SK9 . . . . 34 D3
Caldy Valley Rd
Chester CH3 . . . . 142 B7
Huntington CH3 . . . . 142 A6
Caldy Way CW7 . . . . 126 C1
Cale Rd SK22 . . . . 39 D8
Calico La SK23 . . . . 39 D4
California Cl WA5 . . . . 15 C8
Callands Prim Sch WA5 . . . 7 E2
Callands Rd WA5 . . . . 7 D2
Callender Gdns WA6 . . . . . 73 A2
Callin Ct CH1 . . . . 237 A2
Calmington La WA7 . . . . . . 24 F4
CALROFOLD 88 C2
Calrofold Dr ST5 . . . . 210 D1
Calrofold La SK10 . . . . 88 C2
Calstock Cl WA5 . . . . 14 E3
CALVELEY 169 E2
Calveley Ave CH62 . . . . . . 43 F4
Calveley Cl CW9 . . . . 103 E5
Calveley Green La CW6,
CW7 . . . . 170 C4
Calveley Hall La CW5,
CW6 . . . . 170 A2
Calveley Prim Sch
CW6 . . . . 170 B2
Calveley Rd
Halewood L26 . . . . 21 A6
Macclesfield SK10 . . . . . . 86 F1
Calveley Way CW7 . . . . . . 126 B1
Calverley Cl SK9 . . . . 60 C8
Calverly Cl WA7 . . . . 50 C5
Calver Rd WA2 . . . . 8 A3
Calvers WA7 . . . . 23 E1
Camberley Cl SK7 . . . . 36 A7
Camberwell Park Rd
WA8 . . . . 13 D4
Camborne Ave SK10 . . . . . 111 E8
Camborne Cl
Congleton CW12 . . . . . . 178 E8
Runcorn WA7 . . . . 50 C6
Cambourne Rd WA5 . . . . . . 6 F6
Cambrai Ave WA4 . . . . 16 C2
Cambrian Cl CH66 . . . . 69 A6
Cambrian Ct CH1 . . . . 118 B2
Cambrian Rd CH1 . . . . 118 B2
Cambrian Villas CH3 . . . . 165 C2
Cambrian Way CW7 . . . . . 149 B8
Cambridge Ave
Macclesfield SK11 . . . . . . 112 B4
Wilmslow SK9 . . . . 59 F7
Winsford CW7 . . . . 126 A1
Cambridge Cl
Biddulph ST8 . . . . 179 C1
Warrington WA4 . . . . 26 B7
Cambridge Ct **7** CH65 . . 70 C5
Cambridge Gdns
Helsby WA6 . . . . 73 D4
Warrington WA4 . . . . 26 C6
Cambridge Rd
Bebington CH62 . . . . 43 E8
Chester CH2 . . . . 118 F5
Ellesmere Port CH65 . . . . 70 D5
Macclesfield SK11 . . . . . . 112 B7
Cambridge Road Com
Prim Sch CH65 . . . . 70 C5
Cambridge St
Runcorn WA7 . . . . 23 C2
Widnes WA8 . . . . 23 B7
Camden Ct WA7 . . . . 24 D1
Camden Rd CH65 . . . . 70 A5
Camden St CW1 . . . . 190 C4
Camellia Gdns WA9 . . . . . . 6 B7
Camelot Cl WA12 . . . . 1 F4
Camelot Gr CW2 . . . . 206 C4
Camelot Way WA7 . . . . 50 A8
Cameron Ave
Runcorn WA7 . . . . 48 E8
Shavington CW2 . . . . . . 206 B3
Cameron Ct WA4 . . . . 49 C6
Cameron Rd WA8 . . . . 23 A8
Camm St CW2 . . . . 190 D2
Camomile Wlk **5** M31 . . . 11 F3
Campbell Ave WA7 . . . . . . 49 A8
Campbell Cl
Congleton CW12 . . . . . . 157 A4
Haslington CW1 . . . . 191 C4
Macclesfield SK10 . . . . . . 87 A1
Northwich CW9 . . . . 103 F4
Campbell Cres WA5 . . . . . . 14 F6
Campden Way SK9 . . . . . . 34 D4
Campion Cl
Huntington CH3 . . . . 142 A6
Warrington WA3 . . . . 9 C4
Campsey Ash WA8 . . . . . . 12 F4
Camrose Cl WA7 . . . . 49 C6
Camsley La WA13 . . . . 18 B3
Canaan WA3 . . . . 4 C8
Canada Cl WA2 . . . . 9 A2
Canadian Ave CH2 . . . . . . 119 A3
Canal Bank WA13 . . . . 18 D3
Canal Bridge Ent Pk
CH65 . . . . 70 D6
Canal Cotts CW5 . . . . 187 D6
Canal Rd CW12 . . . . 156 F1
Canal Reach WA7 . . . . 24 C2
Canalside CH65 . . . . 70 D6

Canal Side
Barnton CW8 . . . . 78 B2
Chester CH1 . . . . 237 C3
Macclesfield SK11 . . . . . . 112 F7
Moore WA4 . . . . 25 C5
Runcorn WA7 . . . . 48 D7
Warrington WA4 . . . . 17 C1
Whaley Bridge SK23 . . . . 39 F1
Canalside Cotts
CW11 . . . . 175 C3
Canal Side Cotts WA7 . . . . 50 F6
Canal St
Chester CH1 . . . . 237 A3
Congleton CW12 . . . . . . 156 E2
Macclesfield SK10 . . . . . . 112 E8
Newton-le-W WA12 . . . . . 1 F3
Runcorn WA7 . . . . 23 B2
Whaley Bridge SK23 . . . . 65 E8
Canal Terr CW10 . . . . 151 D8
Canberra Ave WA2 . . . . . . 8 D3
Canberra Rd SK7 . . . . 35 F5
Canberra Sq WA2 . . . . 8 D2
Canberra Way CH1 . . . . . 117 D4
Candelan Way WA16 . . . . . 29 C4
Candle La CW3 . . . . 232 B2
Candleston Cl WA5 . . . . 7 E1
Candy La SK10 . . . . 62 C8
Canford Cl
Crewe CW1 . . . . 190 B8
Warrington WA5 . . . . 15 C6
Cannell Ct WA7 . . . . 50 A6
Cannell St **4** WA5 . . . . . 15 D4
Canning St CH1 . . . . 237 A3
Canniswood Rd WA11 . . . . . 1 A6
Cann La CW9 . . . . 55 A6
Cann La N WA4 . . . . 26 E5
Cann La S WA4 . . . . 26 F4
Cannock Ct CH66 . . . . 94 E8
Cannonbury Cl WA7 . . . . . 50 A8
Cannon St CH65 . . . . 70 A5
Cannon Way CH4 . . . . 161 A7
Canon Dr WA14 . . . . 31 B8
Canons Rd WA5 . . . . 15 D6
Canon St WA7 . . . . 22 F3
Canon Wilson Cl WA11 . . . . 1 D6
Canterbury Cl CH66 . . . . . 94 E8
Canterbury Rd
Blacon CH1 . . . . 117 F5
Widnes WA8 . . . . 22 C8
Canterbury St WA4 . . . . . . 16 C4
Cantilever Gdns WA4 . . . . 16 E2
Cantley Cl WA7 . . . . 49 D6
Canton Pl CW8 . . . . 103 D7
Canton St SK11 . . . . 112 D6
Canton Wlks SK11 . . . . . . 112 D6
Canute Pl **9** WA16 . . . . . 57 A2
Capeland Cl CH4 . . . . 140 E5
Capel Way CW5 . . . . 204 D6
CAPENHURST 94 A8
Capenhurst Ave
Crewe CW2 . . . . 190 A3
Warrington WA2 . . . . 9 A2
Capenhurst CE Prim Sch
CH1 . . . . 94 B8
Capenhurst Ct SK12 . . . . . 36 F4
Capenhurst Gdns
CH66 . . . . 69 D1
Capenhurst Grange Sch
CH66 . . . . 69 E2
Capenhurst La
Capenhurst CH1 . . . . 94 B8
Ellesmere Port CH65 . . . . 70 A3
Woodbank CH1 . . . . 93 F7
Capenhurst Sta CH1 . . . . . 69 C1
Capenhurst Tech Pk
Capenhurst CH1 . . . . 69 B1
Capenhurst CH1 . . . . 94 B1
Capesthorne Cl
Alsager ST7 . . . . 193 C3
Hazel Grove SK7 . . . . 36 F8
Holmes Chapel CW4 . . . . 130 B3
Northwich CW9 . . . . 103 F4
Sandbach CW11 . . . . 175 C7
Widnes WA8 . . . . 22 E8
Capesthorne Hall*
SK11 . . . . 110 A6
Capesthorne Rd
Crewe CW2 . . . . 189 F3
Hazel Grove SK7 . . . . 36 F8
Lymm WA13 . . . . 37 E7
Warrington WA2 . . . . 8 D2
Waverton CH3 . . . . 143 B6
Wilmslow SK9 . . . . 59 E5
Capesthorne Way **16**
SK11 . . . . 112 F7
Capitol Wlk CW12 . . . . . . 156 D2
Cappelle Rise ST7 . . . . . . 209 D1
Capper Cl ST7 . . . . 195 A2
Cappers La CW11 . . . . . . 176 C2
Capper's La CW5,
CW6 . . . . 186 C3
Carden Ave CW7 . . . . 126 B1
Cardenbrook Gr **4**
SK9 . . . . 34 D2
Carden Cl WA3 . . . . 9 D4
Cardeston Cl WA7 . . . . 49 F3
Cardiff Cl CH66 . . . . 94 E8
Cardigan Cl
Macclesfield SK11 . . . . . . 112 A8
Warrington WA5 . . . . 7 D2
Cardinal Newman RC High
Sch WA4 . . . . 16 F5
Cardway Bsns Pk ST7 . . . 193 F3
Carey St WA8 . . . . 13 B1
Carisbrook Ct WA3 . . . . 4 E3
Carisbrook Dr CW7 . . . . . 149 C7
Carisbrooke Cl CW2 . . . . . 205 E8
Carleton Rd SK12 . . . . 37 C4

Carlett Bvd CH62 . . . . 43 F5
Carlingford Rd WA4 . . . . . 26 B7
Carlisle Cl
Macclesfield SK11 . . . . . . 111 F5
Mobberley WA16 . . . . 58 A4
Willaston CW7 . . . . 1E6 A1
Carlisle Rd CH1 . . . . 117 E5
Carlisle St
13 Alderley Edge SK9 . . . 60 A1
Crewe CW2 . . . . 190 B2
Warrington WA4 . . . . 16 A4
Carlow Ct L24 . . . . 21 D2
Carlton Ave
Bramhall SK7 . . . . 35 D5
Handforth SK9 . . . . 34 C2
Runcorn WA7 . . . . 23 D2
Saltney CH4 . . . . 140 D6
Carlton Cl
Mickle Trafford CH2 . . . . 119 E8
Northwich CW9 . . . . 41 C2
Carlton Cres CH66 . . . . . . 69 F8
Carlton Pl CH2 . . . . 119 A4
Carlton Rd
Lymm WA13 . . . . 19 B5
Northwich CW9 . . . . 104 B7
Carlton St
Warrington WA4 . . . . 26 C8
Widnes WA8 . . . . 11 C5
Carlyle Ct ST7 . . . . 193 E8
Carlyle Cres CH66 . . . . . . 69 E4
Carmarthen Cl
Warrington WA5 . . . . 7 D2
3 Winsford CW7 . . . . . 149 C7
Carmel Cl CH1 . . . . 117 D3
Carmel Ct WA8 . . . . 13 B4
Carmenna Dr SK7 . . . . 35 F7
Carmichael Cl **6** M31 . . . 11 E3
Carnegie Cl SK10 . . . . 87 A1
Carnoustie Cl
Wilmslow SK9 . . . . 60 D8
Winsford CW7 . . . . 126 B2
Carnoustie Dr SK10 . . . . . 87 D5
Carnoustie Gr WA11 . . . . . . 1 A5
Carol Dr CH60 . . . . 41 C8
Carolina Rd **2** WA5 . . . . 15 B7
Caroline Ho CH1 . . . . 117 F6
Caroline St
Irlam M44 . . . . 11 F8
Widnes WA8 . . . . 23 B7
Carol St WA4 . . . . 16 D4
Carpenter Gr WA2 . . . . 9 A1
Carpenters Ct SK9 . . . . . . 60 A1
Carr Brook Cl SK23 . . . . . . 65 E5
Carr Brow SK6 . . . . 38 A7
Carrgreen La WA13 . . . . . . 19 F6
Carriage Cl L24 . . . . 21 D1
Carriage Dr
Biddulph ST8 . . . . 179 E1
Frodsham WA6 . . . . 74 A6
Carriage Ho CW1 . . . . 190 A5
Carrick Dr CH65 . . . . 70 B2
Carrick Rd CH4 . . . . 141 B7
Carrington Cl WA3 . . . . 9 C4
Carrington Way CW1 . . . . 190 B8
Carrington Wlk WA1 . . . . . 16 C6
Carr La
Alderley Edge SK9 . . . . . . 59 D2
Audley ST7 . . . . 209 A1
Golborne WA3 . . . . 4 A7
Golborne, Wash End WN7 . . 4 E8
Hale L24, WA8 . . . . 21 E4
Carr Mill Mews SK9 . . . . . 34 B1
Carroll Dr CW2 . . . . 205 F8
Carrs Ct SK9 . . . . 60 B7
Carrs La CH3 . . . . 166 F1
Carr St ST7 . . . . 195 F1
Carrwood
Altrincham WA15 . . . . 32 B7
Knutsford WA16 . . . . 57 C1
Carr Wood Ave SK7 . . . . . 35 E8
Carrwood Cl WA11 . . . . 1 A6
Carrwood Rd SK9 . . . . 59 F8
Carsdale Rd M22 . . . . 33 E8
Car St CH1 . . . . 237 C3
Carter Ave CW6 . . . . 122 D4
Carter Bench Ho SK10 . . . 63 A1
Carter Cl CW5 . . . . 204 D6
Carter La SK11 . . . . 84 B4
Carter St CH1 . . . . 237 C3
Carter Cl
Warrington, Old Hall
WA5 . . . . 7 C1
Warrington WA5 . . . . 15 C8
Cartlake Cl CW5 . . . . 204 C5
Cartledge Cl CW8 . . . . . . 102 A3
Cartmel Ave WA2 . . . . 8 C3
Cartmel Cl
Holmes Chapel CW4 . . . . 130 A3
Macclesfield SK10 . . . . . . 87 B2
Warrington WA5 . . . . 14 F3
Winsford CW7 . . . . 126 D2
Cartmel Dr CH66 . . . . 69 F2
Cartmell Cl WA7 . . . . 49 B6
Cartridge La WA4 . . . . 27 E6
Cartwright Rd CW1 . . . . . 191 D5
Cartwright St
Runcorn WA7 . . . . 23 C2
Warrington WA5 . . . . 15 E4
Carver Ave CW4 . . . . 130 A6
Carver Cl CW7 . . . . 127 A4
Case Rd WA11 . . . . 1 D6
Casey La CW7 . . . . 206 F4
Cassia Green La CW7 . . . . 125 D5
Cassley Rd L24 . . . . 21 A3
Casson St CW1 . . . . 190 B5
Castle Bank CW8 . . . . 103 E7

Castle Cl
Broughton CH5 . . . . 139 B6
Kidsgrove ST7 . . . . 194 D1
Kotsall CW6 . . . . 122 D4
Pulford CH4 . . . . 162 D7
Castle Croft Rd CH4 . . . . . 141 B5
Castle St
Holt LL13 . . . . 196 E8
17 Nantwich CW5 . . . . 204 E5
Northwich CW8 . . . . 103 E7
Castle Dr
Chester CH1 . . . . 237 B1
Ellesmere Port CH65 . . . . 70 A3
Heswall CH60 . . . . 40 F8
Castle Farm SY14 . . . . . . 200 E3
Castle Farm Ct WA7 . . . . . 24 A1
CASTLEFIELDS 23 F2
Castlefields CH3 . . . . 166 C3
Castlefields Ave E
WA7 . . . . 24 A2
Castlefields Ave N
WA7 . . . . 23 F2
Castlefields Ave S
WA7 . . . . 24 A1
Castleford Dr SK10 . . . . . . 86 E6
Castlegate SK10 . . . . 86 E6
Castlegate Mews SK10 . . . 86 F6
Castle Gn WA5 . . . . 7 B2
Castlehill CH4 . . . . 162 C2
Castle Hill
Newton-le-W WA12 . . . . . . 2 E4
Prestbury SK10 . . . . 86 E6
Castle Hill Cl SK10 . . . . . . 86 F7
Castle Hill Farm **3**
CH4 . . . . 103 E8
Castle Inn Rd CW12 . . . . . 179 C7
Castlemead Wlk CW9 . . . . 103 E4
Castlemere Ct CH4 . . . . . 139 A3
Castlemere Dr CW1 . . . . . 190 C7
Castle Mews LL13 . . . . . . 196 E8
Castle Mill La WA15 . . . . . 32 B5
Castle Park Arts Ctr
WA6 . . . . 74 A8
Castle Prim Sch ST7 . . . . 195 D6
Castle Rd
Mow Cop ST7 . . . . 195 D7
Runcorn WA7 . . . . 49 F8
Castle Rise
Prestbury SK10 . . . . 86 F6
Runcorn WA7 . . . . 23 D2
Castle St
Chester CH1 . . . . 237 B1
1 Crewe CW1 . . . . . . 190 C4
Macclesfield SK11 . . . . . . 112 D8
8 Nantwich CW5 . . . . . 204 E5
Northwich CW8 . . . . 103 E8
Widnes WA8 . . . . 13 D1
Castleton Dr SK6 . . . . 37 F6
CASTLETOWN 197 D3
Castletown Cl SK10 . . . . . . 87 C4
Castletown La CH3 . . . . . 197 D2
Castle View Prim Sch
WA7 . . . . 24 D2
Castleview Rd ST7 . . . . . . 195 B3
Castleway WA15 . . . . 32 C7
Castle Way CH4 . . . . 162 A6
Castner Ave WA7 . . . . 48 E7
Catalan Cl CW7 . . . . 127 A1
Catalyst Mus* WA8 . . . . . . 23 A6
Catalyst Trade Pk WA8 . . . 23 A6
Catchpenny La SK11 . . . . 108 F3
Catford Cl WA8 . . . . 12 C2
Catfoss Cl WA2 . . . . 8 E1
Cathcart Gn CH3 . . . . 119 F5
Cathedral Church of
Christ & the Blessed
Virgin Mary* CH1 . . . . . . 237 B2
Catherine Ct/Llys Catrin
CH5 . . . . 139 B6
Catherine St
Chester CH1 . . . . 118 B2
Crewe CW2 . . . . 190 D2
Macclesfield SK11 . . . . . . 112 C8
Warrington WA5 . . . . 15 F7
Widnes WA8 . . . . 23 A7
Catherine Way WA12 . . . . . 2 B2
Catholic High Sch The
CH4 . . . . 141 D6
Catterall Ave WA4 . . . . 8 D2
Caughall Rd CH2 . . . . 95 E2
Caunce Ave
Golborne WA3 . . . . 3 A7
Haydock WA11 . . . . 1 B6
Newton-le-W WA12 . . . . . 2 C1
Causeway Ave WA4 . . . . . . 16 C3
Causeway Pk WA4 . . . . . . 16 C3
Cavalier Dr CH1 . . . . 117 E6
Cavan Dr WA11 . . . . 1 E5
Cavell Dr CH65 . . . . 70 A4
Cavendish Ave WA3 . . . . . . 9 F5
Cavendish Cl
5 Macclesfield SK10 . . . 87 D3
Warrington WA5 . . . . 15 D7
Winsford CW7 . . . . 149 A8
Cavendish Cres ST7 . . . . 193 D5
Cavendish Ct
Chester CH4 . . . . 141 A5
Widnes WA8 . . . . 12 F1
Cavendish Farm Rd
WA7 . . . . 49 A5
Cavendish Gdns CH65 . . . . 70 A4
Cavendish Mews SK9 . . . . 60 A6
Cavendish Mews **7**
WA3 . . . . 3 A8
Cavendish Rd
Chester CH4 . . . . 141 B6
Crewe CW2 . . . . 189 E5

Cavendish Rd continued
Hazel Grove SK7 . . . . 36 E8
Cavendish Sch WA7 . . . . . 49 C5
Cavendish St **7** WA7 . . . 22 F2
Cavendish Way CW4 . . . . 130 A3
Caversham Cl WA4 . . . . . . 26 F6
Cawdor Dr CH3 . . . . 119 A2
Cawdor St
Runcorn WA7 . . . . 22 F3
Warrington WA4 . . . . 26 C8
Cawfield Ave WA8 . . . . 12 D1
Cawley Ave WA3 . . . . 4 E4
Cawley Ct WA3 . . . . 62 E7
Cawley St
8 Macclesfield SK11 . . . 112 E7
Runcorn WA7 . . . . 23 A1
Cawood Cl CH66 . . . . 69 B5
Cawthorne Ave WA4 . . . . . 17 A2
Caxton Cl
Ellesmere Port CH66 . . . . 69 E4
Widnes WA8 . . . . 12 C3
Cecil Rd ST8 . . . . 179 C2
Cecil Rigby Cl **1**
CW11 . . . . 175 B6
Cecil St CH3 . . . . 118 A1
Cedab Rd CH65 . . . . 70 C6
Cedar Ave
Alsager ST7 . . . . 193 D3
Aston WA7 . . . . 50 B4
Connah's Quay, Garden City
CH5 . . . . 116 A7
Ellesmere Port CH66 . . . . 69 D6
Golborne WA3 . . . . 3 F7
Kidsgrove ST7 . . . . 194 D1
Runcorn WA7 . . . . 49 C7
Widnes WA8 . . . . 13 B2
Cedar Cl
Connah's Quay CH5 . . . . 116 A7
Holmes Chapel CW4 . . . . 130 D4
Lostock Gralam CW9 . . . . 80 A3
Middlewich CW10 . . . . . . 151 E6
Poynton SK12 . . . . 36 E3
Sandbach CW11 . . . . 175 C5
Cedar Cres
Audley ST7 . . . . 209 F1
Newton-le-W WA12 . . . . . 2 D2
Cedar Ct
Alsager ST7 . . . . 193 E4
Congleton CW12 . . . . . . 178 F8
Culcheth WA3 . . . . 4 F1
Willaston CW5 . . . . 205 D6
Cedardale Dr CH66 . . . . . . 94 F8
Cedardale Pk WA8 . . . . . . 13 E4
Cedar Dr
Barnton CW8 . . . . 78 A4
Chester CH2 . . . . 119 B4
Cedarfield Rd WA13 . . . . . 19 B4
Cedar Gr
Chester CH2 . . . . 119 B4
Haydock WA11 . . . . 1 E7
Macclesfield SK11 . . . . . . 112 D5
Nantwich CW5 . . . . 205 A5
Neston CH64 . . . . 66 F8
Warrington, Latchford
WA4 . . . . 16 D3
Warrington WA1 . . . . 17 A7
Winsford CW7 . . . . 149 A8
Cedar Ho CH3 . . . . 142 B8
Cedar Lo SK7 . . . . 35 F7
Cedar Mews CH1 . . . . 117 E4
Cedar Pk CH3 . . . . 119 C2
Cedar Rd
Newcastle-u-Lyme
ST5 . . . . 210 D1
Partington M31 . . . . 11 E3
Warrington WA5 . . . . 14 F6
Weaverham CW8 . . . . . . 102 C8
Cedars SK9 . . . . 59 F6
Cedar St WA12 . . . . 2 C2
Cedars The
Alsager ST7 . . . . 193 D3
Mobberley WA16 . . . . 58 E2
Nantwich CW5 . . . . 204 D5
8 Northwich CW9 . . . . 103 E6
Cedarway
Bollington SK10 . . . . 88 A7
Heswall CH60 . . . . 41 B6
Wilmslow SK9 . . . . 59 F5
Cedar Way CW2 . . . . 206 B7
Cedarways WA4 . . . . 26 D5
Cedarwood CW8 . . . . 101 D5
Cedarwood Ct CW6 . . . . . 146 C3
Celandine Cl CH3 . . . . . . 142 A7
Celandine Way WA9 . . . . . 6 B7
Celyn Cres CH4 . . . . 140 D5
Cement Pl CH1 . . . . 237 B3
Cemetery Rd CW2 . . . . . . 207 B5
Cemlyn Cl CH2 . . . . 117 E3
Centenary Ho WA7 . . . . . . 49 C8
Centenary Pl CW12 . . . . . 156 E3
Central Ave
Alsager ST7 . . . . 192 F1
Ellesmere Port CH65 . . . . 70 C4
Warrington, Latchford
WA4 . . . . 16 B3
Warrington WA2 . . . . 16 C8
Central Dr
Barnton CW8 . . . . 78 A3
Gatley SK8 . . . . 34 D8
Haydock WA11 . . . . 1 B6
Central Expressway
WA7 . . . . 49 D6
Central Gr CW9 . . . . 104 D6
Central Pl SK9 . . . . 60 B7
Central Rd
Northwich CW9 . . . . 104 D7
Partington M31 . . . . 11 F3

Central Rd *continued*
 Warrington WA4 . . . . .16 C3
Central St ST7. . . . . .195 B6
Central Trad Pk CH4 . . . . . .140 E7
Central Way
 Newton-le-W WA12. . . . . .2 E2
 Warrington WA2 . . . . .16 B6
Centre Ct ST7 . . . . .193 E4
Centre Park Sq WA1. . . . . . .16 A4
Centre Pk WA1. . . . . .16 A4
Centurion Cl WA3 . . . . .9 D4
Centurion Row WA7 . . . . . . .23 F2
Centurion Way CW10 . . . . .128 D2
Century Rd ST5. . . . . .210 F2
Century Way SK10 . . . . .87 E2
Cestria Cl CW11 . . . . .174 D7
Chads Gn CW5 . . . . .206 A1
Chadwell Cl CW2. . . . . .207 E4
Chadwick Ave
 Croft WA3 . . . . .9 B7
 Warrington WA4 . . . . .16 E1
Chadwick Cl SK9 . . . . .34 C1
Chadwick Cl CW10 . . . . . . .151 D7
Chadwicke Cl CW5 . . . . . . .204 F4
Chadwick Fields Orch
 CW10. . . . . .151 D6
Chadwick Pl WA3. . . . . .9 E5
Chadwick Rd
 Middlewich CW10 . . . . .151 C6
 Runcorn WA7 . . . . .23 E3
Chadwick Terr SK10. . . . . . . .87 E1
Chaffinch Cl
 Congleton CW12 . . . . .156 E1
 Warrington WA3 . . . . .9 F3
Chaffinch Way CW7. . . . . . .149 D6
Chaigeley Sch WA4. . . . . . . .17 E4
Chailey Rise CH3 . . . . .182 D1
Chain Maker's Row
 WA6. . . . . .75 D2
Chamberlain Ct CW1 . . . . . .191 C4
Chamberlain Dr SK9 . . . . . . .34 D1
Chambers St CW2 . . . . .190 D2
Chance Hall La CW12,
 ST7. . . . . .177 C3
Chancel La SK9. . . . . .60 B8
Chancellor Rd WA7 . . . . .24 D5
Chancery La
 Alsager ST7. . . . . .193 B3
 Bollington SK10. . . . . .88 B7
Chandlers Ct WA7 . . . . .22 E1
Chandler Way WA3 . . . . .3 E8
Chandos Cl CW4 . . . . .141 E6
Change La CH64 . . . . .68 B8
Channel The CH1. . . . . .95 B4
Chantler Ave WA4 . . . . .16 E4
Chantry Ave CW8 . . . . .103 B4
Chantry Cl SK12 . . . . .38 E5
Chantry Ct
 Chester CH1 . . . . .117 E2
 Crewe CW1 . . . . .190 D4
Chantry Fold SK12 . . . . .38 E6
Chantry Rd SK12 . . . . .38 E6
Chantry The CW6 . . . . .169 E2
Chantry Wlk CH60 . . . . .41 A6
Chapel Ave WA6. . . . . .75 C2
Chapel Bank ST7 . . . . .195 D6
Chapel Cl
 Northwich CW9. . . . . .103 F7
 Wilmslow SK9 . . . . .60 A6
Chapel Dr WA15. . . . . .32 C7
Chapelfields WA6. . . . . .74 A8
Chapel Gn CW6. . . . . .122 C5
Chapel House La CH64. . . . .93 A7
Chapel La
 Acton Bridge CW8. . . . . .76 E4
 Aldford CH3. . . . . .164 D5
 Allostock WA16. . . . . .106 E3
 Altrincham WA15. . . . . .32 C7
 Appleton Thorn WA4 . . . . . . .27 B4
 Audley ST7. . . . . .209 D2
 Burtonwood WA5. . . . . .6 F6
 Chester CH3 . . . . .119 A1
 Crewe CW1 . . . . .173 D1
 Dutton WA4 . . . . .77 B7
 Hargrave CH3 . . . . .144 A1
 Harriseahead ST7 . . . . .195 E4
 Hollins Green WA3 . . . . .10 F1
 Holt LL13 . . . . .196 D8
 Kelsall CW6 . . . . .122 E2
 Kingsley WA6. . . . . .75 C2
 Ledsham CH66. . . . . .68 F1
 Manley WA6, CH3. . . . . .98 F3

Chapel La *continued*
 Mere WA16. . . . . .30 B4
 Milton Green CH3 . . . . .165 B2
 Moulton CW9. . . . . .126 E8
 Norton in Hales TF9. . . . . . .236 C2
 Partington M31. . . . . .11 F2
 Rainow SK10 . . . . .88 E5
 Ravensmoor CW5 . . . . .203 D2
 Rode Heath ST7. . . . . .193 F7
 Saighton CH3. . . . . .142 E1
 Threapwood SY14 . . . . .222 E8
 Warrington WA4 . . . . .26 C8
 Widnes WA8 . . . . .12 C4
 Wilmslow SK9 . . . . .60 A6
 Windyharbour SK11. . . . . . .109 D2
 Woodbank CH1 . . . . .93 E8
Chapel Lo CH1. . . . . .237 C3
Chapelmere Cl CW11 . . . . .174 E7
Chapelmere Ct CW1 . . . . . .190 C7
Chapel Mews
 Alsager ST7 . . . . .193 C3
 Ellesmere Port CH65 . . . . . . .70 B4
 Elton CH2. . . . . .72 B3
 1 Nantwich CW5 . . . . .204 E5
Chapel Mus* ST7 . . . . .195 D7
Chapel Rd
 Alderley Edge SK9. . . . . .60 A1
 Horwich End SK23. . . . . .65 E5
 Ollerton WA16. . . . . .82 F6
 Warrington WA5 . . . . .14 E3
 Wilmslow SK9 . . . . .61 A8
 Winsford CW7 . . . . .126 F1
Chapel Rise SY14 . . . . .213 B3
Chapel Row
 Barbridge CW5 . . . . .187 D6
 Nantwich CW5 . . . . .204 D5
Chapel St
 7 Alderley Edge SK9. . . . . .60 A1
 Audley ST7. . . . . .209 E3
 Bollington SK10. . . . . .88 B8
 Chester CH3 . . . . .237 C3
 Congleton CW12 . . . . .156 D2
 Crewe CW2 . . . . .190 D3
 Haydock WA11. . . . . .1 E6
 Holt LL13 . . . . .196 D8
 Kidsgrove ST7 . . . . .194 D2
 Macclesfield SK11. . . . . . . .112 D6
 Moulton CW9. . . . . .126 E8
 Mount Pleasant ST7 . . . . . .195 B6
 New Mills SK22 . . . . .39 B6
 Newton-le-W WA12. . . . . .2 B3
 Northwich CW8 . . . . .103 E7
 Sandbach CW11 . . . . .175 B6
 Sandbach, Wheelock
 CW11 . . . . .175 A3
 Weaverham CW8. . . . . .77 C1
 Whaley Bridge SK23 . . . . . . .65 E8
 Widnes WA8 . . . . .23 A7
 Wilmslow SK9 . . . . .79 C3
Chapel Terr WA3. . . . . .4 C3
Chapel View
 Bebington CH62. . . . . .44 A6
 Helsby WA6. . . . . .73 B2
Chapel Wlk WA3. . . . . .4 A8
Chapel Wlks
 Broomedge WA13 . . . . .19 D1
 Cheadle SK8 . . . . .35 B6
Chapel Yd WA2 . . . . .16 A6
Chapman Cl WA8 . . . . .12 D4
Chapterhouse Cl CH65 . . . . .70 E5
Charcoal Rd WA14. . . . . .20 F3
Charity La
 Macclesfield Forest
 SK11. . . . . .114 B6
 Macclesfield SK11. . . . . . . .113 F8
Charlcote Cres CW2 . . . . . .206 C8
Charlcote Rd SK12 . . . . .36 F4
Charles Ave
 Davenham CW9. . . . . .103 F2
 Warrington WA5 . . . . .14 F6
Charles Cres CH4. . . . . .237 C1
Charles Ct CW2. . . . . .190 B3
Charles Darwin Prim Sch
 CW8. . . . . .103 E7
Charles Forbes Ct **7**
 WA1. . . . . .16 B5
Charles Price Gdns **8**
 CH65 . . . . .70 C6
Charles Rd CH2 . . . . .95 C1
Charles Sq CW11. . . . . .175 F2
Charles St
 Chester CH1 . . . . .237 B3
 Chester, Hoole Park
 CH2 . . . . .118 F3
 4 Crewe CW1 . . . . .190 C4
 Irlam M44 . . . . .11 E6
 Widnes WA8 . . . . .23 A8
Charleston Cl CH66. . . . . . . .69 D2
Charleston Gr WA5 . . . . .15 B6
Charlesworth Cl SK23 . . . . . .39 D3
Charlesworth Cres
 SK23. . . . . .39 D3
Charlesworth Ct
 CW11. . . . . .175 C6
Charlesworth Pl **1**
 CW12. . . . . .156 F4
Charlesworth Rd SK23 . . . . .39 D3
Charlesworth St CW11 . . . .190 D6
Charlock Wlk **6** M31 . . . . . .11 F3
Charlotte Ct CH1 . . . . .237 B3
Charlotte Gn **6** WA5 . . . . . .15 C7
Charlotte St W **22**
 SK11. . . . . .112 C8
Charlotte St
 Chester CH1 . . . . .118 B2
 Macclesfield SK11. . . . . . . .112 C8
Charlotte Wlk **2** WA8 . . . . . .23 B7
Charlton Ct WA7 . . . . .50 A7

Charlton Ct CH2. . . . . .119 A4
Charlton St
 22 Macclesfield SK11 . . . . .112 C8
 Warrington WA4 . . . . .16 F3
Charminster Cl WA5. . . . . . .15 B5
Charmouth Cl WA12 . . . . .2 A4
Charnock Ave WA12. . . . . . . .1 F3
Charnock Rd WA3 . . . . .4 F7
Charnwood
 High Lane SK6. . . . . .37 F7
 Kidsgrove ST7. . . . . .195 B1
Charnwood Cl
 Macclesfield SK10. . . . . .87 A1
 Warrington WA3 . . . . .9 F4
Charnwood Cres SK7 . . . . . .36 D8
Charon Way WA5. . . . . .15 B7
Charter Ave WA5. . . . . .16 A8
Charter Cres CH66. . . . . .69 E3
Charterhall Dr CH2 . . . . . . .118 F2
Charter Rd SK10. . . . . .88 A7
Charter Way SK10 . . . . .87 F3
Chartley Gr CW10. . . . . .128 D2
Chartwell Gdns WA4. . . . . . .26 F5
Chartwell Gr CW7 . . . . .149 C5
Chase Dr CH66 . . . . .69 E2
Chaser Ct CH1. . . . . .117 F3
Chase The
 Bebington CH63. . . . . .43 C5
 5 Heswall CH60. . . . . .41 A8
Chasewater WA7 . . . . .24 F4
Chase Way CH66. . . . . .69 E2
Chassagne Sq CW1. . . . . . .189 F7
Chatburn Cl CW3 . . . . .230 A4
Chatfield Dr WA3 . . . . .9 E3
Chatham St **9** SK11. . . . . . .112 D8
Chatham Way CW1 . . . . . . .191 C5
Chatsworth Ave
 Culcheth WA3 . . . . .4 F4
 Macclesfield SK11. . . . . . . .111 E6
Chatsworth Cl
 Ellesmere Port CH66. . . . . . .69 C5
 Northwich CW9 . . . . .104 A5
 Wistaston CW2 . . . . .206 A7
Chatsworth Dr
 Chester CH2 . . . . .119 A5
 Congleton CW12 . . . . .155 F3
 Widnes WA8 . . . . .12 C3
Chatsworth Ho CH1. . . . . . .118 B3
Chatsworth Rd
 Hazel Grove SK7 . . . . .36 F8
 High Lane SK6. . . . . .37 F6
 Wilmslow SK9 . . . . .59 E4
Chatteris Pk WA7 . . . . .24 E2
Chatterton Dr WA7 . . . . .50 E8
Chatterton Ho **16**
 CW5. . . . . .204 E5
Chaucer Cl CH1 . . . . .117 E6
Chaucer Gr CW11. . . . . .174 C5
Chaucer Pl WA4 . . . . .16 B4
Chaucer St WA7 . . . . .23 A1
CHEADLE HULME 35 A8
Cheadle Hulme High Sch
 SK8. .35 B7
Cheadle Hulme Sch
 SK8. .35 A8
Cheadle La WA16. . . . . .81 A1
Cheadle Wood SK8 . . . . .34 F8
CHECKLEY 221 C1
Checkley Dr ST8. . . . . .179 D1
CHECKLEY GREEN 232 B8
Checkley La CW3,
 CW5. . . . . .221 E1
Checkley Rd ST5 . . . . .210 C1
Checkley Row CW5. . . . . . . .232 C8
Cheddar dr WA9. . . . . .6 F7
Cheddington Cl SK8 . . . . . . .35 A7
Chedlee Dr SK8 . . . . .34 E8
Chedworth Dr WA8 . . . . .12 C4
Chedworth Ho **12**
 CH1 . . . . .237 C3
Cheerbrook Rd CW5. . . . . . .205 D4
Cheese Hill La WA6,
 CH66. . . . . .101 B4
Cheethams La WA16 . . . . . . .84 B2
Chelford Ave WA3 . . . . .3 D8
Chelford CE Prim Sch
 SK11. . . . . .84 A3
Chelford Cl
 Chester CH1 . . . . .117 F1
 Warrington WA4 . . . . .26 C8
Chelford Dr CW9 . . . . .103 F5
Chelford La WA16. . . . . .83 C1
Chelford Mews **2**
 CH3 . . . . .119 B1
Chelford Rd
 Chelford, Marthall WA16,
 SK11. . . . . .83 D4
 Chelford SK10, SK11. . . . . . .84 D1
 Congleton CW12 . . . . .155 E6
 Goostrey CW4 . . . . .131 B7
 Handforth SK9 . . . . .34 D5
 Macclesfield SK10,
 SK11. . . . . .111 C8
 Monks Heath SK10 . . . . .85 B1
 Nether Alderley SK9. . . . . . . .84 C7
 Ollerton WA16. . . . . .82 D7
 Prestbury SK10 . . . . .86 D5
 Whisterfield SK11. . . . . .109 F3
Chelford Rdbt SK11 . . . . .84 B1
Chelford Sta SK11 . . . . .84 A2
Chells Hill CW11 . . . . .176 C1
Chell St CW1 . . . . .190 B5
Chelsea Cl ST8 . . . . .179 C1
Chelsea Gdns WA5 . . . . .15 C4
Cholston Dr SK6. . . . . .34 C6

Cheltenham Cl
 2 Macclesfield SK10 . . . . . .87 C4
 Warrington WA5 . . . . .15 A8
Cheltenham Cres
 Crewe CW1. . . . . .190 B7
 Runcorn WA7. . . . . .49 B6
Cheltenham Dr WA12. . . . . . .2 C5
Cheltenham Rd CH65 . . . . . .70 D3
Chemical St WA12 . . . . .2 B3
Cheney Wlk CW2 . . . . .206 D8
Chepstow Cl
 Biddulph ST8. . . . . .179 C1
 Macclesfield SK10 . . . . .87 C4
 Warrington WA5 . . . . .7 E3
 1 Winsford CW7 . . . . .149 C7
Cherington Cl SK9 . . . . .34 F3
Cherington Cres
 SK11. . . . . .112 B7
Cheriton Way CW2. . . . . . . .206 A8
Cherrington Rd CW5. . . . . .204 E3
Cherry Blossom Rd
 WA7. . . . . .49 F4
Cherry Brow Terr
 CH64 . . . . .67 F8
Cherry Cl
 Newcastle-u-Lyme
 ST5. . . . . .210 D1
 Newton-le-W WA12. . . . . .1 F4
 Willaston CH64 . . . . .67 C8
Cherry Cnr WA13 . . . . .28 A7
Cherry Cres CW7 . . . . .149 C8
Cherry Dale Rd CH4 . . . . . .139 A3
Cherryfields Rd SK11 . . . . .111 F8
Cherry Gdns CH3 . . . . .119 A1
Cherry Gr
 Ellesmere Port CH66. . . . . . .70 A1
 Nantwich CW5 . . . . .204 D5
Cherry Grove Prim Sch
 CH3 . . . . .119 A1
Cherry Grove Rd CH3 . . . . .119 A1
Cherry La
 Congleton CW12 . . . . .179 E8
 Cuddington CW8 . . . . .101 F2
 Lawton Heath ST7 . . . . .193 E6
 Warrington WA3 . . . . .18 C1
 Weaverham CW8. . . . . .102 D8
Cherry Orch/Y Berllan
 Geirios LL13 . . . . .196 D8
Cherry Rd CH3 . . . . .119 A1
Cherrysutton WA8 . . . . .12 B3
Cherrysutton Mews
 WA8. . . . . .12 B4
Cherry Tree Ave
 Barnton CW8 . . . . .78 A4
 Lawton-gate ST7 . . . . .194 A5
 Lymm WA13 . . . . .18 D2
 Poynton SK12 . . . . .36 F3
 Runcorn WA7. . . . . .49 C8
 Warrington WA5 . . . . .14 F4
Cherry Tree Cl
 Elton CH2. . . . . .72 B4
 Hale L24 . . . . .21 E1
 Haydock WA11. . . . . .1 A5
 Wilmslow SK9 . . . . .60 E8
Cherry Tree Ct CW5. . . . . . .205 A4
Cherry Tree Dr
 Hazel Grove SK7 . . . . .37 A8
 St Helens WA9. . . . . .1 A2
Cherry Tree Ho SK9 . . . . .85 C8
Cherry Tree La
 Rostherne WA14 . . . . .30 C6
 Woore CW3 . . . . .232 C2
Cherry Tree Mews **3**
 CH60 . . . . .41 A8
Cherry Tree Prim Sch
 WA13. . . . . .18 C2
Cherry Tree Rd
 Audley ST7. . . . . .209 F1
 Crewe CW1 . . . . .190 E6
 Golborne WA3 . . . . .3 F8
 Newcastle-u-Lyme ST5 . . . .210 E1
Cherry Tree Way
 CW12. . . . . .156 D2
Cherry Wlk
 Cheadle SK8 . . . . .35 C8
 Partington M31. . . . . .11 D2
 Swan Green WA16. . . . . . . .106 D7
Cherrywood Cres CW8 . . . . .78 B4
Cherwell Cl
 Cheadle SK8 . . . . .35 A7
 Warrington WA2 . . . . .8 D2
Cheryl Ct CW8. . . . . .102 A4
Cheryl Dr WA8 . . . . .13 D1
Chesford Grange WA1 . . . . .17 F7
Chesham Cl SK9. . . . . .59 F4
Chesham Rd SK9 . . . . .59 F4
Chesham St CH1 . . . . .237 C3
Cheshire Acad CW1. . . . . . .190 E2
Cheshire Candle
 Workshops* CH3 . . . . .184 C5
Cheshire Cl WA12 . . . . .2 E3
Cheshire Farm Ice
 Cream* CH3. . . . . .166 C4
Cheshire Military Mus*
 CH1 . . . . .237 A1
Cheshire Oaks High Sch
 CH65 . . . . .70 C2
Cheshire Oaks Outlet
 Village* CH65. . . . . .70 C2
Cheshire Oaks Way
 CH65. . . . . .70 C2
Cheshire Pk WA6 . . . . .97 D5
Cheshire Rd M31. . . . . .11 D2
Cheshire Row WA16 . . . . . .108 B8
Cheshire St CW3 . . . . .229 F4
Cheshire View
 Audley ST7. . . . . .210 A1

Cheshire View *continued*
 Bollington SK10. . . . . .88 B6
 Chester CH4 . . . . .141 E7
Cheshyre Dr WA7. . . . . .23 F1
Cheshyre's La WA7 . . . . .48 E7
Chessington Cl WA4 . . . . . . .26 F6
CHESTER 237 B2
Chester Aerospace Pk
 CH5 . . . . .139 B6
Chester App
 Aldford CH3. . . . . .163 E7
 Eccleston CH4. . . . . .141 D2
Chester Ave WA3 . . . . .3 D8
Chesterbank Bsns Pk
 CH4 . . . . .140 D7
Chester Bsns Pk CH4 . . . . .141 D8
Chester Castle* CH1 . . . . . .237 A1
Chester Cl
 Handforth SK9. . . . . .34 E2
 Irlam M44 . . . . .11 D5
 Runcorn WA7. . . . . .24 A2
 Talke ST7 . . . . .210 D7
Chester Ent Ctr CH2 . . . . . .237 C4
Chesterfield Cl CW7 . . . . . .125 F1
Chesterfield Rd CH62. . . . . .43 D4
Chestergate SK11
 SK11. . . . . .112 D8
Chester Heritage Ctr*
 CH1 . . . . .237 B2
Chester High Rd
 Neston CH64. . . . . .41 E4
 Willaston CH64 . . . . .67 D7
Chester La CW7 . . . . .125 D2
Chester New Rd WA4 . . . . . .25 F7
Chester Race Course*
 CH1 . . . . .237 A1
Chester Rd
 Acton CW5. . . . . .204 A6
 Aston WA7. . . . . .50 B4
 Audley ST7. . . . . .209 D2
 Barbridge CW5 . . . . .187 D5
 Broughton CH4 . . . . .139 D5
 Churton CH3 . . . . .180 F6
 Connah's Quay CH6. . . . . . . .91 A3
 Cuddington CW8 . . . . .101 D1
 Daresbury WA4 . . . . .25 B1
 Delamere CW6, CH8. . . . . .123 C5
 Dunham-on-t-H CH2,
 WA6. . . . . .97 D5
 Ellesmere Port, Great Sutton
 CH66. . . . . .69 D4
 Ellesmere Port, Whitby CH65,
 CH66. . . . . .70 A2
 Frodsham WA6 . . . . .74 A7
 Gatesheath CH3 . . . . .165 E5
 Grappenhall WA4. . . . . .17 B1
 Hartford CW8 . . . . .102 E3
 Hartford, Greenbank
 CW8 . . . . .103 C6
 Hazel Grove SK7 . . . . .36 D8
 Helsby WA6. . . . . .73 C4
 Heswall CH60, CH64 . . . . . . .41 C6
 Higher Walton WA4 . . . . .26 B1
 Holmes Chapel CW4 . . . . . .130 B2
 Huntington CH3. . . . . .142 A6
 Kelsall CW6. . . . . .122 D5
 Lavister LL12. . . . . .162 C1
 Macclesfield SK11. . . . . . . .112 B8
 Malpas SY14 . . . . .213 B4
 Mere WA16 . . . . .56 B6
 Middlewich CW10 . . . . .128 B2
 Neston CH64. . . . . .66 E7
 Over Tabley WA16. . . . . .56 A2
 Plumley WA16 . . . . .80 E5
 Poynton SK12 . . . . .36 B4
 Rostherne WA14, WA16. . . . .30 C6
 Runcorn WA7. . . . . .50 C4
 Saltney CH4. . . . . .140 C6
 Sandycroft CH5 . . . . .116 A2
 Talke ST7 . . . . .210 D7
 Warrington WA4 . . . . .16 A2
 Whitchurch SY13 . . . . .225 D2
 Winsford CW7 . . . . .125 F2
 Woodford SK7 . . . . .35 E2
Chester Ret Pk CH1 . . . . . . .118 A3
Chester Row WA12 . . . . .2 B8
Chester's Croft Pk SK8. . . . .35 A5
Chester Sq CW1 . . . . .190 C4
Chester St
 Chester CH4 . . . . .140 F7
 Crewe CW1 . . . . .190 C4
 Warrington WA2 . . . . .16 B6
 Widnes WA8 . . . . .13 B1
Chesterton Cl CH3 . . . . .237 C3
Chesterton Cl CW10 . . . . . .151 E6
Chesterton Ct CH2 . . . . . . .118 D4
Chesterton Dr
 Crewe CW2 . . . . .189 F2
 Winwick WA2. . . . . .8 A1
Chesterton Gr CW11 . . . . . .174 D5
Chesterton Way CW2 . . . . .207 E3
Chester Toy & Doll Mus*
 CH1 . . . . .237 B2
Chester Trad Pk CH1. . . . . .117 F2
Chester Way CW9 . . . . .104 A8
Chester West Employment
 Pk CH1 . . . . .117 E2
Chester Zoo* CH2. . . . . .95 E1
Chester Zoological Gdns*
 CH2. . . . . .118 D8
Chestnut Ave
 4 Ellesmere Port
 CH66. . . . . .69 F1
 Irlam M44 . . . . .11 D5
 Macclesfield SK10. . . . . .87 E2

Chestnut Ave continued
Rode Heath ST7 . . . . .193 F7
Shavington CW2 . . . . .206 C5
Warrington WA5 . . . . .14 F6
Widnes WA8 . . . . .13 B2
Chestnut Cl
Chester CH2 . . . . .119 A3
Cuddington CW8 . . . . .101 F7
Middlewich CW10 . . . . .128 B2
Tarporley CW6 . . . . .146 D2
Wilmslow SK9 . . . . .60 E8
Chestnut Ct
Tarporley CW6 . . . . .146 C2
Widnes WA8 . . . . .12 D1
Chestnut Dr
Alsager ST7 . . . . .193 E2
Congleton CW12 . . . . .156 A4
Holmes Chapel CW4 . . . . .130 D3
Poynton SK12 . . . . .36 F3
Chestnut Gr
Barnton CW8 . . . . .78 B4
Bebington CH62 . . . . .43 C8
Crewe CW1 . . . . .190 E5
Golborne WA3 . . . . .3 F8
Newcastle-u-Lyme ST5 . . . . .210 E1
Winsford CW7 . . . . .149 C8
Chestnut Grange CH4 . . . . .141 B7
Chestnut Ho 6 CW11 . . . . .175 B6
Chestnut La WA4 . . . . .73 E4
Chestnut Lodge Specl Sch
WA8 .12 E1
Chestnut Mews WA16 . . . . . .58 E1
Chestnuts The CH64 . . . . . . .67 F8
Chestnut Wlk M31 . . . . .11 D2
Chetham Ct WA2 . . . . .8 A3
Chetton Dr WA7 . . . . .50 E7
Chetwode Mews WA4 . . . . .52 C2
Chetwode St CW1 . . . . .190 C5
Chetwood Cl WA12 . . . . .2 B5
Chetwood Dr WA8 . . . . .12 F4
Cheveley Cl SK10 . . . . .87 C2
Chevin Gdns SK7 . . . . .36 A7
Cheviot Ave WA2 . . . . .8 A3
Cheviot Cl CH66 . . . . .69 A6
Cheviot Ct CW7 . . . . .149 B7
Cheviot Sq CW7 . . . . .149 B7
Chevron Cl CH1 . . . . .117 E4
Chevron Hey CH1 . . . . .117 E4
Cheyne Wlk CW5 . . . . .204 E3
Cheyney Rd CH1 . . . . .118 B3
Chicago Ave M90 . . . . .33 B7
Chichester Cl
Grappenhall Heys WA4 . . . . . .27 A7
Runcorn WA7 . . . . .50 D6
Chichester Ct CH1 . . . . .237 A3
Chichester St CH1 . . . . .237 A3
Chidlow Cl
Hough CW2 . . . . .206 E2
Widnes WA8 . . . . .23 A5
Childer Cres CH66 . . . . .69 B7
Childer Gdns CH66 . . . . .69 B7
CHILDER THORNTON 69 B8
Childer Thornton Prim
Sch CH66 . . . . .69 B8
Child's La CW12 . . . . .177 E6
Childwall Ct CH66 . . . . .69 F8
Childwall Gdns CH66 . . . . . .69 F8
Childwall Rd CH66 . . . . .69 F8
Chilham Cl CW7 . . . . .149 C7
Chilham Pl SK11 . . . . .111 F6
Chilington Ave WA8 . . . . . . .22 D8
Chillingham Cl CW10 . . . . . .128 D2
Chiltern Ave SK11 . . . . .112 A7
Chiltern Cl
Chester CH4 . . . . .141 B5
Chorlton CW2 . . . . .207 B1
Cuddington CW8 . . . . .102 A2
Chiltern Cres WA2 . . . . .8 A3
Chiltern Ct SK10 . . . . .87 D3
Chiltern Pl WA2 . . . . .8 A3
Chiltern Rd
Culcheth WA3 . . . . .4 E4
St Helens WA9 . . . . .1 A3
Warrington WA2 . . . . .8 A3
Chiltern Way CW7 . . . . .149 B7
Chilton Dr CH66 . . . . .69 F7
Chilwell Cl WA8 . . . . .12 D4
Chilworth Cl CW2 . . . . .206 C8
China La WA4 . . . . .16 C2
Chines The CW8 . . . . .101 D5
Chippingdall Cl WA5 . . . . . . .15 C5
Chipstead Cl CW8 . . . . .103 A4
Chirk Cl CH2 . . . . .118 F6
Chirk Gdns CH65 . . . . .70 D3
Chirk Pl CW7 . . . . .126 A1
Chisledon Cl WA11 . . . . .1 D7
Chislet Ct WA8 . . . . .12 E4
Chiswick Cl WA7 . . . . .50 D7
Chiswick Gdns WA4 . . . . . . .26 F6
Chollerton Cl WA16 . . . . . . .29 C4
Cholmley Dr WA12 . . . . .2 E2
Cholmondeley Castle
Gdns* SY14 . . . . .201 A4
Cholmondeley La
SY14 . . . . .200 E7
Cholmondeley Rd
Ellesmere Port CH65 . . . . .69 F4
Hampton Heath SY14 . . . . . . .213 E7
Runcorn WA7 . . . . .49 D4
Wrenbury CW5 . . . . .216 C5
Cholmondeley St
Macclesfield SK11 . . . . .112 D6
Widnes WA8 . . . . .23 A4
CHOLMONDESTON 170 E4

Cholmondeley Rise
SY14 . . . . .214 B4
Cholrugh Grange 6 . . . . .60 A1
CHORLEY 202 B2
CHORLEY BANK 201 F1
Chorley Bank Council Hos
CW5 . . . . .201 E1
CHORLEY GREEN 202 A3
Chorley Green La CW5,
CW5 . . . . .201 E5
Chorley Hall Cl SK9 . . . . .59 F1
Chorley Hall La
Alderley Edge SK9 . . . . .60 A1
Faddiley CW5 . . . . .202 C2
Chorley's La WA8 . . . . .13 E3
Chorley St
Warrington WA2 . . . . .16 B6
Warrington WA2 . . . . .16 C6
Chorley Stock La
CW5 . . . . .202 A2
Chorleywood Cl SK10 . . . . . .87 B4
CHORLTON 207 B1
Chorlton Cl WA7 . . . . .24 D1
Chorlton La CW7 . . . . .207 B2
CHORLTON LANE 212 B4
CHOWLEY 182 F5
Chowley Oak La CH3 . . . . . .182 F6
Chrimes Dr CW8 . . . . .123 F6
Christchurch Ave
CW2 . . . . .190 A1
Christ Church CE Prim
Sch
Ellesmere Port CH65 . . . . .70 B2
Warrington WA2 . . . . .9 A1
Christ Church CE Sch
CW8 .76 B1
Christie Cl CH66 . . . . .44 A2
Christie St WA8 . . . . .13 D1
CHRISTLETON 142 E8
Christleton Ave
Crewe CW2 . . . . .189 D5
Northwich CW9 . . . . .104 A4
Christleton Ct WA7 . . . . .24 C4
Christleton Dr CH66 . . . . .69 E6
Christleton High Sch
CH3 . . . . .142 F7
Christleton Prim Sch
CH3 . . . . .142 E8
Christleton Rd CH3 . . . . .119 A1
Christleton Sports Ctr
CH3 . . . . .142 F8
Christleton Way 15
SK9 . . . . .34 D5
Christopher Dr CH62 . . . . . . .44 A5
Christ The King RC Prim
Sch CH62 . . . . .43 E7
Church Ave SK9 . . . . .34 A2
Church Bank
Audley ST7 . . . . .209 D2
Goostrey CW4 . . . . .107 F1
Kelsall CW6 . . . . .122 D5
Tattenhall CH3 . . . . .166 B2
Church Bk SK23 . . . . .65 D7
Church Cl
Handforth SK9 . . . . .34 D3
Weaverham CW8 . . . . .77 D1
Church College Cl
CH1 .118 B3
Church Cotts
Astle SK11 . . . . .109 B8
Rainow SK10 . . . . .88 E5
Sealand CH1 . . . . .116 E6
Waverton CH3 . . . . .143 C3
Church Croft CH4 . . . . .162 A6
Church Ct
Ashton Hayes CH3 . . . . .121 F8
Farndon CH3 . . . . .180 E2
Church Dr
Newton-le-W WA12 . . . . .2 C1
Warrington WA2 . . . . .9 A1
Church End L24 . . . . .21 D1
Church End Mews L24 . . . . . .21 D1
Church's Ct 15 CW5 . . . . . .204 E5
Church's Mansion*
CW5 . . . . .204 F5
Church Farm CW5 . . . . .216 E4
Church Farm Ct
Hassall CH60 . . . . .40 F7
Willaston CH64 . . . . .67 F8
Churchfield Rd WA6 . . . . .74 C8
Churchfields
Audlem CW3 . . . . .230 A4
Barnton CW8 . . . . .78 B3
Croft WA3 . . . . .9 B7
Cuddington CW8 . . . . .102 B2
Helsby WA6 . . . . .73 C4
Knutsford WA16 . . . . .57 C2
Widnes WA8 . . . . .13 B5
Wybunbury CW5 . . . . .220 B8
Church Fields TF9 . . . . .236 C2
Church Gn WA13 . . . . .19 B8
CHURCH GREEN 18 E2
Church Hall Cl CH1 . . . . .117 F4
CHURCH HILL 149 D6
Church Hill WA16 . . . . .58 A4
Churchill Ave WA3 . . . . .5 B4
Churchill Cl CW12 . . . . .156 A3
Churchill Dr CW6 . . . . .146 D1
Churchill Mans 10
WA7 .23 A3
Churchill Parkway
CW7 . . . . .149 D8
Churchill Way
Macclesfield SK11 . . . . .112 D8
Neston CH64 . . . . .66 E8
Church La
Alderley Edge SK9 . . . . .60 A2

Church La continued
Aldford CH3 . . . . .163 F3
Backford CH1 . . . . .95 D4
Bebington CH62 . . . . .44 A4
Bramhall SK7 . . . . .35 C2
Chester CH2 . . . . .118 D7
Congleton CW12 . . . . .134 F1
Culcheth WA3 . . . . .4 F3
Ellesmere Port CH66 . . . . .69 D3
Farndon CH3 . . . . .180 C1
Golborne WA3 . . . . .3 D7
Guilden Sutton CH3 . . . . .119 F5
Hargrave CH3 . . . . .144 B1
Henbury SK11 . . . . .111 C8
Huxley CH3, CW6 . . . . .167 C6
Lawton-gate ST7 . . . . .194 C4
Mobberley WA16 . . . . .58 C5
Mow Cop ST7 . . . . .195 E7
Nantwich CW5 . . . . .204 E5
Neston CH64 . . . . .66 E7
New Mills SK22 . . . . .39 C8
Rainow SK10 . . . . .88 E5
Sandbach CW11 . . . . .175 E7
Scholar Green ST7 . . . . .194 C7
Smallwood CW11 . . . . .176 E4
Stoak CH2 . . . . .96 A7
Sutton Lane Ends SK11 . . . . .112 F3
Warren SK11 . . . . .134 D8
Warrington WA4 . . . . .17 B1
Weaverham CW8 . . . . .77 D1
Wistaston CW2 . . . . .205 E8
CHURCH LAWTON 194 C3
Church Lawton Prim Sch
ST7 .194 A5
Church Mdw TF9 . . . . .236 C2
Church Mdws
Little Leigh CW8 . . . . .77 D5
Whitchurch SY13 . . . . .226 A1
Church Mead CH4 . . . . .181 A5
Church Meadow La
CH60 .40 F7
Church Meadow Wlk
WA8 .22 B5
Churchmere Cl CW1 . . . . . . .190 C7
Church Mews
Bollington SK10 . . . . .88 B8
Higher Wincham CW9 . . . . .79 E5
Knutsford WA16 . . . . .57 B2
6 Macclesfield SK11 . . . . . .112 D8
CHURCH MINSHULL 172 A6
Church Par 6 CH65 . . . . .70 C6
Church Rd
Alsager ST7 . . . . .193 C4
Ashton Hayes CH3 . . . . .121 F8
Barnton CW8 . . . . .78 B2
Broughton CH4 . . . . .139 C4
Burwardsley CH3 . . . . .184 A5
Cheadle SK8 . . . . .35 B8
Dodleston CH4 . . . . .162 B8
Eccleston CH4 . . . . .141 E2
Frodsham WA6 . . . . .74 C7
Hale L24 . . . . .47 E8
Handforth SK9 . . . . .34 D3
Haydock WA11 . . . . .1 E7
Little Leigh CW8 . . . . .77 D4
Lymm WA13 . . . . .18 E2
Mouldsworth CH3 . . . . .98 F1
New Mills SK22 . . . . .39 C7
Northwich CW9 . . . . .104 A8
Saughall CH1 . . . . .94 A1
Shocklach CH3 . . . . .197 C1
Thornton Hough CH63 . . . . . . .42 B6
Tilston SY14 . . . . .198 B2
Wilmslow SK9 . . . . .59 E4
Worleston CW5 . . . . .188 D6
Church Rise CW8 . . . . .102 B2
Church Row CW6 . . . . .168 F1
Church St N CW6 . . . . .122 C5
Church St W SK11 . . . . .112 C8
Churchside SK10 . . . . .112 D8
Churchside Cl CW1 . . . . .191 D5
Churchside Wlk CH4 . . . . . .140 F7
Church St
Audley ST7 . . . . .209 D2
Audley, Wood Lane ST7 . . . . .210 A1
Bollington SK10 . . . . .88 B8
Chester CH1 . . . . .237 B4
Clanfield Ave WA8 . . . . .12 C3
Connah's Quay CH5 . . . . .91 D1
Davenham CW9 . . . . .104 A3
Ellesmere Port CH65 . . . . .70 C6
Farndon LL13 . . . . .180 E2
Frodsham WA6 . . . . .74 B8
Great Budworth CW9 . . . . .79 A8
Higher Wincham CW9 . . . . .79 E5
Kelsall CW6 . . . . .122 D4
Kidsgrove, Butt Lane
ST7 .194 D1
Kidsgrove, The Rookery
ST7 .195 C4
Macclesfield SK10,
SK11 . . . . .112 D8
Malpas SY14 . . . . .213 B3
Moulton CW9 . . . . .126 F8
Mount Pleasant ST7 . . . . .195 C6
Newton-le-W WA12 . . . . .2 F4
Runcorn WA7 . . . . .23 A3
Sandbach CW11 . . . . .175 C5
Tarvin CH3 . . . . .121 C2
Warrington WA1 . . . . .16 C4
Widnes WA8 . . . . .13 A4
Church Steadings
CH3 .143 C3
Church Terr SK9 . . . . .34 D4
Church View
Audlem CW3 . . . . .230 A4

Church View continued
Handforth SK9 . . . . .34 A2
Higginson CW1 . . . . .191 D5
Kingsley WA6 . . . . .75 B2
16 Knutsford WA16 . . . . .57 A7
Lymm WA13 . . . . .19 B4
New Mills SK22 . . . . .39 C8
Church View Terr
SK11 . . . . .112 F3
Church View Wlk
CW2 . . . . .205 E8
Churchward Cl CH2 . . . . . . .118 D4
Churchway SK10 . . . . .86 F2
Church Way
Alvanley WA6 . . . . .73 A1
Ellesmere Port CH65 . . . . .117 E5
Wybunbury CW5 . . . . .220 B8
Churchway Rd L24 . . . . .21 A2
Church Wlk
Broughton CH4 . . . . .139 C5
Crowton CW8 . . . . .76 C2
2 Ellesmere Port CH65 . . . . .70 C6
Holmes Chapel CW4 . . . . .130 C3
Knutsford WA16 . . . . .57 A2
Lower Peover WA16 . . . . .81 E1
Malpas SY14 . . . . .213 B3
Northwich CW9 . . . . .104 A8
Wilmslow SK9 . . . . .59 F6
Winwick WA2 . . . . .8 A6
Church Wlks
Christleton CH3 . . . . .142 E8
Norton in Hales TF9 . . . . .236 C2
Churchwood View
WA13 . . . . .18 F3
Churchyard Side
CW5 . . . . .204 E5
CHURTON 180 E5
Churton Cl
Hough CW2 . . . . .206 E3
3 Northwich CW9 . . . . .103 E4
Churton Rd
Chester CH3 . . . . .119 A2
Farndon CH3 . . . . .180 E2
Churton St CH3 . . . . .119 A2
Cicely Mill La WA16 . . . . .30 D3
Cinder Cl CH3 . . . . .119 F5
Cinder Hill CW7 . . . . .125 F6
Cinder-Hill La ST7 . . . . .194 F7
Cinder La
Chelford SK11 . . . . .83 E1
Guilden Sutton CH3 . . . . .119 F5
Lostock Green CW9 . . . . .105 A8
Nantwich CW5 . . . . .188 C2
Over Peover WA16 . . . . .108 C7
Warrington WA4 . . . . .17 F1
Cinder Rock Way ST7 . . . . .195 C1
CINNAMON BROW 8 F4
Cinnamon Brow CE Prim
Sch WA2 . . . . .8 F2
Cinnamon La WA2 . . . . .8 F3
Cinnamon La N WA2 . . . . .8 F3
Cinnamon Pk WA2 . . . . .9 B3
Circle Ave CW5 . . . . .205 E5
Circle The
Crewe CW2 . . . . .190 D1
Mere WA16 . . . . .30 C2
Circuit The
Alderley Edge SK9 . . . . .60 B3
Cheadle SK8 . . . . .35 A7
Wilmslow SK9 . . . . .59 D5
Circular Dr CH4 . . . . .140 F4
City Bank ST8 . . . . .179 C2
City Quays 8 CH1 . . . . .237 C3
City Rd CH1 . . . . .237 C3
City Walls Rd CH1 . . . . .237 A2
City Way Apartments 7
CH1 .237 C3
Civic Way
Ellesmere Port CH65 . . . . .70 B4
Middlewich CW10 . . . . .128 C1
Clair Ave CH5 . . . . .116 A3
Clamhunger La WA16 . . . . . .56 D7
Clamley Ct CH 21 A3
Clamley Gdns L24 . . . . .21 E2
Clanbrook Ave WA13 . . . . . . .19 A2
Clanfield Ave WA8 . . . . .12 C3
Clap Gate Cres WA8 . . . . . . .22 B5
Clap Gates Cres WA5 . . . . . .15 E7
Clap Gates Rd WA5 . . . . . . .15 E7
Clare Ave
Chester CH2 . . . . .119 A3
Handforth SK9 . . . . .34 C3
Clare Dr
Crewe CW2 . . . . .189 F1
Ellesmere Port CH65 . . . . .70 B1
Macclesfield SK10 . . . . .87 C3
Clare Ho CH1 . . . . .117 F6
Claremont Ave WA8 . . . . . . .13 C4
Claremont Cl CW9 . . . . .103 F3
Claremont Dr WA8 . . . . .13 B4
Claremont Rd
Cheadle SK8 . . . . .35 A8
Crewe CW2 . . . . .190 B2
Culcheth WA3 . . . . .4 D4
Runcorn WA7 . . . . .23 B2
Clarence Ave
Chester CH3 . . . . .119 B2
Warrington WA5 . . . . .14 D6
Widnes WA8 . . . . .13 A4
Clarence Ct
Newton-le-W WA12 . . . . .2 A4
Clarence Gr CW1 . . . . .190 B5
Clarence Mill Bsns Pk
SK10 .63 A1
Clarence Rd
Bollington SK10 . . . . .63 A1
Warrington WA4 . . . . .17 B2

Clarence St
Newton-le-W WA12 . . . . .1 F4
Runcorn WA7 . . . . .22 F3
Warrington WA1 . . . . .16 F7
Clarence Terr
Bollington SK10 . . . . .63 A1
1 Nantwich CW7 . . . . .33 A4
Clarendon Cl
Chester CH4 . . . . .141 E6
Runcorn WA7 . . . . .50 D7
Clarendon Cotts SK9 . . . . . . .34 A3
Clarendon Ct WA7 . . . . .7 F4
Clarendon Dr SK10 . . . . .88 A1
Clarendon Rd M44 . . . . .11 F7
Clare Pl CW7 . . . . .149 C7
Clares Farm Cl WA1 . . . . . . .17 F7
Clare St
Harrisehead ST7 . . . . .195 E4
Mount Pleasant ST7 . . . . .195 C6
Clarke Ave
Culcheth WA3 . . . . .5 A4
Warrington WA4 . . . . .16 D2
Clarke Gdns 3 WA8 . . . . . . .23 E7
Clarke La
Bollington SK10 . . . . .87 E5
Langley SK11 . . . . .113 D3
Clarke Terr SK11 . . . . .112 D6
CLARK GREEN 63 A3
Clarks Terr WA7 . . . . .48 D8
Clary Mdw CW8 . . . . .78 A4
Clatterbridge Hospl
CH63 .42 D8
Clatterbridge Rd CH63 . . . . .42 D8
Clatterwick La CW8 . . . . .77 D7
Claude St WA1 . . . . .16 C6
Claughton Ave CW2 . . . . . . .190 C1
Claverton Cl WA7 . . . . .49 B6
Claverton Ct CH4 . . . . .237 C1
Claydon Gdns WA3 . . . . .10 F1
Clay Heyes SK11 . . . . .84 A3
Clayhill Gn CH66 . . . . .69 D7
Clayhill Gr WA3 . . . . .4 B8
Clayhill Light Ind Pk
CH64 .41 F2
Clay La
Bickerton SY14 . . . . .200 B7
Burtonwood WA5 . . . . .6 E5
Handforth SK9 . . . . .34 C5
Haslington CW1, CW11 . . . . .191 D7
Over Peover WA16 . . . . .108 B8
Sandbach CW11, CW1 . . . . . .174 B2
Wilmslow SK9 . . . . .59 C4
Winsford CW7 . . . . .125 B4
Claypit Rd CH4 . . . . .141 B5
Claypits La CH3 . . . . .142 F5
Clayton Ave
Congleton CW12 . . . . .157 A5
Golborne WA3 . . . . .3 E8
Clayton-By-Pass
CW12 . . . . .156 C3
Clayton Cl CW1 . . . . .190 A7
Clayton Cres
Runcorn WA7 . . . . .22 F1
Widnes WA8 . . . . .12 F1
Clayton Dr SY13 . . . . .226 B1
Clayton Rd WA3 . . . . .9 F6
Clayton's Row CW5 . . . . . . .204 E7
Cleadon Way WA8 . . . . .12 E4
Cleaver Mews SK11 . . . . . . .112 C5
Cleaver Rd CH1 . . . . .117 E4
Cledford Cres CW10 . . . . . . .151 E6
Cledford Inf Sch
CW10 . . . . .151 C7
Cledford La CW10 . . . . .151 C7
Cledwen Cres 139 D5
Cleethorpes Rd WA7 . . . . . . .50 C7
Cleeves Cl WA1 . . . . .16 C5
Cleeve Way SK8 . . . . .35 B6
Clegge St WA2 . . . . .16 B7
Clelland St WA4 . . . . .16 C3
Clement Dr CW11 . . . . .174 B6
Clemley Cl CW6 . . . . .122 D6
Clerewood Ave SK8 . . . . .34 B7
Clevedon Cl SK11 . . . . .112 A7
Cleveland Dr CH66 . . . . .69 A6
Cleveland Rd WA2 . . . . .8 B3
Cleveland Way CW7 . . . . . . .149 B7
Cleveleys Ave WA8 . . . . .13 D2
Cleveleys Rd WA5 . . . . .15 B4
Cleves Cl CH1 . . . . .117 D6
Cliffbrook Gr 2 SK9 . . . . . . .34 D2
Cliffe Rd
Crewe CW1 . . . . .190 B7
Neston CH64 . . . . .66 F5
Warrington WA4 . . . . .26 C7
Cliffe St 3 WA8 . . . . .13 C1
Cliff La
Acton Bridge CW8 . . . . .76 C4
Warrington WA3 . . . . .28 B6
Macclesfield SK10, SK11 . . . . .88 B1
Warrington WA4 . . . . .17 D1
Clifford Dr CH4 . . . . .140 F5
Clifford Gr CW1 . . . . .191 C4
Clifford Pl 4 CW7 . . . . .149 C7
Clifford Rd
Macclesfield SK11 . . . . .112 A8
Poynton SK12 . . . . .36 D3
Warrington WA5 . . . . .15 A4
Wilmslow SK9 . . . . .59 F6
Cliff Rd
Acton Bridge CW8 . . . . .76 E4
Wilmslow SK9 . . . . .60 B8
Cliff Side SK9 . . . . .60 B8
Cliff View WA8 . . . . .74 A8
CLIFTON 49 D4

Clifton Ave
Bebington CH62........43 E3
Crewe CW2............190 B3
Culcheth WA3..........4 D3
Clifton Cl WA1.........17 C7
Clifton Cres WA6.......49 C1
Clifton St WA7.........49 B6
Clifton Dr
Blacon CH1............117 E3
Northwich CW9.........104 A5
Wilmslow SK9...........59 E4
Clifton Gdns CH65......70 C3
Clifton La WA7.........49 E3
Cliftonmill Mdws WA3....2 F8
Clifton Park Ave CH5....91 D1
Clifton Rd
Runcorn, Clifton WA7....49 E3
Runcorn, Heath WA7.....49 B6
Sandbach CW11........174 D7
Clifton Rdbt WA7........49 E3
Clifton St
Alderley Edge SK9.......60 A1
Crewe CW2............190 B3
Warrington WA4.........16 C4
Cliftonville Rd WA1......17 D6
Clincton Cl WA8.........22 A8
Clincton View WA8.......22 A8
Clipsley Cres WA11......1 B7
Clipsley La WA11........1 C6
Clitheroe Rd CW8........77 E1
CLIVE...............127 D1
Clive Ave WA2..........8 C1
Clive Back La CW7......150 D7
Cliveden Rd CH4........140 F5
CLIVE GREEN..........150 D6
Clivegreen La CW10.....150 E7
Clive La CW7...........150 C8
Clock Face Rd WA8......13 E8
Clocktower The CW4.....130 D2
Clock Twr The WA4.......16 C2
Cloister Way CH65.......70 E5
Clonners Field CW5......205 A4
Closeburn Ave CH60.....40 E6
Close La
Alsager ST7............192 F3
Mow Cop ST7..........195 D7
Close The
Alsager ST7............193 A3
Hartford CW8..........103 D6
Newton-le-W WA12.......2 E1
Saughall CH1...........94 A1
Tarporley CW6.........146 C2
CLOTTON.............145 D4
Cloudberry Wlk M31......11 F3
CLOUD SIDE..........157 F4
Cloud The* CW12.......158 A4
Cloud View CW12.......157 A2
Clough Ave
Handforth SK9..........34 B2
Warrington WA2.........8 B2
Clough Bank SK10.......87 F7
Clough Field Cl SK23....65 D8
CLOUGH HALL.........210 F8
Clough Hall Dr ST7.....210 E6
Clough Hall Rd ST7.....210 F8
Clough Hall Tech Sch
ST7...................194 F1
Clough La CW8.........103 D6
Clough Rd CW7.........126 E1
Cloughside SK12........38 E6
Clough The WA7.........23 F1
Clough Wlk CW2........206 D8
Cloughwood Sch
CW8..................103 D5
Clovelly Ave WA5.......14 E7
Clovelly Gr WA7.........50 C5
Clover Ave WA8.........74 D7
Clover Ct WA7..........50 B5
Cloverdale CW8........103 C7
Cloverdale Rd SK11.....112 B5
Clover Dr
Pickmere WA16.........79 F7
Winsford CW7.........126 D3
Cloverfield
Lymm WA13............18 F4
Runcorn WA7...........50 C7
Cloverfields CW1.......191 B4
Clover La CH4..........140 F5
Clover Pl CH4..........140 F5
Clowes Ave ST7........193 F2
Clowes St SK11........112 B8
Clumber Cl SK12........36 E3
Clumber Rd SK12........36 E3
CLUTTON.............182 D1
Clutton CE Prim Sch
CH3..................182 D1
Clwyd Cl CH5..........139 B6
Clwyd Way CH66........69 A6
Clyde Ave ST8.........179 E1
Clyde Cres CW7........127 B1
Clyde Gr CW2..........190 A3
Clydesdale CH65........70 B3
Clydesdale Ave CW2.....190 B3
Clydesdale Rd WA4......26 D8
Coach Ho The ST7......194 C4
Coach Rd
Broxton CH3...........183 A3
Edge Green SY14.......199 D2
Little Budworth CW6....147 D8
Coachway SK10..........86 F7
Coalbrookdale Rd
CH64..................41 F2
COALPIT HILL.........210 C8
Coalpit Hill ST7.......210 C8
Coalpit La
Clive Green CW10.......150 F7
Langley SK11..........113 C5

Coalpit La continued
Mollington CH1..........94 D4
Coalport Dr CW7.......126 F3
Coare St SK10..........87 D1
Coastguard La CH64....41 B1
Coatings By Pass Rd
CH5...................91 F2
Coatings Two CH5.......91 F2
Cobal Ct WA4...........74 B8
Cobbett's Way SK9......59 F4
Cobblers Cross La
CW6..................146 E2
Cobblers La / Lon Y
Cryddion** LL12.........161 B1
Cobbles The
Chester CH4...........141 D7
Cuddington CW8........101 D4
Lower Peover WA16.....81 E1
Cobblestone Ct CH2....119 E8
COBBS................26 E8
Cobbs Inf Sch The
WA4...................26 E8
Cobbs La
Hough CW2............206 E2
Warrington WA4........26 E8
Cobden St
Newton-le-W WA12.......2 D4
Warrington WA2........16 B6
Cob Hall La WA6........98 D5
Cob Moor Rd ST7.......195 A4
COBSCOT.............235 E3
Cock Hall La SK11......113 D3
Cockhedge La WA1......16 C5
Cockhedge Sh Ctr
WA1...................16 B5
Cockhedge Way WA1.....16 B5
Cockington Cl CW4.....104 A4
Cock La
Great Budworth CW9.....78 F8
Sound CW5............217 F4
Cocklade La L24........21 D1
Cock Lane Ends WA8....22 B4
Cockpit La WA8........102 B1
Cockshades farm
CW5..................206 C2
Cocksheadhey Rd
SK10...................63 C1
Cocksmoss La
Congleton SK11........134 A3
Marton SK11...........133 D3
Cocoa Gdns [11] CW5...204 E5
Cocoa Yd The [10]
CW5..................204 E5
CODDINGTON.........182 A3
Coe La WA14...........30 C7
Cogshall La
Anderton CW9..........78 C5
Comberbach CW9........78 B7
Colchester Ho [10]
CH1..................237 C3
Colchester Sq CH4.....140 F5
COLDHARBOUR........164 F5
Coldmoss Dr CW11......175 C4
COLD MOSS HEATH....175 C5
Coldstream Ct WA2......8 E3
Coldstream Dr CH66.....68 F5
Cole Ave WA12..........2 C4
Colebrook Cl WA3.......10 A4
Coleclough Pl WA3......4 F4
Coleg Glannau Dyfrdwy/
Deeside Coll CH5.......91 B1
Colehill Bank CW12.....156 E2
Colehill Pl CH5.........91 D1
Colemere Ct WA1........17 A8
Colemere Ct CH65.......70 C7
Coleridge Cl
Blacon CH1............118 A5
Sandbach CW11........174 C5
Coleridge Gr WA8.......12 E1
Coleridge Way CW1.....190 F5
Colinwood Ave CH4.....139 B3
Coliseum Way CH5.......70 D2
Collar House Dr SK10....86 E6
College Cl
Warrington, Fearnhead
WA2...................9 B2
Warrington WA1........16 D5
Wilmslow SK9..........59 F8
College Fields
Crewe CW2............190 A1
Widnes WA8............12 F5
College Gn CH4........141 D7
College La CH4.........168 F1
College of Law
(Christleton Hall)
CH3...................142 D8
College Rd ST7.........193 B5
College View CH5.......91 C1
Colley La CW11........175 D5
Colleys La CW5.........205 B7
Colliers La CW9.........54 E2
Collier's Row WA7.......48 E7
Collier St WA7..........22 F3
Collicry Green Cl CH64..66 C5
Colliery Green Ct CH64..66 E5
Colliery Green Dr
CH64..................66 E5
Collinbrook Ave CW2...190 B1
Collingham Gn CH66......69 B5
Collingham Way CW1....126 D1
Collingtree Ave CW7....127 A3
Collingwood Cl
Macclesfield SK10.......87 B2
Poynton SK12..........37 A3
Collingwood Rd WA12....2 B3
COLLINS GREEN.........1 E1
Collins Green La WA3....1 E1
Collinson Ct [2] WA6....74 B8

Collins St CW2.........190 A3
Collin St WA5...........15 F5
Colne Rd WA5............6 F6
Colorado Cl WA5........15 C7
Colshaw Dr SK9.........34 D2
Colshaw Hall Cotts
WA16..................82 F1
Colshaw La SK11.......109 E1
Colson Ct CW2.........237 A4
Coltsfoot Cl CH3.......142 B5
Columbine Cl
Huntington CH3........142 A6
Widnes WA8............12 B4
Columbine Way WA4.....6 B7
Columbine Wlk [8] M31..11 F3
Colville Ct WA2..........8 A3
Colville Rd SK11........111 F8
Colwyn Cl
Ellesmere Port CH65.....70 D3
Warrington WA5.........7 E2
Colwyn Rd SK7..........35 F8
COMBERBACH..........78 C7
Comberbach Dr CW5.....205 A4
Comberbach Prim Sch
CW9...................78 C8
Combermere Pl [8]
CW1..................190 B5
Comber La WA6.........82 A8
Comboy Dr CW9........104 C6
Combs CW9.............104 C6
Combs CI SK22.........39 A8
Commercial Ave SK8....34 F5
Commercial Rd SK10....112 E8
Common Farm La
SK11...................83 E1
Commongate SK10......112 E8
Commonhall St CH1.....237 A2
Common La
Betley CW3............221 F6
Chelford SK11...........83 E1
Culcheth WA3...........4 E4
Duddon CW6...........145 C7
Hapsford WA6...........72 D1
Kelsall CW6............122 C3
Lach Dennis CW9.......105 E5
Norbury SY13..........215 C5
Stretton WA4...........52 E8
Warrington WA4.........16 E2
Waverton CH3..........143 B4
Winsford CW7.........125 B5
Common Rd WA12, WA5....1 E3
COMMONSIDE.........100 B8
Commonside WA6........73 E1
COMMON SIDE........124 D3
Commons Mill CW11....175 B7
Common St WA12........1 E3
Commons The CW11....175 B6
Common The
Kelsall CW6............122 C3
Runcorn WA7...........49 F8
Commonwealth Cl
CW7..................149 D6
Commonwood Rd
LL13..................196 A8
Company's Cl WA7.......48 F6
Compass Ct WA7........50 D5
Compton Cl WA11........1 C7
Compton Pl
Chester CH4...........141 A6
Ellesmere Port CH65.....70 B5
Comrie Rd WA2..........8 D2
Concourse Way WA9.....1 A2
Condliffe Cl CW11......175 C5
Conery Cl WA6..........73 C4
Coney Gr WA7...........50 B5
CONGLETON...........157 A4
Congleton Bsns Ctr
CW12.................156 F3
Congleton Bsns Pk
CW12.................156 C4
Congleton Cl SK9........85 A8
CONGLETON EDGE.....179 B5
Congleton Edge Rd
CW12.................179 B6
Congleton High Sch
CW12.................155 F3
Congleton La SK11.....109 D5
Congleton Mus
CW12.................156 C2
Congleton Rd
Alderley Edge SK9.......60 A1
Biddulph ST8..........179 D2
Broughton CH4.........139 C4
Kidsgrove ST7.........194 D1
Macclesfield SK11......112 B5
Marton SK11...........133 B5
Mow Cop ST7..........178 F1
North Rode SK11.......134 C6
Sandbach, Arclid Green
CW11.................175 B8
Sandbach CW11........175 B8
Scholar Green CW12,
ST7...................177 E3
Siddington SK11.......110 B5
Smallwood CW11.......177 A6
Swettenham CW12......131 F4
Warren SK11...........111 E2
Congleton Rd N ST7....194 E6
Congleton Rd S ST7....194 D3
Congleton Ret Pk
CW12.................156 D4
Congleton Sta CW12....157 A1
Congleton War Meml
Hospl CW12..........156 D4
Conifer Cl
CH66..................95 A8
Conifer Gr
Moore WA4.............25 A7
Warrington WA5.........14 F7
Conifers The ST7.......193 B3

Conifer Wlk M31........11 E3
Coningsby Dr CW7......126 E1
Coningsby Gdns [15] WA3..3 E8
Coniston Ave
Bebington CH63.........43 C4
Congleton CW12........155 F2
Warrington WA5........14 D4
Winsford CW7.........126 C2
Coniston Cl
Alderley Edge SK9.......84 A7
Hooton CH66............44 B2
Nantwich CW5.........205 A6
Runcorn WA7...........49 D6
Coniston Dr
Frodsham WA6..........74 D8
Handforth SK9..........34 C4
Holmes Chapel CW4....130 A3
Coniston Rd
Chester CH2...........118 F5
High Lane SK6..........37 D8
Neston CH64...........66 E6
Partington M31.........11 E4
Coniston Way SK11.....111 F5
CONNAH'S QUAY.......91 B1
Connah's Quay High Sch
CH5...................91 C1
Connaught Ave WA1.....16 E7
Connaught Cl SK9.......60 C8
Connaught Dr WA12.....2 C2
Conrad Cl CW1.........190 E4
Conroy Way WA12.......7 C8
Consort Cl SK10.........87 E7
Constable Dr SK9........60 E8
Constables Cl WA7......24 A1
Constance Rd M31.......11 F3
Constance Way WA8.....23 A5
Convamore Rd SK7......35 D7
Conway Ave
Irlam M44.............11 F8
Warrington WA5.........7 F2
Winsford CW7.........149 C7
Conway Cl
Crewe CW1............190 C8
Knutsford WA16........82 A8
Saltney CH4...........140 D5
Warrington WA5........14 F6
Conway Cres SK10.......87 F1
Conway Ct CH65.........70 D3
Conway Dr WA12.........2 E3
Conway Ct WA7.........24 A2
Coogee Ave WA5........14 E7
Cook Ave WA11..........1 F7
Cookes Cl CH64.........41 E1
Cookes Ct CH3.........166 B1
Cooke's La CW9........104 F6
Cooksmere La
CW11.................175 A8
Cooks Hill WA6.........99 F8
Cooks La SY13.........225 D7
COOKSONGREEN.......76 A1
Cook St CH65...........70 C6
Coole La
Hack Green CW5.......218 E3
Newhall CW3..........229 C5
Coombe Dr WA7.........49 A8
Coombe Park Ct [1]
CH66..................69 C6
Coombe Pk CH66........69 C6
Co-operative St SK12....38 D6
Cooper Ave
Newton-le-W WA12.......1 F3
Warrington WA2.........8 B2
Coope Rd SK10..........87 E6
Cooperis Fold SK8.......34 F6
Cooper La WA11.........1 C6
Cooner's Croft CH3.....142 A7
Cooper's La CH5.........91 D1
Coopers Opening
CW1..................175 B7
Coopers Pl WA4.........16 C1
Cooper St
Congleton CW12........156 E3
Runcorn WA7...........23 A3
Widnes WA8............13 B1
Cooper Terr CW6.......146 D1
Cope Ave CW5.........204 D4
Copeland Gr WA7.......49 E5
Copeland Rd WA5.......14 C5
Copes La CW5.........204 C4
Copeswood Ct CH4.....139 C3
Copgrove Wlk M22......33 E7
Copley Wlk CW5........204 D5
Cop Mdw SK11.........112 F2
COPPENHALL..........190 D7
Coppenhall Gr CW2.....190 A4
Coppenhall Heyes
CW2..................190 A4
COPPENHALL MOSS....173 D1
Copper Beech Cl CH4...139 C3
Copperfield Cl WA3.......9 C5
Copperfield Rd
Cheadle SK8...........35 B5
Poynton SK12..........36 D2
Copperfields
Poynton SK12..........36 D2
Tarporley CW6.........146 D2
Wilmslow SK9..........60 C8
Copperhill Rd CW12.....179 B7
Coppermine La SY14....184 B2
Copper St SK11........112 E6
Copperwood WA7........24 C1
Copper Wood CW8......101 E5
Coppice Ave SK12........38 A6
Coppice Cl
High Lane SK12.........38 A6
Runcorn WA7...........24 A1

Coppice Cl continued
Willaston CW5.........205 D6
Coppice Ct SK8.........34 B8
Coppice Dr CW10......151 E6
Coppice Gn
Elton CH2..............72 C4
Warrington WA5..........7 A1
Coppice Gr WA16........57 A3
Coppice Ho
Poynton SK12..........36 D2
Talke ST7.............210 C8
Coppice La SK12........38 A5
Coppicemere Dr CW1....191 A2
Coppice Rd
Haslington CW11.......192 A8
Poynton SK12..........37 B3
Talke ST7.............210 C8
Willaston CW5.........205 D6
Coppice Rise SK11.....112 D5
Coppice The
Altrincham WA15........32 B8
Cuddington CW8........101 D5
Horwich End SK23.......65 F5
Nantwich CW5.........204 F3
Sandbach CW11........174 E7
Wincham CW9..........79 C3
Coppice Way SK9........34 E3
Coppins Cl
Chester CH3...........119 A2
Helsby WA6.............73 B4
Coppins The
Warrington WA2.........8 C2
Wilmslow SK9...........59 E4
Copse The
Altrincham WA15........32 D7
High Lane SK6..........37 E7
Newton-le-W WA12.......2 B4
Runcorn WA7............50 A6
COPTHORNE...........229 F4
Copthorne Cl CW12.....156 F2
Copthorne Dr CW3......229 F3
Copyhold CH8.........102 D8
Corbet Ave WA2.........16 B8
Corbet Dr TF9.........235 A4
Corbet St WA2..........16 B8
Corbridge Ho [9] CH1...237 C3
Corfe Way CW7.........149 C7
Coriander Cl CW10......128 C3
Corks La SK12..........38 E5
CORLTON.............207 B1
Cormorant Cl CW1......190 F4
Cormorant Dr WA7......22 E2
Cornbrook Rd SK11....112 C4
Corner Croft SK9........60 A4
Cornerhouse La WA8....12 D3
Corners The CW8.......102 E7
Cornfield Cl
Ellesmere Port CH66.....69 F1
Macclesfield SK10.......87 C3
Cornfield Gr WA8.......12 F3
Cornhill Cl ST5........210 D1
Cornish Cl M22..........33 D8
Cornishway M22.........33 D8
Cornishway Ind Est
M22...................33 D8
Cornmill Cl CW11.......173 D7
Cornmill Ct WA3.........9 A8
Cornubia Rd WA8.......23 D7
Cornwall Ave WA7.......23 A2
Cornwall Cl
[3] Congleton CW12....157 A1
High Lane SK6..........37 F8
Macclesfield SK10.......86 E1
Runcorn WA7............23 D1
Cornwall Gr CW1.......190 B5
Cornwall Ho CH1.......237 B3
Cornwall Rd
Chester CH2...........118 F7
Gatley SK8.............34 B8
Irlam M44.............11 D5
Widnes WA8............13 B3
Cornwall St
Chester CH1...........237 B4
Warrington WA1........16 E7
Warrington WA1.........60 D8
Coronation Ave
Alsager ST7............193 A3
Glazebury WA3..........5 C7
Warrington WA4........17 C2
Winsford CW7.........126 E1
Coronation Bldgs
SK10...................88 A8
Coronation Cres
Crewe CW1............190 E6
Kidsgrove ST7.........194 E1
Sandbach CW11........175 A5
Coronation Dr
Frodsham WA6..........49 D1
Haydock WA11..........2 A7
Newton-le-W WA12.......2 E1
Warrington WA5........14 F4
Widnes WA8............22 C8
Coronation Gr CW8.....78 A4
Coronation Ho WA7.....49 C8
Coronation Mill ST7....195 D7
Coronation Rd
Broughton CH4.........139 B3
Congleton CW12........156 F3
Ellesmere Port CH65.....70 C4
Middlewich CW10.......151 D6
Runcorn, Higher Runcorn
WA7...................23 B1
Runcorn, Preston Brook
WA7...................50 F6

Coronation Sq 🔟
WA16 . . . . 57 A2
Coronation St
Chester CH4 . . . . 140 F7
Crewe CW1 . . . . 190 D5
Macclesfield SK11 . . . . 112 D6
Coronation Terr CW6 . . 146 D1
Coroner's La WA8 . . . . . . 13 A4
Coronet Ave CW9 . . . . . . 103 F3
Coronet Way WA8 . . . . . . 22 B8
CORRA COMMON 233 C1
Correction Brow SK12 . . 37 C6
Corridor Rd CH65 . . . . . . 71 B6
Corwen Cl WA5 . . . . 7 E1
Cosgrove Bsns Pk
CW9 . . . . 78 D3
Cossack Ave WA12 . . . . . . 8 C1
COTEBROOK 147 A8
Cotebrook Dr CH2 . . . . . . 118 E7
Cotebrook Rd CW9 . . . . . 104 C8
Cotebrook Shire Horse
Ctr* CW6 . . . . 147 A7
Cote Lea Ct WA7 . . . . 49 F6
Cotes Pl CH1 . . . . 117 E3
Cotgreaves Ct CH4 . . . . . 141 B5
Cotswold Ave WA3 . . . . 3 D6
Cotswold Cl
Chester CH2 . . . . 118 F6
Cuddington CW8 . . . . 102 A2
Macclesfield SK10 . . . . 86 E1
Cotswold Ct 🔟 CH3 . . . . 119 A1
Cotswold Gr WA9 . . . . 1 A3
Cotswold Pl WA2 . . . . 8 B4
Cotswold Rd WA2 . . . . 8 B3
Cotswold Way CW7 . . . . . 149 B7
Cottage Cl
Bebington CH63 . . . . 43 C5
Neston CH64 . . . . 66 F7
Rudheath CW9 . . . . 104 E8
Cottage Dr E CH60 . . . . . . 40 F5
Cottage Dr W CH60 . . . . . 40 F5
Cottage Gr SK9 . . . . 59 F5
Cottage La
Heswall CH60 . . . . 40 F5
Macclesfield SK10 . . . . 112 F7
Cottage Lawns SK9 . . . . . 60 B2
Cottage Rd CH4 . . . . 141 B5
Cottage St SK11 . . . . 112 B8
Cottages The
Lawton Heath ST7 . . . . 193 D6
Sproston Green CW4 . . . . . 129 C2
Warrington WA4 . . . . 17 F4
Cottam Dr WA2 . . . . 9 A3
Cotterdale Cl WA5 . . . . . . 14 F7
Cotterill WA7 . . . . 49 D8
Cotterill Dr WA1 . . . . 17 C7
Cotterill St CW2 . . . . 190 D2
Cottesmore Dr CH60 . . . . 41 D8
Cottesmore Gdns
WA15 . . . . 32 C8
Cotton La
Christleton CH3 . . . . 120 D2
Runcorn WA7 . . . . 49 D8
Sandbach CW11 . . . . 175 A3
Cotton Mews CW3 . . . . . 230 A4
Cottons Bridge WA4 . . . . 50 F5
Cottonwood Gr ST7 . . . . . 195 E4
Cottrell Rd WA15 . . . . 32 C7
Coulton Rd WA8 . . . . 13 F3
Council Hos
Audlem CW3 . . . . 229 E2
Bickerton SY14 . . . . 200 A8
Congleton CW12 . . . . 156 F4
Newhall CW5 . . . . 228 B8
Council Houses CW5 . . . 216 B6
Countess Ave SK8 . . . . . . 34 E5
Countess Cl 🔟 SK11 . . . 111 F7
Countess Ct CH1 . . . . 118 B5
Countess of Chester
Health Pk CH2 . . . . 118 B6
Countess of Chester Hospl
CH2 . . . . 118 B6
Countess Rd SK11 . . . . . . 111 F7
Countess Way CH2 . . . . . 118 C5
Counting House Rd
SK12 . . . . 38 E5
Country Ctr The*
CH3 . . . . 165 E5
County Terr WA16 . . . . 56 F1
Courier Row SK10 . . . . . . 87 F7
Court 2 SK10 . . . . 87 F1
Court Ho The 🔟 CH65 . . . 70 C6
Courtney Gn WA9 . . . . 34 D2
Courtney Rd CH4 . . . . 140 E5
Court No 4 🔟 SK10 . . . . . 112 C8
Court The CH64 . . . . 66 F6
Courtyard The
Bostock Green CW10 . . . . . 127 D5
Chester CH2 . . . . 118 F6
Congleton CW12 . . . . 156 B3
Cuddington CW8 . . . . 101 E2
Elton CH2. . . . . 72 B4
Haughton CW6 . . . . 186 F4
Newton-le-W WA12 . . . . 2 C4
Smallwood CW11 . . . . 177 A7
🔟 Warrington WA1 . . . . 16 B5
Weaverham CW8 . . . . 102 A8
Willaston CH64 . . . . 67 F8
Cousens Way CH1 . . . . . . 118 B4
Covell Rd SK10 . . . . 36 D5
Coventry Ave CH66 . . . . . 94 E8
Coverdale Cl WA5 . . . . 14 F7
Coverdale Fold CW11 . . . 174 D5
Covert Cl WA7 . . . . 149 B8
Covert Gdns ST7 . . . . 210 D8

Covert Rise CH3 . . . . 166 A2
Cavington Pl CH0 . . . . 60 B6
Cowanway WA8 . . . . 12 F5
Cowbrook La SK11 . . . . . . 135 B6
Cowdell St WA2 . . . . 16 B7
Cowfields CW5 . . . . 204 E6
Cowhey Cl CH4 . . . . 141 B5
Cow Hey La WA6, WA7. . . . 49 A5
Cow La
Ashley WA15 . . . . 31 F6
Rollington SK10 . . . . 88 B7
Hargrave CH1 . . . . 144 A2
Macclesfield SK11 . . . . 112 D6
Norley WA6 . . . . 101 A5
Rainow SK10 . . . . 88 D4
Wilmslow SK9 . . . . 60 C7
Winsford CW7 . . . . 149 E8
Cowley Way CW1 . . . . . . 190 E1
Cowper Cl CW2 . . . . 206 A8
Cowthorne Dr CH3 . . . . . 143 A4
COX BANK 234 F8
Crab La WA2 . . . . 9 B3
Crabmill Dr CW11 . . . . . . 174 E7
Crabmill La
Norley WA6 . . . . 100 E6
Warmingham CW11. . . . . . 173 E7
Crabtree Ave
Altrincham WA15. . . . . 32 D7
Disley SK12 . . . . 38 E5
Crabtree Cl WA12. . . . . 2 E3
Crabtree Ct SK12 . . . . 38 D6
Crabtree Fold WA7 . . . . . . 50 C8
Crabtree Gr CW1 . . . . 190 E6
CRABTREE GREEN 101 C1
Crabtree Green Ct
CW8. . . . . 101 C2
Crabtree Green Pk
CW8. . . . . 101 C1
Crabtree La WA13 . . . . 29 A7
Crabwall Pl CH1 . . . . 117 F5
Crackley Bank ST5. . . . . . 210 E1
Crackley Bank Prim Sch
ST5. 210 E1
Craddock Ct SY14 . . . . . . 213 B3
Cradley WA8 . . . . 12 C2
Cragside Way SK9 . . . . . . 60 C6
Craig Cl SK11 . . . . 112 B5
Craig Dr SK23 . . . . 65 E6
Craig Gdns CH66 . . . . 69 E7
Craigleigh Gr CH62 . . . . . 43 F4
Craig Rd
Congleton CW12 . . . . 156 F4
Macclesfield SK11 . . . . 112 B5
Craigside ST9 . . . . 179 C1
Craig Wlk ST7 . . . . 193 F2
Craithie Rd CH3 . . . . 119 A2
Crampton Dr WA15 . . . . . . 32 C8
CRANAGE 130 A6
Cranage Cl WA7. . . . . 49 D7
Cranage Ct 🔟 CW12 . . . 156 F3
Cranage La CW9 . . . . 79 D1
Cranage Rd CW2 . . . . 190 A3
Cranage Way 🔟 SK9 . . . . 34 D5
Cranberry Dr ST5. . . . . . . 210 D1
Cranberry Inf Sch
ST7. 193 A3
Cranberry Jun Sch
ST7. 193 A3
Cranberry La ST7 . . . . 193 A3
Cranberry Moss La
ST7. 193 A3
Cranberry Rd WA11. . . . . . 11 F3
Cranborne Ave WA4 . . . . . 16 B1
Cranborne Rd CW1 . . . . . 190 A8
Cranebrook Cl CW1. . . . . 190 A8
Crane Ho CH1 . . . . 118 B1
Cranfield Dr ST7 . . . . 193 A3
Cranford Ave
Knutsford WA16 . . . . 56 F1
Warrington WA1 . . . . 17 E8
Cranford Mews ST7. . . . . 193 A3
Cranford Rd SK9. . . . . 34 A1
Cranford Sq WA16. . . . . . . 56 F1
Cranham Ave WA3. . . . . 3 E7
Cranleigh Cl WA4 . . . . 26 B7
Cranleigh Cres CH1. . . . . 118 B4
Cranleigh Dr SK7 . . . . 37 A8
Cranmere Cl CW9 . . . . . . 104 A4
Cranshaw La WA8 . . . . 13 B6
Cransley Sch CW9 . . . . . . 53 E1
Cranswick Gn CH66. . . . . 69 C5
Crantock Dr SK8. . . . . 34 C8
Cranwell Ave WA3 . . . . 4 F4
Craufurd Rd CW12 . . . . . 157 A8
Craven Ave WA3 . . . . 3 E7
Craven Ct WA2 . . . . 7 F4
Crawford Ave WA8. . . . . . . 12 B1
Crawford Pl WA7 . . . . 49 B6
Crawford's Wlk CH2 . . . . 118 F3
Crawley Ave WA2 . . . . 8 A3
Crayford Ave CW12 . . . . . 157 A5
Cresanne Cl CW10 . . . . . 151 C7
Crescent Dr
Furness Vale SK23. . . . . 39 D2
Helsby WA6 . . . . 73 B3
Crescent End
Alderley Edge SK9 . . . . 60 B2
Congleton CW12 . . . . 156 C2
Cranage CW4 . . . . 129 F6
Ellesmere Port CH65 . . . . . 70 D6
Rostherne WA16 . . . . 30 B3
Crescent The
Chester CH2 . . . . 118 D4

Crescent The continued
Congleton CW12 . . . . 156 C2
Ellesmere Port CH65. . . . . . 69 F5
Hartford CW8 . . . . 103 A5
Heswall, Gayton CH60. . . . . 41 B6
Lymm WA13 . . . . 18 F2
Macclesfield SK10 . . . . 87 E1
Middlewich CW10 . . . . 128 B1
Mottram St Andrew
SK10 . . . . 61 A1
Nantwich CW5 . . . . 204 F6
New Mills SK22 . . . . 39 B8
Northwich CW9 . . . . 103 F6
Rostherne WA16 . . . . 30 B3
Utkinton CW6 . . . . 146 B7
Weaverham CW8 . . . . 77 D1
Cressbrook Rd 🔟 WA4. . . 16 C1
Cressington Gdns 🔽
CH65 . . . . 70 C6
Cresswell Ave
Newcastle-u-Lyme
ST5 . . . . 210 D1
New Mills SK22 . . . . 39 C8
Cresswell Cl WA5. . . . . 7 D2
Cresswellshawe Rd
ST7. 193 D4
Cresswell St SK22 . . . . . . 39 C8
Cresta Dr WA7 . . . . 48 F6
Crestwood Cl CW2. . . . . . 206 B7
Crew Ave SK10 . . . . 87 E1
CREWE 190 E5
Crewe Bsns Pk CW1 . . . . 190 F2
CREWE-BY-FARNDON 197 A7
Crewe Gates Farm Ind Est
CW1 . . . . 191 B3
Crewe Gates Ind Est
CW1 . . . . 207 A8
CREWE GREEN 191 B3
Crewe Green Ave
CW1 . . . . 191 A3
Crewe Green Rd CW1. . . 191 A3
Crewe Hall Ent Pk
CW1 . . . . 207 D8
Crewe Hill La CH3 . . . . . . 197 A6
Crewe La CW3 . . . . 180 F1
Crewe La S CH3 . . . . 197 A7
Crewe Rd
Alsager CW3 . . . . 193 B3
Crewe, Crewe Green
CW1 . . . . 191 B3
Crewe CW1 . . . . 190 F2
Haslington CW1, CW11. . . 191 D5
Hatherton CW5 . . . . 219 F3
Lawton-gate ST7 . . . . 193 F4
Nantwich CW2, CW5. . . . . 205 D6
Sandbach CW11 . . . . 175 A5
Shavington CW2 . . . . 206 C6
Crewe St
Chester CH1 . . . . 237 C3
Crewe CW1 . . . . 190 D4
Crewe Sta CW1. . . . . 190 E2
Crewood Common Rd
CW8. . . . . 76 A3
Crib La CW6 . . . . 168 A8
Criccieth Ct CH65. . . . . . . 70 D2
Criftin Cl CH66 . . . . 69 C2
Crimes La CH3, CW6. . . . . 167 D4
Crisham Ave CW5. . . . . . . 218 E8
Crispin Rd M22 . . . . 33 E8
Critchley Rd L24 . . . . 21 A3
Croasdale Dr WA7 . . . . 49 E5
Crocus Gdns WA9 . . . . 6 A7
Crocus St CW8 . . . . 78 B3
Croesmere Dr CH66. . . . . 69 E2
CROFT 9 B8
Croft Cl
Altrincham WA15. . . . . 32 C6
Congleton CW12 . . . . 156 F2
Utkinton CW6 . . . . 146 B7
Waverton CH3 . . . . 143 A5
Croft Cotts
Dunham-on-t-H WA6 . . . . . . 97 E6
Ellesmere Port CH66. . . . . . 69 A8
Croft Ct CH65 . . . . 70 E3
Croften Dr CH64 . . . . 66 E5
Crofters Cl
🔟 Ellesmere Port
CH66. . . . . 69 E1
Pickmere WA16. . . . . 80 A7
Wistaston CW2 . . . . 206 B8
Crofters Ct
Holmes Chapel CW4 . . . . . 130 C3
Newcastle-u-Lyme ST5 . . . 210 D3
Crofters Gn SK9 . . . . 59 F6
Crofters Heath CH66. . . . 69 E1
Crofters La WA16 . . . . 103 D7
Crofters Pk CH5 . . . . 116 A3
Crofters Way CH1 . . . . . . 116 F8
Croft Gdns WA4 . . . . 27 A7
Croft Heath Gdns WA3. . . . 9 A8
Croft Ho WA3 . . . . 3 A7
Croft La
Dodleston CH4. . . . . 162 A7
Knutsford WA16 . . . . 82 B8
Crofton Cl WA4. . . . . 27 C5
Crofton Cotts WA6. . . . . . 100 B8
Crofton Gdns WA3. . . . . . . 4 E3
Crofton Rd WA7 . . . . 22 E1
Croft Pk WA16. . . . . 58 F5
Croft Prim Sch WA3 . . . . . 9 A8
Croft Rd SK9 . . . . 59 E4
Croftside WA1 . . . . 17 F7
Croftside Way SK9. . . . . . . 60 C6
Croft St
Golborne WA3 . . . . 3 A8
Widnes WA8 . . . . 23 A6
Crofts The CH3 . . . . 180 F1

Croftsway CH60 . . . . 40 D8
Croft The
Chester CH2 . . . . 118 D5
Norton in Hales TF9 . . . . . 236 B3
Runcorn WA7 . . . . 23 F1
Croftwood Cl 🔟 CW7 . . 149 A8
Cromdale Way WA5. . . . . . 14 E6
Cromer Dr CW1 . . . . 190 B8
Cromford Ct SK23 . . . . . . 65 E6
Cromford Mews SK23 . . . 65 E5
Cromley Rd SK6. . . . . 37 E6
Crompton Cl CW2. . . . . . . 157 A6
Crompton Dr WA2. . . . . 8 A6
Crompton Rd SK11 . . . . . 112 C7
Crompton Way WA3 . . . . . . 4 B8
Cromwell Ave WA5 . . . . . . 15 D6
Cromwell Ave S WA5 . . . . 15 D4
Cromwell Cl WA12. . . . . 2 A4
Cromwell Ct
Irlam M44 . . . . 11 E7
🔟 Nantwich CW5. . . . . . . 204 E5
🔽 Warrington WA1 . . . . . . 16 A5
Cromwell Dr CW2 . . . . . . 206 C4
Cromwell Rd
Bramhall SK7. . . . . 35 D6
Ellesmere Port CH65 . . . . . 70 D5
Irlam M44 . . . . 11 D8
Cromwell St WA8. . . . . 23 A6
Cronkinson Ave CW5 . . . 204 F4
Cronkinson Oak CW5 . . . 204 F4
CRONTON 12 D5
Cronton CE Prim Sch
WA8. . . . . 12 C6
Cronton Farm Ct WA8 . . . 12 C4
Cronton La
Cronton L35. . . . . 12 B8
Widnes WA8 . . . . 12 F5
Cronton Park Ave WA8. . . 12 C6
Cronton Park Cl WA8 . . . . 12 C6
Cronton Rd L35, WA8. . . . . 12 C5
Cronulla Dr WA5 . . . . 14 E7
Crooked La CH3, CW6 . . . 145 C4
Crookedyard Rd SK11 . . 113 E7
Crookenden Cl CH2 . . . . . 95 C1
Crookenden Rd CH2 . . . . . 95 C1
Crook La CW7 . . . . 127 A2
Crook St CH1 . . . . 237 A2
Croppers Rd WA2. . . . . 8 F3
Crosby Ave WA5. . . . . 16 A8
Crosby Gr CH64 . . . . 43 B1
Crosfield Ct WA5. . . . . 15 A5
Crosfield St WA1 . . . . 16 A5
Crossall St SK11 . . . . 112 C7
Crossdale Rd CH62 . . . . . 43 D5
Cross Farm WA2 . . . . 9 A2
Crossfield Ave
Culcheth WA3 . . . . 4 F2
Lymm WA13. . . . . 18 F3
Winsford CW7 . . . . 149 D7
Crossfield Rd
Bollington SK10 . . . . 87 E6
Handforth SK9 . . . . 34 D4
Crossfields CH3 . . . . 121 B2
Crossgates CH3 . . . . 13 F3
Cross Gn CH2 . . . . 118 E6
Cross Hey CH4 . . . . 237 C1
Crossings Ho CW1 . . . . . 190 A5
Crossings The WA12 . . . . . 2 C3
Crosskeys Cl CW6 . . . . . . 145 A6
Cross La
Audley ST7 . . . . 209 E5
Church Minshull CW1,
CW5 . . . . 172 C6
Congleton CW12 . . . . 157 A1
Croft WA3 . . . . 9 D7
Haslington CW11 . . . . 191 F8
Middlewich CW10 . . . . 151 D6
Neston CH64 . . . . 66 E5
Newton-le-W WA12 . . . . 2 B8
Sandbach CW11 . . . . 175 D5
Smallwood CW11 . . . . 176 F5
Smallwood CW11 . . . . 177 B5
Swettenham CW12 . . . . . . 131 F4
Tarvin CH3. . . . . 121 C2
Warrington WA4 . . . . 17 A3
Wilmslow SK9 . . . . 60 F8
Cross La E M31. . . . . 11 F3
Crossland Mews WA13. . . 18 C4
Crosslands
Congleton CW12 . . . . 157 A1
Haslington CW11 . . . . 191 D4
Crossland Terr WA6. . . . . . 73 B2
CROSS LANE 172 D6
Cross Lanes CH3 . . . . 144 C8
Cross Lane S WA3 . . . . 9 A8
Cross La W M31 . . . . 11 F2
Crossledge CW12 . . . . . . 156 B3
Cross Lea CH66 . . . . 69 E6
Crossley Cres CH2 . . . . . 119 B5
Crossley Dr CH60 . . . . 40 D8
Crossley Pk WA6 . . . . 99 C7
Crossley St WA1 . . . . 16 C5
Cross o' th' Hill SY14 . . . 213 D4
Cross o' Th' Hill Rd
SY14 . . . . 214 A4
Cross Rd
Gatley SK8. . . . . 34 B7
Haslington CW11 . . . . 191 D4
Cross St
Alsager ST7 . . . . 193 C3
Barnton CW8 . . . . 78 B3
Chester CH2 . . . . 118 F2
Congleton CW12 . . . . 156 D3
Crewe CW1 . . . . 190 D3
Golborne WA3 . . . . 3 A7
Haslington CW11 . . . . 191 D4
Holt LL13 . . . . 196 E8

Cross St continued
Macclesfield SK11. . . . . 112 E6
Marston CW9 . . . . 79 C3
Neston CH64 . . . . 66 E8
New Mills SK22 . . . . 39 C8
🔟 Runcorn WA7 . . . . 23 A3
Warrington WA3 . . . . 4 D5
Widnes WA8 . . . . 13 C1
Cross The
Holt LL13 . . . . 196 E8
Kingsley WA6. . . . . 75 C2
Lymm WA13 . . . . 18 E3
🔟 Neston CH64 . . . . 66 E8
CROSS TOWN 57 B2
Crossway
Bramhall SK7. . . . . 35 E5
Crewe CW1 . . . . 190 D6
Widnes WA8 . . . . 22 D8
Crossways ST8 . . . . 179 E1
Crossways Rd ST7 . . . . . . 194 A4
Crossway The CH63. . . . . . 42 C4
Cross Wood St 🔽
CW5 . . . . 204 D5
Crosthwaite Ave CH62 . . . 43 F4
Croston Cl
Alderley Edge SK9 . . . . 60 C1
Warrington WA3 . . . . 12 C3
Crotia Ave CW2 . . . . 207 B5
Crouch La CW12 . . . . 157 D4
Crouchley Hall Mews
WA13 . . . . 18 F1
Crouchley La WA13 . . . . . . 18 F1
CROUGHTON 95 F5
Croughton Ct CH66 . . . . . 69 F8
Croughton Rd
Ellesmere Port CH66 . . . . . 69 F8
Stoak CH2 . . . . 96 A7
Stoak, Croughton CH2. . . . . 95 F6
Crowbrook Gr 🔽 SK9 . . 34 E1
Crowder's La CW7 . . . . . . 105 B4
Crowe Ave WA2 . . . . 8 B2
Crowland Gdns SK8. . . . . . 35 B6
Crow Lane E WA12 . . . . 2 C4
Crow Lane W WA12. . . . . . . 2 A4
Crowley La CW9, WA16 . . . 28 A3
Crowmere Ct CW8 . . . . . . 102 A2
Crown Ave WA8 . . . . 22 B8
Crown Bank
🔽 Sandbach CW11 . . . . . 175 B6
Talke ST7 . . . . 210 D6
Crown Bank Cres
ST7. 210 D6
Crown Bldgs WA6 . . . . 73 B1
Crown Cotts CW8 . . . . . . 124 A7
Crown Ctr The 🔟
SK11 . . . . 112 C8
Crown Ctyd CW3 . . . . 229 F4
Crown Dr CW11 . . . . 175 D3
Crownest La CW9 . . . . 78 E8
Crown Fields Cl WA12 . . . . 2 B5
Crown Gate WA7. . . . . 49 F7
Crown Gdns
Newton-le-W WA12 . . . . 2 B4
Talke ST7 . . . . 210 D6
Crown Gn WA13 . . . . 19 B4
Crown La WA16. . . . . 106 D8
Crown Mews CW9 . . . . . . 229 F4
Crown Park Dr WA12 . . . . . 2 B5
Crown St W SK11 . . . . . . 112 C7
Crown St
Newton-le-W WA12 . . . . 2 A3
🔟 Northwich CW9 . . . . . 103 F8
🔽 Warrington WA1 . . . . . . 16 B5
Crow's Nest Cotts
CH3 . . . . 166 C6
CROWTON 76 C1
Crowton Cotts CW7. . . . . 170 F4
CROW WOOD 13 D3
Crow Wood La WA8 . . . . . 13 D2
Crow Wood Pl WA8 . . . . . 13 D3
Croxton Gn SY14 . . . . 201 C6
CROXTON GREEN 201 C6
Croxton La CW10 . . . . 128 A4
Croxton Way CW8 . . . . . . 103 A4
Croyde Cl M22. . . . . 33 F7
Croyde Rd L24 . . . . 21 A3
Crum Hill 🔽 CW9. . . . . . 104 A8
Cryers La
Elton CH2. . . . . 72 A2
Thornton-le-M CH2 . . . . 96 F8
Cty High Sch Leftwich The
CW9. . . . . 104 A4
Cuckoo Clock Mus*
WA16. . . . . 80 F8
Cuckoo La
Acton CW5 . . . . 203 E8
Neston CH64 . . . . 67 C7
CUCKOO'S NEST 162 E5
Cuckstoolpit Hill
SK10. . . . . 112 E8
CUDDINGTON 101 F4
CUDDINGTON GREEN
. . . . 212 B1
CUDDINGTON HEATH
. . . . 212 E2
Cuddington La
Cuddington CW8 . . . . 101 D4
Sandiway CW8. . . . . 102 A6
Cuddington Prim Sch
CW8. . . . . 101 F2
Cuddington Sta CW8 . . . 102 A6
Cuddington Way 🔽
SK9 . . . . 34 D5
CUERDLEY CROSS 13 A2
Cuerdley Gn WA5 . . . . 14 A2
Cuerdley Rd WA5 . . . . 14 C3
Cuerdon Dr WA4 . . . . 17 D1
Culbin Cl WA3. . . . . 10 A3

CULCHETH 4 E3
Culcheth Com Prim Sch
WA3 .4 E3
Culcheth Hall Dr WA3 . . . .4 F4
Culcheth Hall Farm Barns
WA3 .4 F4
Culcheth High Sch WA3. . .5 A3
Culford Cl WA7 . . . . .24 D1
Culland St CW2 . . . . .190 C2
Cullen Cl CH63 . . . . .43 C4
Cullen Rd WA7 . . . . .48 D7
Cumber Cl SK9 . . . . .59 D4
Cumber Dr SK9 . . . . .59 D4
Cumber La SK9 . . . . .59 D4
Cumberland Ave
Irlam M44 . . . . .11 C5
Nantwich CW5 . . . . .204 F6
Cumberland Cl
Crewe CW1 . . . . .190 D5
Talke ST7 . . . . .210 E7
Cumberland Cres WA11 . . . .1 A6
Cumberland Dr
Altrincham WA14 . . . . .31 B8
Bollington SK10 . . . . .88 B8
Cumberland Gr CH66 . . . . .69 C3
Cumberland Rd
Congleton CW12 . . . . .156 A3
Partington M31 . . . . .11 E2
Cumberland St
2 Macclesfield SK10 . . . .112 D8
Warrington WA4 . . . . .16 C3
Cumbermere Dr
CW11 . . . . .174 E7
Cumbers Dr CH64 . . . . .67 A5
Cumbers La CH64 . . . . .67 A5
Cumbrae Dr **6** CH65 . . . .70 C1
Cumbria Cl **2** CH66 . . . . .69 E1
Cundiff Cl SK11 . . . . .112 E6
Cunliffe Ave WA12 . . . . .2 B5
Cunliffe Cl WA7 . . . . .50 A7
Cunningham Cl WA5 . . . . . .14 F5
Cunningham Dr
Bebington CH63 . . . . .43 C7
Gatley M22 . . . . .34 A8
Runcorn WA7 . . . . .22 E1
Cunningham Ho WA7 . . . . .48 E8
Cunningham Rd WA8 . . . . .22 D8
Cuppin St CH1 . . . . .237 A2
Curlender Way L24 . . . . .21 E2
Curlew Cl
Golborne WA3 . . . . .3 D8
Macclesfield SK10 . . . . .87 C5
Winsford CW7 . . . . .149 C5
Curlew Gr WA3 . . . . .7 E2
Curlew Rd ST7 . . . . .195 E1
Currans Rd WA2 . . . . .8 B2
Curzon Ave ST7 . . . . .193 D5
Curzon Cl CH4 . . . . .141 B8
Curzon Ct CH4 . . . . .140 F7
Curzon Mews SK9 . . . . .60 A5
CURZON PARK 141 B7
Curzon Pk N CH4 . . . . .141 B7
Curzon Pk S CH4 . . . . .141 B7
Curzon Rd
Gatley SK8 . . . . .34 B7
Poynton SK12 . . . . .36 E2
Curzon St
Chester CH4 . . . . .140 F7
8 Runcorn WA7 . . . . . . .22 F1
Cwat Erwain CH4 . . . . .140 E7
Cwrt Cwellyn CH5 . . . . . . .139 B7
Cwrt Dinas CH5 . . . . .139 B7
Cwrt Ogwen CH5 . . . . .139 B7
Cygnet Cl CH66 . . . . .69 D4
Cygnet Ct WA1 . . . . .16 A3
Cyman Cl CH1 . . . . .117 D3
Cynthia Ave WA1 . . . . .17 B7
Cynthia Rd WA7 . . . . .22 F1
Cypress Ave
Ellesmere Port CH66 . . . . .69 F1
Widnes WA8 . . . . .13 B2
Cypress Cl WA1 . . . . .17 E2
Cypress Gr WA7 . . . . .49 C2
Cypress Mews CH65 . . . . .102 E7
Cypress Way SK6 . . . . .38 A7
Cyril Bell Cl WA13 . . . . .18 F3
Cyril St WA2 . . . . .16 B7

D

Daffodil Cl WA8 . . . . .13 E4
Daffodil Gdns WA9 . . . . .6 A7
Dagfields Crafts &
Antiques Ctr* CW5 . . .220 A4
Dagnall Ave WA5 . . . . .7 F2
Dahlia Cl WA9 . . . . .6 A7
Daintry St SK11 . . . . .112 E7
Daintry Terr SK10 . . . . .112 E8
Dairy Bank CH2 . . . . .72 B4
Dairybrook Gr **7** SK9 . . .34 E1
Dairy Farm Cl WA13 . . . . . .18 F4
Dairyground Rd SK7 . . . . . .35 F7
Dairy House La SK7 . . . . . . .35 B4
Dairy House Rd SK7 . . . . . . .35 B5
Dairy House Small
Holdings SK7 . . . . .35 B4
Dairy House Way
CW2 . . . . .189 F2
Dairy La CW5 . . . . .188 D6
Dairylands Rd ST7 . . . . . . .193 F4
Daisy Ave WA12 . . . . .2 C2
Daisy Bank
Alsager ST7 . . . . .193 A4
Nantwich CW5 . . . . .204 D5
Daisy Bank Cres CW3 . . . .229 F5

Daisybank Dr
Congleton CW12 . . . . .156 D4
Sandbach CW11 . . . . .175 C6
Daisy Bank La CW9 . . . . . . .78 C3
Daisy Bank Mill Cl WA3 . . .4 E3
Daisy Bank Rd
Lymm WA13 . . . . .18 C3
Warrington WA5 . . . . .14 F4
Daisy Cl WA16 . . . . .79 F6
Daisy Way SK6 . . . . .37 F7
Dakota Dr WA5 . . . . .15 C7
Dalby Cl WA3 . . . . .10 B5
Dalby Ct CW9 . . . . .104 E5
Dale Ave
Bebington CH62 . . . . .43 D8
Bramhall SK7 . . . . .35 F8
Ellesmere Port CH66 . . . . .69 C6
Dale Cl
Warrington WA5 . . . . .15 D4
Widnes WA8 . . . . .22 A8
Dale Cres CW12 . . . . .156 F2
Dale Ct
Heswall CH60 . . . . .40 F8
Middlewich CW10 . . . . . . .151 D7
Dale Dr
Chester CH2 . . . . .118 D8
Ellesmere Port CH65 . . . . .69 F5
Daleford Manor CW8 . . . .125 B8
Daleford Manor Cvn Pk
CW8 . . . . .125 A8
Dalefords La
Cuddington CW8 . . . . .102 A1
Whitegate CW8 . . . . .125 D7
Dale Gdns CH65 . . . . .70 B3
Dale Gr
Congleton CW12 . . . . .157 A2
Irlam M44 . . . . .11 E6
Dale Head Rd SK10 . . . . . . .86 F4
Dale Hey CH66 . . . . .43 E2
Dale House Fold SK12 . . . .37 A4
Dale La WA4 . . . . .26 E7
Dale Pl CW12 . . . . .156 F2
Dale Rd
Bebington CH62 . . . . .43 D6
Golborne WA3 . . . . .3 A7
New Mills SK22 . . . . .39 C7
Dalesford Cl WA7 . . . . .4 C8
Dalesford Cres SK10 . . . . .111 E8
DALES GREEN 195 C5
Dales Green Rd ST7 . . . . . .195 C5
Daleside CH2 . . . . .118 D8
Dale's Sq CW9 . . . . .103 F6
Dale St
Chester CH63 . . . . .119 A1
Macclesfield SK10 . . . . . . .112 E8
Runcorn WA7 . . . . .23 A1
Dalesway CH60 . . . . .40 E8
Dale The
Neston CH64 . . . . .66 E6
Tiverton SK6 . . . . .168 C6
Warrington WA5 . . . . .14 F5
Dale View
Kidsgrove ST7 . . . . .195 C5
Newton-le-W WA12 . . . . . . .2 E4
Dale Way CW1 . . . . .190 A5
Dalewood Cl WA2 . . . . .16 A6
Dalewood Cres CH2 . . . . . .72 A3
DALLAM 7 F2
Dallam Com Prim Sch
WA5 . . . . .7 F1
Dallam La WA2 . . . . .16 A7
Dalmahoy Cl CW7 . . . . . . .126 C2
Dalston Dr SK7 . . . . .35 C5
Dalton Ave
Warrington, Birchwood
WA3 . . . . .9 E6
Warrington WA5 . . . . .15 F7
Dalton Bank WA1 . . . . .16 C6
Dalton Cl CH1 . . . . .117 E3
Dalton Ct
Runcorn WA7 . . . . .23 E3
Sandbach CW11 . . . . .174 E7
Dalton St
Runcorn WA7 . . . . .23 D2
Warrington WA3 . . . . .9 E5
Dalton Way CW10 . . . . . . .128 D1
Dalwood Cl WA7 . . . . .50 E7
Dame Hollow SK8 . . . . .34 D7
Damery Ct SK7 . . . . .35 E8
Damery Rd SK7 . . . . .35 E8
Damhead La CH64 . . . . .67 E7
Dam Head La WA3 . . . . .11 A5
Damian Dr WA12 . . . . .2 A5
Dam La
Hollinfare WA3 . . . . .11 A4
Mobberley WA16 . . . . .58 C3
Warrington WA1 . . . . .17 D7
Winwick WA3 . . . . .8 F7
Dams La WA16 . . . . .106 D5
Damson La WA16 . . . . .58 C3
Damson Wlk M31 . . . . .11 D3
Danby Cl
Runcorn WA7 . . . . .49 D6
Warrington WA5 . . . . .15 E7
Dane Ave WA11 . . . . .11 F4
DANEBANK 38 E5
Dane Bank Ave
Congleton CW12 . . . . .156 E4
Crewe CW2 . . . . .190 A2
Dane Bank Dr SK12 . . . . . .38 D6
Dane Bank Rd
Lymm WA13 . . . . .18 E4
Northwich CW9 . . . . .104 B7
Dane Bank Rd E WA13 . . . .18 E4
Dane Cl
Alsager ST7 . . . . .193 A3
Chester CH4 . . . . .140 F5

Dane Cl *continued*
Sandbach CW11 . . . . .174 E7
Dane Dr
Biddulph ST8 . . . . .179 E1
Wilmslow SK9 . . . . .60 D6
Danefield Ct SK8 . . . . .34 D8
Danefield Rd
Holmes Chapel CW4 . . . . .130 C4
Northwich CW9 . . . . .104 B7
Dane Gdns ST7 . . . . .195 C2
Dane Gr CH2 . . . . .119 F8
Dane Hill Cl SK12 . . . . .38 D5
DANE IN SHAW 179 C8
Dane Mill Bsns Ctr
CW12 . . . . .156 C3
Dane Pl
Crewe CW1 . . . . .190 D6
Winsford CW7 . . . . .127 B1
Danescroft WA8 . . . . .12 B3
Danes Bsns Pk
CW12 . . . . .156 E4
Daneside County Pk
CW12 . . . . .155 B7
Danes Sq SK11 . . . . .112 D5
Dane St
Congleton CW12 . . . . .156 C3
Middlewich CW10 . . . . . . .128 D2
Northwich CW9 . . . . .103 F8
Daneswell Rd L24 . . . . .21 A2
Daniel Adamson Ave
M31 . . . . .11 D3
Daniel Cl WA3 . . . . .10 A4
Daniel Ct M31 . . . . .11 F4
Daniell Way CH3 . . . . .142 A7
Danily Ct SY14 . . . . .213 B3
Dan's Rd WA8 . . . . .13 E2
Dapplecheath Rd CW2 . . .190 A1
Darby Cl CH64 . . . . .66 E4
D'Arcy Cotts CH63 . . . . . . .42 B6
Darent Rd WA11 . . . . .1 B7
DARESBURY 25 B2
Daresbury Cl
Holmes Chapel CW4 . . . . .130 A3
4 Wilmslow SK9 . . . . . .60 C8
Daresbury Ct WA8 . . . . . . .13 C3
DARESBURY DELPH 25 B1
Daresbury Expressway
Daresbury WA4 . . . . .25 A3
Runcorn WA7 . . . . .23 C2
Daresbury La WA4 . . . . .25 D2
Daresbury Pk WA4 . . . . . . .51 A8
Daresbury Prim Sch
WA4 . . . . .25 B2
Deacon Rd WA8 . . . . .33 D8
Dario Gradi Dr CW2 . . . . .190 D1
Dark Ark La CH3, WA6 . . . .99 B3
Darkie Mdw CW6 . . . . .185 E8
Dark La
Henbury SK11 . . . . .111 B8
Higher Whitley WA4 . . . . . .52 D6
Kingsley WA6 . . . . .75 B1
Marston CW9 . . . . .79 C6
Tattenhall CH3 . . . . .183 E7
Warren SK11 . . . . .111 C3
Whitchurch SY13 . . . . .227 B1
Darland La LL12 . . . . .162 C1
Darley Ave
Crewe CW2 . . . . .190 A3
Warrington WA2 . . . . .8 E3
Darley Cl WA8 . . . . .12 B3
Darleydale Dr CH62 . . . . . .43 F5
Darley Rd SK7 . . . . .36 F7
Darlington Ave CW1 . . . . .189 F5
Darlington Ct CH1 . . . . .94 A1
Darlington Ct **3** WA8 . . .23 A7
Darlington St CW10 . . . . .128 C1
Darnaway Cl WA3 . . . . .10 B6
DARNHALL 149 A3
Darnhall Prim Sch
CW7 . . . . .149 C6
Darnhall School La
CW7 . . . . .149 C6
Dart Cl
Alsager ST7 . . . . .193 A4
Biddulph ST8 . . . . .179 D1
Dartnall Cl SK12 . . . . .38 A6
Dart Wlk CW7 . . . . .127 B2
Darwen Gdns WA2 . . . . .8 E1
Darwin Gr SK7 . . . . .35 E6
Darwin Rd CH1 . . . . .117 C4
Darwin St CW8 . . . . .103 E7
Daryl Rd CH60 . . . . .41 A8
Dashwood Cl WA4 . . . . .27 A7
Daten Ave WA3 . . . . .9 E6
Daten Pk WA3 . . . . .9 E6
Dauncey Ct CH2 . . . . .95 C1
Davehall Ave SK9 . . . . .60 A7
DAVENHAM 104 A2
Davenham Ave WA1 . . . . . .16 E8
Davenham CE Prim Sch
CW9 . . . . .103 F2
Davenham Cres CW2 . . . .190 A3
Davenham Ct CW9 . . . . . .104 A3
Davenham Mdws
CW9 . . . . .103 E3
Davenham Rd
Davenham CW9 . . . . .104 E3
Handforth SK9 . . . . .34 D4
Davenham Rdbt CW9 . . . .103 F3
Davenham Way
CW10 . . . . .151 D5
DAVENPORT 154 E7
Davenport Ave
Crewe CW2 . . . . .206 D8
Nantwich CW5 . . . . .204 E7
Warrington WA4 . . . . .16 F5
Wilmslow SK9 . . . . .59 E4
Davenport Cl CW11 . . . . . .175 D8

DAVENPORT GREEN 59 F3
Davenport La
Brereton Green
CW11 . . . . .154 C2
Marton SK11 . . . . .132 F5
Mobberley WA16 . . . . .58 D6
Davenport Park La
CW12 . . . . .131 D2
Davenport Rd CH60 . . . . . .40 E7
Davenport Row WA7 . . . . . .49 D8
Davenport St
Congleton CW12 . . . . .156 C2
Crewe CW1 . . . . .190 C6
Macclesfield SK10 . . . . . . .112 E8
Daven Prim Sch
CW12 . . . . .156 C3
Daven Rd CW12 . . . . .156 F1
Davey La SK9 . . . . .60 B2
Daveylands SK9 . . . . .60 D7
David Lewis Sch SK9 . . . . . .83 F6
David Rd WA13 . . . . .18 C3
David's Ave WA5 . . . . .15 B5
Davidson Ave CW12 . . . . . .157 A5
David St CW8 . . . . .103 E7
Davies Ave
Gatley SK8 . . . . .34 B6
Newton-le-W WA12 . . . . . . .2 C4
Warrington WA4 . . . . .16 F4
Davies St CW9 . . . . .104 B8
Davies Way WA13 . . . . .18 E3
Davis Cl ST7 . . . . .193 E3
Davy Ave WA3 . . . . .9 E5
Davy Rd WA7 . . . . .23 E3
Dawlish Ave SK8 . . . . .34 F7
Dawlish Cl
Bramhall SK7 . . . . .35 F7
Hollinfare WA3 . . . . .11 B3
Dawn Cl CH64 . . . . .67 A5
Dawn Gdns CH65 . . . . .70 B4
Dawpool Cl CH2 . . . . .118 D5
Dawpool Ct CH2 . . . . .118 D5
Dawpool Dr CH62 . . . . .43 C7
Dawson Cl **11** SK11 . . . . .111 F7
Dawson Dr CH2 . . . . .237 A4
Dawson Rd
Bollington SK10 . . . . .88 A7
Gatley SK8 . . . . .34 D8
Macclesfield SK11 . . . . . . .111 F7
Dawstone Cl CH60 . . . . . . .40 F8
Dawstone Ct CH60 . . . . . . .41 A7
Dawstone Rise CH60 . . . . .40 F7
DAY GREEN 192 F8
Deacon Rd WA8 . . . . .13 B1
Deacons Cl WA3 . . . . .10 B3
Deacon Trad Est WA12 . . . .2 A2
Deadman's La CW5 . . . . . .205 B2
Deakin's Rd
Winsford CW7 . . . . .126 F4
Winsford, Wharton Green
CW7 . . . . .127 A4
Dean Bank CW6 . . . . .168 C3
Dean Cl
Bollington SK10 . . . . .88 A7
Handforth SK9 . . . . .34 C1
Partington M31 . . . . .11 F4
Sandbach CW11 . . . . .174 E8
7 Widnes WA8 . . . . .23 B8
Dean Cres WA2 . . . . .8 B2
Dean Ct
Bollington SK10 . . . . .88 B8
Handforth SK9 . . . . .3 A7
Dean Dr SK9 . . . . .34 D2
Deane Ct CW5 . . . . .205 B4
Deanery Cl CH2 . . . . .118 C4
Deangate CW2 . . . . .207 E3
Dean Hollow ST7 . . . . .209 D2
Dean La SK7 . . . . .36 E8
Dean Mdw WA12 . . . . .2 C4
Dean Pk SY14 . . . . .214 A5
Dean Rd
Golborne WA3 . . . . .3 A7
Handforth SK9 . . . . .34 E3
Irlam M44 . . . . .11 E6
DEAN ROW 60 F8
Dean Row St **9** SK9 . . . . .34 D1
Dean Row Jun Sch
SK9 . . . . .34 E1
Dean Row Rd SK9 . . . . .61 A8
Deans Cl
Chester CH2 . . . . .118 D6
Tarvin CH3 . . . . .121 B1
Deansfield Way CH2 . . . . . .72 A3
Deansgate CH65 . . . . .70 A5
DEANSGREEN 29 A8
Deansgreen Cl WA13 . . . . .29 A7
Deans La
Sandbach CW11 . . . . .174 E6
Warrington WA4 . . . . .17 F3
Dean's La
Barthomley CW2 . . . . .208 C4
Newcastle-u-Lyme ST5 . . .210 D2
Deans Rd CH65 . . . . .70 F3
Dean St
Middlewich CW10 . . . . . . .128 C2
Newton-le-W WA12 . . . . . . .3 A8
Widnes WA8 . . . . .23 B8
Winsford CW7 . . . . .126 D1
Deans Way
Higher Kinnerton CH4 . . . .161 A7
Tarvin CH3 . . . . .121 B2
Dean Valley Com Prim Sch
SK10 . . . . .87 E8
Dean View ST7 . . . . .209 D2
Deanwater Cl WA3 . . . . .9 D4
Deanwater Ct SK8 . . . . .34 D7
Deanway SK9 . . . . .34 C1

Deanway Trad Est SK9 . . .34 D3
Dearnford Ave CH62 . . . . . .43 D6
Dearnford Cl CH62 . . . . . . .43 D6
Debra Cl CH66 . . . . .69 C4
Debra Rd CH66 . . . . .69 C4
Decade Cl ST5 . . . . .210 F2
Dee Banks
Chester CH3 . . . . .142 A8
Huntington CH3 . . . . .141 F7
Dee Banks Sch CH3 . . . . .142 A7
Dee Cl
Biddulph ST8 . . . . .179 E1
Sandbach CW11 . . . . .174 E8
Talke ST7 . . . . .210 E7
Dee Cres CH3 . . . . .180 E2
Deefords CH3 . . . . .118 F1
Dee Fords Ave CH3 . . . . . .119 A1
Dee Hills Pk CH3 . . . . .237 C2
De La
Chester CH1, CH3 . . . . . .237 C2
Holt LL13 . . . . .196 D7
Dee Mdws LL13 . . . . .196 D7
Dee Park Cl CH60 . . . . .41 B6
Dee Park Rd CH60 . . . . . . .41 B5
Deepdale WA8 . . . . .12 C3
Deep Dale WA5 . . . . .14 F6
Dee Pk LL13 . . . . .196 D8
Dee Point Prim Sch
CH1 . . . . .117 D3
Dee Rd CH2 . . . . .96 F1
Deer Park Ct WA7 . . . . .49 F6
Deerwood Cl
Ellesmere Port CH65 . . . . .69 D7
Macclesfield SK10 . . . . . . .86 F1
Deerwood Cres CH65 . . . . .69 D7
Deeside
Ellesmere Port CH65 . . . . .70 B2
Holt LL13 . . . . .196 D8
Dee Side CH60 . . . . .40 C8
Deeside Cl CH65 . . . . .70 B2
**Deeside Coll/Coleg
Glannau Dyfrdwy**
CH5 . . . . .91 B1
Deeside Cres CH4 . . . . . . .116 C5
Deeside Ct
Chester CH3 . . . . .237 C2
Neston CH64 . . . . .41 B1
**Deeside Ind Pk/Parc
Ddiwydiannol Glannau
Dyfrdwy** CH5 . . . . .92 E2
Deeside La CH1 . . . . .116 D4
Dee Sq CW7 . . . . .127 B2
Dee View CW7 . . . . .180 E2
Dee View Cotts CH64 . . . . .41 D1
Dee View Ct CH64 . . . . .66 E6
Dee View Rd
Connah's Quay CH5 . . . . . .91 E1
Heswall CH60 . . . . .40 F8
Dee Villas LL13 . . . . .180 E1
Dee Way CW7 . . . . .127 A2
Deirdre Ave WA8 . . . . .13 A1
De Lacy Row WA7 . . . . .24 A2
Delafield Cl WA2 . . . . .8 F3
Delaisy Way CW7 . . . . .127 A1
Delamare Pl **1** WA7 . . . . .22 F1
DELAMERE 123 D6
Delamere Ave
Bebington CH62 . . . . .43 E4
Ellesmere Port CH66 . . . . .69 E5
Golborne WA3 . . . . .3 E6
Widnes WA8 . . . . .12 C1
Delamere CE Prim Sch
CW6 . . . . .123 C1
Delamere Cl
Barnton CW8 . . . . .78 A3
Bebington CH62 . . . . .43 E4
Chorlton CW2 . . . . .207 E4
Sandbach CW11 . . . . .175 F8
Delamere Ct
Alsager ST7 . . . . .192 F4
Bebington CH62 . . . . .43 E4
7 Crewe CW1 . . . . .190 C4
Delamere Dr
Ellesmere Port CH66 . . . . .69 E5
Macclesfield SK10 . . . . . . .87 F2
Delamere Forest Sch
WA6 . . . . .100 C4
Delamere Forest Trail*
WA6 . . . . .100 A4
Delamere Forest Visitor
Ctr* CW8 . . . . .100 B2
Delamere Gn CH66 . . . . . . .69 E5
Delamere Gr CW8 . . . . . . .123 D7
Delamere Ho WA6 . . . . .74 C7
Delamere La CH3 . . . . .99 B2
DELAMERE PARK 101 D5
Delamere Park Way E
CW8 . . . . .101 D5
Delamere Park Way W
CW8 . . . . .101 D5
Delamere Rd
Congleton CW12 . . . . .155 F3
Handforth SK9 . . . . .34 C4
Nantwich CW5 . . . . .204 E7
Norley WA6 . . . . .100 B6
Delamere Rise CW7 . . . . . .126 B1
Delamere Sta
Chester CH1 . . . . .237 A3
Crewe CW1 . . . . .190 C4
Warrington WA3 . . . . .9 E7
Winsford CW7 . . . . .126 B1
Delamere Sta CW8 . . . . . .100 D1
Delamore's Acre CH64 . . . .66 A8
Delavor Cl CH60 . . . . .40 F8
Delavor Rd CH60 . . . . .40 E8

Delenty Dr WA3 . . . . 9 E4
Delcry Dr WA2 . . . . 18 C8
Delhir Rd SK7 . . . . 35 F7
Delhi Rd M44 . . . . 11 F8
Dell Cl CH63 . . . . 43 B6
Dell Dr WA2 . . . . 9 A2
Dell La CH60 . . . . 41 B7
Dell The
  Cuddington CW8 . . . . 101 D5
  Guilden Sutton CH3 . . . . . 119 F5
  Kelsall CW6 . . . . 122 D5
Delmar Rd WA16 . . . . 57 C1
Delphfields Rd WA4 . . . . . . 26 C7
Delphield WA7 . . . . 50 D8
Delph La
  Daresbury WA4 . . . . 25 A2
  Warrington, Houghton Gn
    WA2 . . . . 8 E6
  Winwick WA2 . . . . 8 A5
Delphside ST7 . . . . 209 F2
Delta Cres WA5 . . . . 7 C2
Delta Ct CH4 . . . . 140 B6
Delves Ave WA5 . . . . 15 F7
Delves Broughton Ct
  CW1 . . . . 191 D5
Delves Cl CW2 . . . . 206 B4
Delves Wlk CH3 . . . . 142 B7
Delvine Dr CH2 . . . . 118 D6
Demage Dr CH66 . . . . 69 D3
Demage La
  Backford CH1 . . . . 94 F4
  Chester CH2 . . . . 118 D8
Demage La S CH2 . . . . 118 D7
Denbigh Cl
  Hazel Grove SK7 . . . . 36 C8
  Helsby WA6 . . . . 73 A1
Denbigh Cres CW10 . . . . . . 151 C7
Denbigh Ct CH65 . . . . 70 D3
Denbigh Dr CW7 . . . . 149 B7
Denbigh Gdns CH65 . . . . . . 70 C3
Denbigh St CH1 . . . . 118 B3
Denbury Ave WA4 . . . . 16 F2
Dene Ave WA12 . . . . 1 F4
Dene Dr CW7 . . . . 149 D8
Denehurst Cl WA5 . . . . 14 F4
Denehurst Park Way
  CW8 . . . . 101 D5
Denesgate **1** CW7 . . . . . . 149 D8
Deneside Ave CW1 . . . . 190 C6
Deneway
  Bramhall SK7 . . . . 35 D7
  High Lane SK6 . . . . 37 F8
Denewood Ct **3** SK9 . . . . . 60 A6
Denford Cl CH4 . . . . 139 C4
Denford Pl ST7 . . . . 193 D6
Denhall Cl CH2 . . . . 118 E5
Denhall La CH64 . . . . 67 A3
Denham Ave WA5 . . . . 15 B5
Denham Dr SK7 . . . . 35 D7
Denise Ave WA5 . . . . 14 E5
Dennison Rd SK7 . . . . 36 E8
Den La CW2,CW5 . . . . 221 D4
Dennett Cl WA1 . . . . 17 E6
Dennis Dr CH4 . . . . 141 B6
Dennison Rd SK8 . . . . 35 B8
Dennis Rd WA8 . . . . 23 C7
Dennis Round Ct ST7 . . . . . 193 C3
Densham Ave WA2 . . . . 8 B2
Denston Cl CW2 . . . . 190 B1
Denstone Dr CH4 . . . . 141 A4
Dentdale Wlk M22 . . . . 33 C8
Dentith Dr CH1 . . . . 117 E5
Denton Cl CW7 . . . . 126 C1
Denton Dr CW9 . . . . 79 C1
Denton Drive Ind Est
  CW9 . . . . 79 C2
Denton St WA8 . . . . 13 C1
Denver Ave CW2 . . . . 190 B3
Denver Dr WA5 . . . . 15 B7
Denver Rd WA4 . . . . 17 A3
Denwall Ho **5** CH64 . . . . . 66 E8
Depenbech Cl SY14 . . . . . . 213 B4
Depmore La WA6 . . . . 75 A2
Derby Cl
  Irlam M44 . . . . 11 C5
  Newton-le-W WA12 . . . . . . 2 B3
Derby Dr WA1 . . . . 16 F7
Derby Knoll SK23 . . . . 39 F1
Derby Rd
  Golborne WA3 . . . . 3 C8
  Talke ST7 . . . . 210 D7
  4 Warrington WA4 . . . . . 16 C1
  Widnes, Barrow's Green
    WA8 . . . . 13 D4
  Widnes, Lunts Heath
    WA8 . . . . 13 B4
Derby Row WA10 . . . . 7 D8
DERBYSHIRE HILL 1 A2
Derbyshire Hill Rd WA9 . . . . 1 A2
Derbyshire Rd
  Partington M31 . . . . 11 E2
  Poynton SK12 . . . . 37 D5
Derby St
  Congleton CW12 . . . . 156 D3
  Crewe CW1 . . . . 190 B5
  Newton-le-W WA12 . . . . . . 2 B3
Dereham Way WA7 . . . . 24 D3
Derek Ave WA2 . . . . 8 E1
Derfel Terr **4** WA6 . . . . . . 74 B8
Derrington Ave CW2 . . . . . . 190 C3
Derwen Prim Sch
  CH4 . . . . 161 A7
Derwent Ave CW7 . . . . 127 B1
Derwent Cl
  Alsager ST7 . . . . 193 A4

Derwent Cl continued
    . . . . 6 A0
  Holmes Chapel CW4 . . . . . 130 A3
  Macclesfield SK11 . . . . . . 112 A6
  Partington M31 . . . . 11 F1
  Willaston CW9 . . . . 105 D8
Derwent Cres ST7 . . . . 195 C2
Derwent Dr
  Biddulph ST8 . . . . 179 E1
  Bramhall SK7 . . . . 35 C5
  Congleton CW12 . . . . 156 F1
  Handforth SK9 . . . . 34 C5
  Hooton CH66 . . . . 44 B2
Derwent Rd
  Chester CH2 . . . . 119 A5
  High Lane SK6 . . . . 37 E8
  Warrington WA4 . . . . 16 B2
  Widnes WA8 . . . . 12 C1
Derwent Way
  Alderley Edge SK9 . . . . . . 83 F7
  Neston CH64 . . . . 66 F7
Desoto Rd WA8 . . . . 22 E5
Desoto Rd E WA8 . . . . 22 F6
Desoto Rd W WA8 . . . . 22 F6
De Trafford Mews **9**
  SK9 . . . . 34 D2
Deva Ave CH4 . . . . 140 D6
Deva Bsns Pk CH5 . . . . 116 A8
Deva Cl SK12 . . . . 36 B4
Deva Ct CH2 . . . . 118 F2
Deva Hts CH3 . . . . 141 F7
Deva La CH2 . . . . 118 C6
Deva Link CH1 . . . . 118 B3
Deva Rd CW2 . . . . 189 D4
Deva Ret Pk CH1 . . . . 118 A3
Deva Roman Experience
  Mus* CH1 . . . . 237 B2
Deva Stad (Chester City
  FC) CH1 . . . . 117 E1
Deva Terr CH3 . . . . 237 C2
Devon Cl
  Macclesfield SK10 . . . . . . 86 F2
  Middlewich CW10 . . . . 128 D2
Devon Gr ST8 . . . . 179 C1
Devon Pl
  Congleton CW12 . . . . 156 E4
  Widnes WA8 . . . . 13 B3
Devon Rd
  Chester CH2 . . . . 118 F5
  Irlam M44 . . . . 11 D5
  Partington M31 . . . . 11 E2
Devonshire Dr SK9 . . . . 60 B2
Devonshire Gdns WA12 . . . . 2 C2
Devonshire Pl CH4 . . . . 141 E7
Devonshire Rd
  Broughton CH4 . . . . 139 C4
  Hazel Grove SK7 . . . . 36 F8
  Warrington WA1 . . . . 16 F8
Dewar Ct WA7 . . . . 23 E3
Dewar St WA3 . . . . 9 E5
Dewes St CW1 . . . . 190 B5
Dewhurst Rd WA3 . . . . 9 D2
Dexter Way CW10 . . . . 128 D2
Dial Cotts CH64 . . . . 67 A5
Dial La CW12,SK11 . . . . 158 B1
Dial Rd WA15 . . . . 32 C8
Dial St WA1 . . . . 16 C5
Diamond Ave **3** ST7 . . . . . 195 B2
Dibbinsdale Rd CH63 . . . . . 43 B7
Dibbins Gn CH63 . . . . 43 B7
Dickens Cl
  Cheadle SK8 . . . . 35 B5
  Sandbach CW11 . . . . 174 D6
Dickens La SK12 . . . . 36 E2
Dickenson Ho CW10 . . . . . . 128 C1
Dickenson St WA2 . . . . 16 C7
Dickinson Cl WA11 . . . . 1 A6
Dickinson Way ST7 . . . . 193 A3
Dicklow Cob SK11 . . . . 132 A8
Dickson Cl WA8 . . . . 23 B8
Dickson St
  Widnes, Kingsway
    WA8 . . . . 23 A8
  2 Widnes WA8 . . . . 23 B8
Dierden St CW7 . . . . 127 B1
Dierdens Terr **4**
  CW10 . . . . 128 C1
Dig La
  Acton CW5 . . . . 203 F4
  Frodsham WA6 . . . . 74 A7
  Shavington CW5 . . . . 206 B2
  Warrington WA2 . . . . 9 A5
Diglake Cl ST7 . . . . 210 C6
Diglake Cotts ST7 . . . . 210 A2
Diglake St ST7 . . . . 209 F3
Dilhorne Cl SK23 . . . . 39 C3
Dillors Croft CW1 . . . . 173 A1
Dimelow Ct SY14 . . . . 213 A2
Dinas Cl CH1 . . . . 117 D3
Dingle Ave
  Newton-le-W WA12 . . . . . . 1 F2
  Row-of-Trees SK9 . . . . . . 59 D3
Dingle Bank
  Chester CH4 . . . . 141 C7
  Sandbach CW11 . . . . 175 C6
Dingle Bank Cl WA13 . . . . . 18 E3
Dinglebrook Gr **5** SK9 . . . . 34 D1
Dingle Cl SK10 . . . . 87 B3
Dingle La
  Bridgemere CW5 . . . . 231 F6
  Kelsall CW6 . . . . 122 E6
  Sandbach CW11 . . . . 175 C6
  Warrington WA4 . . . . 26 F6
Dingle Prim Sch The
  CW1 . . . . 191 D6

Dingle The
  Hamilton CW0 . . . . 70 B1
  Haslington CW1 . . . . 191 D5
  Lymm WA13 . . . . 18 C3
Dingleway WA4 . . . . 26 C6
Dingle Way CW8 . . . . 101 E3
Dingle Wlk **4** CW7 . . . . . . 126 D1
Dinnington Ct WA8 . . . . 12 E3
Diploma Dr CW10 . . . . 128 C2
Dipping Brook Ave
  WA4 . . . . 26 F4
DISLEY 38 C5
Disley Prim Sch SK12 . . . . . 38 D6
Disley Sta SK12 . . . . 38 C6
Distaff Rd SK12 . . . . 36 B4
District CE Prim Sch The
  WA12 . . . . 2 A4
Ditchfield La WA16 . . . . 29 D3
Ditchfield Pl WA8 . . . . 22 B8
Ditchfield Rd
  Warrington WA5 . . . . 14 E3
  Widnes WA8 . . . . 22 B8
DITTON 22 C8
Ditton CE Prim Sch
  WA8 . . . . 12 A1
Ditton Prim Sch WA8 . . . . . 12 E1
Ditton Rd WA8 . . . . 22 D6
Dixon Ave WA12 . . . . 2 C5
Dixon Cl WA11 . . . . 2 A8
Dixon Ct SK11 . . . . 84 A2
Dixon Dr SK11 . . . . 84 B3
Dixon St WA10 . . . . 157 A5
Dixon's Hos CH3 . . . . 142 E8
Dixon St
  Irlam M44 . . . . 11 F8
  Warrington WA1 . . . . 16 A5
Dobb Hedge Cl WA15 . . . . . 32 C6
Dobbin Cl WA1 . . . . 17 F7
Dobell's Rd CW9 . . . . 103 F5
Dobers La WA6 . . . . 74 C4
Dobson Ct SY14 . . . . 213 B3
Dock Rd
  Northwich CW9 . . . . 103 F7
  Widnes WA8 . . . . 22 F5
  Widnes WA8 . . . . 23 A5
Dock Road Edwardian
  Pumping Station The*
  CW9 . . . . 103 F7
Dock St
  Ellesmere Port CH65 . . . . . 70 C7
  Widnes WA8 . . . . 23 A5
Dock Yard Rd CH65 . . . . . . 70 E6
Doddington Dr CW11 . . . . . 175 C8
Doddington Rd CW2 . . . . . . 190 A3
Dodgepool Barns
  CW3 . . . . 221 F7
Dodd's Green La CW5,
  SY13 . . . . 228 C4
Dodds La CW12 . . . . 178 C6
Dodd's La SY13,SY14 . . . . . 224 E7
Doddswood Dr **2**
  CW12 . . . . 156 F4
Dodgsley Dr WA6 . . . . 75 C1
DODLESTON 162 A7
Dodleston CE Prim Sch
  CH4 . . . . 162 A7
Dodleston La CH4 . . . . 162 C3
Doeford Cl WA3 . . . . 4 E5
Doe's Meadow Rd
  CH63 . . . . 43 B7
Dog La
  Brereton Green CW4,
    CW11 . . . . 153 E7
  Kelsall CW6 . . . . 122 B5
  Nantwich CW5 . . . . 204 E6
  Tattenhall CH3 . . . . 182 D4
  Threapwood SY14 . . . . . . 223 C7
Dogmore La CW6 . . . . 147 C4
Dolly La SK23 . . . . 39 F3
Dolmans La **9** WA1 . . . . . 16 B5
Dolphin Cres CH66 . . . . 69 E5
Dolphin Ct CH4 . . . . 141 A7
Dombey Rd SK12 . . . . 36 D2
Domestic App M90 . . . . 33 C6
Domville Cl WA13 . . . . 18 E3
Donagh Cl SK10 . . . . 86 F2
DONES GREEN 77 B8
Donkey La SK9 . . . . 60 A5
Donne Pl CH1 . . . . 117 F6
Donnington Way CH4 . . . . . 140 F7
Don Wlk CH65 . . . . 70 A7
Dood's La WA4 . . . . 26 D6
Dooley's Grig SK11 . . . . 108 F1
Dooley's La SK9 . . . . 33 C2
Dorac Ave SK8 . . . . 34 C7
Dorchester Cl
  Kidsgrove ST7 . . . . 195 A3
  Wilmslow SK9 . . . . 60 D8
Dorchester Pk WA7 . . . . 24 C3
Dorchester Rd
  Chester CH4 . . . . 140 F5
  Warrington WA5 . . . . 15 C5
Dorchester Way
  Burtonwood WA5 . . . . 6 F6
  Macclesfield SK10 . . . . . . 87 C4
Doreen Ave CW12 . . . . 179 B8
Dorfold Cl CW11 . . . . 175 C6
Dorfold Dr CW5 . . . . 204 D5
Dorfold Hall* CW5 . . . . 204 B5
Dorfold St CW1 . . . . 190 C4
Dorfold Way CH2 . . . . 118 E6
Doric Ave WA6 . . . . 74 D7
Dorin Park Sch CH2 . . . . . . 118 D6
Dormer Cl CH3 . . . . 143 A5
Dorney Cl WA4 . . . . 26 E5
Dorney Ct CW5 . . . . 204 F3
Dorothea St WA2 . . . . 16 B6
Dorric Way CW1 . . . . 190 C7
Dorrington Cl WA7 . . . . 50 E8

Dorrit Cl SK12 . . . . 36 E2
Dorset Cl CW12 . . . . 156 E4
Dorset Dr ST8 . . . . 179 C1
Dorset Gdns WA7 . . . . 50 A6
Dorset Pl
  Chester CH1 . . . . 117 F6
  Kidsgrove ST7 . . . . 195 A2
Dorset Rd
  Chester CH2 . . . . 118 F7
  Irlam M44 . . . . 11 D5
Dorset Way WA1 . . . . 17 B8
Dorset Wlk SK10 . . . . 86 F2
Douglas Ave WA9 . . . . 6 B6
Douglas Cl
  Northwich CW8 . . . . 103 C5
  Widnes WA8 . . . . 13 F3
Douglas La CW7 . . . . 171 A6
Douglas Pl CH4 . . . . 140 E6
Doulton Cl CW7 . . . . 126 F3
Doune Ct CH65 . . . . 70 D3
Dounrey Cl WA2 . . . . 9 A2
DOVE BANK 195 A2
Dove Bank Prim Sch
  ST7 . . . . 195 A2
Dove Cl
  Ellesmere Port CH66 . . . . . 70 A8
  Elton CH2 . . . . 72 C4
  Helsby WA6 . . . . 73 C5
  Sandbach CW11 . . . . 175 A8
  Warrington WA3 . . . . 9 F4
Dovecote Cl CW2 . . . . 206 B8
Dovecote Dr WA11 . . . . 1 C7
Dovecote Gn WA5 . . . . 7 A1
Dovedale Ave CH62 . . . . . . 43 E5
Dovedale Cl
  Congleton CW12 . . . . 157 A4
  High Lane SK6 . . . . 37 E7
  Warrington WA2 . . . . 8 E3
Dovedale Ct WA8 . . . . 12 B3
Dove Gr ST8 . . . . 179 D1
Dove Ho ST7 . . . . 195 C3
Dove Pl CW7 . . . . 127 B2
Dover Cl WA7 . . . . 50 E6
Dover Ct CH65 . . . . 70 D2
Dover Dr CH4 . . . . 16 F3
Dover Rd
  Chester CH4 . . . . 141 A6
  Macclesfield SK10 . . . . . . 87 F2
  Warrington WA4 . . . . 17 A3
Dover St WA7 . . . . 23 B3
Dovesmead Rd CH60 . . . . . 41 C7
Doward St WA8 . . . . 13 C2
Downes Cl SK10 . . . . 87 A1
Downesway SK9 . . . . 59 F1
Downham Ave WA3 . . . . . . 4 F2
Downham Ct **1** CH60 . . . . 41 A8
Downham Dr CH60 . . . . 41 A8
Downham Pl CH1 . . . . 117 E4
Downham Road S
  CH60 . . . . 41 A8
Downing Cl CW1 . . . . 112 F3
Downs End WA16 . . . . 57 C1
Downsfield Rd CH4 . . . . 141 A6
Downside WA8 . . . . 12 B3
Downs The CW8 . . . . 101 D5
Downswood Ct CH2 . . . . . . 118 C4
Downswood Dr CH2 . . . . . . 118 C4
Downvray La WA9 . . . . 1 A1
Dragon's La
  Middlewich CW11 . . . . 151 F1
  Sandbach CW11 . . . . 152 B1
Dragons Wharf CW11 . . . . . 152 C1
Dragon Yd WA8 . . . . 13 B4
Drake Ave M44 . . . . 11 E6
Drake Cl WA5 . . . . 7 C3
Drake La CW5 . . . . 203 F4
Drakelow La CW10 . . . . 128 F8
Drake Rd CH64 . . . . 41 E1
Drakes Way SY14 . . . . 213 B5
Draycott Dr ST5 . . . . 210 D2
Drayton Cl
  12 Handforth SK9 . . . . . 34 D1
  Runcorn WA7 . . . . 24 C1
Drayton Cres CW1 . . . . 190 F5
Drayton Dr SK8 . . . . 34 B7
Drenfell Rd ST7 . . . . 194 F7
Drew Ct CW7 . . . . 126 C1
Drift Cotts LL12 . . . . 162 C1
Drillfield Ct CW2 . . . . 103 F8
Drillfield Rd CW9 . . . . 104 A8
Drill Field Rd CW9 . . . . 103 F8
Drive A CH5 . . . . 93 A2
Drive B CH5 . . . . 93 A2
Drive C CH5 . . . . 93 A2
Drive D CH5 . . . . 93 A1
Drive The
  Altrincham WA15 . . . . 32 D8
  Bollington SK10 . . . . 87 F7
  Broomedge WA13 . . . . . . 19 D1
  Holmes Chapel CW4 . . . . . 130 C2
Drome Rd CH5 . . . . 93 A2
Drovers Way CW11 . . . . . . 175 A5
Droxford Ct WA4 . . . . 26 B6
Drumber La ST7 . . . . 195 B8
Drumber The CW7 . . . . 126 D1
Drumble Field CH1 . . . . 84 A3
Drummond Ave CH66 . . . . . 69 C4
Drummond La CW12 . . . . . . 13 D2
Drummond Way SK10 . . . . . 86 E1
Druridge Dr WA5 . . . . 14 F4
Drury La
  Knutsford WA16 . . . . 57 A2
  Tallarn Green/Tallwrn Green
    SY13 . . . . 223 E1

Drury La continued
  Warmingham CW1 . . . . . . 173 D4
DRURY LANE 223 D1
Dryden Cl CW2 . . . . 190 A1
Dryden Pl M8 . . . . 8 F7
Dryhurst Ct 118 V2
Dryhurst Dr SK12 . . . . 38 D6
Dryhurst La SK12 . . . . 38 D6
Dublin Croft CH66 . . . . 69 E1
Duchess Pl CH2 . . . . 237 A4
Duchy Rd CW1 . . . . 207 A8
DUCKINGTON 199 C4
Duck La CH3 . . . . 121 F7
Duckworth Gr WA2 . . . . . . 9 A1
DUDDON 145 A6
Duddon Cl
  Duddon CW6 . . . . 145 B6
  6 Northwich CW9 . . . . . 103 F4
Duddon Hall Barns
  CW6 . . . . 144 E8
DUDDON HEATH 144 E7
Duddon Hook La
  CW6 . . . . 144 E8
Duddon Rd CW6 . . . . 145 B5
Duddon St Peter's CE Prim
  Sch CW6 . . . . 145 B6
Dudleston Rd CH66 . . . . . . 69 B6
Dudley Ave WA7 . . . . 23 D2
Dudley Cres CH65 . . . . 44 B3
Dudley Rd
  Ellesmere Port CH65 . . . . . 70 B5
  Irlam M44 . . . . 11 D4
Dudley St WA2 . . . . 16 B7
Dudley Wlk **2** SK11 . . . . . 111 F7
Dudlow Green Rd WA4 . . . . 26 E5
DUDLOW'S GREEN 26 E5
Dufton Wlk M22 . . . . 33 E8
Duke Ave
  Cheadle SK8 . . . . 34 F6
  Glazebury WA3 . . . . 5 C7
Duke Cl WA7 . . . . 23 A2
Dukesbridge Ct **7**
  WA13 . . . . 18 E3
Duke's Cres CW11 . . . . 175 D7
Dukes Ct **2** SK11 . . . . 112 D7
Duke's Ct CH1 . . . . 237 B1
DUKESFIELD 22 E3
Duke St
  Alderley Edge SK9 . . . . . . 60 B2
  Chester CH1 . . . . 237 B1
  Congleton CW12 . . . . 156 D2
  Crewe CW2 . . . . 190 C3
  Macclesfield SK11 . . . . . . 112 D7
  Newton-le-W WA12 . . . . . . 2 B3
Dukesway CH2 . . . . 118 E7
Dukes Way CW9 . . . . 103 E5
Dukes Wharf WA7 . . . . 50 E6
Dulas Ct CH2 . . . . 118 E8
Dulverton Ave CH3 . . . . 119 C2
Dumbah La SK10 . . . . 87 D6
Dumbers SK11 . . . . 112 A8
Dumbill Ho ST7 . . . . 210 C8
Dunbar Cl
  Connah's Quay CH5 . . . . . 91 D1
  Ellesmere Port CH66 . . . . . 69 C5
  Holmes Chapel CW4 . . . . . 130 C2
Dunbar Ct CH66 . . . . 69 C5
Duncan Ave
  Newton-le-W WA12 . . . . . . 2 C5
  Runcorn WA7 . . . . 23 C1
Duncansby Cres WA5 . . . . . 14 E6
Duncansby Dr CH63 . . . . . . 43 C4
Duncan St WA2 . . . . 16 C7
Dundalk Rd WA8 . . . . 22 E8
Dundee Cl WA2 . . . . 8 F4
Dundee Ct CH65 . . . . 70 E3
Dundonald Ave **5**
  WA4 . . . . 16 C1
Dundonald Rd SK8 . . . . 35 A7
Dundrennan Cl SK10 . . . . . . 36 D5
Dunge Valley Gdns*
  SK23 . . . . 89 F8
Dunham Cl
  Alsager ST7 . . . . 193 C3
  Bebington CH62 . . . . 43 F3
  Sandbach CW11 . . . . 175 C6
Dunham Cres CW2 . . . . 206 B8
Dunham Ct
  Dunham-on-t-H WA6 . . . . 97 E6
  Hartford CW8 . . . . 102 F4
DUNHAM HEATH 98 A4
Dunham Hill Prim Sch
  WA6 . . . . 97 E6
Dunham Massey Hall*
  WA14 . . . . 20 D3
DUNHAM-ON-THE-HILL . . . 97 E5
Dunham Pk (Deer Pk)*
  WA14 . . . . 20 D3
Dunham Rd
  Altrincham, Bowgreen
    WA14 . . . . 20 F1
  Handforth SK9 . . . . 34 D5
  Mossbrow WA13 . . . . 19 E7
  Northwich CW9 . . . . 104 A4
Dunham Way CH2 . . . . 118 F6
DUNHAM WOODHOUSES
  . . . . 20 B4
DUNKIRK 94 E6
Dunkirk Ave WA3 . . . . 210 A6
Dunkirk Dr CH65 . . . . 70 B1
Dunkirk La
  Capenhurst CH1 . . . . 94 C7
  Ellesmere Port CH65 . . . . . 70 A1
Dunkirk Trad Est CH1 . . . . . 94 D6
Dunley Cl WA3 . . . . 10 A5
Dunlin Ave WA12 . . . . 2 C4

Dunlin Cl
Poynton SK12 . . . . .36 A4
Runcorn WA7 . . . . .49 F5
Warrington WA2 . . . . .8 E3
Dunlin Rise SK10 . . . . .87 B5
Dunlop St WA4 . . . . .16 B3
Dunmail Gr WA7 . . . . .49 C5
Dunmore Cl CW10 . . . . . . .151 C7
Dunmore Cres CH66 . . . . . .69 B6
Dunmore Rd CH66 . . . . .69 B6
Dunmow Rd WA4 . . . . .17 C3
Dunnillow Field CW5 . . . .205 A4
Dunnock Cl WA2 . . . . .8 E3
Dunnock Gr WA3 . . . . .9 E4
Dunnocksfold Rd ST7 . . .193 A4
Dunnockswood ST7 . . . . .193 A4
Dunn's Cotts CW1 . . . . . .192 C1
Dunn's La CH3 . . . . .121 F7
Dunoon Cl CW4 . . . . .130 B2
Dunraven Rd CH64 . . . . . . .67 A7
Dunscar Cl WA3 . . . . .9 D5
Dunsford WA8 . . . . .12 B3
Dunsmore Cl WA11 . . . . . . .1 C7
Dunstan La CH64 . . . . .67 E3
Dunster Cl CW9 . . . . .104 A4
Dunster Gr CH60 . . . . .41 B7
Dunster Rd SK10 . . . . .87 F1
Dunwood Dr ST7 . . . . . . .193 D6
Dunwoody Way CW1,
CW2 . . . . .190 B4
Durban Ave CH3 . . . . .142 D7
Durber Cl ST7 . . . . .209 D1
Durham Cl
Macclesfield SK10 . . . . . . .86 F2
Warrington WA1 . . . . .17 E7
Durham Ct CH65 . . . . .70 E3
Durham Dr WA7 . . . . .149 C6
Durham Gr WM44 . . . . .11 C6
Durham Rd
Blacon CH1 . . . . .117 F5
Widnes WA8 . . . . .13 B3
Durlston Cl WA8 . . . . .12 C2
Durrell Way WA3 . . . . .3 E8
DUTTON 51 A4
Dutton Ct WA1 . . . . .16 C5
Dutton Dr CH2 . . . . .70 F3
Dutton Hall Ct WA4 . . . . . . .76 E8
Dutton La CW8, WA6 . . . .101 B6
Duttons Bsns Ctr
CW9 . . . . .103 F7
Dutton's La CW6 . . . . .122 C5
Dutton Way
Crewe CW1 . . . . .190 B6
Nantwich CW5 . . . . .204 E3
Duxford Ct WA2 . . . . .8 E1
Dyar Terr CW8 . . . . .78 D1
Dye House La SK22 . . . . . . .39 C8
Dyers Cl WA13 . . . . .19 A4
Dyers Ct SK10 . . . . .88 B8
Dyers La WA13 . . . . .19 A4
Dykin Cl WA8 . . . . .13 E3
Dykin Rd WA8 . . . . .13 E3
Dysart Bldgs CW5 . . . . . .204 E5
Dyserth Rd CH1 . . . . .117 D3
Dystelegh Rd SK12 . . . . . . .38 D6

E

Eadie Gr CW1 . . . . .190 A7
Eaglais Way SK10 . . . . .86 F2
Eagland Pl CW12 . . . . .156 E4
Eagle Brow WA13 . . . . .18 D3
Eagle La CH66 . . . . .69 D7
Eagle Mount WA4 . . . . .16 C2
Eagle Park Dr WA2 . . . . .8 A1
Eaglesfield WA8 . . . . .103 C4
Eagles Way WA7 . . . . .49 E6
Ealing Cl WA7 . . . . .24 D1
Ealing Rd WA5 . . . . .15 B5
Eanleywood Farm Cl
WA7 . . . . .50 C7
Eanleywood La WA7 . . . . . .50 C7
Eardley Cres CW12 . . . . . .156 E4
Eardley Ct WA7 . . . . .190 B5
Eardleyend Rd ST7 . . . . . .209 E7
Eardswick Cl CH2 . . . . . . .237 B4
Eardswick La CW10 . . . . .151 C6
Earle Cl WA12 . . . . .1 C5
Earle Cres CH64 . . . . .41 D1
Earle Dr CH64 . . . . .41 D1
Earle Rd WA8 . . . . .23 C7
Earles La CW9 . . . . .79 E6
Earle's La CW6 . . . . .122 C5
Earle St
Crewe CW1 . . . . .190 D4
Newton-le-W WA12 . . . . . . .2 A2
EARLESTOWN 2 B2
Earlestown Sta WA12 . . . . .2 B3
Earl Rd SK8, SK9 . . . . .34 E5
Earls Gdns CH65 . . . . .70 B5
Earls Oak CH2 . . . . .118 D7
Earl's Port CH1 . . . . .118 B2
Earls Rd WA2 . . . . .16 B7
Earl St WA2 . . . . .16 B7
Earlston Ct CH3 . . . . .237 C2
Earlsway
Chester CH4 . . . . .141 A8
Macclesfield SK11 . . . . . . .111 F7
Earls Way
Northwich CW9 . . . . .103 E4
Runcorn WA7 . . . . .49 E6
Earlswood Mews
CW9 . . . . .103 F3
Easby Cl
Cheadle SK8 . . . . .35 B6
Poynton SK12 . . . . .36 D4

Easby Cl continued
Runcorn WA7 . . . . .23 C2
Easenhall Cl WA8 . . . . .13 C5
East Ave
Bebington SK10 . . . . .87 F7
Gatley SK8 . . . . .34 D8
Northwich CW9 . . . . .104 D6
Warrington, Great Sankey
WA5 . . . . .15 A4
Warrington, Stockton Heath
WA4 . . . . .16 D1
Warrington WA2 . . . . .16 C8
Weston CW2 . . . . .207 C5
Eastbury Cl WA8 . . . . .13 C5
Eastcott Cl CW12 . . . . . . .155 F4
East Ct ST7 . . . . .193 E4
Eastdale WA15 . . . . .31 F8
Eastdale Rd WA1 . . . . .17 A7
East Dam Wood Rd
L24 . . . . .21 A2
East Dudley St CW12 . . . . .126 F1
Easter Ct WA5 . . . . .7 B2
Eastern Pathway CH4 . . . .237 C1
Eastfields Gr CH1 . . . . . . .117 A8
Eastford Rd WA4 . . . . .16 A1
Eastgate SK10 . . . . .112 E8
Eastgate Rd
Holmes Chapel CW4 . . . . .130 D3
Runcorn WA7 . . . . .24 E5
Eastgate Row N CH1 . . . .237 B2
Eastgate Row S CH1 . . . . .237 B2
Eastgate St CH1 . . . . .237 B2
Eastgate Way WA7 . . . . . . .24 D4
East Gn CH5 . . . . .116 A6
EASTHAM 43 F5
**Eastham Ctry Pk*
CH62 . . . . .44 A8
EASTHAM FERRY 44 B8
Eastham Ho CH62 . . . . .44 A4
Eastham Mews CH62 . . . . . .44 A4
Eastham Rake CH62,
CH64 . . . . .43 D3
Eastham Rake Sta
CH63 . . . . .43 D3
Eastham Village Rd
CH62 . . . . .44 A5
Eastham Way 11 SK9 . . . . .34 D5
East La
Cuddington WA8 . . . . . . .102 A3
Runcorn WA7 . . . . .49 F7
East Lancashire Rd WA11,
WA12, WA3 . . . . .2 C7
East Mains L24 . . . . .21 A3
East Millwood Rd L24 . . . .21 A4
East Park Rd SK11 . . . . . .112 B5
East Rd
Halewood L24, L26 . . . . . .21 A5
Middlewich CW10 . . . . . .128 B1
Wythenshawe M90 . . . . . .33 C7
East St WA8 . . . . .13 D1
East Terr WA16 . . . . .57 A2
East View
10 Nantwich CW5 . . . . . . .204 E6
Warrington WA4 . . . . .17 B2
Eastward Ave SK9 . . . . .59 F6
Eastway
Ellesmere Port CH66 . . . . .69 D7
Widnes WA8 . . . . .12 F3
Eastwood WA7 . . . . .24 C2
Eastwood Ave WA12 . . . . . .2 F3
Eastwood Ct CH5 . . . . . . .139 B7
Eastwood Rd WA5 . . . . .6 F7
EATON
Congleton 157 A8
Tarporley 147 A4
Eaton Bank CW12 . . . . . . .156 F4
Eaton Bank Ind Est
CW12 . . . . .156 F5
Eaton Bank Sch
CW12 . . . . .156 F5
Eaton Cl
Broughton CH4 . . . . .139 C4
Poynton SK12 . . . . .37 A3
Sandbach CW11 . . . . .175 C7
Eaton Cres CW9 . . . . .103 E2
Eaton Ct
1 Northwich CW9 . . . . . .103 E5
Wilmslow SK9 . . . . .60 A6
Eaton Dr
Alderley Edge SK9 . . . . . . .59 F2
Middlewich CW10 . . . . . . .151 B8
Eaton Gr CH4 . . . . .140 E6
Eaton La
Davenham CW9 . . . . .103 E2
Eaton CW6 . . . . .147 A5
Goostrey CW4 . . . . .107 C1
Macclesfield SK11 . . . . . . .112 B5
Tarporley CW6 . . . . .168 E8
Eaton Mews CH4 . . . . .141 D7
Eaton Pl CW8 . . . . .102 F4
Eaton Prim Sch CW4 . . . . .147 B3
Eaton Rd
Alsager ST7 . . . . .193 D4
Chester CH4 . . . . .141 E4
Tarporley CW6 . . . . .146 D1
Wettenhall CW7 . . . . .170 B8
Eaton St
Crewe CW2 . . . . .190 C4
13 Runcorn WA7 . . . . . . .23 A2
Eaton View CW9 . . . . .126 E8
Eaton Way CW3 . . . . .230 A4
Eaves Brow Rd WA3 . . . . . .9 B7
Eaves Knoll Rd SK22 . . . . .39 B8
EBNAL 213 D5
Ebnal La SY14 . . . . .213 E4
Ebury Pl CH4 . . . . .141 D7

Eccles Cl SK23 . . . . .65 D8
Eccles Rd SK23 . . . . .65 F6
ECCLESTON 141 E1
Eccleston Ave
Bebington CH62 . . . . .43 C8
Chester CH4 . . . . .141 D6
Ellesmere Port CH66 . . . . .69 E5
Eccleston CE Prim Sch
CH4 . . . . .141 E2
Eccleston Cl WA3 . . . . .9 C5
Eccleston Ct 5 CW9 . . . . .103 E5
Eccleston Dr WA7 . . . . .23 C1
Eccleston Rd CH4 . . . . . . .161 A7
Eccleston Way 3 SK9 . . . . .34 D4
Eccups La SK9 . . . . .59 C8
Echo Cl CH4 . . . . .140 E5
Ecton Ave SK10 . . . . .113 A7
Ecton Cl CW7 . . . . .127 A4
Edale Cl
Bebington CH62 . . . . .43 E5
Gatley SK8 . . . . .34 D7
Edale Dr CW6 . . . . .122 D5
Edburton Ct WA3 . . . . .3 A8
Eddisbury Cl SK11 . . . . . . .112 F7
Eddisbury Dr ST5 . . . . . . .210 D2
Eddisbury Hill CW6,
CW8 . . . . .123 D7
Eddisbury Hill Pk
CW8 . . . . .123 D7
Eddisbury Rd CH66 . . . . . . .69 F1
Eddisbury Sq WA6 . . . . .74 B8
Eddisbury Terr SK11 . . . . .112 F7
Eddisbury Way CW9 . . . . .103 E3
Eddisford Dr WA3 . . . . .4 F4
Edelsten St WA5 . . . . .15 F5
Eden Ave
Fowley Common WA3 . . . . .5 C4
High Lane SK6 . . . . .37 E7
Edenbridge Cl CW2 . . . . . .207 B2
Edenbridge Gdns WA4 . . . .26 E3
Eden Cl
Biddulph ST8 . . . . .179 E1
5 Ellesmere Port CH66 . . .69 C5
Kidsgrove ST7 . . . . .195 B2
Wilmslow SK9 . . . . .59 E5
Edendale WA8 . . . . .12 B2
Eden Dr SK10 . . . . .87 F1
Edenfield Cl WA16 . . . . .58 A3
Edenfield Rd WA16 . . . . . . .58 A4
Edenhall Cl CW4 . . . . .130 A3
Eden Park Rd SK8 . . . . .34 E8
Edgar Ct
Chester CH4 . . . . .237 A2
22 Macclesfield SK11 . . . .112 C8
Edgar Pl CH4 . . . . .237 B1
Edgars Dr WA2 . . . . .9 A1
Edgecroft CH3 . . . . .166 A1
Edge Gr CH2 . . . . .118 F2
EDGE GREEN 199 B2
Edgehill Chase SK9 . . . . . . .60 E7
Edge La SY14 . . . . .199 C1
Edgerley La CH3 . . . . .181 B6
Edgerton Rd WA3 . . . . .3 F8
Edge View La SK9 . . . . .59 B2
Edgeview Rd CW12 . . . . . .179 B7
Edgeway
Henbury SK11 . . . . .111 C8
Wilmslow SK9 . . . . .60 B5
Edgewell La CW6 . . . . .147 A3
Edgewood 3 CH3 . . . . . . .142 A8
Edgewood Dr
Bebington CH62 . . . . .43 D5
Wistaston CW2 . . . . .206 A7
Edgworth St WA2 . . . . .16 A6
Edinburgh Cl CH65 . . . . . . .70 D3
Edinburgh Dr SK10 . . . . . . .87 A1
Edinburgh Pl CW12 . . . . . .156 F2
Edinburgh Rd
Congleton CW12 . . . . . . .156 F2
Widnes WA8 . . . . .22 A8
Warrington CW2 . . . . .205 E8
Edinburgh Way CH4 . . . . . .237 C1
Edison Rd WA7 . . . . .23 D3
Edith St WA7 . . . . .23 A2
Edlestone Gr 2 SK9 . . . . . .34 E1
Edleston Hall La CW5 . . . .203 F2
Edleston Prim Sch
CW2 . . . . .190 C3
Edleston Rd CW2 . . . . .190 D3
Edmund Wright Way
CW5 . . . . .204 C5
Edna St CH2 . . . . .118 F3
Edward Gdns WA1 . . . . . . .17 F6
Edward Rd WA5 . . . . .14 D6
Edwards Ave CW2 . . . . . . .206 C5
Edwards Cl CW2 . . . . .206 C5
Edwards Rd CH4 . . . . .141 A6
Edwards Way
Audley ST7 . . . . .209 F3
Crewe CW2 . . . . .190 D2
Ellesmere Port CH65 . . . . .70 C7
Haydock WA11 . . . . .1 A6
Macclesfield SK11 . . . . . . .112 B7
Northwich CW9 . . . . .104 C8
Widnes WA8 . . . . .13 D1
Edwards Way
Alsager ST7 . . . . .193 E4
Widnes WA8 . . . . .22 C8
Edwin St WA8 . . . . .13 E2
Egdon Cl WA8 . . . . .13 E2
Egerton WA16 . . . . .29 C5
Egerton Ave
Hartford CW8 . . . . .103 A4
Partington WA13 . . . . .19 C8
Warrington WA1 . . . . .16 F7
Egerton Ct CW6 . . . . .122 A5
Egerton Dr CH2 . . . . .118 D5

EGERTON GREEN 200 C5
Egerton Mews 1 WA4 . . . .16 C1
Egerton Moss WA15 . . . . . .31 E5
Egerton Prim Sch
WA16 . . . . .56 F2
Egerton Rd
Blacon CH1 . . . . .117 E5
Handforth SK9 . . . . .34 B1
Lymm WA13 . . . . .18 C2
Egerton Sq 7 WA16 . . . . . .57 A2
Egerton St
Chester CH1 . . . . .237 C3
Congleton CW12 . . . . . . .156 C2
Ellesmere Port CH65 . . . . .70 C6
Runcorn WA7 . . . . .22 F3
Warrington, Howley
WA1 . . . . .16 D5
Warrington, Stockton Heath
WA4 . . . . .16 C1
Egerton Terr CW9 . . . . . . .105 D4
Egerton Wlk CH4 . . . . .162 A7
Eggbridge La CH3 . . . . . . .143 A5
Egremont St WA4 . . . . .16 C3
Egypt St
3 Warrington WA1 . . . . . .16 A5
Widnes WA8 . . . . .22 F7
Eilson Ct CH1 . . . . .237 B3
Elaine Cl
Ellesmere Port CH66 . . . . .69 C4
Widnes WA8 . . . . .13 C1
Elaine Price Ct 3 WA4 . . . .26 E3
Elaine St WA1 . . . . .16 D7
Elanor Rd CW11 . . . . .174 D7
Elcombe Ave WA3 . . . . .3 E7
Elderberry Way SK9 . . . . . .60 E8
Elderberry Wlk M31 . . . . . .11 E3
Elder Dr CH4 . . . . .140 E5
Eldon Rd SK10 . . . . .111 F8
Eldon St WA1 . . . . .16 C5
Eldon Terr CH64 . . . . .66 E7
Eleanor Cl CW1 . . . . .189 F5
Eleanor St
Ellesmere Port CH65 . . . . .70 C6
9 Sandbach CW11 . . . . . .175 B6
Elmore Cl
Holmes Chapel CW4 . . . . .130 B3
Runcorn WA7 . . . . .24 D1
Elm Rd
Congleton CW12 . . . . . . .156 B3
Haydock WA11 . . . . .1 E7
High Lane SK6 . . . . .37 F7
Hollinfare WA3 . . . . .11 A2
Middlewich CW10 . . . . . .151 D7
Runcorn WA7 . . . . .49 C8
Warrington WA5 . . . . .14 F4
Warrington, Winwick Quay
WA2 . . . . .8 B4
Elm Sq WA4 . . . . .140 F6
Elm St
Ellesmere Port CH65 . . . . .70 C7
Northwich CW9 . . . . .79 B1
Elmstead Cres CW1 . . . . .189 F8
Elmstead Rd SK11 . . . . .84 A3
Elms The
Golborne WA3 . . . . .3 F8
Mobberley WA16 . . . . .58 E2
7 Northwich CW9 . . . . . .103 E6
Runcorn WA7 . . . . .24 C2
Tallarn Green/Tallwrn Green
SY14 . . . . .222 F1
Elmsway
Altrincham WA15 . . . . . . .32 B8
Bollington SK10 . . . . .88 A8
Bramhall SK7 . . . . .35 C7
High Lane SK6 . . . . .37 E6
Elm Terr CW1 . . . . .190 C6
Elm Tree Ave
Lymm WA13 . . . . .18 D2
Warrington WA4 . . . . .16 F8
Elm Tree Cotts CH3 . . . . . .167 A7
Elm Tree Ct CW6 . . . . .147 A3
Elm Tree Dr ST7 . . . . .209 F1
Elm Tree La CW11 . . . . . . .174 D8
Elm Tree Rd
Golborne WA3 . . . . .3 F8
Lymm WA13 . . . . .18 D2
Elmuir CH1 . . . . .117 E3
Elmwood WA7 . . . . .24 C2
Elmwood Ave
Chester CH2 . . . . .118 F4
Warrington WA1 . . . . .17 A7
Elmwood Cl ST7 . . . . .194 A4
Elmwood Gr CW7 . . . . . . .149 F8
Elmwood Rd CW8 . . . . .78 B4
Elnor Ave SK23 . . . . .65 E5
Elnor La SK23 . . . . .65 F4
Elphins Dr WA4 . . . . .16 C2
Elsby Rd ST7 . . . . .193 F2
Elston Ave WA12 . . . . .2 C5
Elstree Ave CH3 . . . . .119 B3
Elstree Ct WA8 . . . . .13 D4
Elswick Ave SK7 . . . . .35 E7
Eltham Cl WA3 . . . . .9 D5
Eltham Wlk WA8 . . . . .13 E3
ELTON 72 C3

Elisson St
Warrington, Howley
WA1 . . . . .16 C5
Warrington, Stockton Heath
WA4 . . . . .16 D1
Ellis St
Crewe CW1 . . . . .190 B6
Widnes WA8 . . . . .22 F7
Elloway Rd L24 . . . . .21 A3
Ellwood Cl L24 . . . . .21 E2
Ellwood Gr CW2 . . . . .206 E3
Elm Ave
Newton-le-W WA12 . . . . . . .2 C5
Widnes WA8 . . . . .13 B2
Elm Beds Rd SK12 . . . . . . .37 C2
Elm Cl
Crewe CW2 . . . . .189 E2
2 Partington M31 . . . . . .11 F3
Poynton SK12 . . . . .36 F3
Tarporley CW6 . . . . .146 D2
Elm Cres SK9 . . . . .60 B3
Elm Ct CW1 . . . . .190 D6
Elm Dr
Crewe CW1 . . . . .190 A6
Holmes Chapel CW4 . . . . .130 D4
Macclesfield SK10 . . . . . . .87 E2
Elmfield Cl SK9 . . . . .60 B2
Elmfield Rd SK9 . . . . .60 B2
Elm Gn CH64 . . . . .67 F8
Elm Gr
Alderley Edge SK9 . . . . . . .60 B2
Alsager ST7 . . . . .193 E4
Ellesmere Port CH66 . . . . .70 A1
Handforth SK9 . . . . .34 C3
Saltney CH4 . . . . .140 E5
Warrington WA1 . . . . .16 F7
Widnes WA8 . . . . .13 B1
Winsford CW7 . . . . .127 A1
Elm Ho
Chester CH2 . . . . .118 C5
9 Sandbach CW11 . . . . . .175 B6

Elton Cl

Bebington L.HH? 43 F4
Golborne WA3 . . . . 3 E7
Handforth SK9 . . . . .34 E1
Warrington WA3 . . . . .9 C4
Elton Crossings Rd
CW11 . . . . 174 D6
Elton Dr SK7 . . . . .36 D8
ELTON GREEN 72 A3
Elton La
Elton CH? 72 E4
Haslington CW11, CW1. . 174 D1
Winterley CW11 . . . . 191 F8
Elton Lordship La WA6 . . .73 B7
Elton Prim Sch CH2 . . . . . . 72 B4
Elton Rd CW11 . . . . 174 D5
Elvington Cl
Congleton CW12 . . . . 156 E2
Runcorn WA7 . . . . .49 F4
Elwood Way CW5 . . . . 205 B4
ELWORTH 174 E6
Elworth Ave WA8 . . . . .13 A5
Elworth CE Prim Sch
CW11 . . . . 174 E7
Elworth Ct
12 Congleton CW12 . . . . 156 F3
Sandbach CW11 . . . . 174 D7
Elworth Hall Prim Sch
CW11 . . . . 174 E7
Elworth Rd CW11 . . . . 174 E6
Elworth St CW11 . . . . 175 A7
Elworth Way **6** SK9 . . . .34 D4
Elwyn Dr L26 . . . . .21 A8
Ely Cl CH66 . . . . .94 E8
Ely Pk WA7 . . . . .24 E2
Embassy Cl CH1 . . . . 117 C4
Emberton Pl CW3 . . . . 230 A5
Embleton Ct WA7 . . . . .49 D5
Embridge Cswy SK10 . . . . .90 B5
Emerald Dr CW11 . . . . 175 C8
Emerald Rd M22 . . . . .33 F7
Emily St **7** WA8 . . . . .23 A7
Emmett St CW8 . . . . .78 A3
Empire Ct WA1 . . . . .16 A4
Empress Dr CW2 . . . . 190 B3
Emral Ct SY14 . . . . 211 A1
Emslie Ct CH44 . . . . .66 C7
Enderby Rd CH1 . . . . 237 A3
Endon Ave SK10 . . . . .88 A7
Endon Hall Mews SK10 . . .88 B5
Endsleigh Cl CH2 . . . . 118 E8
Endsleigh Gdns CH2 . . . . . 118 E8
Enfield Cl CW2 . . . . 206 A3
Enfield Park Rd WA2 . . . . . .9 A3
Enfield Rd CH65 . . . . .70 B5
Engineer Pk CH5 . . . . 116 A4
Englefield Ave CH4 . . . . . . 140 D6
Englefield Cl CW1 . . . . 190 A8
ENGLESEA-BROOK 208 A4
Englesea Brook La
CW2 . . . . 208 A3
Englesea Brook Mus of
Primitive Methodism*
CW2 . . . . 208 A3
Englesea Gr CW2 . . . . 190 B1
Ennerdale
Chester CH2 . . . . 118 F5
Macclesfield SK11 . . . . . . 111 F5
Ennerdale Ave
Bebington CH62 . . . . .43 F4
Warrington WA2 . . . . .8 B3
Ennerdale Cl
Alderley Edge SK9 . . . . . . .83 F7
Winsford CW7 . . . . 126 D3
Ennerdale Dr
Congleton CW12 . . . . 156 B2
Frodsham WA6 . . . . .74 C8
Ennerdale Rd
Crewe CW2 . . . . 189 D3
Partington M31 . . . . .11 E3
Ennis Cl L24 . . . . .21 D2
Ensor Way SK22 . . . . .39 C7
Enterprise Ct CW11 . . . . . . 174 D7
Enterprise Ctr The
CW12 . . . . 156 E3
Enterprise Way WA3 . . . . . . .4 A7
Enticott Rd M44 . . . . .11 C5
Enville St WA4 . . . . .16 D2
Epping Dr WA1 . . . . .17 D8
Epsom Ave SK8, SK9 . . . . . .34 E4
Epsom Ct CH1 . . . . 118 B2
Epsom Gdns WA4 . . . . .26 E7
Epworth Cl WA5 . . . . .6 F7
ERF Way CW10 . . . . 151 E8
Eric Ave WA1 . . . . .16 E8
Eric Dr CW11 . . . . 174 D7
Eric Fountain Rd CH65 . . .44 D3
Eric St WA8 . . . . .13 C2
Erindale Cres WA6 . . . . .74 A6
Ermine Rd CH2 . . . . 237 C4
Ernest St CW2 . . . . 190 C1
Ernley Cl CW5 . . . . 204 D6
Errington Ave CH65 . . . . . . .70 C6
Errwood Forest Walks*
SK17 . . . . .90 E2
Erskine Rd M31 . . . . .11 F3
Ervood St WA2 . . . . .16 B6
Eskdale CH65 . . . . .70 B3
Eskdale Ave
Bebington CH62 . . . . .43 E5
Bramhall SK7 . . . . .35 C5
Warrington WA3 . . . . .8 C3
Eskdale Cl WA7 . . . . .49 D5
Esk Dale Cl CW7 . . . . 126 C2
Esk Rd CW7 . . . . 127 A2

Essex Cl CW12 . . . . 156 E3

Essex Dr
Biddulph ST8 . . . . 179 D2
Kidsgrove ST7 . . . . 194 F2
Essex Gdns M44 . . . . .11 C4
Essex Rd CH2 . . . . 119 A5
Essex Wlk SK10 . . . . .86 F1
Esthers La WA8 . . . . 102 D8
Etchells Prim Sch SK8 . . .34 C8
Ethelda Dr CH2 . . . . 119 A5
Etherow Cl CW11 . . . . 174 E7
Ethos Ct CH1 . . . . 237 C3
Eton Cl CH63 . . . . .41 F6
Eton Rd CH65 . . . . .70 D4
Ettiley Ave CW11 . . . . 174 C5
ETTILEY HEATH 174 C6
Ettrick Pk CH3 . . . . 119 A2
Euclid Ave WA4 . . . . .17 B2
Europa Bvd WA5 . . . . .7 D3
Europa Way CH65 . . . . .70 C6
Eustace St WA2 . . . . .16 A4
Evans Bsns Ctr CH5 . . . . . .93 A1
Evans Cl WA11 . . . . .1 F7
Evansleigh Dr CH5 . . . . 116 A3
Evans Pl WA4 . . . . .16 D3
Evans St CW1 . . . . 190 C6
Eva St CW11 . . . . 174 D8
Evelyn St WA5 . . . . .15 E4
Evelyn Street Com Prim
Sch WA5 . . . . .15 E4
Evenwood Cl WA7 . . . . .24 E8
Everdon Cl CW7 . . . . 126 F4
Everest Cl CH66 . . . . .69 F3
Everest Rd ST7 . . . . 195 C3
Everglade Cl SK11 . . . . 112 B5
Evergreens The CW9 . . . . . .80 A3
Evergreen Way WA9 . . . . . . .6 A7
Everite Rd WA8 . . . . .22 B7
Everite Road Ind Est
WA8 . . . . .22 B7
Eversley Cl
Frodsham WA6 . . . . .74 C6
Warrington WA4 . . . . .26 F5
Eversley St CH2 . . . . 118 C4
Eversley Pk CH2 . . . . 118 C4
Evesham Cl
Macclesfield SK10 . . . . . . .87 E4
Warrington WA4 . . . . .26 C8
Evesham Dr SK9 . . . . .34 C2
Evington Ho **2** SK11 . . . . 112 B6
Ewart St WA4 . . . . 140 B7
Ewloe Ct CH65 . . . . .70 D2
Ewrin La SK10 . . . . .89 D5
Excalibur Ind Est ST7 . . . . 193 E3
Excalibur Prim Sch
ST7 . . . . 193 E2
Excalibur Way WA4 . . . . . . .11 F7
Exchange Cl **12** SK11 . . . 112 D8
Exchange St SK11 . . . . 112 D8
Exeter Cl SK8 . . . . .34 F8
Exeter Pl CH1 . . . . 117 F5
Exeter Rd CH65 . . . . .70 C5
Exeter Wlk SK7 . . . . .35 F7
Exit Rd W M90 . . . . .33 B7
Exmouth Cres WA7 . . . . . . .50 E6
Exmouth Way WA5 . . . . .6 F6
Express Ind Est WA8 . . . . . .22 A7
Exton Pk CH1 . . . . 237 A4
Eyam Rd SK7 . . . . .36 E8
Eyebrook Rd WA14 . . . . .20 F2
Eyre Pl CH65 . . . . .70 B6
Eyston Cl CW9 . . . . 103 E5

F

Facit Glen Ind Est
CH4 . . . . 140 F7
Factory La
Warrington WA1, WA5. . . .15 F4
Widnes WA8 . . . . .13 B3
Factory Rd CH5. . . . . 116 A3
FADDILEY 202 D7
FADDILEY BANK 202 C6
Fairacre Dr CW10. . . . . 151 E6
Fairacres Rd SK6 . . . . .37 E8
Fairbourne Ave
Alderley Edge SK9 . . . . . . .60 B3
Wilmslow SK9 . . . . .59 F4
Fairbourne Cl
Warrington WA5. . . . . .7 E3
Wilmslow SK9. . . . . .59 F4
Fairbourne Dr SK9 . . . . .59 F4
Fairbrook CW2 . . . . 189 C2
Fairbrother Cres WA2. . . . . .8 D2
Fairburn Ave CW2 . . . . 189 F4
Fairburn Cl WA8 . . . . .13 E3
Fairclough Ave WA1 . . . . . . .16 C4
Fairclough Cres WA11 . . . .1 A6
Fairclough St
Burtonwood WA5. . . . . .6 E6
Newton-le-W WA12? 2 B3
Fairfax Cl ST8 . . . . 179 C1
Fairfax Ct CW5 . . . . 204 E7
Fairfax Dr
Nantwich CW5 . . . . 204 D6
Runcorn WA7 . . . . .23 D2
Wilmslow SK9 . . . . .59 F4
Fairfield Ave
Bollington SK10. . . . . .88 A8
Ellesmere Port CH65. . . . . .70 A2
Sandbach CW11 . . . . 175 B5
Fairfield Gdns WA4 . . . . . . .16 E2
Fairfield High Sch
WA8 . . . . .13 B3
Fairfield Inf Sch WA8 . . . . . .13 B2
Fairfield Jun Sch WA8 . . . . .13 B2

Fairfield Rd

Broughton CH4 . . . . 139 B4
Chester CH2 . . . . 119 A4
Irlam M44 . . . . .11 C5
Lymm WA13. . . . . .18 F3
Northwich CW9 . . . . 104 A4
Warrington WA4 . . . . .16 E2
Widnes WA8 . . . . .13 B2
Fairfields
Audley ST7 . . . . 209 F2
Whitchurch SY13 . . . . 225 F1
Fairfield St WA1 . . . . .16 D6
Fairford Cl WA5 . . . . .15 B6
Fairford Rd CH4 . . . . 140 F6
Fairford Way SK9 . . . . .60 D7
Fairhaven CW2 . . . . 207 B1
Fairhaven Cl
Bramhall SK7 . . . . .35 F8
Macclesfield SK10 . . . . . . .87 B4
Warrington WA5 . . . . .15 B4
Fairhaven Dr CH63 . . . . .43 C5
Fairhaven Rd WA8 . . . . .13 C2
Fair Haven's Ct WA8 . . . . . .23 B8
Fairhills Ind Est M44 . . . . . .11 F8
Fairhills Rd M44 . . . . .11 F8
Fairholme Ave CH64 . . . . . . .41 D1
Fairholme Cl CW11 . . . . .94 B1
Fairholme Pl **8** CH3. . . . . 119 A1
Fairholme Rd CW9 . . . . 127 A8
Fair Isle Cl CH65. . . . . .70 C1
Fairlawn Cl CH63. . . . . .43 A6
Fair Mead WA16 . . . . .82 B8
Fairmeadow CH4 . . . . 162 D2
Fairoak Cl **12** CW7 . . . . . . 149 A8
Fairoak Ct WA7 . . . . .50 F3
Fairoak La WA7 . . . . .50 F3
Fair Oak Rd ST5 . . . . 210 D1
Fairview CW8 . . . . .77 E8
Fairview LL13 . . . . 196 E8
Fairview Ave
Alsager ST7 . . . . 193 D4
Weston CW2 . . . . 207 B5
Fair View Cl CW8 . . . . .77 F3
Fairview Rd
Ellesmere Port CH65. . . . . .70 A2
Macclesfield SK11 . . . . 112 A6
Fairway
Bramhall SK7 . . . . .35 D6
Sandycroft CH5 . . . . 116 A2
Fairways
Frodsham WA6 . . . . .74 D7
Warrington WA4 . . . . .26 D5
Fairways Dr
Ellesmere Port CH66. . . . . .69 D7
Whitchurch SY13 . . . . 226 A1
Fairways The
Macclesfield SK10 . . . . . . .87 B4
Winsford CW7 . . . . 126 A2
Fairway The ST7 . . . . 193 C4
Fairway Trad Est WA8 . . . . .22 E6
Fairywell Cl SK9 . . . . .34 D1
Falcon Cl
Middlewich CW10 . . . . 151 D5
New Mills SK22 . . . . .39 D8
Winsford CW7 . . . . 149 D6
Falcondale Rd WA2 . . . . .8 B6
Falcon Dr CW1 . . . . 190 B8
Falconers Gn WA5. . . . . .7 B2
Falcon Rd CH66 . . . . .69 F3
Falcons Way WA7 . . . . .49 E6
Falkirk Ave WA8 . . . . .12 F3
Fallbroome Cl SK10 . . . . . . .87 A3
Fallbroome High Sch
SK10. .86 E2
Fallibroome Rd SK10 . . . . . 111 E8
Fallon Ct CW10 . . . . 151 C7
Fallowfield WA7 . . . . .23 D1
Fallowfield Cl CW7 . . . . 125 F1
Fallowfield Ct CW1 . . . . 190 A6
Fallowfield Gr WA2 . . . . .9 B1
Falmouth Cl SK10 . . . . 111 E8
Falmouth Dr WA5 . . . . .14 E3
Falmouth Pl WA7 . . . . .50 E6
Falmouth Rd
Congleton CW12 . . . . 178 E8
Crewe CW1 . . . . 190 A6
Falstone Cl WA3. . . . . .10 B6
Falstone Dr WA7 . . . . .50 E7
Fanner's La WA16 . . . . .28 D5
Fanny's Croft ST7 . . . . 193 D2
FANSHAWE 110 C4
Fanshawe La SK11 . . . . 110 E5
Fanshawe Wlk CW2 . . . . . . 206 C8
Faraday Rd
Ellesmere Port CH65. . . . . .70 A4
Runcorn WA7 . . . . .23 D3
Faraday St WA3 . . . . .9 E6
Farams Rd ST7 . . . . 193 E7
Farbailey Cl CH4. . . . . 141 B5
Farcroft Cl WA13 . . . . .19 C1
Farfields Cl SK11 . . . . 111 C1
Farley Cl CW10 . . . . 151 B8
Farm Cl CW8 . . . . .77 D1
Farmdale Dr CH? 91 C1
Farm Dr CH5 . . . . .91 C1
Farmer Cl CW2 . . . . 190 A4
Farmers Heath CH66. . . . . . .69 D2
Farmer's La WA5. . . . . .7 E4
Farmfield Dr SK10 . . . . .87 C3
Farmfields Rise CW3 . . . . . 232 C1
Farmfold SK9 . . . . .33 F3
Farm Hollow ST7 . . . . 210 A2
Farm La
High Lane SK12 . . . . .38 A6
Warrington WA4 . . . . .26 B8
Withington Green SK11. . . 108 E1
Farmleigh Dr CW1. . . . . 190 E5
Farmleigh Gdns WA5 . . . . . .15 C6

Farm Rd

Northwich CW9 . . . . 104 E7
Oakmere CW8 . . . . 124 A8
Weaverham CW8. . . . . .77 D1
Farmside Cl WA5 . . . . .15 F7
Farmstead Way CH66 . . . . .69 E1
Farm Way WA12 . . . . .2 E1
Farm Wlk WA14 . . . . .20 E1
Farndale WA8 . . . . .13 A5
Farndale Cl
Warrington WA5 . . . . .14 F7
Wistaston CW2 . . . . 206 A6
Farndale Wlk SK11 . . . . 112 D6
FARNDON 180 F2
Farndon Cl
Broughton CH4 . . . . 139 C4
Cuddington CW8 . . . . 102 A3
Farndon Prim Sch
CH3 . . . . 180 E2
Farndon Rd CH66. . . . . .69 E6
Farndon Ct CH65 . . . . .95 C8
Farnham Ave WA3. . . . . .5 C7
Farnham Cl SK11 . . . . 112 A6
Farnham Cl
Cheadle SK8 . . . . .35 A7
Warrington WA4 . . . . .26 E7
Farnhill Cl WA7 . . . . .50 D8
Farnley Cl WA7 . . . . .24 D1
FARNWORTH 13 A3
Farnworth CE Prim Sch
WA8. . . . . .13 A4
Farnworth Cl WA8 . . . . .13 B4
Farnworth Ct WA8 . . . . .13 B3
Farnworth Rd WA5 . . . . .14 C4
Farnworth St WA8 . . . . .13 B4
Farrant St WA8 . . . . .23 B8
Farrell Rd WA4 . . . . .26 C8
Farrell St WA1. . . . . .16 D5
Farr Hall Dr CH60 . . . . .40 E7
Farr Hall Rd CH60 . . . . .40 F8
Farrier Ct CW1 . . . . 190 D7
Farriers Way CW7 . . . . 126 A1
Farringdon Rd WA2 . . . . .8 B6
Farthing La CW9 . . . . .79 B8
Farthings The WA13 . . . . . . .18 D4
Farwood Cl SK10 . . . . .86 F2
Faulkner Dr CW10. . . . . 151 E6
Faulkners Cl CH4 . . . . 161 A7
Faulkners La CH3 . . . . 142 D8
Faulkner's La WA16. . . . . . . .58 E2
Faulkner St CH2 . . . . 118 F3
Fawns Keep SK9 . . . . .60 D7
Fawns Leap CW8 . . . . 101 E5
Fearndown Way SK10 . . . . .87 C4
FEARNHEAD 9 B2
Fearnhead Cross WA2 . . . . .8 F2
Fearnhead La WA2 . . . . .9 A2
Fearnleigh CW8 . . . . 103 C7
Fearnley Way WA12. . . . . . . .2 C1
Feather La CH60 . . . . .40 F8
Feather's La CH1 . . . . 237 B2
Feilden Ct CH1. . . . . .94 F1
Felix Rd CH8 . . . . 103 E8
Felkirk Rd M22. . . . . .33 C8
Fence Ave SK10 . . . . 112 E8
Fence Ave Ind Est
SK10 . . . . 112 E8
Fence Ct SK10 . . . . 112 E8
Fence La CW12 . . . . 178 D4
Fenham Dr WA5 . . . . .14 F4
Fennel St WA1 . . . . .16 C5
Fenton Cl
Congleton CW12 . . . . 157 A1
Widnes WA8 . . . . .12 C3
Weaverham CW8. . . . . .77 C1
Widnes WA8 . . . . .13 E2
Fenwick La WA7. . . . . .49 D6
Fenwick Rd CH66. . . . . .69 E2
Ferguson Ave CH66. . . . . . . .69 E6
Ferguson Dr WA2. . . . . .8 D1
Ferma La CH3 . . . . 120 D6
Fern Ave WA12 . . . . .2 D2
Fernbank Cl
Crewe CW1 . . . . 190 F3
Warrington WA3. . . . . .9 E4
Winsford CW7 . . . . 127 B1
Fernbank Rise SK10 . . . . . . .88 B8
Fern Cl
Mount Pleasant ST7 . . . . . 195 C6
Warrington WA3 . . . . .9 D4
Fern Cres CW12 . . . . 157 A3
Fern Ct CW1 . . . . 190 E3
Ferndale Ave CH2 . . . . .72 A3
Ferndale Cl
Bold Heath WA8 . . . . .13 E7
Sandbach CW11 . . . . 175 C5
Warrington WA1 . . . . .17 C7
Weston CW2 . . . . 207 B5
Ferndale Cres SK11. . . . . . . 111 E7
Ferndale Gdns ST7 . . . . 195 E3
Ferndown Way CW2 . . . . . . 221 C8
Fernhill Rd CH1 . . . . 117 D6
Fernhurst WA7 . . . . .24 D4
FERNILEE 65 E1
Fernilee Cotts SK23. . . . . . . .65 E1
Fernlea Ct CH1 . . . . 116 FR
Fern Lea Dr SK11 . . . . 112 A8
Fernleaf Cl ST7 . . . . 193 F8
Fernlea Rd
Heswall CH60 . . . . .41 A8
Warrington WA3 . . . . .79 B6
Fernleigh Cl
Middlewich CW10 . . . . 151 E6
Winsford CW7 . . . . 126 A1
Fern Rd CH65 . . . . .70 B2
Fernway CW7 . . . . 127 B1
Fernway WA9 . . . . .77 C1
Fernwood WA7 . . . . .24 B1
Fernwood Gr SK9. . . . . .60 C8
Fernyess La CH64 . . . . .67 E7
Ferret Oak La CW6 . . . . 186 B6

Ferrous Way M44. . . . . .11 F6

Ferry Cl CH5 . . . . 116 A6
Ferry La
Sealand CH1 . . . . 117 C1
Warrington WA4 . . . . .17 E1
Ferry Rd CH62. . . . . .44 A6
Festival Ave
Buerton CW3. . . . . 230 E3
Warrington WA2 . . . . .8 D2
Festival Cres WA2 . . . . .8 D2
Festival Dr SK10 . . . . .85 F6
Festival Hill CW12 . . . . 156 F2
Festival Rd CH65 . . . . .69 F5
Festival Terr **1** WA7 . . . . .49 C8
Festival Way WA7 . . . . .49 C8
Ffordd Cledwen/Cledwen
Rd CH4 . . . . 139 D5
Ffordd Smithfield/
Smithfield Dr LL13 . . . . 196 D8
Ffordd Y Blodau/Blossom
Way CH4 . . . . 140 D5
Fiddlers Ferry Rd WA8. . . . .23 C8
Fiddler's Ferry Rd
WA8 . . . . .13 D1
Field Cl CH1 . . . . .94 C1
Field Ave CW2 . . . . 189 F1
Fieldbank Rd SK11. . . . . 112 B8
Field Cl
Bollington SK10 . . . . .87 F7
Bramhall SK7 . . . . .35 D4
Northwich CW8 . . . . 103 C7
Tarvin CH3. . . . . 121 B2
Fieldfare CW7 . . . . 150 A8
Fieldfare Cl
Golborne WA3 . . . . .3 D8
Warrington WA3 . . . . .9 F4
Fieldgate WA8. . . . . .22 B6
Fieldhead Mews SK9 . . . . . .60 E8
Fieldhead Rd SK9 . . . . .60 E8
Field Hey La CH64 . . . . .43 B1
Fieldhouse Row WA7 . . . . . .49 D7
Fielding Ave SK12 . . . . .36 E2
Field La
Crewe CW2 . . . . 189 E2
Tarvin CH3. . . . . 121 B2
Tattenhall CH3 . . . . 166 B1
Warrington WA4 . . . . .26 C6
Fields Cl ST7 . . . . 193 E4
Fields Dr CW11 . . . . 175 A5
Fieldsend Dr WN7 . . . . .4 C8
Fieldside CW6. . . . . 145 B6
Fields The
Bramhall SK7 . . . . .35 D4
Goostrey CW4 . . . . 107 E1
Field Side Cl WA16 . . . . .58 A3
Fieldside Ct CH44 . . . . 139 B4
Fields Rd
Alsager ST7 . . . . 193 E3
Congleton CW12 . . . . 178 E8
Haslington CW1 . . . . 191 D4
Fields The CW5. . . . . 205 D5
Fields View SY13 . . . . 228 D1
Fields View Cl CW5 . . . . 220 B8
Field View WA7 . . . . .49 A6
Field View ST8 . . . . 179 D1
Fieldview Dr WA2 . . . . .8 C1
Field View Dr SK11 . . . . 112 E5
Fieldway
Chester CH2 . . . . 118 E6
Ellesmere Port CH66. . . . . .69 B7
Frodsham WA6 . . . . .74 C7
Saughall CH1. . . . . .94 A2
Weaverham CW8. . . . . .77 C1
Widnes WA8 . . . . .13 E2
Field Way ST7 . . . . 193 E4
Fieldways WA13 . . . . .18 C4
Fifth Ave
Kidsgrove ST7 . . . . 194 F1
2 Runcorn WA7 . . . . .49 F7
Fildon's Ct CH5 . . . . 119 A1
Fillmore Gr WA8. . . . . .12 F3
Finchdale Gdns WA3. . . . . . .4 B8
Finchett Ct CH1 . . . . 118 B3
Finchett Dr CH1. . . . . 118 B3
Finch La L26 . . . . .21 B7
Findlay Cl WA12 . . . . .2 B1
Finger Post La WA6 . . . . 101 A4
Finlan Rd WA8 . . . . .22 F7
Finlay Ave WA5 . . . . .14 E3
Finlow Hill La SK10. . . . . .85 E6
Finney Cl SK9 . . . . .34 C2
Finney Dr SK9 . . . . .34 C2
Finney Gr WA11 . . . . .1 E6
FINNEY GREEN 34 E2
Finney La SK8 . . . . .34 B8
Finney's La CW10 . . . . 128 B2
Finningley Ct WA2 . . . . .8 E1
Finsbury Cl WA5 . . . . .15 C4
Finsbury Pk WA8 . . . . .13 C5
Finsbury Way SK9 . . . . .34 E2
Finsbury Wlk CW7 . . . . 149 A8
Fir Ave
Halewood L26 . . . . .21 A8
Poynton SK12 . . . . .36 F3
Tarporley CW6. . . . . 146 D2
Fir Ct SK10 . . . . .86 F1

Firdale Rd LW8. . . . . .103 D7
Firecrest Ct WA1 . . . . .16 A3
Firemans Sq CH1 . . . . . .237 A3
Fir Gr
 Macclesfield SK11 . . . . . .112 D5
 Warrington WA1 . . . . .16 F7
 Weaverham CW8. . . . . . . .102 E8
Fir La CW8 . . . . .102 A2
Firman Cl WA5 . . . . .15 B8
Fir Rd SK7 . . . . .35 E8
Firrview Pk CW5 . . . . .217 A3
Firs La WA4 . . . . .26 B6
Firs Pottery The*
 CW5. . . . . .217 C1
Firs Sch CH2 . . . . .118 E5
Fir St
 Irlam M44 . . . . .11 D6
 Widnes WA8 . . . . .13 C2
First Ave
 Connah's Quay CH5. . . . . .93 A2
 Crewe CW1. . . . . .190 F2
 Kidsgrove ST7 . . . . .194 E1
 Poynton SK12 . . . . .36 D1
 Sandbach CW11 . . . . . . .175 A5
First Dig La CW5 . . . . . . .219 C8
Firs The SK9. . . . . .60 A5
First Wood St CW5 . . . . .204 D5
Firs View WA6. . . . . .73 D4
Firth Bvd WA2. . . . . .16 C7
Firth Cl CW11 . . . . .175 B7
Firth Fields CW9 . . . . . . .103 F2
Firthfields Cl CW9 . . . . . .103 F2
Firtree Ave WA1 . . . . .17 A8
Fir Tree Ave
 Chester CH4 . . . . .141 B5
 Golborne WA3 . . . . .3 F8
 Knutsford WA16 . . . . .82 C8
Firtree Cl
 Barnton CW8. . . . . .78 B4
 Winsford CW7 . . . . .127 B1
Fir Tree Cl WA4 . . . . .26 D1
Fir Tree Cotts CW2 . . . . .208 C5
Firtree Gr CH66. . . . . .95 A8
Fir Tree La
 Burtonwood WA5. . . . . .7 A7
 Chester CH3. . . . . .119 E2
 Faddiley CW5. . . . . .202 B3
Fir Trees Holiday Pk
 CH1. . . . . .117 C2
Fir Tree Wlk WA3 . . . . .3 F8
Fir Way CH60. . . . . .41 B5
Firwood Rd ST8 . . . . .179 E1
Firwood Wlk CW2 . . . . . .190 C1
Fisher Ave WA2 . . . . .8 B2
Fisherfield Dr CW8 . . . . . .10 A6
Fishermans Cl CW11 . . . .191 F7
Fisher Rd CH1. . . . . .117 E4
Fishers Gn CW6 . . . . .146 B5
Fishers La CW5. . . . . .203 C8
Fisher St WA7 . . . . .23 B3
Fishpool Rd CW8 . . . . . . .123 F3
Fishwicks Ind Est WA11. . . .1 F8
Fistral Ave SK8 . . . . .34 C8
Fitton's Cl CW5. . . . . .217 F5
Fitton St CW9 . . . . .80 A2
Fitz Cl SK10 . . . . .87 D3
Fitz Cres SK10 . . . . .87 D3
Fitzherbert St WA2 . . . . . .16 C7
Fitzwalter Rd WA1 . . . . . .17 D7
Fitzwilliam Ave SK11. . . .112 F3
Fives Ashes Rd CH4 . . . .141 B5
FIVECROSSES 74 D5
Fivelanes End WA6 . . . . . .74 C6
Five Ways CH64. . . . . .41 F3
Fiveways Par SK7. . . . . . . .36 E8
Fiveways Pk CH64 . . . . . . .41 F3
Flacca Ct CH3 . . . . .166 B1
Flag La
 Crewe CW1, CW2. . . . . . .190 C4
 Neston CH64 . . . . .66 F7
 Newhall CW5. . . . . .228 D8
Flag La N CH2 . . . . .118 E8
Flag La S CH2 . . . . .118 E8
Flander Cl WA8 . . . . .12 C2
Flashes La CH64 . . . . .67 B5
Flash La
 Antrobus CW9 . . . . .53 F5
 Bollington SK10 . . . . .87 D7
Flat La
 Kelsall CW6. . . . . .122 C4
 Sandbach CW11 . . . . . . .175 B6
Flatt La CH65. . . . . .70 B5
Flatts La SK23 . . . . .64 F4
Flavian Cl CW10 . . . . . . .128 C2
Flavian St WA7 . . . . .23 E2
Flaxley Cl WA3 . . . . .10 A5
Flaxmere Dr CH3 . . . . . . .142 B8
Flaxyards CW6 . . . . .146 F2
Fleet La WA3 . . . . .1 A2
Fleet St CH65 . . . . .70 A5
Fleetwood Cl WA5. . . . . . .15 B4
Fleetwood Dr WA12 . . . . . .2 B4
Fleetwood Wlk WA7. . . . .50 C6
Fleming Dr WA2. . . . . .8 A6
Fleming St CH65. . . . . .70 C6
Flers Ave WA4 . . . . .16 C3
Fletcher Ct WA16. . . . . . . .56 F1
Fletcher Dr SK12 . . . . .37 F6
Fletcher Gr CW7. . . . . . . .104 C6
Fletcher's Bldgs
 Chester CH1. . . . . .237 B2
  [6] Runcorn WA7. . . . . . . .23 F1
Fletchers La WA13. . . . . . .18 F4
Fletcher's Row [5] WA7. . .23 F1
Fletcher St
 Crewe CW1. . . . . .190 B5
 Warrington WA4 . . . . .16 B3

Fletsand Rd SK9. . . . . .60 D6
Flint Cl CH64 . . . . .66 E6
Flint Cotts 70 D2
Flint Dr CH64. . . . . .66 E6
Flint Gr WA4. . . . . .11 C6
Flint Mdw CH64 . . . . .66 E7
Flint St SK10 . . . . .112 E8
Flittogate La WA16 . . . . . .80 E8
Flixton Dr CW2 . . . . .190 A2
FLOOKERSBROOK 118 E4
Florence St WA4 . . . . .16 D3
Florida Cl WA5 . . . . .15 C7
Flour Mill Way CW1 . . . . .191 A3
Flowcrete Bsns Pk
 CW11. . . . . .152 C1
Flowerscroft CW5 . . . . . . .205 A4
Flowers La CW1 . . . . .172 E1
Flower St CW8 . . . . .103 E7
Fluin La WA6. . . . . .74 E8
Flying Fields Dr SK11. . . .112 A5
Foden Ave ST7 . . . . .194 A3
Foden La
 Alderley Edge SK9. . . . . . .59 C1
 Bramhall SK7. . . . . .35 D3
Foden St SK10. . . . . .87 D1
Fodens Terr CW11 . . . . . .175 A6
Foden Wlk [7] SK9 . . . . . . .34 D2
Fog Cotts CW3 . . . . .221 E4
Fogg's La CW9, WA4. . . . . .53 A6
Fold La
 Biddulph ST8 . . . . .179 E4
 Bosley SK11. . . . . .135 D2
Folds La SK23 . . . . .65 F3
Folds The CH63. . . . . .42 A6
Fold The SK10 . . . . .87 A8
Foley Wlk M22 . . . . .33 E8
Fol Hollow CW12 . . . . . . .156 B1
Folkestone Way WA7 . . . . .50 C7
Folly La WA5 . . . . .15 F7
Forbes Cl WA3 . . . . .9 E3
Forbes Pk SK7 . . . . .35 D7
Ford Cl CW1 . . . . .190 B5
Ford Ct CW7 . . . . .149 C6
Fordington Rd WA5. . . . . .15 B5
Ford La
 Crewe CW1 . . . . .190 B6
 Tattenhall CH3. . . . . .166 F4
Fords La ST7 . . . . .195 D6
Ford's La SK7 . . . . .35 D6
Ford St WA1 . . . . .16 D6
Foregate St CH1 . . . . .237 B2
Foreland Cl WA5 . . . . .14 C7
Forest Ave CW4 . . . . .107 C1
Forest Dr
 Cuddington CW8 . . . . . . .101 F3
 Rainow SK10 . . . . .88 E5
Forest Dr
 Broughton CH4. . . . . .139 C3
 Langley SK11. . . . . .113 C4
Forester Ave WA16 . . . . . .57 C2
Foresters Cl WA5. . . . . . .101 A6
Forest Gate Com Prim Sch
 M31. . . . . .11 D3
Forest Gate La CW6 . . . . .122 E7
Forest Gdns M31 . . . . . . .11 D3
Forest Ho SK10 . . . . .87 F2
Forest La WA6. . . . . .100 C6
Forest Pl [3] CW9 . . . . .79 A1
Forest Rd
 Cuddington CW8 . . . . . . .101 F2
 Delamere CW6 . . . . .124 B1
 Ellesmere Port CH66. . . . .69 E7
 Heswall CH60 . . . . .41 A8
 Macclesfield SK11 . . . . . .113 E6
 Tarporley CW6. . . . . .146 D3
 Winsford CW7 . . . . .149 B8
Forest Road Pk CW8. . . .101 E2
Forest St
 Chester CH1. . . . . .237 C2
 Weaverham CW8. . . . . . .102 C8
Forest Wlk [5] WA7 . . . . . .49 F7
Forge Cl
 Cronton WA8 . . . . .12 C5
 Warren SK11. . . . . .111 D2
Forge Fields CW11. . . . . .174 F3
Forge La
 Congleton CW12 . . . . . . .156 B3
 Norton in Hales TF9 . . . . .236 C1
Forge Mill La CW10. . . . .151 C1
Forge Rd
 Ellesmere Port CH66. . . . .69 C6
 Warrington WA5 . . . . .14 F5
 Whaley Bridge SK23 . . . . .65 E7
Forge Sh Ctr The WA4 . . .16 C1
Forge St CW1. . . . . .190 D4
Forge Way CH4. . . . . .140 F4
Formby Cl WA5. . . . . .14 F4
Formby Dr SK8. . . . . .34 B8
Forrest Way WA5. . . . . . . .15 D3
Forshaw's La WA5 . . . . . . .6 E8
Forshaw St WA2. . . . . .16 C7
Forster Ave CW8 . . . . . . .102 E8
Forster St WA2. . . . . .16 B7
Forsythia Wlk [2] M31. . . .11 E2
Forty Acre La CW1. . . . .
 CW12. . . . . .131 D6
Forum The CH1. . . . . .237 A2
Forwood Rd CH62. . . . . . .43 D8
Fossa Cl CW10 . . . . .128 C2
Foster Rd CW12 . . . . .157 A5
Foster St WA8. . . . . .13 C1
Fothergill St WA1 . . . . . . .16 D7
Fotheringay Ct [3]
 CH65. . . . . .70 D2
Foulkes Ave CW1. . . . . . .189 F6
Foundry Bank CW12 . . . .156 E3
Foundry Ct [1] SK22. . . . . .39 C7

Foundry Ind Est WA8 . . . .23 B7
Foundry La
 Sandbach CW11 . . . . . . .174 D7
 Scholar Green ST7. . . . . .194 F7
 Widnes WA8 . . . . .22 C5
Foundry St
 Bollington SK10. . . . . .88 B8
 Newton-le-W WA12 . . . . . .2 B3
 Warrington WA2 . . . . .16 B6
Fountain Cl SK12 . . . . .36 D4
Fountain Ct
 Biddulph ST8 . . . . .179 D1
 Davenham CW9 . . . . .103 F2
  [2] Winsford CW7. . . . . .126 D1
Fountain Ho SK10 . . . . . .112 E8
Fountain La
 Davenham CW9 . . . . .103 F2
 Frodsham WA6 . . . . .74 B8
Fountain Pl SK12. . . . . .36 D4
Fountains Ave WA11. . . . . .1 F7
Fountains Cl
 Middlewich CW10 . . . . . .128 B1
 Runcorn WA7. . . . . .50 C5
Fountain Sq SK12. . . . . . . .38 D6
Fountains Rd SK8 . . . . . . .35 C6
Fountain St
 Congleton CW12 . . . . . . .156 D2
 Macclesfield SK10 . . . . . .112 E8
Fountains Wlk WA3. . . . . .4 B8
FOURLANE-ENDS 63 A8
FOUR LANE ENDS 168 D7
Four Lane Ends
 Alvanley WA6. . . . . .74 B1
 Warrington WA3 . . . . .9 D3
Four Lanes Ct [3]
 CW7. . . . . .149 B8
FOURLANES END 176 E4
Four Lanes End
 Betley CW2. . . . . .207 F2
 Thornton Hough CH63. . . .42 D5
Fourseasons Cl CW2. . . .206 B8
Fourth Ave
 Connah's Quay CH5. . . . . .92 C4
 Crewe CW1 . . . . .190 F1
  [1] Runcorn WA7. . . . . . .49 F7
Fourways CW2 . . . . .207 B5
Fourways Tech Pk
 CW11. . . . . .176 E4
Fowey Cl SK10. . . . . .86 D1
Fowler Rd CH1 . . . . .117 D4
Fowlers Bench La
 CH3 . . . . .184 C5
Fowler St SK10 . . . . .87 D1
FOWLEY COMMON 5 B8
Fowley Common La
 WA3. . . . . .5 C5
Foxall Way CH66. . . . . . . .69 D2
Fox Bank Cl WA8 . . . . .12 F4
Fox Bench Cl SK7. . . . . . . .35 C6
Foxcote WA8. . . . . .12 B2
Foxcote Cl CH1. . . . . .117 D5
Fox Cover CH3 . . . . .119 F5
Fox Cover Rd CH60 . . . . . .41 D7
Fox Covert WA7 . . . . .50 C7
Foxcovert La WA16 . . . . .106 E7
Fox Covert La
 Hoole Bank CH2 . . . . . . .119 B8
 Picton CH2. . . . . .96 A1
Fox Covert Way CW1. . . .173 A1
Foxdale Ct WA4 . . . . .26 C7
Foxdene CH66 . . . . .69 D5
Foxes Cl CW8 . . . . .78 E1
Foxes Hey CW8 . . . . .101 D5
Foxes Hollow CW1 . . . . . .190 E7
Foxes Wlk CH3 . . . . .142 A7
Foxfield Cl WA2 . . . . .8 E3
Foxfield La CW7 . . . . .126 A1
Fox Gdns
 Lymm WA13 . . . . .18 C4
  [2] Golborne WA3 . . . . .3 D8
 Huntington CH3. . . . . . . .142 A6
 Wistaston CW2. . . . . .206 B7
Foxglove Cl
 Bollington SK10. . . . . .88 C8
  [2] Golborne WA3 . . . . .3 D8
 Huntington CH3. . . . . . . .142 A6
 Wistaston CW2. . . . . .206 B7
Foxglove Ct WA6 . . . . .74 C8
Foxglove Dell WA6 . . . . . .73 D2
Foxglove Way CH64. . . . . .66 E5
Foxglove Wlk M31 . . . . . . .11 F2
Fox Hill WA16 . . . . .57 C1
Fox Hill CW6 . . . . .122 D4
Foxhill Cl CW6 . . . . .146 E1
Foxhill Gr WA6 . . . . .73 D4
Foxhills Cl WA4 . . . . .26 D3
Foxholme Cl CW1 . . . . . . .191 A6
Foxhunter Cl CH3. . . . . . .121 F7
Fox La
 Clutton CH3 . . . . .182 D1
 Waverton CH3 . . . . .143 B5
Foxlea CW9 . . . . .78 C7
Fox Lea CH1. . . . . .117 A8
FOXLEY 209 D7
Foxley Cl WA13. . . . . .19 A2
Foxley Hall Mews
 WA13 . . . . .19 A1
Foxley Heath WA8 . . . . . . .22 E8
Fox's Dr CH5 . . . . .116 A6
Fox St
 Congleton CW12 . . . . . . .156 F3
 Runcorn WA7. . . . . .23 A1
 Warrington WA5 . . . . .16 A3
Foxwist Cl CW7. . . . . .237 B4
Foxwist Green CW8 . . . . .125 F6
FOXWIST GREEN 125 F6
Foxwood Dr WA16 . . . . . .108 A8

Fox Wood Specl Sch
 WA3. . . . . .9 E3
Francesca Ct CH1 . . . . . .237 B2
Frances St
 Crewe CW2 . . . . .190 D2
 Irlam M44 . . . . .11 E5
 Macclesfield SK11 . . . . . .112 B8
Francis Cl WA8 . . . . .22 C8
Francis Ct CH1. . . . . .237 C3
Francis La
 Holt LL13. . . . . .196 D7
 Holt, Ridleywood LL13. . .196 B6
Francis Rd
 Frodsham WA6 . . . . .49 C1
 Irlam M44 . . . . .11 E8
 Warrington WA4 . . . . .16 B1
Francis St CH1 . . . . .237 C3
FRANDLEY 53 A3
Frank Bott Ave CW1 . . . .190 A7
Franklin Cl
 Macclesfield SK11 . . . . . .112 B5
 Warrington WA5 . . . . .15 C8
Franklyn Ave CW2 . . . . . .190 B3
Frank Perkins Way
 M44 . . . . .11 F7
Frank St WA8 . . . . .13 C1
Frank Webb Ave CW1. . . .190 A6
Frappel Ct WA2 . . . . .16 B6
Fraser Ct CH4 . . . . .141 D7
Fraser Rd WA5 . . . . .14 D6
Frawley Ave WA12. . . . . . . .2 C5
Freckleton Cl WA5. . . . . . .15 B4
Frederick St
 Warrington WA4 . . . . .16 E3
 Widnes WA8 . . . . .23 B8
Frederick Terr WA8 . . . . . .22 A4
Fredric Pl WA7 . . . . .23 B3
Freedom Dr ST7. . . . . . . .195 F3
Free Green La WA16 . . . .107 A8
Freeport Shopping Mall
 ST7. . . . . .210 C6
French La CW5 . . . . .218 C5
French Lane End
 CW5. . . . . .218 C5
French St WA8 . . . . .13 D1
Freshfield Dr SK10. . . . . . .87 C3
Freshfields
 Comberbach CW9 . . . . . . .78 C7
 Knutsford WA16 . . . . .56 E3
 Wistaston CW2. . . . . .206 A7
Freshfields Dr WA2. . . . . . .9 C1
Freshmeadow La WA6. . . .73 B2
Freshwater Cl WA5 . . . . . .14 D7
Freshwater Dr CW2. . . . .221 C8
Freshwater View
 CW8. . . . . .103 F8
Friars Ave WA5. . . . . .14 E5
Friars Cl
 Rainow SK10 . . . . .88 D5
 Wistaston CW2. . . . . .205 F8
Friar's Cl SK9 . . . . .59 E8
Friars Ct [1] WA1 . . . . .16 B5
Friars Gate
 Chester CH1. . . . . .237 B2
 Warrington WA1. . . . . . . .16 B4
Friars La WA1 . . . . .16 B4
Friars Way SK10 . . . . .86 F2
Frida Cres CW9. . . . . .103 E6
Friends La WA5 . . . . .14 D6
Friesian Gdns ST5 . . . . . .210 C2
Frith Ave CW8 . . . . .123 D8
Frith La CH3 . . . . .198 C1
Frith Terr SK11 . . . . .112 D4
Frobisher Ct WA5. . . . . . . .15 D8
Frobisher Rd CH64. . . . . . .66 E8
Froda Ave WA6 . . . . .74 B7
FRODSHAM 74 D7
Frodsham Bsns Ctr
 WA6. . . . . .49 C1
Frodsham CE Prim Sch
 WA6 . . . . .74 C7
Frodsham Manor House
 Prim Sch WA6 . . . . .49 C1
Frodsham Marsh 48 E2
Frodsham Rd WA6. . . . . . .73 D1
Frodsham Sch WA6. . . . . .74 B8
Frodsham Sq CH1 . . . . . .237 B3
Frodsham St CH1. . . . . . .237 B3
Frodsham St WA6 . . . . . . .34 E4
Frodsham Weaver Vale
 Prim Sch WA6 . . . . .49 C2
Froghall La
 High Legh WA16 . . . . .29 D7
 High Legh WA16 . . . . .29 E6
 Warrington WA2, WA5. . . .15 F5
Frog La
 Holt LL13. . . . . .196 D8
 Milton Green CH3 . . . . . .165 E2
 Pickmere WA16 . . . . .55 B1
 Worthenbury LL13. . . . .
 SY14 . . . . .211 B1
 Worthenbury SY14. . . . . .211 C2
Frome Ct CH65. . . . . .70 B7
Front St CH11. . . . . .175 C6
Frosts Mews CH65. . . . . . .70 B7
Fryer Rd CW9 . . . . .80 A3
Fryer St [16] WA7 . . . . .23 A3
Fuchsia Cl CH66 . . . . .69 F1
Fulbeck WA8 . . . . .12 C2
Fulbeck Cl CW2 . . . . .206 B8
Fulbrook Dr SK8. . . . . .35 A6
Fuller Dr CW2 . . . . .206 B7
FULLER'S MOOR 183 D1
Fullerton Rd CW8 . . . . . .103 A4
Fulmar Cl SK12. . . . . .36 A4

Fulmards Cl SK9. . . . . .60 C7
Fulshaw Ave SK9 . . . . .60 A6
Fulshaw Cross SK9 . . . . . .60 A5
Fulshaw Ct SK9. . . . . .60 A5
FULSHAW PARK 60 B5
Fulshaw Pk SK9. . . . . .60 A5
Fulshaw Pk S SK9 . . . . . . .60 A4
Fulton Gr CW9 . . . . .103 F2
Fulwood Gdns CH66 . . . . .69 C6
Fulwood Mews CH66. . . . .69 C6
Fulwood Rd
 Ellesmere Port CH66. . . . .69 C5
 Golborne WA3 . . . . .3 E7
Furber St CW1 . . . . .190 C5
Furne Rd CH1 . . . . .117 E4
Furness Cl
 Holmes Chapel CW4 . . . .130 A3
 Poynton SK12 . . . . .36 D4
 Winsford CW7 . . . . .149 B8
Furness Ct WA7 . . . . .24 F4
Furness Lodge Cl
 SK23. . . . . .39 D4
Furness Rd SK8 . . . . .35 C6
FURNESS VALE 39 C3
Furness Vale Bsns Ctr
 SK23. . . . . .39 D4
Furness Vale Prim Sch
 SK23. . . . . .39 D4
Furnival Cl CW11 . . . . . . .175 B7
Furnival St CW2 . . . . .190 C2
Furrocks Cl CH64 . . . . . . .66 F5
Furrocks La CH64. . . . . . . .66 F5
Furrocks Way CH64 . . . . . .66 F5
Furrows The CH66 . . . . . . .94 E8
Fylde Ave SK8 . . . . .34 C8
Fytton Cl SK11. . . . . .111 D1

G

Gable Ave SK9. . . . . .60 A7
Gable Ct [5] CW5. . . . . . . .204 E6
Gables Cl WA2 . . . . .8 F3
Gable St WA12 . . . . .2 B3
Gables The ST7. . . . . .193 C3
Gabriel Bank CW8 . . . . . . .76 A1
Gadbrook Bsns Ctr
 CW9. . . . . .104 D5
Gadbrook Pk CW9 . . . . . .104 D6
Gadbrook Rd CW9 . . . . . .104 D6
Gail Cl SK9 . . . . .60 B2
Gainford Cl WA8. . . . . .12 C3
Gainsborough Cl SK9 . . . .60 D8
Gainsborough Ct WA8 . . .12 B1
Gainsborough Prim Sch
 CW2. . . . . .190 B2
Gainsborough Rd
 Crewe CW2 . . . . .190 B3
 Warrington WA4 . . . . .16 B2
Gairloch Cl WA2. . . . . .8 F4
Gaisgill Ct WA8 . . . . .12 C3
Gala Cl CH4 . . . . .139 C3
Galbraith Cl CW12. . . . . .156 C2
Gale Ave WA5 . . . . .7 F1
Galion Way WA8 . . . . .12 F3
GALLANTRY BANK 200 B8
Galleys Bank ST7 . . . . . . .195 B3
Gallimore Ho ST7. . . . . . .210 D8
Galloway Cl
 Holmes Chapel CW4 . . . .130 C2
 Middlewich CW10 . . . . . .128 E2
Galloway Gn CW12. . . . . .156 E5
Gallowsclough La
 WA6. . . . . .100 F4
Galway Ave WA8. . . . . .12 E3
Galway Gr CW2. . . . . .206 B4
Game St CW11 . . . . .175 A3
Gamul Pl CH1 . . . . .237 B1
Ganton Cl WA8. . . . . .13 B4
Garden Cl SK10. . . . . .87 E1
Garden Ct CH1 . . . . .237 A3
Garden La
 Chester CH1. . . . . .237 A3
 Harthill CH3. . . . . .183 E3
Garden Rd WA16 . . . . .56 F3
Garden St
 Bollington SK10. . . . . .87 F8
 Congleton CW12 . . . . . . .156 C3
 Macclesfield SK10 . . . . . .87 E1
Gardens The
 Holt LL13. . . . . .180 E1
 Lawton-gate ST7. . . . . . .194 C4
 Sandbach CW11 . . . . . . .175 B6
Garden Terr
 Chester, Boughton
  CH2. . . . . .118 F2
 Chester CH1. . . . . .237 A3
Garden Wlk [8] M31 . . . . .11 E3
Gardiner Ave WA11 . . . . . . .1 C6
Garfit St CW10 . . . . .128 C2
Garner St WA2 . . . . .16 C7
Garnett Ave WA4 . . . . .17 A4
Garnett Cl CW5. . . . . .204 F4
Garnett's La WA8 . . . . .22 A3
Garrett Field WA3 . . . . .9 D5
Garrigill Cl WA8 . . . . .13 C5
Garsdale Cl WA5 . . . . .14 F7
Garside Ave WA3 . . . . .3 D7
Garth Dr CH2. . . . . .118 C5
Garth Hts SK9 . . . . .60 C6
Garth Rd CH65 . . . . .71 A5
Garton Dr WA3. . . . . .3 A8
Garven Pl WA1 . . . . .16 A5
Garwood Cl WA5 . . . . .15 C8

Gaskell Ave
Knutsford WA16 . . . . .56 F2
Warrington WA1 . . . . .17 A3
Gaskell St WA4 . . . . .16 L1
Gas Rd SK11 . . . . .112 D8
Gas Works Ind Est
ST7 . . . . .194 E2
Gatcombe Mews **1**
SK9 . . . . .60 A6
Gateacre Ct CH66 . . . . .69 F8
Gatefield St CW1 . . . . .190 C4
Gatehouse The **7**
CW5 . . . . .204 F5
Gateley Cl WA4 . . . . .17 E3
GATESHEATH 165 E5
Gatesheath Dr CH2 . . . . . .118 E7
Gatesheath La CH3 . . . . . .165 F5
Gatewarth Ind Est
WA5 . . . . .15 D3
Gate Warth St WA5 . . . . . . .15 D4
Gateway
Crewe CW1 . . . . .190 F2
Newcastle-u-Lyme ST5 . . . .210 D2
Gateway Trad Pk WA5 . . . . .16 A7
Gathurst Ct WA8 . . . . .22 D8
Gauntlet Birds of Prey
Pk* WA16 . . . . .56 D5
GAUNTONS BANK 215 E4
Gauntons Bank SY13 . . . . .215 E3
Gaunts Way WA7 . . . . .49 E6
Gavin Rd WA8 . . . . .22 B7
Gaw End La SK11 . . . . .112 C2
Gawer Pk CH2 . . . . .118 C4
GAWSWORTH 135 E8
Gawsworth Ave CW2 . . . . .189 F3
Gawsworth Cl
Alsager ST7 . . . . .193 C3
Bramhall SK7 . . . . .35 E6
Holmes Chapel CW4 . . . . . .130 B3
Northwich CW9 . . . . .104 A4
Poynton SK12 . . . . .36 F2
Gawsworth Ct WA3 . . . . .9 F5
Gawsworth Dr CW11 . . . . .175 C7
Gawsworth Hall*
SK11 . . . . .134 E8
Gawsworth Prim Sch
SK11 . . . . .111 D2
Gawsworth Rd
Ellesmere Port CH66 . . . . . .69 E5
Macclesfield SK11 . . . . .111 D5
Gawsworth Way SK9 . . . . . .34 E4
Gayhurst Ave WA2 . . . . .8 F2
Gaymoore Cl CH2 . . . . .237 A4
Gaynor Ave WA11 . . . . .1 F7
GAYTON 41 B6
Gayton Cl CH2 . . . . .118 E5
Gayton Farm Rd CH60 . . . . .41 A5
Gayton La CH60 . . . . .41 B6
Gayton Mill Cl CH60 . . . . . .41 B7
Gayton Parkway CH60 . . . . .41 C5
Gayton Prim Sch CH60 . . . .41 A6
Gayton Rd CH60 . . . . .41 A6
Gelli Dderw/Oak Gr
CH4 . . . . .140 D5
GEMINI 7 D3
Gemini Bsns Pk WA5 . . . . . .7 E3
Gemmull Cl CW3 . . . . .229 F4
General St WA1 . . . . .16 C5
Genesis Ctr The WA3 . . . . . .9 E5
Geneva Rd CW7 . . . . .126 C1
Geo Hampson's Bldgs
WA3 .5 C8
George Bates Cl ST7 . . . . .193 C3
George Cl WA6 . . . . .73 A2
George Ho CW5 . . . . .204 E7
George Kenyon Mews
CH4 . . . . .140 E6
George Rd WA5 . . . . .15 C4
George St W SK11 . . . . . . .112 C8
George's Cl SK12 . . . . .36 E3
Georges Cres WA4 . . . . .17 B2
Georges Ct **15** SK10 . . . . .112 C8
George's La CW9 . . . . .54 D1
George's Prec WA5 . . . . . . .14 D6
George's Rd E SK12 . . . . . .36 E3
George's Rd W SK12 . . . . . .36 E3
George St
Alderley Edge SK9 . . . . .60 A1
Audley ST7 . . . . .209 D1
Barnton CW8 . . . . .78 B3
Chester CH1 . . . . .237 A3
Ellesmere Port CH65 . . . . . .70 C7
Knutsford WA16 . . . . .57 A2
Macclesfield SK11 . . . . .112 D7
Newton-le-W WA12 . . . . .2 A4
Sandbach CW11 . . . . .174 D7
Whaley Bridge SK23 . . . . . . .65 E7
Winsford CW7 . . . . .126 E1
Georges Way ST7 . . . . .209 F2
George's Wlk CW11 . . . . . .175 B6
George VI Ave CW10 . . . . . .151 D6
George VI Cl CW10 . . . . . . .151 D6
Georgia Pl WA5 . . . . .15 C7
Gerard Dr CW5 . . . . .204 C4
Gerosa Ave WA2 . . . . .8 B8
Gerrard Ave
Ellesmere Port CH66 . . . . . .69 C4
Warrington WA5 . . . . .15 F7
Gerrard Dr CW8 . . . . .77 D1
Gerrard Rd WA3 . . . . .9 A7
Gerrards Ave CH3 . . . . .119 A1
Gerrard St WA8 . . . . .23 B8
Giantswood La
Congleton CW12 . . . . .156 C6
Marton CW12 . . . . .132 F1

GIBB HILL 53 D1
Gibb Hill CW9 . . . . .53 D1
Gibbon Dr CW9 . . . . .80 B3
Gibson Cl CW1 . . . . .204 D6
Gibson Cres CW11 . . . . . . .174 D6
Gibson Ct Trad Est
CH65 . . . . .70 C8
Gibson St
Warrington, Howley
WA1 . . . . .16 C5
Warrington, Stockton Heath
WA4 . . . . .17 C2
Gigg La
Moore WA4 . . . . .25 B5
Warrington WA4 . . . . .17 E3
Gig La WA1 . . . . .17 E8
Gilbert Cl **2** ST7 . . . . . . .195 A2
Gilbert Ct WA3 . . . . .4 F3
Gilbert Ho WA7 . . . . .22 E3
Gilchrist Ave SK11 . . . . . . .111 E7
Gilchrist Rd WA4 . . . . .11 F6
Gilderdale Cl WA3 . . . . .10 B5
Gillan Cl WA7 . . . . .50 C5
GILLBENT 34 F6
Gillbent Rd SK8 . . . . .35 A7
Gillow Cl CW1 . . . . .190 A8
GILLOW HEATH 179 C2
Giltbrook Cl WA8 . . . . .13 E4
Gilwell Cl WA4 . . . . .17 C2
Gilvern Cl CH2 . . . . .118 C4
GINCLOUGH 88 F6
Gingerbread La CW5 . . . . .205 A5
Gipsy Cnr SY13 . . . . .224 E2
Girton Cl CH65 . . . . .70 D4
Girton Rd CH65 . . . . .70 D4
Girvin Dr CH64 . . . . .66 F6
Glade Dr CH66 . . . . .66 F6
Gladewood Cl **1** SK9 . . . . .60 C8
Gladstone Ave CH1 . . . . . . .118 B2
Gladstone Mews WA2 . . . . .16 A6
Gladstone Rd
Broughton CH4 . . . . .139 B3
Chester CH1 . . . . .118 B3
Neston CH64 . . . . .66 E8
Gladstone St
Crewe CW1 . . . . .190 C4
Northwich CW8 . . . . .103 E7
Warrington WA2 . . . . .16 A6
8 Widnes WA8 . . . . .23 B8
Willaston CW5 . . . . .205 D6
Winsford CW7 . . . . .149 D8
Gladstone Way WA12 . . . . . .2 B4
Glaisdale Cl CW2 . . . . .206 A6
Glamis Cl
Chester CH3 . . . . .119 A2
Wistaston CW2 . . . . .205 E8
Glanaber Ct CH4 . . . . .141 A7
Glan Aber Dr CH4 . . . . .140 F7
Glan Aber Pk CH4 . . . . . . .141 A7
Glandon Dr SK8 . . . . .35 C8
Glastonbury Ave
Cheadle SK8 . . . . .35 C6
Chester CH2 . . . . .118 F7
Golborne WA3 . . . . .4 C8
Glastonbury Cl WA7 . . . . . .24 F3
Glastonbury Dr
Middlewich CW10 . . . . .128 B1
Poynton SK12 . . . . .36 D5
Glastonbury Mews
WA4 . . . . .16 E2
GLAZEBROOK 11 B6
Glazebrook La WA3 . . . . . . .11 B5
Glazebrook St WA1 . . . . . . .16 D6
Glazebrook Sta WA3 . . . . . .11 A5
GLAZEBURY 5 B7
Glazebury CE Prim Sch
WA3 .5 C7
Glaziers La WA3 . . . . .4 D2
Gleadmere WA8 . . . . .12 C2
GLEADSMOSS 132 B6
Gleaner Cl WA7 . . . . .22 F3
Gleave Ave SK10 . . . . .88 B8
Gleave Rd
Burtonwood WA5 . . . . .6 F6
Weaverham CW8 . . . . .77 D1
Glebe Ave WA4 . . . . .17 C1
Glebe Cl CW5 . . . . .220 A8
Glebecroft Ave CH2 . . . . . . .72 A3
Glebe Ct ST7 . . . . .194 D2
Glebe Farm Mews CH2 . . . .71 E2
Glebe Green Dr CW7 . . . . .149 C6
Glebe La WA8 . . . . .13 B5
Glebeland WA3 . . . . .4 E2
Glebelands Rd WA16 . . . . . .57 A1
Glebe Mdws CH2 . . . . .96 F1
Glebe Rd CW8 . . . . .102 A4
Glebe St ST7 . . . . .194 D2
Glebe The WA7 . . . . .23 E1
Glebeway Rd CH65 . . . . .70 F5
Gleggs Cl CH3 . . . . .142 B7
Glegg St SK11 . . . . .112 E7
Glenathol Rd CH66 . . . . .69 C4
Glenbourne Pk SK7 . . . . . . .35 D5
Glenburn Ave CH62 . . . . . . .43 E4
Glen Cl WA3 . . . . .11 B2
Glencoe Cl CW4 . . . . .130 C2
Glencoe Rd CH66 . . . . .69 C4
Glencourse Rd WA8 . . . . . . .13 A5
Glendale Ave
Elton CH2 . . . . .72 A3
Sandycroft CH5 . . . . .116 A3
Glendale Bsns Pk
CH5 . . . . .116 A3
Glendale Cl
Buerton CW3 . . . . .230 F4
Crewe CW2 . . . . .189 D3
Glendale Pk CH5 . . . . .116 A3
Glendene Ave SK7 . . . . .35 D5

Glendyke Rd CH66 . . . . .69 C4
Gleneagles Cl
Bramhall SK7 . . . . .36 A7
Chester CH3 . . . . .119 D3
Golborne WA3 . . . . .3 F7
Wilmslow SK9 . . . . .60 D8
Gleneagles Dr
Haydock WA11 . . . . .1 A5
Holmes Chapel CW4 . . . . . .130 B2
Macclesfield SK10 . . . . .87 C4
Widnes WA8 . . . . .13 B5
Winsford CW7 . . . . .126 C2
Gleneagles Rd CH66 . . . . . .69 C4
Glenesk Rd CH66 . . . . .69 C4
Glenfield Dr SK12 . . . . .36 D3
Glenholme Rd SK7 . . . . .35 D7
Glenmaye Rd CH66 . . . . . . .69 C4
Glenn Pl WA8 . . . . .12 E1
Glenorchy Cl CW4 . . . . . . .130 C2
Glen Rd CH66 . . . . .69 C4
Glenside Cl CH1 . . . . .117 D5
Glenside Dr SK9 . . . . .60 C6
Glen The
Blacon CH1 . . . . .117 E5
Runcorn WA7 . . . . .49 F5
Glenton Pk CH64 . . . . .66 F6
Glenville Cl WA7 . . . . .49 B6
Glenwood WA7 . . . . .24 C1
Glenwood Cl CH66 . . . . .69 C6
Glenwood Gdns CH66 . . . . .69 C6
Glenwood Rd CH66 . . . . . . .69 C6
Gleyve WA16 . . . . .29 C5
Gloucester Ave WA3 . . . . . . .3 B8
Gloucester Cl
Ellesmere Port CH66 . . . . . .94 E8
Macclesfield SK10 . . . . .87 E4
Warrington WA1 . . . . .17 D7
Gloucester Ho **14**
CH1 . . . . .237 C3
Gloucester Rd
Gatley SK8 . . . . .34 C7
Kidsgrove ST7 . . . . .195 A3
Knutsford WA16 . . . . .81 F8
Poynton SK12 . . . . .36 D4
Widnes WA8 . . . . .13 B3
Gloucester St CH1 . . . . . . .237 B4
Glover Rd WA3 . . . . .9 C4
Glovers Loom CH3 . . . . . . .142 B7
Glover St
Crewe CW1 . . . . .190 A5
Newton-le-W WA12 . . . . .2 C3
Gloverstone Ct CH1 . . . . . .237 B1
Glyn Ave CH62 . . . . .43 E7
Glyn Garth CH1 . . . . .117 D3
Go Ape Delamere*
CW8 . . . . .100 B2
Goathland Way SK11 . . . . .112 D6
Goddard Cl **15** CW1 . . . . .190 B5
Goddard Rd WA7 . . . . .23 E3
Goddard St CW1 . . . . .190 B5
Godfrey St WA2 . . . . .16 D7
Godscroft La WA6 . . . . .73 E6
Godshill Cl WA5 . . . . .14 D7
Godstall La CH1 . . . . .237 B2
Godstow WA7 . . . . .50 D7
Godward Rd SK22 . . . . .39 B8
GOLBORNE 3 B7
Golborne Dale Rd WA3,
WA12 . . . . .3 A5
Golborne Jun & Inf Sch
WA3 .3 A3
Golborne La WA16 . . . . .28 F3
Golborne Rd
Golborne WA3 . . . . .3 A7
Winwick WA12, WA2 . . . . . . .8 A7
Golborne St WA12 . . . . .2 B3
Goldcliff Cl WA5 . . . . .7 D3
Goldcrest Cl
Runcorn WA7 . . . . .49 F5
Winsford CW7 . . . . .149 C5
Golden Hill CW2 . . . . .207 E4
Golden Sq WA1 . . . . .16 B5
Goldfinch Cl CW12 . . . . . . .156 E1
Goldfinch Dr ST7 . . . . .193 B3
Goldfinch La WA3 . . . . .9 E4
Goldfinch Rd ST7 . . . . .195 F1
Goldford La SY14 . . . . .199 F6
Goldsmith Dr CW11 . . . . . .174 D6
Gold Triangle Complex
WA8 . . . . .22 C5
Golftyn Dr CH5 . . . . .91 C1
Golftyn La CH5 . . . . .91 C1
GOLLY 161 B1
Gongar La
Ashton Hayes CH3 . . . . . . .121 E8
Mouldsworth CH3 . . . . .98 E1
Gonsley Cl CH2 . . . . .237 B4
Gonville Ave SK11 . . . . . . .112 F3
Gooch Dr WA12 . . . . .2 D2
Goodall's Cnr CW2 . . . . . . .206 C3
Goodall St WA3 . . . . .3 C8
Goodall St CW11 . . . . .112 E7
Goode Way CW2 . . . . .190 D1
Goodier Ct WA7 . . . . .49 C7
Goodrington Rd WA9 . . . . . .34 E3
Goodwin Cres CW2 . . . . . . .206 C4
Goodwood Cl
Barnton CW8 . . . . .78 B3
Chester CH1 . . . . .118 B2
Goodwood Ct ST7 . . . . .193 F6
Goodwood Gr CH66 . . . . . . .69 D3
Goodwood Rise
CW10 . . . . .128 A2
Gooseberry La
Kelsall CH3 . . . . .122 A4
Runcorn WA7 . . . . .24 D1
Goosebrook Cl WA3 . . . . .9 F5
Goosebrook La WA4,
CW9 . . . . .52 F2

Goose La WA4 . . . . .26 A2
Goosetrey Cl SK9 . . . . .34 E1
GOOSTREY 107 D1
Goostrey Com Prim Sch
CW4 . . . . .130 F8
Goostrey Com Prim Sch
(The Annexe) CW4 . . . . . .107 F1
Goostrey Ct **4** CW12 . .156 F3
Goostrey La
Goostrey CW4 . . . . .130 B8
Holmes Chapel CW4 . . . . . .131 A6
Goostrey Sta CW4 . . . . . . .131 A8
Goostry La WA16 . . . . .108 A7
Gordale Cl
Congleton CW12 . . . . .157 A5
Northwich CW8 . . . . .103 D8
Warrington WA5 . . . . .14 F7
Winnington CW8 . . . . .78 D1
Gordon Ave
Bebington CH62 . . . . .43 E7
Haydock WA11 . . . . .1 F7
Warrington WA1 . . . . .17 B7
Gordon La CH1 . . . . .95 B5
Gore La SK9 . . . . .59 C3
Gorran Haven WA7 . . . . .50 C5
Gorse Bank Rd WA15 . . . . .32 C7
Gorse Cl WA6 . . . . .101 A6
GORSE COVERT 10 B5
Gorse Covert CW9 . . . . .79 C3
Gorse Covert Prim Sch
WA3 . . . . .10 B5
Gorse Covert Rd WA3 . . . . .10 B6
Gorsefield CH3 . . . . .166 A1
Gorsefield Ave CH62 . . . . . .43 D5
Gorsefield Cl CH62 . . . . . . .43 D5
Gorsefield Hey SK9 . . . . . . .60 E8
Gorse Hill Hostel CH1 . . . .117 E2
Gorse La CW12 . . . . .178 D5
Gorselands WA8 . . . . .35 B5
Gorse Sq M31 . . . . .11 D3
Gorse Stacks CH1 . . . . .237 B3
Gorse The WA14 . . . . .31 B8
Gorse Way CH3 . . . . .142 A5
Gorsewood Prim Sch
WA7 . . . . .50 D7
Gorsewood Rd WA7 . . . . . . .50 D6
GORSEY BANK 231 F2
Gorsey Bank Cres
CW5 . . . . .220 A8
Gorsey Bank Prim Sch
SK9 . . . . .59 F7
Gorsey La
Partington WA13 . . . . .20 B7
St Helens WA5, WA9 . . . . . . .6 C5
Warrington WA1, WA2 . . . . .16 D7
Widnes WA8 . . . . .13 E1
Gorsey Rd SK9 . . . . .59 F8
Gorseywell La WA7 . . . . . . .50 F6
GORSTAGE 102 C6
Gorstage La CW8 . . . . .102 C7
GORSTELLA 140 A1
Gorsthills Com Prim Sch
CH66 . . . . .69 C3
Gorstons La CH64 . . . . .67 A6
Gorston Wlk M22 . . . . .33 C8
GORSTYHILL 207 E2
Gorsty Hill Cl CW2 . . . . . . .207 F2
Gorsty Hill Ct CW2 . . . . . . .207 F2
Gosberryhole La
CW12 . . . . .158 A2
Gosforth Ct WA7 . . . . .49 E7
Gosforth Pl CH2 . . . . .118 F3
GOSLAND GREEN 169 B1
Gosling Cl WA5 . . . . .26 A1
Gosling Rd WA3 . . . . .9 B7
Gosling Way CW12 . . . . . . .156 A3
Gosport Cl WA2 . . . . .8 F1
Goss St CH1 . . . . .237 A2
Gough Ave WA2 . . . . .8 B2
Gough's La WA16 . . . . .82 C7
Goulden St
Crewe CW1 . . . . .190 A5
Warrington WA5 . . . . .15 E6
Goulders Ct WA7 . . . . .50 B5
GOWHOLE 39 E4
Gowy Cl
Alsager ST7 . . . . .192 F3
Sandbach CW11 . . . . .174 E8
Gowy Cres CH3 . . . . .121 B2
Gowy Ct
Calveley CW6 . . . . .169 E2
Ellesmere Port CH66 . . . . . .69 E8
Gowy Rd CH2 . . . . .96 F1
Gowy Wlk CW7 . . . . .127 A8
Goyt Forest Walks*
SK11 . . . . .115 E7
Goyt Pl SK23 . . . . .65 E7
Goyt Rd
Disley SK12 . . . . .38 D5
Horwich End SK23 . . . . .65 E6
New Mills SK22 . . . . .39 D6
Goyt Valley Ind Est
SK23 . . . . .39 D4
Goyt View SK22 . . . . .39 B6
Grace Ave WA3 . . . . .16 B8
Grace Cl CW1 . . . . .191 C4
Grace Rd CH5 . . . . .70 C7

Graham Ave CH66 . . . . .69 D5
Graham Cl WA8 . . . . .12 C1
Graham Cres M44 . . . . .11 C3
Graham Dr
Disley SK12 . . . . .38 C6
Halewood L26 . . . . .21 A8
Graham Rd
Blacon CH1 . . . . .117 F3
Widnes WA8 . . . . .22 C8
Grainger's Rd CW9 . . . . . . .103 F5
Grammar School Ct
WA4 . . . . .16 F3
Grammar School Rd
Lymm WA13 . . . . .18 F2
Warrington WA4 . . . . .16 F3
Grampian Way
Bebington CH62 . . . . .43 E4
Neston CH64 . . . . .66 E5
Winsford CW7 . . . . .149 A8
Granary Mews SK12 . . . . . . .36 E3
Granary Mill WA7 . . . . .50 E6
Granby Cl WA7 . . . . .50 C5
Granby Rd
Cheadle SK8 . . . . .35 B8
Warrington WA4 . . . . .26 B8
Grandford La CW5 . . . . .217 D2
Grand Junction Ret Pk
CW1 . . . . .190 D3
GRANGE
Runcorn 49 D7
Warrington 17 E8
Grange Ave
Barnton CW8 . . . . .78 A3
Warrington WA4 . . . . .16 E4
Grangebrook Dr CW7 . . . . .126 C1
Grange Cl
Chorlton CW2 . . . . .207 E4
Crewe CW1 . . . . .190 E3
Golborne WA3 . . . . .3 C6
Sandbach CW11 . . . . .174 F7
Grange Com Prim Sch
CW7 . . . . .126 B1
Grange Comp Sch
WA7 . . . . .23 C1
Grange Cres CH66 . . . . .44 A1
Grange Ct
Biddulph ST8 . . . . .179 D2
12 Knutsford WA16 . . . . .57 A2
Winsford CW7 . . . . .126 B2
Grange Dr
Hartford CW8 . . . . .103 A6
Thornton Hough CH63 . . . . .42 A7
Warrington WA5 . . . . .15 A4
Widnes WA8 . . . . .12 D1
Grange Farm Cl WA5 . . . . .15 D6
Grangefields ST8 . . . . .179 E4
Grange Green Manor
WA4 . . . . .25 E7
Grange Inf Sch The
WA7 . . . . .23 C1
Grange Jun Sch The
Hartford CW8 . . . . .103 A6
Runcorn WA7 . . . . .23 C1
Grange La
Tilston SY14 . . . . .198 E3
Weaverham CW8 . . . . .102 A7
Whitegate CW8 . . . . .125 C1
Winsford CW7 . . . . .126 B4
Grangelands SK10 . . . . .86 F2
Grange Lea CW10 . . . . .128 B1
Grangemoor WA7 . . . . .49 D8
Grange Park Ave
Warrington WA1 . . . . .17 D7
Wilmslow SK9 . . . . .60 A8
Grange Park Dr ST8 . . . . . .179 E3
Grange Pl M44 . . . . .11 E5
Grange Rd
Barnton CW8 . . . . .78 A3
Biddulph ST8 . . . . .179 E3
Chester CH2 . . . . .118 C5
Chester, Vicarscross
CH3 . . . . .119 C2
Cuddington CW8 . . . . .101 F3
Ellesmere Port CH65 . . . . . .70 C4
Haydock WA11, WA12 . . . . . .1 D5
Macclesfield SK11 . . . . .112 C6
Mouldsworth CH3 . . . . .99 B1
Northwich, Rudheath
CW9 . . . . .104 D6
Runcorn WA7 . . . . .23 C2
Grange Rd N WA7 . . . . .23 C2
Grange Rd W CH3 . . . . .119 C2
Grange Sch The CW8 . . . . .103 B6
Grangeside CH2 . . . . .118 D7
Grange The
Congleton CW12 . . . . .179 B8
Hartford CW8 . . . . .103 B5
Macclesfield SK11 . . . . .112 A6
Grange Valley WA11 . . . . . . .1 D6
Grange Valley Prim Sch
WA11 . . . . .1 D5
Grange Villas CW11 . . . . . .142 F6
Grangeway
Handforth SK9 . . . . .34 D4
Runcorn WA7 . . . . .49 C8
Grange Way CW11 . . . . . . .174 F7
Grangewood CW9 . . . . .79 C8
Grangewood Dr SK11 . . . . .83 F3
Granston Cl WA5 . . . . .7 E2
Grant Cl WA5 . . . . .7 D1
Grantham Ave
Warrington, Bruche
WA1 . . . . .16 E7
Warrington WA4 . . . . .16 E7
Grantham Cl CW9 . . . . .104 C7
Granville Dr CH66 . . . . .69 B7
Granville Rd
Chester CH1 . . . . .118 B3

Granville Rd *continued*
Northwich CW9 . . . . 104 A5
Wilmslow SK9 . . . . 59 F5
Granville Sq CW7 . . . . 149 E8
Granville St
15 Runcorn WA7 . . . . 23 A3
Warrington WA1 . . . . 16 D6
Winsford CW7 . . . . 149 E8
Grapes St 9 SK11 . . . . . . 112 D7
GRAPPENHALL 17 A1
Grappenhall Hall Sch
WA4 . . . . 17 B1
GRAPPENHALL HEYS 27 A8
Grappenhall La WA4 . . . . . 27 E6
Grappenhall Rd
Ellesmere Port CH65 . . . . . . 69 F3
Warrington WA4 . . . . 16 D1
Grappenhall St Wilfrid's
CE Prim Sch WA4 . . . . . . 17 B1
Grasmere SK11 . . . . 112 A6
Grasmere Ave
Congleton CW12 . . . . 155 F2
Crewe CW2 . . . . 189 F5
Warrington WA2 . . . . 8 C3
Grasmere Cl CW7 . . . . . . 126 D2
Grasmere Cres
Bramhall SK7 . . . . 35 E8
High Lane SK12 . . . . 37 E8
Grasmere Dr
Holmes Chapel CW4 . . . . . 130 A3
Runcorn WA7 . . . . 49 D5
Grasmere Rd
Alderley Edge SK9 . . . . 60 A1
Chester CH2 . . . . 118 F5
Ellesmere Port CH65 . . . . . . 70 C2
Frodsham WA6 . . . . 74 C8
Lymm WA13 . . . . 18 E4
Neston CH64 . . . . 66 E6
Partington M31 . . . . 11 E3
Grason Ave SK9 . . . . 34 C1
Grassfield Way WA16 . . . . 82 A8
Grassmoor Cl CH62 . . . . . . 43 E8
Grassgreen La ST7 . . . . . 209 E1
Gratrix Rd CH62 . . . . 43 D8
GRAVEL 127 A1
Gravel La SK9 . . . . 59 E5
Gravel Wlk SY14 . . . . 213 D7
Gravenhunger La
CW3 . . . . 232 D1
GRAVENHUNGER MOSS
. . . . 232 D2
Graveyard La WA16 . . . . . 58 F5
Gray Ave WA11 . . . . 1 D6
Grayfag Cl WA7 . . . . 49 F5
Graymarsh Dr SK12 . . . . . 36 E2
Gray's Cl ST7 . . . . 195 B7
Greasby Dr CH66 . . . . 69 E4
Great Ashfield WA8 . . . . . 12 D3
GREAT BARROW 120 E6
GREAT BUDWORTH 79 A7
Great Budworth CE Prim
Sch CW9 . . . . 79 B8
Great Delph WA11 . . . . 1 D7
Greater Grace Sch
CH1 . . . . 95 B4
Great King St SK11 . . . . . 112 C8
Greatoak Rd ST7 . . . . 209 F4
Great Oak Sq WA16 . . . . . 58 A4
Great Queen St SK11 . . . . 112 C8
Great Riding WA7 . . . . 50 C7
GREAT SANKEY 15 A6
Great Sankey High Sch
WA5 . . . . 14 E7
Great Sankey Prim Sch
WA5 . . . . 15 A5
GREAT SUTTON 69 D3
Greaves La SY14 . . . . 222 E6
Greaves La E SY14 . . . . . . 222 E7
Greaves Rd SK9 . . . . 59 E7
Grebe Cl
Knutsford WA16 . . . . 57 B3
Poynton SK12 . . . . 36 B4
Greeba Ave WA4 . . . . 16 B3
Greek St WA7 . . . . 22 F3
Greenacre St SK8 . . . . 34 C7
Green Acre Cl WA16 . . . . . 82 B8
Greenacre Dr CH63 . . . . . . 43 C7
Greenacre Rd CH4 . . . . . . 140 F4
Greenacres
Crewe CW1 . . . . 190 D6
Duddon CW6 . . . . 145 A6
Frodsham WA6 . . . . 74 C6
Sandbach CW11 . . . . 175 A7
Greenacres Cl WA3 . . . . . . 4 B8
Greenacres Ct CH2 . . . . . . 95 F1
Greenacres Rd CW12 . . . . 155 F2
Greenacres The WA13 . . . . 19 A4
Greenall Ave WA5 . . . . 14 D4
Greenall Rd CW9 . . . . 104 B8
Greenall's Ave WA4 . . . . . . 16 C2
Green Ave
Alpraham CW6 . . . . 169 D4
Barnton CW8 . . . . 78 A3
Davenham CW9 . . . . 103 F3
GREENBANK 103 C7
Greenbank
Chester CH4 . . . . 141 E6
Dunham-on-t-H WA6 . . . . . 97 E6
Green Bank
Adderley TF9 . . . . 235 A5
Chester CH4 . . . . 141 E6
Greenbank Ave CH66 . . . . 69 C7
Greenbank Cl CW5 . . . . . . 205 D6
Greenbank Dr SK10 . . . . . . 88 A8
Greenbank Gdns CW4 . . . . 16 F2
Greenbank La CW8 . . . . . 103 D6

Greenbank Pk CW11 . . . . 175 A2
Greenbank Rd
Chester CH2 . . . . 119 A4
Warrington WA4 . . . . 16 F2
Greenbank Residential
Sch CW8 . . . . 103 D6
Greenbank St CW4 . . . . . . 16 C2
Greenbank Sta CW8 . . . . . 103 D6
Green Bridge Cl WA7 . . . . . 24 A2
Greenbridge Rd WA7 . . . . . 24 B2
Green Coppice WA7 . . . . . . 50 C8
Greencourts Bsns Pk
M22 . . . . 34 A8
GREENDALE 86 E7
Greendale Dr
Middlewich CW10 . . . . 151 B7
Newcastle-u-Lyme ST5 . . . . 210 D1
Greendale Gdns CW1 . . . . 190 E5
Greendale La SK10 . . . . . . 86 D8
Green Dr
Alsager ST7 . . . . 193 D4
Handforth SK9 . . . . 34 D2
Green Farm CH4 . . . . 163 B2
Greenfield Ave CH4 . . . . . 161 A7
Greenfield Cl SK22 . . . . . . 39 A8
Greenfield Cres
Chester CH2 . . . . 119 B5
Waverton CH3 . . . . 143 B6
Greenfield Farm Ind Est
CW12 . . . . 156 B3
Greenfield Gdns CH2 . . . . . 72 B3
Greenfield La
Chester CH2 . . . . 119 B5
Frodsham WA6 . . . . 49 B1
Greenfield Rd
Bollington SK10 . . . . 88 A7
Broughton CH4 . . . . 139 C4
Congleton CW12 . . . . 156 B3
Ellesmere Port CH66 . . . . . . 69 B7
Waverton CH3 . . . . 143 B6
Greenfields
Chester CH2 . . . . 95 F1
Winsford CW7 . . . . 127 B1
Greenfields Ave
Bebington CH62 . . . . 43 C7
Shavington CW2 . . . . 206 B4
Warrington WA4 . . . . 26 D8
Greenfields Cl
Chester CH4 . . . . 66 F5
Newton-le-W WA12 . . . . 2 C4
Warrington WA1 . . . . 17 C7
Greenfields Cres CH62 . . . . 43 C7
Greenfields Croft
CH64 . . . . 66 E5
Greenfields Dr
Alsager ST7 . . . . 193 E3
Neston CH64 . . . . 66 F5
Greenfields La
Malpas SY14 . . . . 213 B4
Rowton CH3 . . . . 142 F5
Greenfields Lo CH3 . . . . . 120 D6
Greenfields Prim Sch
CW7 . . . . 126 A1
Greenfield Way CW8 . . . . 102 A4
Greengate WA15 . . . . 32 D7
Greengate Rd ST7 . . . . . . 193 F5
Greengates Cres CH4 . . . . 66 E5
Green Hall Mews SK9 . . . . 60 B6
Greenhaven Ct CW5 . . . . . 219 E5
Greenhill La WA4 . . . . 52 A5
Greenhills Cl SK11 . . . . . . 112 E7
Greenhill Wlk SK12 . . . . . . 38 D6
Greenhouse Farm Rd
WA7 . . . . 50 B6
Greenhythe Rd SK8 . . . . . . 34 C6
Greenlow Brow WA5 . . . . . . 6 F6
Green La
Acton CW5 . . . . 204 B3
Alderley Edge SK9 . . . . 59 F1
Audlem CW3 . . . . 229 F2
Barbridge CW5 . . . . 187 A7
Bollington SK10 . . . . 63 B1
Burtonwood WA5 . . . . 6 E7
Chester CH4 . . . . 140 E4
Chester, Vicarscross
CH3 . . . . 119 B3
Christleton CH3 . . . . 120 C2
Davenham CW9 . . . . 103 F3
Disley SK12 . . . . 38 D4
Ellesmere Port, Great Sutton
CH66 . . . . 69 C4
Ellesmere Port, Great Sutton
CH66 . . . . 69 D4
Ellesmere Port, Wolverham
CH65 . . . . 70 C4
Higher Kinnerton CH4 . . . . 161 B6
Higher Wincham CW9 . . . . . 79 F4
Irlam M44 . . . . 11 C5
Kelsall CW6 . . . . 122 D4
Knutsford WA16 . . . . 56 D4
Lindow End SK9 . . . . 84 F8
Over Peover WA16 . . . . 83 D1
Picton CH2 . . . . 96 C3
Plumley WA16 . . . . 80 E6
Poynton SK12 . . . . 37 C4
Sandbach CW11 . . . . 173 F7
Saughall CH1 . . . . 117 C7
Shocklach SY14 . . . . 211 C7
Tattenhall CH3 . . . . 182 F5
Tilston SY14 . . . . 212 B8
Warrington, Dudlow's Green
WA4 . . . . 26 F5
Warrington, Paddington
WA1 . . . . 17 A8
Widnes WA8 . . . . 12 E1
Willaston CW5 . . . . 205 E5
Wilmslow SK9 . . . . 60 B7
Winwick WA2 . . . . 8 A7

Green Lake La CH3 . . . . . 163 F3
Greenland Cl CW6 . . . . . . 146 D1
Greenlands CH3 . . . . 166 B3
Greenlands Cl 3 SK8 . . . . . 34 E8
Green Lane CW2 . . . . 8 A7
Green Lane Com Specl
Sch WA1 . . . . 17 B8
Green Lane E
Connah's Quay CH5 . . . . . . 93 C1
Sealand CH5 . . . . 116 D7
Green Lane Est
Connah's Quay CH5 . . . . . . 93 C1
Sealand CH5 . . . . 116 C8
Green Lane W CH5 . . . . . . 93 B3
Greenlaw Cl CW9 . . . . 104 A5
Green Lawns Dr 8
CH66 . . . . 94 F8
Greenlea Cl CH65 . . . . 70 B2
GREENLOOMS 143 F4
Green Mdws
Golborne WA3 . . . . 3 E5
Macclesfield SK11 . . . . 111 F6
Greenoaks Ctr WA8 . . . . . . 23 B8
Greenoaks Farm Ind Est
WA8 . . . . 23 C8
Green Oaks Path WA8 . . . . 23 C8
Green Oaks Way WA8 . . . . 23 C8
Greenock Mews WA8 . . . . . 12 E3
Greenore Dr L24 . . . . 21 D2
Green Pk CW8 . . . . 102 E7
Green Rd M31 . . . . 11 F2
Greensbridge La L26 . . . . . 21 A8
Greenshall La SK12 . . . . . . 38 F5
Greenshank Cl WA12 . . . . . . 2 C4
Greenside Ave WA6 . . . . . . 74 D7
Greenside Cl CW9 . . . . . . 105 D5
Greenside Dr CW9 . . . . . . 105 A8
Green St
5 Alderley Edge SK9 . . . . . 60 A1
Holt LL13 . . . . 180 E1
Knutsford WA16 . . . . 57 A2
Macclesfield SK10 . . . . 112 E7
Sandbach CW11 . . . . 175 B6
Warrington WA5 . . . . 15 E5
Warrington WA5 . . . . 15 F5
Greens The WA15 . . . . 32 D7
Greensway CH4 . . . . 141 A7
Green The
Cheadle SK8 . . . . 34 F8
Congleton CW12 . . . . 156 C2
Ellesmere Port CH65 . . . . . . 70 B2
Hale L24 . . . . 21 D1
Handforth SK9 . . . . 34 E3
Hartford CW8 . . . . 103 B5
Harthill CH3 . . . . 183 E3
Higher Kinnerton CH4 . . . . 161 B7
Lawton-gate ST7 . . . . 194 A4
Middlewich CW10 . . . . 151 D6
Nantwich CW5 . . . . 204 D8
Neston CH64 . . . . 66 D8
Neston, Little Neston
CH64 . . . . 66 F6
Partington M31 . . . . 11 F4
4 Runcorn WA7 . . . . 23 F1
Saughall CH1 . . . . 94 A2
Tarvin CH3 . . . . 121 F2
Thornton Hough CH63 . . . . 42 C4
Woore CW3 . . . . 232 C1
Green View WA13 . . . . 19 A4
Green Villa Pk SK9 . . . . 59 E4
Greenway
Alsager ST7 . . . . 193 B5
Bramhall SK7 . . . . 35 D6
Congleton CW12 . . . . 156 B3
Crewe CW1 . . . . 190 D7
Farndon CH3 . . . . 180 F1
Neston CH64 . . . . 41 F2
Saughall CH1 . . . . 94 A1
Tilston SY14 . . . . 198 C3
Warrington, Great Sankey
WA5 . . . . 14 E7
Warrington, Paddington
WA1 . . . . 16 F7
Warrington WA4 . . . . 26 D7
Wilmslow SK9 . . . . 60 B6
Greenway Cl
Helsby WA6 . . . . 73 B3
Rode Heath ST7 . . . . 193 F8
Greenway Dr CW9 . . . . . . 104 C7
Greenway Rd
Biddulph ST8 . . . . 179 E2
Gatley SK8 . . . . 34 C6
Runcorn WA7 . . . . 23 A1
Speke L24 . . . . 21 A3
Widnes WA8 . . . . 13 B1
Greenways ST7 . . . . 209 F2
Greenways Ct CH62 . . . . . . 43 C6
Greenway St CH4 . . . . 237 B1
Greenway Wlk CW9 . . . . . 104 C7
Greenwell Rd WA11 . . . . . . 1 C6
Greenwich Ave WA8 . . . . . . 13 D4
Green Wlk
Cuddington CW8 . . . . 102 B4
Partington M31 . . . . 11 E3
Greenwood Ave
Chester CH4 . . . . 141 D7
Congleton CW12 . . . . 156 F3
Greenwood Cl
Greenwood CW8 . . . . 77 D1
Greenwood Cres WA2 . . . . . 8 E2
Greenwood Ct WA4 . . . . 4 F1
Greenwood Dr
Newton-le-W WA12 . . . . 2 D7
Runcorn WA7 . . . . 24 F4
Wilmslow SK9 . . . . 60 B6
Greenwood Rd WA13 . . . . . 18 F2
Greenwood Terr WA16 . . . . 58 A4
Greenwood The CW6 . . . . 168 D8
Grove Ave
Chester CH3 . . . . 119 B3

Greg Mews SK9 . . . . 34 B2
Gregory Cl WA5 . . . . 15 C7
Gregorys Row WA3 . . . . 4 A8
Gregson Rd WA8 . . . . 13 C1
Grenfell Cl CH64 . . . . 41 C1
Grenfell Ct CH64 . . . . 66 C8
Grenfell Pk CH64 . . . . 41 C1
Grenfell St 11 WA8 . . . . . . 23 B8
Grenville Cl CW1 . . . . 191 C5
Grenville Cres CH63 . . . . . . 43 C7
Grenville Rd CH64 . . . . 41 F1
Gresford Ave CH2 . . . . . . 237 C4
Gresford Cl WA5 . . . . 7 E1
Gresham Cl WA5 . . . . 15 C7
Gresty Bldgs 33 CW5 . . . . 204 E6
Gresty Green Rd
CW2 . . . . 206 D7
Gresty La CW2 . . . . 206 B7
Gresty Rd CW2 . . . . 190 D2
Gresty Road Football Gd (
Crewe Alexandra FC)
CW2 . . . . 190 D2
Gresty Side CW5 . . . . 204 C5
Gresty Terr CW1 . . . . 190 E4
Greta Ave SK8 . . . . 34 C6
Greville Dr CW7 . . . . 127 A1
Grey Friars CH1 . . . . 237 A2
Greyfriars Cl WA2 . . . . 8 D1
Greyhound Park Rd
CH1 . . . . 118 A3
Greyhound Pk CH1 . . . . . . 118 A3
Greyhound Rd SK10 . . . . . . 86 B5
Greymist Ave WA1 . . . . 17 C7
Greys Ct WA1 . . . . 9 C1
Greysfield Flats CH3 . . . . . 120 D6
Grey St WA1 . . . . 16 C6
Greystoke Dr SK9 . . . . 60 A2
Greystoke Rd SK10 . . . . . . 87 F2
Greystone Pk CW1 . . . . . . 190 D4
Greystone Rd WA5 . . . . 14 F4
Greystones CH66 . . . . 69 D4
Greystones Rd CH3 . . . . . 119 C1
Grice St WA4 . . . . 16 C1
Griffin Cl
Blacon CH1 . . . . 117 F6
New Mills SK22 . . . . 39 D6
Norton in Hales TF9 . . . . . 236 C2
Griffin La SK8 . . . . 34 D7
Griffin Mews WA8 . . . . 13 B3
Griffith Ave WA3 . . . . 9 E5
Griffiths Dr CW9 . . . . 104 D6
Griffiths Rd
Lostock Gralam CW9 . . . . . 79 F1
Northwich CW9 . . . . 104 E8
Griffiths St WA4 . . . . 16 F4
Higher Kinnerton CH4 . . . . 161 B7
Grig Pl ST7 . . . . 193 C5
Grimsditch La WA4 . . . . . . 52 B5
Grimshaw Ave SK10 . . . . . . 88 A7
Grimshaw La SK10 . . . . 88 A7
Grindley Bank CH2 . . . . . . 119 F8
GRINDLEY BROOK 225 C3
Grindley Gdns CH65 . . . . . . 70 C2
Grindley Gn SY13 . . . . 228 B3
Grisedale Ave WA2 . . . . 8 B3
Grisedale Cl WA7 . . . . 49 E5
Grisedale Rd CH62 . . . . . . 43 F8
Grisedale Way SK11 . . . . . 112 A5
Gritstone Dr SK10 . . . . . . 112 A8
Grizedale WA8 . . . . 12 D2
Grizedale Cl CW2 . . . . 189 D2
Groarke Dr WA5 . . . . 14 D5
Groby Rd CW1 . . . . 190 E8
Grocotts Row 12 CW5 . . . . 204 E5
Grosvenor Ave
Alsager ST7 . . . . 193 D5
3 Golborne WA3 . . . . 3 D8
Hartford CW8 . . . . 103 A4
Warrington WA1 . . . . 16 F7
Grosvenor Cl
Warrington WA5 . . . . 15 C5
Wilmslow SK9 . . . . 60 A4
Grosvenor Cotts CH4 . . . . 141 D7
Grosvenor Ct
Chester CH1 . . . . 237 C2
12 Crewe CW1 . . . . 190 B5
Winsford CW7 . . . . 149 C7
Grosvenor Ctr SK11 . . . . . 112 D8
Grosvenor Dr SK12 . . . . . . 36 D3
Grosvenor Gdns WA12 . . . . 2 C6
Grosvenor Grange WA1 . . . . 9 B1
Grosvenor Mus*
CH1 . . . . 237 A1
Grosvenor Nuffield Hospl
CH4 . . . . 141 C6
Grosvenor Pk Rd CH1 . . . . 237 C2
Grosvenor Pk Terr CH1,
CH3 . . . . 237 C2
Grosvenor Pl CH1 . . . . 237 B1
Grosvenor Rd
Chester CH4 . . . . 141 C7
Congleton CW12 . . . . 156 A3
Haydock WA11 . . . . 1 B7
Tarvin CH3 . . . . 121 A2
Widnes WA8 . . . . 13 B5
Grosvenor Sh Ctr The
CH1 . . . . 237 B2
Grosvenor St
Chester CH1 . . . . 237 A2
Crewe CW1 . . . . 190 B5
3 Macclesfield SK10 . . . . 112 C8
Runcorn WA7 . . . . 23 B3
Winsford CW7 . . . . 149 E8
Grotsworth La SY14 . . . . . 214 E8
Grotto La WA16 . . . . 108 B7
Grounds St WA2 . . . . 16 B7
Grove Arc SK9 . . . . 60 A2
Grove Ave
Chester CH3 . . . . 119 B3

Grove Ave *continued*
Kidsgrove ST7 . . . . 194 E1
Lawton-gate ST7 . . . . 194 A4
Lostock Gralam CW9 . . . . . 80 A3
Lymm WA13 . . . . 18 C3
Wilmslow SK9 . . . . 60 B7
Grove Cl 1 CW7 . . . . 149 B8
Grove Cres CW3 . . . . 232 C1
Grove Ct
Alsager ST7 . . . . 193 E4
Lymm WA13 . . . . 18 C3
Grove Gdns CH3 . . . . 119 E2
Grove Ho SK8 . . . . 35 B6
Grove La SK8 . . . . 35 A6
Grovemount CW9 . . . . 103 F2
Grove Park Ave ST7 . . . . . 194 A4
Grove Pk WA16 . . . . 57 A1
Grove Rd CH1 . . . . 94 E4
Grove Rise WA13 . . . . 18 E3
Grove St
New Mills SK22 . . . . 39 B7
Runcorn WA7 . . . . 22 F3
Warrington WA4 . . . . 16 C4
Wilmslow SK9 . . . . 60 B7
Groves The
Chester CH1 . . . . 237 B2
Ellesmere Port CH66 . . . . . . 95 A8
Grove Terr WA6 . . . . 73 C4
Grove The
Cheadle SK8 . . . . 35 A6
Knutsford WA16 . . . . 57 C4
Lawton-gate ST7 . . . . 194 A4
Lymm WA13 . . . . 18 E3
Tarporley CW6 . . . . 146 C2
Warrington WA5 . . . . 14 F4
Whitchurch SY13 . . . . 225 F1
Grove Way SK9 . . . . 60 B7
Growewood Mews
SK11 . . . . 112 C6
Grub La CW6 . . . . 122 C5
Grundy Cl WA8 . . . . 12 F3
Grundy St WA3 . . . . 3 A7
Guardian St WA5 . . . . 15 F6
Guardian Street Ind Est
WA5 . . . . 15 F6
Guernsey Cl
Congleton CW12 . . . . 157 A2
Middlewich CW10 . . . . 128 D2
Warrington WA4 . . . . 26 D3
Guernsey Dr CH65 . . . . 70 C1
Guernsey Ho CH2 . . . . 119 B5
Guernsey Rd WA8 . . . . 13 E3
Guests Slack WA6 . . . . . . 100 B8
Guest St WA8 . . . . 23 A7
Guilden Gn CH3 . . . . 119 E4
GUILDEN SUTTON 119 E5
Guilden Sutton CE Prim
Sch CH3 . . . . 119 F5
Guilden Sutton La
CH3 . . . . 119 D5
Guildford Ave SK8 . . . . 35 A6
Guildford Cl
1 Chester CH4 . . . . 140 F6
Warrington WA2 . . . . 9 A1
Guillemot Cl CW1 . . . . 190 F5
Gullane Cl SK10 . . . . 87 B4
Gull Cl SK12 . . . . 36 B3
Gullet The CW5 . . . . 204 E5
Gullivers World Theme
Pk* WA5 . . . . 7 E1
Gulls Way CH60 . . . . 40 E7
Gunco La
Macclesfield SK11 . . . . 112 E6
Prestbury SK10 . . . . 87 C8
Gunn Gr CH64 . . . . 66 F8
GURNETT 112 F4
Gutterscroft CW1 . . . . 191 D5
Gutticar Rd WA8 . . . . 12 B1
Guy La CH3 . . . . 143 D5
Gypsy La CH1 . . . . 94 F2

H

Hacked Way La SK11 . . . . . 113 F6
HACK GREEN 218 D5
Hack Green Secret
Nuclear Bunker*
. . . . 218 D4
Haddon Cl
Alderley Edge SK9 . . . . 59 F2
High Lane SK6 . . . . 37 E6
Holmes Chapel CW4 . . . . . 130 B3
Macclesfield SK11 . . . . 112 B5
Wistaston CW2 . . . . 206 B7
Haddon Dr WA8 . . . . 12 C3
Haddon Ho 4 CH64 . . . . . . 66 E8
Haddon La CH64 . . . . 67 C4
Haddon Rd
Burton CH64 . . . . 67 D2
Gatley SK8 . . . . 34 C7
Hadfield Cl WA8 . . . . 13 E2
Hadfield St CW9 . . . . 79 B1
Hadleigh Cl WA5 . . . . 14 E5
Hadley Ave CH62 . . . . 43 C8
Hadley Dr CW2 . . . . 207 E4
Hadlow La CH64 . . . . 67 F6
Hadlow Rd CH64 . . . . 67 F6
Hadlow Terr CH64 . . . . 67 F7
Hadrian Dr CH1 . . . . 117 E6
Hadrian Way
Cuddington CW8 . . . . 102 B2
Middlewich CW10 . . . . 128 C2
Hadyn Jones Dr CW5 . . . . 204 F4

Hafod Cl
Blacon CH1 . . . . .117 D3
Connah's Quay CH5 . . . . .91 C1
Hag Bank La SK12 . . . . .38 D7
HAGUE BAR 38 F8
Hague Bar Prim Sch
SK22 . . . . .38 E8
Hague Bar Rd SK22 . . . . .39 A7
Hague Fold Rd SK22 . . . . . . .38 F8
Haig Ave
Irlam M44 . . . . .11 C4
Warrington WA5 . . . . .15 A5
Haig Ct WA16 . . . . .57 C4
Haighton Ct 11 CW5 . . . . . .204 E6
Haig Rd
Knutsford WA16 . . . . .57 C4
Widnes WA8 . . . . .13 A1
Hailwood Ho SK10 . . . . .88 B8
HALE
Altrincham 32 B8
Liverpool 21 D1
Hale Ave SK12 . . . . .36 D2
HALE BANK 22 A4
Hale Bank CE Prim Sch
WA8 . . . . .22 A5
Halebank Rd WA8 . . . . .21 F5
Hale Bank Terr WA8 . . . . . . .22 A4
HALE BARNS 32 E7
Hale CE Prim Sch L24 . . . . .21 E1
Hale Ct WA8 . . . . .22 A4
Hale Gate Rd
Hale WA8 . . . . .21 F3
Widnes WA8 . . . . .22 A3
Hale Gr WA5 . . . . .6 E5
HALE HEATH 21 A1
Hale Rd
Hale L24 . . . . .21 B2
Widnes WA8 . . . . .22 C7
Hale Road Ind Est WA8 . . . .22 B4
Hale St WA2 . . . . .16 B7
Hale View WA7 . . . . .48 E8
Hale View Rd WA46 . . . . .73 C4
HALEWOOD 21 B7
Halewood Lane Ends
L26 .21 A8
HALEWOOD VILLAGE 21 A8
Haley Rd N WA5 . . . . .6 E6
Haley Rd S WA5 . . . . .6 E5
Halfacre La WA4 . . . . .17 F2
Half St SK11 . . . . .112 D6
Halghton La LL13 . . . . .222 B2
Halifax Cl WA2 . . . . .8 D2
Halkett Cl CH4 . . . . .140 E5
Halkyn Rd CH2 . . . . .237 C4
Hall Acres La SK8 . . . . .34 E8
Hallams Dr CW5 . . . . .205 B4
Hallastone Rd WA6 . . . . .73 C4
Hall Ave WA8 . . . . .12 A1
Halla-Way WA4 . . . . .16 E3
Hall Bank WA16 . . . . .58 C4
Hall Bank N WA16 . . . . .58 C4
Hall Bank S WA16 . . . . .58 C4
Hall Cl SK10 . . . . .87 D4
Hallcroft M31 . . . . .11 F4
Hallcroft Pl WA4 . . . . .17 A2
Hall Dr
Alsager ST7 . . . . .193 C3
Marston CW9 . . . . .79 B6
Warrington WA4 . . . . .26 D6
Willaston CW5 . . . . .205 C6
Hallefield Cres 5
SK11 . . . . .112 E7
Hallefield Dr 4 SK11 . . . . . .112 E7
Hallefield Rd SK10,
SK11 . . . . .112 E7
Hall Farm CH62 . . . . .44 A4
Hall Farm Cl SK23 . . . . .65 D8
Hallfield Dr CH2 . . . . .72 B3
Hallfield Pk CH66 . . . . .69 D4
Hallfields Rd
Tarvin CH3 . . . . .121 C2
Warrington WA2 . . . . .8 D1
Hall Gr SK10 . . . . .87 D3
HALL GREEN
Scholar Green 194 E5
Whitchurch 224 E1
Hallgreen La CW12 . . . . .155 D8
Hall Hill SK10 . . . . .87 E7
Halliday Cl WA3 . . . . .9 F3
Halliwel Jones Stad
(Warrington Wolves
RLFC) The WA2 . . . . .16 A6
Halliwell's Brow WA16 . . . . . .29 B3
Hall La
Appleton Thorn WA4 . . . . . . .27 B8
Audlem CW3 . . . . .230 C7
Brown Knowl CH3 . . . . .199 C7
Cronton L35 . . . . .12 C7
Daresbury WA4 . . . . .25 D2
Haughton CW6 . . . . .186 D5
Kelsall CW6 . . . . .122 D6
Little Leigh CW9 . . . . .77 F8
Lostock Gralam CW9 . . . . . . .79 F3
Mobberley WA16 . . . . .58 D4
Newton-le-W WA5 . . . . .7 B8
Ollerton WA16 . . . . .83 B5
Partington M31 . . . . .11 F4
Pickmere WA16 . . . . .55 B1
Sandbach CW11 . . . . .174 B5
Shotwick CH1 . . . . .93 B5
St Helens WA9 . . . . .6 A4
Stretton WA4 . . . . .52 D8
Sutton Lane Ends SK11 . . . . .112 F3
Utkinton CW6 . . . . .146 C6
Winsford CW7 . . . . .149 B3

Hall La The CW6 . . . . .147 D2
Hall Moss La SK7 . . . . .35 C4
Hall Nook WA5 . . . . .14 F3
Hall O'shaw St CW1 . . . . . . .190 E4
Hallows Ave WA2 . . . . .16 D8
Hallows Cl CW6 . . . . .122 C4
Hallows Dr CW6 . . . . .122 C4
HALLOWSGATE 122 C4
Hallowsgate Ct CW6 . . . . . .122 C4
Hall Rd
Handforth SK9 . . . . .34 E3
Haydock WA11 . . . . .1 E7
Warrington WA1 . . . . .17 C7
Winsford SK9 . . . . .60 A7
Hallsgreen La CH2 . . . . .96 F7
Hallshaw Ave CW1 . . . . .190 E5
Hallside Pk WA16 . . . . .57 C1
Halls Rd
Biddulph ST8 . . . . .179 C1
Mow Cop ST7 . . . . .195 C7
Hall St
Audley ST7 . . . . .209 D2
Macclesfield SK10 . . . . .112 C8
New Mills SK22 . . . . .39 B8
Warrington WA1 . . . . .16 C5
Hall Terr WA5 . . . . .14 E7
Hall View CH3 . . . . .166 B1
Hall View Cl CW8 . . . . .102 A7
Hall Wood Ave WA11 . . . . .1 E8
Hallwood Cl WA7 . . . . .49 B6
Hallwood Ct CH64 . . . . .66 E7
Hallwood Dr CH66 . . . . .68 D4
Hallwood Link Rd WA7 . . . . .49 F6
HALLWOOD PARK 49 F6
Hallwood Park Ave
WA7 .49 E6
Hallwood Park Prim Sch
WA7 .49 E6
Hallwood Rd SK9 . . . . .34 D2
Halsall Ave WA2 . . . . .16 D8
Halsall Cl WA7 . . . . .50 C5
Halsall's Cotts WA8 . . . . .21 E5
Halstone Ave SK9 . . . . .59 E4
HALTON BROOK 23 D1
Halton Brook Ave WA7 . . . . .23 D1
Halton Brow WA7 . . . . .23 E1
Halton Castle * WA7 . . . . . . .23 F1
Halton Cres CH66 . . . . .69 F2
Halton Ct WA7 . . . . .23 D1
Halton Dr CW2 . . . . .189 D5
Halton General Hospl
WA7 .49 F7
Halton High Sch WA7 . . . . . .50 C6
Halton Lea S Ctr WA7 . . . . . .49 E8
Halton Link Rd WA7 . . . . .49 E8
HALTON LODGE 49 D7
Halton Lodge Ave
WA7 .49 D7
Halton Lodge Prim Sch
WA7 .49 D8
Halton Rd
Chester CH2 . . . . .118 F6
Ellesmere Port CH66 . . . . . . .69 E2
Runcorn WA7 . . . . .23 D2
Warrington WA5 . . . . .14 F3
Halton Station Rd WA7 . . . . .49 F3
HALTON VIEW 13 C1
Halton View Rd WA8 . . . . . . .13 C1
HALTON VILLAGE 49 F8
Halton Way CH66 . . . . .69 E1
Hambledon Cl CH66 . . . . .69 A6
Hamble Dr WA5 . . . . .14 F3
Hambleton Cl WA8 . . . . .12 C3
Hambleton Rd SK8 . . . . .34 C8
Hambleton Way CW7 . . . . . .149 A7
Hambletts Hollow
WA6 . . . . .100 F6
Hamble Way SK10 . . . . .86 E1
Hamilton Ave
Irlam M44 . . . . .11 D4
Sandycroft CH5 . . . . .116 A3
Hamilton Cl
Haslington CW1 . . . . .191 C4
Macclesfield SK10 . . . . .113 A8
Neston CH64 . . . . .41 B2
Hamilton Ct CH64 . . . . .66 F8
Hamilton Pl CH1 . . . . .237 A2
Hamilton Rd CH5 . . . . .91 D1
Hamilton St CH2 . . . . .118 F3
Hamlin Cl WA7 . . . . .49 A6
Hammersmith Way
WA8 .13 D4
Hammond Sch CH2 . . . . .119 B7
Hammond St CW2 . . . . .190 C3
Hamnett Ct WA3 . . . . .9 E3
Hampshire Cl CW12 . . . . . . .156 D4
Hampshire Gdns ST7 . . . . . .194 F2
Hampshire Rd M31 . . . . .11 D2
Hampshire Wlk SK10 . . . . . . .86 F2
Hampson Ave WA3 . . . . .4 F3
Hampson Cres SK9 . . . . .34 C4
Hampstead Ct 7
CW7 . . . . .149 A8
Hampstead Dr CW2 . . . . . . .221 C8
Hampton Cl
Neston CH64 . . . . .66 E6
Widnes WA8 . . . . .13 E3
Hampton Court Way
WA8 .13 D4
Hampton Cres
Neston CH64 . . . . .66 E6
No Man's Heath SY14 . . . . . .214 A5
Hampton Ct
Gatley SK9 . . . . .34 D5
Runcorn WA7 . . . . .24 C4
Hampton Dr
Cronton WA8 . . . . .12 C5

Hampton Dr *continued*
Warrington WA5 . . . . .15 C4
Hampton Gdns CH65 . . . . . . .70 A5
HAMPTON GREEN 214 B7
HAMPTON HEATH 213 C7
Hampton Heath Ind Est
SY14 . . . . .213 D7
Hampton Rd
Chester CH4 . . . . .140 F6
Irlam M44 . . . . .11 D4
Hamson Dr SK10 . . . . .63 B1
Hamsterley Cl WA3 . . . . .10 B6
Hanbury Cl CW2 . . . . .206 B7
Hancock Cl WA4 . . . . .16 C4
Hancock Rd CW12 . . . . .156 F4
Handa Dr CH65 . . . . .95 B8
HANDBRIDGE 141 E7
Handbridge CH4 . . . . .237 B1
Handford Ave CH62 . . . . .43 F5
Handford Rd CH2 . . . . .118 F6
HANDFORTH 34 C4
Handforth Cl WA4 . . . . .17 C3
Handforth La WA7 . . . . .49 D6
Handforth Rd
Crewe CW2 . . . . .189 E3
Handforth SK9 . . . . .34 E1
Handforth Sta SK9 . . . . .34 D3
HAND GREEN 168 B6
HANDLEY 182 D8
Handley Dr WA2 . . . . .8 E1
Handley Hill CW7 . . . . .149 C8
Handley Hill Prim Sch
CW7 . . . . .149 C8
Handley St WA7 . . . . .22 F3
Hand St SK11 . . . . .112 B8
Hangman's La
Lostock Green CW9 . . . . .105 C7
Smallwood CW11 . . . . .177 B5
HANKELOW 230 C7
Hankelow Cl
Chester CH2 . . . . .237 B4
Middlewich CW10 . . . . .151 C6
Hankey St 2 WA7 . . . . .22 F2
Hankins Heys La CW3 . . . . .231 A1
Hankinson Cl M31 . . . . .11 E2
Hanley Cl
Disley SK12 . . . . .38 D5
Widnes WA8 . . . . .12 C1
Hanley Rd WA8 . . . . .12 C1
Hannah's Wlk 2
CW10 . . . . .151 C8
Hanns Hall Farm CH64 . . . . .67 D8
Hanns Hall Rd CH64 . . . . . . .67 D8
Hanover Cl WA7 . . . . .50 A6
Hanover Dr 2 CW7 . . . . .149 D6
Hanover Ho 8 CW8 . . . . . . .103 E8
Hanover St WA1 . . . . .16 A4
Hapsdale View WA6 . . . . .72 E1
HAPSFORD 72 F1
Hapsford Cl WA3 . . . . .9 C4
Hapsford La
Dunham-on-t-H WA6 . . . . . . .97 E8
Elton CH2 . . . . .72 D4
Hapsford Mews WA6 . . . . . . .72 E2
Harbord St WA1 . . . . .16 C4
Harbour Cl
Chester CH2 . . . . .118 E7
Runcorn WA7 . . . . .50 D6
Harbour La SK11 . . . . .111 C1
Harburn Wlk M22 . . . . .33 E8
Harcourt Cl WA3 . . . . .9 E3
Harden Pk SK9 . . . . .60 A3
Harding Ave
Tattenhall CH3 . . . . .166 C2
Warrington WA2 . . . . .8 E1
Harding Rd
Chester CH2 . . . . .118 B8
Nantwich CW5 . . . . .204 C4
Hardings Mdw ST7 . . . . .194 F2
Hardings Row ST7 . . . . .195 D7
Hardings Wood ST7 . . . . . . .194 E2
HARDING'S WOOD 194 E2
Hardingswood Rd
ST7 .194 E2
Hardknott Rd CH62 . . . . .43 E8
Hardwick Cl SK6 . . . . .37 F6
Hardwick Dr SK11 . . . . .112 B5
Hardwicke Ct CW1 . . . . .190 E4
Hardwicke Rd SK12 . . . . .36 F4
Hardwick Grange WA1 . . . . .17 E8
Hardwick Rd WA7 . . . . .23 D3
Hardy Cl
Ellesmere Port CH66 . . . . . . .69 F3
Wistaston CW2 . . . . .205 F8
Hardy Dr SK7 . . . . .35 D7
Hardy Rd WA13 . . . . .18 C2
Hardy St WA2 . . . . .16 B6
Harebell Cl
Huntington CH3 . . . . .142 A6
Widnes WA8 . . . . .12 E4
Harebell Gr ST7 . . . . .195 F1
Harecastle Ave ST7 . . . . . . .194 E1
Harecastle Villas ST7 . . . . .194 E2
Harefield Dr SK9 . . . . .60 B5
Harefield Rd SK9 . . . . .34 E4
Hare Hill Gdn * SK10 . . . . . . .86 B6
Hare La CH3 . . . . .119 D3
Hare's La WA6 . . . . .73 F7
Harewood Ave CH66 . . . . . . .69 C4
Harewood Cl
Northwich CW9 . . . . .103 F4
Winsford CW7 . . . . .126 A1
Harewood Way SK11 . . . . . .112 B5
Harfield Gdns CH66 . . . . .69 C5
Harford Cl WA5 . . . . .14 F4
HARGRAVE 144 A1

Hargrave Ave CW2 . . . . .189 F3
Hargrave Dr CH66 . . . . .69 E5
Hargrave La
Dodleston CH64 . . . . .43 A4
Thornton Hough CH63,
CH4 .42 F5
Hargreave Ho 7 CH64 . . . . .66 E8
Hargreaves Ct WA8 . . . . .13 D1
Hargreaves Ho 5
WA8 .13 D1
Hargreaves Rd CW9 . . . . . . .104 C8
Harington Cl CH12 . . . . .118 C8
Harland Gn L24 . . . . .21 A3
Harlech Cl WA5 . . . . .7 E2
Harlech Ct CH65 . . . . .70 D3
Harlech Gr 3 WA7 . . . . .23 F1
Harlech Way CH65 . . . . .70 D3
Harlow St WA4 . . . . .17 C3
Harlyn Ave SK7 . . . . .35 F7
Harlyn Gdns WA5 . . . . .14 D3
Harn The CH66 . . . . .69 B8
Haroldgate SY13 . . . . .225 F1
Harold Rd WA11 . . . . .1 F7
Harper Cl CH66 . . . . .69 D4
Harper Gr CW12 . . . . .156 E4
Harpers Rd WA2 . . . . .9 B2
Harpur Cl SK11 . . . . .112 D6
Harpur Cres ST7 . . . . .193 B5
Harrier Rd WA2 . . . . .8 F2
Harriet St M44 . . . . .11 E5
Harrington Dr SK11 . . . . .111 D1
Harris Cl CW1 . . . . .173 B1
HARRISEAHEAD 195 E4
Harriseahead La ST7 . . . . . .195 D4
Harrison Cl WA1 . . . . .16 C6
Harrison Dr
Crewe CW1 . . . . .190 B4
Goostrey CW4 . . . . .107 B1
Haydock WA11 . . . . .1 A6
Harrison Gr CH5 . . . . .116 A3
Harrison Pl 4 CW8 . . . . .103 E8
Harrison Sq WA5 . . . . .7 F1
Harrison St WA8 . . . . .22 B6
Harrisons Terr CH66 . . . . . . .69 C6
Harrison Way WA12 . . . . .2 C4
Harris Rd CW9 . . . . .80 A2
Harris St WA8 . . . . .13 C1
Harrogate Cl
Bebington CH62 . . . . .43 D4
Warrington WA5 . . . . .7 A1
Harrogate Rd CH62 . . . . .43 D4
Harrop La SK10 . . . . .62 E5
Harrop Rd
Bollington SK10 . . . . .88 C8
Runcorn WA7 . . . . .23 B1
Harrow Cl
Crewe CW2 . . . . .190 A1
Warrington WA4 . . . . .26 E6
Wilmslow SK9 . . . . .60 D8
Harrow Dr WA7 . . . . .23 E2
Harrow Gr CH62 . . . . .43 E8
Harrow Rd CH65 . . . . .70 D4
Harrow Way CW9 . . . . .103 E3
HARTFORD 103 C4
Hartford Ave SK9 . . . . .59 F5
HARTFORDBEACH 103 A6
Hartford Bsns Ctr
CW8 . . . . .102 F4
Hartford Cl CW11 . . . . .175 C7
Hartford Dr CH65 . . . . .69 F4
Hartford Manor Com Prim
Sch CW8 . . . . .103 C5
Hartford Mews 3
CH3 .119 B1
Hartford Prim Sch
CH3 .183 D3
Hartford Rd CW9 . . . . .103 B4
Hartford Sta CW8 . . . . .103 B4
Hartford Way CH1 . . . . .118 A2
HARTHILL 183 E3
Harthill Cl CW9 . . . . .103 E5
Harthill La CH3 . . . . .183 E4
Harthill Prim Sch
CH3 .183 D3
Harthill Rd
Blacon CH1 . . . . .117 E6
Burwardsley CH3 . . . . .184 A6
Hartington Dr SK7 . . . . .36 E8
Hartington Rd
Bramhall SK7 . . . . .35 E6
Gatley SK8 . . . . .34 D8
High Lane SK12, SK6 . . . . . . .37 F7
Hartington St CH4 . . . . .141 E7
Hartland Cl
Poynton SK12 . . . . .36 D5
Widnes WA8 . . . . .13 E4
Hartley Cl WA13 . . . . .18 F3
Hartley Gdns CW12 . . . . .179 B8
Hartley Gn SK10 . . . . .87 F8
Harton Cl WA8 . . . . .12 E3
Hartswood Cl WA4 . . . . .26 E3
Hartwell Gr CW7 . . . . .126 F4
Harty Rd WA11 . . . . .1 A5
Harvard Cl WA7 . . . . .24 D2
Harvard Gr WA2 . . . . .8 A3
Harvard Way CW2 . . . . .126 F8
Harvest Rd SK10 . . . . .86 F2
Harvey Ave
Nantwich CW5 . . . . .205 A6
Newton-le-W WA12 . . . . .1 F3
Harvey Cl WA2 . . . . .8 B3
Harvey La WA3 . . . . .3 E8
Harvey Rd CW12 . . . . .157 A5
Harwood Gdns WA4 . . . . .17 A2
Haryngton Ave WA5 . . . . .15 F7
Haseley Cl SK12 . . . . .36 E5

Haslemere Ave WA15 . . . . . .32 C6
Haslemere Dr WA5 . . . . .14 D4
Haslemere Way CW11 . . . . . .190 D6
Haslin Cres CH3 . . . . .142 D7
HASLINGTON 191 D4
Haslington Cl ST5 . . . . .210 D1
Haslington Gr L26 . . . . .21 A6
Haslington Prim Sch
CW1 . . . . .191 D4
HASSAL 192 C7
HASSALL GREEN 176 A2
Hassall Rd
Alsager ST7 . . . . .193 B5
Haslington CW11 . . . . .192 B7
Sandbach CW11 . . . . .175 C4
Winterley CW11 . . . . .191 F8
Hassall Way 7 SK9 . . . . .34 E5
Hassals La CH2 . . . . .96 F3
Hastings Ave WA2 . . . . .8 B4
Hastings Rd CW5 . . . . .204 F5
Hasty La
Altrincham WA15 . . . . .32 E8
Hale WA15 . . . . .32 E8
Wythenshawe WA15 . . . . .32 F8
Hatchery Cl WA4 . . . . .27 B4
Hatchings The WA13 . . . . .18 E2
HATCHMERE 100 C4
Hatch Mere * WA6 . . . . .100 C4
Hatchmere Cl
Sandbach CW11 . . . . .174 F7
Warrington WA5 . . . . .15 C5
Hatchmere Dr CH3 . . . . .142 B8
Hatchmere Pk WA6 . . . . .100 C5
Hatfield Cl CW4 . . . . .130 B3
Hatfield Gdns WA4 . . . . .26 E4
Hathaway Cl SK8 . . . . .34 B7
Hathaway Dr SK11 . . . . .112 C5
HATHERTON 219 E3
Hatherton Cl
Newcastle-u-Lyme
ST5 .210 D2
5 Northwich CW9 . . . . .103 F4
Hatherton Gr L26 . . . . .21 A6
Hatherton Way CH2 . . . . .237 B4
Hatley La WA6 . . . . .73 F7
Hatter St CW12 . . . . .156 E3
HATTON 26 A2
Hatton Ave CH62 . . . . .43 E3
Hatton Bldgs CH2 . . . . .237 C4
Hatton Brow Terr
SK11 . . . . .112 F4
HATTON HEATH 143 B1
Hatton La
Hartford CW8 . . . . .103 D6
Stretton WA4 . . . . .26 B1
Hatton Rd CH1 . . . . .117 E6
Hatton St SK11 . . . . .112 C7
HAUGHTON 186 C6
Haughton Cl SK10 . . . . .86 F1
HAVANNAH 157 A6
Havannah Bsns Ctr 6
CW12 . . . . .157 A6
Havannah La
Congleton CW12 . . . . .156 F6
St Helens WA9 . . . . .1 B3
Havannah Prim Sch
CW12 . . . . .157 A6
Havannah St CW12 . . . . .156 F4
Haven The
Crewe CW1 . . . . .190 D7
Sandbach CW11 . . . . .174 E7
Havergal St 1 WA7 . . . . .22 F1
Haverhill Cl CW7 . . . . .207 C3
Haverty Prec WA12 . . . . .2 B1
Havisham Cl WA3 . . . . .9 D5
Hawarde Cl WA12 . . . . .2 A4
Hawarden Airport CH4,
CH5 .139 D7
Hawarden Gdns CH65 . . . . . .70 D2
Hawarden Ind Pk
CH5 .139 B6
Haweswater Ave
Crewe CW1 . . . . .173 B1
Haydock WA11 . . . . .1 A6
Haweswater Cl WA7 . . . . .50 A5
Haweswater Dr CW7 . . . . . . .126 D2
Hawick Cl CH66 . . . . .69 A5
Hawker Cl CH4 . . . . .139 C4
Hawkes Cl WA3 . . . . .10 A6
Hawkins Cl CH64 . . . . .41 F1
Hawkins View CH3 . . . . .120 E6
Hawk Rd SK22 . . . . .39 E8
Hawks Ct WA7 . . . . .49 E6
Hawksey Dr CW5 . . . . .204 F4
Hawkshaw Cl WA3 . . . . .9 C4
Hawkshead Cl WA7 . . . . .50 A4
Hawkshead Rd WA5 . . . . .6 E6
Hawkshead Way CW7 . . . . . .126 D2
Hawk St CW11 . . . . .175 B6
Hawkstone Gr WA6 . . . . .73 C4
Hawks Way CH60 . . . . .40 E8
Hawley Dr WA15 . . . . .32 B8
Hawley La WA15 . . . . .32 B8
Hawley's Cl WA5 . . . . .7 F1
Hawley's La WA2, WA5 . . . . . . .8 A1
Hawley's Lane Trad Pk
WA2 . . . . .8 A1
Haworth Ave CW12 . . . . .157 A5
Haworth Cl SK11 . . . . .112 B5
Hawthorn Ave
3 Nantwich CW5 . . . . .204 F5
Newton-le-W WA12 . . . . .2 D3
Runcorn WA7 . . . . .23 A1
1 Widnes WA8 . . . . .13 A1
Wilmslow SK9 . . . . .60 A7
Hawthorn Bank SK22 . . . . . . .39 B6
Hawthorn Cl
Holmes Chapel CW4 . . . . . . .130 D3

Hawthorn Cl *continued*
Winsford CW7. . . . . **126** C3
Hawthorn Cotts CH60. . . . . **40** F8
Hawthorn Dr M44 . . . . **11** D5
Hawthorne Ave
 Audley ST7. . . . . **209** F1
 Fowley Common WA3. . . . . . **5** C4
 Warrington WA5 . . . . **15** A6
 Warrington, Woolston
  WA1 . . . . **17** B7
Hawthorne Bsns Pk
 WA5. . . . . **16** A8
Hawthorne Cl
 Congleton CW12 . . . . **156** A4
 Haydock WA11. . . . . **1** A5
Hawthorne Ct ST7 . . . . **193** E4
Hawthorne Dr
 Sandbach CW11 . . . . **175** D6
 Willaston CH64 . . . . **43** B1
Hawthorne Gr
 Barnton CW8. . . . . **77** F4
 Poynton SK12 . . . . **37** C4
 Warrington, Bruche WA1. . . **16** F7
 Warrington WA4 . . . . **16** D3
 Winsford CW7 . . . . **127** A1
Hawthorne Rd
 Frodsham WA6 . . . . **49** B1
 Warrington WA4 . . . . **26** C8
Hawthorne St WA5 . . . . **16** A8
Hawthorn Gdns ST7 . . . . . **210** D8
Hawthorn Gn SK9 . . . . **60** A7
Hawthorn Gr
 Bramhall SK7. . . . . **35** C6
 Crewe CW1 . . . . **190** D7
 Warrington WA4 . . . . **16** D1
 Wilmslow SK9 . . . . **60** B7
Hawthorn La
 Bebington CH62. . . . . **43** D8
 Congleton CW12 . . . . **155** C6
 Crewe CW2 . . . . **189** F2
 Wilmslow SK9 . . . . **60** A7
Hawthorn Pk SK9. . . . . **60** A7
Hawthorns The
 Bunbury CW6. . . . . **185** G8
 Ellesmere Port CH66. . . . . . . **69** F7
 Haslington CW1. . . . . **191** D5
 Northwich CW8 . . . . **103** C7
 Tarporley CW6. . . . . **146** D1
Hawthorn View
 Connah's Quay CH5. . . . . . . **116** A7
 Lindow End WA16 . . . . **59** B2
 Wilmslow SK9 . . . . **60** A7
Hawthorn Villas CW4. . . . . **130** C3
Hawthorn Way SK10 . . . . . . **87** E2
Hawthorn Wlk
 3 Partington M31 . . . . **11** E3
 Wilmslow SK9 . . . . **60** A7
 Wincham CW9. . . . . **79** C3
Haycroft SK8 . . . . **34** E8
Haycroft Cl CH66 . . . . **69** D2
Haydan Ct CH7 . . . . **118** D4
Haydan Mews WA6. . . . . **73** E6
Haydn Jones Dr CW5 . . . . . **204** F3
HAYDOCK **1** D6
Haydock Cl
 Chester CH1 . . . . **118** B2
 Macclesfield SK10. . . . . **87** C3
Haydock English Martyrs'
 RC Prim Sch WA11. . . . . . . **1** C7
Haydock La WA11 . . . . **1** C7
Haydock La Ind Est
 WA11. . . . . **1** E8
Haydock Park Racecourse
 WA3. . . . . **2** E8
Haydock Sports Coll
 WA11. . . . . **1** C6
Haydock St
 Newton-le-W WA12. . . . . **2** A3
 Warrington WA2 . . . . **16** B6
Hayes Cl CW5. . . . . **204** E2
Hayes Cres WA6. . . . . **49** C1
Hayes Dr CW8. . . . . **78** C3
Hayes Pk CH1 . . . . **237** A4
Haye's Rd M44 . . . . **11** E5
Hayfield Cl SK10. . . . . **87** B3
Hayfield Rd
 New Mills SK22 . . . . **39** D8
 Warrington WA1 . . . . **17** C7
Hayfields WA16. . . . . **57** C3
Hayfields Gr CW3. . . . . **229** F3
Haygarth Hts **5** CH1. . . . . **237** C3
Hayhead Cl ST7 . . . . **195** B2
Hayhurst Ave CW10 . . . . . . **151** C8
Hayhurst Cl CW9 . . . . **103** F8
Hayle Cl SK10 . . . . **86** D1
Hayling Cl CW1. . . . . **190** B8
Haymakers Cl CH4. . . . . **140** F4
Haymakers Way CH1. . . . . . **117** A8
HAYMOOR GREEN **205** E2
Haymoor Green Rd
 CW5. . . . . **205** E3
Hayscastle Cl WA5. . . . . **7** E1
Hayside Wlk SY14 . . . . **213** A3
Hayton St WA16 . . . . **56** F1
Haywood Cres WA7. . . . . **24** D2

Hazel Ave
 Macclesfield SK11. . . . . **112** A5
 Runcorn WA7. . . . . **48** E8
Hazelbadge Cl SK12 . . . . . . **36** C4
Hazelbadge Rd SK12. . . . . . **36** C4
Hazelbank CH65. . . . . **69** F3
Hazelborough Cl WA3. . . . . **10** B5
Hazel Cl
 1 Ellesmere Port
  CH66. . . . . **69** F1
 Kidsgrove ST7 . . . . **195** B3
Hazelcroft SK9 . . . . **85** A8
Hazelcroft Gdns SK9. . . . . . **85** A8
Hazeldean Ct **1** SK9 . . . . . . **34** E1
Hazel Dr
 Gatley M22 . . . . **34** A8
 Lymm WA13. . . . . **18** F2
 Poynton SK12 . . . . **36** F3
 Weaverham CW8. . . . . **102** D7
 Winsford CW7 . . . . **149** C8
Hazel Gr
 Alsager ST7. . . . . **194** A3
 Crewe CW1 . . . . **190** C7
 Golborne WA3 . . . . **3** B8
 Warrington WA1 . . . . **17** A8
Hazel Grove High Sch
 SK7. . . . . **36** C8
Hazelhurst Dr SK10 . . . . **88** A8
Hazelmere Cl CW8. . . . . **103** C5
Hazel Rd CH4 . . . . **140** F6
Hazel St WA1. . . . . **16** D7
Hazel Wlk M31. . . . . **11** E3
Hazelwood Cl WA8 . . . . **22** A8
Hazelwood Mews WA4. . . . . **17** C1
Hazelwood Rd
 Barnton CW8 . . . . **78** B4
 Wilmslow SK9 . . . . **60** D8
 Wythenshawe M22 . . . . **33** D8
Hazlehurst Rd WA6. . . . . **74** D6
Hazlemere Ave SK11 . . . . . **112** A6
Headland Cl WA3. . . . . **3** E6
Headlands The CH1,
 CH3 . . . . **237** C2
Headworth Cl CW9. . . . . . . **103** F4
HEALD GREEN **34** B8
Heald Green Sta M22 . . . . . **34** A8
Heald St WA12 . . . . **1** F3
Healey Cl CW1. . . . . **190** A8
Heapy St SK11 . . . . **112** E6
Hearn's La CW5 . . . . **202** E5
HEATH **49** A6
Heath Ave
 Ellesmere Port CH65. . . . . . . **70** A1
 Rode Heath ST7. . . . . **193** F7
 Sandbach CW11 . . . . **175** E6
Heath Bank CH3. . . . . **119** D5
Heathbank Rd SK8. . . . . **34** F8
Heathbrook Cotts
 CW9. . . . . **104** E7
Heath Bsns & Technical
 Pk The WA7. . . . . **49** A7
Heath Cl
 Chester CH3 . . . . **142** B8
 Sandbach CW11 . . . . **175** D6
 Tarvin CH3 . . . . **121** B1
Heathcote Cl CH2 . . . . **118** C8
Heathcote Gdns CW8. . . . . **104** D7
Heathcote St ST7. . . . . **195** A2
Heath Ct
 Alsager ST7. . . . . **193** F6
 Ellesmere Port CH66. . . . . . . **69** B6
Heath Dr
 Knutsford WA16 . . . . **56** F2
 Runcorn WA7. . . . . **49** A7
 Tarvin CH3 . . . . **121** B1
Heath End Rd ST7 . . . . **193** B5
Heather Ave M44 . . . . **11** D6
Heather Brae WA12. . . . . **2** A4
Heather Brae Mews
 CW12. . . . . **156** A3
Heather Cl
 Ellesmere Port CH66. . . . . . . **69** E3
 Macclesfield SK11. . . . . **112** C3
 Runcorn WA7. . . . . **49** E4
 Warrington WA3 . . . . **9** D5
Heather Ct CH3. . . . . **142** A8
Heather Falls SK22 . . . . **39** B8
Heatherfield Ct SK9 . . . . . . **60** E8
Heathergate Pl CW2 . . . . . **206** B8
Heatherside ST7. . . . . **195** C6
Heatherways CW4. . . . . **130** C3
Heather Wlk M31. . . . . **11** E3
Heathfield SK9 . . . . **60** A5
Heathfield Ave CW1. . . . . . **190** C4
Heathfield Cl
 Congleton CW12 . . . . **155** F3
 Nantwich CW5. . . . . **204** F6
Heathfield Ct
 Ellesmere Port, Whitby
  CH65. . . . . **70** B5
 Ellesmere Port, Whittymheath
  CH66. . . . . **95** A8
Heathfield Dr ST5 . . . . **210** D1
Heathfield Pk
 Warrington WA4 . . . . **17** A2
 Widnes WA8. . . . . **12** D3
Heathfield Rd
 Audlem CW3 . . . . **230** A5
 Ellesmere Port CH66. . . . . . . **70** B5
Heathfields Cl CH2 . . . . **237** B4
Heathfield Sq WA16 . . . . . . **56** F2
Heathgate Ave L24 . . . . **21** A2
Heath Gn CW6. . . . . **146** C4
Heath La
 Chester CH3 . . . . **142** A8
 Culcheth WA3 . . . . **4** A1

Heath La *continued*
 Ellesmere Port, Little Sutton
  CH66. . . . . **69** B7
 Golborne, Kenyon WA3 . . . . . **3** F2
 Golborne WA3 . . . . **3** C6
 Great Barrow CH3. . . . . . . **120** E6
 Great Budworth CW9 . . . . . . **54** A1
 High Legh WA16 . . . . **28** D5
 Little Leigh WA4, CW8. . . . . **77** B7
 Marbury SY13 . . . . **226** E6
 Stoak CH2 . . . . **95** E7
 Stoak CH2 . . . . **95** F7
 Swan Green WA16. . . . . . . **106** F6
 Willaston CH64, CH66. . . . . **68** D7
 Wincham CW9 . . . . **79** C3
Heathlands Ho WA16. . . . . . **56** F2
Heathlands Rd CH66. . . . . . . **69** B7
Heathland Trail *
 CW6. . . . . **147** E7
Heathmoor Ave WA3. . . . . . . **3** D6
Heath Park Gr WA7. . . . . **48** F8
Heath Rd
 Bollington SK10. . . . . **87** E6
 Chester CH2 . . . . **118** E7
 Congleton CW12 . . . . **156** A2
 Runcorn WA7. . . . . **23** B2
 Sandbach CW11 . . . . **175** D6
 Warrington WA5 . . . . **14** F5
 Weaverham CW8. . . . . **77** E1
 Widnes WA8 . . . . **12** D2
Heath Rd S WA7. . . . . **48** F6
Heath Road Cres WA7 . . . . . **49** B8
Heath Sch The WA7. . . . . . . **49** B7
Heathside CW5 . . . . **204** F6
Heaths La CW6 . . . . **123** D2
Heath St
 Crewe CW1 . . . . **190** D4
 Golborne WA3 . . . . **3** A8
 Warrington WA4 . . . . **26** D8
Heath Terr
 Chester CH2 . . . . **118** E8
 Smallwood CW11 . . . . **154** B1
Heathview CW1 . . . . **191** D3
Heath View
 Alsager ST7. . . . . **193** E5
 Weston CW2 . . . . **207** B5
Heathview Cl WA8. . . . . **22** A5
Heathview La CW8 . . . . **22** A5
Heath Way CW6. . . . . **168** D8
Heathwood ST7 . . . . **193** F7
Heathwood Dr ST7 . . . . **193** B5
Heathwood Gr WA1. . . . . **17** B7
HEATLEY **19** C5
Heatley Cl WA13. . . . . **19** A4
Heatley La CW5 . . . . **217** F3
Heatley Way **5** SK9. . . . . **34** D1
HEATON **159** E2
Heaton Cl CW10 . . . . **151** C6
Heaton Ct WA3 . . . . **9** F6
Heaton Sq CW7 . . . . **149** C8
Heaton Way CW2 . . . . **207** E4
Heaward Cl CW2 . . . . **206** B4
Hebden Ave WA3 . . . . **5** B5
HEBDEN GREEN **148** F7
Hebden Green Com Sch
 CW7. . . . . **149** A7
Heber's Cl SY14 . . . . **213** C5
Heber Wlk CW9 . . . . **104** A8
Hedge Hey WA7 . . . . **24** A1
Hedge Row SK10 . . . . **63** E1
Hedgerow Dr CW9. . . . . **79** C3
Hedgerows The WA11. . . . . . **1** F7
Hedingham Cl **7**
 SK10. . . . . **111** F8
Hefferston Grange Dr
 CW8 . . . . **102** A7
Hefferston Rise CW8. . . . . . **102** A7
Heights The WA6 . . . . **73** C4
Helena Cl WA16 . . . . **57** C2
Hellath Wen CW5. . . . . **204** E2
Hellyar-Brook Rd
 ST7. . . . . **193** B4
Helmdon Cl CW7 . . . . **127** A3
Helmsdale Cl CW1. . . . . **190** B6
Helmsdale La WA5. . . . . **15** C6
Helmsley Cl WA5 . . . . **15** C6
HELSBY **73** C3
Helsby Ave CH62 . . . . **43** F3
Helsby High Sch WA6. . . . . **73** D5
Helsby Hillside Prim Sch
 WA6. . . . . **73** D4
HELSBY MARSH **73** B5
Helsby Pk WA6. . . . . **73** C5
Helsby Rd WA6. . . . . **73** C1
Helsby St WA1. . . . . **16** C6
Helsby Sta WA6 . . . . **73** B4
Helsby Way **4** SK9 . . . . **34** D1
Helston Cl
 Bramhall SK7. . . . . **35** F7
 Runcorn WA7. . . . . **50** B5
 Warrington WA5 . . . . **14** E5
Helston Gr SK8 . . . . **34** C8
Helton Cl CW4. . . . . **130** A3
Hemingford Cl CH66. . . . . . . **69** D2
Hemleigh Vale WA6 . . . . **73** B2
Hemmingshaw La
 CW11. . . . . **176** B8
Hemming St CW1 . . . . **190** D1
Hemswell Cl CW7 . . . . **149** E8
Hemsworth Ave CH66. . . . . . **69** C5
HENBURY **111** B8
Henbury Cl CW10 . . . . **151** C7
Henbury Gdns WA4 . . . . **26** E3
Henbury High Sch
 SK10. . . . . **111** C8
Henbury La SK8 . . . . **34** F2
HENBURY MOSS **110** D5

Henbury Pl WA7. . . . . **49** B6
Henbury Rd SK9 . . . . **34** D4
Henbury Rise SK11 . . . . . . **111** C8
Henderson Cl WA5 . . . . **14** D6
Henderson Rd
 Widnes, Lower House
  WA8 . . . . **22** F8
 2 Widnes WA8. . . . . **13** A1
Henderson St SK11 . . . . . . **112** C7
Hendon Cl CW1. . . . . **190** F5
Henley Ave M44 . . . . **11** E6
Henley Cl
 Macclesfield SK10. . . . . **87** B4
 Neston CH64 . . . . **66** E6
 Warrington WA4 . . . . **26** E6
Henley Ct WA7 . . . . **23** D2
Henley Dr CW7 . . . . **126** F1
Henley Rd
 Chester CH4 . . . . **140** F6
 Chorlton CW2 . . . . **207** B1
 Neston CH64 . . . . **66** E6
Henrietta St CW12. . . . . . . **156** C3
Henry Pl CH1. . . . . **237** B3
Henry St
 Crewe CW1 . . . . **190** D5
 Haslington CW1. . . . . **191** D4
 2 Lymm WA13 . . . . **18** E3
 Tarporley CW6. . . . . **146** C2
 Warrington WA1 . . . . **16** A5
 4 Widnes WA8. . . . . **13** C1
Henry Wood Ct CH4 . . . . . **140** E6
Henshall Ave WA4 . . . . **16** F4
Henshall Dr CW11. . . . . **175** D8
Henshall Hall Dr
 CW12. . . . . **157** B1
Henshall La WA14 . . . . **20** C6
Henshall Rd SK10. . . . . **87** F7
Henshall St CH1. . . . . **237** A4
Henshaw La SK11. . . . . **110** E2
Hepherd St WA5. . . . . **15** D4
Hepley Rd SK12 . . . . **37** A3
Herald Dr CW1. . . . . **190** E3
Herald Pk CW1 . . . . **190** E3
Heralds Cl WA8. . . . . **22** C8
Heralds Gn WA5. . . . . **7** A2
Herberts La CH60. . . . . **40** F8
Herbert St
 Burtonwood WA5. . . . . **6** E6
 Congleton CW12 . . . . **156** F3
 Crewe CW1 . . . . **191** A5
 Lostock Gralam CW9. . . . . . . **80** A2
Herbert Swindells Cl
 CW2. . . . . **190** D1
Herdman St CW2 . . . . **190** D2
Hereford Ave
 Ellesmere Port CH66. . . . . . . **94** E8
 Golborne WA3 . . . . **3** A8
Hereford Cl
 Macclesfield SK10. . . . . **86** F1
 Warrington WA1 . . . . **17** D7
Hereford Dr SK9. . . . . **34** E3
Hereford Pl CH1. . . . . **118** A5
Hereford Rd CH3 . . . . **119** B1
Heritage Ct CH1 . . . . **237** B2
Hermitage Cl
 Holmes Chapel CW4 . . . . . . **130** D3
 Saughall CH1. . . . . **117** A8
Hermitage Dr CW4 . . . . **130** D3
Hermitage Green La WA2,
 WA12. . . . . **8** A8
Hermitage La CW4 . . . . **130** C7
Hermitage Prim Sch
 CW4. . . . . **130** D4
Hermitage Rd CH1. . . . . . . **117** B7
Hermitage The CH60. . . . . . **40** F7
Heron Cl
 Broughton CH4 . . . . **139** C4
 Farndon CH3 . . . . **180** F1
 Knutsford WA16 . . . . **57** B3
 Runcorn WA7. . . . . **50** D8
 Winsford CW7 . . . . **149** D5
Heron Cres CW1. . . . . **190** F5
Heron Ct
 Neston CH64 . . . . **66** C7
 Northwich CW9 . . . . **79** C2
Heron Dr SK12 . . . . **36** A3
Heron Pl CH2 . . . . **237** B4
Herons Reach WA3 . . . . **5** C6
Herons Way
 Chester CH4 . . . . **141** B2
 Runcorn WA7. . . . . **24** F4
Herrick Cl CW2 . . . . **206** A8
Hertford Apartments
 WA2 . . . . **9** A3
Hertford Cl
 Congleton CW12 . . . . **156** E4
 Warrington WA1 . . . . **17** E7
Hertford Gr M44 . . . . **11** C6
Hesketh Cl WA5 . . . . **14** F4
Hesketh Croft CW1 . . . . . . **190** A8
Hesketh Dr CW9 . . . . **80** A3
Hesketh Grange Cotts
 CH63 . . . . **42** A7
Hesketh Meadow La
 WA3. . . . . **3** F8
Hesketh Rd L24. . . . . **21** E2
Hesketh St N WA5 . . . . **15** D4
Hesketh St S WA5 . . . . **15** C4
Hesnall Cl WA3. . . . . **5** C8
Heswall Ave WA3 . . . . **4** F8
Heswall Point **7** CH60. . . . . **41** A8
Heswall St Peter's CE Prim
 Sch CH60. . . . . **40** F8

Haw–Hig **259**

Heswall Sta CH60. . . . . **41** D8
HETHERSON GREEN **214** D8
Hetherson Green La
 SY14. . . . . **214** D8
Hevetson Cres SK11. . . . . . **111** E7
Hewitt Dr CW7 . . . . **150** D8
Hewitt Gr CW9 . . . . **79** F5
Hewitt St
 Chester CH2 . . . . **118** F3
 Crewe CW2 . . . . **190** D2
 Northwich CW9 . . . . **79** D2
 Warrington WA4 . . . . **16** C3
Hexham Ct CH1. . . . . **118** B2
Hexham Way **4** SK10 . . . . . . **87** C4
Heybridge La SK10 . . . . **87** B6
Heydon Cl
 Congleton CW12 . . . . **156** C3
 Halewood L26 . . . . **21** A7
Heyes Ave WA11. . . . . **1** D5
Heyes Dr WA13. . . . . **18** C2
Heyes Farm Rd SK11. . . . . **111** E8
Heyes La WA16 . . . . **111** E8
Heyes La
 Alderley Edge SK9. . . . . **60** B3
 Warrington WA4 . . . . **26** E8
Heyes Pk CW8. . . . . **102** F4
Heyes Rd WA8. . . . . **22** C8
Heyeswood La CW8. . . . . . . **103** A4
Heyfield Park Rd CH66. . . . . **69** B7
Heygarth Prim Sch
 CH62. . . . . **43** E5
Heygarth Rd CH62 . . . . **43** E5
Hey Lock Cl WA12 . . . . **7** C8
Heys Ave CH62 . . . . **43** D8
Heysbank Rd SK12. . . . . **38** D5
Heysham Cl WA7 . . . . **50** D6
Hey Shoot La WA3. . . . . **5** C5
Heysoms Ave CW8 . . . . **103** D7
Heysoms Cl CW8 . . . . **103** D7
Heys The
 Bebington CH62. . . . . **43** F5
 Runcorn WA7. . . . . **23** E1
Heythrop Dr CH60. . . . . **41** D8
Heywood Cl SK9. . . . . **60** B2
Hey Wood Cl WA12. . . . . **7** C8
Heywood Gn CW2 . . . . **206** C8
Heywood La CW3,
 SY13. . . . . **234** C7
Heywood Rd
 Alderley Edge SK9. . . . . **60** B2
 Ellesmere Port CH66. . . . . . . **69** D5
Heywoods Ridge
 CW3. . . . . **229** E3
Heywood St CW12 . . . . **156** C2
Heywoods The CH2 . . . . . . **118** C4
Hibbert St
 New Mills SK22 . . . . **39** B6
 6 Widnes WA8. . . . . **23** B8
Hibel Rd SK10 . . . . **87** D1
Hickhurst La CW6 . . . . **147** D3
Hickmore Heys CH3 . . . . . . **119** F5
Hickory Cl WA1. . . . . **17** E7
Hickson St CW8 . . . . **78** B3
Hidcote Cl CW2 . . . . **206** B8
HIDEBANK **39** C8
Hield Brow CW9 . . . . **79** C7
Hield Gr CW9. . . . . **79** C8
Hield La CW9. . . . . **79** C8
Higginbotham Gn
 SK11. . . . . **112** C6
Higginson Cl CW12 . . . . . . **179** C8
Higham Ave WA5 . . . . **7** F1
Highbank Cl CW8. . . . . **78** B3
High Bank Cl M44 . . . . **11** D6
Highbank Rd
 Kingsley WA6. . . . . **75** C2
 Northwich CW8 . . . . **103** D7
High Bent Ave SK8. . . . . **35** A6
HIGH CARR **210** F3
High Carr Bsns Pk
 ST5. . . . . **210** F2
High Carr Network Ctr
 ST5. . . . . **210** F2
Highcliffe Ave CH1. . . . . . . **118** B4
Highcroft Ave CW12 . . . . . . **156** F2
High Cross La CH3. . . . . . . **182** D1
High Ct SK10 . . . . **88** B8
High Elm Dr WA15. . . . . **32** C8
High Elm Rd WA15 . . . . **32** D7
High Elms SK8 . . . . **35** B5
Higher Ash Rd ST7 . . . . . . **210** D8
Higher Ashton WA8 . . . . **12** F3
HIGHER BUNBURY **185** F1
HIGHER BURWARDSLEY
 . . . . **184** C5
HIGHER CARDEN **198** D7
Higher Carden La
 SY14. . . . . **198** D6
HIGHER DISLEY **38** B4
Higher Downs WA16. . . . . . . **57** C2
HIGHERFENCE **113** A8
Higher Fence Rd SK10. . . . . **87** F1
HIGHER FERRY **140** C8
Higher Heyes Dr WA6. . . . . . **75** C1
HIGHER HURDSFIELD **88** A2
HIGHER KINNERTON
 . . . . **161** B8
Higher Knutsford Rd
 WA4. . . . . **16** F2
Higher La
 Bollington SK10 . . . . **88** B6
 Disley SK12 . . . . **38** E1
 Dutton WA4 . . . . **51** D4
 Kettleshulme SK23 . . . . **64** E6
 Lymm WA13. . . . . **19** B1

Highland Ct **6** ST7 .... 195 A2
HIGHER MARSTON 79 C6
HIGHER POYNTON 37 B2
Higher Rd L76, WA8 ...21 C5
HIGHER RUNCORN 23 A1
HIGHER SHURLACH ...104 E6
HIGHER WALTON 25 F7
HIGHER WHITLEY ...52 D5
HIGHER WINCHAM ...779 C4
Higher Works Cotts
SK11................158 C6
HIGHER WYCH 224 D4
Highfield
Elton CH2...........72 B4
Prestbury SK10.......87 A5
High Field WA14.......20 B2
Highfield Ave
Audlem CW3 ....230 A4
Golborne WA3........2 F8
Kidsgrove ST7 ....195 D8
Lostock Gralam CW9...80 A3
Warrington, Dudlow's Green
WA4 ....26 D4
Warrington WA5 ......15 A5
Highfield Cl CH64.....66 E8
Highfield Com Prim Sch
CH1 ....117 F4
Highfield Cres
Handforth SK9........34 C1
Widnes WA8 ....13 A2
Highfield Dr
Lymm WA13..........18 C2
Macclesfield SK10.....87 A1
Nantwich CW5........205 A6
Highfield Est SK9......34 C1
Highfield La
Coddington CH3......181 E4
Golborne WA3 ....3 C5
Winwick WA2.........8 C7
Highfield Parkway
SK7................35 D8
Highfield Pl **1** CW8 ...103 E8
Highfield Rd
Blacon CH1 ....117 D5
Bollington SK10.......88 A8
Cheadle SK8 ....34 F8
Congleton CW12 ......156 E2
Ellesmere Port CH65...70 C5
Ellesmere Port, Little Sutton
CH66..............69 B6
Lymm WA13..........18 C2
Macclesfield SK11 .....112 C7
Neston CH64 ....66 F8
Northwich CW8 ....103 F7
Poynton SK12 ....36 A4
Widnes WA8 ....13 A2
Highfield Rd N 11
CH65...............70 C6
Highfields SY13........224 A2
Highfield Sch L26 .....21 A7
Highfields Com Prim Sch
CW5................204 F6
Highfield Terr SK22 ...39 D8
Highgate Cl
Crewe CW1 ....190 A8
Runcorn WA7.........24 D1
High Gates Cl WA5 ....15 E7
High Gates Lo WA5....15 E7
Highgrove Mews 2
SK9................60 A6
High Hill Rd SK22......39 D8
Highlands Rd WA7.....48 F8
Highlands The CW6....185 E8
Highland Way WA16...82 A7
HIGHLANE 134 C6
HIGH LANE 37 E8
High Lane Prim Sch
SK6................37 F8
High Lea Rd SK22 .....39 A8
HIGH LEGH 29 B5
High Legh Prim Sch
WA16..............29 C5
High Legh Rd WA13 ...29 C8
High Lowe Ave CW12 ..157 A4
Highmarsh Cres WA12...2 B4
High Mdw **2** SK8.......34 E8
High Mount CH60......40 F8
High St
Audley ST7...........210 A1
Bollington SK10.......88 B8
Clotton CW6 ....145 D4
Congleton CW12 ......156 D2
Crewe CW2 ....190 D3
Farndon CH3 ....180 E2
Frodsham WA6 ....49 B1
Golborne WA3 ....3 A8
Great Budworth CW9 ...79 A7
Hale L24 ....21 D1
Harriseahead ST7 ....195 E5
Kidsgrove, The Rookery
ST7................195 C4
Macclesfield SK11 .....112 D6
Malpas SY14 ....213 B3
Mow Cop ST7.........195 D7
Nantwich CW5........204 E5
Neston CH64 ....66 E7
Newchapel ST7 ....195 C8
New Mills SK22 ....39 C8
Newton-le-W WA12.....2 D4
Norley WA6 ....100 F5
Northwich CW9 ....103 F8
Runcorn WA7.........23 A2
Saltney CH4..........140 E7
Sandbach CW11 ......175 B6
Talke ST7............210 D6

High St *continued*
Tarporley CW6.........146 C2
Tarvin CH3............121 B2
Tattenhall CH3.........166 B1
Warrington WA1 ......16 C5
Weaverham CW8.......77 C1
Winsford CW7.........126 D1
Hightown
Crewe CW1 ....190 C4
Middlewich CW10 .....128 C1
Sandbach CW11 ......175 B6
Hightown Appts 6
CW1................190 C4
Hightree Dr SK11 .....111 C8
High View
Helsby WA6..........73 C4
Mount Pleasant ST7 ...195 B5
HIGH WARREN 26 C6
High Warren Cl WA4...26 C5
Highwood Rd WA4.....26 C7
Hignett Ave WA9 ......1 B2
Hilary Ave SK8 ....34 D8
Hilary Cl
Chester CH3 ....119 B1
Warrington WA5 ......14 D6
Widnes WA8 ....13 E3
Hilbre Ave CH60.......40 E6
Hilbre Bank CW6 ......169 D4
Hilbre Dr CH65 ....70 C1
Hilden Pl WA2.........16 D8
Hilden Rd WA2........8 E1
Hillary Ave CW12 .....157 A2
Hillary Dr CW3 ....230 A4
Hillary Rd
Bebington CH62.......43 E5
Kidsgrove ST7 ....195 B3
Hillberry Cres WA4....16 B3
Hillbre Way **1** SK9 ....34 D4
Hillbrook Rd SK7......35 D6
Hill Cl
Bunbury CW6.........185 E7
Neston CH64 ....67 B5
HILLCLIFFE 26 C8
Hill Cliffe Rd WA4 .....26 B8
Hill Cotts CH3 ....164 A4
Hillcourt Rd SK6.......37 F7
Hillcrest WA7 ....23 D1
Hillcrest Ave CW4.....130 B3
Hillcrest Dr CH66 .....69 A6
Hillcrest Rd
Bollington SK10.......87 F7
Ellesmere Port CH66...69 B6
Kelsall CW6...........122 E6
Warren SK11..........112 A4
Hill Ct CH64 ....67 B5
Hill Dr
Handforth SK9........34 E3
Whaley Bridge SK23 ...65 D8
Hillesden Rise CW12...156 F2
Hillfield
Frodsham WA6 ....74 B7
Runcorn WA7.........50 D8
Hillfield Gdns CW5 ....204 E4
Hillfield Pl CW5 ....204 E4
Hillfield Rd CH66 ......69 D7
Hillfields CW12 ....156 D4
Hill Fields CW12.......156 D4
Hillfields CH12 CW12 ..156 D4
Hillfield View CW5.....204 E4
Hillfoot Cres WA4 .....26 B7
Hillfoot La WA4 ....74 E3
Hilliards Ct CH4 ....141 B3
Hillingden Ave L26 ....21 A7
Hill La
Brown Knowl CH3 .....199 C8
Peckforton CW6 ......184 E6
Hillock La WA1........17 C8
Hill Rd CH4 ....141 E2
Hill Rd N WA6.........73 D3
Hill Rd S WA6.........73 C3
Hillsboro Ave WA6.....74 C7
Hillsdown Way CH66...69 C2
Hillside
Broomedge WA13 .....19 E1
Northwich CW8 ....103 C7
Hillside Ave
Newton-le-W WA12.....1 F2
Runcorn WA7.........48 E8
Hillside Cl
Bramhall SK7.........36 A7
Chorlton CW2 ....207 E3
Helsby WA6..........73 D4
Mow Cop ST7.........195 D7
Hill Side Cl SK12 ......38 E6
Hillside Ct
Macclesfield SK10.....88 A1
Warrington WA4 ......26 D3
Hillside Dr
Crewe CW1 ....190 E5
Ellesmere Port CH66...69 E7
Macclesfield SK10.....88 A1
Hillside Gr WA5 ....14 F4
Hillside Ho **1** CW8 ....103 C5
Hillside La CW8 ....126 E7
Hillside Rd
Blacon CH1 ....117 C4
Frodsham WA6 ....74 C7
Heswall CH60 ....41 A7
Kelsall CW6...........122 D4
Knutsford WA16 ......57 A2
Warrington WA4 ......26 D3
Hillside View SK22 ....39 A8
Hill St
Crewe CW1 ....190 D4
Macclesfield SK11 .....112 D6
Runcorn WA7.........23 A2
Sandbach CW11 ......174 D7
Warrington WA1 ......16 B5

Hill St *continued*
Winsford CW7.........126 F1
Hill Terr ST7...........209 D2
Hill The
Buckworth WA16 ......82 B8
Sandbach CW11 ......175 D5
HILLTOP 60 B8
Hilltop WA7 ....50 C7
Hill Top
Altrincham WA15......32 A8
Barnton CW8.........78 B2
Hill Top Ave
Cheadle SK8 ....35 B8
Wilmslow SK9 ....60 B8
Winsford CW7.........126 C1
Hilltop Com Prim Sch
ST7................210 D7
Hill Top La
Heswall CH60 ....41 B8
Neston CH64 ....67 B5
Hilltop Pk WA16.......79 F7
Hilltop Rd
Guilden Sutton CH3....119 F5
Lymm WA13..........18 C2
Hill Top Rd
Acton Bridge CW8.....76 F2
Dutton WA4 ....51 C1
Runcorn WA7.........50 F6
Warrington, Stockton Heath
WA4 ....16 F2
Warrington, Woolston
WA4 ....17 C7
Hill Top Rise SK23 ....65 D8
Hill View
Bollington SK10.......87 F7
Whaley Bridge SK23 ...65 C8
Widnes WA8 ....12 F5
Hill View Ave WA6.....73 A1
Hillview Cl WA6.......74 C7
Hill View Prim Sch
WA7................49 E4
Hillview Rise CW8.....78 E1
Hilton Ave WA5.......15 B5
Hilton Cl
9 Macclesfield SK11 ....111 F7
Middlewich CW10 .....151 B8
Hilton Dr M44 ....11 C5
Hilton Gr SK12 ....36 D4
Hilton Rd
Disley SK12...........38 B7
Poynton SK12 ....37 C5
Himalayan Birch Cl
CH66..............69 E6
Hinchley Cl CW8......103 A5
Hinckley Ct CW12.....156 A3
Hinderton Dr CH60 ...40 F6
Hinderton Gn CH64...66 F8
Hinderton La CH64....67 A8
Hinderton Rd CH64...66 F8
Hinderton Sch CH65...69 F3
Hinde St CW5 ....204 D4
Hind Heath La CW11...174 F4
Hind Heath Rd CW11...174 E4
Hindle Ave WA5 ......7 F1
Hindley Cres CW8 ....78 A3
Hinton Cres WA4.....26 E8
Hinton Rd
Crewe CW2 ....206 D8
Runcorn WA7.........23 A1
Hirsch Cl CW5........205 A4
Hitchen's Cl WA7......50 D7
Hitchens La SY14.....184 D1
Hitch Lowes SK11.....84 A3
Hobart Cl SK7 ....35 F4
Hobart Way CW1......117 D4
Hobb La WA4.........25 C5
Hobbs Cl CW1 ....191 D4
Hobbs Hill La WA16...28 E1
Hobby Ct WA7.........49 E6
Hobcroft La WA16....58 A7
Hob Hey La WA3......4 D3
Hob La
Chorlton CH3 ....180 F5
Dunham-on-t-H WA6...97 C6
Hobson St SK11 ....112 D6
Hockenhall Ave CH3...121 B2
Hockenhull Cres CH3...121 B2
Hockenhull La
Tarvin, Broom Bank
CH3...............121 B1
Tarvin CH3............121 B2
Hocker La
Adder's Moss SK10.....85 F4
Nether Alderley SK10 ...85 C4
Hockerley Ave SK23....65 D8
Hockerley Cl SK23.....65 D8
Hockerley La SK23.....65 D8
Hockerley New Rd
SK23...............65 D8
HOCKLEY 37 A2
Hockley Cl SK12 ......37 A3
Hockley Paddock SK12...36 F3
Hockley Rd SK12......37 A3
HODGEHILL 132 E8
Hodgehill La SK11.....132 E5
Hodge La
Hartford CW8 ....103 A6
Weaverham CW8......102 D5
Hodgkin Cl CW5......204 F4
Hodgkinson Ave WA5...7 F1
Hoghton Rd L24 ....21 E2
Hogshead La CW8.....124 C7
Holbein Cl CH4 ....50 C7
Holbein Cl CH4 ....141 E6
Holborn Ct WA8.......12 F3
Holbrook Cl WA5 .....18 D5
Holbury Cl CW1.......190 B8
Holcombe Ave WA3....3 C8

Holcombe Dr SK10.....87 B3
Holcot Ct CW7 ....127 A4
Holcroft La WA3.......5 D2
Huldings La CW3......232 F4
Holehouse La
Langley SK11.........113 C4
Scholar Green ST7....194 D8
Whiteley green SK10...62 D2
Hole House La CW8 ...77 E4
Hole La WA16 ....106 E4
Holes La WA1 ....17 B7
Holford Ave
Lostock Gralam CW9...80 A3
Warrington WA5 ......15 F8
Holford Cres WA16....57 B1
Holford Moss 24 D3
Holford St CW12 ......156 D3
Holford Way WA12....2 F3
Holgrave Cl WA16 ....29 C4
Holkam Cl CW9.......103 F5
Holker Cl SK12 ....36 F4
Holkham Cl WA8 .....12 F1
Holkham The CH3.....119 B1
Holland Cl CW11......175 C5
Holland Ct SK12 ......36 E3
Holland Rd SK7.......35 E7
Hollands La CW6 .....122 C5
Hollands Pl SK11......112 F7
Hollands Rd CW9.....103 F7
Holland St
Crewe CW1 ....190 B6
5 Macclesfield SK11 ....112 C7
Holland Wlk CW5.....204 D6
Hollies La SK9.........60 F7
Hollies The
Moulton CW9.........126 E8
1 Northwich CW9 ....103 E6
Runcorn WA7.........49 D8
Shavington CW2 ......206 E4
HOLLINFARE 11 A3
Hollingford Pl WA16...82 A8
HOLLIN GREEN 202 F6
Hollingreen La CW5 ...229 B7
Hollin Green La CW5...202 E6
Hollinhey Prim Sch
SK11...............112 F3
Hollin La
Langley SK11.........113 A1
Newhall CW5.........228 D8
Styal SK9.............33 F5
Sutton Lane Ends SK11...136 C6
Hollin Rd SK10 ....88 A7
Hollins Cres ST7......194 E1
Hollins Dr WA2.......8 D3
Hollins Grange ST7 ...210 D8
HOLLINSGREEN 152 D4
HOLLINS GREEN 11 B2
Hollins Green St Helens
CE Prim Sch WA3....11 B2
Hollinshead Cl ST7 ...194 F7
Hollins Hill CW6......146 F8
Hollins La
Antrobus CW9........53 F4
Marbury SY13 ....226 E7
Winwick WA2.........7 E6
HOLLINS-LANE 226 E6
Hollins Park Hospl WA2...7 F6
Hollins Rd SK11 ......112 F6
Hollins Terr SK11......112 F6
Hollins Way WA8 .....22 B5
Hollinwood Cl ST7....210 E8
Hollinwood Rd
Disley SK12...........38 D6
Talke ST7.............210 E8
Holloway WA7 ....22 F1
Hollow Dr WA4........16 E1
Hollow La
Kingsley WA6.........75 B3
Knutsford WA16 ......57 B1
Hollowmoor Heath
CH3 ....121 A6
Hollow Oak La CW8...101 D4
Hollowood Rd SY14...213 B5
Hollow The ST7.......195 B5
Holly Ave WA12.......2 D3
Hollybank
Audlem CW3 ....229 E3
Moore WA4 ....25 B5
Holly Bank
Chester CH1 ....237 A4
Frodsham WA6 ....74 C8
Helsby WA6..........73 D2
Lymm WA13..........18 D2
Hollybank Cl CW8 ....78 D1
Hollybank Ct WA8 ....12 F1
Holly Bank Cvn Pk
WA3 ....11 A1
Hollybank Rd WA7....49 F8
Holly Bank Rd SK9....34 B1
Hollybush Cres CW5...205 D5
Holly Bush La WA3 ...10 C2
Holly Cl
Connah's Quay CH5....91 C1
Hale L24 ....21 D2
Mickle Trafford CH2....119 F8
Holly Cotts CW12 .....132 C1
Holly Croft CW12 .....154 F6
Holly Ct
Helsby WA6..........73 C5
Middlewich CW10 .....128 B2
Holly Dr CW7.........149 D8
Holly Farm Ct WA8 ...12 E4
Hollyfield Rd CH65....70 B5
Hollyfields CW9 ......191 F8
Holly Gr
Over Tabley WA16.....56 A3
Warrington WA1 ......17 A7

Holly Heath Cl CW11...175 C5
Holly Hedge La WA4...25 D6
Holly House Est
CW10..............129 C6
HOLLYHURST 227 A5
Hollyhurst Rd SY13...227 B7
Holly La
Alsager ST7..........193 C3
Harriseahead ST7 ....195 F5
Wythenshawe SK9....33 E5
Holly Mount CW2.....206 E5
Holly Rd
Bramhall SK7.........35 E5
Chester CH4 ....140 F5
Ellesmere Port CH65...70 C5
Golborne WA3........3 C8
Haydock WA11........1 A6
High Lane SK6........37 F7
Lymm WA13..........19 B5
Macclesfield SK11.....112 B7
Newcastle-u-Lyme ST5...210 D1
Poynton SK12 ....36 E3
Warrington WA5 ......14 E5
Weaverham CW8......102 C8
Holly Rd N SK9........60 B5
Holly Rd S SK9........60 B5
Holly Terr
Tilston SY14..........198 C3
Warrington WA5 ......14 F5
Hollythorn Ave SK8 ...35 C7
Holly Tree Dr
Biddulph ST8 ....179 C2
Swan Green WA16....106 D7
Hollytree Rd WA16....80 F3
Holly Wlk
Northwich CW8 ....103 C7
Partington M31.......11 D3
Holm Dr CH2..........72 C3
Holmes Chapel Bsns Pk
CW4 ....130 D3
Holmes Chapel Comp Sch
CW4 ....130 A2
Holmes Chapel Prim Sch
CW4 ....130 D2
Holmes Chapel Rd
Allostock WA16 ......106 C3
Brereton Green CW4,
CW12..............154 D8
Congleton CW12 .....155 C4
Knutsford WA16 ......82 C3
Lach Dennis CW9.....105 E4
Middlewich CW10 .....128 E2
Sandbach CW11 ......153 E1
Sproston Green CW4,
CW10..............129 B2
Withington Green SK11...109 A7
Holmes Chapel Sta
CW4 ....130 D2
Holmes Ct WA3........9 C4
Holme St CH3 ....120 F2
Holmesville Ave
CW12..............156 B3
Holmeswood Cl SK9...60 C8
Holmfield SK9.........85 A8
Holmfield Ave WA7....23 C2
Holmfield Dr
Cheadle SK8 ....35 B8
Ellesmere Port CH66...69 D3
Holmlea Dr CW5......190 F3
Holmlee Way SK10....86 D6
Holm Oak Way CW8...94 F8
Holmsfield Rd WA1....16 A1
Holmshaw La CW1....192 B3
Holmwood Dr CH65...70 B2
HOLT 58 E6
Holt Gdns WA16......58 E6
Holt Hey CH64........67 A5
Holtis La SK9..........33 F3
Holt La WA7..........49 F8
HOLTRIDGE 215 E6
Holt Ridge La SY13...215 E6
Holt's Com Prim Sch
LL13 ....196 D8
Holt St CW1 ....190 B4
Holy Family RC Prim Sch
WA8 ....12 D5
Holyhead Cl WA5 .....7 F2
Holyrood Ave WA8....13 A4
Holyrood Dr CW2.....205 E8
Holyrood Way CH3....119 B2
Holy Spirit RC Prim Sch
WA9 ....1 A3
Holy Spirit RC Prim Sch
The WA7.............49 D8
Holywell Cl CH64 .....41 B1
Holywell Dr WA1......16 C5
Holywell La CH3.......182 D2
Home Cl CH3..........142 E7
Homecrofts CH64.....66 E5
Homedee Ho CH1 ....237 A3
Home Farm Ct WA8 ...56 B8
Home Farm Ave SK10...86 F1
Home Farm Pk CW8...172 A8
Home Pk CH1 ....94 F1
Homeshire Ho ST7....193 D3
Homestead Ave WA11...1 E6
Homestead Ct CW9 ...104 D7
Homestead Rd SK12...38 C6
Homesteads The
CW5...............172 A6
Homeway WA3........4 B4
Homewood Cres CW8...103 B5
Honey Fields CW6 ....146 C1
Honeysuckle Cl
Broughton CH4 ....139 C3
Widnes WA8 ....13 B4

Honey Suckle Cl 3
CH66 . . . . 94 F8
Hong Kong Ave M90 . . . . 33 A8
Honister Ave WA2 . . . . 8 C2
Honister Gr WA7 . . . . 49 E5
Honiton Way
Middlewich CW10 . . . . 128 D2
Warrington WA5 . . . . 14 E4
HONKLEY 161 C3
Hood La WA5 . . . . 15 C4
Hood La N WA5 . . . . 15 C6
HOOD MANOR 15 D5
Hood Rd WA8 . . . . 12 F1
HOOFIELD 145 A2
Hoofield La CH3 . . . . 145 A1
HOO GREEN 29 F2
Hoo Green La WA16 . . . . 29 E1
Hooker St CW8 . . . . 103 E7
Hook La CW6 . . . . 145 A6
Hookstone Dr CH66 . . . . 69 C6
HOOLE 119 A3
HOOLE BANK 119 C7
Hoole CE Prim Sch
CH2 . . . . 119 A3
Hoole Gdns CH2 . . . . 119 B3
Hoole Ho CH2 . . . . 119 B4
Hoole La CH2 . . . . 119 A3
HOOLE PARK 118 F3
Hoole Pk CH2 . . . . 118 F2
Hoole Rd CH2 . . . . 118 F3
Hoole Way CH1 . . . . 237 B3
Hooleyhey La SK10,
SK11 . . . . 89 D4
Hoolpool La WA6 . . . . 72 F5
Hooten Hey CH66 . . . . 69 D5
HOOTON 44 A1
Hooton Gn CH66 . . . . 44 B2
Hooton La CH66 . . . . 44 B1
Hooton Rd CH64, CH66 . . . . 43 D1
Hooton Sta CH66 . . . . 43 D1
Hooton Way
14 Handforth SK9 . . . . 34 D5
Hooton CH66 . . . . 44 A2
Hooton Works CH66 . . . . 43 E1
Hope Ave SK9 . . . . 34 C3
Hope Croft CH66 . . . . 69 F2
Hope Farm Prec CH66 . . . . 69 F2
Hope Farm Rd CH66 . . . . 69 E2
Hopefield Rd WA13 . . . . 19 B4
Hope Green Way SK10 . . . . 36 D2
Hope La
Midway SK10 . . . . 36 D1
Wardsend SK10 . . . . 36 E1
Hope Rd CH4 . . . . 139 B3
Hope St W SK10 . . . . 112 C8
Hope St
Audley ST7 . . . . 209 F3
Chester CH4 . . . . 140 F7
Crewe CW2 . . . . 190 D2
Macclesfield SK10 . . . . 112 E8
Newton-le-W WA12 . . . . 2 B3
Northwich CW8 . . . . 103 E7
Sandbach CW11 . . . . 175 B6
Hopkins Cl CW12 . . . . 156 B3
Hopkinson Ct CH1 . . . . 118 B1
Hopwood Cl 5 WA3 . . . . 3 F8
Hopwood St WA1 . . . . 16 C6
Horace Black Gdns
CH65 . . . . 70 C6
Horace Lawton Ct 2
CW12 . . . . 156 D3
Horbury Gdns CH66 . . . . 69 C5
Hornbeam Ave CH66 . . . . 69 F1
Hornbeam Cl
Chester CH2 . . . . 119 B3
Runcorn WA7 . . . . 24 C1
Hornbeam Dr CW8 . . . . 102 E4
Hornbeam Rd L26 . . . . 21 A7
Hornby Dr
Congleton CW12 . . . . 156 A3
Nantwich CW5 . . . . 205 A5
Hornby La WA2 . . . . 8 A6
Horncastle Cl 4 WA3 . . . . 3 F8
Horn's Mill Prim Sch
WA6 . . . . 73 A1
Hornsmill Way WA6 . . . . 73 A3
Horridge Ave WA12 . . . . 2 C5
Horrocks La WA1 . . . . 16 B5
Horrocks Rd CH2 . . . . 118 E5
Horsemarket St WA1 . . . . 16 B5
Horseshoe Cl WA6 . . . . 75 B2
Horseshoe Cres WA2 . . . . 8 E3
Horseshoe Dr SK11 . . . . 112 B7
Horseshoe La SK9 . . . . 60 A2
Horsley La CW6 . . . . 167 E1
Horstone Cres CH66 . . . . 69 F2
Horstone Gdns CH66 . . . . 70 A2
Horstone Rd CH66 . . . . 69 F2
HORTON GREEN 212 A8
Horton Way CW5 . . . . 205 A4
HORWICH END 65 D5
Hoscar Ct WA8 . . . . 22 D7
Hospital La CW5 . . . . 203 E2
Hospital of St John
Almhouses CH1 . . . . 237 A3
Hospital St
Crewe CW1 . . . . 190 D6
Nantwich CW5 . . . . 204 E5
Hospital Way WA7 . . . . 49 F7
Hotel Rd M90 . . . . 33 C7
Hotel St WA12 . . . . 2 B3
Hothershall Cl CW1 . . . . 173 B1
HOUGH
Alderley Edge 60 D1
Crewe 206 F3
Hough Cl SK10 . . . . 88 D5
HOUGH COMMON 206 F2
Hough Cotts CW2 . . . . 206 E3
Hougher Wall Rd ST7 . . . . 209 D1
Hough Gn
Ashley WA15 . . . . 31 E5
Chester CH4 . . . . 141 B7
HOUGH GREEN 12 B2
Hough Green Rd WA8 . . . . 12 B3
Hough Green Sta WA8 . . . . 12 B2
Hough La
Alderley Edge SK9 . . . . 60 D3
Barnton CW8, CW9 . . . . 78 B4
Comberbach CW9 . . . . 78 A7
Norley WA6 . . . . 100 F5
Houghley Cl SK10 . . . . 87 C2
Hough's La WA4 . . . . 26 A6
Houghton Cl
Chester CH2 . . . . 118 F3
Newton-le-W WA12 . . . . 2 B3
9 Northwich CW9 . . . . 103 F4
Widnes WA8 . . . . 13 D2
Houghton Croft WA8 . . . . 12 C5
HOUGHTON GREEN 8 E4
Houghton St
Newton-le-W WA12 . . . . 2 B3
Warrington WA2 . . . . 16 B6
Widnes WA8 . . . . 13 D2
Houndings La CW11 . . . . 175 B4
Hourd Way CH66 . . . . 94 E8
Housesteads Dr CH2 . . . . 118 F3
Housman Cl CH1 . . . . 118 A5
Houston Gdns WA5 . . . . 15 A8
Hove Cl CW1 . . . . 190 B8
Hove The WA7 . . . . 50 D6
Hovis Mill SK11 . . . . 112 E7
Howard Ave
Bebington CH62 . . . . 43 D8
Lymm WA13 . . . . 19 B4
Howard Ct
Neston CH64 . . . . 41 F1
Runcorn WA7 . . . . 24 C4
Howard Rd
Culcheth WA3 . . . . 5 A2
Saltney CH4 . . . . 140 D6
Howard St CW1 . . . . 191 A5
Howards Way CH64 . . . . 67 A6
Howarth Ct 4 WA7 . . . . 23 B2
HOWBECK BANK 219 E8
Howbeck Cres CW5 . . . . 220 A8
Howbeck Wlk CW2 . . . . 206 D8
Howells Ave CH66 . . . . 69 D3
Howe Rd CH4 . . . . 141 B7
Howe St SK10 . . . . 87 F1
Howey Hill CW12 . . . . 156 D1
Howey La
Congleton CW12 . . . . 156 D2
Frodsham WA6 . . . . 74 B7
Howey Rise WA6 . . . . 74 B7
Howgill Cl CH66 . . . . 68 F6
HOWLEY 16 D5
Howley La WA1 . . . . 16 E5
Howley Quay Ind Est
WA1 . . . . 16 D5
Howson Rd WA2 . . . . 8 C3
Howty Cl SK9 . . . . 34 D1
Hoylake Cl WA7 . . . . 50 C6
Hoyle St WA5 . . . . 15 F7
Hubert Dr CW10 . . . . 151 C8
Hubert Worthington Ho 9
SK9 . . . . 60 A1
Hudson Cl WA5 . . . . 15 D8
Hudson Gr 9 WA3 . . . . 3 E8
Hudson Rd WA2 . . . . 8 E2
Hughes Ave WA2 . . . . 8 D2
Hughes Dr CW2 . . . . 189 F4
Hughes Pl WA2 . . . . 8 D2
Hughes St WA4 . . . . 16 C3
Hugh St CH4 . . . . 141 D7
Hulley Pl SK10 . . . . 87 F1
Hulley Rd SK10 . . . . 87 F2
Hullock's Pool Rd
ST7 . . . . 209 E5
HULME 8 B3
Hulme Hall Ave SK8 . . . . 35 B8
Hulme Hall Cres SK8 . . . . 35 A8
Hulme Hall Gram Sch
SK8 . . . . 35 A8
Hulme Hall La WA16 . . . . 106 B4
Hulme Hall Rd SK8 . . . . 35 A8
Hulme La WA16 . . . . 106 C7
Hulme Sq SK11 . . . . 112 D5
Hulme St CW1 . . . . 189 F5
HULME WALFIELD 156 B7
HULSEHEATH 30 A4
Hulseheath La WA16 . . . . 30 A3
Hulse La CW9 . . . . 105 D6
Hulton Cl CW12 . . . . 157 B1
Humber Cl WA8 . . . . 13 F3
Humber Dr ST8 . . . . 179 E1
Humber Rd
Ellesmere Port CH66 . . . . 69 F2
Warrington WA2 . . . . 8 E2
Humble Bee Bank Cotts
CW5 . . . . 187 C8
Hume St WA1 . . . . 16 D6
Humphrey's Cl WA7 . . . . 50 D7
Hungerford Ave CW1 . . . . 190 E4
Hungerford Pl
Barthomley CW2 . . . . 208 D5
Sandbach CW11 . . . . 175 A5
Hungerford Prim Sch
CW1 . . . . 190 E4
Hungerford Rd CW1 . . . . 190 F4
Hungerford Terr CW1 . . . . 190 F4
Hungerford Villas
CW1 . . . . 190 F4
HUNSTERSON 220 B1
Hunsterson Rd
Bridgemere CW5 . . . . 231 D8
Hatherton CW5 . . . . 220 B3
Hunt Cl WA5 . . . . 15 B8
Hunter Ave
Shavington CW2 . . . . 206 D7
Warrington WA2 . . . . 8 B3
Hunters Cl SK9 . . . . 34 F1
Hunter's Cres CH3 . . . . 121 C1
Hunters Ct
Helsby WA6 . . . . 73 D4
Runcorn WA7 . . . . 49 E6
Hunter's Dr CH3 . . . . 121 C1
Huntersfield CW2 . . . . 206 B3
Hunters Field CW8 . . . . 103 D7
Hunters Hill
Kingsley WA6 . . . . 75 C1
Weaverham CW8 . . . . 77 C1
Hunters Lo SK9 . . . . 34 F1
Hunters Mews SK9 . . . . 60 C7
Hunters Pointe CW12 . . . . 155 C6
Hunters Pool La SK10 . . . . 86 C8
Hunters Rise CW7 . . . . 126 C1
Hunter St CH1 . . . . 237 A3
Hunter's View SK9 . . . . 34 C3
Hunters Way
Neston CH64 . . . . 66 C8
Talke ST7 . . . . 210 D8
Hunters Wlk CH1 . . . . 237 A2
Hunting Lodge Mews
CW8 . . . . 102 A4
HUNTINGTON 142 A5
Huntington Com Prim Sch
CH3 . . . . 142 A5
Huntley St WA5 . . . . 15 C4
Huntly Chase SK9 . . . . 60 C7
Hunt Rd WA11 . . . . 1 E6
Huntsbank Bsns Pk
CW2 . . . . 205 E7
Huntsbank Dr ST5 . . . . 210 D1
Hunts Cl CH3 . . . . 119 B1
Hunts Field Cl WA13 . . . . 18 D2
Hunts La WA4 . . . . 16 F2
Huntsman Dr M44 . . . . 11 F7
HURDSFIELD 87 E2
Hurdsfield Cl CW10 . . . . 151 C7
Hurdsfield Com Prim Sch
SK10 . . . . 87 F2
Hurdsfield Gn SK10 . . . . 87 E2
Hurdsfield Ind Est
SK10 . . . . 87 E3
Hurdsfield Rd SK10 . . . . 87 E1
Hurford Ave CH65 . . . . 69 F3
Hurlbote Cl SK9 . . . . 34 D5
Hurleston Bldgs CW5 . . . . 204 E6
Hurlestone Cl CH2 . . . . 96 F1
Hurley Cl WA5 . . . . 15 C5
Hurn Cl CW1 . . . . 190 B8
HURST 179 F3
Hurst Ave SK8 . . . . 35 C6
Hurst Cl
Bunbury CW6 . . . . 185 E8
Talke ST7 . . . . 210 D6
Hurst Ct CW6 . . . . 185 F8
Hursthead Inf Sch SK8 . . . . 35 C6
Hursthead Jun Sch
SK8 . . . . 35 C7
Hursthead Rd SK8 . . . . 35 B7
Hurst La
Bollington SK10 . . . . 88 A8
Glazebury WA3 . . . . 5 C7
Hurst Lea Ct SK9 . . . . 60 A2
Hurst Lea Rd SK22 . . . . 39 C7
Hurst Mews WA6 . . . . 75 C2
Hurst Mill La WA3 . . . . 5 C8
Hurst Rd ST8 . . . . 179 F4
Hurst St WA8 . . . . 23 A4
Hurst The WA6 . . . . 75 C2
Hurstwood CH3 . . . . 143 A4
Hush Ho CH1 . . . . 237 A2
Huskisson Way WA12 . . . . 2 B4
Hutchins' Cl CW10 . . . . 151 E6
Hutchinson St WA8 . . . . 22 F6
Huttfield Rd L24 . . . . 21 A4
Hutton Cl WA3 . . . . 4 E5
Hutton Dr CW12 . . . . 157 A2
HUXLEY 167 A8
Huxley CE Prim Sch
CH3 . . . . 167 A7
Huxley Cl
Bramhall SK7 . . . . 35 E7
Macclesfield SK10 . . . . 87 B2
Huxley Ct CH66 . . . . 69 F8
Huxley Dr SK7 . . . . 35 E7
Huxley La CW6 . . . . 168 B6
Huxley St CW8 . . . . 103 E7
Hyacinth Cl WA11 . . . . 1 F6
Hyde Bank Ct SK22 . . . . 39 C7
Hyde Bank Mill SK22 . . . . 39 C8
Hyde Bank Rd SK22 . . . . 39 C8
Hyde Cl
Ellesmere Port CH65 . . . . 69 F4
Runcorn WA7 . . . . 49 D6
Hydrangea Way WA9 . . . . 6 A7
Hylton Ct CH65 . . . . 70 E2
Hylton Dr SK8 . . . . 35 C8
Hythe Ave CW1 . . . . 190 B8

I

Ian Rd ST7 . . . . 195 D3
Iberis Gdns WA9 . . . . 6 A7
Ibis Ct WA1 . . . . 16 A3
Ikey La CW5 . . . . 202 F6
Ikins Dr ST7 . . . . 209 F2
Ilex Ave WA2 . . . . 8 B7
Ilford Way WA16 . . . . 58 A4
ILLIDGE GREEN 154 C4
Imperial Ave CH1 . . . . 117 C4
Imperial Mews
Crewe CW2 . . . . 190 D3
Ellesmere Port CH65 . . . . 70 B6
INCE 71 F6
Ince Ave CH62 . . . . 43 E3
Ince Dr CH3 . . . . 180 F1
Ince & Elton Sta CH2 . . . . 72 B4
Ince La
Elton CH2 . . . . 72 B3
Wimbolds Trafford CH2 . . . . 96 F5
Ince Orchards CH2 . . . . 72 B4
Indigo Rd CH65 . . . . 70 F6
Ingersley Ct SK10 . . . . 88 B8
Ingersley Rd SK10 . . . . 88 C8
Ingersley Vale SK10 . . . . 88 B8
Ingham Ave WA12 . . . . 2 C1
Ingham Cl CH3 . . . . 119 A1
Ingham Rd WA8 . . . . 12 F4
Inglegreen CH60 . . . . 41 B8
Inglenook Rd WA5 . . . . 14 F4
Ingleton Cl
Holmes Chapel CW4 . . . . 130 A3
Newton-le-W WA12 . . . . 2 B4
Ingleton Gr WA7 . . . . 49 D5
Inglewood Ave CW10 . . . . 151 D5
Inglewood Cl
Partington M31 . . . . 11 F4
Warrington WA3 . . . . 10 B6
Inglewood Cvn Pk M31 . . . . 11 F4
Inman Ave WA9 . . . . 1 B2
Inner Gosling Cl WA4 . . . . 25 F1
Innisfree Cl 4 CH66 . . . . 69 C5
Innovation Ho CW7 . . . . 149 A7
Insall Rd WA2 . . . . 8 F2
Intack La WA16 . . . . 28 B3
Intake Cl CH64 . . . . 68 A8
International App M90 . . . . 33 C7
Int Peace Ctr WA5 . . . . 15 D5
Inveresk Rd SY14 . . . . 198 C3
Inward Way CH65 . . . . 70 B7
Ion Path CW7 . . . . 127 C1
Irby Cl CH66 . . . . 69 E4
Ireland Blackburne Ho
WA1 . . . . 16 E7
Ireland Rd
Hale L24 . . . . 21 E1
Haydock WA11 . . . . 1 C6
Ireland St
Warrington WA2 . . . . 16 B8
Widnes WA8 . . . . 13 D2
Iris Cl WA8 . . . . 12 C2
Iris Wlk 7 M31 . . . . 11 E2
Irlam & Cadishead Com
High Sch M44 . . . . 11 E7
Irlam Ind Est M44 . . . . 11 E7
Irlam Sta M44 . . . . 11 E7
Ironbridge Dr CW4 . . . . 130 C2
Irons La CH3 . . . . 120 F7
Irvin Dr M22, SK8 . . . . 34 A8
Irving's Cres CH4 . . . . 140 E6
Irwell La WA7 . . . . 23 B3
Irwell Rd WA4 . . . . 16 B2
Irwell Rise SK10 . . . . 87 F7
Irwell St WA8 . . . . 23 A4
Irwin Dr SK9 . . . . 34 C5
Isabella Ct CH4 . . . . 140 E6
Isherwood Cl WA2 . . . . 8 F3
Isis Cl CW12 . . . . 156 F1
Islay Cl CH65 . . . . 70 C1
Islington Gn WA8 . . . . 13 D4
ISYCOED 196 C1
Iveagh Cl WA7 . . . . 50 A7
Iver Cl
Chester CH2 . . . . 118 E7
Cronton WA8 . . . . 12 C6
Iver Rd CH2 . . . . 118 E7
Ivy Ave WA12 . . . . 2 C2
Ivy Bank Prim Sch
SK11 . . . . 112 A5
Ivychurch Mews WA7 . . . . 23 D2
Ivy Cotts SY13 . . . . 225 A8
Ivy Ct CH4 . . . . 162 D2
Ivy Dr CW8 . . . . 102 A2
Ivy Farm Ct L24 . . . . 21 D1
Ivy Farm Dr CH64 . . . . 66 F6
Ivy Farm Gdns WA3 . . . . 4 D4
Ivy Farm La CH3 . . . . 183 C1
Ivy Gdns CW12 . . . . 156 C2
Ivy Ho
Macclesfield SK11 . . . . 112 A7
Nether Alderley SK9 . . . . 84 C7
Ivy House Rd ST8 . . . . 179 C2
Ivy La
Alsager ST7 . . . . 193 E2
Macclesfield SK11 . . . . 112 A6
Ivy Meade Cl 10 SK11 . . . . 111 F7
Ivy Meade Rd SK11 . . . . 111 F6
Ivy Mews CH2 . . . . 119 A5
Ivy Rd
Golborne WA3 . . . . 3 B8
Macclesfield SK11 . . . . 112 A7
Poynton SK12 . . . . 36 E3
Warrington WA1 . . . . 17 E7
Ivy St WA7 . . . . 23 A1
Ivy Wlk M31 . . . . 11 D3

J

Jackie Stewart Bsns Ctr
CW6 . . . . 147 D6
Jack La
Moulton CW9, CW10 . . . . 127 A7
Weston CW2 . . . . 207 D6
Jackson Ave
Culcheth WA3 . . . . 4 F3
Nantwich CW5 . . . . 204 F5
Warrington WA1 . . . . 16 F6
Jackson Ct CH5 . . . . 139 B7
Jackson La SK10 . . . . 88 B7
Jackson Rd CW12 . . . . 156 E5
Jacksons Cl SK10 . . . . 88 B7
Jacksons Edge Rd
SK12 . . . . 38 B6
Jackson's La SK7 . . . . 36 C8
Jackson St
Burtonwood WA5 . . . . 6 E6
Haydock WA11 . . . . 1 A7
Macclesfield SK11 . . . . 112 D6
Jacobs Way WA16 . . . . 79 F7
Jamage Ind Est ST7 . . . . 210 C5
Jamage Rd ST7 . . . . 210 D5
James Atkinson Way
CW1 . . . . 189 F7
James Ave CH66 . . . . 69 C3
James Cl WA8 . . . . 23 A4
James Hall St CW5 . . . . 204 E6
James Pl CH2 . . . . 118 F2
James Rd WA11 . . . . 1 F7
James St
Chester CH1 . . . . 237 B3
Macclesfield SK11 . . . . 112 D6
Northwich CW9 . . . . 104 C8
5 Warrington WA1 . . . . 16 B5
Jamieson Cl
Alsager ST7 . . . . 193 E4
Chester CH3 . . . . 119 A2
Jane Maddock Homes
ST7 . . . . 193 B3
Jan Palach Ave CW5 . . . . 204 F4
Japonica Gdns WA9 . . . . 6 A7
Jarman SK11 . . . . 112 F4
Jasmine Cres ST7 . . . . 195 D2
Jasmine Gdns WA9 . . . . 6 A7
Jasmine Gr WA8 . . . . 22 D8
Jasmine Wlk M31 . . . . 11 F2
Jasmin Way ST7 . . . . 195 F2
Jay Cl WA3 . . . . 10 A4
Jays Cl WA7 . . . . 50 E7
Jedburgh Ave CH66 . . . . 69 A6
Jefferson Dr WA5 . . . . 15 B7
Jefferson Gdns WA8 . . . . 12 F3
Jellicoe Ave M44 . . . . 11 E6
Jennet's La WA3 . . . . 5 C8
Jenny La SK7 . . . . 35 E4
Jensen Ct WA7 . . . . 23 C3
Jersey Ave CH65 . . . . 70 C1
Jersey Cl CW12 . . . . 157 A2
Jersey Way CW10 . . . . 128 D2
Jervis Cl WA2 . . . . 9 A3
Jesmond Cres CW2 . . . . 190 B2
Jesmond Gr SK8 . . . . 35 B8
Jesmond Rd CH1 . . . . 118 B2
Jessop Ho WA7 . . . . 22 E3
Jessop Way CW1 . . . . 191 C4
JH Godwin Prim Sch
CH1 . . . . 117 D4
Jockey St WA2 . . . . 16 B7
JODRELL BANK 108 D2
Jodrell Bank Obsy*
CW4 . . . . 108 C3
Jodrell Bank Visitor Ctr*
SK11 . . . . 108 D3
Jodrell Cl
Holmes Chapel CW4 . . . . 130 A3
Macclesfield SK11 . . . . 112 E7
Jodrell Dr WA4 . . . . 27 A7
Jodrell Mdw SK23 . . . . 65 E8
Jodrell Rd SK23 . . . . 65 D8
Jodrell St
Macclesfield SK11 . . . . 112 E7
New Mills SK22 . . . . 39 B7
John Brunner Cres
CW9 . . . . 103 E6
John Ford Way CW11 . . . . 154 B1
John Fryer Ave CW9 . . . . 80 A5
John Gresty Dr CW5 . . . . 205 D6
John Lloyd Ct M44 . . . . 11 F8
John May Ct SK10 . . . . 87 B2
John Middleton Cl L24 . . . . 21 E2
John Nicholas Cres
CH65 . . . . 70 C6
John Rd WA13 . . . . 18 C3
Johns Ave
Haydock WA11 . . . . 1 E7
Runcorn WA7 . . . . 48 F8
Johns Cl SK10 . . . . 88 D5
Johnson Ave WA12 . . . . 2 B5
Johnson Cl CW12 . . . . 157 B1
Johnsons Cl CH4 . . . . 141 B5
Johnson's La WA8 . . . . 13 E1
Johnson St SK23 . . . . 65 E8
John St
Bollington SK10 . . . . 88 B8
Congleton CW12 . . . . 156 C2
Crewe CW1 . . . . 190 C5
Ellesmere Port CH65 . . . . 70 B6
Golborne WA3 . . . . 3 A8
Irlam M44 . . . . 11 E5
Macclesfield SK11 . . . . 112 D6
1 Northwich CW9 . . . . 104 A8
Utkinton CW6 . . . . 146 B7
Warrington WA2 . . . . 16 B6
Winsford CW7 . . . . 126 C1
John Street Com Prim Sch
CH65 . . . . 70 B6
Jonathan's Way CH1 . . . . 117 E5
Jones's La CW10 . . . . 152 D6
Jonson Rd CH64 . . . . 66 E8
Jordangate SK10 . . . . 112 D8
Joseph Cres ST7 . . . . 193 F2
Joseph Groome Twrs 10
CH65 . . . . 70 C6

Joseph St WA8 ... 13 C2
Joyce Ave CW7 ... 126 C2
Joy La WA5 ... 6 F4
Jubilee Almshouses
 CW5 ... 204 E6
Jubilee Ave
 Crewe CW2 ... 190 B3
 Warrington, Padgate
  WA1 ... 16 F8
 Warrington WA4 ... 14 E4
Jubilee Cres WA11 ... 1 F7
Jubilee Ct
 2 Handforth SK9 ... 34 E5
 Holmes Chapel CW4 ... 130 A3
Jubilee Gdns
 Nantwich CW5 ... 204 E4
 New Mills SK22 ... 39 C7
Jubilee Gn CH65 ... 70 C4
Jubilee Gr WA13 ... 18 C4
Jubilee Rd CW12 ... 156 E2
Jubilee St SK22 ... 39 C7
Jubilee Terr CW5 ... 204 E4
Jubilee Villas CH1 ... 175 C2
Jubilee Way
 Widnes WA8 ... 12 E1
 5 Winsford CW7 ... 126 D1
Jubits La WA8 ... 13 A8
Juddfield St WA11 ... 1 A7
Judy La SK11 ... 113 A3
Julian Way WA8 ... 12 F4
July Bglws CH4 ... 141 E2
Jumper La SK10 ... 88 F7
Junction Eight Bsns Ctr
 CH65 ... 70 A7
Junction Ho CW1 ... 190 A5
Junction La WA12 ... 2 B3
June Ave CH60 ... 43 E8
Juniper Cl ST5 ... 210 E1
Juniper Ct CH2 ... 119 B4
Juniper Dr CH66 ... 69 E1
Juniper Gr CH66 ... 69 F1
Juniper La WA3 ... 18 A7
Juniper Rise SK10 ... 86 E1
Jupiter Dr CH1 ... 117 E2
Jurby Ct WA2 ... 8 F1
Justice St SK10 ... 87 D1

K

Kansas Pl WA5 ... 15 B7
Karen Cl WA5 ... 7 A6
Karen Way CH66 ... 69 D3
Kaye Ave WA3 ... 4 F3
Kay La WA13 ... 29 B8
Keats Cl
 Ellesmere Port CH66 ... 94 E8
 Widnes WA8 ... 22 F8
Keats Dr
 Macclesfield SK10 ... 86 F1
 Rode Heath ST7 ... 193 E8
 Warrington CW2 ... 206 A8
Keats Gr WA2 ... 8 C2
Keats La CW9 ... 80 A5
Keats Terr CH1 ... 118 A5
Keble St WA8 ... 23 B7
KECKWICK ... 25 A3
Keckwick La WA4 ... 25 A3
Keele Cres SK11 ... 112 B6
Keel Hey CH64 ... 43 A2
Keepers Cl WA16 ... 57 D3
Keepers La CW9 ... 53 D4
Keeper's La CW8 ... 102 E8
Keeper's Rd WA4 ... 27 A7
Keepers Wlk WA7 ... 23 F2
Keith Ave WA5 ... 14 E6
Keith Dr CH63 ... 43 D5
Kelburn Ct WA3 ... 9 F6
Kelmscott Cl CH66 ... 69 D2
KELSALL ... 122 C4
Kelsall Ave CH62 ... 43 F3
Kelsall Cl
 Bebington CH62 ... 43 E3
 Warrington WA3 ... 9 C3
 Widnes WA8 ... 12 D1
Kelsall Com Prim Sch
 CW6 ... 122 C4
Kelsall Rd CH3 ... 121 C4
Kelsall St CW12 ... 156 E3
Kelsall Way
 Audley ST7 ... 209 D1
 6 Handforth SK9 ... 34 D5
Kelsborrow Cl CW9 ... 103 E3
Kelsborrow Way
 CW6 ... 122 D4
Kelso Way WA3 ... 9 C4
Kelstern Cl **2** CW9 ... 104 B8
KELSTERTON ... 91 B2
Kelsterton Ct CH5 ... 91 C1
Kelsterton La CH6 ... 91 B1
Kelsterton Rd
 Connah's Quay CH5,
  CH6 ... 91 C2
 Kelsterton CH6 ... 91 A3
Kelton Cl CW3 ... 9 D6
Kelvin Gr CH2 ... 118 E4
Kelvin St WA3 ... 9 F5
Kemberton Dr WA8 ... 13 A5
Kemble Cl CW2 ... 206 B8
Kemmel Ave WA4 ... 16 C3
Kempsell Way L26 ... 21 A7
Kempsell Wlk L26 ... 21 A7
Kempton Ave CW1 ... 190 C7
Kempton Cl
 Chester CH1 ... 118 B2

Kempton Cl continued
 Newton-le-W WA12 ... 2 D5
 Runcorn WA7 ... 49 C6
Kempton Way SK10 ... 87 C4
Kendal Ave WA2 ... 8 C2
Kendal Cl
 Chester CH2 ... 119 A6
 Ellesmere Port CH66 ... 69 D2
 Macclesfield SK10 ... 111 E6
Kendal Ct CW12 ... 156 A2
Kendal Dr
 Bramhall SK7 ... 35 C5
 Ellesmere Port CH66 ... 69 E2
Kendal Rd
 Macclesfield SK11 ... 111 F6
 Widnes WA8 ... 12 C1
Kendal Rise WA7 ... 49 D5
Kendal Way CW2 ... 207 C1
Kendrick Cl CW8 ... 77 D1
Kendrick St WA1 ... 16 A5
Kenilworth Ave
 Handforth SK9 ... 34 D3
 Knutsford WA16 ... 57 C2
 Runcorn WA7 ... 49 B8
Kenilworth Cl
 Macclesfield SK11 ... 111 F6
 Wistaston CW2 ... 206 A7
Kenilworth Ct CH65 ... 70 E2
Kenilworth Dr
 Hazel Grove SK7 ... 36 D8
 Warrington WA1 ... 16 F8
Kenilworth Gdns WA12 ... 2 C1
Kenilworth Gn SK11 ... 111 F6
Kenilworth Ho **6**
 CH1 ... 237 C3
Kenilworth Rd
 Golborne WA3 ... 3 E7
 Macclesfield SK11 ... 111 F6
 Neston CH64 ... 66 E5
Kenley Ave WA8 ... 12 D5
Kenmare Bank CW9 ... 104 A5
Kenmore Gr M44 ... 11 D6
Kennedy Ave SK10 ... 86 F2
Kennedy Cl CH2 ... 119 A5
Kennedy Ct **4** WA5 ... 15 B7
Kennel La
 Cuddington CW8 ... 102 A1
 Little Budworth CW8 ... 124 E7
Kennelwood Rd CW9 ... 78 C7
Kennerley's Ct SK9 ... 60 A7
Kennerley's La SK9 ... 60 A7
Kennet Cl SK9 ... 34 D2
Kennet Dr CW12 ... 156 F1
Kenneth Rd WA8 ... 22 C8
Kennet Rd WA11 ... 1 C6
Kennet Way **1** SK11 ... 111 F8
Kensington Pk WA8 ... 12 E4
Kenrick Cl CW3 ... 232 C1
Kensington Ave WA4 ... 17 C2
Kensington Cl
 Chester CH4 ... 141 A6
 Widnes WA8 ... 13 D4
Kensington Ct
 Alsager ST7 ... 192 F3
 8 Nantwich CW5 ... 204 E6
 Wilmslow SK9 ... 60 A6
 Winsford CW7 ... 149 C7
Kensington Dr
 Congleton CW12 ... 156 F4
 Willaston CW5 ... 205 D4
Kensington Gn CH4 ... 140 F6
Kensington Rd
 Chester CH4 ... 141 A6
 Ellesmere Port CH65 ... 70 A5
Kensington Sq **11**
 SK10 ... 111 F8
Kensington Way CW9 ... 103 E3
Kent Ave SK10 ... 87 E6
Kent Cl CH63 ... 43 B8
Kent Dr CW12 ... 156 D4
Kent Gdns CH2 ... 118 F5
Kent Gr WA7 ... 23 B1
Kent Ho ST7 ... 210 D6
Kentmere Ave CW7 ... 126 D2
Kentmere Pl WA2 ... 8 A3
Kenton Rd L26 ... 21 A7
Kent Rd
 Chester CH2 ... 118 F5
 Irlam M44 ... 11 C5
 Padgate M31 ... 11 E2
 Warrington WA5 ... 15 C4
Kentridge Dr CH66 ... 69 D3
Kent's Green La CW1,
 CW11 ... 191 E7
Kent's La CW1 ... 173 C1
Kent St
 Warrington WA4 ... 16 C4
 Widnes WA12 ... 2 C1
Kentwell Dr SK10 ... 87 C3
Kent Wlk SK10 ... 86 F1
Kenview CW4 WA4 ... 22 A4
Kenwick Cl CH66 ... 69 C3
Kenwood Ave SK7 ... 35 D5
KENYON ... 3 F3
Kenyon Ave WA5 ... 14 E5
Kenyon Ct WA8 ... 23 A6
Kenyon La
 Culcheth WA3 ... 4 A4
 Golborne, Kenyon WA3 ... 3 F3
 Golborne WA3 ... 3 F5
Kenyons La N WA11 ... 1 F8
Kenyon's La S WA11 ... 1 F7
Kerfoot Bsns Pk WA2 ... 16 A8
Kerfoot St WA2 ... 16 A7
Keristal Ave CH3 ... 142 A7
KERRIDGE ... 88 A6
Kerridge Cl CW10 ... 151 B8

KERRIDGE-END ... 88 D3
Kerridge Rd SK10 ... 88 B3
Kerry Croft CH66 ... 69 C1
Kershaw Cl **3** CH11 ... 110 B0
Kershaw St WA8 ... 12 D1
Kershaw Way WA12 ... 2 C5
Kestrel Ave WA16 ... 57 B3
Kestrel Cl
 Congleton CW12 ... 156 E1
 Middlewich CW10 ... 151 D6
 Winsford CW7 ... 149 D5
Kestrel Dr CW1 ... 190 B8
Kestrel La WA3 ... 9 E4
Kestrel Rd
 Heswall CH60 ... 41 C7
 Northwich CW8 ... 103 C2
Kestrels Way WA7 ... 49 F6
Keswick Ave
 Bebington CH63 ... 43 C4
 Macclesfield SK11 ... 111 F5
 Warrington WA2 ... 8 C2
Keswick Cl
 Chester CH2 ... 119 A5
 Crewe CW2 ... 189 E3
 Irlam M44 ... 11 D4
 Macclesfield SK11 ... 111 F6
 Widnes WA8 ... 12 C1
 Winsford CW7 ... 126 D2
Keswick Cres WA2 ... 8 C2
Keswick Ct CW12 ... 156 A2
Keswick Dr
 Bramhall SK7 ... 35 C5
 Frodsham WA6 ... 74 D8
Keswick Rd CH63 ... 43 C5
Keswick Rd SK6 ... 37 E8
Ketlan Ct CH4 ... 140 E7
Kettell Ave CW1 ... 190 A6
Kettle La CW3 ... 230 C2
KETTLESHULME ... 64 F4
Kettleshulme St James CE
 Prim Sch SK23 ... 64 F4
Kettleshulme Way
 SK12 ... 37 A3
Kettleshulme Wlk **4**
 SK9 ... 34 E1
Kew Gardens Cl WA8 ... 13 D4
Keyes Cl WA3 ... 9 F4
Keyes Gdn WA3 ... 9 F4
KEY GREEN ... 157 E4
Keysbrook CH3 ... 166 C2
Keysbrook Ave CH3 ... 166 C2
Kidderton Cl CW5 ... 202 E7
Kidderton La CW5 ... 202 F7
KIDNAL ... 212 E8
KIDSGROVE ... 195 B1
Kidsgrove Sta ST7 ... 194 F1
Kidston Dr CW1 ... 189 F7
Kilbuck La WA11 ... 2 A8
Kilburn Ave CH62 ... 43 E6
Kilburn Cl SK8 ... 34 B7
Kildare Cl L24 ... 21 D2
Kildonan Rd WA4 ... 17 A2
Kilford Cl WA5 ... 7 E2
Killingworth La WA3 ... 10 B5
Kilmorey Park Rd
 CH2 ... 118 F3
Kilmorey Pk CH2 ... 118 F4
Kilmorey Pk Ave CH2 ... 237 C4
Kilncroft WA7 ... 50 B5
Kiln Croft La SK9 ... 34 E4
Kiln La CW5 ... 220 B8
Kilsby Dr WA8 ... 13 E2
Kilshaw Rd WA5 ... 6 F6
Kilsyth Cl WA2 ... 9 A8
Kimberley Dr WA4 ... 16 C1
Kimberley St WA5 ... 15 E5
Kimberley Terr CH2 ... 118 F2
Kinder Dr CW2 ... 189 D3
Kinderton Cl WA16 ... 29 C4
Kinderton Mobile Home
 Pk CW10 ... 152 A7
Kinderton St CW10 ... 128 D1
Kinder View SK22 ... 39 C7
King Arthur's Wlk WA7 ... 24 A1
King Charles Ct CH1 ... 237 A3
King Edward Bldgs **4**
 CH3 ... 119 A1
King Edward Cl CW9 ... 103 F5
King Edward Rd
 Knutsford WA16 ... 57 A2
 3 Widnes WA8 ... 112 D8
King Edward St
 Macclesfield SK10 ... 112 D8
 Middlewich CW10 ... 128 C1
 Warrington WA1 ... 16 E7
Kingfisher Cl
 Congleton CW12 ... 156 E1
 Farndon CH3 ... 180 F1
 Newton-le-W WA12 ... 2 B3
 Nantwich CW5 ... 204 E8
 Runcorn WA7 ... 49 F5
 Sandbach CW11 ... 174 E8
 3 Warrington WA3 ... 9 F4
Kingfisher Ct
 Chester CH2 ... 237 A4
 Northwich CW9 ... 79 C2
Kingfisher Dr **5** CW7 ... 149 D6
Kingfisher Gr WA7 ... 49 E6
Kingfisher Way
 ST7 ... 195 C1
Kingham Cl **3** WA8 ... 13 D1
King Ho ST7 ... 210 D5
King George Ave
 CW9 ... 104 B8
King George Cres WA11 ... 16 E7
King George Rd WA11 ... 2 A8
King George Way
 ST7 ... 195 C1
King's Ave WA3 ... 3 F7
King's Bldgs CH1 ... 237 A3

Kingsbury Cl WA4 ... 26 D3
Kingsbury Dr **14** SK9 ... 34 D1
Kingsbury Rd WA8 ... 13 D4
King Cl
 Chester CH4 ... 140 F5
 Wilmslow SK9 ... 60 A6
King's Cres CW10 ... 128 C2
King's Cres CH13 ... 119 A1
King's Cres W CH3 ... 119 A1
Kings Croft ... 91 D1
Kings Ct
 Nantwich CW5 ... 204 D5
 Runcorn WA7 ... 24 D4
King's Ct
 Chester CH1 ... 237 A3
 Middlewich CW10 ... 128 D2
Kingsdale Rd WA5 ... 14 F7
Kingsdown Cl CW2 ... 207 C1
Kings Dr
 Helsby WA6 ... 73 B3
 Westaston CW2 ... 205 E8
Kingsfield Ct CH4 ... 141 C3
King's Gate CW8 ... 102 A2
Kings Grove Sch
 CW2 ... 190 A3
Kingshead Cl WA7 ... 24 A2
Kings La CW6 ... 147 D4
King's La
 Allostock CW10,
  WA16 ... 106 C1
 Nantwich CW5 ... 204 D5
Kingsland Grange WA1 ... 9 D1
Kingslawn Cl **4** CW9 ... 103 F5
Kings Lea Ho CH3 ... 142 A8
KINGSLEY ... 75 C2
Kingsley Ave
 Bebington CH62 ... 43 E3
 Handforth SK9 ... 34 C2
Kingsley Cl
 Northwich CW8 ... 103 C5
 Talke ST7 ... 210 D6
Kingsley Com Prim Sch
 WA6 ... 74 F3
Kingsley Cres WA7 ... 23 A1
Kingsley Ct CW11 ... 174 D8
Kingsley Dr
 Northwich CW9 ... 104 A6
 Warrington WA4 ... 26 C7
Kingsley Gdns CH3 ... 142 B8
Kingsley Gn WA6 ... 74 E5
Kingsley Rd
 Chester CH3 ... 142 B8
 Congleton CW12 ... 157 A3
 Crowton CW8 ... 76 B1
 Ellesmere Port CH65 ... 70 C5
 Frodsham WA6 ... 74 E4
 Haslington CW11 ... 191 C4
 Runcorn WA7 ... 23 A1
 Talke ST7 ... 210 D6
Kingsley St John's CE
 Prim Sch WA6 ... 75 C2
Kingsley Wlk CW7 ... 126 B2
Kings Mdw
 Hough CW2 ... 206 E2
 Runcorn WA7 ... 50 C8
KINGSMEAD ... 103 E5
Kingsmead
 Chester CH2 ... 118 C8
 Northwich CW9 ... 103 F5
Kingsmead Crossroads **16**
 CW9 ... 9 A8
Kingsmead Dr WA3 ... 9 A8
Kingsmead Prim Sch
 CW9 ... 103 E4
Kingsmead Sq CW9 ... 103 E4
Kings Mews CH66 ... 69 C7
Kings Rd
 Connah's Quay CH5 ... 91 D1
 Ellesmere Port CH66 ... 69 C7
 Golborne WA3 ... 3 A7
 Irlam M44 ... 16 E6
 Warrington WA2 ... 9 A2
 Sandbach CW11 ... 174 E8
 Talke ST7 ... 210 D6
King's Rd SK9 ... 59 E8
King's Sch The
 Chester CH4 ... 141 B4
 Macclesfield SK10 ... 87 C1
 Macclesfield SK10 ... 112 E8
King St
 Audley ST7 ... 209 D1
 Chester CH1 ... 237 A3
 Congleton CW12 ... 156 F4
 Ellesmere Port CH65 ... 70 C6
 Hartford CW8 ... 103 B5
 Kidsgrove ST7 ... 195 A2
 Knutsford WA16 ... 57 A2
 Macclesfield SK10 ... 128 E5
 Middlewich CW10 ... 128 E5
 Newton-le-W WA12 ... 2 B3
 Runcorn WA7 ... 23 A3
 Sandbach CW11 ... 174 E8
 Talke ST7 ... 210 D5

Kingsway continued
 Crewe CW2 ... 190 B2
 Frodsham WA6 ... 74 B8
 Heswall CH60 ... 41 C6
 Newton-le-W WA12 ... 2 C2
 Northwich CW9 ... 104 B8
 Widnes WA8 ... 13 A1
 Winsford CW7 ... 126 F1
Kingsway Ho WA4 ... 16 F4
Kingsway N WA1 ... 16 F6
Kingsway S WA1, WA4 ... 16 F4
Kingsway W CH2 ... 118 E4
KINGSWOOD ... 74 C1
Kingswood ST7 ... 195 B1
KINGSWOOD ... 7 B2
Kingswood WA5 ... 7 B2
Kingswood Ave
 Chorlton CW2 ... 207 B3
 Saughall CH1 ... 94 C1
Kingswood Cres
 CW10 ... 151 E5
Kingswood La CH1 ... 94 C1
Kingswood Rd WA5 ... 7 A2
Kings Wood Wlk
 CW6 ... 122 D5
Kinloch Cl
 Crewe CW1 ... 190 B6
 Halewood L26 ... 21 A7
Kinnerley Rd CH65 ... 70 A3
Kinnersley Ave CT2 ... 63 A1
Kinnersley St **1** ST7 ... 195 A2
Kinnerton Cl CH4 ... 140 E5
Kinnerton Hts CH4 ... 161 A7
Kinnerton La CH4 ... 161 A8
Kinnerton Rd CH4 ... 162 A7
Kinnington Way CH1 ... 94 F7
Kinnock Pk WA5 ... 6 E6
Kinross Cl WA2 ... 8 F4
Kinsale Dr WA3 ... 9 C4
KINSEY HEATH ... 230 B1
Kinsey Rd CH65 ... 70 D1
Kinsey's La CW7 ... 71 F6
Kinsey St CW12 ... 156 E2
Kintore Cl
 Bebington CH63 ... 43 C4
 Winsford CW7 ... 127 A3
Kintore Dr WA5 ... 14 D6
Kintyre Cl CH65 ... 70 C1
Kipling Ave WA2 ... 8 D2
Kipling Cres WA8 ... 22 F8
Kipling Rd CH1 ... 117 F5
Kipling Way WA1 ... 190 F4
Kirby Cl CH2 ... 118 D5
Kirkacre Ave WA12 ... 7 C8
Kirkby Rd WA3 ... 4 F3
Kirkcaldy Ave WA5 ... 14 C6
Kirkfell Dr SK6 ... 37 E8
Kirkham Ave WA3 ... 9 E7
Kirkham Cl WA5 ... 15 B4
Kirkham Rd
 Gatley SK8 ... 34 C8
 Widnes WA8 ... 13 A4
Kirkstall Cl
 Macclesfield SK10 ... 87 B2
 Poynton SK12 ... 36 D4
Kirkstead Rd SK8 ... 35 C6
Kirkstead Way WA3 ... 3 A8
Kirkstone Ave WA2 ... 8 C2
Kirkstone Cres WA7 ... 50 A4
Kirkstone Ct CW12 ... 156 A1
Kirkwall Dr WA5 ... 15 A3
Kirkwood Cl CH3 ... 119 A2
Kishfield La SK23 ... 65 A6
Kitchener Ave M44 ... 11 C4
Kitchen St CH1 ... 118 B1
Kite Gr ST7 ... 195 D3
Kitfield Ave CW10 ... 151 D7
KITT'S MOSS ... 35 D6
Kitt's Moss La SK7 ... 35 D6
Knap The CH60 ... 41 A6
Knebworth Ct CW12 ... 179 B8
Knight Rd WA5 ... 6 F6
Knightsbridge Ave
 1 Northwich CW9 ... 103 E3
 Warrington WA1 ... 17 C2
Knightsbridge Cl
 13 Handforth SK9 ... 34 D1
 Widnes WA8 ... 13 D4
Knightsbridge Ct
 Chester CH4 ... 237 C2
 Warrington WA1 ... 16 A5
Knight's Cl SK11 ... 112 E7
Knights Grange (Sports
 Complex) CW7 ... 126 B3
Knights La CW6 ... 123 E3
Knights Mdw CW7 ... 126 C3
Knight St SK11 ... 112 E7
Knights Way CW2 ... 206 B3
Knightwake Rd SK22 ... 39 A4
Knole Ave SK12 ... 36 F4
KNOLLS GREEN ... 58 E3
Knoll St SK22 ... 39 B8
Knoll The WA7 ... 49 F7
KNOTBURY ... 159 F2
Knottingley Dr CH66 ... 69 C5
Knott's Hos WA7 ... 4 B8
Knotty La CW12 ... 179 F8
Knowe The CH60 ... 41 A6
Knowle Cl CH66 ... 69 E3
Knowle Gn WA3 ... 3 A8
Knowle Pk SK9 ... 34 C3
Knowles Ind Est SK23 ... 39 D3
Knowles St **2** WA8 ... 13 C2
Knowl Hey Rd L26 ... 21 A6
Knowl La CH3 ... 180 F5
Knowl The CH3 ... 180 F5
Knowsley Ave WA3 ... 3 B8

Knowsley Ct CH2 ....118 F4
Knowsley Expressway L35,
  WA8 .... E3
Knowsley La ST7 ....194 F4
Knowsley Rd
  Chester CH2 ....118 F4
  Hazel Grove SK7 ....36 F8
  Macclesfield SK11 .....112 C5
KNUTSFORD 57 A3
Knutsford & Dist Hospl
  WA16 ....56 F1
Knutsford High Sch
  (Lower Sch) WA16 ......56 E1
Knutsford High Sch
  (Upper Sch) WA16 ......56 F1
Knutsford Old Rd WA4 ...17 A2
Knutsford Rd
  Alsager ST7 ....193 F6
  Antrobus CW9 ....53 D4
  Chelford SK11 ....84 A2
  Grappenhall WA4 ....17 C1
  Great Budworth CW9 .....54 A2
  Holmes Chapel CW4 .....130 B5
  Mobberley WA16 ....57 C4
  Row-of-Trees SK9,
    WA16 ....59 D3
  Warrington WA4 ....16 D3
Knutsford Road Wlk 12
  SK11 ....112 F7
Knutsford Sta WA16 .....57 A1
Knutsford View WA16 ....32 C8
Knutsford Way CH1 .....117 F2
Kohima Cres CH3 ....142 B5
Kronsbec Ave CH66 .....69 D6
KUS Ind Est CH5 ....139 A6
Kynaston Dr CH4 ....140 C7

L

Laburnum Ave
  Crewe CW2 ....189 F2
  2 Nantwich CW5 ....204 F5
  Warrington WA1 ....17 C7
Laburnum Cl
  Congleton CW12 ....156 A4
  Talke ST7 ....210 E8
Laburnum Cres CW8 .....78 B3
Laburnum Ct
  Lymm WA13 ....19 B4
  Wistaston CW2 ....205 F7
Laburnum Farm Cl
  CH64 ....67 A5
Laburnum Gr
  Crewe CW1 ....190 D6
  Ellesmere Port CH66 ...95 A8
  Runcorn WA7 ....49 C7
  Saltney CH4 ....140 E6
  Weaverham CW8 ....102 D8
Laburnum La
  Altrincham WA15 ....31 E8
  Warrington WA5 ....14 C5
Laburnum Pl ST5 ....210 D1
Laburnum Rd
  Davenham CW9 ....103 F3
  Golborne WA3 ....3 F7
  Irlam M44 ....11 D5
  Macclesfield SK11 ....112 E5
  Northwich CW9 ....104 C6
Laburnum Way LL13 ....180 D1
Lacey Ave SK9 ....34 B1
Lacey Ct
  Handforth SK9 ....34 B1
  Widnes WA8 ....23 B7
Lacey Gn SK9 ....34 B1
Lacey Gr SK9 ....34 C1
LACEY GREEN 34 B1
Lacey Green Prim Sch
  SK9 ....34 B1
Lacey St WA8 ....23 A7
LACH DENNIS 105 D5
LACHE 140 F5
Lache Hall Cres CH4 ...140 F4
Lache La
  Chester, Westminster Park
    CH4 ....141 B5
  Roughhill CH4 ....140 E3
Lache Park Ave CH4 ....141 A6
Lache Prim Sch CH4 ....141 A5
Lacy Ct CW12 ....156 F2
Ladies Mile WA16 ....56 F2
Ladies Wlk CH64 ....66 E8
Lady Acre CW13 ....18 D2
Ladybarn Ave WA3 ....2 F7
Ladybarn Cres SK7 .....35 F6
Ladybarn Manor SK7 ....35 E8
Ladybrook Gr 6 SK9 ....34 D2
Ladybrook Prim Sch
  SK7 ....35 F7
Ladycroft Cl WA1 ....17 E2
Ladyfield St SK9 ....60 B7
Ladyfield Terr SK9 .....60 C7
Lady Helen Wlk CW5 ...204 E6
Lady Heyes Craft &
  Antique Restoration
  Ctr* WA6 ....74 F4
Lady La
  Croft WA3 ....9 C8
  Culcheth WA3 ....4 C1
  Mobberley WA16 ....58 C6
Lady Mary's Sq WA16 ...30 E3
Ladypit Rd SK23 ....39 E4
Ladypool L24 ....21 C2
Lady Richeld Cl WA7 ...24 D3
Ladys Cl SK12 ....36 E4
Ladythorn Cres SK7 ....35 F6
Ladythorn Gr SK7 ......35 F6
Ladythorn Rd SK7 ......35 E6

Ladywood Rd WA5 ....7 D1
Lagos Gr CW7 ....126 E2
Laidon Ave CW2 ....206 A7
Laira Ct WA3 ....16 C2
Laira St WA2 ....16 C7
Lake House Cl CW8 .....77 D1
Lake La WA4 ....52 F5
Lakelands Cl SK10 ....112 F7
Lakemore Ctry Pk*
  CW1 ....174 C1
Lakeside
  Bosley SK11 ....158 D8
  Chester CH4 ....141 B2
Lakeside Cl
  Chester CH2 ....118 F7
  Widnes WA8 ....22 A8
Lakeside Cvn Pk CW7 ..149 F7
Lakeside Dr
  Poynton SK12 ....36 E5
  Warrington WA1 ....16 A3
Lakeside Rd WA13 ......18 D2
Lakeside View
  Moulton CW7 ....126 F7
  Nantwich CW5 ....204 E3
Lake View
  Alsager ST7 ....193 C2
  Congleton CW12 ....156 B2
  Furness Vale SK23 .....39 D4
Lakewood CH4 ....141 B2
Laleston Cl WA8 ....22 E8
Lamb Cottage Cvn Pk
  CW8 ....125 C7
Lambert Cres CW5 .....204 C6
Lambert's La CW12 ....156 E1
Lambert Way CW8 .....103 A4
Lamb La WA14 ....31 D4
Lambourn Ave WA8 .....12 C5
Lambourn Cl SK12 .....36 D4
Lambourn Dr CW1 .....173 B1
Lambourne Cl
  4 Ellesmere Port
    CH66 ....94 F8
  Wythenshawe M22 ......33 D8
Lambourne Gr
  1 Middlewich CW10 ...128 C1
  St Helens WA9 ....1 A4
Lambs House Sch
  CW12 ....156 F4
Lambsickle Cl WA7 .....48 F6
Lambsickle La WA7 .....49 A6
Lambs La
  Warrington, Padgate
    WA1 ....17 A8
  Warrington WA1 ....17 A7
Lamb St ST7 ....195 A2
Lamerton Cl WA5 ....14 D4
Lamerton Way SK9 .....34 E2
Lampeter Cl WA3 ....7 E2
Lampits La CH3 ....120 E6
Lamport Cl WA8 ....13 E3
Lanark Gdns WA8 ......12 E3
Lanark Wlk SK10 ......86 F2
Lancashire Rd M31 ....11 E2
Lancaster Ave
  Golborne WA3 ....3 C8
  Runcorn WA7 ....48 E8
  Widnes WA8 ....12 A2
Lancaster Cl
  Hazel Grove SK7 ....36 D8
  Newton-le-W WA12 ......1 F4
  Warrington WA2 ....8 F2
  Winsford CW7 ....126 D2
Lancaster Ct 3 WA4 ....16 E1
Lancaster Dr CH3 .....119 B2
Lancaster Fields CW1 .191 A2
Lancaster Gdns CH66 ...70 D3
Lancaster Pk CH4 .....139 A3
Lancaster Rd
  Handforth SK9 ....34 E1
  Irlam M44 ....11 D5
  Widnes WA8 ....13 B3
Lancaster St WA5 ......15 E5
Lanceley Ct SY14 .....213 B3
Lancelyn Dr SK9 ......60 D8
Lancer Cl WA7 ....23 E3
Lancers Croft CH66 ...69 E1
Lancing Ave WA2 ....8 A4
Lancing Rd CH65 ......70 D4
Land Cut La WA3 ....9 D3
Lander Cl WA5 ....15 D7
Land La SK9 ....60 C6
Landor Cl WA3 ....3 E8
Landscape Dr WA6 .....73 D4
Landseer Ave
  Neston CH64 ....66 F7
  Warrington WA4 ....16 B2
Landswood Cl SK10 ...111 E8
Landswood Pk CW8 ....103 B4
LANE ENDS 173 D3
Lane Ends WA8 ....21 D5
LANE HEAD 3 E6
Lane Head Ave WA3 .....3 F8
Lanehead Rd SK23 .....65 C5
Laneside Rd SK22 .....39 E7
Lane The SY13, SY14 ..223 C3
Langcliffe Cl WA3 .....3 E4
Langdale Ave WA13 ....18 F4
Langdale Cl
  High Lane SK6 ....37 D8
  Macclesfield SK11 ....111 F5
  Warrington WA3 ....9 B8
  Widnes WA8 ....22 C8
Langdale Ct CW12 ....156 A1
Langdale Rd
  Bramhall SK7 ....35 C5
  Crewe CW2 ....189 D2
  Partington M31 ....11 E3

Langdale Rd continued
  Runcorn WA7 ....23 B1
Langdale Way WA6 .....49 C1
Langden Ho CH4 ......141 B7
Langfield WA3 ....3 E7
Langfield Gr CH62 .....43 A5
Langford L24 ....21 C2
Langford Ct CH3 .....121 C2
Langford Rd CW9 ......80 A3
Langford St 4 SK11 ..112 C8
Langford Way WA4 .....27 D4
Langland Cl WA5 ....7 E2
LANGLEY 113 C3
Langley Ave WA12 ......2 C1
Langley Cl
  Newcastle-u-Lyme
    ST5 ....210 D2
  Sandbach CW11 ......175 C8
Langley Ct CH65 ......70 E3
Langley Dr
  Crewe CW2 ....190 A2
  Handforth SK9 ....34 E3
  Macclesfield SK11 ....112 B4
Langley Hall Cl SK11 .113 B4
Langley Hall Cotts
  SK11 ....113 B4
Langley Rd
  Langley SK11 ....113 A3
  Northwich CW9 ....104 A6
Langport Dr CH3 .....119 C2
Langton Cl
  Newton-le-W WA12 .....2 A4
  Widnes WA8 ....13 F3
Langwell Cl WA3 ......10 A5
Lanreath Cl SK10 .....86 D1
Lansdowne
  Culcheth WA3 ....4 E2
  Frodsham WA6 ....74 D6
Lansdowne Gr CW4 ....141 A7
Lansdowne Rd
  Connah's Quay CH5 ....91 D1
  Crewe CW2 ....190 F5
  Great Barrow CH3 ....120 D3
Lansdowne St CH66 ....87 E1
Lansdown Rd CH4 .....139 B4
Lanyard Way CW11 ....175 C3
Lapwing Cl
  Golborne WA3 ....3 D8
  Newton-le-W WA12 .....2 C3
  Packmoor ST7 ....195 E1
  Winsford CW7 ....149 C5
Lapwing Gr WA7 ....50 A6
Lapwing La
  Moore WA4 ....25 A8
  Whisterfield SK11 ...109 C4
  Whisterfield SK11 ...109 C6
Lapwing Rd ST7 ......195 D3
Lapwing Rise CH60 ....40 F6
Larch Ave
  Hough CW2 ....206 F5
  Macclesfield SK11 ....112 A5
  Newton-le-W WA12 .....2 C1
  Warrington WA5 ....14 E5
  Widnes WA8 ....13 B2
Larch Cl
  Golborne WA3 ....3 F8
  Poynton SK12 ....36 F3
  Runcorn WA7 ....49 C7
  Weaverham CW8 ....102 D7
Larchdale Cl CH66 ....94 F8
Larches The WA16 .....58 E2
Larchfields CH1 .....117 A8
Larch Rd
  Crewe CW1 ....189 E2
  Haydock WA11 ....1 E7
  Partington M31 ....11 E3
  Runcorn WA7 ....49 C7
Larch Rise SK10 .....86 D6
Larchtree Cl CW8 ....78 B4
Larchway
  Bramhall SK7 ....35 C7
  High Lane SK6 ....37 F7
Larch Way CH4 ....140 E6
Larchways WA4 ....26 D5
Larchwood Dr SK9 ....60 E8
LARDEN GREEN 202 D4
Lark Ave ST7 ....195 D3
Larkfield WA4 ....17 A7
Lark Hall Cl SK10 ...113 A7
Lark Hall Cres SK10 .113 A8
Lark Hall Rd SK10 ...113 A7
Lark Hill Cotts SK22 ..39 A8
Larkspur Cl
  Chester CH4 ....140 F4
  Nantwich CW5 ....204 E8
  Runcorn WA7 ....49 F4
Larkspur Gr WA5 .....15 E3
Larkstoke Cl WA4 ....26 E6
Larksway CH60 ....41 B8
Larkwood Way SK10 ...87 E5
Larne Cl WA4 ....12 E2
Larne Dr CH4 ....139 C4
Laskey La WA4 ....17 E4
LATCHFORD 16 C3
Latchford CE Prim Sch
  WA4 ....16 B4
Latchford Rd CH60 ...41 B6
Latchford St WA4 ....16 B3
Latham Ave
  Helsby WA6 ....73 B1
  Newton-le-W WA12 ....2 C4
  Runcorn WA7 ....23 B1
Latham Ho WA12 ....2 B4

Latham Rd CW11 ......175 A5
Latham St CW7 ....126 C1
Lathom Ave WA2 ......16 B8
Lathom Dr WA11 ......11 F8
Lathom Way SK10 .....87 F2
Latimer Dr CW2 .....190 A4
Launceston Cl
  Runcorn WA7 ....50 C6
  Winsford CW7 ....149 B7
Launceston Dr
  Bramhall SK7 ....35 F7
  Warrington WA5 ......14 E3
Laura St CW7 ....190 D1
Laurel Ave
  Newton-le-W WA12 ....2 D3
  Warrington WA1 ......17 D7
Laurel Bank
  Warrington WA4 ......17 C1
  Widnes WA8 ....13 A3
  Winsford CW7 ....149 D8
Laurel Cl
  Barnton CW8 ....78 A4
  Middlewich CW10 ....128 B2
  Sandbach CW11 ......175 C5
Laurel Dr
  Crewe CW2 ....189 F2
  Ellesmere Port CH65 .70 B2
  Harriseahead ST7 ...195 E4
  Willaston CH64 ......43 B1
Laurel Gr
  Chester CH2 ....119 A3
  Golborne WA3 ....3 D8
Laurel Pk CW6 ......145 A6
Laurels Farm Ct CH2 .72 B3
Laurels The
  High Lane SK6 ....37 E8
  Milton Green CH3 ...165 C2
Laurel Way SK8 ......35 C8
Laurel Wlk M31 ......11 E2
Laurelwood Dr 4
  CH66 ....69 E1
Laureston Ave CW1 ..190 F4
Lavender Cl WA7 .....23 C1
Lavender Dr CW9 ....104 E7
Lavender Gdns WA9 ...6 A7
Lavender Wlk M31 ....11 E2
Lavenham Cl
  Hazel Grove SK7 .....36 E8
  Macclesfield SK10 ...87 C2
Lavenham Gr
LAVISTER 162 C1
Lavister Ct 6 CW9 ..103 F4
Lavister Wlks LL12 .162 C1
Lawford Cl CW1 .....189 F8
Lawford Dr CH60 ....41 C8
Lawn Ave WA5 ....16 F8
Lawn Cl CH2 ....118 D7
Lawns Ave CH63 .....43 B6
Lawnsdale CW8 .....101 D5
Lawns The WA4 ......59 E4
Lawnswood Gr CH2 ..72 B3
Lawrence Ave
  3 Middlewich CW10 .128 C1
  Moulton CW9 ....126 E8
Lawrence Ave E 2
  CW10 ....128 C1
Lawrence Cl
  Cranage CW4 ....130 A5
  3 Sandbach CW11 ..174 D6
Lawrence Pl SK12 ...36 D2
Lawrence St
  Crewe CW1 ....190 C4
  Sandycroft CH5 ....116 A3
Laws Gdns CH3 .....142 A8
Lawson Cl WA1 ......17 E7
Law St CH2 ....118 F3
Lawton Ave
  Bramhall SK7 ....35 E8
  Lawton-gate ST7 ...194 D3
Lawton Cl WA3 ....4 E3
Lawton Coppice ST7 .194 E4
LAWTON-GATE 194 A4
Lawtongate Est ST7 .194 A5
Lawton Hall ST7 ...194 C4
Lawton Hall Dr ST7 .194 C4
LAWTON HEATH 193 E6
LAWTON HEATH END
  ....193 E6
Lawton Heath Rd ST7 193 F5
Lawton Rd ST7 ....193 E4
Lawton St
  Congleton CW12 ....156 E2
  Crewe CW2 ....190 C3
  Kidsgrove ST7 .....195 C4
Lawton Way CW11 ...174 E7
Laxey Ave WA1 ......17 D6
Laxton Cl CH66 .....94 F8
Laxton Way CW10 ...128 C2
Layland Ave WA3 ....4 E4
Layton Cl WA3 ......9 E3
Lea Ave
  Crewe CW1 ....190 F4
  Goostrey CW4 ......107 C1
Lea Bank Cl SK11 ..112 A8
Lea Cl CW11 ....175 C5
Leacroft Rd WA3 ...10 A7
Lea Cross Gr WA8 ..12 C3
Leadbeaters Cl SK11 112 F7
Leadbeaters Rd SK11 112 F7
Leadgate La CH3 ...144 F2
Lea Dr
  Nantwich CW5 .....204 C4
  Wimboldsley CW10 .151 A4
Leadsmithy St CW10 .128 C1
Leadworks La CH1 ..237 C3
Leaf Gr CW7 ......126 B1
Leafield Dr SK8 ...34 F6
Leafield Rd SK12 ..38 C6
Leaf La CW7 ......127 A2

Leaf Lane Inf Sch
  CW7 ....127 A2
Leafy Way CW8 ....102 D7
LEA GREEN 172 A8
Lea Hall Barns CW5 .220 E6
Lea Hall Pk CH1 ...95 A3
Lea Homes CW5 ....217 B7
Leahurst Cl CH2 ..118 F4
Lea La CH3 ....164 C3
Leamington Ave WA12 .2 C1
Leamington Cl
  Neston CH64 ....66 E6
  Warrington WA5 ....15 A8
Leamington Rd
  Congleton CW12 ...155 F3
  Macclesfield SK10 ..86 F1
Lear Dr CW2 ......205 F8
Leas Cl 3 CH66 ....69 C5
Leaside WA7 ......23 D1
Leaside Rd CH1 ...117 E6
Leaside Way WA5 ..60 C6
Lea's Pas CW10 ...128 B1
Lea St SK22 ......39 A8
Leatham Cl WA3 ....9 E3
Leathers La L26 ...21 A7
Lea Way ST7 .....193 D3
Leawood Cl CW8 ..103 A6
Ledbury Dr CW2 ..206 A7
Ledge Ley SK8 ....34 E8
Ledger Rd WA11 ....1 A5
Ledley St CH4 ....87 F7
LEDSHAM 68 F2
Ledsham Cl WA3 ....9 C3
Ledsham Ct CH66 ..69 B6
Ledsham Hall La CH66 68 E4
Ledsham La CH66 ..68 F3
Ledsham Park Dr
  CH66 ....69 A6
Ledsham Rd CH66 ..69 B6
Ledsham Village CH66 68 F2
Ledston Cl WA7 ...24 D1
Ledward St CW7 ..127 A1
Ledyard Cl WA5 ..15 D7
Leech Rd SY14 ...213 B3
Lee Cl WA16 ......56 F1
Lee Ct
  Runcorn WA7 ....23 D2
  Warrington WA2 ....8 C2
Lee Dr CW8 ......103 E7
Lee Green La CW5 .150 A1
Leek Old Rd SK11 .112 E2
Leek Rd CW12 ....179 A8
Leen La CH1 .....237 B2
Lee Rd WA5 ......15 B6
Lees La
  Ellesmere Port CH65 70 E4
  Mottram St Andrew
    SK10 ....61 B7
  Neston CH64 ....67 A7
Lees Mill 4 SK22 ..39 C7
Lees Rd SK7 ......35 D5
Lees The WA5 ....15 A8
LEFTWICH 104 B5
Leftwich Com Prim Sch
  CW9 ....104 A4
Leftwich Warehouse
  CW9 ....103 F7
Legh Cl SK12 ....36 E4
Legh Ct
  Golborne WA3 ......3 A8
  Knutsford WA16 ...57 D4
Legh Gdns WA16 ..57 B1
Legh Ho 3 WA16 ..57 B1
Legh Rd
  Adlington SK10 ...62 C5
  Haydock WA11 ......1 B6
  High Lane SK12 ...38 A6
  Knutsford WA16 ...82 B8
  Prestbury SK10 ...87 A8
Legh St
  Golborne WA3 ......3 A8
  3 Lymm WA13 .....18 E3
  Newton-le-W WA12 .2 A3
  Warrington WA1 ...16 A5
Legh Vale Prim Sch
  WA11 ....1 B6
Leicester Ave ST7 193 D5
Leicester St
  Northwich CW9 ....79 A1
  Warrington WA5 ...15 F5
Leigh Ave
  Knutsford WA16 ...57 C3
  Widnes WA8 ....13 A1
Leigh Green Cl 4
  WA8 ....22 C8
Leigh La CW8 .....77 C5
Leigh Rd
  Congleton CW12 ..157 B5
  Wilmslow SK9 .....59 D5
Leigh's Brow CW8 .77 F3
Leigh St SK11 ...112 E8
Leighstone Ct CH2 237 A4
Leighton Chase CH64 41 D1
Leighton Cotts CH64 41 D5
Leighton Ct CH64 .66 D8
Leighton Dr WN7 ..4 B8
Leighton Hospl CW1 172 E1
Leighton Pk CH64 .66 D8
Leighton Prim Sch
  CW1 ....190 A7
Leighton Rd CH64 .41 D2
Leighton St 11 CW1 190 B5
Leightons The CH64 66 D8
Leighton View CW1 190 A8
Leigh Way CW8 ...77 C1

Leinster Gdns WA7 . . . . . . .22 F3
Leinster St WA7 . . . . .22 F1
Leiria Way WA7 . . . . .23 B2
Lenham Wlk M22 . . . . .33 D8
Lenthall Ave CW12 . . . . . . .178 F8
Leonard St
 Chester CH1 . . . . .118 B3
 Runcorn WA7 . . . . .48 D7
 Warrington, Stockton Heath
 WA4 . . . . .16 C1
 Warrington WA2 . . . . .16 C7
Leon Cl WA5 . . . . .14 D7
Leslie Rd CW7 . . . . .149 A7
Lessingham Rd WA8 . . . . . . .12 F3
Lester Cl ST7 . . . . .193 D4
Leven Ave CW7 . . . . .126 F2
Levens Cl WA5 . . . . .15 F6
Levens Way 1 WA8 . . . . . . .22 C8
Leven Wlk CH66 . . . . .70 A7
Leveret Rd L24 . . . . .21 A3
Levisham Gdns WA5 . . . . . . .15 E7
Lewin St CW10 . . . . .128 C1
Lewis Ave WA5 . . . . .7 F2
Lewis Cl
 Ellesmere Port CH65 . . . . . . .95 C8
 Nantwich CW5 . . . . .205 A5
Lewis Cres WA4 . . . . .23 A7
Lewis Gr WA8 . . . . .12 D1
Lewis St CW1 . . . . .190 C3
Lexden St WA5 . . . . .15 E6
Lexington Wlk 2 WA5 . . . . . .15 C7
Leycester Cl WA16 . . . . .82 C8
Leycester Dr WA16 . . . . .57 F7
Leycester Rd WA16 . . . . .82 B8
Leyfield Ct CH4 . . . . .140 F5
Leyland Dr CH4 . . . . .140 C6
Leyland Gr
 Haslington CW1 . . . . .191 C4
 Haydock WA11 . . . . .1 B6
Leyland Wlk CW7 . . . . .149 C6
Leyton St WA7 . . . . .49 B6
Libris Ho 1 WA16 . . . . .57 A1
Libris Pk 2 WA16 . . . . .57 A1
Libris Pl 3 WA16 . . . . .57 A1
Libson Cl WA2 . . . . .9 A3
Lichfield Ave
 Golborne WA3 . . . . .3 D8
 Grappenhall Heys WA4 . . . . . .27 A7
Lichfield Cl WA16 . . . . .57 D2
Lichfield Ct CW7 . . . . .149 D7
Lichfield Dr CH66 . . . . .94 E8
Lichfield Rd
 Blacon CH1 . . . . .117 F5
 Talke ST7 . . . . .210 D7
Lichfield St CW10 . . . . .128 D2
Lidgetts La SK10 . . . . .88 C3
Lift La CW9 . . . . .78 D3
Light Alders La SK12 . . . . . . .38 A6
Lightburn St 4 WA7 . . . . . . .22 F1
Lightfoot Cl CH60 . . . . .41 B7
Lightfoot La
 Eaton CW6 . . . . .147 A4
 Heswall CH60 . . . . .41 B7
Lightfoot St CH2 . . . . .118 F2
Lighthouse Rd L24 . . . . .47 E7
Lightley Cl CW11 . . . . .175 A4
Lightley Ct CW11 . . . . .175 A4
Light Oaks Rd WA3 . . . . .5 C6
LIGHTWOOD GREEN 229 B3
Lightwood Green Ave
 CW3 . . . . .229 A2
Lightwood Rd ST5 . . . . .210 D1
Lilac Ave
 Knutsford WA16 . . . . .56 L1
 Warrington WA5 . . . . .15 A5
 Widnes WA8 . . . . .13 E2
Lilac Cl
 Kelsall CW6 . . . . .122 E2
 Newcastle-u-Lyme ST5 . . . . .210 D1
Lilac Cres WA7 . . . . .49 C8
Lilac Ct CW12 . . . . .156 E2
Lilac Dr CW8 . . . . .103 D6
Lilac Gr
 Ellesmere Port CH66 . . . . . . .95 A8
 Warrington WA4 . . . . .16 E1
Lilac Wlk M31 . . . . .11 E3
Lilford Ave WA5 . . . . .15 F8
Lilford Dr WA5 . . . . .15 A8
Lilford La SK11 . . . . .112 D5
Lilford St WA5 . . . . .15 F7
Lillyfield CH60 . . . . .40 F6
Lily Ave WA12 . . . . .2 D2
Lilybrook Dr WA16 . . . . .57 B1
Lily La CW10 . . . . .129 B6
Limbrick Rd ST7 . . . . .209 A1
Lime Ave
 Frodsham WA6 . . . . .74 C8
 Northwich CW9 . . . . .103 F5
 Weaverham CW8 . . . . .102 D8
 3 Widnes WA8 . . . . .13 B2
Lime Cl
 Hollinfare WA3 . . . . .11 A2
 Middlewich CW10 . . . . .128 B2
 Sandbach CW11 . . . . .175 A4
 Tarporley CW6 . . . . .146 D2
Lime Ct
 Leftwich CW9 . . . . .104 A5
 Northwich CW9 . . . . .103 F5
Limefield Ave WA13 . . . . . . .18 F2
Lime Gr
 Alsager ST7 . . . . .193 E2
 Chester CH2 . . . . .119 A3
 Elton CH2 . . . . .72 A3
 Golborne WA3 . . . . .3 E8
 Macclesfield SK10 . . . . .112 E8

Lime Gr continued
 Runcorn WA7 . . . . .49 C8
 Saltney CH4 . . . . .140 D6
Stavington LW2 . . . . .206 C4
 Winsford CW7 . . . . .177 A1
Limehurst Gr CH62 . . . . .43 D6
Limekiln La WA5 . . . . .6 E3
Lime Kiln La ST7 . . . . .194 E2
Limekiln Row WA7 . . . . .50 A8
Limerick Cl WA8 . . . . .12 E3
Limes Cl CW1 . . . . .191 C4
Limes La WA4 . . . . .52 D6
Lime St
 Congleton CW12 . . . . .156 D2
 Crewe CW1 . . . . .190 C6
 Ellesmere Port CH65 . . . . . . .70 C7
Limes The
 Culcheth WA3 . . . . .4 D4
 Golborne WA3 . . . . .3 D6
 Middlewich CW10 . . . . .128 B1
Limetree Ave
 Warrington, Stockton Heath
 WA4 . . . . .16 L1
 Warrington WA1 . . . . .17 A8
Lime Tree Ave
 Congleton CW12 . . . . .156 B3
 Crewe CW1 . . . . .190 E6
Lime Tree Cl
 Ellesmere Port CH66 . . . . . . .95 A8
 Winsford CW7 . . . . .149 C8
Lime Tree Dr CH3 . . . . .180 F1
Lime Tree Gr CH60 . . . . .41 C8
Lime Tree La WA16 . . . . .29 D6
Limeways WA4 . . . . .26 E5
Lime Wlk
 6 Handforth SK9 . . . . .34 D1
 Partington M31 . . . . .11 D3
Lime Wood Cl CH3 . . . . .118 F4
Limewood Cres CW8 . . . . . . .78 B4
Limewood Gr CW8 . . . . .78 B4
Linacre La WA8 . . . . .12 E5
Lincoln Ave
 Gatley SK8 . . . . .34 B7
 Irlam M44 . . . . .11 C4
Lincoln Cl
 Golborne WN7 . . . . .4 C8
 Macclesfield SK10 . . . . .86 F2
 Rainow SK10 . . . . .88 E5
 Runcorn WA7 . . . . .49 C6
 Warrington WA1 . . . . .17 E6
Lincoln Ct
 Helsby WA6 . . . . .73 B3
 5 Warrington WA5 . . . . . . .15 B7
Lincoln Dr CH2 . . . . .119 A5
Lincoln Ho 12 CH1 . . . . . . .237 C3
Lincoln Pl SK10 . . . . .86 F2
Lincoln Rd
 Blacon CH1 . . . . .117 F5
 Ellesmere Port CH66 . . . . . . .69 D3
 Handforth SK9 . . . . .34 E1
 Kidsgrove ST7 . . . . .194 F2
Lincoln Sq WA8 . . . . .13 B2
Lincoln St 3 CW1 . . . . .190 B5
Lincoln Wlk SK10 . . . . .86 F2
Lincombe Hey SK10 . . . . .87 C8
Lincombe Rd M22 . . . . .33 D8
Lindale Cl CW12 . . . . .157 A5
Linden Ct
 Congleton CW12 . . . . .179 A8
 Ellesmere Port CH66 . . . . . . .94 F8
 Lymm WA13 . . . . .19 A4
 Warrington WA1 . . . . .17 D7
Linden Ct
 Macclesfield SK10 . . . . .87 B2
 Sandbach CW11 . . . . .174 F3
 Widnes WA8 . . . . .12 F4
Linden Dr
 Biddulph ST8 . . . . .179 C1
 Crewe CW1 . . . . .190 F4
 Helsby WA6 . . . . .73 B1
 Mickle Trafford CH2 . . . . . . .96 F1
Linden Gr
 Biddulph ST8 . . . . .179 C1
 Bramhall SK7 . . . . .35 D4
 Chester CH2 . . . . .119 A4
 Saltney CH4 . . . . .140 D6
Linden Way
 High Lane SK6 . . . . .38 A7
 Widnes WA8 . . . . .12 F4
Lindfield Cl WA4 . . . . .25 A5
Lindfield Est N SK9 . . . . .60 A6
Lindfield Est S SK9 . . . . .59 F6
Lindfields CH4 . . . . .140 F5
Lindi Ave WA4 . . . . .17 C2
Lindisfarne Ave
 Ellesmere Port CH65 . . . . . . .70 C2
 Golborne WA3 . . . . .4 C8
Lindisfarne Cl CW10 . . . . . .128 B1
Lindisfarne Ct WA8 . . . . .12 F4
Lindisfarne Dr SK12 . . . . . . .36 D4
Lindley Ave WA4 . . . . .16 F4
Lindop Cl WA16 . . . . .57 C2
Lindow Com Prim Sch
 SK9 .59 D3
Lindow Court Pk WA16 . . . . .59 B5
Lindow Ct SK9 . . . . .59 E8
LINDOW END 59 D5
Lindow Fold Dr SK9 . . . . . . .59 D5
Lindow La SK9 . . . . .59 E6
Lindow Par SK9 . . . . .59 F6
Lindrick Cl SK10 . . . . .87 C4
Lindrum Ave SK11 . . . . .112 D2
Lindsay Way ST7 . . . . .193 A4
Lindsay Wlk CW8 . . . . .102 A4
Lindsworth Cl WA5 . . . . .15 C6
Linear View WA12 . . . . .2 C1
Linen Hall Pl CH1 . . . . .237 A2
Lines Rd M44 . . . . .11 F8

Lingdale Wlk SK11 . . . . . . .112 D5
Lingfield Cl SK10 . . . . .87 C4
Lingfield Dr CW1 . . . . .190 C7
Lingfield Ho WA7 . . . . .48 E8
Lingfield Rd WA7 . . . . .22 F1
LINGLEY GREEN 14 C7
Lingley Green Ave
 WA5 . . . . .14 D8
Lingley Rd WA5 . . . . .14 D6
Linglongs Ave SK23 . . . . . . .65 C5
Linglongs Rd SK73 . . . . .65 C5
Lingmell Gdns CW4 . . . . . . .129 F3
Lingwell Ave WA8 . . . . .12 D2
Lingwell Pk WA8 . . . . .12 E2
Lingwood Rd WA5 . . . . .14 F6
Links Ave CH66 . . . . .69 C7
Links Cl CH63 . . . . .43 B6
Linkside Ave WA2 . . . . .8 B6
Linkside Way CH66 . . . . .94 F8
Links Rd SK9 . . . . .59 E4
Links Way CH66 . . . . .69 C7
Linksway
 Chester CH2 . . . . .118 C7
 Congleton CW12 . . . . .178 E8
Linksway Cl CW12 . . . . .178 F8
Link The SK9 . . . . .34 D3
Linkway WA7 . . . . .49 B6
Link Wlk M31 . . . . .11 D2
Linley Gr ST7 . . . . .193 F3
Linley La ST7 . . . . .194 A2
Linley Rd
 Alsager ST7 . . . . .193 F2
 Cheadle SK8 . . . . .35 B8
 Talke ST7 . . . . .210 C8
Linley Trad Est ST7 . . . . . . .194 C1
Linnards La CW9, WA16 . . . .80 B5
Linnet Cl
 Newton-le-W WA12 . . . . .2 C3
 Warrington WA2 . . . . .8 D3
 Winsford CW7 . . . . .150 B8
Linnet Gr
 Macclesfield SK10 . . . . .87 A1
 Warrington WA3 . . . . .9 E4
Linnet's Way WA7 . . . . .23 C2
Linnets Way CH60 . . . . .40 E8
Linnett Cl CW1 . . . . .190 A7
Linnett Gr ST7 . . . . .195 E1
Linton Ct CW7 . . . . .127 A3
Linum Gdns WA9 . . . . .6 B7
Linwood CW7 . . . . .150 B8
Linwood Cl WA7 . . . . .50 C5
Lion Salt Works Mus *
 WA9 . . . . .79 C3
Lip Car St CW10 . . . . .156 D2
Liskeard Cl WA7 . . . . .50 B6
Liskeard Dr SK7 . . . . .35 F7
Lismore Wlk M22 . . . . .33 E8
Lister Cl CW10 . . . . .151 D6
Lister Rd WA7 . . . . .23 D2
Little Abbey Gateway
 CH1 . . . . .237 A3
Little Aston Cl SK10 . . . . .87 C4
Little Bollington 20 B2
Little Bollington CE Prim
 Sch WA14 . . . . .20 B2
Littlebourne WA7 . . . . .50 E7
LITTLE BUDWORTH 147 F8
Little Budworth Ctry Pk *
Littlecote Gdns WA4 . . . . . . .26 D4
Littledale Rd WA5 . . . . .14 F7
Littledales La CW8 . . . . .102 E4
Little Delph WA11 . . . . .1 F7
Littlegate WA7 . . . . .49 E8
Little Gn CH66 . . . . .69 D3
LITTLE HEATH 230 A5
Little Heath Cl CW3 . . . . . . .230 A5
Little Heath La WA14 . . . . . . .20 D5
Little Heath Rd
 Chester CH3 . . . . .119 E1
 Christleton CH3 . . . . .142 E8
Little La CH64 . . . . .41 C1
Little Lakes CW2 . . . . .207 D2
LITTLE LEIGH 77 A2
Little Leigh Prim Sch
 CW8 . . . . .77 D5
Little Meadow Cl SK10 . . . . . .87 B7
Little Mere CH3 . . . . .142 E8
Little Moreton Hall *
 CW12 . . . . .177 E2
LITTLE-MOSS 194 E6
Little Moss Cl ST7 . . . . .194 E5
Little Moss La ST7 . . . . .194 E5
LITTLE NESTON 66 D6
LITTLER 126 A2
Little Rake La CH2 . . . . .95 D5
Littler Grange Ct
 CW7 . . . . .126 A1
Littler La CW7 . . . . .125 F1
Little Roodee CH1 . . . . .139 B7
Little Row 6 ST7 . . . . .195 B2
Littler Rd WA11 . . . . .1 F6
Little St John St CH1 . . . . . .237 B2
Little St
 Congleton CW12 . . . . .156 D2
 4 Macclesfield SK10 . . . . . .112 D8
LITTLE STANNEY 70 E1
Little Stanney La CW2 . . . . . .95 F8
Littlestone Cl WA8 . . . . .13 A4
LITTLE SUTTON 69 B5
Little Sutton CE Prim Sch
 CH66 . . . . .69 A6
Little Sutton Sta CH66 . . . . . .69 B6
LITTLETON 119 E1
Littleton Cl
 1 Northwich CW9 . . . . .103 F4

Littleton Cl continued
 Warrington WA5 . . . . .15 D4
Littleton La CH3 . . . . .119 E2
LITTLE TOWN 4 L1
Little Wissage CH66 . . . . . .69 E7
Littondale Cl CW12 . . . . . . .157 A5
Liverpool Pl WA8 . . . . .12 C1
Liverpool Rd
 Backford CH1, CH2 . . . . .95 B4
 Chester CH2 . . . . .118 C6
 Haydock, Stanley Bank
 WA11 . . . . .1 A7
 Haydock WA11 . . . . .1 B8
 Irlam, Cadishead M44 . . . . . .11 D4
 Kidsgrove ST7 . . . . .195 A1
 Neston CH64 . . . . .41 F1
 Newcastle-u-Lyme ST5 . . . .210 D2
 Warrington, Great Sankey
 WA5 . . . . .14 E6
 Warrington, Penketh
 WA5 . . . . .15 B4
 Warrington WA5, WA1 . . . . . .15 F5
 Widnes WA8 . . . . .12 C1
Liverpool Rd E ST7 . . . . . . .194 E2
Liverpool Rd W ST7 . . . . . . .194 B4
Liverpool Row WA12 . . . . .7 D8
Liverpool St CW9 . . . . .104 C8
Livingstone Cl
 Macclesfield SK10 . . . . .111 F8
 Warrington WA5 . . . . .15 D7
Livingstone Rd CH65 . . . . . . .70 C7
Livingstone Way
 CW10 . . . . .151 D6
Liz Kaye Ho SK11 . . . . .112 E7
Llandaff Cl CH66 . . . . .69 E1
Llandovery Cl CW7 . . . . .149 B7
Lloyd Cl CH3 . . . . .180 E2
Lloyd Cres WA12 . . . . .1 F3
Lloyd Dr CH65 . . . . .70 D1
Lloyd Pl CH1 . . . . .117 E4
Lloyd La CH1 . . . . .162 B1
Llys Bernsdale/Bernsdale
 Ct CH5 . . . . .116 A3
Llys Cadnant/Cadnant Ct
 CH4 . . . . .139 D5
Llys Caer CH4 . . . . .139 A3
Llys Catrin/Catherine Ct
 CH5 . . . . .139 B6
Llys Derwen CH4 . . . . .161 A8
Llys Maes Y Ffynnon /
 Springfield Ct CH4 . . . . . . .161 A8
Llys Perenna/Perenna Ct
 CH6 . . . . .91 B2
Llys Rhuddlan/Rhuddlan
 Cl 5 CH4 . . . . .140 F6
Llys Sant Iago/St James
 Ct CH5 . . . . .91 D1
Llys Y Faenol CH5 . . . . .139 B7
Loachbrook Ave
 CW12 . . . . .156 A2
Lobelia Gr WA7 . . . . .49 F4
Lobelia Wlk 6 M31 . . . . .11 E2
Lochinvar Ave CH66 . . . . . . .68 F6
Lochleven Rd CW2 . . . . .206 A7
Lochmaben Cl CW4 . . . . . . .130 B2
Loch St
 4 Runcorn WA7 . . . . .23 A2
 14 Runcorn WA7 . . . . .23 A3
Locke Ho CW1 . . . . .190 B4
Locker Ave WA2 . . . . .8 B2
Lockerbie Cl
 Holmes Chapel CW4 . . . . . .130 C2
 Warrington WA2 . . . . .8 E3
Lockett Rd WA8 . . . . .13 B3
Lockett St WA4 . . . . .16 F3
Lockgate E WA7 . . . . .24 C2
Lockgate W WA7 . . . . .24 C2
LOCKING STUMPS 9 C3
Locking Stumps Com Prim
 Sch WA3 . . . . .9 B4
Locking Stumps La WA3 . . . . .9 B4
Lockitt St CW2 . . . . .190 D3
Lock La M31 . . . . .11 E3
Lock Rd
 Bebington CH62 . . . . .44 A8
 Warrington WA1 . . . . .16 F6
Locks The
 Grappenhall WA4 . . . . .17 B3
 Middlewich CW10 . . . . .151 D8
Lockton La WA5 . . . . .15 E7
Lockwood View WA7 . . . . . . .50 F5
Lodge Brow SK10 . . . . .63 A1
Lodgebury Ct SY14 . . . . . . .211 C2
Lodge Cl WA13 . . . . .19 B4
Lodge Dr
 Culcheth WA3 . . . . .4 F3
 Moulton CW9 . . . . .126 F7
 Winsford CW7 . . . . .127 A1
Lodgefields Com Prim Sch
 CW2 . . . . .189 E4
Lodgefields Dr CW2 . . . . . . .189 E4
Lodge Gdns CH2 . . . . .118 D6
Lodge Hollow WA6 . . . . .73 B4
Lodge La
 Antrobus CW9 . . . . .54 A6
 Dutton WA4 . . . . .76 C8
 Hartford CW8 . . . . .103 B4
 Hatherton CW5 . . . . .220 A4
 Haydock WA11, WA12,
 WN4 . . . . .2 B8
 Lostock Gralam CW9 . . . . . . .80 A2
 Runcorn WA7 . . . . .49 F8
 Saughall CH1 . . . . .94 A2
 Warrington WA5 . . . . .15 F7
 Widnes WA8 . . . . .12 B4
Lodge Rd
 Alsager ST7 . . . . .193 C4
 Knutsford WA16 . . . . .57 C3

Lodge Rd continued
 Sandbach CW11 . . . . .174 E5
 Talke ST7 . . . . .210 D6
 Widnes WA8 . . . . .22 B8
Lodmore La SY13 . . . . .233 C6
Lofthouse Gate WA8 . . . . . . .12 F4
Lomas Sq SK11 . . . . .112 D5
Lomax Rd CW9 . . . . .205 D6
Lomond Gr CH66 . . . . .69 F3
London Rd
 Adlington SK10 . . . . .62 C5
 Alderley Edge SK9 . . . . .60 A1
 Allostock WA16 . . . . .106 F3
 Bridgemere CW5, CW3 . . . . .232 A5
 Davenham CW9 . . . . .104 A1
 Frodsham WA6 . . . . .74 B8
 Hatherton CW5 . . . . .220 D4
 Holmes Chapel CW4 . . . . . .130 C2
 Macclesfield SK11 . . . . .112 D3
 Nantwich CW5 . . . . .204 F5
 Northwich CW9 . . . . .103 F7
 Northwich, Leftwich
 CW9 . . . . .104 A5
 Sandbach CW11 . . . . .174 D8
 Stapeley CW5 . . . . .205 B3
 Warrington WA4 . . . . .26 D5
 Woore CW3 . . . . .232 C1
London Rd N SK12 . . . . .36 E5
London Rd S SK12 . . . . .36 D3
London Road Terr
 SK11. . . . . .112 D5
London Row WA12. . . . . .7 D8
Loney St SK11 . . . . .112 C7
Long Acre
 Cuddington CW8 . . . . .101 D4
 Weaverham CW8 . . . . .77 C1
Longacres Rd WA15 . . . . .32 D7
Long Acres Rd CH64 . . . . . . .41 E2
Longacre St SK10 . . . . .112 C8
LONGBARN 9 B1
Longbarn Bvd WA2 . . . . .9 B2
Longbarn Com Prim Sch
 WA2 .9 B1
Long Barn La
 Warrington WA2 . . . . .9 B2
 Warrington, Woolston
 WA1 . . . . .17 D8
Longbenton Way WA7 . . . . . .24 B4
Longburgh Cl CH2 . . . . .118 F3
Longbutt La WA13 . . . . .19 A2
Longbutts La SK11 . . . . .111 E2
Longclough Rd ST5 . . . . . . .210 D2
Long Croft La SK8 . . . . .34 E8
Longcross Ct CW10 . . . . . . .128 C1
Longdale Dr CH1 . . . . .117 C5
Longden Ct SK7 . . . . .35 E5
Longden La SK11 . . . . .113 A6
Longden St SK10 . . . . .112 E8
Longdin St WA4 . . . . .16 F3
Longdown Rd CW12 . . . . . . .155 F4
Longfield Ave
 Chester CH2 . . . . .118 E7
 Gatley SK8 . . . . .34 C7
Longfield Rd WA2 . . . . .8 C1
LONGFORD 8 B1
Longford Dr WA8 . . . . .12 C2
Longford St
 4 Crewe CW2 . . . . .190 D2
 Warrington WA2 . . . . .16 B7
Long Gn CH3 . . . . .97 E1
LONG GREEN 97 F1
LONGHILL 230 E5
Long Hill SK3 . . . . .65 F2
Longhill La CW3 . . . . .230 E5
Longhorn Cl CW10 . . . . .128 D2
Long La
 Alpraham CW6 . . . . .169 E4
 Bickerton SY14 . . . . .199 F4
 Bollington SK10 . . . . .63 B2
 Burland CW5 . . . . .203 A8
 Chester CH2 . . . . .118 F7
 Hargrave CH3 . . . . .143 D2
 Harriseahead ST7 . . . . .195 E4
 Haughton CW6 . . . . .186 C2
 Horwich End SK23 . . . . .65 F3
 Huxley CH3 . . . . .166 C8
 Middlewich CW10 . . . . .151 C7
 Saughall CH1 . . . . .94 B2
 Swan Green WA16 . . . . .107 D7
 Swettenham CW12 . . . . . . .131 F5
 Tilston SY14 . . . . .198 B3
 Warrington WA2 . . . . .8 B1
 Wettenhall CW6, CW7 . . . . .170 C6
Longlands Dr SK22 . . . . .39 B8
Longlands Rd SK22 . . . . .39 B8
Long La S CW10 . . . . .151 D7
Longley La CW9 . . . . .122 D6
Longley La CW6 . . . . .99 D1
Long Looms CH3 . . . . .120 D6
Longlooms Rd CH65 . . . . . . .70 D1
Long Marl Dr SK9 . . . . .34 F4
Long Mdw CH60 . . . . .40 F6
Longmeade Gdns SK9 . . . . . .60 C6
Longmeadow
 Cheadle SK8 . . . . .35 C7
 Weaverham CW8 . . . . .102 C8
LONGMOSS 86 C1
Longmoss Cl CW10 . . . . . . .151 B8
Longmynd Rise SK10 . . . . . .149 B8
Longnor Rd
 Gatley SK8 . . . . .34 B7
 Hazel Grove SK7 . . . . .36 E7
Longridge WA16 . . . . .57 D3
Longridge Trad Est
 WA16 . . . . .57 D3
Long Row WA12 . . . . .195 A1
Longsdon Cl ST5 . . . . .210 C1

Longshaw St
　Warrington, Bewsey
　WA5 . . . . .15 F8
　Warrington, Dallam WA5. . . . .7 F1
Long Shoot CW4 . . . . .130 D8
Long Shoot Rd SK11. . . . . .108 E1
Longsides Rd WA15. . . . . . . .32 C7
Longsight La SK8. . . . . .34 F6
Long Spinney WA7 . . . . .50 C8
Longster Cl WA6 . . . . .73 B2
Longstone La CW6. . . . . . . .124 E3
Longton Ave WA3. . . . . .3 C7
Long Valley Rd ST8 . . . . . . .179 C2
Longview Ave ST7 . . . . .193 E4
Long Wlk M31. . . . . .11 D3
Longwood Cl CW10 . . . . . . .151 C7
Longwood Rd WA4 . . . . .26 E5
Lonsdale Cl
　Warrington WA5 . . . . .14 F8
　3 Widnes WA8. . . . . .22 C8
Lonsdale Ct CH4. . . . . .140 F4
Lon Y Cryddion / Cobblers
　La LL12. . . . . .161 B1
Lon yr Orsaf / Station App
　CH1 . . . . .1 A1
Lon yr Ywen / Yew Tree
　Ave CH1 . . . . .116 F7
Looe Cl WA8 . . . . .12 E2
Looms The CH64. . . . . .41 B2
Loont The CW7 . . . . .149 C7
Lord Nelson St WA1 . . . . . . .16 C5
Lordship La WA6. . . . . .73 B7
Lordshire Pl ST7. . . . . .195 F2
Lords La WA3 . . . . .9 C4
Lords Mill Rd CW2. . . . . . . .206 B4
Lord's St M44 . . . . .11 C5
Lord St
　Bollington SK10 . . . . .88 B8
　Chester CH3 . . . . .118 F2
　Crewe CW2 . . . . .190 D3
　Croft WA3 . . . . .9 B1
　Macclesfield SK11. . . . . . .112 D6
　Macclesfield SK11. . . . . . .112 D7
　Newton-le-W WA12. . . . . . . .2 A3
　Runcorn WA7. . . . . .22 F3
　Warrington WA4 . . . . .16 B4
Lorne St CH1 . . . . .237 A3
Lorraine St ST7. . . . . .195 F1
Lostock Ave
　Poynton SK12 . . . . .36 B4
　Warrington WA5 . . . . .15 F8
Lostock Cl **2** CW9. . . . . . . .103 E5
Lostock Gn CW9. . . . . .80 A1
LOSTOCK GRALAM 80 A3
Lostock Gralam CE Prim
　Sch CW9. . . . . .80 A2
Lostock Gralam Sta
　CW9. . . . . .80 A2
LOSTOCK GREEN 105 B8
Lostock Hall Prim Sch
　SK12. . . . . .36 B3
Lostock Hall Rd SK12. . . . . .36 B3
Lostock Hollow CW9. . . . . . .80 A2
Lostock Rd SK12. . . . . .36 D2
Lostock Way SK9 . . . . .34 D4
Lotus Gdns WA9. . . . . .6 A7
Louise St CH1 . . . . .237 A3
Loushers La WA4 . . . . .16 D2
Lovage Cl WA2 . . . . .9 C1
Lovat Dr WA16 . . . . .82 B7
Lovatt Cl WA13 . . . . .19 B4
Lovatts The ST7 . . . . .195 A1
Love La
　Hassall Green CW11 . . . . .176 C3
　Nantwich SW14. . . . . .213 A4
　Nantwich CW5. . . . . .204 E5
Lovell Ct CW4 . . . . .130 C3
Lovel Terr WA8 . . . . .22 B5
Lovely La WA5. . . . . .15 E6
Love St CH1 . . . . .237 B2
Lowcross Rd SY14 . . . . . . .198 D3
Lowe Ave
　Congleton CW12 . . . . .156 E2
　Warrington WA4 . . . . .16 F4
Lowe Cres CW9. . . . . .53 C4
Lowe Dr WA16. . . . . .57 B2
Lower Appleton Rd
　WA8. . . . . .13 B1
Lower Ash Rd ST7 . . . . .194 E1
Lower Bank St **10**
　SK11. . . . . .112 E7
Lower Beech Cotts
　SK10. . . . . .87 D2
Lower Bridge St CH1 . . . . . .237 B1
Lower Brook St CH5. . . . . . .91 D1
LOWER BUNBURY 185 F8
LOWER CARDEN 198 C6
Lower Church St WA8 . . . . . .23 A5
Lower Cl L26. . . . . .21 A8
Lower Darwin St
　CW9. . . . . .103 E6
Lower Exchange St **13**
　SK11. . . . . .112 D7
Lower Farm Mews
　CW6. . . . . .147 B3
Lowerfield Rd SK10. . . . . . . .87 E1
Lower Field Rd CH4 . . . . . . .141 A5
Lower Fold Cott SK6. . . . . . .37 D7
Lower Greenhall La
　SK12. . . . . .38 F6
Lower Hague WA3 . . . . .38 A8
Lower Haigh St **3**
　CW7. . . . . .149 C8
Lower Hall La CH3. . . . . . . .182 D2
Lower Hall Mews
　CH3 . . . . .182 D2
Lower Hall Rd SY13. . . . . . .215 D4
LOWER HEATH 156 E5

Lower Heath CW12 . . . . . . .156 E4
Lower Heath Ave
　CW12. . . . . .156 E4
Lower Heath Terr
　CW12. . . . . .156 E4
Lower High St ST7. . . . . . . .195 D7
LOWERHOUSE 87 E8
Lowerhouse SK10. . . . . .87 E8
LOWER HOUSE 22 E8
Lower House La WA8 . . . . . .22 F8
LOWER KINNERTON 139 D1
Lower La
　Aldford CH3. . . . . .164 A2
　Churton CH3. . . . . .181 A7
　Eaton CW6. . . . . .147 A3
Lowerlea SK12 . . . . .38 C6
Lower Macclesfield Rd
　SK23. . . . . .65 E6
Lower Meadow Dr
　CW12. . . . . .156 C3
Lower Meadow Rd
　SK9. . . . . .34 E4
Lower Mews SK5. . . . . .70 C7
Lower Park Cres SK12 . . . . .36 C6
Lower Park Prim Sch
　SK12. . . . . .36 C4
Lower Park Rd
　Chester CH4 . . . . .237 C2
　Poynton SK12. . . . . .36 B5
Lower Park St CW12. . . . . . .156 E3
LOWER PEOVER 81 E1
Lower Peover CE Prim
　Sch WA16. . . . . .81 E1
Lower Rake La WA6 . . . . . . .73 B4
Lower Rd L26, WA8. . . . . . . .21 C7
Lower Robin Hood La
　WA6. . . . . .73 B3
Lower Rock St **2** SK22 . . . .39 C7
Lower Sandy La CH3. . . . . .199 C7
LOWER STRETTON 52 F8
LOWER THREAPWOOD
　. . . . . .222 A6
LOWER WALTON 26 A8
Lower Wash La WA4. . . . . . .16 E3
LOWER WHITLEY 53 D3
LOWER WITHINGTON
　. . . . . .132 A8
LOWER WYCH 224 B6
Lowes La SK11 . . . . .111 F2
Lowe St
　Golborne WA3 . . . . .3 A8
　Macclesfield SK11. . . . . . .112 D7
Loweswater Cl WA2. . . . . . . .8 B3
Loweswater Cres WA11. . . . .1 A6
Lowfield Gdns WA3. . . . . .5 C7
Lowfields Ave CH62. . . . . . . .43 E3
Lowfields Cl CH62 . . . . .43 E3
Low Hill WA6. . . . . .97 D5
Lowlands Rd **6** WA7. . . . . . .22 F2
Lowland Way WA16. . . . . . . .82 A8
LOW LEIGHTON 39 D8
Low Leighton Rd SK22 . . . . .39 D8
Low Mdw SK23. . . . . .65 D8
Lownorth Rd M22 . . . . .33 E8
Lowry Cl WA7. . . . . .15 D6
Low St ST7. . . . . .193 E8
Lowther Ave WA3. . . . . .4 F4
Lowther St SK10. . . . . .88 C8
LOWTON 4 A7
LOWTON COMMON 4 A8
Lowton Com Sports Coll
　WA3. .4 B8
Lowton Gdns WA3 . . . . .3 B5
LOWTON HEATH 3 C4
Lowton Jun & Inf Sch
　WA3. .1 A7
Lowton Rd WA3 . . . . .3 C8
LOWTON ST MARY'S 3 F8
Lowton St Mary's CE Prim
　Sch WA3. . . . . .3 D8
Lowton West Prim Sch
　WA3. .3 D8
Loxdale Dr CH65. . . . . .69 F4
Loxley Cl
　Macclesfield SK11. . . . . . .112 B7
　Warrington WA5 . . . . .15 A8
Loyola Hey L35 . . . . .12 E8
Lucerne Cl CH3. . . . . .142 B6
Ludford Cl ST5 . . . . .210 D2
Ludford St CW1 . . . . .190 C5
Ludlow Ave CW1. . . . . .190 F3
Ludlow Cl
　Macclesfield SK10. . . . . . . .87 E2
　Warrington, Paddington
　WA1 . . . . .17 B8
　Winsford CW7. . . . . .149 B7
Ludlow Cres WA7. . . . . .49 B8
Ludlow Dr CH65 . . . . .70 E3
Ludlow Rd CH1 . . . . .118 A5
Ludwell Cl CH4. . . . . .141 B6
LUGSDALE 23 C7
Lugsdale Rd WA8 . . . . .23 B7
Lulworth Cl CW7 . . . . .149 B7
Lumb Brook Mews **5**
　WA4. . . . . .16 E1
Lumb Brook Rd
　Appleton Thorn WA4. . . . . .27 A5
　Warrington WA4 . . . . .26 F8
Lumb Cl SK7 . . . . .35 E6
Lumber La WA5 . . . . .6 F8
Lumb La SK7. . . . . .35 E6
Lumley Pl CH1 . . . . .237 B2
Lumley Rd
　Chester CH2 . . . . .118 C4
　Macclesfield SK11. . . . . . .111 F7
Lumley Wlk L24 . . . . .21 F1
Lumpy St CW12 . . . . .156 C3

Lundy Dr CH65 . . . . .95 C8
Lune Cl **1** CW12. . . . . .157 A1
Lunehurst **12** WA3 . . . . .3 E8
Lune Way WA8 . . . . .12 C1
Lunt Ave CW2 . . . . .190 C2
LUNTS HEATH 13 A5
Lunts Heath Prim Sch
　WA8. . . . . .13 B5
Lunt's Heath Rd WA8 . . . . . .13 B5
Lunts Moss ST7 . . . . .194 C6
Luntswood Gr WA12 . . . . .2 A4
Lupin Dr
　Haydock WA11. . . . . .1 F6
　Huntington CH3. . . . . .142 B6
Lupus Way CH66. . . . . .69 F3
Luscombe Cl L26 . . . . .21 A8
Luther Gr WA9. . . . . .1 B2
Luton Rd CH65. . . . . .70 A5
Luton St WA8 . . . . .23 A7
Lutyens Cl SK10 . . . . .111 F8
Lyceum Cl CW1. . . . . .190 A8
Lyceum Way CW1 . . . . .190 A8
Lychgate WA4. . . . . .26 D5
Lycroft Cl WA7 . . . . .49 B6
Lydbury Cl WA5 . . . . .7 D2
Lydden Rd CH65 . . . . .70 B7
Lydgate Cl CW2. . . . . .205 F8
Lydiate La
　Runcorn WA7. . . . . .48 D7
　Willaston CH64 . . . . .42 E1
Lydiate The
　Heswall CH60. . . . . .40 F7
　Willaston CH64 . . . . .42 D1
Lydiat La WA5 . . . . .60 A1
Lydney Ave SK8 . . . . .34 C7
Lydstep Ct WA5 . . . . .14 D3
Lydyett La CW9. . . . . .78 B3
Lymcote Dr CW8 . . . . .103 A4
Lyme Ave
　Handforth SK9. . . . . .34 B1
　Macclesfield SK11. . . . . . .112 A6
Lyme Com Prim Sch
　WA13. . . . . .1 F4
LYME GREEN 112 C2
Lyme Green Bsns Pk
　SK11. . . . . .112 C3
Lyme Green Settlement
　SK11. . . . . .112 D2
Lyme Lea Cl SK8 . . . . .35 B8
Lyme Park Ctry Pk*
　SK12. . . . . .38 B2
Lyme Pk* SK12. . . . . .38 B1
Lyme Rd
　High Lane SK12. . . . . .38 A6
　Poynton SK12. . . . . .37 C3
Lyme St
　Haydock WA11. . . . . .1 E6
　Newton-le-W WA12. . . . . . . .1 F4
　13 Warrington WA1 . . . . . .16 B5
Lymewood Dr
　Disley SK12 . . . . .38 C6
　Wilmslow SK9 . . . . .60 E8
LYMM .18 E4
Lymm Brook **1** WA13. . . . . .18 E3
Lymm Hall WA13 . . . . .18 E3
Lymmhay La WA13. . . . . . . .18 E4
Lymm High Sch WA13 . . . . .19 B3
Lymmington Ave
　WA13. . . . . .18 C3
Lymm Rd
　Little Bollington WA14. . . .20 B1
　Warrington WA4 . . . . .17 F3
Lynalls Cl CW12 . . . . .155 F3
Lynbrook Rd CW1. . . . . .190 F4
Lyncastle Rd WA4 . . . . .27 D4
Lyncastle Way WA4. . . . . . . .27 D4
Lyncombe Cl SK8 . . . . .35 B6
Lyncroft Cl CW1. . . . . .190 F3
Lyndale **2** CW7 . . . . .149 C8
Lyndale Ave WA4 . . . . .49 C8
Lyndale
　Bebington CH62. . . . . .43 E4
　Warrington, Fearnhead
　WA2. .8 F2
　Warrington WA2 . . . . .16 D8
Lyndale Ct CW7 . . . . .127 A3
Lyndale Sch The CH62 . . . . .43 F5
Lyndhurst Cl SK9 . . . . .59 D5
Lyndon Gr WA7. . . . . .49 B8
Lyneal Ave CH66. . . . . .69 C3
Lyngard Cl SK9 . . . . .34 E1
Lynham Ave WA5 . . . . .15 B5
Lynn Ave ST7. . . . . .210 C8
Lynn Cl WA7. . . . . .49 C7
Lynndene CH66. . . . . .69 D7
Lynn Gr SK11. . . . . .112 C6
Lynside Wlk M22 . . . . .33 E8
Lynthorpe Ave M44 . . . . .11 D6
Lynton Ave M44 . . . . .11 E6
Lynton Cl
　Chester CH4 . . . . .140 F6
　Heswall CH60. . . . . .41 B6
　Knutsford WA16 . . . . .57 C1
　Warrington WA5 . . . . .14 E4
Lynton Cres WA8 . . . . .12 E2
Lynton Dr CH6 . . . . .37 D2
Lynton Gdns WA4. . . . . .26 D4
Lynton Gr CW1 . . . . .191 D5
Lynton La SK9 . . . . .60 A2
Lynton Mews WA5. . . . . .60 A3
Lynton Park Rd SK8 . . . . . . .34 F8
Lynton Pl
　Alsager ST7 . . . . .193 D4
　Broughton CH4 . . . . .139 B4
Lynton Way CW2 . . . . .206 A8
Lynwood
　Altrincham WA15. . . . . . . .32 A8

Lynwood continued
　Wilmslow SK9 . . . . .60 A6
Lynwood Ave
　Golborne WA3 . . . . .3 E6
　Warrington WA4 . . . . .26 C7
Lynwood Rd CH1 . . . . .117 F5
Lyon Ct WA4 . . . . .16 F3
Lyon's La WA4. . . . . .26 E6
Lyons Rd WA5. . . . . .15 A4
Lyon St
　Chester CH1 . . . . .237 B3
　Crewe CW1 . . . . .190 D4
　Macclesfield SK11. . . . . . .112 C7
　Warrington WA4 . . . . .16 F3
Lysander Dr WA2 . . . . .8 E2
Lyster Cl WA3 . . . . .9 F3
Lytham Cl WA5 . . . . .15 B3
Lytham Dr
　Chester SK7 . . . . .36 A7
　Winsford CW7. . . . . .126 C2
Lytham Rd WA8 . . . . .13 C2
Lytherton Ave M44. . . . . . . .11 D4
Lythgoes La WA2. . . . . .16 B6

M

Mableden Cl SK8. . . . . .34 D8
Mablins La CW1 . . . . .190 B8
Mablins Lane Com Prim
　Sch CW1. . . . . .190 B8
Macbeth Ho ST7. . . . . .210 C8
McCarthy Cl WA3 . . . . .10 A3
Mc Clellan Pl WA8. . . . . .13 B1
MACCLESFIELD 112 B4
Macclesfield Coll
　SK11. . . . . .112 B6
Macclesfield District
　General Hospl SK10 . . . . .112 B8
MACCLESFIELD FOREST
　. . . . . .114 D5
Macclesfield Forest
　Walks* SK11. . . . . .114 A3
Macclesfield Rd
　Alderley Edge SK9. . . . . . .85 D7
　Congleton CW12 . . . . .156 F6
　Eaton CW12. . . . . .134 B2
　Hazel Grove SK7 . . . . .36 F8
　Holmes Chapel CW4 . . . .130 E4
　Kettleshulme SK23,
　SK10. . . . . .64 D3
　Prestbury SK10 . . . . .86 F4
　Rainow SK10. . . . . .89 B7
　Wilmslow SK9 . . . . .60 E8
Macclesfield Sta
　SK11. . . . . .112 D8
Macdermott Rd WA8. . . . . . .22 F5
Macdonald Rd M44. . . . . . . .11 E8
McEllin Cl ST7. . . . . .209 E2
McGarva Way CH65. . . . . . . .70 C4
McGowan Ho ST7 . . . . .210 D8
McKeagney Gdns WA8 . . . . .22 C7
McKee Ave WA2. . . . . .8 B2
McKinley St WA5. . . . . .15 A7
Mckinley Way WA8 . . . . .12 F3
McLaren St CW1 . . . . .190 C7
McMinnis Ave WA9 . . . . .1 B2
McNeill Ave CW1 . . . . .190 A5
Macon Ct CW1 . . . . .190 E3
Macon Ind Pk CW1 . . . . . . .190 E3
Macon Way CW1 . . . . .190 E3
Maddocks Hill WA6. . . . . . . .100 F5
Maddock St ST7 . . . . .209 D1
Madeley Cl
　Altrincham WA14. . . . . .31 E8
　Broughton CH4 . . . . .139 C4
Madeley St CW2. . . . . .190 C1
Madeline McKenna Ct
　WA8. . . . . .12 C3
Madron Ave SK10. . . . . .86 D1
Maelor Cl CH63. . . . . .43 C6
Maes-y-Coed CH4. . . . . . . .140 E6
Magdala Pl CW2 . . . . .190 C8
Magdalen Ct CW2 . . . . .190 A1
Magecroft CW1. . . . . .173 B1
Magenta Ave M44 . . . . .11 E6
Maggoty La SK11 . . . . .111 D1
Magnolia Cl
　3 Ellesmere Port
　CH66. . . . . .69 F1
　5 Partington M31 . . . . . . .11 E2
　Warrington WA1 . . . . .17 E7
Magnolia Dr WA7. . . . . .49 F4
Magnolia Rise SK10. . . . . . .86 E6
Magpie Cres **8** ST7 . . . . . .195 B2
Maiden Est CW5 . . . . .228 C8
Maiden Gdns CH65 . . . . .70 D3
Maidenhills CW10 . . . . .128 D1
Maidstone Cl SK10. . . . . .87 B2
Maidwell Cl CW7. . . . . .127 A4
Main Cl WA11 . . . . .1 A6
Main Rd
　Knutsford WA16 . . . . .57 D7
　Warrington WA5 . . . . .14 A3
Main La WA3 . . . . .3 F3
Main Rd
　Betley CW2, CW3 . . . . . . .221 F8
　Broughton CH4 . . . . .139 B4
　Goostrey CW4 . . . . .107 E1
　Higher Kinnerton CH4 . . .161 A8
　Langley SK11 . . . . .113 C4
　Moulton CW9. . . . . .126 E7
　Norton in Hales TF9. . . . .236 C1
　Shavington CW2 . . . . .206 B4
　Weston CW2 . . . . .207 C6
　Worleston CW5. . . . . .188 F5
　Wybunbury CW5 . . . . . . .220 B8
Main St
　Frodsham WA6 . . . . .74 B8

Lon–Man

Main St continued
　Great Barrow CH3. . . . . . .120 E5
　Runcorn WA7. . . . . .49 F8
Maintree Cres L24. . . . . .21 A4
Mainwaring Cl CW5 . . . . . . .205 A4
Mainwaring Dr
　Saltney CH4. . . . . .140 C7
　Wilmslow SK9 . . . . .60 D8
Mainwaring Rd
　Bebington CH62. . . . . .43 D8
　Over Peover WA16 . . . . . .108 A8
Mairesfield Ave WA4. . . . . . .17 B2
Maisterson Ct **7**
　CW5. . . . . .204 E5
Maitland Way CH1. . . . . . . .117 D4
Maitland-Wood Cl
　CW9. . . . . .104 D7
Major Cross St **6** WA8 . . . .23 A7
Makepeace Cl CH3 . . . . . . .119 C3
Makerfield Dr WA12 . . . . .2 A5
Malaga Ave M90. . . . . .33 B7
Malahide Ct WA8. . . . . .12 C2
Malam Dr CW9. . . . . .104 D6
Malbank CW5 . . . . .204 E6
Malbank Rd CW2 . . . . .189 E4
Malbank Sch & Sixth Form
　Coll CW5 . . . . .204 C6
Malcolm Ave WA3 . . . . .8 D1
Malcolm Cres CH63. . . . . . . .43 C6
Malcolm St WA7. . . . . .23 B2
Malham Cl WA5 . . . . .14 D4
Malhamdale Rd
　CW12. . . . . .157 A5
Malin Cl L24. . . . . .21 D2
Malston Rd WA5 . . . . .13 B5
MALKINS BANK 175 C3
Mallaig Cl CW4 . . . . .130 C2
Mallard Cl
　Knutsford WA16 . . . . .57 B3
　Warrington WA2 . . . . .9 F3
Mallard Cres SK12. . . . . .36 A4
Mallard Ct
　Chester CH2 . . . . .118 F7
　Crewe CW1 . . . . .191 A2
　Gatley SK8 . . . . .34 B8
Mallard La WA3 . . . . .9 F3
Mallard Way
　Crewe CW1 . . . . .191 A2
　Winsford CW7. . . . . .149 D6
Mallory Cl WA16. . . . . .58 A4
Mallory Ct
　Congleton CW12 . . . . .155 F3
　Mobberley WA16. . . . . .58 A4
Mallory Rd CH65. . . . . .70 A4
Mallory Wlk CH4 . . . . .162 A7
Mallow Cl CH3 . . . . .142 A6
Mallowdale Cl CH62 . . . . . . .43 F5
Mallow Wlk M31. . . . . .11 F2
Mall The WA1. . . . . .16 A5
Malmesbury Cl
　Middlewich CW10 . . . . . . .128 B1
　Poynton SK12. . . . . .36 D4
Malmesbury Pk WA7. . . . . . .24 E2
Malmesbury Rd SK8. . . . . . .35 B6
Malory Cl CW1 . . . . .190 F5
MALPAS 213 B4
Malpas Alport Prim Sch
　SY14. . . . . .213 B4
Malpas Cl
　Handforth SK9. . . . . .34 E1
　Northwich CW9 . . . . .104 B7
Malpas Dr WA5. . . . . .15 C4
Malpas Rd
　Ellesmere Port CH65 . . . . .69 F4
　Northwich CW9 . . . . .104 C7
　Runcorn WA7. . . . . .49 C7
Malpas Way WA5 . . . . .14 E4
Malta Rd CH2 . . . . .95 B1
Malt Kiln Rd WA16. . . . . .80 F4
Malt Kiln Way CW11 . . . . . .175 B7
Maltmans Rd WA13. . . . . . . .18 D3
Malton Ave WA3. . . . . .3 E7
Malton Cl WA8 . . . . .12 C5
Malton Dr SK7. . . . . .36 D7
Malt St WA16. . . . . .57 A2
Malvern Ave CH65 . . . . .70 D3
Malvern Cl
　Congleton CW12 . . . . .155 F3
　Shavington CW2 . . . . .206 B4
　Warrington WA5 . . . . .15 C4
Malvern Dr SK10 . . . . .87 E4
Malvern Rd
　Blacon CH1 . . . . .118 A5
　Haydock WA9. . . . . .1 A4
　Knutsford WA16 . . . . .81 F8
Malvern Way CW7. . . . . . . .149 B7
Manchester Airport Sta
　M90. . . . . .33 B7
Manchester Bridge
　CW1. . . . . .190 D4
Manchester Bsns Pk
　M22. . . . . .33 D8
Manchester International
　Airport M90. . . . . .33 A7
Manchester Met Univ
　(Alsager Campus)
　ST7. . . . . .193 A5
Manchester New Rd
　M31. . . . . .11 F4
Manchester Rd
　Congleton CW12. . . . . . . .156 E5
　Knutsford WA16 . . . . .34 C2
　Hollinfare WA3 . . . . .11 A2
　Mullins Green WA3 . . . . . .11 A3
　Knutsford WA16 . . . . .56 E4

Manchester Rd continued
Macclesfield SK10 . . . . **.87** D4
Warrington, Bruche WA1. . . . **.16** E6
Warrington WA3 . . . .**.18** D/
Warrington, Woolston
WA1 . . . .**.17** C/
Wincham CW9 . . . .**79** D1
Manchester Row WA12 . . **.7** D8
Mancroft Ct WA1 . . . .**.17** E7
Mandarin Ct WA1 . . . .**.16** A3
Manhattan Gdns ❶
WA5 . . . .**15** B7
Manifold Cl CW11 . . . .**174** E8
Manifold Dr SK6 . . . .**.37** F6
MANLEY **99** A4
Manley Cl
Antrobus CW9 . . . .**.53** C4
Holmes Chapel CW4 . . . . . .**130** A3
Northwich CW9 . . . .**104** A5
MANLEY COMMON . . . . . **.99** C5
Manley Gdns WA5 . . . .**15** F5
Manley Gr SK/ **35** E6
Manley La
Dunham-on-t-H WA6 . . . . . .**97** F5
Manley WA6 . . . .**.98** C4
Manley Mere* WA6 . . . .**98** B5
Manley Rd
Frodsham WA6 . . . .**.74** B3
Manley WA6 . . . .**.98** E2
Warren SK11 . . . .**112** A5
Manley View CH2 . . . .**72** C3
Manley Village Sch
WA6 . . . .**99** A5
Manna Dr CH2 . . . .**.72** C3
Manners La CH60 . . . .**40** E6
Mannings La CH2 . . . .**119** B6
Mannings La S CH2 . . . . . .**119** A5
Manning St CW2 . . . .**190** D1
Manora Rd CW9 . . . .**104** A8
Manor Ave
Crewe CW2 . . . .**190** A1
Golborne WA3 . . . .**3** D8
Goostrey CW4 . . . .**107** F1
Marston CW9 . . . .**79** B6
Newton-le-W WA12 . . . .**1** F4
Manor Bsns Pk CW4 . . . . .**130** D3
Manor Cl
Broughton CH5 . . . .**139** C7
Cheadle SK8 . . . .**35** C8
Congleton CW12 . . . .**157** A1
Great Barrow CH3 . . . .**120** E6
Lymm WA13 . . . .**18** D2
Neston CH64 . . . .**66** C7
Warrington WA1 . . . .**.17** D7
Wilmslow SK9 . . . .**59** F8
Manor Cres
Broughton CH4 . . . .**139** C8
Knutsford WA16 . . . .**57** B2
Macclesfield SK10 . . . .**.87** D3
Middlewich CW10 . . . .**151** C7
Manor Ct
Acton CW5 . . . .**204** B4
Crewe CW2 . . . .**190** B1
Golborne WA3 . . . .**3** C8
Knutsford WA16 . . . .**57** B1
❷ Nantwich CW5 . . . .**204** E6
Manor Dr
Barnton CW8 . . . .**.78** B2
Chester CH3 . . . .**119** C1
Northwich, Rudheath
CW9 . . . .**104** C7
Manor Farm Cl CH2 . . . . .**119** F8
Manor Farm Cres CH1 . . .**.94** B8
Manor Farm Ct
Broughton CH5 . . . .**139** B7
❺ Frodsham WA6 . . . .**49** C1
Manor Farm Mews
WA7 . . . .**24** D4
Manor Farm Rd WA7 . . . . .**24** D4
Manor Fell WA7 . . . .**50** B7
Manorfield Cl CH11 . . . .**69** A1
Manor Fields CW10 . . . . . .**151** C7
Manor Gdns
Nantwich CW5 . . . .**204** E6
Wilmslow SK9 . . . .**60** D7
Manor Gr CW8 . . . .**103** C6
Manor Ho
Bebington CH62 . . . .**43** D8
Ellesmere Port CH65 . . . . . .**69** D2
Row-of-Trees SK9 . . . .**59** D3
Manorial Rd CH64 . . . .**66** C8
Manorial Rd S CH64 . . . . . .**66** C7
Manor Ind Est WA4 . . . . . .**16** E4
Manor La
Broughton CH5 . . . .**139** B7
Davenham CW9 . . . .**104** D2
Ellesmere Port CH66 . . . . . .**69** D3
Holmes Chapel CW4 . . . . . .**130** D3
❸ Middlewich CW10 . . . . .**151** C8
Ollerton WA16 . . . .**82** E6
MANOR PARK
Middlewich **151** B7
Runcorn . . . .**.24** B3
Manor Park Ave WA4 . . . .**24** C4
Manor Park Dr CH66 . . . . .**69** D2
Manor Park N WA16 . . . . . .**57** C2
Manor Park Prim Sch
WA16 . . . .**57** C2
Manor Park Rd CW12 . . . .**134** D2
Manor Park S WA16 . . . . . .**57** C1
Manor Pk CH5 . . . .**139** B7
Manor Pk CH3 . . . .**120** E6
Manor Pl
Hatherton CW5 . . . .**220** B1
Widnes WA8 . . . .**12** B1

Manor Rd
Bebington CH62 . . . .**43** E6
Chester CH4 . . . .**141** B5
Cuddington CW8 . . . .**101** F/
Frodsham WA6 . . . .**49** C1
Haydock WA11 . . . .**1** F7
Horwich End SK23 . . . .**65** E5
Lymm WA13 . . . .**18** F7
Mow Cop ST7 . . . .**195** D7
Nantwich CW5 . . . .**204** E6
Runcorn WA7 . . . .**23** D2
Sandbach CW11 . . . .**175** D6
Sealand CH5 . . . .**116** A6
Thornton Hough CH63 . . . . .**42** A7
Widnes WA8 . . . .**12** B1
Wilmslow SK9 . . . .**59** E8
Manor Rd N CW5 . . . .**204** E7
Manor Sq CW7 . . . .**149** A8
Manor St CW8 . . . .**103** D6
Manor Terr SK11 . . . .**113** B3
Manor The WA1 . . . .**17** F7
Manor Way
Crewe CW2 . . . .**190** C1
Sandbach CW11 . . . .**175** C6
Manse Field Rd WA6 . . . . .**75** B1
Manse Gdns WA12 . . . .**2** D4
Mansell Cl WA8 . . . .**13** D4
Mansfield Apartments
WA1 . . . .**9** A3
Mansfield Cl WA3 . . . .**10** A4
Mansfield Prim Sch
CH65 . . . .**69** F3
Mansfield Rd CH65 . . . .**70** A2
Mansion Ct S CW5 . . . . . .**204** F5
Mansion Dr WA16 . . . .**57** B2
Manston Rd WA5 . . . .**14** F3
Manuel Perez Rd WA5 . . . .**15** B6
Manx Rd WA4 . . . .**16** B3
Maori Dr WA4 . . . .**74** A8
Maple Ave
Alsager ST7 . . . .**193** E2
Aston WA7 . . . .**50** A4
Disley SK12 . . . .**39** A6
Ellesmere Port CH66 . . . . . .**69** D6
Golborne WA3 . . . .**3** F7
Haydock WA11 . . . .**2** F7
Macclesfield SK11 . . . .**112** D5
Newcastle-u-Lyme ST5 . . . .**210** E1
Newton-le-W WA12 . . . .**2** D2
Poynton SK12 . . . .**36** F3
Runcorn WA7 . . . .**49** C8
Talke ST7 . . . .**210** D8
❺ Widnes WA8 . . . .**13** B2
Maple Cl
Brereton Green
CW11 . . . .**153** F5
Congleton CW12 . . . .**155** F4
Holmes Chapel CW4 . . . . . .**130** D4
Sandbach CW11 . . . .**175** C6
Maple Cres WA5 . . . .**14** F3
Maple Ct CW7 . . . .**127** A3
Maple Gr
Barnton CW8 . . . .**.78** B4
Bebington CH62 . . . .**43** C8
Chester CH2 . . . .**119** B4
Crewe CW1 . . . .**190** E6
Ellesmere Port CH66 . . . . . .**95** A8
Northwich, Greenbank
CW8 . . . .**103** C7
Saltney CH4 . . . .**140** D5
Warrington WA4 . . . .**16** D3
Winsford CW7 . . . .**127** A1
Maple La CH8 . . . .**101** F2
Maple Pl ST7 . . . .**193** F7
Maple Rd
Alderley Edge SK9 . . . .**60** B3
Bramhall SK7 . . . .**35** E6
Partington M31 . . . .**11** E3
Warrington WA1 . . . .**17** E7
Winwick WA2 . . . .**8** B6
Maples SK9 . . . .**59** F6
Maples The
Mobberley WA16 . . . .**58** E1
Winsford CW7 . . . .**127** A3
Mapleton Dr WA7 . . . .**49** F3
Maplewood SK11 . . . .**112** D5
Maplewood Cl WA8 . . . .**22** A7
Maplewood Gr CH1 . . . . . .**117** B8
Maplewood Rd SK9 . . . .**60** E8
Mapplewell Cres WA5 . . . .**15** A6
Marble Arch ❺ WA16 . . . . .**57** A2
MARBURY **226** D8
Marbury Gdns CH65 . . . . . .**69** F6
Marbury House Farm
WA4 . . . .**52** E5
Marbury La CW9 . . . .**78** E5
Marbury Park Ctry Pk*
CW9 . . . .**78** E5
Marbury Rd
Chester CH3 . . . .**119** C2
Comberbach CW9 . . . .**78** D6
Handforth SK9 . . . .**34** B1
Norbury SY13 . . . .**215** D3
Marbury St WA4 . . . .**16** D3
March St CW1 . . . .**190** E4
Marchwiel Rd CH65 . . . .**70** D4
Marcien Way WA8 . . . .**12** F3
Marcliff Gr WA16 . . . .**57** A1
Marcross Cl WA5 . . . .**7** E1
Mardale Ave WA1 . . . .**8** C3
Mardale Cl CW12 . . . .**157** B5
Mardale Cres WA13 . . . .**18** F3
Mardale Ct CW4 . . . .**130** A2
Mardon Cl WA16 . . . .**57** D3
Marfield Ave WA13 . . . .**19** A2
Marford Cl CW9 . . . .**103** E5
Marfords Ave CH63 . . . .**43** C7
Margaret Ave WA1 . . . .**17** B7

Margaret Ct WA8 . . . .**23** B/
Margaret's La CH66 . . . .**69** A7
Margery Ave ST7 . . . .**194** E7
Marian Ave WA12 . . . .**1** F3
Marian Dr CH3 . . . .**142** B8
Marian Rd WA11 . . . .**1** E7
Marie Cl CW5 . . . .**216** F4
Marie Dr WA4 . . . .**17** D2
Marigold Cl SK11 . . . .**111** F8
Marigold Pl WA5 . . . .**15** D3
Marigold Way WA9 . . . .**6** A7
Marina Ave WA5 . . . .**15** C4
Marina Cl SK9 . . . .**34** D5
Marina Dr
Chester CH2 . . . .**118** E7
Ellesmere Port CH65 . . . . . .**70** B5
Warrington WA2 . . . .**8** C1
Marina Flats CH3 . . . .**142** E7
Marina Gr WA7 . . . .**23** B1
Marina La WA7 . . . .**50** E7
Marina Village WA7 . . . .**50** E7
Marina Wlk CH65 . . . .**70** B5
Marine App 19 CW9 . . . . .**103** F8
Marine Ave M31 . . . .**11** D3
Marine Dr CH60 . . . .**40** D6
Mariner Cl WA7 . . . .**50** D6
Marion Dr
Mobberley WA16 . . . .**58** A4
Runcorn WA7 . . . .**48** F6
Maritime Cl WA12 . . . .**2** C5
Mark Ave CH66 . . . .**69** C4
Mark Cl CH2 . . . .**118** F2
Market Cl CW1 . . . .**190** D5
Market Ct CW6 . . . .**146** C2
Market Ctr The CW1 . . . . .**190** D4
Market Gate WA1 . . . .**16** B5
Market Pl
Bollington SK10 . . . .**88** B8
Hampton Heath SY14 . . . . .**213** D7
Macclesfield SK10,
SK11 . . . .**112** D8
Winsford CW7 . . . .**126** F1
Market Sq
Chester CH1 . . . .**237** A2
Congleton CW12 . . . .**156** D2
Crewe CW1 . . . .**190** D4
❹ Sandbach CW11 . . . . . .**175** B6
Market St
Congleton CW12 . . . .**156** D3
Crewe CW1 . . . .**190** D4
Crewe CW1 . . . .**190** D5
Disley SK12 . . . .**38** D6
Kidsgrove ST7 . . . .**195** A1
Macclesfield SK11 . . . .**112** D8
Nantwich CW5 . . . .**204** E5
New Mills SK22 . . . .**39** B7
Newton-le-W WA12 . . . .**2** A3
❾ Northwich CW9 . . . . . .**103** F8
Whaley Bridge SK23 . . . .**65** E7
Widnes WA8 . . . .**23** A7
Market Way ❼ CW9 . . . . .**103** F8
Marlborough Ave
Alderley Edge SK9 . . . .**60** B2
Winsford CW7 . . . .**126** C3
Marlborough Cl
Knutsford WA16 . . . .**57** C4
Macclesfield SK10 . . . .**.87** D4
Wistaston CW2 . . . .**205** E8
Marlborough Cres
Warrington WA4 . . . .**16** F2
Widnes WA8 . . . .**13** A5
Marlborough Ct
❶ Chester CH3 . . . .**119** B2
❸ Macclesfield SK10 . . . .**112** D7
Marlborough Dr
Helsby WA6 . . . .**73** B2
Macclesfield SK10 . . . .**.87** D4
Sandbach CW11 . . . .**175** B8
Marlborough Ho ❽
SK11 . . . .**111** F8
Marlborough Prim Sch
The SK10 . . . .**.87** D4
Marlborough Rd CH65 . . . .**70** D3
Marlborough Way WA11 . . .**1** E8
Marlborough Wlk
CH65 . . . .**70** C3
Marl Cl CW8 . . . .**102** A4
Marl Croft CH3 . . . .**142** B7
Marl Edge SK10 . . . .**87** A5
Marley Ave CW1 . . . .**190** B7
Marley Gn SY13 . . . .**227** C8
MARLEY GREEN **227** C8
Marley Rd SK12 . . . .**36** E2
Marley Way CH4 . . . .**140** E7
Marlfield Rd
Altrincham WA15 . . . .**32** D7
Warrington WA4 . . . .**17** A2
Marl Heys CH2 . . . .**118** E7
Marline Ave CH63 . . . .**43** C6
Marling Cl WA6 . . . .**74** D6
Marling Pk WA8 . . . .**12** B1
Marlow Ave CH2 . . . .**118** F7
Marlow Cl
Sandbach CW11 . . . .**174** D5
Warrington WA3 . . . .**9** C5
Marlow Dr
Altrincham WA14 . . . .**20** F2
Handforth SK9 . . . .**34** C5
Marlowe Cl
Blacon CH1 . . . .**118** A5
Widnes WA8 . . . .**12** F1
Wistaston CW2 . . . .**206** A8
Marlowe Ct SK11 . . . .**112** C5
Marlowe Dr CW5 . . . .**204** F3
Marlowe Rd
❶ Neston CH64 . . . .**66** E8
Northwich CW9 . . . .**104** C6

Marlston Ave CH4 . . . .**141** A0
Marlston Ct CH4 . . . .**140** F1
Marlston Pl WA7 . . . .**49** B6
Marlwood Pl CH4 . . . .**139** A3
Maroon Rd M22 . . . .**33** F/
Marple Cres CW2 . . . .**189** E2
Marple Rd CW9 . . . .**104** C8
Marquis Dr SK8 . . . .**34** D7
Marratt Rd CW11 . . . .**174** A5
Marron Ave WA2 . . . .**8** B2
Marryat Cl WA2 . . . .**8** A6
Marsden Ave WA4 . . . .**17** A4
Marsden Ct WA8 . . . .**12** E4
Marsden Terr ❸
SK11 . . . .**112** C7
Marshall Ave CW2 . . . .**189** F2
Marshall Gr CW12 . . . .**179** B8
Marshall La CW8 . . . .**103** D6
Marshall Rd WA1 . . . .**17** D7
Marshalls Ct ❷ CW8 . . . .**103** C5
Marsh Ave ST7 . . . .**195** E2
Marsh Brook Cl WA3 . . . . . .**11** A2
Marshbrook Cl WA4 . . . . . .**17** D3
Marsh Gr ST8 . . . .**179** C3
Marsh Gr ST7 . . . .**193** A3
MARSH GREEN
Biddulph **179** D3
Frodsham **74** A8
Marsh Green Cl ST8 . . . . .**179** D2
Marshgreen Rd ST8 . . . . . .**179** D3
Marsh Green Rd
CW11 . . . .**174** E8
Marsh Hall Pad WA8 . . . . . .**13** B4
Marsh House La WA1,
WA2 . . . .**16** C7
Marsh La
Alsager ST7 . . . .**193** A3
Barton CH3, SY14 . . . .**181** E3
Churton CH3 . . . .**181** B5
Dutton WA4 . . . .**51** E3
Elton CH2 . . . .**72** B4
Frodsham WA6 . . . .**74** A8
Holmes Chapel CW4 . . . . . .**130** E2
Ince CW7 . . . .**72** D6
Mere WA16 . . . .**30** F3
New Mills SK22, SK23 . . . . .**39** D6
Norley CW8, WA6 . . . .**101** B7
Ravensmoor CW5 . . . .**203** F2
Runcorn WA7 . . . .**23** F3
Warrington, Penketh
WA5 . . . .**14** C2
Marshlands Rd CH64 . . . . . .**66** E5
Marsh Lane Trad Est
SK12 . . . .**39** D7
Marsh Rd WA4 . . . .**27** B4
Marsh St
Warrington WA1 . . . .**16** D7
Widnes WA8 . . . .**23** A6
Marshway Dr WA12 . . . .**2** B5
Marson St WA2 . . . .**16** A6
MARSTON **79** B4
Marston Cl CH62 . . . .**43** B8
Marston Gdns CH65 . . . . . .**69** F6
Marston La CW9 . . . .**79** C6
Marten Ave CH63 . . . .**43** C7
Martens Rd M44 . . . .**11** E5
MARTHALL **83** E4
Marthall La WA16 . . . .**83** B7
Marthall Way ❽ SK9 . . . . .**34** E5
Martham Cl WA4 . . . .**17** A3
Martin Ave
Newton-le-W WA12 . . . .**2** C5
Warrington WA2 . . . .**8** E1
Martin Cl
Chester CH2 . . . .**118** C8
Runcorn WA7 . . . .**50** A7
Martindale Gr WA7 . . . .**49** D5
Martin Rd
Chester CH2 . . . .**118** C8
Frodsham WA6 . . . .**74** B8
MARTIN'S ASH **227** B2
MARTINSCROFT **17** F7
Martinscroft Gn WA1 . . . . .**17** F7
Martinsfields CW8 . . . .**77** A5
Martin's La CH3 . . . .**143** F3
Martins Mill CW12 . . . .**179** C8
MARTIN'S MOSS **176** E6
Martland Ave WA3 . . . .**3** E7
Martlet Ave SK12 . . . .**38** C6
MARTON **133** B5
Marton Cl
Congleton CW12 . . . .**156** C5
Culcheth WA3 . . . .**4** E4
Hough CW2 . . . .**206** E3
Macclesfield SK10 . . . .**.87** B2
Marton & District CE Prim
Sch SK11 . . . .**133** C5
MARTON GREEN **125** C4
Marton Hall La SK11 . . . . .**133** B3
Marton La
Marton SK11 . . . .**133** D7
Warren SK11 . . . .**111** B1
Marton Rd CH4 . . . .**139** C3
MARTONSANDS **125** F4
Marton Way ❽ SK9 . . . . . .**34** E5
Marubi Cl WA16 . . . .**57** B2
Maryhill Cl WA7 . . . .**49** A3
Maryhill High Sch
ST7 . . . .**195** A3

Marjorie Pilkington
ST7 . . . .**195** A3
Maryhill Rd WA7 . . . .**49** A8
Maryland Cl WA5 . . . .**.13** C7
Marys Gate BWB **065** C0
Mary St
Crewe CW1 . . . .**190** E5
Warrington WA4 . . . .**23** D7
Maryville Cl ❸ CH65 . . . . . .**70** CG
Masefield Ave WA8 . . . .**22** F8
Masefield Dr
Blacon CH1 . . . .**117** E6
Crewe CW1 . . . .**190** F4
Winwick WA2 . . . .**8** A5
Masefield Way CW11 . . . . .**174** D5
Maskery Pl CW12 . . . .**156** E4
Mason Ave
Warrington WA1 . . . .**16** E8
Widnes WA8 . . . .**13** B4
Mason Cl CH66 . . . .**69** D2
Masons La SK10 . . . .**87** F1
Mason's Row CW6 . . . .**169** E2
Mason St
Chester CH2 . . . .**237** A3
Warrington WA7 . . . .**23** C3
Warrington WA1 . . . .**16** C5
Massey Ave
Hartford CW8 . . . .**103** A4
Lymm WA13 . . . .**18** B2
Warrington WA5 . . . .**7** F2
Winsford CW7 . . . .**126** F1
Massey Brook La
WA13 . . . .**18** B2
Massey Cl CW5 . . . .**205** A4
Masseyfield Rd WA7 . . . . . .**50** B5
Massey Hall Sch WA4 . . . .**17** F2
Massey St ❻ SK9 . . . .**60** A1
Masters Ct WA16 . . . .**56** F1
Mastiff La SY14 . . . .**213** B1
Mates La SY14 . . . .**213** B6
Mather Ave
Golborne WA3 . . . .**3** E6
Warrington WA1 . . . .**48** D7
Mather Cl CW10 . . . .**151** C7
Mather Dr
Comberbach CW9 . . . .**78** C8
Northwich CW9 . . . .**104** D7
Mathers Cl WA4 . . . .**.9** A4
Mathieson Rd WA8 . . . .**22** E5
Matlock Cl WA5 . . . .**15** A8
Matlock Dr SK7 . . . .**36** E8
Matlock Rd SK8 . . . .**34** C7
Matterdale Cl WA6 . . . .**74** D7
Matthew Cl CH2 . . . .**118** F2
Matthews Pl CW12 . . . .**157** A2
Matthews St WA1 . . . .**16** D7
Matty's La WA6 . . . .**74** A7
Mavor Ct CW1 . . . .**190** B4
Mawdsley Ave WA1 . . . .**.17** E7
Mawdsley Cl ST7 . . . .**193** A3
MAW GREEN **190** E7
Maw Green Cl CW1 . . . . . .**190** E7
Maw Green Rd CW1 . . . . . .**190** F7
Maw La CW1 . . . .**191** C7
Mawson Cl WA5 . . . .**15** D8
Maxfield Cl SK11 . . . .**111** F8
Maxwell Cl CH65 . . . .**70** A2
Maxwell Rd CW12 . . . .**179** A8
Maxwell St
Crewe CW2 . . . .**190** C3
Warrington WA3 . . . .**9** E6
May Ave SK8 . . . .**35** B6
Mayberry Gr WA2 . . . .**9** A1
Maybrook Pl WA4 . . . .**16** F3
Maydor Ave CH4 . . . .**140** C7
Mayfair Cl
Poynton SK12 . . . .**36** E4
Warrington WA5 . . . .**14** E7
Mayfair Ct CW4 . . . .**162** E5
Mayfair Dr
Crewe CW1 . . . .**190** F6
Northwich CW9 . . . .**103** F3
Mayfair Gr WA8 . . . .**22** D1
Mayfield Ave
Macclesfield SK11 . . . .**112** C5
Widnes WA8 . . . .**12** B1
Mayfield Cl CW4 . . . .**130** D3
Mayfield Ct WA8 . . . .**13** A2
Mayfield Dr
Bebington CH62 . . . .**44** B6
Cuddington CW8 . . . .**102** A4
Golborne WN7 . . . .**4** C8
Winsford CW7 . . . .**127** A3
Mayfield Gdns CH64 . . . . . .**41** E1
Mayfield Gr
Cuddington CW8 . . . .**102** A4
Wilmslow SK9 . . . .**59** E5
Mayfield Mews CW1 . . . . .**189** F6
Mayfield Rd
Blacon CH1 . . . .**117** D5
Bramhall SK7 . . . .**35** F4
Mobberley WA16 . . . .**58** D7
Northwich CW9 . . . .**104** C8
Warrington WA4 . . . .**17** A2
Mayfield Terr SK11 . . . . . .**112** C5
Mayfield View WA13 . . . . . .**18** F2
Mayflower Rd CW5 . . . . . .**204** E3
May Rd
Cheadle SK8 . . . .**35** B6
Heswall CH60 . . . .**41** A8
Maythorn Ave WA3 . . . .**9** A7
Maytree Ave CH3 . . . .**119** B2
May Wlk ❷ M31 . . . .**11** E3
Mead Ave ST7 . . . .**194** E7
Mead Cl WA16 . . . .**56** F1
Meade The SK9 . . . .**60** C8
Meadow Ave
Congleton CW12 . . . .**156** C1

Meadow Ave continued
Goostrey CW4 . . . . **107** C1
Warrington WA4 . . . . **16** B2
Weston CW7 . . . . **207** B5
MEADOWBANK **126** D5
Meadow Bank
Adderley TF9 . . . . **235** A4
Kelsall CW6 . . . . **122** C4
Meadow Bank Cvn Pk
WA4 . . . . **25** C6
Meadowbank Dr CH66 . . **69** A6
Meadowbank Gdns
WA3 . . . . **5** C7
Meadow Brow SK9 . . . . . **60** A2
Meadow Cl
Cuddington CW8 . . . . **102** A4
Farndon CH3 . . . . **180** F1
Goostrey CW4 . . . . **107** E1
Helsby WA6 . . . . **73** B3
High Lane SK6 . . . . **37** F8
Neston CH64 . . . . **66** E6
Newton-le-W WA12 . . . . **1** F3
Shavington CW2 . . . . **206** D5
Tarvin CH3 . . . . **121** B2
Whaley Bridge SK23 . . . . . **65** C8
Widnes WA8 . . . . **12** D3
Willaston CH64 . . . . **67** F8
Wilmslow SK9 . . . . **59** E4
Winsford CW7 . . . . **126** C3
Meadow Com Prim Sch
CH66 . . . . **69** E2
Meadow Cotts [5]
CW12 . . . . **156** D3
Meadowcroft
Higher Kinnerton CH4 . . . . **161** A7
Saughall CH1 . . . . **94** B1
Meadow Croft
Alsager ST7 . . . . **193** E2
Nantwich CW5 . . . . **204** E7
Meadowcroft Ct WA7 . . . **50** A8
Meadow Ct
Frodsham WA6 . . . . **49** C1
Mollington CH1 . . . . **94** F1
Newchapel ST7 . . . . **195** E2
No Man's Heath SY14 . . . . **214** A5
Meadow Dr
Barnton CW8 . . . . **78** A3
Knutsford WA16 . . . . **81** F8
Prestbury SK10 . . . . **87** B7
Wistaston CW2 . . . . **205** F7
Meadowfield
Tarporley CW6 . . . . **146** C1
Whaley Bridge SK23 . . . . . **65** D8
Meadow Field Rd
CH4 . . . . **141** A5
Meadow Gate CW9 . . . . . **79** F5
Meadowgate Cl
CW11 . . . . **174** D5
Meadowgate Farm
WA7 . . . . **49** F2
Meadow Gr
Northwich CW9 . . . . **104** B5
Winsford CW7 . . . . **126** E5
Meadow Home Pk
CW7 . . . . **126** D6
Meadow House Pk
CW6 . . . . **185** D5
Meadow La
Comberbach CW9 . . . . **78** C7
Disley SK12 . . . . **38** D6
Ellesmere Port CH65 . . . . . **70** D6
Huntington CH3 . . . . **142** A5
Moulton CW9 . . . . **126** F8
Warrington WA2 . . . . **9** A2
Willaston CH64 . . . . **67** F8
Meadow Lane Ind Pk
CH3 . . . . **70** D3
Meadow Mill Ct
CW12 . . . . **156** E3
Meadow Rd
Broughton CH4 . . . . **139** B4
Weaverham CW8 . . . . **102** E7
Meadow Rise
Clutton CH3 . . . . **182** D2
Winsford CW7 . . . . **126** A1
Meadow Row WA7 . . . . . **24** A1
Meadowside
Disley SK12 . . . . **39** A6
Fourlane-ends SK10 . . . . . **63** B8
Frodsham WA6 . . . . **74** A8
Northwich CW8 . . . . **103** D7
Whaley Bridge SK23 . . . . . **65** D8
Meadowside Ave ST7 . . . **209** D2
**Meadowside Com Prim
Sch** WA2 . . . . **8** B1
Meadowside La ST7 . . . . **195** B7
Meadowside Mews
CH1 . . . . **118** B4
Meadowside Rd CH62 . . . **43** D8
Meadows La
Chester CH4 . . . . **237** C1
Saughall CH1 . . . . **117** A8
Tilston SY14 . . . . **212** B6
Meadows Pl CH4 . . . . . . **141** E7
Meadows Rd
Cheadle SK8 . . . . **34** F8
Kidsgrove ST7 . . . . **194** F1
Meadow St
New Mills SK22 . . . . **39** C8
[3] Northwich CW9 . . . . . . **104** A8
Meadows The
Ashton Hayes CH3 . . . . . . **121** E8
Bebington CH62 . . . . **43** D7
Congleton CW12 . . . . **156** E3
Irlam M44 . . . . **11** E6
Neston CH64 . . . . **66** F6
Meadowsway CH2 . . . . . **118** D8

Meadowsweet Rd
WA16 . . . . **57** F3
Meadow The CW4 . . . . . **130** D8
Meadowvale Cl CW5 . . . . **204** E7
Meadow View
Chester CH3 . . . . **118** F1
Ellesmere Port CH2 . . . . . . **70** E1
Elton CH2 . . . . **72** A3
Lymm WA13 . . . . **18** D4
Middlewich CW10 . . . . . . **128** B2
Sealand CH5 . . . . **116** A6
Meadow View Dr WA6 . . **74** A7
Meadow Way
Lawton-gate ST7 . . . . **194** A5
Macclesfield SK10 . . . . **87** E2
Wilmslow SK9 . . . . **59** E4
Meadow Wlk
Partington M31 . . . . **11** E3
[4] Runcorn WA7 . . . . **49** F7
Mead Rd WA1 . . . . **17** A8
Meadscroft Dr SK9 . . . . . **59** F1
Meadway Rd ST7 . . . . . . **193** D4
Meadway
Bramhall SK7 . . . . **35** E5
Ellesmere Port CH66 . . . . . **69** B7
Golborne WA3 . . . . **3** D8
Heswall CH60 . . . . **40** F6
High Lane SK6 . . . . **37** F8
Poynton SK12 . . . . **36** B4
Prestbury SK10 . . . . **87** A5
Runcorn WA7 . . . . **49** E8
Widnes WA8 . . . . **12** A1
Meakin Cl CW12 . . . . **157** B1
Mealors New Cotts
CH64 . . . . **67** A4
Mealors Weint CH64 . . . . **41** B1
Meal St SK22 . . . . **39** C8
Meddings Cl SK9 . . . . **85** A8
Medina Ave CW7 . . . . . . **126** F2
Medina Way ST7 . . . . . . **195** B2
Medlar Cl CH4 . . . . **140** F5
Medway Cl
Golborne WN7 . . . . **4** C8
Handforth SK9 . . . . **34** D2
Warrington WA3 . . . . **8** E2
Medway Dr ST8 . . . . **179** D1
Medway Rd WA3 . . . . **5** A2
Mecanee Dr CW5 . . . . . . **204** D4
Mee St SK11 . . . . **112** E5
Meeting House La
WA6 . . . . **74** E2
Meeting La WA5 . . . . **14** E5
MEGACRE **210** A1
Megacre ST7 . . . . **210** A1
Meg La
Langley SK11 . . . . **113** D1
Macclesfield SK10 . . . . . . **111** E8
Megs La CW9 . . . . **53** B4
Melbourne Ave CW1 . . . **191** C5
Melbourne Rd
Blacon CH1 . . . . **117** D4
Bramhall SK7 . . . . **35** F5
Melbury Ct WA3 . . . . **9** F6
Melbury Rd SK8 . . . . **35** B6
Melchett Cres CW9 . . . . **104** D7
Melford Cl CW2 . . . . **206** C8
Melford Ct WA1 . . . . **17** D8
Melford Dr
Macclesfield SK10 . . . . **87** C2
Runcorn WA7 . . . . **23** C1
Meliden Gr WA6 . . . . **73** B1
Melkridge Cl CH2 . . . . . . **119** A3
Melksham Cl SK11 . . . . . **112** A7
Mellard St ST7 . . . . **209** D1
Mellock Cl CH64 . . . . **66** F6
Mellock La CH64 . . . . . . **66** F7
Mellor Cl WA7 . . . . **24** A1
Mellor Cres WA16 . . . . . . **56** E1
Mellors Bank ST7 . . . . . **195** D6
Mellor St
Crewe CW1 . . . . **190** D5
Packmoor ST7 . . . . **195** F2
Mellor View SK12 . . . . . . **38** E6
Melrose Ave
Burtonwood WA5 . . . . **6** F7
Chester CH3 . . . . **119** B2
Warrington WA4 . . . . **26** D8
Melrose Cres SK10 . . . . . **87** C2
Melrose Ct [15] SK9 . . . . . **34** E1
Melrose Dr
Crewe CW1 . . . . **190** B8
Ellesmere Port CH66 . . . . . **94** F8
Melton Ave WA4 . . . . **26** B8
Melton Cl CW12 . . . . **155** F3
Melton Dr CW12 . . . . **155** F3
Melton Rd WA7 . . . . **49** C7
Melverly Dr CH1 . . . . **117** C4
Melville Cl
Warrington WA2 . . . . **16** B7
[3] Widnes WA8 . . . . **13** D1
Melville Rd M44 . . . . **11** C5
Mendell Cl CH62 . . . . **43** E8
Mendell Prim Sch
CH62 . . . . **43** E8
Mendip Ave WA2 . . . . **8** B3
Mendip Cl
Ellesmere Port CH66 . . . . . **69** E3
Gatley SK8 . . . . **34** B7
Winsford CW7 . . . . **149** B8
Menin Ave WA4 . . . . **16** C3
Menlow Cl WA4 . . . . **17** C1
Mentmore Gdns WA4 . . . **26** F5
Meols Cl
Ellesmere Port CH66 . . . . . **69** E4
Hale L24 . . . . **21** A2
Mercer Cl SY14 . . . . **213** B3
Mercer Rd WA11 . . . . **1** D6

Mercer St
Burtonwood WA5 . . . . **6** E6
Newton-le-W WA12 . . . . **2** D4
Mercer Way
Chester CH4 . . . . **140** F6
Nantwich CW5 . . . . **204** E7
Mercer Wlk CH65 . . . . . . **70** C4
Merchants Ct CW2 . . . . . **190** C7
Mercian Cl CW2 . . . . **206** B4
Mercury Ct CH1 . . . . **117** E2
MERE **56** B8
Mere Ave CH63 . . . . **43** B6
Mere Bank CW9 . . . . **127** A8
Merebank Rd CW2 . . . . . **190** B1
Merebrook Cl SK11 . . . . . **112** A8
Merebrook Rd SK11 . . . . **111** F8
Mere Brook Wlk CW2 . . . **190** C1
Mere Cl
Ellesmere Port CH66 . . . . . **69** D2
Haslington CW1 . . . . **191** D4
Pickmere WA16 . . . . **80** A7
Mere Cres CW8 . . . . **123** F6
Merecroft [1] CH3 . . . . . . **119** A1
Mere Ct
Alsager ST7 . . . . **193** D4
Chelford SK11 . . . . **83** F3
[6] Knutsford WA16 . . . . . . **57** A2
Weston CW2 . . . . **207** B5
Meredith Ave WA4 . . . . . **17** B2
Meredith St CW1 . . . . . . **190** C5
Mere Hall WA16 . . . . **56** A8
Merehaven Cl WA16 . . . . **80** A7
MERE HEATH **127** A8
Merehearth La WA16 . . . **56** E5
Merehearth Pk WA16 . . . **56** F4
Mere Ho ST7 . . . . **193** C3
Mere La
Cuddington CW8 . . . . **102** A2
Pickmere WA16 . . . . **79** F7
Merelake Rd ST7 . . . . . . **210** B8
Meremore Dr ST5 . . . . . **210** D2
Mere Rd
Marston CW9 . . . . **79** B6
Newton-le-W WA12 . . . . **2** D2
Warrington WA2 . . . . **9** A2
Weston CW2 . . . . **207** B5
Mereside Ave CW12 . . . **156** B3
Mereside Cl SK10 . . . . . . **87** A1
Mereside Gdns SK23 . . . . **65** D6
Mereside Rd WA16 . . . . . **30** C2
Mere St CW1 . . . . **191** D4
Merevale Cl WA7 . . . . **49** E6
Mere View WA6 . . . . **73** A2
Mere View Gdns WA4 . . . **26** E5
Merewood Cl WA7 . . . . . **49** C7
Mereworth Dr CW9 . . . . **103** F5
Meridian Ho CW7 . . . . . **127** B3
Meriton Rd SK9 . . . . **34** D4
Merlin Ave WA16 . . . . **57** B3
Merlin Cl
Runcorn WA7 . . . . **24** A1
Winsford CW7 . . . . **150** A8
Merlin Way
Crewe CW1 . . . . **190** A8
Kidsgrove ST7 . . . . **195** D3
Merrick Cl WA3 . . . . **9** E3
Merridale The WA15 . . . . **32** A8
Merriden Rd SK10 . . . . . . **87** B2
Merrill's Ave CW7 . . . . . **189** E5
Merriman Ave WA16 . . . . **57** C3
Merrivale Rd CW2 . . . . . **206** B8
Merrydale Cl SK10 . . . . . **86** F1
Merryman's La SK9 . . . . . **84** B7
Mersey Pl CW7 . . . . **127** B1
Mersey Rd
Runcorn WA7 . . . . **23** A3
Widnes WA8 . . . . **23** A4
Mersey St
St Helens WA9 . . . . **1** A3
Warrington WA1 . . . . **16** B5
Merseyton Rd CH65 . . . . . **70** B8
**Merseyton Road
Workshops** CH65 . . . . **70** C7
Mersey View WA7 . . . . . . **48** D7
Mersey View Rd WA8 . . . **22** B4
Mersey Wlk WA4 . . . . **16** F5
Mersham Ct WA8 . . . . . . **12** F4
Merton Ave SK7 . . . . **36** F8
Merton Cl CH64 . . . . **66** E5
Merton Dr CH4 . . . . **141** A4
Merton House Sch
CH2 . . . . **118** C4
Merton Rd
Bebington CH65 . . . . **44** B3
Ellesmere Port CH66 . . . . . **69** F3
Poynton SK12 . . . . **36** B4
Mertoun Rd WA16 . . . . . . **16** B1
Mervyn Rd WA5 . . . . **14** F2
Merwood Ave SK8 . . . . . . **34** D8
Messuage La CW12 . . . . **132** E4
Meteor Cres WA2 . . . . **8** D2
Mevagissey Rd WA7 . . . . **50** C5
Mevril Rd SK23 . . . . **65** E5
Mevril Springs Way
SK23 . . . . **65** E5
Mews The
Barnton CW8 . . . . **78** B2
Burtonwood WA5 . . . . **6** E6
Mottram St Andrew SK10 . . **60** E1
New Mills SK22 . . . . **39** D8
Tarporley CW6 . . . . **168** C8
Willaston CH64 . . . . **68** A8
Wilmslow SK9 . . . . **33** D4
Meynell Cl CW2 . . . . **190** A1
Meynell Pl CH1 . . . . **118** A5
Meyrick Cl WA12 . . . . **2** A1
Miami Cl [5] WA5 . . . . **15** E7
Micawber Rd SK12 . . . . . **36** E2

Micklegate
Mickle Trafford CH2 . . . . . **119** E8
Runcorn WA7 . . . . **50** D7
MICKLE TRAFFORD . . . **119** E8
**Mickle Trafford Village
Sch** CH2 . . . . **119** E8
Micklewright Ave
CW1 . . . . **190** D5
Mickley Hall La CW5 . . . **218** A4
**Mid-Cheshire Coll
(Hartford Campus)**
CW8 . . . . **103** C6
**Mid Cheshire Coll (London
Road Studios)** CW9 . . . . **103** F6
**Mid Cheshire Coll (Verdin
Ctr)** CW7 . . . . **126** D1
Middlecroft CH3 . . . . **119** E5
Middlehills SK11 . . . . **113** A6
Middlehurst Ave CW8 . . . **102** E8
Middlehurst Rd WA4 . . . . **17** A2
Middle La
Aldford CH3 . . . . **163** F3
Congleton CW12 . . . . **157** D4
Kingsley WA6 . . . . **74** F2
MIDDLEWICH **128** D3
Middlewich High Sch
CW10 . . . . **151** C8
Middlewich Prim Sch
CW10 . . . . **151** B8
Middlewich Rd
Allostock WA16 . . . . **106** D5
Church Minshull CW1,
CW10 . . . . **172** E5
Cranage CW4, CW10 . . . . **129** E6
Crewe CW1 . . . . **189** D6
Delamere CW6, CW8 . . . . **123** D5
Holmes Chapel CW4 . . . . **130** B3
Knutsford WA16 . . . . **82** A3
Lower Peover WA16 . . . . . . **81** F2
Nantwich CW5 . . . . **189** B1
Nantwich CW5 . . . . **204** F7
Northwich CW9 . . . . **126** D8
Sandbach CW11 . . . . **174** E7
Winsford CW7, CW10 . . . . **127** E1
Middlewich Road Ind Est
CW10 . . . . **129** A6
Middlewich St CW1 . . . . **190** D6
Middle Wlk
Frodsham WA6 . . . . **74** B7
Knutsford WA16 . . . . **57** B2
MIDDLEWOOD **37** C5
Middlewood Rd
Hazel Grove SK7, SK12 . . . **37** C7
High Lane SK6 . . . . **37** D7
Poynton SK12 . . . . **37** B4
Middlewood Sta SK12 . . . . **37** D6
Middlewood View SK6 . . . . **37** D7
Midfield Cl ST8 . . . . **179** D2
Midhurst Cl SK8 . . . . **34** F8
Midland St WA8 . . . . **13** B1
Midland Terr SK22 . . . . . **39** C7
Midland Way WA1,
WA5 . . . . **16** B5
Midlothian Ho [4]
CH1 . . . . **237** C3
**Midpoint 18 Motorway Ind
Est** CW10 . . . . **128** E1
MIDWAY **36** D2
Midway SK8 . . . . **35** B5
Midway Dr SK12 . . . . **36** D2
Milborne Cl CH2 . . . . **118** E5
Mildenhall Cl WA5 . . . . . . **15** B6
Mile Bank Rd SY13 . . . . . **226** D3
Miles Cl WA3 . . . . **9** F3
Milford Gdns WA4 . . . . . . **26** C8
Milk Cl CW12 . . . . **156** D3
Millar Cres WA8 . . . . **23** A7
Mill Ave WA5 . . . . **14** E7
Millbank WA13 . . . . **18** E3
Mill Bank CH64 . . . . **67** A5
Millbank Cl SK11 . . . . **84** A3
Millbank Cotts CH3 . . . . **166** C2
Millbank Cl WA4 . . . . **74** A8
Millbank Dr SK10 . . . . **86** F1
Millbeck Cl CW2 . . . . **207** B5
Mill Bridge Cl CW1 . . . . **190** F3
Millbridge Gdns WA12 . . . **2** E3
Millbrook Cl
Fowley Common WA3 . . . . . **5** C5
Winsford CW7 . . . . **148** F8
Millbrook Ct
Middlewich CW10 . . . . . . **128** D1
Warrington WA2 . . . . **8** B2
Millbrook End CH3 . . . . **166** A2
Millbrook Fold SK7 . . . . . **36** F8
Millbrook Gr [1] SK9 . . . . **34** D1
Mill Brow WA8 . . . . **13** C1
Millbuck Pk CW11 . . . . . **174** C5
Millbuck Way CW11 . . . . **174** C6
Mill Cl
Chester CH2 . . . . **118** D6
Knutsford WA16 . . . . **57** D4
Warrington WA2 . . . . **8** E4
Mill Cotts
Bollington SK10 . . . . **88** B8
Christleton CH3 . . . . **142** D8
Willaston CH64 . . . . **42** F1
Millcroft
Neston CH64 . . . . **41** E1
Mill Cross CH3 . . . . **143** B5
Mill Ct CH65 . . . . **69** F6
Milldale Rd WN7 . . . . **4** B8
MILLEND **209** C5
Millend La ST7 . . . . **209** C5
Millenium Way [8] WA5 . . **15** B7

Millennium Ct CH64 . . . . **41** E2
Millennium Way ST5 . . . **210** F2
Millers Cl CH3 . . . . **143** A4
Millers Croft [8] SK10 . . **112** C8
Millers Ct [6] SK10 . . . . **112** C8
Millersdale Cl CH62 . . . . . **43** F5
Millersdale Gr WA7 . . . . . **49** D6
Millers La WA13 . . . . **19** B5
Millers Mdw SK10 . . . . . . **88** E5
Miller St WA4 . . . . **16** C4
Millers View ST7 . . . . . . **195** A1
Millers Wharf ST7 . . . . . **193** E7
Milley La WA16 . . . . **80** C7
Mill Farm Cl WA2 . . . . **8** E3
Mill Farm Cotts CW7 . . . **149** B3
Mill Farm Est CW5 . . . . **217** A3
Millfield
Holt LL13 . . . . **196** D7
Neston CH64 . . . . **41** E1
Millfield Bsns Ctr WA11 . . **1** E8
Mill Field Cl CH3 . . . . **180** F2
Millfield La
Haydock WA11 . . . . **1** E8
Saighton CH3 . . . . **142** F1
Tarporley CW6 . . . . **146** C2
Millfield Rd WA8 . . . . **13** C2
Millfields CW5 . . . . **204** D4
Millfields Prim Sch
Bebington CH62 . . . . **43** E4
Nantwich CW5 . . . . **204** D5
Millfield Terr CH66 . . . . . **69** C7
Millgate CW8 . . . . **101** F4
Mill Gn
Congleton CW12 . . . . **156** D3
Willaston CH64 . . . . **67** F8
Mill Gr
Bulkeley SY14 . . . . **184** E2
Kidsgrove ST7 . . . . **194** D1
Mill Green La WA8 . . . . . . **13** E5
Mill Green Sch WA12 . . . . **2** E3
Mill Hill Ave SK12 . . . . . . **36** D7
Mill Hill Dr CW11 . . . . . . **175** A5
Mill Hill Hollow SK12 . . . **36** D7
Mill Hill La CW11 . . . . . . **175** A4
Mill Ho CW5 . . . . **204** D5
Millhouse Ave WA4 . . . . . **26** D1
Millhouse La WA3 . . . . **9** A6
Milling Field The
CW4 . . . . **130** C2
Millingford Ind Est WA3 . . **3** A8
Millington Cl
Runcorn WA7 . . . . **49** F3
Widnes WA8 . . . . **22** F8
Millington Hall La
WA14 . . . . **30** B5
Millington La
Rostherne WA14 . . . . **30** B6
Weaverham CW8 . . . . **102** B6
Mill La
Adlington SK10 . . . . **62** B6
Aldford CH3 . . . . **163** F3
Alsager CW11 . . . . **192** E8
Altrincham WA15 . . . . **32** E4
Audlem, Little Heath
CW3 . . . . **230** A4
Audlem, Swanbach
CW3 . . . . **229** E2
Barthomley CW2 . . . . **208** C7
Blakenhall CW5 . . . . **221** B4
Bold Heath WA8 . . . . **13** D6
Bollington SK10 . . . . **88** C8
Brereton Green CW4 . . . . **153** E8
Bulkeley SY14 . . . . **184** E2
Durten CH3 . . . . **147** C8
Chester CH2 . . . . **118** D6
Christleton CH3 . . . . **120** D2
Congleton CW12 . . . . **179** C8
Cronton WA8 . . . . **12** D6
Cuddington CW8 . . . . **101** F4
Duddon CW6 . . . . **145** A7
Eaton CW6 . . . . **147** B2
Ellesmere Port CH66 . . . . . **69** E5
Frodsham WA6 . . . . **49** E2
Goostrey CW4 . . . . **107** E2
Great Barrow CH3 . . . . . . **120** E5
Hazel Grove SK7 . . . . **36** F8
Heswall CH60 . . . . **41** B8
Higher Walton WA4 . . . . . . **25** E7
Holmes Chapel CW4 . . . . **154** A8
Huxley CH3 . . . . **144** C1
Kelsall CW6 . . . . **122** C1
Kingsley WA6 . . . . **75** E3
Lindow End SK9 . . . . **84** A8
Little Budworth CW6 . . . . **148** A8
Lymm WA13 . . . . **19** C4
Macclesfield SK11 . . . . . . **112** D1
Marton CW12 . . . . **132** F2
Middlewich CW10 . . . . . . **128** D1
Middlewich, Newtonia
CW10 . . . . **128** B1
Middlewich, Stud Green
CW11 . . . . **152** C1
Mobberley WA16 . . . . **58** B4
Mottram St Andrew
SK10 . . . . **61** C5
Neston CH64 . . . . **67** C5
Newton-le-W WA12 . . . . **2** E3
Over Peover WA16,
SK11 . . . . **108** D8
Prestbury SK10 . . . . **61** F6
Sandbach CW11 . . . . **174** C8
Sandbach, Wheelock
CW11 . . . . **175** B2
Siddington SK11 . . . . **109** F6
Smallwood CW11 . . . . **176** D7

Mill La continued

Tarvin CH3	121 C4
The Bank ST7	195 A7
Warrington, Houghton Gn WA2	8 E4
Warrington, Stockton Heath WA1	16 E1
Warrington WA2	7 F4
Weston CW2	207 B6
Whitegate CW7, CW8	126 B6
Willaston CH64	42 F1
Mill Lane Cotts CH3	120 E5
Mill Lane End CW5	221 C4
Mill Mdw WA12	2 E3
Millmead ST7	193 F7
Mill Park Dr CH62	43 E3
Mill Pool La CW5	187 C6
Millport Cl WA2	9 A2
Millrace Dr CW2	206 B8
Mill Rd	
Macclesfield SK11	112 D6
Wilmslow SK9	60 B7
Mill Rise	
Helsby WA6	73 C4
Kidsgrove ST7	195 A1
Mill Row CH1	175 C6
Mill St	
Chester CH4	237 B1
Congleton, Buglawton CW12	156 F4
Congleton CW12	156 D3
Crewe CW2	190 D3
Golborne WA3	3 A8
Macclesfield SK11	112 D7
Nantwich CW5	204 E5
Neston CH64	66 D8
Wilmslow SK9	60 B7
Millstone Ave ST7	194 E1
Millstone Cl SK12	36 F5
Millstone La CW5	204 F5
Millstone Pas SK11	112 E6
Mill Stream Cl CW4	107 E1
Mills Way CW1	173 B1
Mill The ST7	195 C5
Mill View Cl SY14	184 E2
Mill View Prim Sch CH2	118 E6
Millway	
Altrincham WA15	32 C7
Waverton CH3	143 B5
Mill Way CW5	204 F2
Millway Rd L24	21 A4
Mill Wharf CH3	143 B5
Millwood WA7	24 C1
Millwood Cl 4 SK8	34 E8
Millwood Ct L24	21 A4
Millyard The CH4	162 C1
Milne Cl CW2	189 F1
Milner Cop CH60	41 A8
Milner Rd	
Heswall CH60	41 A8
Northwich CW8	103 C6
MILNERS GREEN	143 C2
Milner St WA5	15 F5
Milnthorpe Rd WA5	6 E6
Milton Ave	
Irlam M44	11 E6
Newton-le-W WA12	2 B3
Widnes WA8	22 F8
Milton Cl	
Ellesmere Port CH65	70 D4
Higher Wincham CW9	80 A5
Middlewich CW10	151 D5
Milton Cres ST7	210 C8
Milton Ct SK7	35 F6
Milton Dr	
Poynton SK12	36 D4
Wistaston CW2	206 A8
Milton Gr	
Helsby WA6	73 A1
Warrington WA4	16 D3
MILTON GREEN	165 C2
Milton Rd	
Blacon CH1	117 F6
Bramhall SK7	35 E7
Ellesmere Port CH65	70 D4
Golborne WA3	3 D7
Widnes WA8	23 A8
Milton Rough CW8	76 E2
Milton St	
Chester CH4	237 B3
Widnes WA8	23 A5
Milton Way CW11	174 D6
Milvain Dr WA2	8 C1
Milverton Dr SK7	35 B5
Mimosa Cl CH2	72 C4
Miners Way	
Speke L24	21 A3
Widnes WA8	23 A7
Minerva Ave CH1	117 E2
Minerva Cl WA4	16 D2
Minerva Ct CH1	117 E2
Mine Way WA11	1 F7
Minn-End-La SK11	159 B6
Minor Ave SK11	112 D3
Minshull La CW5, CW7	171 D1
Minshull New Rd CW1	189 F7
Minshull St WA16	57 A2
MINSHULL VERNON	172 E5
Minster Cl CW7	149 D5
Minster Ct	
Runcorn WA7	48 E8
Wistaston CW2	205 E8

Minster Dr WA14	31 A8
Minton Cl CW12	157 B1
Minton Way WA8	13 B5
Mirfield Cl WA3	3 D7
Mirion St CW1	190 D4
Mission Mews CH2	118 F2
Misty Cl WA8	12 C2
Mitchell Ave	
Burtonwood WA5	6 E5
Kidsgrove ST7	194 D1
Mitchell Dr ST7	194 D1
Mitchell Fold	
Fourlane-ends SK10	63 D8
High Lane SK6	37 D1
Mitchell St	
Golborne WA3	3 A8
Warrington WA4	26 C8
Mithril Cl WA8	13 E3
Mitton Cl WA3	4 E5
MMU Cheshire (Crewe Campus) CW1	190 F3
Moat Ho 17 WA8	103 F8
Moat La	
Audley ST7	209 B3
Bickerton Green WA3	10 E2
MOBBERLEY	58 A4
Mobberley CE Prim Sch WA16	58 C5
Mobberley Cl WA4	17 D4
Mobberley Rd	
Ashley WA14, WA15, WA16	31 E3
Knutsford WA16	57 B3
Wilmslow SK9	33 D1
Mobberley Sta WA16	57 F7
MOBLAKE	230 D4
Modyn CH2	118 C4
Moelfre Dr SK8	35 C7
Moggie La SK10	36 F1
Mold Rd CH4	139 A3
MOLLINGTON	94 F2
Mollington Ct CH1	94 F2
Mollington Grange Bsns Pk CH1	117 F8
Mollington Rd M22	33 E8
Molly Potts Cl WA16	82 B8
Molyneux Ave CW5	15 F8
Monarch Cl	
Crewe CW2	189 F4
Irlam M44	11 E6
Monarch Dr CW9	103 E5
Monck Dr CW5	204 D6
Mond Rd WA8	23 A8
Mond St WA8	78 B3
Monica Dr WA8	13 A5
Monks Coppenhall Prim Sch CW1	190 E7
Monks Gr CH65	70 B6
MONKS HEATH	85 A1
Monk's Heath Crossroads SK10	85 A1
Monks Heath Hall Wrkshps SK10	85 B1
Monks La	
Acton CW5	203 F7
Crewe CW1	189 F5
Nantwich CW5	204 E5
Monk's Orch CW5	204 F5
Monks Pl WA2	16 C7
Monks St WA5	15 E6
Monk St CW1	190 A5
Monks Way CW8	103 B4
Monkswood Cl WA5	7 E2
Monmouth Cl WA1	17 E7
Monroe Cl WA1	17 B8
Monsall Cl SK11	112 D7
Monsall Dr SK11	112 F7
Montague Rd WA8	22 A6
Montana Cl 3 WA5	15 C7
Montclare Cres WA4	16 F2
Montcliffe Cl WA3	9 C5
Montgomery Cl	
Knutsford WA16	57 C4
Warrington WA5	15 A8
Montgomery Rd WA8	22 D8
Montgomery Way CW7	149 B7
Montmorency Rd WA16	57 D3
Montpelier Ave WA7	48 F6
Montrose Cl	
Macclesfield SK10	87 A1
Shavington CW2	206 B3
Warrington WA2	8 F4
Montrose Ct	
Chester CH4	140 F7
Holmes Chapel CW4	130 B2
Monument Rd ST7	210 D6
Monument View ST7	209 F2
Moody St CW12	156 D2
Moor Cl ST8	179 E1
Moor Cres CW4	139 D1
Moorcroft WA16	80 F3
Moorcroft Ave CH3	119 B1
Moorcroft Cres CH3	119 C4
Moorcroft Ct CH3	119 B1
Moorcroft Mews CH4	140 D6
Moordale Rd WA16	57 B2
Moorditch La	
Frodsham WA6	48 D1
Frodsham WA6	48 F1
MOORE	25 B6
Moore Ave	
St Helens WA9	1 B3
Warrington WA3	17 D3
Moore Cl WA8	13 D2
Moore Dr WA11	1 F6

Moore Gr WA13	19 B5
Moore La WA4	25 C7
Moore Prim Sch WA4	25 A5
Moorfield Cres WA3	4 A7
Moorfield	
Neston CH64	41 C1
Wilmslow SK9	59 E5
Moorfield Prim Sch WA8	13 D3
Moorfield Rd WA8	13 D3
Moorfields CW5	205 E6
Moorhead La CW11	154 D3
Moorhill Rd SK11	112 C4
Moor Ho WA6	74 B8
Moorhouse Ave ST7	193 E4
Moorhouse Cl CH2	118 D5
Mooring Cl WA7	50 D6
Moorings CW12	156 E1
Moorings Cl CH64	41 B1
Moorings The	
Christleton CH3	142 E7
Disley SK12	38 E6
Heswall CH60	40 C8
Middlewich CW10	128 C1
Moor La	
Bramhall SK7	35 E3
Elton WA6	72 E1
Frodsham WA6	74 B8
Heswall CH60	40 F8
Higher Kinnerton CH4	161 D8
Lower Kinnerton CH4	161 C6
Sandycroft CH5	116 A2
Waverton CH3	143 A6
Widnes WA8	22 F7
Widnes WA8	23 A7
Wilmslow SK9	59 E5
Moorland Cl CH60	41 A7
Moorland Dr	
Cheadle SK8	34 F8
Runcorn WA7	50 E7
Moorland Pk CH60	41 A7
Moorland Rd	
Biddulph ST8	179 D1
Ellesmere Port CH66	69 E8
Mow Cop ST7	195 D7
Moorlands Ave CW8	102 A4
Moorlands Cl SK10	87 C3
Moorlands Dr CW5	206 A1
Moorlands Pk CW8	102 A4
Moor Lane Bsns Ctr 9 WA8	23 A7
Moor La S WA8	22 F7
Moor-Park Way CW9	103 F4
Moorsbrook Gr 9 SK9	34 E1
Moorsfield Ave CW3	229 F3
MOORSIDE	66 C7
Moorside	
Knutsford WA16	57 A2
Warrington WA4	16 E4
Moorside Ave CH66	66 C8
Moorside Ct WA8	22 F7
Moorside La	
Neston CH64	66 D8
Pott Shrigley SK10	63 E4
Moors La CW7	149 D5
Moorson Ave ST7	194 F8
Moor St CW12	156 F2
Moorview Gdns ST7	195 E6
Moorway CH60	41 B8
Moran Cl SK9	34 E2
Moran Cres SK11	112 B7
Moran Dr WA5	15 A6
Moran Rd SK11	112 B7
Morcott La L24	21 D2
Moresby Cl WA7	50 E7
Moreton Cl WA3	4 F3
Moreton Ct CW11	175 C7
Moreton Dr	
Alsager ST7	193 C3
Handforth SK9	34 E3
Holmes Chapel CW4	130 B3
Poynton SK12	36 F4
Moreton Pl ST7	194 E6
Moreton Rd CW2	189 F3
Moreton St CW8	78 D1
Moreton Terr WA6	74 A8
Moreville Cl CW9	103 E3
Morgan Ave WA2	8 C2
Morgan Cl	
Blacon CH1	117 F6
Crewe CW2	190 A4
Morgans Way WA3	4 A8
Morgan Wlk CW5	204 D6
Morland Ave	
Bebington CH62	43 D6
Neston CH64	66 F7
MORLEY	33 C2
Morley Cl CH2	119 F8
MORLEY COMMON	15 F1
Morley Dr CW12	157 A1
MORLEY GREEN	33 C1
Morley Green Rd SK9	33 C1
Morley Rd	
Runcorn WA7	23 A1
Warrington WA4	16 B1
Morley St WA1	16 D6
Mornant Ave CW8	103 A4
Mornington Ave CH65	70 C5
Mornington Cl CW11	174 D7
Morphany La WA4	51 E6
Morreys La CW6	122 F6
Morris Ave WA4	16 F4
Morris Cl WA11	1 A5
Morris Dr CW8	78 B1
Morrison Cl WA5	15 A5
Morris Pk CW8	103 B4
Mort Ave WA4	17 A5
Mortimer Ave WA2	16 B8

Mortimer Dr CW11	175 C5
Mortlake Cl WA8	12 C3
Mortlake Cres CH3	119 A1
Morton Ave WA6	73 B1
Morton Cl WA5	15 C8
Morton Dr SK11	112 F3
Morton Gdns CH1	117 E4
Morton Rd	
Blacon CH1	117 E4
Runcorn WA7	50 D0
Morval Cres WA7	23 D1
Morven Cl WA2	8 E3
Mosedale Gr WA7	49 E5
Moseley Ave WA4	17 A3
Moses Ct CH1	237 C3
MOSS BANK	23 D8
Moss Bank	
Bramhall SK7	35 C5
Chester CH2	118 C4
Winsford CW7	126 C1
Moss Bank Rd SK11	112 C4
Moss Bower Rd SK11	112 C4
MOSSBROW	19 E7
Moss Brow SK10	87 E7
Moss Brow La WA16	28 D4
Moss Cl	
Warrington WA4	16 E2
Willaston CH64	68 A8
Moss Croft CW1	190 A8
Mossdale Cl	
Crewe CW2	189 E4
Warrington WA5	15 A7
Moss Dr	
Manley WA6	98 F4
Middlewich CW10	151 D6
MOSSEND	154 E1
MOSS END	54 C2
Moss End La CW11	176 E8
Moss Farm Barns CH8	102 D4
Moss Farm Recn Ctr CW8	103 D8
Mossfield Cres 4 ST7	195 B2
Moss Fields	
Alsager ST7	193 A3
Crewe CW1	173 A1
Mossford Ave CW1	190 B7
Moss Gate WA4	10 A5
Moss Gr	
Lymm WA13	19 B4
Newcastle-u-Lyme ST5	210 D3
Saltney CH4	140 D6
Moss Green Way WA9	1 A1
Moss Hall La WA4	26 F1
Moss Hall La CW6	147 C4
Moss Hey Prim Sch SK7	35 C5
MOSS HOUSES	111 F2
Moss La	
Alderley Edge SK9	60 B1
Bollington SK10	87 E8
Bramhall SK7	35 D5
Brereton Green CW12	154 F5
Byley CW10	129 B7
Congleton CW12	156 E6
Crewe CW1	173 A2
Cuddington CW8	102 A3
Dunham Woodhouses WA13	20 B8
Fowley Common WA3	5 D5
Golborne WA3	3 B5
Higher Wincham CW9	79 E6
High Legh, Sink Moss WA16	28 D4
High Legh WA16	29 E6
Hollins Green WA3	10 E5
Irlam M44	11 D5
Lawton-gate ST7	194 F4
Lostock Green CW9	105 D8
Macclesfield SK11	112 C4
Manley WA6	99 A4
Mere WA16	56 F4
Mobberley WA16	58 F4
Moore WA4	25 A6
Mottram St Andrew SK10	61 A2
Norbury SY13	215 C5
Norley WA6	101 B5
Northwich CW8	103 D7
Over Peover WA16	83 C3
Partington M31	11 F3
Partington, Mossbrow WA13	11 F1
Sandbach CW11	174 C7
Siddington SK11	109 E2
St Helens, Moss Nook WA9	1 A1
Tarporley CW6	146 B2
Warmingham CW11	173 C3
Warrington WA3	9 E1
Wythenshawe SK9	206 A1
Wythenshawe SK9	33 E6
Mosslands Cl CH66	69 E2
Moss Lane Bsns Ctr WA11	174 D6
Moss Lane Ind Est CW11	174 D7
MOSSLEY	179 A8
Mossley Ave CH62	43 D8
Mossley CE Prim Sch CW12	179 B8
Mossley Ct CW12	178 F8
Mossley Garth Cl 4 CW12	157 A1
Moss Mere CW11	176 F7
MOSS NOOK	33 F7
Moss Pl ST7	195 B3

Moss Rd	
Alderley Edge SK9	60 C2
Congleton CW12	178 F7
Irlam M44	
Northwich CW8	103 D6
Warrington WA4	17 A3
Moss Rose SK9	60 B2
Moss Rose Football Gnd SK11	112 D4
Moss Side La	
Antrobus CW9	53 D7
Hollins Green WA3	10 F3
Warrington WA4	24 F7
Moss Side Rd M44	11 E6
Moss Sq	
Crewe CW1	190 D3
Macclesfield SK11	112 D4
Moss St	
Weaverham CW8	77 D1
Widnes WA8	23 D7
Moss Terr	
Warren SK11	112 A5
Wilmslow SK9	60 F8
Winnington CW8	78 D1
Moss The CW9	78 D7
Mossvale CH66	69 D8
Moss View Rd SK11	112 A4
Moss Way ST7	193 A3
Mossways Pk SK9	59 C7
Mosswood Rd SK9	34 C1
MOSTON	95 L1
Moston Ct 5 CW12	156 F3
Moston Gr WA13	18 D3
MOSTON GREEN	174 B8
Moston Rd	
Chester CH2	118 D8
Sandbach CW11	174 D6
Moston Way CH66	69 F3
Mostyn Ave CH60	40 C8
Mostyn Gdns CH64	41 B1
Mostyn House Sch CH64	66 C8
Mostyn Pl CH1	117 C6
Mostyn Sq CH64	41 B1
Mote Hill Ct WA1	16 D6
Motherwell Cl WA8	13 A5
Mottershead Cl 1 WA8	23 A8
Mottershead Rd WA8	23 A8
Mottram Cl	
Middlewich CW10	151 B7
Warrington WA4	17 B3
Mottram Dr CW5	205 A4
Mottram Rd SK9	60 D1
MOTTRAM ST ANDREW	61 B2
Mottram St Andrew Prim Sch SK10	61 B1
Mottram Way SK10	87 E2
Moughland La WA7	49 A8
Moulders La WA1	16 B4
MOULDSWORTH	99 E3
Mouldsworth Cl 2 CW9	103 E4
Mouldsworth Motor Mus* CH3	99 E1
Mouldsworth Sta CH3	99 A2
MOULTON	126 F7
Moulton Cl	
Knutsford WA16	57 C1
Northwich CW9	103 E4
Runcorn WA7	49 F4
Moulton Sch CW9	126 F8
Mountain View	
Helsby WA6	73 B3
Saltney CH4	140 E6
Mount Ave CH60	40 F8
Mount Barns CH2	95 C6
Mountbatten Ct CW2	190 A3
Mountbatten Way CW12	156 E3
Mount Cl CW5	204 F6
Mount Ct 3 CH60	40 F8
Mount Dr CW5	204 F6
Mount Farm Way CH66	69 C2
Mountfield Rd SK7	35 E5
Mount Mews CH60	40 F8
Mount Pl CH2	118 F2
Mount Pleasant	
Audlem CW3	230 B4
Chester CH4	140 F7
Congleton CW12	156 B2
Crewe CW1	190 B6
Elton CH2	72 A4
Haslington CW1	191 D4
Kidsgrove ST7	195 A1
Macclesfield SK10	87 B1
MOUNT PLEASANT	195 B6
Mount Pleasant	
Rainow SK10	88 D3
Widnes WA8	13 B2
Wilmslow SK9	60 B8
MOUNT PLEASANT	149 A7
Mount Pleasant Ave WA9	1 B3
Mount Pleasant Dr CW7	149 A7
Mount Pleasant Rd	
Davenham CW9	103 F2
The Bank ST7	195 B4
Mount Pleasant Residential Pk CW4	130 D8
Mount Rd	
Kidsgrove ST7	195 B2
Runcorn WA7	49 F8
Mount St WA8	13 B1
Mount Terr SK11	112 F7

Mount The
Chester CH3 . . . . .118 F1
Congleton CW12 . . . . 156 A2
Great Budworth CW9 . . . . .79 A7
Hale WA15 . . . . .32 C8
Heswall CH60 . . . . .40 F8
Kidsgrove ST7 . . . . .195 A1
Scholar Green ST7 . . . . . . .194 E7
Mount Way CH3 . . . . 143 A4
Mourne Cl CH66 . . . . .69 A6
MOW COP 195 C7
Mow Cop Rd ST7 . . . . 195 D6
Mowcroft La WA5 . . . . . .14 B3
Mow La
Mount Pleasant ST7 . . . . . 195 A5
Mow Cop ST7 . . . . .179 B2
Mowpen Brow WA16 . . .29 B6
Moxon Ave WA4 . . . . .16 F5
Moyles Cl WA8 . . . . 12 D2
Mudhouse La CH64 . . . . . .67 F2
Mudhurst La SK12 . . . . . . .38 E3
Muirfield Cl
Northwich CW9 . . . . 104 A5
Warrington WA2 . . . . .9 A3
Wilmslow SK9 . . . . .60 D8
Muirfield Dr
Macclesfield SK10 . . . . .87 D4
Winsford CW7 . . . . .126 C2
Muirfield Mews CW7 . . 126 C2
Muir Rd CH1 . . . . .117 E3
Mulberry Ave WA3 . . . . . . .3 F7
Mulberry Cl
Elton CH2 . . . . .72 C3
Gatley SK8 . . . . .34 C7
Warrington WA1 . . . . .17 E7
Mulberry Ct
Macclesfield SK11 . . . . 112 D4
Warrington WA1 . . . . .16 D1
Mulberry Dr SK10 . . . . . . .87 E1
Mulberry Gdns CW11 . . 174 D7
Mulberry Rd CW2 . . . . . . 189 E2
Mulberry Rise CW8 . . . . 103 C7
Mulcaster Ct CW1 . . . . . . 191 D5
Mull Cl CH65 . . . . .70 C1
Mullein Cl WA3 . . . . .3 D8
Mullen Cl WA5 . . . . .7 F1
Mullins Ave WA12 . . . . .2 C5
Mullion Cl WA7 . . . . .50 B6
Mullion Gr WA2 . . . . .9 A1
Mulsford Ct LL13 . . . . 222 A8
Mulsford La LL13,
SY14 . . . . 222 B8
MURDISHAW 50 D7
Murdishaw Ave WA7 . . . .50 D6
Murdishaw West Com
Prim Sch WA7 . . . . .50 D6
Muriel Cl WA5 . . . . .14 D6
Murray Cl SK10 . . . . .87 A1
Murrayfield SK10 . . . . .87 A5
Murrayfield Dr CW5 . . . . 205 D5
Museum St WA1 . . . . .16 A4
Music Hall Pass CH1 . . . 237 B2
Muslin Row CW5 . . . . 172 A5
Mustard La WA3 . . . . .4 B1
Myddleton La WA2 . . . . . . .8 C6
Myrica Gr CH2 . . . . 119 B3
Myrtle Ave
Haydock WA11 . . . . .1 B7
Higher Kinnerton CH4 . . . 161 A7
Newton-le-W WA12 . . . . .2 C2
Myrtle La
Warrington WA4 . . . . .16 D3
Widnes WA8 . . . . .22 D8
Myrtle Rd M31 . . . . 11 D3
Myrtle St
Crewe CW2 . . . . 190 C3
Ellesmere Port CH65 . . . . . .70 C7
Mytholme Ave M44 . . . . . 11 C3
Mytton Dr CW5 . . . . 204 D6

N

Nabbs Cl ST7 . . . . 195 B2
Nabbswood Rd ST7 . . . . . 195 B2
Nab Cl SK10 . . . . .63 C1
Nab La SK10 . . . . .63 C1
Nairn Ave CW4 . . . . 130 B2
Nairn Cl
Bebington CH63 . . . . .43 D4
Warrington WA2 . . . . .9 B3
Nancy View SK10 . . . . .88 B8
Nansen Cl WA5 . . . . .15 D7
Nansmoss La SK9 . . . . .33 D1
Nant Peris CH1 . . . . 117 D3
NANTWICH 204 D6
Nantwich Mus* CW5 . . . 204 E5
Nantwich Rd
Audley ST7 . . . . 209 B1
Barbridge CW5 . . . . 187 B8
Betley ST7 . . . . 208 E1
Broxton CH3 . . . . 183 C1
Chorley Bank CW5 . . . . 201 E2
Crewe CW2 . . . . 190 C2
Ellesmere Port CH66 . . . . . .69 F3
Middlewich CW10 . . . . 151 A2
Sound CW5 . . . . 217 B5
Tarporley CW6 . . . . 168 D7
Wimboldsley CW10 . . . . . 150 F5
Wistaston CW2, CW5 . . . 189 C2
Woore CW3 . . . . 232 B1
Nantwich Sta CW5 . . . . . 204 E4
Nantwich Trade Yd
CW5 . . . . 204 F7
Nantwich Way ⑥ SK9 . . .34 E5
Naomi Cl CH1 . . . . 117 D5
Napier Gdns ① ST7 . . . . 195 A1
Napier Rd CH2 . . . . 118 C8

Napier St WA1 . . . . .16 C5
Napley Dr TF9 . . . . 236 C2
NAPLEY HEATH 236 F1
Napley Rd TF9 . . . . 236 D1
Nares Cl WA5 . . . . .7 C1
Narrow La
Crewe, Crewe Green
CW1 . . . . 191 C3
Wardsend SK10 . . . . .37 A1
Naseby Rd CW12 . . . . 156 A3
Nathan Dr WA11 . . . . .1 E6
Nathans Mdw CW12 . . . 179 C7
Nat La CW7 . . . . 126 F2
Nat Lane Ret Pk CW7 . . 126 F2
Naughton Lea WA8 . . . . .12 D3
Naughton Rd ③ WA8 . . . .23 A8
Navan Ct CW1 . . . . 190 B5
Navigation Cl WA7 . . . . . .50 D6
Navigation Ho ⑯
CW9 . . . . 103 F8
Navigation Rd WA8 . . . . 103 F7
Navigation St WA1 . . . . . .16 D5
Naylor Ave WA3 . . . . .3 B8
Naylor Cl CH66 . . . . .69 F8
Naylor Cres
Ellesmere Port CH66 . . . . . .69 F8
Nantwich CW5 . . . . 205 A4
Naylor Ct
Ellesmere Port CH66 . . . . . .69 E6
Warrington WA9 . . . . .103 F8
Warrington WA9 . . . . .69 F8
Naylor Pl CH66 . . . . .69 F8
Naylor Rd
Overpool CH66 . . . . .69 F7
Widnes WA8 . . . . .13 D1
Naylor St WA1 . . . . .16 B5
Naylor Wlk CH66 . . . . .69 F8
Nazareth House La
WA8 . . . . .22 C7
Neal Ave SK8 . . . . .34 A8
Neath Cl SK12 . . . . .36 D5
Needham Cl WA7 . . . . .23 D2
Needham Dr
Cranage CW4 . . . . 130 A5
Hartford CW8 . . . . 103 A4
Needhams Bank
CW11 . . . . 174 C6
Needhams Wharf Cl
SK10 .88 A1
Neills Rd WA5 . . . . .6 B6
Neil St WA8 . . . . .13 C2
Nelson Ave SK12 . . . . .37 A3
Nelson Bldgs ST7 . . . . . . 195 A1
Nelson Cl SK12 . . . . .37 A3
Nelson Dr M44 . . . . 11 E6
Nelson Gr ST7 . . . . 193 F2
Nelson Ind Est ST7 . . . . 194 C1
Nelson Rd CH65 . . . . .70 C7
Nelson St
Chester CH1 . . . . 237 C3
Congleton CW12 . . . . 156 D2
Crewe CW2 . . . . 190 C2
Macclesfield SK11 . . . . 112 D7
Newton-le-W WA12 . . . . .2 A3
③ Runcorn WA7 . . . . .23 A2
Widnes WA8 . . . . .23 A6
Nemos Cl WA6 . . . . .73 C2
Neptune Cl WA7 . . . . .50 D7
Nesfield Cl CW11 . . . . 191 F7
Nesfield Ct CW11 . . . . 191 F7
NESS .67 B4
Ness Acre La CH64 . . . . . .67 E8
Ness Botanic Gdns*
CH64 .67 A3
Nesse Ho CH64 . . . . .66 D8
NESS HOLT 66 F5
Nessina Gr CW2 . . . . 205 F8
NESTON 66 E7
Neston Dr CH2 . . . . 118 E5
Neston Gn CH66 . . . . .69 D4
Neston High Sch CH64 . .41 F1
Neston Prim Sch CH64 . .66 E7
Neston Rd
Heswall CH63, CH64 . . . . . .41 F5
Neston CH64 . . . . .67 B3
Willaston CH64 . . . . .67 F8
Neston Road Cotts
CH63 .42 A6
Neston Sta CH64 . . . . .66 E8
Neston Way SK9 . . . . .34 D3
NETHER ALDERLEY 85 A6
Nether Alderley Mill*
SK10 .85 A5
Nether Alderley Prim Sch
SK10 .85 A6
Netherfield WA8 . . . . .22 E8
Netherfields SK9 . . . . .85 A8
Nether Fold SK10 . . . . .87 A8
Nether Lea CW4 . . . . 130 C8
Netherley Rd WA8 . . . . . . .12 F3
Netherpool Rd CH66 . . . .69 F8
NETHER TABLEY 80 F8
NETHERTON 74 A6
Netherton Dr WA6 . . . . . .74 A7
Netherton Farm Cotts
WA6 . . . . .74 A7
Neumann St CW9 . . . . . . 104 B8
Nevada Cl WA5 . . . . .15 C8
Neville Ave
St Helens WA9 . . . . .1 B2
Warrington WA4 . . . . .8 D1
Neville Cres WA5 . . . . .15 A3
Neville Dr CH3 . . . . 119 B1
Neville Rd
Bebington CH62 . . . . .43 E8
Chester CH1 . . . . 119 B1
Neville St
Crewe CW2 . . . . 190 D1

Neville St continued
Newton-le-W WA12 . . . . .2 A3
Nevin Cl SK7 . . . . .36 A7
Nevin Rd CH1 . . . . 117 D3
Nevis Dr CW7 . . . . 189 D3
New Albert Terr WA7 . . .23 B3
Newall Ave CW11 . . . . 175 A5
Newall Cl CH3 . . . . 166 B1
Newall Cres CW7 . . . . 127 A1
Newarth Dr WA13 . . . . . . .19 A2
New Bank Pl WA8 . . . . . . .12 B1
New Bank Rd WA8 . . . . . . .12 B1
New Barnet WA8 . . . . .12 F4
Newbiggin Way ⑯
SK10 . . . . 112 C8
Newbold Cl ⑨ WA9 . . . . . . .6 A7
New Bold Ct WA9 . . . . .6 A7
Newbold Way CW5 . . . . 204 E3
Newborough Cl WA5 . . . . .7 E2
NEW BOSTON 1 E7
Newbridge Cl
Runcorn WA7 . . . . .50 C6
Warrington WA5 . . . . .7 D2
Newbridge Rd CH65 . . . . .70 F4
New Bridge Rd CH65,
CH2 . . . . .71 B4
Newburgh Cl WA7 . . . . . . .24 D1
Newbury Ave
Crewe CW1 . . . . 190 C7
⑤ Winsford CW7 . . . . 149 A8
Newbury Cl
Cheadle SK8 . . . . .35 A6
Widnes WA8 . . . . .13 A3
Newbury Ct SK9 . . . . .60 A6
Newbury Rd
Chester CH4 . . . . 140 F6
Gatley SK8 . . . . .34 C7
Newby Ct CW12 . . . . 156 A1
Newcastle Rd
Astbury CW12 . . . . 178 A7
Brereton Green CW11 . . . . 153 F4
Congleton CW12 . . . . 156 A2
Hassall Green CW11 . . . . . . 176 A3
Nantwich CW5 . . . . 205 B4
Shavington CW2, CW5 . . . 206 C3
Smallwood CW11 . . . . 176 D6
Talke ST7 . . . . 210 E7
Willaston CW5 . . . . 205 E4
Woore CW3 . . . . 232 E1
Newcastle Rd N
CW11 . . . . 153 E5
Newcastle Rd S CW11 . . 153 F5
Newcastle Road Cvn Pk
CW11 . . . . 175 E5
Newcastle St CW1 . . . . . . 190 A5
NEWCASTLE-UNDER-
LYME 210 D3
NEWCHAPEL 195 E2
Newchapel Obsy*
ST7 . . . . 195 E2
Newchapel Rd ST7 . . . . . 195 C3
New Chester Rd CH62 . . .43 E7
Newchurch Com Prim Sch
WA3 . . . . .4 F2
Newchurch La WA3 . . . . . . .4 F2
Newcombe Ave WA2 . . . .16 E8
New Cotts
Hampton Heath SY14 . . . . 213 E7
Manley WA6 . . . . .99 C7
New Crane Bank CH1 . . 118 B1
New Crane St CH1 . . . . . . 118 B1
Newcroft CH1 . . . . .94 B2
New Cut Ind Est WA1 . . 17 C7
New Cut La WA1 . . . . .17 B7
Newdigate St
Crewe CW1 . . . . 190 C4
Crewe CW1 . . . . 190 C6
New Farm Cotts WA3 . . .11 A7
New Farm Ct
Great Barrow CH3 . . . . 120 E5
Malpas SY14 . . . . 213 A5
NEWFIELD 172 E8
Newfield Ct WA13 . . . . . . .19 A5
Newfield Dr CW1 . . . . 190 E5
Newfield Rd WA13 . . . . . . .18 D3
Newfield St CW11 . . . . . . 175 B7
Newfield Terr WA6 . . . . . .73 B2
Newgate
① Macclesfield SK11 . . . . 112 D7
Wilmslow SK9 . . . . .59 E7
Newgate Rd SK9 . . . . .59 D7
Newgate St CH1 . . . . 237 B2
Newgate Wlk CH1 . . . . . . 237 B2
New Grosvenor Rd
CH65 .70 B7
NEWHALL 228 C8
New Hall Ave SK8 . . . . . . .34 B7
Newhall Ct CH2 . . . . 118 E6
New Hall La
Culcheth WA3 . . . . .5 A2
Culcheth, Wigshaw WA3 . . .4 F1
New Hall Manor CH64 . . .41 E6
Newhall Rd CH2 . . . . 118 F6
New Hall St SK10 . . . . .87 D1
Newham Cl WA1 . . . . .16 E8
New Hampshire Cl ⑦
WA5 . . . . .15 B7
Newhaven Ct CW5 . . . . . 204 F5
Newhaven Rd WA2 . . . . . . .8 A3
New Heyes CH64 . . . . .41 E1
New Hey La CH64 . . . . .68 A6
New Home Farm Cotts
CH64 .93 A7
NEW HORWICH 65 E7
New Horwich Rd SK23 . .65 E7
New Hos CW5 . . . . 187 D6
New Houses CH3 . . . . 143 B7
New Inn Cotts WA16 . . . 108 C8

New Inn La CW11 . . . . 176 A2
New King St
Audley ST7 . . . . 209 C1
Middlewich CW10 . . . . 128 C2
New La
Appleton Thorn WA4 . . . . . .27 B5
Churton CH3 . . . . 180 F6
Croft WA3 . . . . .9 B7
Harthill CH3 . . . . 183 F3
Winsford CW7 . . . . 149 F4
Newland Cl WA8 . . . . .12 C3
Newland Mews WA3 . . . . . .4 E5
Newlands Ave
Bramhall SK7 . . . . .35 F8
Cheadle SK8 . . . . .35 A7
Newlands Cl
Cheadle SK8 . . . . .35 A7
Frodsham WA6 . . . . .74 C6
Newlands Dr
Golborne WA3 . . . . .3 D8
Wilmslow SK9 . . . . .59 E5
Newlands Rd
Macclesfield SK10 . . . . 111 E7
Warrington WA4 . . . . .16 F2
Newland Way CW5 . . . . . 205 B4
NEW LANE END 4 A2
New Lane End WA3 . . . . . . .4 A2
Newlyn Ave
Congleton CW12 . . . . 178 F8
Macclesfield SK10 . . . . .86 D1
Newlyn Cl WA7 . . . . .50 B6
Newlyn Gdns WA5 . . . . . . .14 D3
New Manchester Rd
WA1 . . . . .17 A7
Newman Cl CW12 . . . . . . 156 B3
New Manor Rd WA4 . . . . .51 B6
Newman's La CW5 . . . . . 219 D8
Newmans Way WA4 . . . . .16 F3
Newmarket Cl ② SK10 . .87 C4
New Market Wlk ⑯
WA1 . . . . .16 B5
New Meadowside
Residential Cvn Pk
WA5 . . . . 217 E5
NEW MILLS 39 D7
New Mills Central Sta
SK22 .39 B7
New Mills Heritage Ctr*
SK22 .39 B7
New Mills Newtown Sta
SK22 .39 B6
New Mills Prim Sch
SK22 .39 B8
New Mills Sch & Sixth
Form Ctr SK22 . . . . .39 C8
Newmoore La WA7 . . . . . .24 F4
New Moss Rd M44 . . . . . . .11 C6
Newnham Dr CH65 . . . . . .70 C4
New Pale Rd WA6 . . . . .99 C6
New Park Ct SK22 . . . . .39 D7
New Platt La CW4 . . . . . . 107 B1
Newport Gr ST5 . . . . 210 E2
Newquay Cl WA7 . . . . .50 B6
Newquay Ct CW12 . . . . . 178 E8
Newquay Dr
Bramhall SK7 . . . . .35 F7
Macclesfield SK10 . . . . 111 D8
New Rd
Anderton CW9 . . . . .78 D4
Antrobus CW9 . . . . .27 D1
Astbury CW12 . . . . 178 B4
Audley ST7 . . . . 209 E3
Duddon CW6 . . . . 145 B6
Ellesmere Port CH66 . . . . . .69 A8
Horwich End SK23 . . . . .65 E6
Lymm WA13 . . . . .18 E3
Marton CW12 . . . . 132 D1
Mossend CW11 . . . . 154 F2
Prestbury SK10 . . . . .87 A7
Rostherne WA16 . . . . .30 E3
Warrington WA4 . . . . .16 C4
Whaley Bridge, Bridgemont
SK23 .39 F1
Winsford CW7 . . . . 126 E2
Wrenbury CW5 . . . . 216 D3
New Road Bsns Ctr
CW7 . . . . 126 E2
New Russia Hall Craft
Ctr* CH3 . . . . 165 E5
Newry Ct CH2 . . . . 118 D4
Newry Pk CH2 . . . . 118 D4
Newry Pk E CH2 . . . . 118 D4
NEWSBANK 132 F1
New School La CH66 . . . . .44 B1
Newsham Cl WA8 . . . . .12 B4
Newsholme Cl WA3 . . . . . . .4 F3
Newspaper Ho WA5 . . . . .14 D3
New St
Congleton CW12 . . . . 156 E2
Haslington CW1 . . . . 191 C5
Neston CH64 . . . . .66 E8
New Mills SK22 . . . . .39 D7
③ Runcorn WA7 . . . . .23 A2
Sandbach CW11 . . . . 174 D7
Widnes WA8 . . . . .23 B8
Wilmslow SK9 . . . . .59 E5
Newstead Rd SK10 . . . . . . .36 D5
Newstead Rd WA16 . . . . . .21 F6
New Street Cotts
CW12 . . . . 157 A6
Newtech Sq CH5 . . . . .92 F2
NEWTON
Chester 118 F5
Frodsham 74 D3
Tattenhall 166 E4
Newton Ave WA3 . . . . .9 E5
Newton Bank
Middlewich CW10 . . . . 128 B1

Newton Bank continued
Preston on t H WA4 . . . . . . .51 B8
Newton Bank Sch WA12 . . .2 E4
Newton Com Hospl
WA12 .2 B2
Newton Cotts CH3 . . . . . . 166 C4
Newton Gdns WA3 . . . . . . .4 A8
Newton Gr WA2 . . . . .8 F3
Newton Hall Ct CH2 . . . . 118 F5
Newton Hall Dr CH2 . . . . 118 F5
Newton Hall La WA16 . . . .58 E5
Newton Hall Mews ①
CW10 . . . . 151 C8
Newton Heath CH10 . . . . 128 B1
Newton Ho CH2 . . . . 118 F5
Newton Hollow WA6 . . . .74 D1
NEWTONIA 128 B1
Newton La
Chester CH2 . . . . 118 F4
Daresbury WA4 . . . . .51 C8
Daresbury WA4 . . . . .51 E7
Golborne WA2 . . . . .2 E6
Tattenhall CH3 . . . . 166 D4
NEWTON-LE-WILLOWS 2 B2
Newton-le-Willows Com
High Sch WA12 . . . . .2 D5
Newton-le-Willows Prim
Sch WA12 . . . . .2 C3
Newton-le-Willows Sta
WA12 .2 E3
Newton Park Dr WA12 . . . .2 F3
Newton Park View
CH2 . . . . 118 D4
Newton Pl CW12 . . . . 156 F2
Newton Prim Sch
CH2 . . . . 118 E4
Newton Rd
Ellesmere Port CH65 . . . . . .70 C5
Golborne, Lowton Common
WA3, WN7 . . . . .4 A8
Golborne, Town of Lowton
WA12, WA3 . . . . .3 D5
Handforth SK9 . . . . .34 A1
St Helens WA9 . . . . .1 A3
Winwick WA2 . . . . .8 A5
Newtons Cres CW11 . . . . 191 F7
Newtons Gr CW11 . . . . . . 191 E7
Newtons La CW11 . . . . . . 191 F7
Newton St
Crewe CW1 . . . . 190 D5
Macclesfield SK11 . . . . 112 C7
NEWTOWN
Burwardsley 183 E8
Frodsham 49 D1
Newtown
Neston CH64 . . . . .66 F7
Newchapel ST7 . . . . 195 F2
NEWTOWN
New Mills 39 B6
Poynton 37 A3
Sound 217 E4
Widnes 23 A6
Newtown Cl CH1 . . . . 118 B3
Newtown Prim Sch
SK22 .39 B6
New Warrington Rd
CW9 . . . . .79 C2
New William Cl M31 . . . . 11 F4
New York Cotts WA16 . . .29 F2
Nicholas Ave CW9 . . . . . . 104 C6
Nicholas Ct CH1 . . . . 237 A7
Nicholas Rd
Weaverham CW8 . . . . .77 D1
Widnes WA8 . . . . .13 C1
Nicholas St Mews
CH1 . . . . 237 A2
Nicholas St CH1 . . . . 237 A2
Nicholls St WA4 . . . . .17 B2
Nicholson Ave SK10 . . . . . .87 E1
Nicholson Cl SK10 . . . . .87 E1
Nicholson St WA1 . . . . .15 F5
NICK I' TH' HILL 179 B4
Nickleby Rd SK12 . . . . .36 E3
Nickleford Hall Dr
WA8 . . . . .12 F6
Nickolson Cl CW12 . . . . . 119 F8
Nicol Ave WA1 . . . . .17 F8
Nidderdale Cl CW12 . . . . 157 A5
Niddries Cl CW9 . . . . 126 F7
Niddries La CW9 . . . . 126 F7
Nield Ct CH2 . . . . 118 D7
Nigel Gresley Cl CW1 . . 191 A4
Nigel Rd CH60 . . . . .41 C8
Nightingale Cl
Farndon CH3 . . . . 180 F1
Handforth SK9 . . . . .34 B1
Middlewich CW10 . . . . 151 D6
Runcorn WA7 . . . . .49 F5
Warrington WA3 . . . . .9 F4
Nightingale Ct ④
CW7 . . . . 149 D6
Nightingale Way ST7 . . . 193 B3
Nile St CW2 . . . . 190 D2
Nine Hos The CH3 . . . . . . 166 B1
Nixon Dr CW7 . . . . 126 B2
Nixon Rd CW8 . . . . 101 F3
Nixon's Row CW5 . . . . . . 204 C5
Nixon St
Crewe CW1 . . . . 189 F5
Macclesfield SK11 . . . . 112 D7
No 1 Road N CW2 . . . . . . 192 F1
No 1 Road S CW2 . . . . . . 192 F1

No 2 Road N CW2 . . . . .192 F1
No 2 Road S LW2 . . . . .192 F1
No 156 CH1 . . . . .237 C2
Noalis Ark La WA10 . . . . . .53 F1
Noble Cl WA3 . . . . .9 E3
NO MAN'S HEATH 214 B4

Nook La
Antrobus CW9 . . . . .53 E6
Golborne WA3 . . . . .3 B8
Warrington, Fearnhead
WA2 .9 B2
Warrington WA4 . . . . .17 A3

Nook The
Backford CH1 . . . . .95 B4
Bramhall SK7 . . . . .35 D5
Chester CH2 . . . . .118 E4
Guilden Sutton CH3 . . . . . . .119 C4
Hankelow CW3 . . . . .230 C8
Saltney CH4 . . . . .140 E6
Noon Ct WA12 . . . . .2 B1
Noonsun Farm WA16 . . . . . .58 E1
Nora St WA1 . . . . .16 C5
Norbreck Ave CW2 . . . . . . .190 B2
Norbreck Cl WA5 . . . . .15 A4
NORBURY 215 D4
Norbury Ave WA2 . . . . .16 D8

Norbury Cl
Hough CW2 . . . . .206 E3
Knutsford WA16 . . . . .57 C3
Widnes WA8 . . . . .13 E1
NORBURY COMMON

. . . . .215 C6

Norbury Dr
Congleton CW12 . . . . .156 E4
Middlewich CW10 . . . . .151 B8
Norbury Hollow Rd
SK7 .37 B8

Norbury St
Macclesfield SK11 . . . . .112 C7
Northwich CW9 . . . . .104 B8
Norbury Town La
SY13 . . . . .215 C3
Norbury Way █ SK9 . . . . . . .34 D5
Norcott Ave WA4 . . . . .16 D2
NORCOTT BROOK 52 C6
Norcott Dr WA5 . . . . .6 F6
Norden Cl WA3 . . . . .9 C5
Norfolk Cl WA4 . . . . .11 C5
Norfolk Dr WA5 . . . . .14 E6
Norfolk Gr ST8 . . . . .179 C1
Norfolk Ho ST7 . . . . .210 D6
Norfolk House Prep Sch
CW1 . . . . .175 B7
Norfolk Pl WA8 . . . . .22 C8

Norfolk Rd
Chester CH2 . . . . .118 F4
Congleton CW12 . . . . .156 E4
Ellesmere Port CH65 . . . . . . .70 C5
Kidsgrove ST7 . . . . .194 F2
Norfolk St WA7 . . . . .23 B3
Norfolk Wlk SK10 . . . . .86 F2
Norgrove Cl WA7 . . . . .50 E8
Norlands Pk WA8 . . . . .12 F6
Norland St WA8 . . . . .13 D1
Norleane Cres WA7 . . . . . . .49 B8
NORLEY 100 F6

Norley Ave
Bebington CH62 . . . . .43 E3
Ellesmere Port CH65 . . . . . . .69 F6
Norley CE Prim Sch
WA6 . . . . .100 F5
Norley Cl WA5 . . . . .15 E6
Norley Dr CH3 . . . . .119 C1
Norley La CW8 . . . . .101 A8
Norley Pl CW9 . . . . .103 E5

Norley Rd
Cuddington CW8,
WA6 . . . . .101 E4
Kingsley WA6 . . . . .75 A1
Norley WA6 . . . . .100 D7
Sandiway CW8 . . . . .102 A3

Norman Ave
Haydock WA11 . . . . .2 A7
Newton-le-W WA12 . . . . .2 E3
Normanby Cl WA5 . . . . .15 E7
Norman Cl CH66 . . . . .94 F8
Norman Dr CW7 . . . . .149 C6
Normandy Ave █
CW7 . . . . .149 D8
Normandy Rd CH2 . . . . .95 C1
Norman Ho █ CW8 . . . . . . .103 C5
Norman Rd WA7 . . . . .23 A1
Normans Cotts █
CH64 . . . . .66 F7
Norman's Hall Farm
SK10 . . . . .63 B5
Norman's La WA4 . . . . .52 F4
Norman St WA2 . . . . .16 B6
Norman Way CH1 . . . . .117 E5
Norreys Ave WA5 . . . . .15 F8
Norris Rd CH1 . . . . .117 E5
Norris St WA2 . . . . .16 D8
North Ave WA2 . . . . .16 F1
Northbank Ind Pk M44 . . . .11 F6
Northbank Wlk CW2 . . . . . .206 C8
North Brook Rd CW6 . . . . .146 B7
Northbury Rd CH66 . . . . . . .69 E1
North Cheshire Coll
(Museum St Ctr)
WA1 .16 A4
North Cheshire Hospl
WA4 .26 D1
Northcote Rd SK7 . . . . .35 F7
North Crofts CW5 . . . . .204 E5

Northdale Rd WA1 . . . . .17 A8
North Downs WA16 . . . . . . .57 D2
North Dr
Heswall CH60 . . . . .41 A7
High Legh WA16 . . . . .29 C4
Northwich CW9 . . . . .104 E7
Northern La WA8 . . . . .12 A3
Northern Pathway
CH4 . . . . .237 C1
Northern Rise CH66 . . . . . . .69 E4
Northfield Dr
Biddulph ST8 . . . . .179 E2
Wilmslow SK9 . . . . .60 D8
Northfield Pl CW2 . . . . .206 C5
Northfields WA16 . . . . .57 C3
NORTH FLORIDA 1 D8
North Florida Rd WA11 . . . . .1 D8
Northgate CW6 . . . . .146 B7
Northgate Ave
Chester CH2 . . . . .237 B4
Macclesfield SK10 . . . . .87 C1
Northgate Row CH1 . . . . . .237 B2
Northgate St CH1 . . . . .237 A3
North Gn CH5 . . . . .116 A6
Northlands CW3 . . . . .232 C1
Northmead SK10 . . . . .87 A5
Northolt Ct WA8 . . . . .8 E1
North Par CH64 . . . . .41 B2
North Park Brook Rd
WA5 .7 E1
North Rd
Altrincham WA15 . . . . .32 A8
Bebington CH65 . . . . .44 E3
Connah's Quay CH5 . . . . .91 F2
Ellesmere Port CH65 . . . . . . .70 B8
Halewood L26 . . . . .21 A5
NORTH RODE 134 E2
North St
Chester CH3 . . . . .119 A1
Congleton CW12 . . . . .156 D3
Crewe CW1 . . . . .190 C7
Haydock WA11 . . . . .1 E6
Mount Pleasant ST7 . . . . . . .195 B6
Newton-le-W WA12 . . . . .1 F4
Saltney CH4 . . . . .140 B7
Sandycroft CH5 . . . . .116 A3
North Stafford St
CW1 . . . . .190 D4
Northumberland Rd
M31 .11 E2
North View
Crewe CW1 . . . . .190 A6
Ellesmere Port CH66 . . . . . . .69 C7
Middlewich CW10 . . . . .128 B2
Warrington WA5 . . . . .14 E7
Northward Rd SK9 . . . . .59 F6
Northway
Chester CH4 . . . . .141 A7
Lymm WA13 . . . . .18 D4
Runcorn WA7 . . . . .49 F8
Warrington WA2 . . . . .8 B2
Widnes WA8 . . . . .12 D1
Winnington CW8 . . . . .78 D1
North Way
Holmes Chapel CW4 . . . . . .130 C3
Shavington CW2 . . . . .206 D5
NORTHWICH 103 D8
Northwich Rd
Allostock CW4, WA16 . . . . . .106 E1
Antrobus CW9 . . . . .53 B2
Dutton WA4 . . . . .51 B2
Great Budworth CW9 . . . . . . .78 F8
Knutsford WA16 . . . . .57 B3
Runcorn, Brookvale WA7 . . . .50 C5
Weaverham CW8 . . . . .102 E7
Northwich Ret Pk CW9 . . . .79 C1
Northwich Sta CW9 . . . . . .104 B8
Northwood Ave
Middlewich CW10 . . . . .151 E5
Newton-le-W WA12 . . . . .2 F3
Northwood La WA16 . . . . . . .28 F1
Northwood Rd WA7 . . . . . . .23 E2
NORTON 24 C1
Norton Ave
Saltney CH4 . . . . .140 D6
Warrington WA5 . . . . .14 E5
Norton Cotts WA7 . . . . .50 E7
Norton Gate WA7 . . . . .50 C8
Norton Hill WA7 . . . . .24 C2
NORTON IN HALES 236 C1
Norton in Hales CE Prim
Sch TF9 . . . . .236 C2
Norton La
Runcorn, Norton WA7 . . . . . .24 D1
Runcorn, Town Park
WA7 . . . . .50 A8
Runcorn WA7 . . . . .50 B8
Norton Priory Mus*
WA7 .24 B3
Norton Priory Walled
Gdn* WA7 . . . . .24 B3
Norton Rd CH3 . . . . .119 C2
Nortons La CW6 . . . . .122 F7
Norton's La CH3 . . . . .98 B2
Norton St SK10 . . . . .112 E8
Norton Station Rd
WA7 .50 D8
Norton View WA7 . . . . .50 A8
Norton Village WA7 . . . . . . .24 D1
Norton Way CW11 . . . . .174 D7
Nortonwood La WA7 . . . . . .24 C1
Norville CH66 . . . . .69 D7
Norwich Ave WA3 . . . . .3 D8
Norwich Dr CH66 . . . . .94 E8
Norwood Ave
Bramhall SK7 . . . . .35 D5
Golborne WA3 . . . . .3 F7
High Lane SK6 . . . . .37 D7

Norwood Dr CH4 . . . . .141 B8
Nottingham Cl WA1 . . . . . . .17 E6
Nova Cl █ CW1 . . . . .190 B5
NOVA SCOTIA 125 C6
Nun House Cl CW7 . . . . . . .127 B2
Nun House Dr LW7 . . . . . . .127 B2
Nunsmere Cl CW7 . . . . .127 B1
Nuns Rd CH1 . . . . .237 A1
Nursery Ave WA15 . . . . .31 FR
Nursery Cl
Crewe CW7 . . . . .190 A2
Kidsgrove ST7 . . . . .194 D1
Shavington CW2 . . . . .206 C3
Widnes WA8 . . . . .13 D3
Nursery Dr
Biddulph ST8 . . . . .179 C2
Poynton SK12 . . . . .36 D4
Nursery Gr M31 . . . . .11 F4
Nursery La
Congleton CW12 . . . . .156 E2
Nether Alderley SK10 . . . . . . .84 D5
Siddington SK11 . . . . .110 A3
Wilmslow SK9 . . . . .59 F5
Nursery Pk WA6 . . . . .100 B7
Nursery Rd
Barnton CW8 . . . . .78 B3
Bollington SK10 . . . . .87 F7
Oakhanger CW1, ST7 . . . . . .192 D3
Scholar Green ST7 . . . . .194 E5
Nursery The CW8 . . . . .103 C6
Nutfield Ave CW2 . . . . .190 B7
Nuthurst Gdns █
CW5 . . . . .204 F5
Nuttall Ct WA3 . . . . .9 C4
Nuttall St M44 . . . . .11 E6

O

Oak Ave
Alsager ST7 . . . . .193 E2
Disley SK12 . . . . .39 A6
Golborne WA3 . . . . .3 B8
Haydock WA11 . . . . .1 E7
Irlam M44 . . . . .11 D5
Macclesfield SK11 . . . . .112 A5
Newton-le-W WA12 . . . . .2 D3
Wilmslow SK9 . . . . .59 F5
Winsford CW7 . . . . .149 D7
Oak Bank
Alderley Edge SK9 . . . . .60 A2
Disley SK12 . . . . .39 A6
Oak Bank Cl CW5 . . . . .205 E4
Oak Bank Dr SK10 . . . . .63 B1
Oak Bank La CH2 . . . . .119 C6
Oak Brow Cotts SK9 . . . . . .33 E4
Oak Cl SK9 . . . . .59 F6
Oak Cotts
Styal SK9 . . . . .33 E4
Wrenbury CW5 . . . . .216 F4
Oakdale Ave
Frodsham WA6 . . . . .74 D6
Warrington WA4 . . . . .16 D1
Oakdale Cl
Broughton CH4 . . . . .139 B3
Chorlton CW2 . . . . .207 B3
Oakdene Ave
Ellesmere Port CH66 . . . . . . .69 C5
Gatley SK8 . . . . .34 C7
Warrington WA1 . . . . .17 C7
Oakdene Cl CH2 . . . . .43 D5
Oakdene Ct SK9 . . . . .34 B1
Oakdene Way CW6 . . . . . . .168 D8
Oak Dr
Cheadle SK7 . . . . .35 C7
Higher Kinnerton CH4 . . . . . .161 A7
Middlewich CW10 . . . . .151 D7
Runcorn WA7 . . . . .49 C7
Scholar Green ST7 . . . . .194 E6
Oakenbank La SK10 . . . . . . .88 D7
Oakenclough Cl SK9 . . . . . .34 E2
Oakes Cnr CW5 . . . . .219 E3
Oak Farm CW6 . . . . .186 C5
Oakfield Ave
Chester CH2 . . . . .118 E8
Knutsford WA16 . . . . .57 C3
Wrenbury CW5 . . . . .216 F3
Oakfield Cl
Alderley Edge SK9 . . . . .60 B3
Bramhall SK7 . . . . .35 C6
Wrenbury CW5 . . . . .216 F3
Oakfield Com Prim Sch
WA8 .22 B8
Oakfield Dr
Chester CH2 . . . . .118 E8
Widnes WA8 . . . . .22 B8
Oakfield Rd
Alderley Edge SK9 . . . . .60 B2
Bebington CH62 . . . . .43 C8
Blacon CH1 . . . . .117 D4
Ellesmere Port CH66 . . . . . . .68 E8
Plumley WA16 . . . . .80 F3
Poynton SK12 . . . . .36 F4
Oakfield Rise CW4 . . . . . . .130 B3
Oakfield Terr CH66 . . . . .68 E8
Oakfold SK10 . . . . .88 A6
Oak Gr
Ellesmere Port CH65 . . . . . . .70 A3
Nantwich CW5 . . . . .204 E3
Poynton SK12 . . . . .36 D4
Oak Gr/Gelli Dderw
CH4 . . . . .140 D5
OAKGROVE 135 D7
Oak Grove Sch SK8 . . . . . . .34 C7
OAKHANGER 192 C2
Oakhill Cl SK10 . . . . .87 B4
Oak Ho
Chester CH2 . . . . .118 C5

Oak Ho continued
█ Sandbach CW11 . . . . . . .175 B6
Oak House La CW7 . . . . . . .149 D8
Oakhurst Chase SK9 . . . . . .60 A2
Oakhurst Dr CW2 . . . . .206 B7
Oak La
Astbury CW12 . . . . .178 B4
Cuddington CW8 . . . . .101 F2
Kerridge SK10 . . . . .88 A6
Marton SK11 . . . . .133 C5
Wilmslow SK9 . . . . .59 F6
Oakland Ave CW2 . . . . .191 C4
Oakland Cl SK12 . . . . .36 D4
Oakland Gdns WA1 . . . . . . .16 E7
Oaklands
Bebington CH62 . . . . .43 D6
Guilden Sutton CH3 . . . . . . .119 F4
Oaklands Ave CH3 . . . . . . .166 B2
Oaklands Cl SK9 . . . . .34 E1
Oaklands Cres CH3 . . . . . . .166 B2
Oaklands Dr WA3 . . . . .18 D2
Oaklands Inf Sch SK9 . . . . .34 E1
Oaklands Rd
Golborne WA3 . . . . .3 F7
Ollerton WA16 . . . . .82 F6
Oaklands Sch CW7 . . . . . . .149 B7
Oakland St
Warrington WA1 . . . . .16 E7
Widnes WA8 . . . . .23 A4
Oaklea Ave CH2 . . . . .118 F4
Oak Lea Ave SK9 . . . . .60 A5
Oakleaf Lo SK11 . . . . .112 D5
Oakleigh WA16 . . . . .82 C7
Oakleigh Ct CW12 . . . . .155 F3
Oakleigh Ho SK10 . . . . .88 B8
Oakleigh Rd SK8 . . . . .34 E8
Oakleigh Rise CW8 . . . . .78 F1
Oakley Cl CW1 . . . . .175 A8
Oakley Ct CH65 . . . . .70 C4
Oakley St CW1 . . . . .190 C5
Oak Lo SK7 . . . . .35 F7
Oakmere Barns CW8 . . . . . .124 A7
Oakmere Cl CW11 . . . . .174 F7
Oakmere Dr
Chester CH3 . . . . .142 B8
Ellesmere Port CH66 . . . . . . .69 F1
Warrington WA5 . . . . .14 F3
Oakmere Hall CW8 . . . . . . .101 E1
Oakmere Pl █ CW1 . . . . . . .190 B5
Oakmere Rd
Handforth SK9 . . . . .34 D5
Winsford CW7 . . . . .149 B8
Oak Mews █ WA7 . . . . .23 A2
Oak Mews SK9 . . . . .34 C1
Oakmoore WA7 . . . . .24 F4
Oak Rd
Chelford SK11 . . . . .84 A3
Chester CH4 . . . . .140 F6
Hooton CH66 . . . . .43 E1
Lymm WA13 . . . . .18 C3
Mottram St Andrew
SK10 . . . . .86 B7
Paddockhill WA16 . . . . .59 B5
Partington M31 . . . . .11 D2
Warrington WA5 . . . . .14 F3
Oaks Com Prim Sch The
CH65 . . . . .70 D3
Oaks Dr The CH2 . . . . .118 D7
Oaks Gdns WA5 . . . . .14 E4
Oaks Pl WA8 . . . . .23 A7
Oak St
Crewe CW2 . . . . .190 D3
Croft WA3 . . . . .9 A7
Ellesmere Port CH65 . . . . . . .70 C7
Northwich CW9 . . . . .79 A1
Rode Heath ST7 . . . . .193 E8
Sandbach CW11 . . . . .174 D8
Oaks The
Bebington CH62 . . . . .43 C8
Goostrey CW4 . . . . .130 D8
Mobberley WA16 . . . . .58 E1
█ Northwich CW9 . . . . . . .103 E6
Widnes WA8 . . . . .13 D4
Oaksway CH60 . . . . .41 C6
Oakthorn Gr WA11 . . . . .1 C6
Oaktree Cl
Barnton CW8 . . . . .78 B4
Tarporley CW6 . . . . .146 D2
Oak Tree Ct CW8 . . . . .190 F5
Oaktree Ct CH2 . . . . .119 A3
Oak Tree Dr CW5 . . . . .190 F5
Oak Tree Gate CW3 . . . . . . .229 F3
Oaktree La ST7 . . . . .210 D5
Oak Tree La CW10 . . . . .129 E7
Oak View
Knutsford WA16 . . . . .57 C1
Martin SK11 . . . . .133 C5
Speke L24 . . . . .21 A3
Oak Villas CW5 . . . . .216 F4
Oakways WA4 . . . . .26 D5
OAKWOOD 9 F4
Oakwood Ave
Warrington WA1 . . . . .16 E7
Wilmslow SK9 . . . . .59 E6
Oakwood Avenue Com
Prim Sch WA1 . . . . .16 E7
Oakwood Cl CH66 . . . . .69 D1
Oakwood Cres
Crewe CW2 . . . . .189 E4
Sandbach CW11 . . . . .175 E6
Oakwood Ct WA14 . . . . .31 B8
Oakwood Dr SK10 . . . . .87 C6
Oakwood Gate WA3 . . . . .9 D4

Oakwood Ho
Alderley Edge SK9 . . . . .85 B8
Barnton CW8 . . . . .78 A2
Oakwood La
Altrincham WA14 . . . . .31 B8
Barnton CW8 . . . . .78 A2
Sandbach CW11 . . . . .174 B8
Oakwoo Pk CH62 . . . . .43 D5
Oakwood Rd
Disley SK12 . . . . .38 D6
Rode Heath ST7 . . . . .193 F8
Oak Wood Rd WA16 . . . . . . .29 F2
Oakworth Cl CW12 . . . . . . .156 C3
Oathills SY14 . . . . .213 B5
Oathills Cl CW6 . . . . .146 D1
Oathills Dr CW6 . . . . .146 D1
Oathills Lea CW6 . . . . .146 D1
Oatlands SK9 . . . . .85 B8
Oat Market █ CW5 . . . . . . .204 E5
Oban Dr CH60 . . . . .41 A8
Oban Gr WA2 . . . . .9 A3
Obelisk Way CW12 . . . . . . .156 C3
OCCLESTONE GREEN

. . . . .151 B2
O'Connell Cl WA11 . . . . .1 C6
Oddfellows Pas CW10 . . . .128 B1
Odeon Bldg CH1 . . . . .237 A3
Offal Pit La WA6 . . . . .74 F2
Offley Ave CW1 . . . . .175 B7
Offley Prim Sch
CW11 . . . . .175 B7
Offley Rd CW11 . . . . .175 B7
Off Spring Bank SK22 . . . . .39 C8
Ogden Rd SK7 . . . . .35 D5
Oglet La L24 . . . . .45 C6
Oil Sites Rd CH65 . . . . .71 C5
Okell St WA7 . . . . .23 A2
Old Albert Terr WA7 . . . . . . .23 B3
Old Alder La WA2, WA5 . . . . .7 D5
Old Applecroft CW11 . . . . . .174 C5
OLD BOSTON 2 A8
Old Boston WA11 . . . . .2 A7
Old Boston Trad Est
WA11 .2 B8
Old Brickworks Ind Est
SK10 . . . . .63 E4
Old Butt La ST7 . . . . .194 D2
OLDCASTLE HEATH 223 E8
Oldcastle La SY14 . . . . .222 E8
Old Cherry La WA13 . . . . . . .28 A7
Old Chester Ct CW5 . . . . . .187 D6
Old Chester Rd
Barbridge CW5 . . . . .187 D6
Ellesmere Port CH66 . . . . . . .69 D4
Helsby WA6 . . . . .73 C4
Higher Walton WA4 . . . . .25 F7
Old Church Cl CH65 . . . . . . .70 C7
Old Coach Rd
Brown Knowl SY14,
CH3 . . . . .199 B6
Kelsall CW6 . . . . .122 D5
Runcorn WA7 . . . . .22 F3
Old Constabulary The █
CW5 . . . . .204 D5
Old Court Ho The █
WA16 . . . . .57 A2
Olde George The CH1 . . . .237 B3
Old Farm Cl
Macclesfield SK10 . . . . .87 A2
Willaston CH64 . . . . .68 A8
Old Farm Cotts CH1 . . . . . .116 E3
Old Farm Mews SK8 . . . . . . .35 C7
Oldfield Cres CH4 . . . . .140 F5
Oldfield Dr
Chester CH3 . . . . .119 C2
Mobberley WA16 . . . . .58 A4
Oldfield La WA14 . . . . .20 F4
Oldfield Prim Sch
CH3 . . . . .119 C3
Oldfield Rd
Ellesmere Port CH65 . . . . . . .70 B5
Lymm WA13 . . . . .18 C4
Sandbach CW11 . . . . .174 F3
Oldgate WA8 . . . . .22 C7
Old Gate Cl CW10 . . . . .151 B7
Old Gorse Cl CW2 . . . . .189 E3
OLD HALL 15 C8
Old Hall Cl WA4 . . . . .26 A8
Old Hall Cres SK9 . . . . .34 E1
Old Hall Ct
Ashton Hayes CH3 . . . . .121 F7
Malpas SY14 . . . . .213 B3
Old Hall Dr
Ellesmere Port CH65 . . . . . . .70 B4
Horwich End SK23 . . . . .65 E4
Old Hall Gdns CW7 . . . . . . .237 C4
Old Hall La
Elton CH2 . . . . .72 B3
Hargrave CH3 . . . . .144 A1
Over Tabley WA16 . . . . .55 E4
Woodford SK7 . . . . .35 C2
Old Hall Pk CH3 . . . . .119 F5
Old Hall Pl CH1 . . . . .237 A2
Old Hall Rd
Northwich CW9 . . . . .104 A5
Warrington WA5 . . . . .15 D7
Oldhall St SY14 . . . . .213 B3
Old Hall St SK10 . . . . .87 D1
Oldhams Hill
Kingsmead CW8 . . . . .103 F8
Winnington CW8 . . . . .78 F1
Oldham's Rise SK10 . . . . . . .87 D3
Oldham St
Bollington SK10 . . . . .88 B8
Warrington WA4 . . . . .16 D3
Oldham Ct SK10 . . . . .88 B8
Old Hey Wlk WA12 . . . . .2 C1
Old Higher Rd WA8 . . . . . . .21 D5
Oldhill Cl ST7 . . . . .210 E6

Old Hutte La L26 . . . . .21 A6
Old Knutsford Rd
 ST7. . . . . .194 A6
Old La
 Acton Bridge CW8. . . . . . . .76 F3
 Antrobus CW9. . . . . .53 C3
 Davenham CW9. . . . . .104 D2
 Heswall CH60. . . . . .41 D8
 Mouldsworth CH3 . . . . .99 C2
 Pulford CH4. . . . . .162 E2
Old Library The CW7. . . . . .126 E1
Old Liverpool Rd WA5. . . . . .15 E4
Old Man of Mow *
 ST7. . . . . .195 D8
Old Market Pl
 ⓵ Knutsford WA16. . . . . . .57 A2
 ⓬ Warrington WA1 . . . . . . .16 B5
Old Marsh Farm Ho
 CH5 . . . . .116 A8
Old Mill Cl
 Heswall CH60. . . . . .41 B7
 Lymm WA13. . . . . .19 C6
Old Mill Ct CH2. . . . . .118 D6
Old Mill La
 Hazel Grove SK7 . . . . .37 A8
 Higher Whitley WA4. . . . . . .52 F3
 Macclesfield SK11. . . . . . . .112 E6
Old Mill Pl CH3. . . . . .166 B1
Old Mill Rd CW11. . . . . . . .175 C6
Old Mill The
 Crowton CW8. . . . . .76 B2
 Ellesmere Port CH66. . . . . .69 C7
OLD MOSS 144 D7
Old Moss La
 Fowley Common WA3 . . . . . .5 E6
 Tarvin CH3. . . . . .144 D7
Old Newcastle Rd
 CW5. . . . . .205 D4
Old Orch SK9. . . . . .60 A7
Old Orchard The
 Antrobus CW9. . . . . .53 C4
 Cuddington CW8 . . . . .101 F4
Old Paddock The
 CW4 . . . . .130 F8
Old Pale Cotts CW8. . . . . .123 C7
Old Pale Hts CW8 . . . . . . .123 C7
Old Park Rd CW1. . . . . . . .207 D8
Old Pearl La CH3. . . . . . . .119 B1
Old Penny La WA11. . . . . . .2 B8
Old Pewterspear La
 WA4. . . . . .26 E4
Old Port Sq CH1. . . . . .118 B2
Old Pump Ho The
 CH66 . . . . .68 E8
Old Quay Cl CH64. . . . . . . .66 C7
Old Quay La CH64. . . . . . . .66 D7
Old Quay St WA7. . . . . .23 B3
Old Quays The WA4. . . . . . .16 E3
Old Rd
 Anderton CW9. . . . . .78 D3
 Audley ST7. . . . . .209 E3
 Furness Vale SK23. . . . . . . .39 D4
 Handforth SK9. . . . . .34 D3
 Horwich End, New Horwich
  SK23. . . . . .65 E6
 Horwich End SK23. . . . . . . .65 F3
 Warrington WA4 . . . . .16 B4
 Wilmslow SK9 . . . . .60 B8
Old Ribbon Mill The
 SK11. . . . . .112 D6
Old School Cl
 Barnton CW8. . . . . .78 B2
 Farndon CH3 . . . . .180 E2
 Kidsgrove ST7 . . . . .195 A1
 Neston CH64. . . . . .66 F5
Old School House La
 WA2. . . . . .8 A7
Old School Sk8 . . . . .35 A8
Old Seals Way CH1 . . . . . .118 A3
Old Smithy La WA13. . . . . .18 C2
Old Smithy Row SK22. . . . .39 C7
Old Stack Yd CH3. . . . . . . .120 E6
Old Upton La WA8. . . . . . . .12 E4
Old Vicarage Gdn
 CW3. . . . . .230 A3
Old Vicarage La CW8. . . . .103 C5
Old Vicarage Rd CH64. . . . .68 A8
Old Wargrave Rd WA12 . . . .2 C3
Old Warrington Rd
 CW9. . . . . .79 A2
Old Wesleyan
 Schoolhouse The
 SK22. . . . . .39 B6
Old Whint Rd WA11. . . . . . . .1 A6
Old Woman's La CH3 . . . .142 D7
OLD WOODHOUSES 227 C2
Old Wrexham Rd CH4. . . . .141 C7
O'leary St WA2. . . . . .16 C7
Olive Dr CH64. . . . . .66 E4
Olive Gr ST5. . . . . .210 D1
Oliver Cl SK10. . . . . .87 F7
Olive Rd CH66. . . . . .66 E8
Oliver Ho CH66. . . . . .69 D4
Oliver La CH66. . . . . .69 D4
Oliver St WA2. . . . . .16 B6
Ollersett Ave SK22. . . . . . . .39 D8
Ollersett Dr SK22. . . . . .39 D8
Ollersett Ho SK22. . . . . .39 D8
Ollershaw La CW9. . . . . . . .79 C4
OLLERTON 83 C6
Ollerton Cl WA4. . . . . .17 B3
Ollerton Pk WA5. . . . . .6 E7
Ollerton Rd SK9. . . . . .34 E5
Ollier St ⓵ WA8. . . . . .23 A7
Olympia Pl WA5. . . . . .15 B7
Omega Bvd WA5. . . . . .6 D1
One Oak La SK9. . . . . .60 F7

ONNELEY 232 F3
Onslow Rd CH1. . . . . .117 D4
ONSTON 76 E1
Onston La CW8. . . . . .101 E8
On The Air The
 Broadcasting Mus &
 Vintage Sound Shop*
 CH1. . . . . .237 B2
Openshaw La WA44. . . . . . .11 E6
Orange Gr WA2. . . . . .8 E2
Orchard Ave
 Acton Bridge CW8. . . . . . . .76 E4
 Lymm WA13. . . . . .18 F3
 Partington M31. . . . . .11 F4
 Whaley Bridge SK23 . . . . . .65 D7
Orchard Brow WA3 . . . . . . .11 A2
Orchard Cl
 Barnton CW8. . . . . .78 B3
 Bunbury CW6. . . . . .185 F8
 Cheadle SK8 . . . . .35 C7
 Chester CH2 . . . . .118 D5
 Ellesmere Port CH66. . . . . .69 F1
 Frodsham WA6. . . . . .74 A6
 Goostrey CW4. . . . . .107 E1
 Higher Wincham CW9 . . . . .80 A6
 Macclesfield SK11. . . . . . . .112 B6
 Middlewich CW10 . . . . .151 D7
 Poynton SK12 . . . . .36 E3
 Weaverham CW8. . . . . .77 D1
 Wilmslow SK9 . . . . .59 F5
 Winsford CW7. . . . . .149 D7
Orchard Cotts CW6. . . . . .146 D1
Orchard Cres
 Kidsgrove ST7 . . . . .194 D1
 Nantwich CW5. . . . . .204 E3
 Nether Alderley SK10 . . . . . .84 F6
Orchard Croft CH3. . . . . . .119 E5
Orchard Ct
 Alsager ST7. . . . . .193 E4
 ⓷ Chester CH3. . . . . .119 A1
 Croft WA3 . . . . .9 A8
 Frodsham WA6. . . . . .74 A8
 Haslington CW1. . . . . .191 D4
Orchard Dene CW8 . . . . . .101 D5
Orchard Dr
 Handforth SK9. . . . . .34 E2
 Little Leigh CW8 . . . . .77 D5
 Neston CH64. . . . . .66 E5
Orchard Gdns
 Congleton CW12 . . . . .156 A3
 Tarporley CW6. . . . . .168 D8
 Weaverham CW8. . . . . .77 B1
Orchard Gn SK9. . . . . .60 B1
Orchard Gr CH3 . . . . .180 F1
Orchard Haven CH66. . . . . .69 E1
Orchard Ho SK10 . . . . .86 E1
Orchard La CH66 . . . . .69 A8
Orchard Park La CH2 . . . . . .72 B4
Orchard Pk CH2 . . . . .72 B4
Orchard Rd
 Helsby WA6. . . . . .73 C4
 Poynton SK12 . . . . .36 D4
Orchard Rd
 Ellesmere Port CH65. . . . . .70 B2
 Lymm WA13. . . . . .19 B5
 Whaley Bridge SK23 . . . . . .65 D7
Orchard Rise CW9 . . . . . . .126 E8
Orchard St
 Chester CH1 . . . . .237 A3
 Crewe CW1. . . . . .190 C5
 Northwich CW9 . . . . .104 B8
 Warrington, Fearnhead
  WA2. . . . . .9 A2
 Warrington, Stockton Heath
  WA4. . . . . .26 C8
 Warrington WA1. . . . . .16 C5
 Willaston CW5. . . . . .205 D6
Orchards The
 Holt LL13. . . . . .196 D8
 Pickmere WA16. . . . . .79 F7
 Saltney CH4. . . . . .140 D6
 Shavington CW2 . . . . .206 C4
Orchard The
 Alderley Edge SK9. . . . . . . .85 B8
 Chester CH3 . . . . .142 A8
 Disley SK12. . . . . .38 D6
 Helsby WA6. . . . . .73 B2
Orchard Way
 Congleton CW12 . . . . .156 A3
 Kelsall CW6. . . . . .122 D5
 Widnes WA8 . . . . .12 A3
Orchard Wlk
 Neston CH64. . . . . .66 E8
 ⓷ Runcorn WA7. . . . . .49 F7
Orchid Cl
 Huntington CH3. . . . . .142 A6
 Irlam M44 . . . . .11 E8
Orchid Way WA9 . . . . .6 B7
Orchil Cl CH66. . . . . .69 A6
Ordnance Ave
 Warrington, Birchwood
  WA3 . . . . .10 A5
 Warrington WA3 . . . . .9 F4
Ordsall Cl WA13. . . . . .174 F3
ORFORD 8 D2
Orford Ave
 Disley SK12. . . . . .38 D6
 Warrington WA1, WA2. . . . .16 C7
Orford Cl
 Golborne WA3. . . . . .3 A7
 High Lane SK6. . . . . .37 E7
Orford Gn WA2. . . . . .8 D1
Orford La WA2 . . . . .16 B7
Orford Rd WA1. . . . . .16 E8
Orford St WA1. . . . . .16 B5
Organsdale Cotts
 CW6. . . . . .123 B5

Oriel Ho CH2. . . . . .118 C4
Orion Bvd WA5. . . . . .6 E1
Orkney Cl
 ⓷ Ellesmere Port
  CH65. . . . . .70 C1
 Widnes WA8 . . . . .13 E3
Orlando Dr WA5. . . . . .15 C7
Orme Cl
 Macclesfield SK10. . . . . . . .87 D3
 Prestbury SK10 . . . . .87 A8
Ormerod Cl CW11 . . . . . . .175 C5
Ormesby Gr CH63. . . . . . . .43 B6
Orme St SK9. . . . . .60 A1
Ormond Cl WA8 . . . . .12 C2
Ormonde Rd CH2 . . . . .118 C4
Ormonde St CH1. . . . . .237 C3
Orrell Cl WA5. . . . . .15 A6
Orton Cl CW7 . . . . .127 A4
Orwell Cl WA7 . . . . .34 D2
Osborne Ave WA2. . . . . .8 D1
Osborne Cl CW11 . . . . .174 D5
Osborne Gr CW2 . . . . .206 C5
Osborne Rd
 Crewe CW2. . . . . .190 C2
 Northwich CW9 . . . . .104 B8
 Warrington WA2 . . . . .16 A7
Osborne Cl
 Bebington CH62. . . . . .43 E7
 Wilmslow SK9 . . . . .60 D6
OSCROFT 121 E2
Osier Cl CH2 . . . . .72 C3
Osmere Cl SY13 . . . . .226 B1
Osnath Wks WA7. . . . . .16 B6
Osprey Ave CW7 . . . . .149 D5
Osprey Cl
 Middlewich CW10 . . . . .151 D5
 Runcorn WA7. . . . . .49 F5
 Warrington WA2 . . . . .8 E3
Osprey Ct CH2. . . . . .237 A4
Osprey Dr SK9 . . . . .60 C8
Osprey View ST7. . . . . .195 D3
Ossett Cl WA7 . . . . .50 D8
Ostler's La WA16 . . . . .174 F8
Ostler's La WA16. . . . . .58 E7
Otelay Ave CH62. . . . . .43 D8
Otters Bank ⓶ CW7 . . . . .126 A1
Ottersbank Mews
 CW8. . . . . .123 F3
OUGHTRINGTON 19 C4
Oughtrington Com Prim
 Sch WA13. . . . . .19 B4
Oughtrington Cres
 WA13. . . . . .19 B4
Oughtrington La WA13. . . . .19 A2
Oughtrington View
 WA13. . . . . .19 B4
Oulton Ave CH2 . . . . .118 E7
Oulton Cl WA4 . . . . .17 B2
Oulton Ct CW11 . . . . .155 F3
Oulton Mill La CW6. . . . . .147 B7
Oulton Pl CH1. . . . . .237 B3
Our Lady Mother of the
 Saviour RC Prim Sch
 WA7. . . . . .50 A6
Our Lady of Lourdes RC
 Prim Sch M31. . . . . .11 E3
Our Lady of Perpetual
 Succour RC Prim Sch
 WA8 . . . . .22 A8
Our Lady's RC Inf & Jun
 Sch CH65. . . . . .70 A3
Our Lady's RC Prim Sch
 WA4. . . . . .16 E3
Ousel Nest CW8 . . . . .101 D4
Out La CH3. . . . . .184 C6
Outwood Dr SK8. . . . . .34 A8
Outwood La WA4. . . . . .33 C/
Outwood La W M50 . . . . . . .33 B8
Outwood Prim Sch
 SK8. . . . . .34 D7
Outwood Rd SK8 . . . . .34 B7
Oval The
 Ellesmere Port CH65. . . . . .70 C3
 Gatley SK8. . . . . .34 B8
Ovenhouse La SK10. . . . . . .87 E7
Oven La SK11. . . . . .114 D5
OVER 149 B8
Overdale La CW8 . . . . .101 D1
Overdale Rd
 New Mills SK12. . . . . .38 F6
 Willaston CH64 . . . . .43 A1
Overdene Rd CW7 . . . . . . .149 D8
Overfields WA16. . . . . .57 D7
Over Hall Com Prim Sch
 CW7. . . . . .149 B7
Over Hall Dr CW7. . . . . . . .149 C7
Overhill Dr SK9. . . . . .60 E7
Overhill La SK9. . . . . .60 E7
Overhill Rd SK9. . . . . .60 D7
OVER KNUTSFORD 57 C1
OVER LEIGH 65 F6
Overleigh Cl CH4. . . . . .141 D7
Overleigh Rd CH4. . . . . . . .141 C7
Overleigh St Mary's CE
 Prim Sch CH4 . . . . .141 D6
Overleigh Terr CH4 . . . . . . .141 C7
OVER PEOVER 83 A1
Over Pl WA8. . . . . .82 C8
OVERPOOL 69 F7
Overpool Gdns CH66. . . . . .69 F3
Overpool Rd
 Ellesmere Port CH66. . . . . .70 A2
 Ellesmere Port, Great Sutton
  CH65, CH66. . . . . .69 F5
Overpool Sta CH66 . . . . . . .69 E6
Over Rd
 Church Minshull CW5 . . . .172 A7
 Winsford CW7. . . . . .149 F1

Over St John's CE Prim
 Sch CW7. . . . . .126 B1
OVER TABLEY 56 A5
OVERTON 74 C7
Overton Cl
 Congleton CW12 . . . . .156 C3
 Middlewich CW10 . . . . .151 B8
Overton Dr WA6. . . . . .74 C6
Overton Heath La
 SY14 . . . . .212 F5
Overton Rd ST8 . . . . .179 F6
Overton Way ⓶ SK9 . . . . . .34 D5
Overway CW7. . . . . .126 E1
Overwood Ave CH1 . . . . . . .94 E1
Overwood La
 Blacon CH1 . . . . .117 C4
 Mollington CH1. . . . . .94 E1
Ovington Cl WA7 . . . . .49 F3
Owen Cl CH1 . . . . .117 E6
Owens Cnr WA4. . . . . .26 D3
Owen St
 Crewe CW2. . . . . .190 C2
 Northwich CW9 . . . . .104 B8
 Warrington WA2 . . . . .16 A7
Owlers The SK23. . . . . .65 E6
Owley Wood Rd CW8 . . . . .77 E1
Owlhurst The CW8 . . . . .88 B8
Owl Ind Est The CH5 . . . . .116 B6
Owlsfield WA12. . . . . .2 E3
Oxborough Cl WA8 . . . . . . .12 F4
Oxenham Rd WA2 . . . . .8 A3
Oxford Cl CH66. . . . . .94 E8
Oxford Cl WA1 . . . . .16 D6
Oxford Dr
 Halewood L26 . . . . .21 A8
 Heswall CH63. . . . . .41 F6
Oxford Gr M44 . . . . .11 C6
Oxford Rd
 Chester CH4 . . . . .140 F6
 Macclesfield SK11. . . . . . . .112 B7
 Runcorn WA7. . . . . .49 A8
Oxford St
 Crewe CW1. . . . . .190 B5
 Newton-le-W WA12. . . . . . . .2 B3
 Warrington WA4 . . . . .16 C4
 Widnes WA8 . . . . .23 B7
Ox-Hey Cres ST8 . . . . .179 D1
Ox-Hey Dr ST8 . . . . .179 D1
Oxhey Fast Sch ST8. . . . . .179 E1
Oxheys WA7. . . . . .50 C8
Oxheys La CW6. . . . . .169 C8
Oxmead Cl WA7 . . . . .49 F4
Oxmoor Cl WA7 . . . . .50 A5
Oxney Cl SK11. . . . . .111 F8
Oxton Cl WA8 . . . . .12 C4
Oxton Gn CH66. . . . . .69 D4

P

PACKMOOR 195 F1
Packmoor Prim Sch
 ST7. . . . . .195 F1
Packsaddle Pk SK10 . . . . . .86 E5
Padarn Cl CH4 . . . . .140 D5
PADDINGTON 17 A8
Paddington Bank WA1. . . . .16 F6
Paddock Brow SK10. . . . . . .87 A5
Paddock Chase SK12 . . . . . .36 F6
Paddock Cl SK23 . . . . .64 F4
Paddock Dr CH64. . . . . .41 D2
PADDOCKHILL 59 A4
Paddock Hill La WA16 . . . . .59 A3
Paddock La
 Audlem CW3 . . . . .230 B2
 Horwich End SK23. . . . . . . .65 F5
 Kettleshulme SK23 . . . . . . .64 F4
 Lymm WA13. . . . . .19 C7
 Partington WA13, WA14 . . .20 B5
Paddock Rd CH4. . . . . .141 E1
Paddock Rise WA7 . . . . .49 E4
Paddock Row CH1 . . . . . . .237 B2
Paddocks Gn CW12 . . . . . .178 F8
Paddocks The
 Prestbury SK10 . . . . .87 A5
 Whitegate CW8 . . . . .125 B6
Paddock The
 Chester CH4 . . . . .141 B7
 Ellesmere Port CH66. . . . . .69 D3
 Elton CH2. . . . . .72 A3
 Hartford CW8 . . . . .103 C3
 Hassall Green CW11 . . . . .175 F2
 Helsby WA6. . . . . .73 C2
 Heswall CH60. . . . . .41 C8
 Horwich End SK23. . . . . . . .65 F6
 Lymm WA13. . . . . .19 C4
 Sandbach CW11 . . . . .175 B7
 Tarporley CW6. . . . . .146 D1
 Willaston CW5. . . . . .205 D4
Paddock View CW10 . . . . .128 C2
Paddock Way CH4. . . . . . . .161 A7
Paddock Wlk CW8. . . . . . .156 B4
PADGATE 8 F1
Padgate Bsns Ctr WA1. . . .17 B8
Padgate Com High Sch
 WA2 .8 F1
Padgate La
 Warrington, Padgate
  WA1. . . . . .16 F8
 Warrington WA1. . . . . .16 D7
Padgate Sta WA1. . . . . .9 A1
Padgbury Cl CW12. . . . . . .156 A1
Padgbury La CW12. . . . . . .156 A1
Padge La CH3. . . . . .183 C2
Padmore Cl WA1 . . . . .190 A7
Padston Dr ST7. . . . . .193 B3

Padstow Cl
 Crewe CW1. . . . . .190 C8
 Macclesfield SK10. . . . . . . .111 E8
 Warrington WA5 . . . . .14 E3
Padstow Dr SK7 . . . . .35 F7
Padstow Sq WA7. . . . . .50 B5
Padworth Pl CW1. . . . . . . .173 B1
Page Gr CW2. . . . . .206 B3
Page La WA8. . . . . .13 C1
Paignton Cl WA5 . . . . .14 E4
Painswick Rd CH66 . . . . . . .69 E2
Paisley Ave CH62. . . . . .43 E4
PALACE FIELDS 50 A6
Palace Fields Ave WA7. . . .50 A6
Palace Fields Local Ctr
 WA7. . . . . .50 A6
Palace Fields Prim Sch
 WA7. . . . . .50 A6
Palace Hey CH64 . . . . .67 A5
Palatine Cl CH1 . . . . .117 D6
Palatine Ind Est WA4 . . . . .16 C3
Palgrave Cl CH1. . . . . .118 A5
Palin Dr WA5. . . . . .14 F5
Palliser Cl WA3. . . . . .10 A3
Pall Mall CW5. . . . . .204 E5
Palma Ave M90. . . . . .33 B8
Palmer Cl ⓷ CW9 . . . . . . .103 F5
Palmer Cres WA5. . . . . .15 D8
Palmer Rd CW11 . . . . .175 C5
Palmerston Cl CW1 . . . . . .191 C5
Palmerston Cl WA1. . . . . . . .16 E3
Palmerston Rd SK11. . . . . .112 A7
Palmerston St CW8. . . . . . .88 B8
Palmerston Way ST8. . . . .179 D1
Palm Gr CH66 . . . . .70 A1
Palmyra Sq N WA1. . . . . . . .16 A5
Palmyra Sq S WA1. . . . . . . .16 A5
PANDY 222 A3
Pangbourne Cl WA4 . . . . . .26 E6
Panton Pl CH2. . . . . .118 F3
Panton Rd CH2 . . . . .118 F3
Parade Rd M90. . . . . .33 C7
Parade The
 ⓵ Alderley Edge SK9. . . . . .60 A1
 Blacon CH1 . . . . .117 C5
 Culcheth WA3. . . . . .4 E3
 Neston CH64. . . . . .41 B1
Paradise CH4. . . . . .237 B1
PARADISE GREEN 171 E6
Paradise La CW5. . . . . .171 E7
Paradise Row ⓷
 SK11. . . . . .112 D7
Paradise St SK11 . . . . .112 C7
Paragon Cl WA8 . . . . .13 B5
Parbold Ct WA8. . . . . .22 D8
Parc Ddiwydiannol
 Glamau Dyfrdwy/
 Deeside Ind Pk CH5. . . . .92 E2
Parc Ddiwydiannol Y Ffin/
 Borders Ind Pk The
 CH4 . . . . .140 C7
Parchments The WA12. . . . .2 D4
Parish Cl ST7. . . . . .193 B4
Park Ave
 Bramhall SK7. . . . . .35 D5
 Furness Vale SK23. . . . . . . .39 D3
 Haydock WA11. . . . . .1 A6
 Poynton SK12 . . . . .36 E4
 Saltney CH4. . . . . .140 E6
 Saughall CH1. . . . . .94 A2
 Talke ST7. . . . . .210 E8
 Tattenhall CH3. . . . . .166 B2
 Warrington WA4 . . . . .16 D3
 Weaverham CW0. . . . . .77 D1
 Widnes WA8 . . . . .13 B1
 Wilmslow SK9 . . . . .60 C8
 Winsford CW7. . . . . .127 A3
Park Ave N WA12. . . . . .2 C2
Park Ave S WA12. . . . . .2 C2
Park Bank CW12. . . . . .156 F2
Park Brook Rd SK11 . . . . .112 A8
Park Bvd WA1 . . . . .16 B4
Park Cl CH3. . . . . .121 B2
Park Cres
 Cuddington CW8 . . . . .101 F4
 Furness Vale SK23. . . . . . . .39 D3
 Handforth SK9. . . . . .34 B1
 Warrington WA4 . . . . .16 C3
Park Ct
 Chester CH1 . . . . .237 C2
 Frodsham WA6. . . . . .74 A8
 Runcorn WA7. . . . . .49 A4
 ⓵ Warrington WA1. . . . . . .16 A5
Parkdale Ind Est WA1. . . . .16 C4
Parkdale Rd WA1. . . . . .17 A7
Park Dr
 Chester CH2 . . . . .119 A4
 Ellesmere Port CH65. . . . . .70 B3
 Handforth SK9. . . . . .34 B1
 Wistaston CW2. . . . . .205 F8
Park Drive Gdns CW2. . . .205 F8
Park Dr S CH2. . . . . .119 A4
PARK END 209 A4
Parker Ave CW8 . . . . .103 A6
Parker Dr CH3. . . . . .180 E1
Parker Dr S CH3. . . . . .180 F1
Parker's Bldgs CH1. . . . . .237 C3
Parker's Ct WA7 . . . . .49 E6
Parker's Rd CW7. . . . . .190 A8
Parker's Row CH3. . . . . . . .166 B2
Parker St
 Macclesfield SK11. . . . . . . .112 E7
 Runcorn WA7. . . . . .23 B8
 Warrington WA1. . . . . .16 A5
Parker Way CW12. . . . . . . .156 A3

Park Est CW2 . . . . 206 D5
Parkctt Heyes Rd
SK11. . . . . 111 E7
Parkfield CW1 . . . . 173 A1
Parkfield Ave WA4. . . . . . . 17 A4
Parkfield Dr
Ellesmere Port CH65. . . . . . 70 A3
Helsby WA6 . . . . 73 D1
Nantwich CW5. . . . . 204 E4
Parkfield Rd
Broughton CH4 . . . . 139 C3
Knutsford WA16 . . . . 82 B8
Northwich CW9 . . . . 104 C8
Parklands La WA2. . . . . 8 F2
Parkgate WA16 . . . . 57 C3
PARKGATE
Neston 41 C1
Over Peover. 108 B8
Parkgate Ave WA16. . . . . . 108 B8
Parkgate Ct
Chester CH3 . . . . 118 B4
Warrington WA4 . . . . 16 C2
Parkgate Ho
Neston CH64 . . . . 41 B1
Neston CH64 . . . . 41 B2
Parkgate La
Heswall CH64 . . . . 41 F5
Knutsford WA16 . . . . 57 C3
Parkgate Prim Sch
CH64 . . . . 41 C1
Parkgate Rd
Blacon CH1 . . . . 118 A6
Macclesfield SK11. . . . . . . 112 C4
Neston CH64 . . . . 66 D8
Puddington CH66. . . . . 68 C2
Saughall CH1 . . . . 94 C3
Warrington WA4 . . . . 16 D1
Woodbank CH1. . . . . 93 E7
Parkgate Trad Est
WA4. . . . . 57 C4
Parkgate Way
7 Handforth SK9. . . . . . . 34 D4
Runcorn WA7. . . . . 50 D7
Park Gn SK11. . . . . 112 D7
Park Gr SK11. . . . . 112 C6
Parkhill Ct WA16 . . . . 57 B1
Park House Dr
Prestbury SK10 . . . . 87 A8
Sandbach CW11 . . . . 175 C8
Parkhouse Ind Est
ST5. . . . . 210 F1
Park House La SK10 . . . . . . 87 A8
Parkhouse Mews
CW11. . . . . 175 D8
Parkhouse Rd E ST5. . . . . 210 F1
Parkhouse Rd W ST5. . . . . 210 E1
Park La
Audley ST7. . . . . 209 B4
Congleton CW12 . . . . 156 F2
Frodsham WA6 . . . . 74 B8
Hargrave CH3 . . . . 144 E3
Hartford CW8 . . . . 103 B4
Hatherton CW5. . . . . 219 E4
Higher Walton WA4. . . . . . . 25 F5
Little Bollington WA14. . . . . 20 B2
Littleton CH3 . . . . 119 F3
Macclesfield SK11. . . . . . . 112 C6
Macclesfield SK11. . . . . . . 112 D7
Moulton CW9. . . . . 126 F7
Pickmere CW9, WA16 . . . . . 79 E8
Poynton SK12 . . . . 36 F3
Pulford CH4. . . . . 162 E5
Sandbach CW11 . . . . 174 F6
Warrington WA4 . . . . 27 B4
Parkland Dr CH2 . . . . 72 B3
Parklands
Ellesmere Port CH66. . . . . . 69 D6
Kidsgrove ST7 . . . . 195 B1
Widnes WA8 . . . . 12 C3
Parklands Com Prim Sch
CH66 . . . . 69 D5
Parklands Dr
Chorlton CW2 . . . . 207 E3
Heswall CH60 . . . . 41 C6
Parklands Gdns CH66. . . . . 69 D6
Parklands The
Congleton CW12 . . . . 157 A2
Middlewich CW10 . . . . 151 B7
Parklands View CH66 . . . . . 69 D5
Parklands Way SK12. . . . . . 36 E4
Park Lane CW5 . . . . 204 D4
Park Lane Sch SK11 . . . . . 112 B6
Parklea CH66. . . . . 69 D6
Parkleigh CW12 . . . . 156 E2
Park Mills Cl CW5 . . . . 205 D5
Park Mount Cl SK11 . . . . . 112 A6
Park Mount Dr SK11 . . . . . 112 A6
Park Prim Sch The
WA7. . . . . 24 A1
Park Rd
Bebington, Eastham
CH62. . . . . 43 F6
Congleton CW12 . . . . 156 E3
Ellesmere Port CH65. . . . . . 70 C4
Golborne WA3 . . . . 3 A7
Haslington CW1. . . . . 191 D5
Heswall CH60 . . . . 41 B8
High Lane SK12. . . . . 38 A6
Horwich End SK23. . . . . 65 D6
Little Budworth CW6. . . . . . 124 F1
Lymm WA13. . . . . 29 D8
Middlewich CW10 . . . . 128 C1
Nantwich CW5. . . . . 204 E3
New Mills SK22. . . . . 39 C7
North Rode CW12 . . . . 134 F2

Park Rd *continued*
Partington, Warburton
WA13 . . . . 19 C8
Runcorn WA7. . . . . 49 A8
Tarporley CW6. . . . . 146 D2
Thornton-le-M CH2 . . . . 71 F1
Warrington, Orford WA2. . . . 8 D1
Warrington WA1. . . . . 14 E4
Widnes WA8 . . . . 13 B1
Willaston CH64 . . . . 68 B8
Willaston(in Nantwich)
CW5. . . . . 205 C5
Wilmslow SK9 . . . . 59 F7
Winnington CW8 . . . . 78 D1
Park Rd N WA12. . . . . 2 E4
Park Rd S WA12 . . . . 2 D2
Park Rd W CH4. . . . . 141 A7
Park Road Com Prim Sch
WA5. . . . . 14 E6
Parkroyal Com Sch
SK11. . . . . 112 C7
Parkside Bsns Pk WA3. . . . . 3 A8
Parkside Cl
High Lane SK6 . . . . 37 D8
Neston CH66 . . . . 66 D8
Parkside Ct WA8 . . . . 13 A2
Parkside Rd WA12, WA2 . . . 3 B2
Park St
Bollington SK10 . . . . 88 B8
Chester CH1 . . . . 237 B2
Congleton CW12 . . . . 156 E2
Haydock WA11. . . . . 1 A6
Macclesfield SK11. . . . . . . 112 D7
Neston CH64 . . . . 66 E8
Northwich CW8 . . . . 103 E7
Parkstone Dr CW1 . . . . 190 B8
Parksway WA1 . . . . 17 D7
Park The
Christleton CH3 . . . . 142 E8
Warrington WA5 . . . . 14 D3
Park Vale Rd SK11 . . . . 112 C6
Park View
Audlem CW3 . . . . 230 C8
Bebington CH62. . . . . 43 C8
Congleton CW12 . . . . 156 E3
Hazel Grove SK7 . . . . 37 B8
Little Bollington WA14. . . . . 20 B2
Nantwich CW5. . . . . 204 F6
Newton-le-W WA12. . . . . 2 E3
Warrington WA5 . . . . 14 D3
Parkview Ct CH60 . . . . 40 F8
Park View Ct SK12 . . . . 36 E4
Parkview Pk WA13. . . . . 29 D8
Park View Rd ST7. . . . . . . 195 B3
Park W CH60 . . . . 40 E7
Parkway
Connah's Quay CH5. . . . . . . 92 E1
Holmes Chapel CW4 . . . . . 130 C3
Wilmslow SK9 . . . . 60 B6
Park Way CH1 . . . . 94 A2
Parkway Bsns Ctr CH5. . . . . 92 E1
Park Wlk CH2 . . . . 118 C4
Parkwood Cl
Bebington CH62. . . . . 43 E8
Lymm WA13. . . . . 18 D2
Parliament St 4
CW8. . . . . 103 E7
Parliament Way 9
CH66 . . . . 94 F8
Parlington Cl WA8 . . . . 22 C7
Parnell Sq CW12 . . . . 157 A2
PARRAH GREEN 231 E7
Parr Gr WA11 . . . . 1 A6
Parr St
Macclesfield SK11. . . . . . . 112 C8
Warrington WA1 . . . . 16 C4
1 Widnes WA8. . . . . 13 C1
Parrs Wood View WA4. . . . . 17 B1
Parry Dr WA4 . . . . 17 E3
Parsonage Gn
Hale L24 . . . . 21 E1
Wilmslow SK9 . . . . 60 B7
Parsonage Rd WA8 . . . . 23 A4
Parsonage St SK11 . . . . . . 112 D7
Parsonage Way WA5. . . . . . 15 A5
Parsons La CH2 . . . . 118 B7
Parson St CW12 . . . . 156 C2
PARTINGTON 11 F4
Partington Prim Sch
M31. . . . . 11 F3
Partington Sh Ctr M31. . . . . 11 F3
Partridge Cl
Congleton CW12 . . . . 156 E1
4 Warrington WA3 . . . . 9 E4
Winsford CW7 . . . . 149 D5
Partridge Way CW9 . . . . 79 F5
Parvey La SK11. . . . . 112 E2
Pasture Cl
Kelsall CW6 . . . . 122 C4
Macclesfield SK10. . . . . 87 C3
Pasture Dr WA3 . . . . 9 B7
Pasture La WA2 . . . . 9 B3
Pastures Dr CW7 . . . . 207 D3
Pastures The WA9 . . . . 6 A7
Patch La SK7. . . . . 35 D5
Patmos La WA16 . . . . 105 F8
Patrivale Cl WA1 . . . . 16 F6
Patten La WA1. . . . . 16 B5
Patterdale Ave WA2 . . . . 8 C2
Patterdale Cl CW7 . . . . 189 D3
Patterdale Rd M31. . . . . 11 E3
Patterson Cl WA3 . . . . 9 E3
Patterson St WA12. . . . . 2 B3
Patton Dr WA5 . . . . 15 B6
Paul Cl WA5. . . . . 14 D6
Paulden Rd CW9 . . . . 80 A2
Paul St WA2. . . . . 16 A6
Pavement La WA16 . . . . 57 F3

Pavilion Ct WA12 . . . . 2 A3
Pavilions The
Chester CH4 . . . . 141 B3
Davenham CW9 . . . . 103 E2
Pavilion Way
Congleton CW12 . . . . 156 C3
Macclesfield SK10. . . . . 86 F1
Paxford PI SK9 . . . . 60 A5
Payne Cl WA5 . . . . 15 D6
Paythorne Cl WA3 . . . . 4 F3
Peace Dr WA5. . . . . 15 D5
Peach Field CH3. . . . . 142 B7
Peach Gr WA11. . . . . 1 E7
Peach La CW5. . . . . 189 A1
Peach Tree Cl L24 . . . . 21 E2
Peacock Ave
Warrington WA1 . . . . 16 E6
Winsford CW7 . . . . 149 C5
Peacock Dr SK8 . . . . 34 B6
Peacock Hay Rd ST7. . . . . 210 F4
Peacock La WA16. . . . . 29 E6
Peacock Way 5 SK9. . . . . . . 34 D5
Peak Rd SK22 . . . . 39 D8
Pearle St SK10 . . . . 87 D1
Pearlings The CH3. . . . . . . 119 B1
Pearl La
Chester CH3 . . . . 119 C1
Littleton CH3 . . . . 119 D1
Pearl St SK10. . . . . 87 A7
Pearson Ave WA4. . . . . 16 D2
Pearson St 9 SK11. . . . . . . 112 E7
Pear Tree Ave
Crewe CW1. . . . . 190 B7
Runcorn WA7. . . . . 49 C7
Pear Tree Bank CW12 . . . . 156 E2
Peartree Cl CW11. . . . . 175 E6
Pear Tree Cl
Frodsham WA6 . . . . 49 D1
Hale L24 . . . . 21 E1
Weaverham CW8. . . . . 77 C1
Winsford CW7 . . . . 149 D7
Pear Tree Dr CW9. . . . . 80 A6
Pear Tree Farm Cotts
CW9 . . . . 104 F4
Pear Tree Field CW5. . . . . . 205 A4
Peartree La SY14 . . . . 222 D1
Pear Tree La
Acton Bridge CW8. . . . . 76 E4
Whitchurch SY13. . . . . 225 D1
Peartree Pl WA4. . . . . 16 C4
Pear Tree Rd ST7 . . . . 209 F1
Pear Tree Sch CW5 . . . . . . 205 A4
Pear Tree Way
Chester CH2 . . . . 118 F6
5 Ellesmere Port CH66 . . . 69 E1
Pearwood Cl CW6 . . . . 146 D1
Peasley Cl WA2. . . . . 9 B1
Pebble Brook Prim Sch
CW2. . . . . 190 C1
Peckfield Cl WA7. . . . . 50 A5
PECKFORTON 184 F5
Peckforton Castle*
CW6. . . . . 167 E1
Peckforton Cl CW11 . . . . . 174 E7
Peckforton Dr
Ellesmere Port CH66. . . . . . 69 E3
Runcorn WA7. . . . . 49 F4
Peckforton Hall Farm
CW6 . . . . 185 A6
Peckforton Hall La
CW6. . . . . 185 B6
Peckforton Rd CW6. . . . . . . 168 A2
Peckforton Way
Chester CH2 . . . . 118 F6
2 Northwich CW9 . . . . 103 E7
Peckforton Wlk 11 SK9 . . . . 34 E1
Peckmill Cl SK9 . . . . 34 E2
Peck Mill La WA6. . . . . 98 A7
Peckmill Rdbt CW9 . . . . 127 B8
Pedley Hill
Booth Green SK10. . . . . 62 F7
Rainow SK10 . . . . 88 E4
Pedley House La WA16. . . . . 58 E1
Pedley La
Chelford WA16. . . . . 83 D8
Congleton CW12 . . . . 157 F4
Pedley St CW2 . . . . 190 D2
Peebles Cl
Ellesmere Port CH66. . . . . . 68 F6
Holmes Chapel CW4 . . . . . 130 B2
Peel Cl WA1. . . . . 17 D6
Peel Cres CH3. . . . . 121 E7
Peel Cl 4 ST7. . . . . 195 A2
Peel Dr CW12 . . . . 178 B7
Peel Hall La CH3 . . . . 121 E7
Peel Hall Pk CH3 . . . . 121 D8
Peel Hollow ST7. . . . . 209 A2
Peel House La WA8. . . . . . . 13 B2
Peel La CW12 . . . . 178 D7
Peel Sq 1 CW1 . . . . 190 B5
Peel St
Crewe CW1. . . . . 190 B5
Macclesfield SK11. . . . . . . 112 D6
Newton-le-W WA12. . . . . 2 A3
Runcorn WA7. . . . . 22 F3
Peel Terr CH1 . . . . 237 C3
Peerswood Ct CH64. . . . . . . 66 E5
Peewit Cl CW7 . . . . 149 D5
Peggie's La SK10 . . . . 62 D2
Pelham Cl CW1 . . . . 191 C5
Pelham Rd WA4 . . . . 17 C3
Pelican Cl CW1 . . . . 191 A5
Pemberton Cl CH64. . . . . . . 68 A8
Pemberton Rd CH1 . . . . . . 237 A3
Pembridge Ct CH65. . . . . . . 70 E3
Pembridge Gdns CH65. . . . . 70 E3
Pembroke Apartments
WA2. . . . . 9 A3

Pembroke Cl CH4. . . . . 141 E6
Pembroke Ct WA7 . . . . 24 D5
Pembroke Dr CH65. . . . . 70 A3
Pembroke Gdns WA4 . . . . . . 26 D4
Pembroke Gr WA4 . . . . 11 C6
Pembroke Rd SY11 . . . . 113 F7
Pembroke Way CW7 . . . . . . 149 B7
Penare WA7. . . . . 50 C6
Penbrook Cl CW2. . . . . 189 D3
Pendine Way CW11. . . . . . . 175 B6
Pendine Cl WA5 . . . . 7 C2
Pendlebury Gdns
SK11. . . . . 112 D2
Pendlebury St WA4 . . . . 17 A3
Pendle Cl
Crewe CW1. . . . . 191 A5
Ellesmere Port CH66. . . . . . 68 F6
Pendle Gdns WA3 . . . . 4 E2
Penfold Cl CH1 . . . . 94 B8
Penfold Hey CH2 . . . . 118 D7
Penfolds WA7. . . . . 23 D1
Penfold Way CH4 . . . . 162 A7
Penhale Mews SK7 . . . . 35 F7
Peninsula Ho WA2. . . . . 16 C7
Penistone Dr CH66. . . . . 69 B5
PENKETH 14 D4
Penketh Ave WA5. . . . . 15 F8
Penketh Bsns Pk WA5 . . . . . 15 B4
Penketh Com Prim Sch
WA5. . . . . 14 D4
Penketh Ct
1 Runcorn WA7. . . . . 23 B2
Warrington WA5 . . . . 14 D4
Penketh High Sch
WA5. . . . . 15 A5
Penketh Rd WA5 . . . . 15 A4
Penketh's La 19 WA7 . . . . . . 23 A3
Penketh South Com Prim
Sch WA5. . . . . 14 E3
Penkford La WA5. . . . . 1 D2
Penkford Sch WA12 . . . . 1 E2
Penkford St WA12. . . . . 1 E3
Penkmans La WA6. . . . . 74 C6
Penlington Ct CW5 . . . . 204 F6
Penmann Cres L26 . . . . 21 A7
Penmark Cl WA5 . . . . 7 C2
Penmon Cl CH1 . . . . 117 D3
Pennant Cl WA3 . . . . 10 A3
Penn Bridge SK11. . . . . . . 158 E6
Penn Gdns CH65. . . . . 70 B5
Penn House Cl SK7 . . . . 35 E8
Pennine Cl SK10. . . . . 87 E2
Pennine Rd WA2 . . . . 8 E2
Pennine Way
Biddulph ST8 . . . . 179 E1
Winsford CW7 . . . . 149 B8
Pennine Wlk CH66. . . . . 69 B6
Pennington Cl WA6. . . . . 49 D2
Pennington Dr WA12 . . . . 2 E3
Pennington Gn CH66. . . . . . . 69 C3
Pennington La WA5,
WA9 . . . . 1 D2
Penningtons La SK11 . . . . . 111 F5
Penn La WA7. . . . . 22 F1
Penny Bank Cl CH4 . . . . . . 139 A3
Pennyfields Rd ST7 . . . . . . 195 D2
Penny La
Collins Green WA5. . . . . 1 D1
Cronton L35, WA8 . . . . 12 B6
Haydock WA11. . . . . 2 B7
Rainow SK10 . . . . 88 D3
Pennymoor Dr CW10. . . . . . 128 D2
Pennypleck La CW9 . . . . 28 A2
Penny's La
Northwich CW9 . . . . 104 F7
Rudheath CW9 . . . . 105 B5
Penrhyn Cres
Hazel Grove SK7 . . . . 36 C8
Runcorn WA7. . . . . 49 B7
Penrhyn Rd CW8 . . . . 103 E8
Penrith Ave
Macclesfield SK11. . . . . . . 111 F5
Warrington WA2 . . . . 8 C2
Penrith Cl
Frodsham WA6 . . . . 49 D1
Partington M31. . . . . 11 E4
Penrith Ct CW12 . . . . 156 A2
Penrose Gdns WA5 . . . . 14 D3
Penry Ave M44 . . . . 11 E6
Penryn Cl WA5 . . . . 14 E3
Pensarn Gdns WA5 . . . . 7 D2
Pensby Ave CH2 . . . . 118 D5
Pensby Dr CH66. . . . . 69 D4
Pensby Rd CH60. . . . . 40 F8
Penshaw Ct WA7 . . . . 49 E7
Pentland Ave WA2. . . . . 8 B3
Pentland Cl
Chester CH3 . . . . 119 A2
Winsford CW7 . . . . 149 B8
Pentland Pl WA2 . . . . 8 B3
Pentre Cl CH3 . . . . 121 F7
Pentre La CH3. . . . . 121 F7
Penzance Cl SK10 . . . . 111 C0
Peony Gdns WA9 . . . . 6 B7
Peover Hall & Gdns*
WA16. . . . . 107 E8
PEOVER HEATH 108 C8
Peover La
Chelford SK11 . . . . 108 F8
Congleton CW12 . . . . 157 F6
Peover Rd SK9 . . . . 34 E5
Pepper Cl SK9. . . . . 60 A6
Pepper St
Appleton Thorn WA4 . . . . . . 27 B3
Ashley WA16 . . . . 31 F1
Chelford SK11 . . . . 83 E2

Pepper St *continued*
Chester CH1 . . . . 237 B2
Christleton CH3. . . . . 142 D8
Hale L24 . . . . 21 D1
Henbury SK11 . . . . 111 B8
Lymm WA13. . . . . 18 F3
Middlewich CW10 . . . . 128 C1
Nantwich CW5. . . . . 204 E5
Peppers The WA13. . . . . . . 18 F3
Percival Cl CH2 . . . . 118 C8
Percival La WA7. . . . . 22 E2
Percival Rd
Chester CH2 . . . . 118 C8
Ellesmere Port CH65. . . . . . 70 B6
Percivals La WA16. . . . . 83 B3
Percival St WA1 . . . . 16 C5
Percy James Cl ST7 . . . . . 193 E4
Percy Rd CH4 . . . . 141 D7
Percy St
Northwich CW9 . . . . 104 A8
Warrington WA5 . . . . 15 E5
Percyvale St SK10 . . . . 112 E8
Peregrine Cl CW7 . . . . 149 D5
Perenna Ct/Llys Perenna
CH6 . . . . 91 B2
Perimeter Rd CH2 . . . . 72 D5
Perrin Ave WA7 . . . . 48 E8
Perrins Rd WA5. . . . . 6 F6
Perry Fields CW1 . . . . 173 B1
Perry St WA7. . . . . 23 B2
Perth Cl
Bramhall SK7. . . . . 35 F5
Holmes Chapel CW4 . . . . . 130 B2
Warrington WA2 . . . . 8 F3
Peterborough Cl
Ellesmere Port CH66. . . . . . 94 F7
Macclesfield SK10. . . . . 86 F1
Peter Destapleigh Way
CW5. . . . . 205 A3
Peter Ellson Cl CW2 . . . . . 190 D1
Peter House Rd SK11. . . . . 112 F3
Peter Pl 7 CW1. . . . . 190 B5
Peter St W 1 SK11 . . . . . . 112 C7
Peters Cl SK10 . . . . 87 A7
Petersfield Gdns WA3 . . . . . . 4 E4
Petersfield Way CW7 . . . . . 207 D3
Petersgate SK9 . . . . 59 D7
Petersham Dr WA4 . . . . 26 E5
Peter St
Golborne WA3 . . . . 3 A8
Macclesfield SK11. . . . . . . 112 C7
Northwich CW9 . . . . 79 B1
Peterstone Cl WA5 . . . . 7 D2
Petham Ct WA8 . . . . 12 E4
Petrel Ave SK12 . . . . 36 B4
Petrel Cl CW7 . . . . 149 D5
Petunia Cl
Macclesfield SK11. . . . . . . 112 B5
St Helens WA9 . . . . 6 A7
Petworth Ave WA2. . . . . 8 B8
Petworth Cl CW2 . . . . 206 B8
Pevensey Dr WA16. . . . . 82 A8
Peveril Cl WA4 . . . . 26 D8
Peveril Dr SK7 . . . . 36 F8
Peveril Gdns CW8 . . . . 39 A6
Peveril Rd CH65. . . . . 70 A6
Peveril Wlk 3 SK11 . . . . . . 111 F7
Pewithall Prim Sch
WA7. . . . . 49 B7
Pewit La CW5 . . . . 231 C7
PEWTERSPEAR 26 E4
Pewterspear Green Rd
WA4. . . . . 26 E3
Pewterspear La WA4 . . . . . . 26 E4
Pexall Rd SK11 . . . . 134 C3
Pex Hill Ct WA8 . . . . 12 E5
Pexhill Dr SK10 . . . . 111 E7
Pexhill Rd SK11 . . . . 111 C5
Pex Hill Visitor Ctr*
WA8. . . . . 12 E6
Pheasant Cl WA3 . . . . 9 F4
Pheasant Dr CW9. . . . . 79 F5
Pheasant Field L24 . . . . 21 C2
Pheasant Way CW7 . . . . . . 149 D5
Pheasant Wlk WA16 . . . . . . 29 C4
Philip Rd WA8. . . . . 22 B8
Philips Dr WA5. . . . . 14 E7
Philips La CH66. . . . . 69 C4
Philip St CH5. . . . . 116 A3
Phillips Rd CH1. . . . . 117 D3
Phillip St CH2 . . . . 118 F3
Phillips Way CH60 . . . . 40 E8
Phipps' La WA5. . . . . 7 A1
Phoenix Ave WA5. . . . . 7 F2
Phoenix Cl ST7 . . . . 195 C2
Phoenix Ctr The CW7 . . . . . 127 C1
Phoenix St CH5. . . . . 116 A3
Phythian Cres WA5 . . . . 14 F4
Pichael Nook WA4. . . . . 17 A4
Pickenham Cl SK11 . . . . . . 111 F6
Pickering Cres WA4 . . . . 17 D3
Pickerings Cl WA7 . . . . 49 C6
Pickerings Lock Cvn PK
CW8. . . . . 76 A5
Pickerings O The Boat
CW8. . . . . 76 B5
Pickering's Pasture
(Nature Reserve)*
WA8. . . . . 22 B8
Pickerings Rd WA8 . . . . 22 B5
Pickering St CH2 . . . . 237 C4
Pickering Way CW5. . . . . . . 204 F4
Pickford St SK11 . . . . 112 D7
PICKMERE 80 A7
Pickmere Cl CW11. . . . . . . 174 F7
Pickmere Ct
Crewe CW1. . . . . 190 C5
10 Handforth SK9. . . . . . . 34 D5

Pic–Pri 273

Pickmere Dr
Bebington CH62 43 F3
Bebington CH62 43 F4
Chester CH3 142 B8
Runcorn WA7 50 C5
Pickmere La
Higher Wincham CW9 79 F6
Pickmere WA16 55 D2
Pickmere Rd SK9 34 D5
Pickmere St WA5 15 E5
Pickwick Cl CW11 175 C8
Pickwick Pl ST7 194 D2
Pickwick Rd SK12 36 D3
Picow Farm Rd WA7 22 E1
Picow St 2 WA7 22 F1
PICTON 96 C3
Picton Ave
Ellesmere Port CH65 70 C5
Runcorn WA7 23 B2
Picton Cl
Bebington CH62 43 E3
2 Northwich CW9 103 F4
Warrington WA3 9 C4
Picton Dr
Handforth SK9 34 E2
Winsford CW7 126 B2
Picton Gorse La CH2 119 B7
Picton La CH2 96 C4
Picton Sq CW4 130 C3
Piele Rd WA11 1 E8
Pierce St SK11 112 C8
Pierpoint La CH1 237 B2
Pierpoint St WA5 15 F7
Pigginshaw SK9 59 E8
Pigot Pl WA4 16 F5
Pike La WA6 75 A3
Pikemere Prim Sch
ST7 193 B5
Pikemere Rd ST7 193 B5
Pikenall La CW8 76 D3
Pike Rd SK10 89 B6
Pike St WA4 16 D1
Pike The CW5 204 E3
Pilgrim Cl WA2 8 A6
Pilgrims Way WA7 24 D2
Pillar Box La CW11 153 B3
Pillmoss La WA4 52 B8
Pillory St CW5 204 E5
Pimblett Rd WA11 1 E7
Pimblett St WA3 3 A7
Pimlico Rd WA7 22 E2
Pinders Farm Dr WA1 16 C5
Pineapple Pk CW7 127 B2
Pine Ave
Newton-le-W WA12 2 D2
4 Widnes WA8 13 B2
Pine Cl
Haydock WA11 1 C6
Macclesfield SK10 87 F1
Talke ST7 210 D7
Pine Ct ST7 193 E4
Pinedale Cl CH66 95 A8
Pine Gdns CH2 118 C6
Pine Gr
Chester CH2 119 B4
Ellesmere Port CH66 70 A1
Golborne WA3 3 C8
Sandbach CW11 175 C6
Warrington WA1 17 A7
Winsford CW7 127 A1
Pinehey CH64 41 D1
Pine Ho CH2 118 C5
Pinehurst SK10 86 E6
Pinellas WA7 23 B3
Pine Lo SK7 35 F7
Pine Rd
Bramhall SK7 35 F8
Heswall CH60 41 C8
Macclesfield SK10 87 F1
Poynton SK12 36 F3
Runcorn WA7 49 C8
Pines The
Mobberley WA16 58 E1
6 Northwich CW9 103 E6
Widnes WA8 13 D4
Pinetree Cl
Barnton CW8 78 B4
Winsford CW7 127 A1
Pine Tree Cl CH4 139 C3
Pine Trees WA16 57 F8
Pineways WA4 26 D5
Pine Wlk
Nantwich CW5 204 F4
1 Partington M31 11 E3
Pinewood Ave WA1 16 E7
Pinewood Cl CH2 72 C3
Pinewood Ct CW2 206 B7
Pinewood Dr CH60 41 B8
Pinewood Gr ST5 210 E1
Pinewood Rd
Burtonwood WA5 6 F7
Wilmslow SK9 60 E8
Winsford CW7 126 B1
Pinfold Cl WA15 32 D7
Pinfold Craft Ctr*
CW5 188 B3
Pinfold Ct CH4 141 E6
Pinfold La
Alpraham CW6 169 D5
Chelford WA16 83 D6
Chester CH4 141 D6
Chester CH4 141 E7
Little Budworth CW6 147 E7
Middlewich CW10 128 B1
Plumley WA16 81 B4
Wythenshawe M90,
WA15 32 F6
Pinfold St 18 SK11 112 C8
Pinfold The LL13 196 D8
Pinfold Way CW8 77 D1
Pingard's La CW8 101 C6
Pingate Dr SK8 35 A6
Pingate La SK8 35 A6
Pingate La S SK8 35 A6
Pingot Croft CH3 142 B7
Pingot La WA6 99 A5
Pingot Rd SK22 39 D8
Pinmill Brow WA6 74 B7
Pinmill Cl WA6 74 C7
Pinners Brow WA2 16 B6
Pinners Brow Ret Pk
WA2 16 B6
Pinners Fold WA7 24 B1
PINSLEY GREEN 216 D2
Pinsley Green Rd
CW5 216 E2
Pinsley View CW5 216 E4
Pintail Pl CW7 149 D6
Pinwood Ct 13 SK9 34 E1
Pipers Ash CW7 126 A1
PIPER'S ASH 119 D4
Piper's Cl CH60 40 D8
Pipers Ct CH2 119 B4
Piper's End CH60 40 D8
Pipers La
Chester CH2 119 B4
Puddington CH64 93 A8
Piper's La CH60 40 D8
Pipers The
Golborne WA3 3 F8
Heswall CH60 40 D8
Pipit Ave WA12 2 C3
Pipit La WA3 9 E3
Pippin Cl CW10 151 C7
Pippits Row WA7 49 E4
Pirie Cl CW12 157 A4
Pirie Rd CW12 157 A4
Pitcher La CW11 177 A8
Pit La
Hough CW2 206 E2
Talke ST7 210 C6
Widnes WA8 13 A4
Pitt La SK11 132 B8
Pitts Cl CH3 121 C2
Pitts Heath La WA7 24 E3
Pitt St
Macclesfield SK11 112 D6
Warrington WA5 15 F7
Widnes WA8 23 A5
Pitville Terr WA8 22 C7
Plaistow Ct WA7 49 E7
Plane Gr ST5 210 E1
Plane Tree Dr CW1 190 E6
Plane Tree Gr WA11 2 A7
Plane Tree Rd M31 11 D3
Plantagenet Cl 3
CW7 149 D6
Plantation Cl WA7 24 A1
Plantation Dr CH66 69 E7
Plant La CW11 174 B7
Plant St CW11 175 A7
Plas Dinas CH1 117 D3
Plas Newton La CH2 118 F5
Plas Newydd CH4 161 B6
Platt Ave CW11 175 A7
Platts La
Christleton CH3 143 D8
Duddon CH3, CW6 144 E7
Tarvin, Broom Bank
CH3 144 B8
Tarvin CH3 121 B2
Tattenhall CH3 183 F7
Platt's La CH3 164 E5
Platts St WA11 1 A6
Pleasance Way WA12 2 D4
Pleasant St
Macclesfield SK10 87 F1
Northwich CW8 103 E7
Pleasant View SK10 111 C8
Pleasant Way SK8 35 C6
Pleck Rd CH65 70 A2
PLEMSTALL 97 B1
Plemstall Cl CH2 119 F8
Plemstall La CH2 97 A1
Plemstall Way CH2 96 F1
Plemston Ct CH66 69 F8
Plex The ST7 193 D4
Plinston Ave WA4 16 F4
Plough Croft ST7 193 A3
Plough Inn Pk The
CW8 125 E5
Plough La CH3 143 B7
Ploughmans Cl CH66 94 E8
Ploughmans Way
Ellesmere Port CH66 94 E8
Macclesfield SK10 87 B3
Plover Ave CW7 149 D5
Plover Cl
Farndon CH3 180 F1
Macclesfield SK10 87 B4
Newton-le-W WA12 2 C3
Plover Dr WA7 50 D8
Plovers La WA6 73 C5
Plover Way WA3 3 E8
Plumbs Fold CW8 78 A2
PLUMLEY 80 F3
Plumley Cl
Chester CH3 119 C1
16 Macclesfield SK11 112 E7
Plumley Gdns WA8 12 A1
PLUMLEY MOOR 81 C2
Plumley Moor Rd
WA16 81 C2
Plumley Rd SK9 34 D5
Plumley Sta WA16 81 A3
Plumpstons La WA6 49 B1
Plumpton Cross 6
WA8 13 B2
Plum Terr CH1 237 A3
Plumtree Ave WA5 15 F8
Plymouth Cl WA7 50 E6
Plymouth Dr SK7 35 F7
Plymyard Ave CH62 43 D5
Plymyard Cl CH62 43 D5
Plymyard Ct CH62 43 C6
Poachers' La WA4 16 F3
Pochard Ave CW7 149 D6
Pochard Dr SK12 36 A4
Pochard Rise WA7 50 D8
Pochin Way CW10 128 E1
Pocket Nook La WA3 4 B7
Pocklington Ct WA2 8 F1
Points Ho CW1 190 A5
Polden Cl CH66 69 A6
Poleacre Dr WA8 12 D2
Pole La CW9 53 E2
Pole Lane Ends CW9 53 C4
Pollard Ave WA6 74 D7
Pollard Dr CW5 205 B4
Polperro Cl
Macclesfield SK10 86 D1
Warrington WA5 14 E3
Pond Cotts CH2 72 A3
Pond St WA3 4 A8
Pond View Cl CH60 41 C8
Pond Wlk WA9 1 A1
Pool Bank Bsns Pk
CH3 121 C3
Pool Bank Cotts CH3 121 C3
Poole Ave WA2 8 B2
Poole Cres WA2 8 B2
Poole Hall La CH66 69 E8
Poole Hall Rd CH66 69 F8
POOLEHILL 188 A2
Poole Hill Rd CW5 188 A2
Poole La CH2 71 E2
Pool End Cl SK10 87 D4
Pool End Rd SK10 87 D4
Poole Old Hall La
CW5 188 D4
Pooles La CW11 177 A6
POOLFOLD 179 F4
Poolford La CW4 129 E2
Pool Hall Ind Est CH65,
CH66 70 A8
Pool House Rd SK12 37 D5
Pool La
Cuddington CW8 102 B2
Haslington CW11 192 A7
Ince CH2 71 F4
Lymm WA13 18 B4
Malpas SY14 212 D1
Runcorn WA7 23 B3
Tarvin CH3 121 C4
Warrington WA4 16 A1
Pool Meadows Rd
CW1 191 B4
Pool Rd WA3 11 A3
Pool Side ST7 194 A8
Poolside Ct ST7 193 E4
Poolside Rd WA7 23 B1
Pools Platt La CW9 53 E6
Pool St
Macclesfield SK11 112 E6
Widnes WA8 23 B7
Pooltown Rd CH65 69 F5
Pool View CW11 191 F7
Poplar Ave
Culcheth WA3 4 F3
Moulton CW9 126 F8
Newton-le-W WA12 2 D3
Runcorn WA7 49 C7
Warrington WA5 14 E3
Wilmslow SK9 59 F5
Poplar Cl
Congleton CW12 156 A4
Cuddington CW8 102 A3
Ellesmere Port CH65 70 B4
Runcorn WA7 49 C7
Winsford CW7 149 B8
Poplar Ct CW5 205 A4
Poplar Dr
Alsager ST7 193 E2
Kidsgrove ST7 195 A1
Middlewich CW10 151 D7
Poplar Gr
Bollington SK10 88 A8
Crewe CW1 190 E5
Elton CH2 72 A3
Haydock WA11 1 C6
Irlam M44 11 D6
Poplar Hall La CH2 95 C6
Poplar La TF9 236 F5
Poplar Rd
Chester CH4 140 F5
Haydock WA11 1 C6
Macclesfield SK11 112 D6
Weaverham CW8 102 D8
Poplars Ave
Warrington, Hulme WA2 8 C3
Warrington, Winwick Quay
WA2 8 A4
Poplars Pl WA2 8 D2
Poplars The
Golborne, Wash End
WN7 4 C8
Lymm WA13 18 D4
Wistaston CW2 205 F7
Poplar View WA4 25 A7
Poplar Way SK6 38 A7
Poplar Weint 2 CH64 66 E8
Poplar Wlk M31 11 D3
Poppy Cl CW2 207 C5
Poppyfields ST7 193 B3
Porlock Cl
Heswall CH60 41 B6
Warrington WA5 14 E4
Port Arcades The
CH65 70 C5
Porter Ave WA12 2 C5
Porter Dr CW9 104 C6
Porters Croft CH3 119 F5
Porter St WA7 23 C2
Porter Way CW9 104 C6
Portford Cl SK10 86 F1
Porthcawl Cl WA8 12 C3
Porthleven Rd WA7 50 B5
Portland Dr
Biddulph ST8 179 D2
Scholar Green ST7 194 E6
Winsford CW7 149 B8
Portland Gr CW1 191 D5
Portland Pl WA6 73 C4
Portland Rd WA5 15 A8
Portland St
Newton-le-W WA12 1 F4
Runcorn WA7 22 F3
Portland Trad Pk WA2 16 A6
Portland Wlk 4 SK11 111 F7
Portloe Rd SK8 34 B7
Portman Pl 3 CW7 149 A8
Portmarnock Cl SK10 87 B3
Portola Cl WA4 17 C2
Portree Ave CH63 43 D5
Portree Dr CW4 130 B2
Portrush Cl
Macclesfield SK10 87 C4
Widnes WA8 12 E3
Portside WA7 50 E7
Portside Bsns Pk CH65 70 B8
Portsmouth Pl WA7 50 E6
Portway M22 33 E8
Postles Pl CW9 103 F6
Post Office La
Betley CW2 207 F1
Hampton Heath SY14 213 D7
Norley WA6 100 E5
Runcorn WA7 48 D7
Post Office Pl 1 CW9 79 A1
Potter Cl CW5 205 D4
Potters Barn The*
CW11 176 A1
Potters End ST8 179 C1
Potters La WA8 21 F5
Pott Hall SK10 63 D3
POTT SHRIGLEY 63 D3
Pott Shrigley Church Sch
SK10 63 C3
POULTON 163 B2
Poulton Cres WA1 17 D8
Poulton Dr WA8 22 D8
Poulton Hall Rd CH63 43 A7
Poulton Rd CH63 43 A8
Pound Rd CH66 69 C7
Povey Rd WA2 8 D1
Powell's Orch CH4 141 C7
Powell St WA4 16 F3
Powey La CH1 94 B5
Pownall Ave SK7 35 F7
Pownall Ct SK9 59 E8
POWNALL GREEN 35 E6
Pownall Green Prim Sch
SK7 35 E7
Pownall Hall Sch SK9 59 F8
POWNALL PARK 59 F7
Pownall Pl SK7 35 E7
Pownall Rd SK9 59 F8
Pownall Sq SK11 112 C8
Pownall St SK10 87 D1
Powy Dr ST7 195 B2
Powys Ct CH1 237 A3
Powys St WA5 15 F5
POYNTON 36 E4
Poynton Cl WA4 17 B3
Poynton High Sch
SK12 36 F2
Poynton Ind Est SK12 36 D1
Poynton St 15 SK10 112 C8
Poynton Sta SK12 36 C4
Pratchitts Row CW5 204 E5
Precinct The CW2 189 F2
Preece Cl WA8 12 D4
Preece Ct CW1 190 B5
Preesall Ave SK8 34 B8
Premier Pk CW7 127 B3
Prenton Pl CH4 141 E7
Prescot Rd WA8 12 D2
Prescot St CH2 118 F3
Prescott Rd SK9 34 B1
Prescott St WA4 16 E3
PRESTBURY 87 B7
Prestbury CE Prim Sch
SK10 86 F7
Prestbury Cl
8 Northwich CW9 103 F4
Widnes WA8 22 E8
Prestbury Ct SK10 86 F6
Prestbury Dr WA4 17 D4
Prestbury La SK10 87 B7
Prestbury Pk SK10 86 E6
Prestbury Rd
Adder's Moss SK10 85 F6
Macclesfield SK10 87 B1
Nether Alderley SK10 86 A5
Wilmslow SK9 60 E5
Prestbury Sta SK10 87 A7
Preston Ave M44 11 F7
PRESTON BROOK 50 F5
PRESTON ON THE HILL
51 A6
Preston St W SK11 112 D6
Prestwich Ave WA3 4 E3
Prestwick Cl
Macclesfield SK10 87 C5
Widnes WA8 12 F3
Winsford CW7 126 C2
Prestwood Ct WA3 10 A7
Pretoria St CH4 141 D7
Price Ave CW11 175 A5
Price Dr CW11 175 A5
Price Gr WA9 1 A2
Pride Cl WA12 2 E2
Priestfield Rd CH65 70 C5
Priest La SK10 61 B1
Priestley Bsns Ctr WA5 15 F5
Priestley Coll WA4 16 C3
Priestley Ct WA4 16 C2
Priestley St WA5 15 F5
Priestly Ct 13 CW5 204 E5
Priestner Dr WA6 73 B4
Priestway La CH64 67 E1
Priesty Ct CW12 156 D2
Priesty Fields CW12 156 D2
Primary Cl M44 11 D5
Primitive St ST7 195 C7
Primrose Ave
Haslington CW1 191 C5
Macclesfield SK11 112 B5
Primrose Chase CW4 130 D8
Primrose Cl
Huntington CH3 142 A6
Runcorn WA7 50 A8
Warrington WA2 8 D2
Widnes WA8 12 E1
Primrose Gr WA11 1 E7
PRIMROSE HILL 28 C6
Primrose Hill
Crewe CW2 189 E5
Cuddington CW8 101 F4
Kelsall CW6 122 E6
Primrose La WA6 73 B1
Primula Cl WA9 6 A7
Primula Dr WA3 3 D8
Prince Albert St CW1 190 D4
Prince Edward St
CW5 204 E6
Prince Henry Sq 3
WA1 16 B5
PRINCE HILL 231 F6
Prince Rd SK12 37 C5
Princes Ave
Bebington CH62 43 E6
Chester CH1 237 C3
Northwich CW9 104 B8
Princes Cl WA7 23 F1
Princes Ct CW5 204 E7
Princes Pk CW8 78 A2
Princes Pl WA8 12 E1
Princes Rd CH65 70 B6
Princess Ave
Audley ST7 209 D1
Haydock WA11 2 A7
Warrington, Bruche WA1 16 F6
Warrington, Great Sankey
WA5 14 E7
Warrington, Padgate
WA1 17 A8
Princess Cl CW2 205 F8
Princess Cres
Middlewich CW10 151 D6
Warrington WA1 16 F6
Princess Ct ST7 210 D5
Princess Dr
Bollington SK10 87 E7
Nantwich CW5 205 A6
Sandbach CW11 175 A7
Wistaston CW2 205 F8
Princess Gr CW2 205 F8
Princess Rd
Allostock WA16 106 E3
Lymm WA13 18 C3
Wilmslow SK9 59 F5
Princess St
Bollington SK10 87 F7
Chester CH1 237 A2
Congleton CW12 156 D3
Crewe CW1 190 C6
Knutsford WA16 57 A2
Northwich CW9 79 E2
13 Runcorn WA7 23 A3
Talke ST7 210 D5
2 Warrington WA5 15 D4
Winsford CW7 127 A2
Princes St WA12 2 B3
Prince's St WA8 23 A8
Princess Wlk SK7 36 A7
Princes Way SK11 111 E7
Princeway WA6 74 B8
Prince William Ave
CH5 116 B3
Prior Cl CW2 189 F1
Priory Ave CW9 103 F4
Priory Cl
Chester CH2 118 C4
Congleton CW12 179 B7
Crewe CW1 190 A8
Runcorn WA7 24 A1
Winsford CW7 126 C3
Priory Ct SK10 86 F1
Priory Dr SK10 86 E2
Priory La SK10 86 E2
Priory Pl
Chester CH1 237 B2
Kidsgrove ST7 195 B3
Priory Rd
Altrincham WA14 31 D8
Runcorn WA7 24 C2

Priory Rd *continued*
Wilmslow SK9 . . . . 59 E8
Priory St
Northwich CW9 . . . . 104 A8
Warrington WA4 . . . . 16 B3
Priory The
Neston LH64 . . . . 41 E1
Winwick WA2 . . . . 8 A7
Priory Way CW8 . . . . 103 B4
Pritchard Dr CW9 . . . . 103 E2
Private Wlk CH3 . . . . 142 A8
Probert Cl CW2 . . . . 190 A4
Proctors Cl WA8 . . . . 13 D2
Proctors La CW11 . . . . . . 174 C5
Proffitts La WA6 . . . . 73 E4
Promenade Cvn Pk
WA4 . . . . 25 B7
Promised Land La
CH3 . . . . 142 E5
Prospect Ave M44 . . . . . . 11 E6
Prospect Dr
Altrincham WA15 . . . . 32 D8
Davenham CW9 . . . . 103 E2
Prospect La WA3 . . . . 10 D3
Prospect Rd M44 . . . . 11 E6
Prospect Row WA7 . . . . . . 48 F7
Prospect St CW2 . . . . 156 C2
Prosperity Ct CW10 . . . . . 128 D1
Prosperity Way CW10 . . . 128 D1
Prosser Rd CH2 . . . . 95 C1
Protector Way M44 . . . . . . 11 F8
Provan Way CH1 . . . . 117 D5
Provident St WA9 . . . . 1 A3
Prunus Rd CW1 . . . . 190 E6
Pryors The CH3 . . . . 121 C3
Ptarmigan Pl CW7 . . . . . . 149 D5
Public Hall St [18] WA7 . . . 23 A3
Pudding La CW6 . . . . 168 A7
PUDDINGLAKE 129 A8
PUDDINGTON 92 F8
Puddington La CH64 . . . . . 92 E5
Puddle Bank La CW12 . . . 178 F5
Puffin Ave SK12 . . . . 36 B4
Puffin Cl CH65 . . . . 95 C8
PULFORD 162 D3
Pulford App
Aldford CH3 . . . . 163 D3
Pulford CH4 . . . . 162 E2
Pulford Cl
Northwich CW9 . . . . 103 E4
Runcorn WA7 . . . . 49 E6
Pulford Ct CH4 . . . . 162 D2
Pulford La CH4 . . . . 162 A6
Pulford Rd
Blacon CH1 . . . . 117 E5
Ellesmere Port CH65 . . . . . . 69 F4
Winsford CW7 . . . . 126 C1
Pullman Cl CH60 . . . . 41 D8
Pullman Dr CW9 . . . . 104 C8
Pump Ct ST7 . . . . 209 E2
Pumping Station Hos
CW6 . . . . 184 B3
Pump La
Churton CH3 . . . . 181 A5
Runcorn WA7 . . . . 49 F8
Tattenhall CH3 . . . . 182 C6
Pumptree Mews
SK11 . . . . 111 E7
Purdy Cl WA5 . . . . 7 D1
Puritan Bridge WA7 . . . . . 23 C2
Purley Dr M44 . . . . 11 C5
Purser La SY14 . . . . 211 E4
Puss Bank Sch SK10 . . . . 112 F8
Putney Ct WA7 . . . . 49 F7
Pye Cl WA11 . . . . 2 B8
Pyecroft Cl WA5 . . . . 14 E4
Pyecroft Rd WA5 . . . . 14 D6
Pyecroft St CH4 . . . . 141 D7
Pye Rd CH60 . . . . 41 A8
Pym's La CW1 . . . . 189 E6
Pyrus Ave CW1 . . . . 190 E6
Pyrus Gr WA6 . . . . 73 C4
Pytcheley Hollow
WA6 . . . . 100 F6

Q

Quadrant Cl WA7 . . . . 50 D6
Quadrant The CH1 . . . . . . 117 E2
Quadrant The WA3 . . . . 9 F5
Quad The CH1 . . . . 117 E2
Quail Cl WA2 . . . . 8 D3
Quaintways CW8 . . . . 103 C4
Quakers Coppice
CW1 . . . . 191 A2
Quakers Way LL13 . . . . . . 180 E1
Quantock Cl
Ellesmere Port CH66 . . . . . . 69 A6
Winsford CW7 . . . . 149 A7
Quarry Ave CH3 . . . . 180 F1
QUARRYBANK 146 C8
Quarrybank CW6 . . . . 184 F6
Quarry Bank CW6 . . . . . . 146 C8
Quarry Bank Cotts
CW6 . . . . 184 F6
Quarry Bank Mill *
SK9 . . . . 33 F2
Quarry Bank Rd SK9 . . . . . 33 F3
Quarry Bank Rise
CW7 . . . . 149 B8
Quarry Cl
Chester CH4 . . . . 141 C7
Runcorn WA7 . . . . 23 D1

Quarry Ct
Farndon CH3 . . . . 180 F1
Widnes WA8 . . . . 12 C1
Quarry Hill CH3 . . . . 180 F1
Quarry La
Christleton CH3 . . . . 142 C1
Kelsall CW6 . . . . 122 D5
Warrington WA4 . . . . 26 C6
Quarry Rd
Neston LH64 . . . . 42 C1
New Mills SK22 . . . . 39 D7
Quarry Terr ST7 . . . . 195 A1
Quarter The CH1 . . . . 237 B3
Quay Fold WA5 . . . . 15 F4
Quayle Cl WA11 . . . . 1 C6
Quay Pl WA7 . . . . 50 E7
Quayside
Congleton CW12 . . . . 156 E1
Neston CH64 . . . . 66 E5
Quay Side WA6 . . . . 49 D1
Quayside Mews WA13 . . . . 18 F3
Quayside Way SK11 . . . . . 112 E7
Quay The WA6 . . . . 49 D2
Queastybirch La
Hatton WA4 . . . . 25 F1
Hatton WA4 . . . . 26 A1
Quebec Rd WA2 . . . . 16 D7
Queen Anne St WA6 . . . . . 60 C6
Queen Annes Ct [5]
SK11 . . . . 112 B6
Queen Elizabeth Ho
CW9 . . . . 79 A2
Queens Ave
Ellesmere Port CH65 . . . . . . 70 A3
Warrington WA1 . . . . 16 E7
Queen's Ave CH4 . . . . 237 C3
Queen's Ave CH5 . . . . 91 D1
Queen's Ave
Glazebury WA3 . . . . 5 C7
Macclesfield SK10 . . . . 87 E2
Sandycroft CH5 . . . . 116 A3
Widnes WA8 . . . . 22 B8
Queensbury Cl
[15] Handforth SK9 . . . . . . 34 D1
Wilmslow SK9 . . . . 60 D8
Queensbury Way WA8 . . . . 12 E3
Queens Cl SK10 . . . . 87 E6
Queen's Cl
Macclesfield SK10 . . . . 87 E2
Runcorn WA7 . . . . 22 F1
Queens Cres
Chester CH2 . . . . 118 E7
Warrington WA1 . . . . 17 A8
Queen's Cres CW12 . . . . . 172 E2
Queens Ct
Chester CH4 . . . . 237 C1
Winsford CW7 . . . . 126 D1
Queen's Ct CW10 . . . . 128 D1
Queens Dr
Golborne WA3 . . . . 3 C8
Helsby WA6 . . . . 73 B3
Heswall CH60 . . . . 40 E8
Newton-le-W WA12 . . . . 2 C5
Warrington WA4 . . . . 17 A2
Queen's Dr
Chester CH4 . . . . 237 C1
Middlewich CW10 . . . . 151 D7
Nantwich CW5 . . . . 204 D4
Sandbach CW11 . . . . 175 A8
Queensford LL13 . . . . 222 A8
Queensgate
Bramhall SK7 . . . . 35 E5
Northwich CW8 . . . . 103 E8
Queensgate Prim Sch
SK7 . . . . 35 E4
Queens Gdns
Ellesmere Port CH65 . . . . . . 70 B5
Talke ST7 . . . . 210 D5
Queen's Par [4] CW1 . . . . 126 D1
QUEEN'S PARK 141 F8
Queen's Park Dr CW1 . . . . 189 F3
Queen's Park Gdns
CW2 . . . . 189 F4
Queens Park High Sch
CH4 . . . . 237 B1
Queen's Park Ho CH4 . . . 237 B1
Queen's Park Rd CH4 . . . 237 B1
Queen's Park View
CH4 . . . . 237 B1
Queens Pk CH60 . . . . 40 D8
Queen's Pl CH1 . . . . 237 B3
Queens Rd
Chester CH3 . . . . 119 B3
Ellesmere Port CH66 . . . . . . 69 C7
Haydock WA11 . . . . 2 A7
Queen's Rd
Chester CH1 . . . . 237 C3
Runcorn WA7 . . . . 22 F1
Wilmslow SK9 . . . . 60 A6
Queen's Sch (Lower) The
CH2 . . . . 118 C4
Queen's Sch The CH1 . . . 237 A2
Queen St
Audley ST7 . . . . 209 C1
Bollington SK10 . . . . 88 B8
Bunbury CW6 . . . . 185 E8
Chester CH1 . . . . 237 B2
Congleton, Buglawton
CW12 . . . . 156 F4
Congleton CW12 . . . . 156 C2
Crewe CW1 . . . . 190 E5
Ellesmere Port CH65 . . . . . . 70 C7
Golborne WA3 . . . . 3 A8
Kidsgrove ST7 . . . . 195 A2
Knutsford WA16 . . . . 57 F2
Macclesfield SK10 . . . . . . 112 D8
Middlewich CW10 . . . . 128 C1
Nantwich CW5 . . . . 204 E5

Queen St *continued*
Newton-le-W WA12 . . . . 2 B3
Northwich CW9 . . . . 103 F7
[8] Runcorn WA7 . . . . 23 A3
Shavington CW2 . . . . 206 C4
Queens Terr CW9 . . . . 79 D3
Queensway
Alsager ST7 . . . . 193 B5
Chester CH2 . . . . 118 F5
Crewe CW1 . . . . 190 C4
Frodsham WA6 . . . . 74 B8
Gatley SK8 . . . . 34 C8
Heswall CH60 . . . . 41 C6
Knutsford WA16 . . . . 56 E3
Partington M31 . . . . 11 F4
Poynton SK12 . . . . 36 D3
Runcorn WA7 . . . . 22 F3
Widnes WA8 . . . . 22 F6
Winsford CW7 . . . . 149 D8
Queen's Way CH4 . . . . 139 B4
Queensway Trad Est
WA8 . . . . 23 A5
Queen Victoria St [14]
SK11 . . . . 112 D8
Quill Ct M44 . . . . 11 E6
Quillet The CH64 . . . . 66 F7
Quinn St WA8 . . . . 23 B7
Quinta Prim Sch The
CW12 . . . . 156 A2
Quinta Rd CW12 . . . . 156 A3
QUOISLEY 226 B8

R

RABY 42 C4
Raby Ave CH63 . . . . 43 B6
Raby Cl
Bebington CH63 . . . . 43 A7
Heswall CH60 . . . . 40 F7
Widnes WA8 . . . . 13 E2
Raby Ct CH65 . . . . 70 D3
Raby Gdns CH64 . . . . 66 E8
Raby Hall Rd CH63 . . . . . . 43 A6
RABY MERE 43 B7
Raby Mere Rd CH63 . . . . . 42 D5
Raby Park Cl CH64 . . . . . . 66 E8
Raby Park Rd CH64 . . . . . . 41 F1
Raby Rd
Neston CH64 . . . . 66 E8
Thornton Hough CH63 . . . . . 42 B5
Racecourse La CW6 . . . . . 124 A1
Racecourse Pk SK9 . . . . . . 59 F6
Racecourse Rd SK9 . . . . . . 59 E6
Racefield Cl WA13 . . . . 18 F3
Racefield Rd WA16 . . . . . . 56 F2
Race The SK9 . . . . 34 D2
Radbroke Cl CW11 . . . . . . 175 D8
Radcliffe Ave WA3 . . . . 4 E3
Radcliffe Cl CH3 . . . . 121 C3
Radcliffe Rd
Sandbach CW11 . . . . 174 F3
Sutton Lane Ends SK11 . . . 135 D7
Winsford CW7 . . . . 149 B6
Raddel La WA4 . . . . 52 C5
Raddle Wharf CH65 . . . . . . 70 C7
Raddon Pl WA4 . . . . 16 E3
Radford Cl WA8 . . . . 12 D3
Radlett Cl WA5 . . . . 14 E3
Radley Dr CH63 . . . . 41 F6
Radley La WA2 . . . . 8 E4
RADMORE GREEN 186 E3
RADNOR 155 E6
Radnor Cl
Congleton CW12 . . . . 156 B3
Sandbach CW11 . . . . 174 E7
Radnor Dr
Chester CH4 . . . . 141 A4
Widnes WA8 . . . . 12 D2
Radnor Park Ind Ctr
CW12 . . . . 156 A4
Radnor Park Trad Est
CW12 . . . . 156 A4
Radnor St WA5 . . . . 15 E6
RADWAY GREEN 192 F1
Radway Green Bsns &
Tech Ctr CW2 . . . . 192 F1
Radway Green Rd
Alsager CW2 . . . . 208 E8
Barthomley CW2 . . . . 208 D6
Raeburn Ave
Bebington CH62 . . . . 43 E6
Neston CH64 . . . . 66 F7
Raeburn Prim Sch
CH62 . . . . 43 D6
Raglan Ct WA3 . . . . 9 F6
Raglan Rd SK10 . . . . 87 F2
Ragley Cl SK12 . . . . 36 F4
Railbrook Ct CW2 . . . . 190 D2
Railton Ave CW1 . . . . 190 A2
Railway Age Mus The *
CW1 . . . . 190 D3
Railway Cotts
Congleton CW12 . . . . 157 A1
Hollinfare WA3 . . . . 11 B5
Hooton CH66 . . . . 43 E1
Wimboldsley CW10 . . . . . . 150 F5
Railway St
Crewe CW2 . . . . 190 D2
Newton-le-W WA12 . . . . 2 B3
Railway Terr
Disley SK12 . . . . 38 D6
Sandycroft CH5 . . . . 116 B3
Railway View WA5 . . . . 1 D1
Rainbow Cl WA8 . . . . 12 C3
Rainbow St CW1 . . . . 190 D4

Rainford Cl ST7 . . . . 195 F1
RAINOW 88 D5
Rainow Cl CW10 . . . . 151 B7
Rainow Dr SK12 . . . . 37 A2
Rainow Prim Sch SK10 . . . 88 D4
Rainow Rd CH10 . . . . 88 A8
Rainow View SK10 . . . . . . 63 C1
Rainow Way [6] SK9 . . . . . 34 E1
Rajar Cotts WA16 . . . . 57 F4
Rajar Wlk WA16 . . . . 58 A4
Rake House Mews
WA6 . . . . 73 B4
Rake La
Backford CH2 . . . . 95 D6
Broughton CH5 . . . . 139 A8
Christleton CH3 . . . . 143 A7
Dunham-on-t-H WA6 . . . . . . 97 B7
Dunham-on-t-H WA6 . . . . . . 97 E7
Eccleston CH4 . . . . 141 C1
Helsby, Helsby Marsh
WA6 . . . . 73 A5
Helsby WA6 . . . . 73 C4
Rake The
Bebington CH62 . . . . 43 C8
Heswall CH60 . . . . 67 D1
Rake Way CH1 . . . . 94 A1
Raleigh Cl WA5 . . . . 7 D1
Raleigh Rd CH64 . . . . 41 F1
Rampit Cl WA11 . . . . 1 F7
Ramp Rd E M90 . . . . 33 C2
Ramp Rd S M90 . . . . 33 C2
Ramp Rd W M90 . . . . 33 B7
Ramsay Cl WA3 . . . . 9 E3
Ramsbottom St [2]
CW1 . . . . 190 B5
Ramsbrook La L24, ...
WA8 . . . . 21 C3
Ramsdale Rd SK7 . . . . 35 E8
Ramsden Ct CH4 . . . . 140 F4
Ramsey Cl WA8 . . . . 13 E3
Ramsey Rd CH65 . . . . 72 C1
Ramsfield Rd L24 . . . . 21 A4
Randal Cres SK23 . . . . 65 E5
Randall Cl WA12 . . . . 2 B4
Randle Bennett Cl
CW11 . . . . 174 E7
Randle Mdw CH66 . . . . 69 F1
Randle Meadow Ct
CH66 . . . . 69 F2
Randle's View CW12 . . . . . 179 C8
Range Ct SK10 . . . . 87 E1
Rangemoor Cl WA3 . . . . . . 10 A6
Rannoch Cl CH66 . . . . 69 F3
Ranulph Ct WA6 . . . . 74 C7
Ranwonath Ct CH2 . . . . . . 237 B4
Ranworth Dr WA3 . . . . 3 E2
Ranworth Rd WA5 . . . . 14 E6
Rappax Rd WA15 . . . . 32 B8
Raquets Ct The CW10 . . . 127 D5
Rathbone Pk CW6 . . . . 146 D2
Rathlin Cl WA8 . . . . 13 E3
Rathmell Cl WA3 . . . . 9 F3
Rathvale Dr M22 . . . . 33 C8
Ravenbank Com Prim Sch
WA13 . . . . 18 F3
Raven Cl CW11 . . . . 175 A8
Raven Cotts YP6 . . . . 235 A5
Ravendale Cl CW7 . . . . . . 149 E8
Ravenfield Dr WA8 . . . . . . 12 C3
Ravenho La SK10 . . . . 88 D4
Ravenhurst St WA3 . . . . 9 F2
Ravenoak Park Rd SK8 . . . 35 B8
Ravenoak Rd SK8 . . . . 35 B8
Ravenscar Cres M22 . . . . . 33 D8
Ravens Cl ST7 . . . . 209 E3
Ravenscliffe Rd ST7 . . . . . 195 A1
RAVENSCLOUGH 101 E3
Ravens Cnr CW5 . . . . 203 E2
Ravenscroft CW4 . . . . 130 A3
Ravenscroft Cl CW11 . . . . 175 C7
Ravenscroft Rd CW2 . . . . . 189 E3
Ravensdale Cl WA2 . . . . 8 D3
Ravensfield CW8 . . . . 101 D4
Ravensholme Cl CH3 . . . . 166 A2
Ravensholme La CH3 . . . . 166 A2
Ravenslea Cl CW5 . . . . . . 203 E5
Raven's La CW7 . . . . 209 F3
Ravensmead Com Prim
Sch ST7 . . . . 209 E3
RAVENSMOOR 203 E2
Ravenswood CW8 . . . . 103 B4
Ravenswood Dr SK8 . . . . . 35 B8
Ravenswood Rd SK9 . . . . . 59 E4
Rawcliffe Dr WA15 . . . . 32 D7
Rawcliffe Cl WA8 . . . . 12 F4
Rawdon Cl WA7 . . . . 50 A7
Rawlings Cl WA3 . . . . 9 F3
Rawlinson Cres L26 . . . . . . 21 B8
Rawson Rd CH1 . . . . 117 E3
Ray Ave CW5 . . . . 204 F7
Raycliffe Cl WA7 . . . . 49 D5
Rayleigh Ave CW7 . . . . . . 127 A8
Rayleigh Way SK10 . . . . . . 86 C1
Raymond Ave WA4 . . . . . . 16 D2
Raymond St CH1 . . . . 237 A3
Raymond Way CH64 . . . . . 67 A7
Rays Brow CW8 . . . . 78 B2
Readesdale Ave CW2 . . . . 189 F2
Reade's La CW12 . . . . 157 C6
Reading Room La SY14, . . .
CW5 . . . . 199 D8
Rean Mdw CW5 . . . . 166 D6
Reaper Cl WA5 . . . . 15 D6
REASE HEATH 188 D1
Reaseheath Coll CW5 . . . . 188 D1
Reay St WA8 . . . . 13 C1
Rectory Ave WA3 . . . . 3 C8

Rectory Cl
Farndon CH3 . . . . 180 E1
Heswall CH60 . . . . 40 F7
[8] Nantwich CW5 . . . . . . 204 E5
Winwick WA2 . . . . 8 A6
Wistaston CH2 . . . . 105 D3
Rectory Gdns
Lymm WA13 . . . . 18 E3
Talke ST7 . . . . 210 D6
Rectory La
Adderley TF9 . . . . 235 B5
Capenhurst CH1 . . . . 94 A8
Heswall CH60 . . . . 40 E7
Lymm WA13 . . . . 18 E3
Warrington WA2 . . . . 8 A6
Rectory View ST7 . . . . 210 D6
Redacre SK12 . . . . 36 F6
Redacre Cl WA4 . . . . 51 A3
Red Bank Ave WA12 . . . . . . 2 F1
Redbourne Dr
Chorlton CW2 . . . . 207 D3
Widnes WA8 . . . . 12 B4
Redbrook Cl CH62 . . . . 43 D6
Redbrook Gr [2] SK9 . . . . . 34 D1
Redbrook Rd M31 . . . . 11 E2
Redbrook Way SK10 . . . . . 62 C5
Red Brow La WA7, WA4. . . 50 F8
RED BULL 194 E3
Redcar Dr CH62 . . . . 43 D5
Red Cow Yd [11] WA16 . . . 57 A2
Reddish Ave SK23 . . . . 65 D6
Reddish Cres WA13 . . . . . . 18 F4
Reddish La
Horwich End SK23 . . . . 65 D6
Lymm WA13 . . . . 18 F4
Reddish Rd SK23 . . . . 65 D6
Reddy La WA14 . . . . 30 B8
Redesdale Cl WA2 . . . . 8 E2
Redesmere Cl
Macclesfield SK10 . . . . 87 A1
Northwich CW9 . . . . 104 A5
Sandbach CW11 . . . . 174 F7
Redesmere Dr SK9 . . . . . . 60 A1
Redesmere La SK11 . . . . . 110 B3
Redesmere Rd SK9 . . . . . . 34 D5
Redfern Ave CW12 . . . . . . 156 F4
Red Gables WA4 . . . . 27 B3
Redgate CW8 . . . . 103 D7
Redhill Mews CH65 . . . . . . 70 B6
Redhill Rd
Chester CH4 . . . . 140 F6
Kelsall CW6 . . . . 122 C5
Red Ho SK10 . . . . 87 E1
Redhouse La SK12 . . . . . . 38 E7
Red House La WA14 . . . . . . 20 C8
Redhouses SK11 . . . . 113 D3
Red La
Disley SK12 . . . . 38 C5
Frodsham WA6 . . . . 74 C7
Huxley CH3 . . . . 166 D6
Lower Whitley WA4 . . . . 52 C1
Sandbach CW11 . . . . 174 A2
Warrington WA4 . . . . 26 C7
Redland Cl CH4 . . . . 141 A7
Redland Ho CH4 . . . . 141 B7
Red Lion Cl
Ellesmere Port CH66 . . . . . . 69 C7
Nantwich CW5 . . . . 204 D5
Red Lo SK12 . . . . 38 A6
Redmain Gr WA3 . . . . 3 E8
Redmayne Cl WA12 . . . . 2 B4
Redmere Dr CH60 . . . . 41 D8
Redmoor La
Disley SK12 . . . . 39 A4
New Mills SK22 . . . . 39 A4
Red Pike CH66 . . . . 69 D8
Redpoll La WA3 . . . . 9 E4
Redrock Cres ST7 . . . . 195 C1
Red Row SK7 . . . . 37 B8
Redruth Ave SK10 . . . . 86 E1
Redruth Cl WA7 . . . . 50 B6
Redshank Ave CW7 . . . . . . 149 C5
Redshank Cl WA12 . . . . 2 C4
Redshank Dr SK10 . . . . 87 C5
Redshank La WA3 . . . . 9 F4
Redshaw Cl CW10 . . . . . . 151 C6
Redstart Cl [7] WA3 . . . . . . 3 E8
Redstone Dr [3] CW7 . . . . 126 A1
Red Stone Hill WA6 . . . . . . 73 C4
RED STREET 210 D3
Redtail Cl WA7 . . . . 22 F3
Redvales Ct WA3 . . . . 9 C4
Redvers Ave CH66 . . . . 44 A2
Redway La SK10 . . . . 88 B7
Redwing Cl ST7 . . . . 195 F1
Redwood Cl
Barnton CW8 . . . . 78 B4
Holt LL13 . . . . 196 D8
Saltney CH4 . . . . 140 E6
Warrington WA1 . . . . 17 E7
Redwood Cl SK10 . . . . 87 E5
Redwood Dr
Crewe CW1 . . . . 189 F7
Ellesmere Port CH66 . . . . . . 69 F1
Elton CH2 . . . . 72 C4
Reece Cl CW2 . . . . 119 E8
Reedgate La CW9 . . . . 27 F1
Reed La CW9 . . . . 78 E4
Reedsmere Cl WA4 . . . . . . 16 E2
Reedsmere Wlk CW9 . . . . . 78 D8
Reeman St CW4 . . . . 34 B2
Rees Cres CW4 . . . . 130 C3
Reeves Rd CH3 . . . . 142 B8
Reeve St WA3 . . . . 4 B8
Regal Cl
Ellesmere Port CH66 . . . . . . 69 E3
Northwich CW9 . . . . 103 E4

Regal Cres WA8 . . . . 22 B8
Regency Cl ST7 . . . . 210 D5
Regency Ct
  Chester CH2 . . . . .119 E8
  Winsford CW7 . . . . 149 C7
Regency Gdns Sk8 . . . . 34 E8
Regency Hospl SK11 . . . . . .112 B8
Regency Pk SK9 . . . . 59 F5
Regency Sq WA5 . . . . .15 F6
Regency Way CW9 . . . . 103 E4
Regency Wlk CW10 . . . . . . 128 D1
Regent Ave
  Haydock WA11 . . . . .1 B7
  Macclesfield SK11 . . . . . . .112 B6
  Warrington WA1 . . . . .17 A8
Regent Bank SK9 . . . . 59 F5
Regent Cl
  Bramhall SK7 . . . . .35 D4
  Shavington CW2 . . . . 206 B3
  Wilmslow SK9 . . . . 59 F5
Regent Ct WA15 . . . . 32 C8
Regent & Foundry Ct **19**
Regent St
  Ellesmere Port CH65 . . . . . .70 A5
  Moulton CW9 . . . . .126 F8
  Newton-le-W WA12 . . . . 2 A3
  12 Runcorn WA7 . . . . .23 A3
Regents The Sk9 . . . . 60 C8
Regents Theological Coll
  CW5 . . . . 205 A5
Regents Way **4** CW7 . . 149 A8
Reginald Mitchell Prim
  Sch The ST7 . . . . 194 D1
Registry Cl CW9 . . . . 103 E4
Reid Ave WA5 . . . . .15 F8
Reid Ct CW6 . . . . .147 C4
Reid St CW11 . . . . .190 C6
Reins Croft CH64 . . . . 41 E1
Rembury Pl WA4 . . . . .51 A3
Remer St CW1 . . . . 190 D7
Renaissance Way
  CW1 . . . . 191 A3
Rendel Cl WA12 . . . . 2 D2
Rendlesham Cl WA3 . . . . . . 10 B6
Renfrew Ave CH62 . . . . 43 E5
Renfrew Cl SK10 . . . . .86 F2
Renown Cl WA3 . . . . 9 D4
Renshaw St CW9 . . . . 79 D2
Rensherds Pl WA16 . . . . . . 29 C5
Renton Ave WA7 . . . . .23 D2
Repton Cl WA16 . . . . .29 C4
Repton Dr CW1 . . . . 191 D5
Repton Rd CH65 . . . . .70 D2
Reservoir Rd SK23 . . . . 65 D7
Reservoir Terr CH2 . . . . . . .118 F2
Retreat The CW1 . . . . 190 C6
Revesby Cl WA8 . . . . .12 D2
Rex Bldgs Sk9 . . . . 60 B6
Reynolds Ave
  St Helens WA9 . . . . 1 B2
  Warrington WA3 . . . . 9 E5
Reynold's La CW11 . . . . . .175 F6
Reynolds Mews Sk9 . . . . . . 60 E8
Reynolds St WA4 . . . . 16 F3
Rhoden St CW1 . . . . 191 A6
Rhodes Cl CW1 . . . . 191 D4
Rhodes St WA2 . . . . 16 C7
Rhodesway CH60 . . . . 41 B7
Rhona Cl CH63 . . . . 43 C4
Rhona Dr WA5 . . . . .14 C6
Rhone Ct CH3 . . . . .142 A8
RHUDDALL HEATH 146 E1
Rhuddlan Cl CH65 . . . . .70 D2
Rhuddlan Ct/Llys
  Rhuddlan **5** CH4 . . . . .140 F6
Rhuddlan Rd CH1 . . . . . . .117 D3
Rhum Cl CH65 . . . . .70 C1
Rhyl St WA8 . . . . .22 F7
Ribble Ave CW7 . . . . 127 B1
Ribble Cl
  Culcheth WA3 . . . . 4 F2
  Widnes WA8 . . . . .13 F3
Ribble Dr ST8 . . . . .179 E1
Ribble Pl CW7 . . . . .127 B1
Ribblesdale CH65 . . . . .70 B3
Ribblesdale Ave
  CW12 . . . . .157 A5
Ribblesdale Cl CH62 . . . . . .43 F5
Ribchester Gdns WA3 . . . . . 5 A3
Richard Cl WA24 . . . . 24 A2
Richard Moon St
  CW1 . . . . 190 B4
Richard Reynolds Ct
  M44 . . . . .11 E6
Richards Croft CH3 . . . . . . 142 A7
Richards Gr CW12 . . . . . . .156 A3
Richardson Cl
  4 Sandbach CW11 . . . .174 D6
  Shavington CW2 . . . . 206 D5
Richardson St WA2 . . . . . . .16 C8
Richard St
  Crewe CW1 . . . . .190 B5
  Northwich CW9 . . . . 104 C7
Richbell Cl WA4 . . . . .17 C1
Richmond Ave
  Grappenhall WA4 . . . . .17 C3
  Handforth SK9 . . . . .34 D4
  Haydock WA11 . . . . 1 B7
  Warrington WA4 . . . . .17 A4
Richmond Cl
  Chorlton CW2 . . . . 207 D1
  Culcheth WA3 . . . . 4 D4

Richmond Cl continued
  Lymm WA13 . . . . .19 B4
  Sandbach CW11 . . . . .174 E7
Richmond Cres CH3 . . . . . 119 C2
Richmond Ct
  Chester CH3 . . . . .118 F2
  Ellesmere Port CH65 . . . . . .70 D3
  Warrington WA4 . . . . .17 A3
  Widnes WA8 . . . . .13 D4
Richmond Dr
  Lymm WA13 . . . . .19 B4
  Northwich CW9 . . . . 104 A4
Richmond Gdns WA12 . . . . . 2 C2
Richmond Gr SK7 . . . . .35 F6
Richmond Hill
  1 Knutsford WA16 . . . . . . .57 B1
  Macclesfield SK11 . . . . . . .112 E6
Richmond Mews CH2 . . . . .118 F2
Richmond Pl SK11 . . . . . . .112 E6
Richmond Rd CW1 . . . . . . .190 E5
Richmond St
  Warrington WA4 . . . . .17 A3
  Widnes WA8 . . . . .13 C1
Richmond Village
  CW5 . . . . 205 A5
Rickaby Cl CH3 . . . . .43 C8
Ridding La WA7 . . . . 50 B5
Riddings Ct CW8 . . . . .103 B4
Riddings La
  Hartford CW8 . . . . .103 B4
  Wybunbury CW5 . . . . 220 A8
Riddings The CH65 . . . . 70 B4
Rides The WA11 . . . . 1 D6
Ridge Ave WA15 . . . . .32 D6
Ridgeborne Cl WA5 . . . . 7 D2
Ridge Hill
  Langley SK11 . . . . .113 B2
  Utkinton CW6 . . . . .146 B5
Ridge Pk SK7 . . . . .35 D6
Ridge The CW8 . . . . 123 D7
Ridge View SK11 . . . . .112 C5
Ridgeway
  Golborne WA3 . . . . .3 E7
  Wilmslow SK9 . . . . 60 F7
Ridgeway Cl CH66 . . . . .69 C2
Ridgeway Ho CH3 . . . . 121 C3
Ridgeway The
  Alvanley WA6. . . . . .74 C1
  Cronton WA8 . . . . .12 C6
  Disley SK12 . . . . .38 C6
  Heswall CH60 . . . . .41 B7
  Runcorn WA7 . . . . .50 D6
  Tarvin CH3 . . . . .121 C3
Ridgewell Ave **4** WA3 . . . . 3 D8
Ridgmont Rd SK7 . . . . .35 E5
RIDGWARDINE 235 E1
Ridgway Gdns WA13 . . . . . .18 D3
Ridgway St
  Crewe CW1 . . . . .190 D5
  Warrington WA2 . . . . .16 D8
Ridings Com Inf Sch The
  CH1 . . . . .94 A1
Ridings The
  Saughall CH1 . . . . .117 B8
  Wilmslow SK9 . . . . 59 D4
Ridley Cl CW2 . . . . 206 E2
Ridley Dr WA5 . . . . 15 C4
Ridley Gn CW6 . . . . 185 D1
Ridley Hill Farm CW6 . . . . 185 C3
Ridley Rd SK10 . . . . .87 E8
Ridley Wood Rd LL13 . . . . 196 C3
Ridsdale **2** WA8 . . . . .22 C8
Rigby Ave CW1 . . . . .190 A7
Rigby Rd ST7 . . . . 195 B3
Rigby's Row CW5 . . . . 204 E5
Rigby St WA3 . . . . 3 A8
Rigg St **5** CW2 . . . . 190 B5
Riley Bank Mews WA6 . . . . .74 B1
Riley Cl CW11 . . . . .174 E5
Riley Dr WA7 . . . . .49 A8
Rileys Way ST7 . . . . 209 F2
Rilshaw La CW7 . . . . 150 B8
Rimington Cl WA3 . . . . 4 E3
Rimsdale Cl CW2 . . . . .206 A7
Ring-o-Bells La SK12 . . . . . .38 D6
Ring Rd
  Chester CH2, CH3 . . . . . . 119 C3
  Connah's Quay CH5 . . . . . . .91 E2
Ringsfield Rd LL24 . . . . .21 A2
Ringstead Cl SK9 . . . . 34 D1
Ringstead Dr SK9 . . . . 34 D1
Ringstone Way SK23 . . . . . .65 D8
Ringway
  Ellesmere Port CH66 . . . . . .69 E4
  Neston CH64 . . . . .41 E1
  Waverton CH3 . . . . 143 B5
Ringway Cl SK10 . . . . .87 B4
Ringway Prim Sch
  M22 . . . . .33 D8
Ringway Rd
  Runcorn WA7 . . . . .50 E6
  Wythenshawe M22, M90 . . .33 D7
Ringway Rd W M22,
  M90 . . . . .33 D8
Ringway Trad Est M22 . . . . 33 E8
Ringwood Cl WA3 . . . . .10 B5
Ripley Ave SK8 . . . . .35 B5
Ripley Cl SK7 . . . . .36 E8
Ripley Rd WA3 . . . . .4 D1
Ripon Ave
  Ellesmere Port CH66 . . . . . .69 C5
  Golborne WA3 . . . . .3 D8
Ripon Cl
  Macclesfield SK10 . . . . 87 C3
  Newton le W WA12 . . . . 2 C5
Ripon Dr CW2 . . . . 206 A7

Ripon Row WA7 . . . . .49 D6
Riseley St SK10 . . . . .112 C8
Rise The SK23 . . . . .65 C6
Rising Sun Cl SK11 . . . . . . 112 A5
Rising Sun Rd SK11 . . . . . .112 A4
RISLEY 9 E6
Risley Moss Local Nature
  Reserve Visitor Ctr*
  WA3 . . . . .10 B5
Risley Rd WA3 . . . . 9 F6
Rivacre Brow CH66 . . . . . . .69 E8
Rivacre Bsns Ctr CH66 . . . .69 E5
Rivacre Rd CH62, CH65,
  CH66 . . . . .44 C2
Rivacre Valley Ctry Pk*
  CH66 . . . . .69 D8
Rivacre Valley Prim Sch
  CH66 . . . . .69 D8
Riverbank Cl
  Bollington SK10 . . . . .87 F8
  Heswall CH60 . . . . .40 F6
  Nantwich CW5 . . . . 204 E8
Riverbank Rd CH60 . . . . . . .40 E6
Riverdane Rd CW12 . . . . . .156 F4
River La
  Chester CH4 . . . . 141 C7
  Farndon CH3 . . . . .180 E2
  Partington M31 . . . . 11 F4
  Saltney CH4 . . . . .140 E7
Rivermead Ave WA15 . . . . . 32 C7
River Rd
  Connah's Quay CH5 . . . . . . .91 F1
  Warrington, Latchford
  WA4 . . . . .16 B3
  Warrington, Wilderspool
  WA4 . . . . .16 C2
Riversdale
  Frodsham WA6 . . . . .49 C1
  Warrington WA1 . . . . .17 F7
Riversdale Rd WA7 . . . . 49 E8
Rivershill Gdns WA15 . . . . . 32 D6
Riverside
  Nantwich CW5 . . . . 204 D5
  Northwich CW9 . . . . 104 B5
Riverside Bsns Pk 60 B7
Riverside Cl WA1 . . . . .16 D4
Riverside Coll Halton
  (Kingsway Campus)
  WA8 . . . . .23 A8
Riverside Coll Halton
  Runcorn Campus
  WA7 . . . . .22 E3
Riverside Cres CW4 . . . . . .130 C4
Riverside Ct
  Huntington CH3 . . . . 141 F7
  Langley SK11 . . . . .113 C4
Riverside Dr SK10 . . . . .87 A5
Riverside Gr CW2 . . . . 189 D3
Riverside Pk CW9 . . . . 103 E6
Riverside Ret Pk WA1 . . . . .16 C4
Riverside Trad Est
  Northwich CW8 . . . . .103 F7
  Warrington WA5 . . . . .14 D1
Riverside Trad Pk
  CH4 . . . . 140 E7
Riverside Wlk CH66 . . . . . . .66 D5
Riversmead CH3 . . . . .142 A6
River St
  Congleton CW12 . . . . 156 D3
  Macclesfield SK11 . . . . . . .112 E6
  Wilmslow SK9 . . . . 60 B8
River View CW7 . . . . .126 E1
Riverview Rd CH64 . . . . 66 F5
River Wlk **8** WA7 . . . . .49 F7
Rivington Cl WA11 . . . . 17 E8
Rivington Gr M44 . . . . .11 D6
Rivington Rd
  Ellesmere Port CH65 . . . . . .70 C5
  Runcorn WA7 . . . . .50 F3
Rixton Ave WA5 . . . . 15 F8
Rixton Park Homes
  WA3 . . . . .10 F2
Roaches The SK11 . . . . . . .112 B5
Road Beta CW10 . . . . .151 D8
Road Five CW7 . . . . 127 C2
Road Four CW7 . . . . 127 B2
Road One
  Weston CW1 . . . . 207 D8
  Winsford CW7 . . . . .127 B3
Roadside Ct WA3 . . . . 3 C8
Road Three CW7 . . . . 127 D1
Road Two
  Anderton CW9 . . . . 78 C3
  Weston CW1 . . . . 207 C8
  Winsford CW7 . . . . .127 B2
Roan Ct SK11 . . . . 112 F7
Roan House Way
  SK11 . . . . 112 F7
Roan Mews SK11 . . . . .112 F7
Roan Way SK9 . . . . 85 B8
Robert Moffat WA16 . . . . . .29 C5
Roberts Ave WA11 . . . . 1 A5
Roberts Cl WA7 . . . . 49 F6
Roberts Dr CW9 . . . . 104 D6
Roberts Fold WA3 . . . . 9 D4
Roberts Rd CW9 . . . . .80 A2
Robert St
  Northwich CW9 . . . . .103 E6
  Runcorn WA7 . . . . .23 C2
  Warrington WA5 . . . . .15 F6
  Widnes WA8 . . . . .13 B1
Robert's Terr CH1 . . . . .118 B1
Robin Cl
  Chelford SK11 . . . . .84 A2
  Rainow SK10 . . . . 88 E5
  Runcorn WA7 . . . . .50 D7
  Sandbach CW11 . . . . .175 A8
Robin Cres SK11 . . . . .112 D2

Robin Hood Ave
  SK11 . . . . 112 D5
Robin Hood La WA6 . . . . . . .73 B2
Robin La
  Chelford SK11 . . . . .84 A3
  Sutton Lane Ends SK11 . . . .112 D2
Robinsbay Rd M22 . . . . 33 E8
Robins Cl SK7 . . . . .35 E7
Robins Croft CH66 . . . . .69 F2
Robins La WA3 . . . . 3 A8
Robin's La SK7 . . . . 35 E7
Robinsons Croft CH3 . . . . .142 B7
Robins Way SK10 . . . . 88 A7
Rob La WA12 . . . . 2 E5
Robson St WA1 . . . . .16 D6
Robson Way **3** WA3 . . . . . . 3 F8
Roby Gr WA5 . . . . .15 A6
Roche Gdns SK8 . . . . .35 B6
Rochester Cl
  Golborne WA3 . . . . 3 A8
  Warrington WA5 . . . . .15 C5
Rochester Cres CW1 . . . . . .190 F6
Rochester Dr CH65 . . . . . . .70 D3
Rochester Ho SK10 . . . . . . .86 F1
Rock Bank WA3 . . . . 65 E6
Rock Bank Rise SK10 . . . . . 63 A1
Rock Cotts CH5 . . . . .91 D1
Rock Dr WA6 . . . . .49 C1
Rock Farm Cl CH64 . . . . . . 67 A6
Rock Farm Dr CH64 . . . . . . 67 A6
Rock Farm Gr CH64 . . . . . . 67 A6
Rockfield Cl WA8 . . . . .12 D2
Rockfield Dr WA6 . . . . .73 C2
Rockfield Mews WA4 . . . . . .16 F2
Rockford Gdns WA5 . . . . . . 15 A8
Rockford Lo WA16 . . . . .57 C1
Rockhouse La ST7 . . . . 210 C7
Rockingham Cl WA3 . . . . . . 10 C6
Rock La
  Burwardsley CH3 . . . . 184 C6
  Chester CH2 . . . . 237 A4
  Widnes WA8 . . . . .12 F4
Rocklands La CH63 . . . . . . .42 C8
Rocklee Gdns CH64 . . . . . . 67 A6
Rockliffe La CH6 . . . . 91 A3
Rock Mill La SK22 . . . . .39 B7
Rock Rd
  Connah's Quay CH5 . . . . . . .91 E1
  Warrington WA4 . . . . .16 E4
ROCKSAVAGE 49 B4
Rock Savage Rdbt
  WA7 . . . . .49 E4
Rockside ST7 . . . . 195 C6
Rock St SK22 . . . . .39 C7
Rock The WA6 . . . . .73 C2
Rockwood Ave CW2 . . . . . . 190 A3
Rockwood Cl CW2 . . . . 190 A3
Rocky La
  Heswall CH60 . . . . .40 F8
  Tattenhall CH3 . . . . .182 F7
Rocky La S CH60 . . . . .41 A8
Roddy La WA6 . . . . .75 E2
Rode Ct **7** CW12 . . . . 156 F3
Rode Hall* ST7 . . . . .194 B7
RODEHEATH 134 B3
Rode Heath Prim Sch
  ST7 . . . . .193 F7
Rodehouse Cl ST7 . . . . . . .193 F7
Rodepool Cl SK9 . . . . .34 D2
Rode St CW6 . . . . .146 A3
Rode The ST7 . . . . .193 D4
Rodgers Cl WA6 . . . . 49 B1
Rodney St SK11 . . . . .112 D7
Roebourne Rise CH1 . . . . . .117 D4
Roebuck St CW11 . . . . 190 C5
Roeburn Way WA5 . . . . 14 C3
Roedean Wlk CW6 . . . . . . .190 D6
Roehampton Dr WA7 . . . . . . 49 E7
Roehurst La CW7 . . . . .126 D2
Roemarsh Ct WA7 . . . . 49 E6
Roe Pk CW12 . . . . 178 E1
Roe St
  Congleton CW12 . . . . 156 E2
  Macclesfield SK11 . . . . . . .112 D7
Roewood La
  Higher Hurdsfield
  SK10 . . . . 88 A1
  Macclesfield SK10 . . . . . . .113 A8
Roften Ind Est CH66 . . . . . .43 D1
Rokeby Ct WA7 . . . . .24 D5
Rokeden WA12 . . . . 2 D4
Roklis Grange **10** CH64 . . . . 66 E8
Roland Ave WA7 . . . . 22 F1
Rolands Wlk WA7 . . . . .23 A2
Rolleston St WA2 . . . . .16 C8
Rolls Ave CW1 . . . . .190 A6
Rolt Cres CW10 . . . . .151 C7
Roman Cl
  Newton-le-W WA12 . . . . 2 C2
  Runcorn WA7 . . . . .23 D2
Roman Ct CH64 . . . . 66 F7
Roman Dr CH1 . . . . .117 D6
Romanes St CW8 . . . . 103 E7
Roman Rd WA11 . . . . 16 C1
Roman Way CW11 . . . . . . .174 E7
Romiley Rd CH66 . . . . 69 E6
Romney Cl
  Neston CH64 . . . . .66 E7
  Widnes WA8 . . . . .13 E2
Romney Croft CH64 . . . . . . 66 E7
Romney Way CH64 . . . . 66 E7
Romsey Dr SK8 . . . . .35 C6
Rona Ave CH65 . . . . .70 C1
Ronald Dr WA2 . . . . 9 B2
Ronaldshay WA8 . . . . .13 E2

Ronaldsway
  Halewood L26 . . . . .21 A8
  Heswall CH60 . . . . 40 F6
Ronan Rd WA8 . . . . 22 E5
ROODEE 237 A1
Rood Hill CW12 . . . . 156 D3
Rood La CW12 . . . . .156 E4
Rookery Cl
  11 Nantwich CW5 . . . . . . .204 F5
  Sandbach CW11 . . . . .174 C5
Rookery Ct CW11 . . . . .174 C5
Rookery Dr
  Nantwich CW5 . . . . 204 E4
  Tattenhall CH3 . . . . .166 B2
Rookery Farm Rd
  CW6 . . . . .169 A6
Rookery Gdns CW9 . . . . . . 103 E3
Rookerypool Cl SK9 . . . . . . 34 D2
Rookery Rd
  Kidsgrove ST7 . . . . 195 C3
  Tilston SY14 . . . . .198 B3
Rookery Rise CW7 . . . . . . .150 A8
Rookery The
  Broughton CH4 . . . . .139 B3
  Newton-le-W WA12 . . . . 2 D4
Rook St CW2 . . . . .190 C2
Rooks Way CH60 . . . . 40 E8
Roome St WA2 . . . . 16 C7
Rope Bank Ave CW2 . . . . . 206 A7
Rope La
  Shavington CW2 . . . . 206 A5
  Wistaston CW2 . . . . .205 F7
Ropewalk The CH64 . . . . . . 66 C8
Rope Wlk CW12 . . . . .156 D3
Ropeworks The CH1 . . . . . .118 B2
Rosam Ct WA7 . . . . 49 E6
Roscoe Ave
  Newton-le-W WA12 . . . . 2 E3
  Warrington WA2 . . . . .16 D8
Roscoe Cres WA7 . . . . .48 E7
Roscoe Rd M44 . . . . 11 F8
Roscoes Yd **4** WA16 . . . . . 57 A2
Roscommon Way WA3 . . . . 12 E3
Roscote Cl CH60 . . . . .40 F7
Roscote The CH60 . . . . 40 F7
Rose Ave WA11 . . . . 1 E6
Rose Bank
  Bollington SK10 . . . . .87 F7
  Lymm WA13 . . . . .18 E3
Rosebank Cl CW7 . . . . .149 E8
Rosebank Mews
  CW10 . . . . 129 E5
Rosebank Rd M44 . . . . .11 C4
Rosebank Sch CW8 . . . . . . 78 A3
Rosebank Wlk CW8 . . . . . . 78 A4
Rosebery Way CW1 . . . . . . 191 C4
Rose Cl
  Blacon CH1 . . . . .117 D4
  Halewood L26 . . . . 21 A7
  Runcorn WA7 . . . . .50 D5
Rose Cnr CH3 . . . . .166 A1
Rose Cotts CW12 . . . . .154 F6
Rose Cres WA8 . . . . .22 E5
Rosecroft CH62 . . . . .43 C6
Rosedale Ave
  Golborne WA3 . . . . .3 C7
  Warrington WA1 . . . . .17 C7
Rosedene Cl CH2 . . . . .118 E8
Rose Farm Cl CW9 . . . . . . .79 E4
Rose Farm Mews WA6 . . . . 73 B4
Rose Gdns CH64 . . . . .66 F6
Rosehsath Dr L26 . . . . .21 A6
Roseheill Ave WA9 . . . . 6 B5
Rosehill Rd CW2 . . . . .190 D1
Roselands Ct LL12 . . . . . . .162 C1
Rose Lea Cl WA8 . . . . 13 A4
Rosemary Ave
  Runcorn WA7 . . . . .49 F4
  Warrington WA4 . . . . .16 E2
Rosemary Cl
  Broughton CH4 . . . . .139 C3
  Warrington WA5 . . . . .15 C6
Rosemary Dr WA12 . . . . 2 F3
Rosemary La LL12 . . . . . . .161 D1
Rosemary Row CH3 . . . . . .166 A1
Rosemary Wlk M31 . . . . . . 11 F2
Rosemere Dr CH1 . . . . 94 F7
Rosemoor Gdns WA4 . . . . . 26 F5
Rosemount CW10 . . . . 128 C1
Rosemount Cotts WA2 . . . . . 8 B8
Rose St WA8 . . . . 22 F7
Rose Terr
  Blacon CH1 . . . . .117 D4
  Crewe CW1 . . . . .190 C5
Rosetree Mdw CW9 . . . . . . 80 A2
Rosevale Rd ST5 . . . . .210 F1
Rose View Ave WA8 . . . . . . 13 A2
Roseville Dr CW12 . . . . . . .179 B8
Roseway ST5 . . . . 112 D5
Rose Wharf SK11 . . . . .112 F7
Rose Wlk **5** M31 . . . . .11 E3
Rosewood Ave
  Chester CH2 . . . . 118 D5
  Frodsham WA6 . . . . .74 D7
  Warrington WA1 . . . . .16 E7
Rosewood Cl CW1 . . . . . . .190 E6
Rosewood Dr CW7 . . . . . . .126 A1
Rosewood Farm Ct
  WA8 . . . . .12 E4
Rosewood Gr
  Saughall CH1 . . . . .117 B8
  Widnes WA8 . . . . .22 B8
Rosewood Ho CW12 . . . . . 156 A3
Rossall Cl L24 . . . . .21 E2
Rossall Ct SK7 . . . . 35 E6

Rossall Dr SK7 . . . . .35 E6
Rossall Gr CH60 . . . . .69 D6
Rossall Rd
  Warrington WA5 . . . . .15 B4
  Widnes WA8 . . . . .13 D2
Rossbank Rd CH65 . . . . .70 A7
Ross Cl WA3 . . . . .13 C7
Rosscliffe Rd CH65 . . . . .70 A6
Ross Dr CH66 . . . . .69 C5
Rossenclough Rd SK9 . . . . . .34 D1
Rossendale Dr WA3 . . . . .10 A6
Rossendale Rd SK8 . . . . .34 C8
Rossett Ave ■ M22 . . . . .33 D8
Rossett Bsns Village
  LL12 . . . . .162 B1
Rossett Cl
  Northwich CW9 . . . . .103 E4
  Warrington WA5 . . . . .7 E2
Rossett Pk LL12 . . . . .162 C1
Rossett Rd LL13 . . . . .180 A1
Rossfield Rd CH65 . . . . .70 A6
Rossfield Rd N CH65 . . . . . . .70 B7
Rosslyn Cl CH5 . . . . .116 A8
Rosslyn La WA16 . . . . .102 A3
Rosslyn Rd CH3 . . . . .119 B3
Rossmill La WA15 . . . . .32 B7
Rossmore Bsns Pk
  CH65 . . . . .70 B7
Rossmore Ct CH66 . . . . .69 E6
Rossmore Gdns CH66 . . . . . .69 D6
Rossmore Ind Est
  CH65 . . . . .70 A6
Rossmore Rd E CH65 . . . . . . .69 F7
Rossmore Rd W CH65 . . . . . .69 D7
Rossmore Sch CH66 . . . . . . .69 C7
Rossmore Terraced
  Factories CH65 . . . . .70 A6
Rossmount Rd CH65 . . . . . . .70 A6
Ross Rd CH65 . . . . .70 A6
Ross St WA8 . . . . .13 B1
Rosswood Rd CH65 . . . . .70 A6
ROSTHERNE 30 E4
Rostherne Ave
  Ellesmere Port CH66 . . . . . .69 E4
  Golborne WA3 . . . . .3 D8
  High Lane SK6 . . . . .37 E8
Rostherne Cl ■ WA5 . . . . . . .15 D4
Rostherne Cres 12 D2
Rostherne La WA16 . . . . .30 E4
Rostherne Rd SK9 . . . . .59 F4
Rostherne Way ■ 174 F7
Rosyth Cl WA2 . . . . .8 F3
Rothay Dr WA5 . . . . .14 D3
Rothbury Cl WA7 . . . . .49 D6
Rother Dr CH65 . . . . .70 A7
Rother Dr Bsns Ctr
  CH65 . . . . .70 A7
Rotherhead Dr SK11 . . . . . .112 B5
Rotherwood Rd SK9 . . . . . . .59 D6
Rothesay Cl WA7 . . . . .22 E2
Rothesay Dr CH62 . . . . .43 E4
Rothesay Rd CH4 . . . . .141 A7
Rough Bank CW12 . . . . .179 E8
Rough Heys La SK11 . . . . . .111 A8
ROUGHHILL 140 E1
Roughlea Ave WA3 . . . . .4 D4
Roughley Ave WA5 . . . . .15 D4
Roughlyn Cres CH4 . . . . . . .140 E1
Roughwood La
  Alsager CW11, ST7 . . . . . .193 B7
  Hassall Green CW11 . . . . . .176 A1
Roundabout The WA8 . . . . . .12 D6
Round Gdns SK10 . . . . .88 A8
Roundhey SK8 . . . . .34 C8
Round Hill Mdw CH2 . . . . . .142 B7
Round Mdw SK10 . . . . .88 E5
Round Thorn WA3 . . . . .9 A8
Roundway SK7 . . . . .35 D6
Round Way SK22 . . . . .39 D8
Roundy La SK10 . . . . .62 F6
Routledge St WA8 . . . . .13 B1
Rowan Ave WA3 . . . . .3 F7
Rowan Cl
  Alsager ST7 . . . . .193 D3
  Delamere CW8 . . . . .123 D7
  Lawton Heath ST7 . . . . . . .193 D6
  Middlewich CW10 . . . . . . .151 E6
  Runcorn WA7 . . . . .49 C7
  Sandbach CW11 . . . . .174 F7
  Warrington WA5 . . . . .14 F6
  Winsford CW7 . . . . .126 D3
Rowan Ct SK8 . . . . .60 B7
Rowan Dr SK8 . . . . .35 C8
Rowan Gr CH5 . . . . .91 C1
Rowan Ho CH2 . . . . .237 C4
Rowan Lo SK7 . . . . .35 F7
Rowan Pk CH3 . . . . .142 E7
Rowan Pl CH2 . . . . .119 B4
Rowan Rd CW8 . . . . .102 D8
Rowan Rise CW8 . . . . .78 A3
Rowans Cl CW1 . . . . .189 F7
Rowanside SK10 . . . . .86 E6
Rowanside Dr SK9 . . . . .60 E8
Rowans The
  Broughton CH4 . . . . .139 B3
  ■ Northwich CW9 . . . . . . .103 E6
  Widnes WA8 . . . . .13 D4
Rowan Tree Rd WA16 . . . . . .59 B5
Rowan Way SK10 . . . . .87 E1
Rowan Wlk M31 . . . . .11 E2
Rowcliffe Ave CH4 . . . . .141 A4
Rowena Cl CH2 . . . . .118 F3
Rowland Cl WA2 . . . . .9 A3
Rowlands Hts ■ CH1 . . . . . .237 C3
Rowlands View CW6 . . . . . .146 B7

Rowley Bank La WA16 . . . . . .29 B1
ROWLEYHILL 181 B1
Rowley Rd SK7 . . . . .36 E8
Rowley Way WA16 . . . . .82 B7
ROWLINSON'S GREEN
  . . . . .28 C5
ROW-OF-TREES 59 D3
Rowson Dr M44 . . . . .11 D6
Rowswood Ctyd WA4 . . . . . . .25 E5
Rowswood Farm WA4 . . . . . .25 E5
Row The
  ■ Winsford CW7 . . . . .126 D1
  Wrenbury CW5 . . . . .217 B5
Rowthorn Cl WA8 . . . . .22 E8
Rowton Bridge Rd
  CH3 . . . . .142 E7
Rowton Cl ■ CW7 . . . . .126 D1
Rowton La CH3 . . . . .103 F4
Rowton La CH3 . . . . .142 F6
Rowton Rd CW2 . . . . .189 D4
Roxborough Cl WA5 . . . . .7 A6
Roxburgh Cl SK10 . . . . .87 A1
Roxburgh Rd CH66 . . . . .68 F6
Roxby Way WA16 . . . . .82 A7
Roxholme Wlk M22 . . . . .33 C8
Royal Arc ■ CW1 . . . . .190 C4
Royal Ave ■ WA16 . . . . .12 A1
Royal Ct ■ WA16 . . . . .57 A2
Royal Gdns
  Altrincham WA14 . . . . .20 F2
  Northwich CW9 . . . . .103 E3
Royal La CW6 . . . . .147 A3
Royal Mdws SK10 . . . . .87 A1
Royal Mews CW9 . . . . .104 D5
Royal Pl WA8 . . . . .22 B8
Royal Rd SK12 . . . . .38 D5
Royal Schools for The
  Deaf & Communication
  Disorders SK8 . . . . .34 D6
ROYAL'S GREEN 228 E1
Royal Sh Arc The ■
  CH64 . . . . .66 E8
Royce Cl CW1 . . . . .190 A7
Royce Ct WA16 . . . . .56 F2
Royden Ave
  Irlam M44 . . . . .11 F8
  Runcorn WA7 . . . . .49 A8
Royds Cl CW8 . . . . .103 A8
Royds Ct CW11 . . . . .174 D5
Roylance Dr CW10 . . . . .151 C8
Royleen Dr WA6 . . . . .74 D6
Royle Pk CW12 . . . . .156 D3
Royle's Pl CH1 . . . . .103 D6
Royles Sq ■ SK9 . . . . .60 A1
Royle St
  Congleton CW12 . . . . .156 D3
  Northwich CW9 . . . . .104 B8
  Winsford CW7 . . . . .126 E1
Royston Ave WA1 . . . . .17 A7
Royston Cl
  Ellesmere Port CH66 . . . . . .69 F3
  ■ Golborne WA3 . . . . .3 E8
Rozel Cres WA5 . . . . .15 B5
Rubin Dr CW1 . . . . .189 F7
Rudd Ave WA9 . . . . .1 B2
RUDHEATH 104 D6
Rudheath Cl CW2 . . . . .189 D5
Rudheath Com High Sch
  CW9 . . . . .104 D7
Rudheath Com Prim Sch
  CW9 . . . . .104 D6
Rudheath La CW9 . . . . .24 D3
Rudheath Way CW9 . . . . . . .104 E5
Rudloe Ct WA4 . . . . .8 F1
Rudstone Cl CH66 . . . . .69 B5
Rudyard Cl SK11 . . . . .112 B6
Rue De Bohars CW6 . . . . . . .168 D8
Rufford Cl
  Widnes WA8 . . . . .12 C2
  Wistaston CW2 . . . . .206 B8
Rufford Ct WA1 . . . . .17 E8
Rufus Ct CH1 . . . . .237 A3
Rugby Cl SK10 . . . . .87 E4
Rugby Dr SK10 . . . . .87 E4
Rugby Ho SK10 . . . . .87 D3
Rugby Rd CH65 . . . . .70 D3
Rugby Wlk CH65 . . . . .70 D3
Ruislip Ct WA2 . . . . .8 F1
RULOE 101 D7
RUNCORN 23 C1
Runcorn All Saints CE
  Prim Sch WA7 . . . . .23 A3
Runcorn Docks Rd
  WA7 . . . . .22 E2
Runcorn East Sta WA7 . . . . . .50 D7
Runcorn Mkt WA7 . . . . .23 A3
Runcorn Rd
  Barnton CW8 . . . . .78 B2
  Higher Walton WA4 . . . . . . .25 D6
  Little Leigh CW8 . . . . .77 D5
Runcorn Spur Rd WA7 . . . . . .23 B1
Runcorn Sta WA7 . . . . .22 F2
Runger La M90, WA15 . . . . . .32 F8
Runnell The CW4 . . . . .41 D4
Runnymede WA1 . . . . .17 D7
Runnymede Ct ■ 13 C1
Runnymede Dr WA11 . . . . . . .1 A6
Runnymede Gdns ■
  WA8 . . . . .13 C1
Runnymede Wlk ■
  WA8 . . . . .13 C2
Rupert Row WA7 . . . . .50 A8
Ruscoe Ave CW11 . . . . .174 E6
Ruscolm Cl WA5 . . . . .14 D7
Rushes Mdw WA13 . . . . .19 B5
Rushey Cl WA15 . . . . .32 D7
Rushfield Cres WA7 . . . . .50 B5

Rushfield Rd
  Cheadle SK8 . . . . .35 A6
  Chester CH4 . . . . .141 B5
Rush Gdns WA13 . . . . .19 A4
RUSHGREEN 19 A4
Rushgreen Rd WA13 . . . . . . .19 A4
Rushmere Cl SK10 . . . . .62 F2
Rushmere La CH3 . . . . .163 F3
Rushmore Gr WA1 . . . . .17 A7
Rusholme Cl L26 . . . . .21 A6
Rushside Rd SK8 . . . . .35 A6
RUSHTON 147 C5
Rushton Ave WA12 . . . . .2 B4
Rushton CE Prim Sch
  SK11 . . . . .159 B2
Rushton Cl
  Burtonwood WA5 . . . . .6 F7
  Northwich CW9 . . . . .104 C7
  Widnes WA8 . . . . .12 F3
Rushton Dr
  Chester CH2 . . . . .118 E7
  Hough CW2 . . . . .206 E2
  Middlewich CW10 . . . . . . .151 C7
Rushton Fold SK10 . . . . .61 A2
Rushton La CW6 . . . . .147 D6
Rushton Rd SK8 . . . . .35 A6
RUSHTON SPENCER 159 B2
Rushy View WA12 . . . . .2 A4
Ruskin Ave
  Newton-le-W WA12 . . . . . . .2 C4
  Warrington WA2 . . . . .8 C2
Ruskin Cl WA10 . . . . .57 A2
Ruskin Ct CH65 . . . . .70 D3
Ruskin Rd
  Congleton CW12 . . . . .156 C2
  Crewe CW2 . . . . .190 C2
Ruskin Sports Coll & Com
  High Sch CW2 . . . . .190 C2
Ruskin Way WA16 . . . . .57 A3
Russel Ct WA8 . . . . .13 B4
Russell Ave
  Alsager ST7 . . . . .193 D5
  Warrington WA5 . . . . .14 F4
Russell Cl CW12 . . . . .179 A8
Russell Dr CW1 . . . . .191 C5
Russell Rd
  Runcorn WA7 . . . . .48 E8
  Winsford CW7 . . . . .149 C8
Russell St CH1, CH3 . . . . . . .237 C3
Russet Cl CW10 . . . . .152 D6
Russet Rd CW8 . . . . .102 D8
Russett Sch & Cheshire
  MSI Unit The CW8 . . . . . .102 E8
Russet Way SK9 . . . . .59 E3
Rutherford Dr WA16 . . . . . . .82 C7
Ruthin Cl WA7 . . . . .7 F3
Ruthin Ct CH65 . . . . .70 D3
Ruthin Wlk WA6 . . . . .73 A1
Rutland Ave
  Golborne WA3 . . . . .3 D7
  Halewood L26 . . . . .21 A8
  Warrington WA4 . . . . .26 B8
Rutland Cl
  Congleton CW12 . . . . .156 E4
  Sandbach CW11 . . . . .174 C5
Rutland Dr
  Middlewich CW10 . . . . . . .151 C7
  Weaverham CW8 . . . . .77 C1
Rutland Pl CH2 . . . . .119 A5
Rutland Rd
  Hazel Grove SK7 . . . . .36 E8
  Irlam M44 . . . . .11 D5
  Kidsgrove ST7 . . . . .195 A2
  Macclesfield SK11 . . . . . . .112 D4
  Partington M31 . . . . .11 E2
Rutland St ■ WA7 . . . . .22 F2
Rutter Ave WA5 . . . . .7 F2
Ryburn Cl CW2 . . . . .207 B3
Ryburn Rd SK11 . . . . .112 A5
Rydal Ave
  High Lane SK6 . . . . .37 E8
  Warrington WA4 . . . . .16 C1
Rydal Cl
  Ellesmere Port CH65 . . . . . .70 C2
  Holmes Chapel CW4 . . . . .130 B2
  Neston CH64 . . . . .66 F6
  Winsford CW7 . . . . .126 D3
Rydal Ct CW12 . . . . .156 A2
Rydal Dr WA15 . . . . .32 D8
Rydal Gr
  Chester CH4 . . . . .141 A6
  Helsby WA6 . . . . .73 B1
  Runcorn WA7 . . . . .49 B8
Rydal Mount CW1 . . . . .173 B1
Rydal Pl SK11 . . . . .112 A6
Rydal St WA12 . . . . .2 C3
Rydal Way
  Alsager ST7 . . . . .193 C5
  Widnes WA8 . . . . .12 C1
Ryde Cl CW1 . . . . .190 B8
Ryder Rd
  Warrington WA1 . . . . .17 C7
  Widnes WA8 . . . . .13 B1
Ryders St CW8 . . . . .103 E8
Ryebank Ave CW1 . . . . .190 B7
Ryebank Rd SK10 . . . . .87 C3
Rye Cl ST7 . . . . .195 A2
Ryecroft CH2 . . . . .72 B3
Ryecroft Cl CW10 . . . . .151 B7
Ryecroft La
  Duddon CH3, CW6 . . . . . .144 C6
  Mobberley WA16 . . . . .57 E4
Ryecroft Rd CH60 . . . . .41 C7
Ryedale Way WA7 . . . . .50 B5
Ryehills WA7 . . . . .209 E1
RYE HILLS 209 E1
Rylands Cl SY14 . . . . .213 B4
Rylands Dr WA2 . . . . .16 C7

Rylands St
  Warrington WA1 . . . . .16 B5
  ■ Widnes WA8 . . . . .23 B8
Ryles Cl SK11 . . . . .112 C5
Ryles Cres SK11 . . . . .112 C5
Ryles Ho SK11 . . . . .112 C6
Ryle St SK11 . . . . .112 D6
Ryleys Farm SK9 . . . . .59 F1
Ryleys La SK9 . . . . .59 F1
Ryleys Sch The SK9 . . . . .59 F1

S

Sabre Cl WA7 . . . . .50 D7
Sack La CW9 . . . . .54 F6
Sacred Heart RC Prim Sch
  WA5 . . . . .15 E5
Saddleback Dr SK10 . . . . . . .86 F7
Saddlers Rise WA7 . . . . .50 C8
Saddlery Way CH1 . . . . .118 B1
Sade Ct ■ CW1 . . . . .190 B5
Sadler Cl CW7 . . . . .126 D1
Sadler Rd CW7 . . . . .126 D1
Sadler's Cl CW4 . . . . .130 B3
Sadlers La CW6 . . . . .124 A1
Sadler St WA8 . . . . .13 C1
Sadlers Wells CW6 . . . . .185 E8
Saffron Cl
  Golborne WA3 . . . . .3 E8
  Warrington WA2 . . . . .9 B1
Saffron Wlk M31 . . . . .11 F2
Sagars Rd
  Handforth SK9 . . . . .34 C3
  Styal SK9 . . . . .34 B4
Sage Cl WA3 . . . . .9 C2
SAIGHTON 142 E1
Saighton CE Prim Sch
  CH3 . . . . .142 E1
Saighton La CH3 . . . . .142 F2
St Aelred's RC Tech Coll
  WA12 . . . . .2 D4
St Aidans Dr WA8 . . . . .12 F6
St Alban Rd WA5 . . . . .14 E5
St Albans Cl WA11 . . . . .2 A7
St Albans Dr CW5 . . . . .204 F3
St Alban's RC Prim Sch
  Macclesfield SK10 . . . . .86 F1
  Warrington WA5 . . . . .15 F6
St Albans St SK22 . . . . .39 C8
St Ambrose Coll WA15 . . . . .32 B8
St Ambrose Ct WA4 . . . . .16 B2
St Ambrose RC Prim Sch
  L24 . . . . .21 A2
St Ambrose Rd WA8 . . . . .13 C1
St Andrew's Ave CW2 . . . . .190 C1
St Andrew's CE Prim Sch
  WA2 . . . . .9 A4
St Andrews Ct
  Crewe CW2 . . . . .190 C1
  Ellesmere Port CH65 . . . . . .70 E2
  Macclesfield SK11 . . . . . . .112 B7
St Andrews Dr
  Holmes Chapel CW4 . . . . .130 B2
  Kidsgrove ST7 . . . . .195 C3
St Andrew's Gdns
  ST7 . . . . .193 E2
St Andrew's Rd
  Ellesmere Port CH65 . . . . . .70 E2
  Macclesfield SK11 . . . . . . .112 B7
St Andrews Wlk
  Mickle Trafford CH2 . . . . . .96 F1
  New Mills SK22 . . . . .39 D8
St Annes CH1 . . . . .237 B3
St Annes Ave WA4 . . . . .17 B2
St Anne's Ave CW10 . . . . . .151 D8
St Annes Ave E WA4 . . . . . . .17 B2
St Anne's Fulshaw CE
  Prim Sch SK9 . . . . .59 F6
St Anne's La CW5 . . . . .204 D5
St Anne's RC Prim Sch
  CW5 . . . . .204 E3
St Anne's Rd WA8 . . . . .13 B2
St Anne St CH1 . . . . .237 B3
St Ann's Rd CW10 . . . . .151 C8
St Ann's Rd S SK8 . . . . .34 C8
St Ann's Sq SK8 . . . . .34 C8
St Anthony Pl WA2 . . . . .9 B8
St Anthony's RC Prim Sch
  CH4 . . . . .140 E6
St Asaph Dr WA5 . . . . .14 E5
St Asaph Rd CH66 . . . . .94 E8
St Augustine's Ave
  WA4 . . . . .17 C1
St Augustines Dr
  CW2 . . . . .207 E3
St Augustine's RC Prim
  Sch
  Runcorn WA7 . . . . .24 A2
  Warrington WA4 . . . . .16 F4
St Austell Cl WA5 . . . . .14 D7
St Austell Ave SK10 . . . . .86 E1
St Austell Cl
  Macclesfield SK10 . . . . .86 E1
  Runcorn WA7 . . . . .50 B6
St Austell Dr SK8 . . . . .34 B8
St Austins La WA1 . . . . .16 B4
St Barnabas CE Prim Sch
  Macclesfield SK11 . . . . . . .112 D6
  Warrington WA5 . . . . .15 E6
St Barnabas Ct SK11 . . . . . .112 D6
St Barnabas Pl WA5 . . . . .15 E6
St Bartholomews Ct
  CH5 . . . . .116 E6

St Basil's RC Prim Sch
  WA8 . . . . .12 A2
St Bede's Ave CW8 . . . . .77 D1
St Bede's RC Inf Sch
  WA8 . . . . .13 A1
St Bede's RC Jun Sch
  WA8 . . . . .13 A1
St Bede's RC Prim Sch
  CW8 . . . . .102 F7
St Benedicts Cl WA2 . . . . . . .16 B7
St Benedict's RC Prim Sch
  Handforth SK9 . . . . .34 E3
  Warrington WA2 . . . . .16 D7
St Bernard's RC Prim Sch
  CH65 . . . . .70 D3
St Berteline's CE Prim Sch
  WA7 . . . . .50 C8
St Brannocks Rd SK8 . . . . . .35 B7
St Brides Cl WA5 . . . . .14 E3
St Bridgets Cl
  Warrington WA2 . . . . .8 F3
  Widnes WA8 . . . . .23 A5
St Bridgets Ct CH4 . . . . . . .141 B6
St Bridget's RC Prim Sch
  WA2 . . . . .8 E3
St Catherine Dr CW8 . . . . . .103 A4
St Catherine's RC Prim
  Sch WA3 . . . . .9 D7
St Chad's CE Prim Sch
  Newcastle-u-Lyme
  ST5 . . . . .210 D2
  Winsford CW7 . . . . .149 E8
St Chads Cl CW5 . . . . .220 A8
St Chad's Fields CW7 . . . . . .149 C5
St Chad's RC High Sch
  WA7 . . . . .49 D7
St Chad's Rd CH1 . . . . .117 F4
St Chad's Terr ST5 . . . . .210 D2
St Chads Way TF9 . . . . .236 C2
St Christophers Cl
  CH2 . . . . .118 D8
St Clair St CW2 . . . . .190 D1
St Clare's RC Prim Sch
  CH4 . . . . .141 A5
St Clements Ct CW2 . . . . . . .207 B1
St Clement's RC Prim Sch
  WA7 . . . . .49 A8
St David Rd CH62 . . . . .44 A6
St Davids Dr
  ■ Ellesmere Port
  CH66 . . . . .94 F8
  Warrington WA5 . . . . .7 E2
St David's High Sch
  CH4 . . . . .140 C6
St Davids' Ret Pk
  CH4 . . . . .140 D7
St David's Terr CH4 . . . . . . .140 C6
St Edwards Cl SK11 . . . . . . .112 D6
St Edward's RC Prim Sch
  Macclesfield SK11 . . . . . . .112 C5
  Runcorn WA7 . . . . .23 B3
St Elmo Pk SK12 . . . . .37 C4
St Elphins Cl WA1 . . . . .16 C5
St Elphin's (Fairfield) CE
  Prim Sch WA1 . . . . .16 D6
SS Peter & Paul RC High
  Sch WA8 . . . . .12 F2
St Gabriels CE Prim Sch
  ST7 . . . . .193 C3
St Gabriel's RC Prim Sch
  ST7 . . . . .193 C3
St George's CH1 . . . . .237 B3
St Georges Ave ■
  CH66 . . . . .94 F8
St George's CE Prim Sch
  CH66 . . . . .39 C8
St Georges Cl WA4 . . . . .26 E3
St George's Cl WA16 . . . . . . .82 C8
St George's Cres
  Chester CH4 . . . . .237 C1
  Waverton CH3 . . . . .143 A5
St George's Pl ■
  SK11 . . . . .112 D7
St Georges Rd CW2 . . . . .39 C8
St George's Rd CW7 . . . . . .149 C8
St George's St SK11 . . . . . . .112 D6
St George's Way
  Northwich CW9 . . . . .103 F5
  Thornton Hough CH63 . . . . .42 A7
St Gerard's RC Prim Sch
  WA8 . . . . .23 B7
St Gregory's RC High Sch
  WA5 . . . . .15 D5
St Gregory's RC Prim Sch
  SK10 . . . . .87 F8
ST HELENS 1 A1
St Helens Ct WA3 . . . . .11 B3
St Helens Coll Newton
  Campus WA12 . . . . .2 B4
St Helens Rd
  ■ Northwich CW9 . . . . . . .104 A8
St Hilarys Pk WA9 . . . . .4 B8
St Hilda's Dr WA6 . . . . .49 C1
St Ives Cl SK10 . . . . .86 E1
St Ives Pk CH5 . . . . .116 A3
St Ives Way CH5 . . . . .116 A3
St James Ave
  Chester CH2 . . . . .118 F7
  Congleton CW12 . . . . .156 C2
  Warren SK11 . . . . .111 E2
St James' CE Prim Sch
  WA11 . . . . .1 E6
St James Cl
  Audlem CW3 . . . . .230 A4
  ■ Frodsham WA6 . . . . .49 C1
St James Ct
  Audley ST7 . . . . .209 D2

St James Ct continued
Cheadle SK8 . . . .**34** F6
Chester CH2 . . . .**118** F3
St James' Ct
Biddulph ST8 . . . .**179** E3
Warrington WA4 . . . .**16** B3
**St James Ct/Lys Sant
Iago** CH5 . . . .**91** D1
St James' Dr SK9 . . . .**60** A6
St James' RC High Sch
SK8 . . . .**34** F6
St James' Sq SK22 . . . .**39** C8
St James St CH1 . . . .**237** B3
St James Terr 🟦
CW7 . . . .**149** A8
St James' Way SK8 . . . .**34** F6
St James Wlk 🟦 CW8 . . . . . .**103** E7
St John Ave WA4 . . . .**16** B2
**St John Fisher RC Prim
Sch** WA8 . . . .**13** D1
St John's Ave
Knutsford WA16 . . . .**56** F1
Lostock Gralam CW9 . . . .**79** F3
St John's Brow WA7 . . . .**23** B3
St John's CE Prim Sch
Bollington SK10 . . . .**88** A7
Sandbach CW11 . . . .**175** E6
St John's Cl CW9 . . . .**104** E8
St Johns Ct
Chester CH1 . . . .**237** B2
Winsford CW7 . . . .**126** B1
St John's Ct
Knutsford WA16 . . . .**57** C2
Warrington WA1 . . . .**16** F7
St Johns Dr CW7 . . . .**149** A8
St John's Rd
Bebington CH62 . . . .**44** A5
Chester CH4 . . . .**237** C1
Congleton CW12 . . . .**157** A5
Knutsford WA16 . . . .**57** A1
🟦 Macclesfield SK11 . . . .**112** C7
Wilmslow SK9 . . . .**59** E3
St John's Rear Rd
CH4 . . . .**237** C1
St John's St WA7 . . . .**23** B3
St John St
Chester CH1 . . . .**237** B2
Newton-le-W WA12 . . . .**2** A3
St John's Way
Cuddington CW8 . . . .**102** B2
Sandbach CW11 . . . .**175** E6
St John's Wood ST7 . . . .**194** F1
St John's Wood Com Sch
WA16 . . . .**57** D2
**St John The Evangelist CE
Prim Sch** SK11 . . . .**112** A7
**St John The Evangelist RC
Prim Sch** ST7 . . . .**194** F1
St Joseph's CE WA15 . . . .**14** E5
St Joseph's RC Prim Sch
Warrington WA5 . . . .**14** E5
Winsford CW7 . . . .**149** B8
St Josephs Way CW5 . . . . . .**205** A5
St Katherines Way
WA1 . . . .**16** D5
St Kilda Cl CH65 . . . .**70** C1
St Lawrence Cres CW5 . . . .**204** F6
St Lawrence Rd WA6 . . . .**74** B8
St Leonard's Way
CW3 . . . .**232** C1
St Lewis RC Prim Sch
WA3 . . . .**4** B1
St Luke's Ave WA3 . . . .**3** D8
St Luke's CE Prim Sch
WA3 . . . .**3** E7
St Lukes Cl CH4 . . . .**130** D3
St Luke's Cres WA8 . . . .**13** R4
St Luke's Ho 🟦 SK10 . . . . .**111** F8
St Luke's RC Prim Sch
WA6 . . . .**74** C8
St Margaret's Ave WA4 . . . .**8** D1
St Margaret's CE Prim Sch
WA2 . . . .**8** C1
St Mark's CE Prim Sch
CW9 . . . .**53** C4
St Marks Cres CH66 . . . .**94** F8
St Mark's RC Prim Sch
L26 . . . .**21** A8
St Marks Rd CH4 . . . .**140** F6
St Mark's St WA11 . . . .**1** A6
St Martins Dr CH66 . . . .**69** D2
St Martins La WA7 . . . .**50** D7
St Martins RC Prim Sch
WA7 . . . .**50** D7
St Martin's Rd ST7 . . . .**210** E6
St Martin's Way CH1 . . . .**237** A3
**St Mary of the Angels RC
Prim Sch** CH66 . . . .**69** D6
St Mary's Ave CW8 . . . .**77** D1
St Mary's CE Prim Sch
Bebington CH62 . . . .**44** A5
Bosley SK11 . . . .**158** D8
Irlam M44 . . . .**11** C5
Runcorn WA7 . . . .**50** A8
St Mary's Cl
Alsager ST7 . . . .**193** C5
Hale L24 . . . .**21** E2
Warrington WA4 . . . .**26** C6
St Mary's Ct CW5 . . . .**204** A7
St Mary's Ct CW12 . . . .**156** A2
St Mary's Dr
Golborne WA3 . . . .**4** B8
Partington M31 . . . .**11** F4
St Mary's Dr CW8 . . . .**126** A8
St Mary's Hill CH1 . . . .**237** B1
St Mary's Hospl The
Phineas Gage Ctr WA2 . . .**8** B1

St Mary's RC Inf Sch
WA12 . . . .**2** C4
St Mary's RC Jun Sch
WA12 . . . .**2** DJ
St Mary's RC Prim Sch
Congleton CW12 . . . .**156** D3
Crewe CW2 . . . .**190** A1
Middlewich CW10 . . . .**151** C8
New Mills SK22 . . . .**39** B8
St Mary's Rd
Disley SK12 . . . .**38** D5
Dodleston CH4 . . . .**162** A7
Nantwich CW5 . . . .**204** E7
New Mills SK22 . . . .**39** B8
Runcorn WA8 . . . .**23** F1
Warrington WA5 . . . .**14** F5
Widnes WA8 . . . .**23** A4
St Mary's St
Crewe CW1 . . . .**190** C4
Warrington WA4 . . . .**16** D3
St Mary's Way CH4 . . . .**139** C5
St Matthews CE Prim Sch
WA4 . . . .**26** E2
St Matthews Cl
Haslington CW1 . . . .**191** D4
Warrington WA4 . . . .**26** D7
St Mawes Cl WA8 . . . .**12** E2
St Mawes Ct SK10 . . . .**86** E1
St Mawgan Ct WA2 . . . .**8** F2
St Michael's Ave SK7 . . . .**35** E8
St Michael's Cl
Little Leigh CW8 . . . .**77** D5
Widnes WA8 . . . .**22** C7
St Michael's Cotts
CW12 . . . .**156** B7
St Michael's Ind Est
WA8 . . . .**22** C7
St Michael's RC Prim Sch
WA8 . . . .**22** C7
St Michael's Rd WA8 . . . .**22** C7
St Michael's Row
CH1 . . . .**237** B2
St Michael's Sq CH1 . . . . . .**237** B2
St Michaels Terr 🟦
SK11 . . . .**112** D8
St Michael's View
CW1 . . . .**190** B5
St Michael's Way
CW10 . . . .**128** C1
St Monicas Cl WA4 . . . .**26** D7
St Monica's RC Prim Sch
WA4 . . . .**26** D7
St Nicholas Cl CW5 . . . .**204** F5
St Nicholas RC High Sch
CW8 . . . .**103** D6
St Nicholas Rd WA3 . . . .**4** A8
St Olave St CH1 . . . .**237** B1
St Oswalds CH1 . . . .**237** B3
St Oswald's CE Prim Sch
CH1 . . . .**94** F2
St Oswalds Cl
Malpas SY14 . . . .**213** B3
Winwick WA2 . . . .**8** B6
St Oswald's Cres
CW11 . . . .**153** F5
St Oswald's Rd
WA1 . . . .**16** F8
St Oswalds Way CH1,
CH2 . . . .**237** B3
**St Oswald's Worleston CE
Prim Sch** CW5 . . . .**188** E6
St Patricks Cl WA8 . . . .**23** A5
**St Paul of the Cross RC
Prim Sch** WA5 . . . .**6** E5
St Paul's Cl CW1 . . . .**190** C4
St Paul's Ct
🟦 Macclesfield SK11 . . . . . .**112** F7
Warrington WA2 . . . .**16** A6
St Pauls Gdns CH66 . . . .**69** B7
St Pauls Pl 🟦 CW9 . . . .**79** A1
St Paul's RC Prim Sch
SK12 . . . .**36** E2
St Paul's Rd
🟦 Macclesfield SK11 . . . . . .**112** E7
Widnes WA8 . . . .**23** A7
St Paul's St CW1 . . . .**190** C4
St Peter's Ave WA16 . . . .**56** F1
St Peter's CE Prim Sch
WA12 . . . .**2** E4
St Peter's Cl
Heswall CH60 . . . .**40** F7
Lymm WA13 . . . .**19** A4
St Peter's Ct WA2 . . . .**16** C6
St Peter's Dr CW6 . . . .**147** F7
St Peter's Ho SK11 . . . .**112** E6
St Peters Rd
WA1 . . . .**17** C7
St Peters Rd CW12 . . . .**156** E1
St Peter's Rise SK11 . . . . . .**174** E7
St Peters Way CH2 . . . .**119** F8
St Peter's Way WA2 . . . .**16** B6
**St Philip (Westbrook) CE
Prim Sch** WA5 . . . .**7** B1
St Saviour's CE Prim Sch
ST7 . . . .**194** D1
St Saviour's RC Inf Sch
CH66 . . . .**69** E3
St Saviour's RC Jun Sch
CH66 . . . .**69** E3
St Stephen's St ST7 . . . . . .**194** D1
St Stephen Rd WA5 . . . .**14** F5
St Stephen's Ave WA2 . . . .**8** B3
St Stephens Cl CH60 . . . .**41** C6
St Stephens Ct
🟦 Congleton CW12 . . . .**156** F3
Sandbach CW11 . . . .**174** D7
St Stephen's RC Prim Sch
WA2 . . . .**8** B2

St Teresa's RC Prim Sch
M44 . . . .**11** E8
St Theresa's RC Prim Sch
CI/1 . . . .**117** F5
St Thomas CE Prim Sch
ST7 . . . .**195** A1
St Thomas Ct WA8 . . . .**12** E1
**St Thomas More RC High
Sch** CW2 . . . .**190** A2
**St Thomas of Canterbury
Blue Coat CE Jun Sch**
CH1 . . . .**237** A4
St Thomas's CE Prim Sch
WA4 . . . .**16** C2
St Thomas's Pathway
CH1 . . . .**237** B2
St Thomas St ST7 . . . .**195** E7
St Thomas Terr WA4 . . . .**12** E1
St Thomas' View CH65 . . . . . .**70** B4
St Vincent Dr CW8 . . . .**102** F3
St Vincent Rd WA5 . . . .**14** F5
St Vincent's RC Prim Sch
Knutsford WA16 . . . .**57** C1
Warrington WA5 . . . .**14** F3
St Wenefredes Gn
SY13 . . . .**214** F6
**St Werburgh's &
St Columba's RC Prim Sch**
CH2 . . . .**118** F2
St Werburgh St CH1 . . . .**237** B2
St Wilfrids Cl CW9 . . . .**104** A3
St Wilfrid's Dr WA4 . . . .**17** C1
St Wilfrid's RC Prim Sch
CW8 . . . .**103** D5
**St Winefride's RC Prim
Sch** CH64 . . . .**66** F7
Salander Cres CW2 . . . .**206** A7
Salerno Rd CH2 . . . .**95** B1
Salesbrook La CW5 . . . .**228** C7
Salford CW3 . . . .**230** A4
Salford Pl CW12 . . . .**156** E3
Salisbury Ave
Crewe CW2 . . . .**190** C1
Saltney CH4 . . . .**140** E6
Salisbury Cl
Crewe CW2 . . . .**190** C1
🔟 Ellesmere Port CH66 . . . . .**94** F8
Salisbury Pl SK10 . . . .**87** E4
Salisbury Rd WA11 . . . .**1** B8
Salisbury St
Chester CH1 . . . .**118** B3
Golborne WA3 . . . .**3** A8
Runcorn WA7 . . . .**23** A1
Warrington WA1 . . . .**16** D6
🟦 Widnes WA8 . . . .**23** B8
Salkeld St 🟦 CW9 . . . .**104** B8
Salmon Leap CH4 . . . .**237** B1
Salop Pl ST7 . . . .**195** A3
Salop Wlk SK10 . . . .**86** F2
Saltash Cl WA7 . . . .**50** B6
Saltersbrook Gr 🟦
SK9 . . . .**34** E1
Salters Ford CW8 . . . .**77** F3
Saltersford Cnr CW4 . . . . . .**130** E3
Saltersgate CH66 . . . .**69** F2
Salters La
Lower Withington
SK11 . . . .**132** B8
Windyharbour SK11 . . . .**109** D1
Salter's La
Bickerton SY14 . . . .**199** F8
Broxton CH3, SY14 . . . .**183** E1
Hoole Bank CH2 . . . .**119** C8
SALTERSWALL **125** F3
Salt Line Way CW11 . . . .**174** D6
Salt Mdws CW5 . . . .**204** C5
SALTNEY **140** D6
Saltney Bsns Ctr CH4 . . . . .**140** F7
Saltney Ferry Rd
CH4 . . . .**140** B6
Saltney Ferry Rd CH4 . . . . .**140** B7
Saltney Terr CH4 . . . .**140** B7
Salton Gdns WA5 . . . .**15** E7
Saltwood Dr WA7 . . . .**50** C5
Saltworks Cl WA6 . . . .**49** D2
Samian Cl CW10 . . . .**128** C2
Samphire Gdns WA9 . . . .**6** B7
Samuel St
Chester CH1 . . . .**237** C3
Crewe CW1 . . . .**190** B5
Macclesfield SK11 . . . .**112** D7
Packmoor ST7 . . . .**195** F1
Warrington WA5 . . . .**15** E4
Sanbec Gdns WA8 . . . .**12** D5
Sandalwood WA7 . . . .**24** C1
Sandalwood Cl WA2 . . . .**8** D2
SANDBACH **175** B5
Sandbach Com Prim Sch
CW11 . . . .**175** B6
Sandbach Dr CW9 . . . .**103** E6
SANDBACH HEATH **175** D6
**Sandbach High Sch &
Sixth Form Coll**
CW11 . . . .**175** A7
Sandbach Rd
Congleton CW12 . . . .**156** A3
Rode Heath ST7 . . . .**193** E7
Sandbach Rd N ST7 . . . .**193** C4
Sandbach Rd S ST7 . . . .**193** D3
Sandbach Sch CW11 . . . . . .**175** A6
Sandbach Sta CW11 . . . . . .**174** DB
Sanderling Rd WA12 . . . .**2** C4
Sanders Hey Cl WA7 . . . .**50** D5
Sanderson Cl
Crewe CW2 . . . .**206** C8

Sanderson Cl continued
Warrington WA5 . . . .**14** D2
Sanderson Way CW10 . . . . .**128** E1
Sanders Sq SK11 . . . .**112** D5
Sandfield Ave CW5 . . . .**216** F3
Sandfield Cl 🟦 WA3 . . . .**3** E8
Sandfield Cres WA3 . . . .**5** C7
Sandfield Ct
🟦 Frodsham WA6 . . . .**74** B8
Wrenbury CW5 . . . .**216** F4
Sandfield Hall WA3 . . . .**3** A4
Sandfield La
Acton Bridge CW8 . . . .**76** E1
Hartford CW8 . . . .**103** C4
Sandfield Pk CH60 . . . .**40** D8
Sandfields WA6 . . . .**74** B8
Sandfield Terr CW8 . . . .**76** F1
Sandford Cres CW7 . . . .**207** D2
Sandford Rd CW5 . . . .**204** F7
Sandgate Rd SK10 . . . .**87** F2
Sandham Gr CH60 . . . .**41** D7
Sandham Rd L24 . . . .**21** A4
Sandheys CH64 . . . .**41** C1
Sandhill Terr WA4 . . . .**16** E3
Sandholme Cotts 🟦
CW7 . . . .**149** B8
Sandhole La
Chelford WA16 . . . .**83** D4
Crowton CW8 . . . .**101** B7
Sandhurst Ave CW2 . . . .**190** A1
Sandhurst Dr 🟦 SK9 . . . .**60** C8
Sandhurst Rd L26 . . . .**21** A6
Sandhurst St WA4 . . . .**16** F3
Sandicroft Cl WA3 . . . .**9** C5
Sandiford Rd CW4 . . . .**130** C3
Sandiford Sq CW9 . . . .**104** A8
Sandileigh Ave WA14 . . . .**56** F2
Sandington Dr CW8 . . . .**101** F2
SANDIWAY **102** B3
Sandiway
Bebington CH63 . . . .**43** C6
Knutsford WA16 . . . .**57** B2
Sandiway Ave WA8 . . . .**12** A1
Sandiway Cl CW8 . . . .**102** A2
Sandiway La CW9 . . . .**53** A2
Sandiway Pk CW8 . . . .**102** E4
Sandiway Prim Sch
CW8 . . . .**102** B3
Sandiway Rd
Crewe CW1 . . . .**190** A7
Handforth SK9 . . . .**34** D5
Sand La SK10 . . . .**84** F5
Sandlebridge Farm
SK9 . . . .**83** F6
Sandle Bridge La WA16,
SK9 . . . .**83** E5
Sandle Bridge Rise
WA16 . . . .**83** F6
SANDLOW GREEN **131** B1
Sandmoor Pl WA13 . . . .**19** A2
Sandon Cres CH64 . . . .**66** E5
Sandon Park Gdns
CW2 . . . .**189** D4
Sandon Pl WA8 . . . .**13** D1
Sandon Rd CH2 . . . .**118** E4
Sandon St WA1 . . . .**190** D4
Sandown Cl
Culcheth WA3 . . . .**4** F4
Middlewich CW10 . . . .**151** C8
Runcorn WA7 . . . .**49** C6
Wilmslow SK9 . . . .**60** D8
Sandown Cres CW8 . . . .**102** A3
Sandown Dr WA15 . . . .**32** D6
Sandown Pl SK11 . . . .**111** F7
Sandown Rd CW1 . . . .**190** C7
Sandown Reach CW5 . . . . . .**229** D7
Sandown Terr CH3 . . . .**118** F1
Sandpiper Cl
Chester CH4 . . . .**141** B2
Kidsgrove ST7 . . . .**195** C2
Sandpiper Way CH4 . . . .**141** B3
Sandra Dr WA12 . . . .**2** E3
Sandringham Ave
Chester CH3 . . . .**119** A2
Helsby WA6 . . . .**73** B4
Sandringham Cl
Altrincham WA14 . . . .**20** F1
Northwich CW9 . . . .**103** E4
Winsford CW7 . . . .**126** C3
Sandringham Ct
Golborne WA3 . . . .**3** E7
🟦 Wilmslow SK9 . . . .**60** A6
Sandringham Dr
Poynton SK12 . . . .**36** D3
Warrington WA5 . . . .**15** C4
Wistaston CW2 . . . .**205** E8
Sandringham Gdns 🟦
CH65 . . . .**70** D2
Sandringham Rd
Congleton CW12 . . . .**156** F4
Macclesfield SK10 . . . .**87** F1
Widnes WA8 . . . .**13** A4
Sandringham Way 🟦
SK9 . . . .**60** A6
Sandrock Rd CH3 . . . .**142** E7
Sandsdown Cl ST8 . . . .**179** C1
Sandside Rd ST7 . . . .**193** B3
Sands Rd ST7 . . . .**195** C6
Sandstone Mews WA8 . . . . . .**12** E4
Sandstone Wlk CH60 . . . .**41** A7
Sandwich Dr SK10 . . . .**87** C4
Sandwood Ave CH4 . . . .**139** B3
Sandybank CW8 . . . .**78** D1
Sandy Brow La WA3 . . . .**3** F7
Sandy Cl SK10 . . . .**87** F7

St J–Sax 277

SANDYCROFT **116** B2
Sandyfield Ct ST8 . . . .**179** C1
Sandyhill Pl 🟦 CW7 . . . . . .**149** C6
Sandyhill Rd CW7 . . . .**149** C6
Sandy La
Allostock CW4 . . . .**106** C1
Astbury CW12 . . . .**177** E6
Aston CW5 . . . .**217** C2
Bold Heath WA8 . . . .**14** B6
Brown Knowl CH3 . . . .**199** C7
Bulkeley SY14 . . . .**184** C1
Chester CH3 . . . .**119** A1
Congleton, Astbury Marsh
CW12 . . . .**177** E6
Congleton CW12 . . . .**155** D3
Croft WA3 . . . .**9** A8
Cronton WA8 . . . .**12** D5
Gohorne, Lowton Common
WA3 . . . .**4** A8
Golborne WA3 . . . .**2** F8
Goostrey CW4 . . . .**107** D1
Haslington CW11 . . . .**192** B7
Hatherton CW5 . . . .**219** F5
Helsby WA6 . . . .**73** B2
Higher Kinnerton CH44 . . . . . .**161** A6
Huntington CH3 . . . .**141** F8
Knutsford WA16 . . . .**57** A1
Lymm WA13 . . . .**19** B4
Macclesfield SK10 . . . .**86** C2
Neston CH64 . . . .**67** A7
Runcorn, Preston Brook
WA7 . . . .**50** F6
Runcorn WA7 . . . .**48** E7
Saighton CH3 . . . .**142** C3
Saltney CH4 . . . .**140** D6
Sandbach CW11 . . . .**174** D5
Swan Green WA16 . . . .**106** E6
Swettenham CW12 . . . .**131** F3
Tarvin CH3 . . . .**121** C4
Threapwood SY14 . . . .**222** E8
Warrington, Longford
WA2 . . . .**8** C2
Warrington, Penketh
WA5 . . . .**15** A4
Warrington, Stockton Heath
WA4 . . . .**26** D8
Weaverham CW8 . . . .**77** C2
Whitegate CW8 . . . .**125** D6
Wilmslow SK9 . . . .**59** E8
Sandylands Cres CW7 . . . . .**193** F5
Sandylands Pk CW2 . . . .**205** D7
Sandylane Mews
CW12 . . . .**156** C5
Sandy La W WA2 . . . .**8** B3
Sandymere Ct CW7 . . . .**126** B1
Sandymoor La WA7 . . . .**24** D3
Sandy Moor La WA7 . . . .**24** D3
Sandy Rd ST8 . . . .**179** C2
Sandy Way CW7 . . . .**149** B8
SANKEY BRIDGES **15** C4
Sankey Bridges Ind Est
WA5 . . . .**15** C4
Sankey for Penketh Sta
WA5 . . . .**14** F6
Sankey La WA4 . . . .**25** F1
Sankey St
Golborne WA3 . . . .**3** A8
Newton-le-W WA12 . . . .**2** A3
Warrington WA1 . . . .**16** A5
Widnes WA8 . . . .**23** A6
Sankey Valley Ind Est
WA12 . . . .**2** A2
Sankey Valley Pk
Newton le W WA5 . . . .**1** DJ
Warrington WA5 . . . .**15** D5
**Sankey Valley St James
CE Prim Sch** WA5 . . . .**15** C6
Sankey Way WA5 . . . .**15** D5
Santon Dr WA3 . . . .**3** E8
Sapling La CW6 . . . .**146** F3
Sark Ave CH65 . . . .**95** B8
Sark Ho CH2 . . . .**119** B4
Sarl Williams Ct CH1 . . . . . .**237** A3
Sarn Bank Rd SY14 . . . .**222** E6
Sarn Rd SY14 . . . .**222** D8
Sarra La CH3 . . . .**184** B5
Sarsfield Ave 🟦 WA3 . . . .**3** D8
Sarus Ct WA7 . . . .**24** B4
SAUGHALL **117** B8
Saughall Cl CW9 . . . .**103** E4
Saughall Hey CH1 . . . .**94** A1
Saughall Rd
Blacon, Abbot's Meads
CH1 . . . .**118** A4
Blacon CH1 . . . .**117** E5
Saundersfoot Cl WA5 . . . .**7** E2
Saunders St CW1 . . . .**190** B4
Saunderton Cl WA11 . . . .**1** C7
Savannah Pl 🟦 WA5 . . . .**15** C7
Saville Ave WA5 . . . .**15** F7
Saville St SK11 . . . .**112** E7
Savoy Rd CH4 . . . .**207** A8
Sawley Cl
Culcheth WA3 . . . .**5** A2
Runcorn WA7 . . . .**156** B2
Sawley Dr SK8 . . . .**35** C6
Sawpit St WA13, WA14 . . . . . .**20** A6
Sawyer Dr ST8 . . . .**179** C1
Saxon Cl WA4 . . . .**26** B5
Saxon Crossway CW7 . . . . .**126** B1
Saxon Rd WA7 . . . .**23** C2
Saxons La CW8 . . . .**103** D7
Saxon Terr 🟦 WA8 . . . .**23** B7

Saxon Way
Blacon CH1 . . . . .117 E6
6 Ellesmere Port CH66 . . 94 F8
Sandbach CW11 . . . . . . .175 C6
Sayce St WA8 . . . . .13 B1
Scafell Ave WA2 . . . . .8 C3
Scafell Cl
Bebington CH62 . . . . .43 D3
High Lane SK6 . . . . .37 E8
Scaife Rd CW5 . . . . .204 F5
Scaliot Cl SK22 . . . . .39 B8
Scar La SY14 . . . . .198 F1
Sceptre Cl WA12 . . . . .2 A3
SCHOLAR GREEN 194 E8
Scholar Green Prim Sch
ST7 . . . . .194 E6
Scholar Rise CW7 . . . . . .127 A7
Scholars Cl
Macclesfield SK10 . . . . . . .111 D8
Saltney CH4 . . . . .140 E6
Scholar's Ct 3 CH64 . . . . .66 E8
Scholars Green La
WA13 . . . . .18 F2
School Ave CH44 . . . . .66 F6
School Bank
Norley WA6 . . . . .101 A6
Wybunbury CW5 . . . . . . .220 B8
School Brow WA1 . . . . . . .16 C6
School Cl
Audley ST7 . . . . .210 A1
Knutsford WA16 . . . . .56 E1
Marbury SY13 . . . . .226 E8
Poynton SK12 . . . . .36 F3
School Cotts
Bradwall Green
CW11 . . . . .153 B4
Wimboldsley CW10 . . . . . .150 F4
School Cres CW1 . . . . . . .190 E4
School Dr
Barnton CW8 . . . . .78 A3
Lymm WA13 . . . . .19 C5
School Field Cl CW3 . . . . .230 F4
Schoolfold La SK10 . . . . . .63 A7
School Gn CH3 . . . . .182 C1
SCHOOL GREEN 149 C5
School Hos SK11 . . . . .109 A1
School House Cotts
CH66 . . . . .69 B6
School La
Aldford CH3 . . . . .163 F2
Antrobus CW9 . . . . .53 C3
Astbury CW12 . . . . .178 B8
Audlem CW3 . . . . .230 A4
Bold Heath WA8 . . . . .13 E7
Brereton Green CW11 . . . .153 F5
Bunbury CW6 . . . . .168 E1
Burwardsley CH3 . . . . . . .184 B6
Cuddington CW8 . . . . .102 A2
Eaton (nr Congleton)
CW12 . . . . .156 E8
Ellesmere Port CH66 . . . . . .69 A8
Elton CH2 . . . . .72 B3
Frodsham WA6 . . . . .74 C7
Great Budworth CW9 . . . . .79 B8
Guilden Sutton CH3 . . . . . .119 E5
Hartford CW8 . . . . .103 C4
Henbury SK11 . . . . .111 B6
Higher Whitley WA4 . . . . . .52 E6
Hollinfare WA3 . . . . .11 A2
Hooton CH66 . . . . .43 F1
Irlam, Cadishead M44 . . . . .11 D5
Lostock Gralam CW9 . . . . . .80 A2
Marbury WA16 . . . . .29 A4
Marton SK11 . . . . .133 C5
Mickle Trafford CH2 . . . . . .119 E8
Moulton CW9 . . . . .126 F8
4 Nantwich CW5 . . . . . . .204 E6
Neston CH64 . . . . .42 B2
Neston, Little Neston
CH64 . . . . .66 F6
Neston, Parkgate CH64 . . . .41 B1
Nether Alderley SK10 . . . . .86 A6
Norbury SY13 . . . . .215 E2
Norley WA6 . . . . .100 D5
Ollerton WA16 . . . . .83 B4
Onneley CW3 . . . . .232 F3
Partington WA14 . . . . .20 D5
Poynton SK12 . . . . .36 F4
Runcorn WA7 . . . . .49 F8
Sandbach CW11 . . . . .49 A2
Sandbach Heath CW11 . . . .175 E6
Smallwood CW11 . . . . . . .176 F5
Warmingham CW11 . . . . . .173 E7
Warrington WA3 . . . . .10 D5
School Mews SK7 . . . . . . .35 E7
School Rd
Ellesmere Port CH65 . . . . . .70 B5
Handforth SK9 . . . . .34 D4
Higher Shurlach CW9 . . . . .104 D5
Warrington WA2 . . . . .8 C1
Winsford, Meadowbank
CW7 . . . . .126 C5
Winsford, Wharton
CW7 . . . . .127 A2
School Rd N CW9 . . . . . . .104 E6
School Rd S CW9 . . . . . . .104 E6
School St
Chester CH2 . . . . .118 F3
Golborne WA3 . . . . .3 A8
Haslington CW1 . . . . .191 D5
Newton-le-W WA12 . . . . . . .2 B3
Warrington WA4 . . . . .16 B4
School Terr WA3 . . . . .3 A8

School Way
Northwich CW9 . . . . .104 A8
Widnes WA8 . . . . .13 D3
Schooner Cl WA7 . . . . .50 D6
Scilly Cl CH5 . . . . .70 C1
Scope Ho CW1 . . . . .190 C1
Scotch Hall La CW9 . . . . . .53 A3
Scotia Wlk 1 WA3 . . . . . . .3 F8
Scotland Rd WA1 . . . . .16 B5
Scott Ave
Crewe CW1 . . . . .190 F4
Widnes WA8 . . . . .22 F8
Scott Cl
Macclesfield SK10 . . . . . . .113 A7
Rode Heath ST7 . . . . .193 E8
2 Sandbach CW11 . . . . .174 D6
Scott Ct WA2 . . . . .16 B6
Scotthope Cl SK11 . . . . . .111 F6
Scotton Ave CH66 . . . . . . .69 B5
Scott Rd SK10 . . . . .87 A7
Scotts Ind Est WA5 . . . . . .16 A7
Scott St WA2 . . . . .16 C6
Scott Wlk WA12 . . . . .2 C1
Scroggins La M31 . . . . .11 F4
Sea Bank CW10 . . . . .128 D1
Seabank Rd CH60 . . . . . . .40 E6
Seabury St WA4 . . . . .17 A3
Seacombe Dr CH66 . . . . . . .69 E3
Seafield Ave CH60 . . . . . . .40 E6
Seaford Cl WA7 . . . . .24 D1
Seaford Pl WA2 . . . . .8 A4
Seagrave Cl CW9 . . . . . . .103 F5
Seagull Cl CW11 . . . . .190 F5
Seahill Rd CH1 . . . . .116 F8
Sea La WA7 . . . . .23 D2
SEALAND 116 E6
Sealand Cl WA2 . . . . .8 E1
Sealand Ind Est CH1 . . . . .117 F2
Sealand Rd
Blacon CH1 . . . . .117 C3
Chester CH1 . . . . .118 A2
Sealand CH1, CH5 . . . . . .116 D6
Sealand Trad Pk CH1 . . . . .117 F2
Sealand Way 2 SK9 . . . . . .34 D4
Seal Rd SK7 . . . . .36 A7
Seathwaite Cl WA7 . . . . . . .49 E5
Seaton Cl CW1 . . . . .190 B8
Seaton Pk WA7 . . . . .24 E3
Seaton St CW7 . . . . .127 D1
Seattle Cl 3 WA5 . . . . .15 B7
Sea View CH64 . . . . .66 E4
Seaview Ave CH62 . . . . .44 B6
Seaville St CH3 . . . . .237 C3
Secker Ave WA4 . . . . .16 D2
Secker Cl WA4 . . . . .16 D2
Second Ave
Connah's Quay CH5 . . . . . .92 F3
Crewe CW1 . . . . .190 F2
Kidsgrove ST7 . . . . .194 E1
Poynton SK12 . . . . .36 D1
Runcorn WA7 . . . . .49 F8
Sandbach CW11 . . . . .175 A5
Second Dig La CW5 . . . . .219 C8
Second Wood St
CW5 . . . . .204 D5
Sedbergh Cl CW4 . . . . . . .130 A3
Sedbergh Gr WA7 . . . . .49 E5
Seddon St CW10 . . . . .128 C2
Sedgefield Cl 3 SK10 . . . .87 C4
Sedgefield Rd CH1 . . . . . .118 B2
Sedgeford Cl SK9 . . . . .34 D1
Sedgewick Cres WA5 . . . . . .6 E6
Sedgmere Ave CW1 . . . . .190 A8
Sedum Cl CH3 . . . . .142 A6
Sefton Ave
Congleton CW12 . . . . .157 A1
Widnes WA8 . . . . .13 A3
Sefton Dr SK9 . . . . .34 C2
Sefton Rd CH2 . . . . .119 A4
Sefton St WA12 . . . . .1 F3
Selby Cl
Poynton SK12 . . . . .36 D5
Runcorn WA7 . . . . .24 F4
Selby Gdns SK8 . . . . .35 C6
Selby Gn CH66 . . . . .69 B5
Selby St WA5 . . . . .15 E5
Selkirk Ave
Bebington CH62 . . . . .43 E4
Warrington WA4 . . . . .17 A3
Selkirk Dr
Ellesmere Port CH66 . . . . . .68 F5
Macclesfield SK10 . . . . . . .86 F2
Selkirk Rd
Chester CH4 . . . . .141 A7
Holmes Chapel CW4 . . . . .130 B2
Selkirk Rd CH4 . . . . .141 A7
Seller St CH1 . . . . .237 C3
Selsdon Ct CH4 . . . . .141 C7
Selsey Cl CW11 . . . . .190 B8
Selworthy Dr
Crewe CW1 . . . . .190 B7
Warrington WA4 . . . . .17 D3
Selwyn Cl
Newton-le-W WA12 . . . . . . .2 B5
Widnes WA8 . . . . .13 E3
Selwyn Dr
Cheadle SK8 . . . . .35 C7
Sutton Lane Ends SK11 . . .112 F3
Semper Cl CW12 . . . . .157 A4
Seneschal Ct WA7 . . . . . . .49 E6
Senna La CW9 . . . . .78 C8
Sennen Cl WA7 . . . . .50 C5
Sens Cl CH1 . . . . .237 A2
Sephton Ave WA3 . . . . .4 E3
Serin Cl WA12 . . . . .2 C3
Serpentine The CH4 . . . . .141 B7
Servite Cl CH65 . . . . .69 F6
Servite Pl CH64 . . . . .66 E7

Sell Cl SK22 . . . . .39 B0
Sevenoaks Cl SK10 . . . . . .87 B2
Seven Row CH64 . . . . .66 E5
Seven Sisters La WA16 . . .82 E5
Severn Cl
Biddulph ST8 . . . . .179 E1
Congleton CW12 . . . . .156 F1
Macclesfield SK10 . . . . . . .86 F2
Warrington WA2 . . . . .8 E5
Widnes WA8 . . . . .13 F3
Severn Dr SK7 . . . . .35 C6
Severn Rd WA3 . . . . .4 F7
Severnvale CH65 . . . . .70 B3
Severn Wlk CW7 . . . . .127 A2
Sewell St 7 WA7 . . . . .23 B2
Sextant Cl WA7 . . . . .50 D6
Sexton Ave WA9 . . . . .1 B4
Seymour Chase WA16 . . . .82 A8
Seymour Cl WA7 . . . . .24 C4
Seymour Dr
Ellesmere Port CH66 . . . . . .69 E6
Warrington WA1 . . . . .17 A8
Seymour Ho 10 SK9 . . . . . .34 E1
Sgt York Loop WA5 . . . . . .15 B6
Shackleton Cl WA5 . . . . . . .15 D8
Shade Terr SK6 . . . . .37 F7
Shadowood Cres WA4 . . . .17 B2
Shadowood Rd SK11 . . . . .112 A6
Shadowmoss Rd M22 . . . . .33 E8
Shady Brook La CW8 . . . . .77 C1
Shady Gr ST7 . . . . .193 D4
Shaftesbury Ave
Chester CH3 . . . . .119 C2
Warrington WA5 . . . . .14 E2
Shaftesbury Way WA5 . . . . .6 F7
Shaftway Cl WA11 . . . . .1 F7
Shakerley Ave CW12 . . . . .156 F3
Shakespeare Cl CW9 . . . .104 C7
Shakespeare Dr CW1 . . . .191 A4
Shakespeare Rd
Neston CH64 . . . . .41 E1
Widnes WA8 . . . . .13 A1
Shalcombe Cl L26 . . . . . . .21 A7
Shallacres CH65 . . . . .69 F7
Shallcross Ave SK23 . . . . . .65 F4
Shallcross Cres SK23 . . . . .65 F4
Shallcross Hall Barns
SK23 . . . . .65 E4
Shallcross Mill Rd
SK23 . . . . .65 E5
Shambles The WA16 . . . . . .57 B1
Shanklin Cl WA5 . . . . .14 C6
Shannon Cl
Chester CH4 . . . . .140 E5
Willaston CW5 . . . . .205 D6
Shannon Gr WA8 . . . . .12 E2
Shargate Cl SK9 . . . . .34 C1
Sharnbrook Dr CW2 . . . . .189 D4
Sharon Park Cl WA4 . . . . . .17 C1
Sharpley St 11 SK10 . . . . .112 C8
Sharp St
Warrington WA2 . . . . .16 C6
Widnes WA8 . . . . .23 A8
Sharston Cres WA16 . . . . . .57 B1
SHAVINGTON 206 C5
Shavington Ave CH2 . . . . .118 F4
Shavington High Sch
CW2 . . . . .206 A5
Shavington Prim Sch
CW2 . . . . .206 A5
Shavington Way CW9 . . . .103 F4
Shawbury Gr WA1 . . . . .17 A8
Shaw Cl CH66 . . . . .69 E4
Shaw Dr WA16 . . . . .57 C3
Shawell St WA8 . . . . .13 E2
Shaw Entry L35, WA8 . . . . .12 A7
SHAW HEATH 57 D3
Shaw Heath View
WA16 . . . . .57 C3
Shaw's Ave WA2 . . . . .16 C8
Shaws Fold SK9 . . . . .33 F3
Shaws La
Winsford CW7 . . . . .126 F4
Winsford, Wharton
CW7 . . . . .127 A3
Shaw St
Culcheth WA3 . . . . .5 A3
Haydock WA11 . . . . .1 E6
Macclesfield SK11 . . . . . . .112 C8
Runcorn WA7 . . . . .22 F2
Shay La
Ashton Hayes CH3 . . . . . . .121 F7
Hampton Heath SY14 . . . .200 A1
Tarvin CH3 . . . . .121 E3
Shay's La CW6 . . . . .124 E4
Sheaf Cl CH3 . . . . .121 C2
Shearbrook La CW4 . . . . . .107 E1
Sheardhall Ave SK12 . . . . .38 E5
Sheath St CW9 . . . . .104 A8
Shed La CH3 . . . . .183 C7
Sheepfield Cl CH66 . . . . . .69 C7
Sheerwater Cl WA1 . . . . . . .17 A7
Sheffield Cl WA5 . . . . .15 C5
Sheffield Row WA12 . . . . . .7 D8
Sheilings The WA3 . . . . .3 F8
Shelagh Ave WA8 . . . . .13 A1
Shelbourne Mews 2
SK10 . . . . .111 F8
Shelburne Dr CW1 . . . . . .191 C5
Sheldon Ave
Chester CH3 . . . . .119 B2
Congleton CW12 . . . . .157 A1
Sheldon Cl M31 . . . . .11 F3
Sheldon Dr SK11 . . . . .112 B4
Sheldon Pl SK10 . . . . .88 B8

Sheldon Rd
Hazel Grove SK7 . . . . .36 E8
Poynton SK12 . . . . .37 C2
Sheldrake Gr CH64 . . . . . . .66 F5
Shellbrook Dr 3 SK9 . . . . .34 D1
Shelley Ave CW9 . . . . .80 A5
Shelley Cl
Crewe CW1 . . . . .190 F4
Middlewich CW10 . . . . . . .151 E5
Rode Heath ST7 . . . . .193 E8
Shelley Ct 5 CW11 . . . . . .174 D6
Shelley Dr CW2 . . . . .189 F1
Shelley Gr WA4 . . . . .16 F4
Shelley Rd
Blacon CH1 . . . . .117 F6
Widnes WA8 . . . . .13 A1
SHELL GREEN 13 E1
Shell Green Est WA8 . . . . . .23 E8
Shellow La CW12,
SK11, ...134 C5
Shellway Rd CH2 . . . . .71 A3
Shelton Cl WA8 . . . . .13 F3
Shenhurst Cl WA9 . . . . .59 E4
Shepcroft La WA4 . . . . .26 C3
Shepherds Fold Dr
CW7 . . . . .126 C3
Shepherd's La CH2 . . . . . .118 D5
Shepherds Row WA7 . . . . .23 F2
Shepherds View CW8 . . . . .78 B2
Shepley Cl SK7 . . . . .36 D8
Sheppard Cl CW1 . . . . . . .190 D5
Sheppenhall Gr CW5 . . . . .217 C1
Sheppenhall La CW5,
SY13 . . . . .228 D5
Shepperton Cl WA4 . . . . . . .26 E6
Shepsides Cl CH66 . . . . . . .69 C3
Shepton Rd CH66 . . . . .69 E2
Sheraton Rd CH3 . . . . . . .143 B5
Sherborne Cl WA7 . . . . . . .24 F3
Sherborne Cl SK8 . . . . .35 B6
Sherbourne Rd
Ellesmere Port CH65 . . . . . .70 D3
Macclesfield SK11 . . . . . . .111 F7
Sherbourne Way WA5 . . . . . .6 F6
Sherbrooke Rd SK12 . . . . .38 D6
Sherbrook Rise SK9 . . . . . .60 C6
Sheridan Ave WA3 . . . . .3 A8
Sheridan Cl CW1 . . . . .173 B1
Sheridan Pl WA2 . . . . .8 A5
Sheridan Way WA7 . . . . . . .24 D2
Sheri Dr WA12 . . . . .2 C3
Sheringham Cl CH4 . . . . . .140 E5
Sheringham Dr CW1 . . . . .190 B8
Sheringham Rd WA5 . . . . . .14 E6
Sherlock Ave WA11 . . . . . . .1 E7
Sherratt Cl
Congleton CW12 . . . . .156 E2
Nantwich CW5 . . . . .204 F4
Sherrington's La CH3 . . . . .199 D8
Sherwin St CW2 . . . . .190 C1
Sherwood Cl WA8 . . . . .12 C1
Sherwood Cres WA5 . . . . . . .6 E6
Sherwood Gr WA6 . . . . .73 A3
Sherwood Rd
Chester CH4 . . . . .117 E5
Macclesfield SK11 . . . . . . .112 D5
Shetland Cl
Warrington WA2 . . . . .8 E4
Widnes WA8 . . . . .13 E3
Shetland Dr
Bebington CH62 . . . . .43 E8
Ellesmere Port CH65 . . . . . .70 C1
Shevington Cl WA8 . . . . . . .13 E3
Shevington Wlk WA8 . . . . .13 E3
Shiggins Cl WA5 . . . . .15 D6
Shillingford Cl WA4 . . . . . . .26 E5
Shilton Cl CW10 . . . . .151 E5
Shipbrook Rd
Chester CH2 . . . . .118 F6
Davenham CW9 . . . . .104 C3
Northwich CW9 . . . . .104 C6
Shipgate St CH1 . . . . .237 B1
Shipgate The CH1 . . . . . . .237 B1
Shipley Gdns ST7 . . . . . . .210 D6
Ship St WA6 . . . . .49 C1
Shipton Cl
Warrington WA5 . . . . .15 B8
Widnes WA8 . . . . .12 D3
Shirley Ave SK8 . . . . .34 C6
Shirley Dr WA4 . . . . .17 D2
Shirley Gr SK10 . . . . .87 A6
Shirleys Dr SK10 . . . . .87 A6
SHOCKLACH 211 D7
SHOCKLACH GREEN 211 C7
Shocklach Oviatt CE Prim
Sch SY14 . . . . .211 C7
Shocklach Rd CH2 . . . . . .118 F6
Shones Croft CH64 . . . . . . .67 A5
Shop La
Congleton CW12 . . . . .156 E1
Little Budworth CW6 . . . . .124 F2
Shopping Precinct The
CH2 . . . . .72 B3
Shoreham Dr WA5 . . . . . . .15 A3
Shores Green Dr CW9 . . . .79 F5
Shores La CW5 . . . . .203 D7
Short Cl WA12 . . . . .2 C3
Shorthorn Cl CW10 . . . . . .128 D2
Short St
Haydock WA11 . . . . .1 E6
11 Macclesfield SK11 . . . .112 D8
Newton-le-W WA12 . . . . . . .1 E3
Widnes WA8 . . . . .23 A5
Shot Tower Cl CH1 . . . . . .237 C3
SHOTWICK 93 B4

Shotwick La CH1 . . . . .93 D6
Shotwick Rd CH5 . . . . .92 F3
SHRALEYBROOK 209 A1
Shrewbridge Cres
CW5 . . . . .204 E4
Shrewbridge Rd CW5 . . . .204 D4
Shrewsbury Dr SY5 . . . . . .210 E2
Shrewsbury Gdns SK8 . . . .35 C6
Shrewsbury Rd 4
CH65 . . . . .70 C5
Shrewsbury St WA4 . . . . . .16 D3
Shrewsbury Way CH44 . . .140 F6
Shrigley Cl SK9 . . . . .34 D1
Shrigley Cl SK10 . . . . .88 B8
Shrigley Rd SK10 . . . . .63 B5
Shrigley Rd N SK12 . . . . . .37 C3
Shrigley Rd S SK10,
SK12 . . . . .37 C2
Shrigley Rise SK10 . . . . . . .63 C1
Shropshire Cl
Middlewich CW10 . . . . . . .151 C8
Warrington WA1 . . . . .17 E1
Shropshire La SY13 . . . . . .227 E2
Shropshire Rd CH2 . . . . . . .70 F3
Shropshire St CW3 . . . . . .229 F4
Shuldham Cl CH64 . . . . . . .66 E8
Shurlach Rd CW9 . . . . . . .104 D6
Shutley La CW8 . . . . .77 D6
Shutlingsloe Way
SK10 . . . . .112 A8
Sibberdsfield La CH3 . . . . .180 F4
Sibell St CH1 . . . . .237 C3
Siddall St 1 CW9 . . . . . . .104 B8
Siddals Ct CW5 . . . . .204 C5
Siddeley Cl CH4 . . . . .139 C4
Siddeley Dr WA12 . . . . .1 F4
SIDDINGTON 110 A4
Siddington Ave CW9 . . . . .104 A4
SIDDINGTON HEATH
. . . . .109 E1
Siddington Rd
Handforth SK9 . . . . .34 D5
Poynton SK12 . . . . .36 F2
Siddorn St CW7 . . . . .126 E1
Side End La SK23 . . . . .64 F3
Side La CW6 . . . . .144 E6
Sidings Ct WA1 . . . . .16 C6
Sidings The SK23 . . . . .65 C8
Sidlaw Cl CH66 . . . . .69 A6
Sidmouth Cl WA5 . . . . .14 E4
Sidmouth Gr SK8 . . . . .34 F7
Sidney Cl CH64 . . . . .41 F1
Sidney Rd CH64 . . . . .41 F1
Siemens Rd M44 . . . . .11 E5
Sienna Cl M44 . . . . .11 E6
Signal Ct CH2 . . . . .118 F2
Silk Hill SK23 . . . . .65 F8
Silk Mill
Macclesfield SK11 . . . . . . .112 D6
Poynton SK12 . . . . .36 C4
Silk Mill WA16 . . . . .57 A2
**Silk Mus Heritage Ctr*
SK11 . . . . .112 D7
Silk Rd The
Bollington SK10 . . . . .87 E4
Macclesfield SK10 . . . . . . .112 E7
Silk St CW12 . . . . .156 C2
Silkstone Cres WA7 . . . . . .50 B7
Silsden Ave WA3 . . . . .4 B8
Silvan Ct SK10 . . . . .87 B1
Silver Ave WA11 . . . . .1 A5
Silverbirch Croft CH4 . . . .139 B3
Silverbirch Way CH66 . . . . .94 F8
Silverdale CW8 . . . . .103 D7
Silverdale Cl
Chorlton CW2 . . . . .207 C2
Frodsham WA6 . . . . .74 C7
High Lane SK6 . . . . .37 E8
Silverdale Dr SK9 . . . . .60 A4
Silverdale Rd
Newton-le-W WA12 . . . . . . .2 B4
Warrington WA4 . . . . .16 B2
Silvergate Ct WA12 . . . . . .178 E8
Silver La
Croft WA3 . . . . .9 F7
Warrington WA3 . . . . .10 C6
Silvermine Cl 8 ST7 . . . . .195 B2
Silvermuir CH1 . . . . .117 E3
Silverne Dr CH65 . . . . .70 A2
Silver St
Bollington SK10 . . . . .88 B8
Congleton CW12 . . . . .156 E2
Warrington WA2 . . . . .16 B6
Silver Terr CW13 . . . . .175 D6
Silverwood ST7 . . . . .195 B1
Simkin Ave WA4 . . . . .16 F4
Simmonds Cl CW9 . . . . . .103 E3
SIMM'S CROSS 23 B8
Simms Cross Prim Sch
WA8 . . . . .23 A8
Simonside WA8 . . . . .12 C2
Simons La WA6 . . . . .74 B5
Simonstone Rd CH4 . . . . .139 D4
Simonswood Cl CW10 . . .151 B8
Simpson Cl CW2 . . . . .95 C1
Simpson Ct CW1 . . . . .173 B1
Simpson La SK10 . . . . .63 D7
Simpson Rd CH2 . . . . .95 C1
Simpson's Ct 17 SK11 . . . .112 C8
Simpson St WA9 . . . . .59 F6
Simpson Way CW4 . . . . . .139 B3
Sinclair Ave
Alsager ST7 . . . . .193 B3
Warrington WA2 . . . . .8 B2
Widnes WA8 . . . . .23 A8
Sinderland La
Partington WA13 . . . . .20 B8
Partington WA13 . . . . .20 B8

Singleton Ave M90 . . . . . . .33 A8
Singleton Ave CW1 . . . . . . 190 C6
Singleton Rd CH65. . . . . . . .69 F4
SINK MOSS 28 D3
Sir John Deane's Coll
CW9 . . . . 103 F6
Sir Thomas Boteler CE
High Sch WA4 . . . . .16 E3
Siskin Cl WA12 . . . . .2 C3
Six Acre Gdns WA4 . . . . . . .25 A5
Six Acre La WA4 . . . . .25 A5
Sixth Ave CH5 . . . . 92 E1
Skeath Cl CW11 . . . . 175 E6
Skellern St ST7 . . . . 194 D2
SKELLORN GREEN 62 E8
Skellorn Green La
SK10. . . . . .62 F8
Skiddaw Cl WA7 . . . . .50 A4
Skip's La CH3 . . . . 142 F7
Skipton Cl
Hazel Grove SK7 . . . . .36 C8
Runcorn WA7 . . . . .23 F1
Skipton Dr CH66. . . . . .69 C5
Skye Cl
Ellesmere Port CH65. . . . .70 C1
Widnes WA8 . . . . 13 E3
Skylark Cl CW1. . . . . 189 F7
Sky Lark Rise WA9. . . . . .1 A3
Slacken La ST7 . . . . 194 D2
Slack St SK11 . . . . 112 E6
Slade La
Mobberley WA16. . . . . . . .58 A7
Nether Alderley SK10 . . . .85 E5
Slade St **5** CW9. . . . . . . 104 B8
Slag La
Golborne WA3 . . . . 3 D8
Haydock WA11 . . . . 1 B7
Slater St
Macclesfield SK11 . . . . . . 112 C6
Warrington WA4 . . . . 16 D3
Slicks Bsns Ctr CW8 . . . . . .78 C2
Slindon Cl ST5 . . . . 210 D1
Slutchers La WA1 . . . . .16 A3
Small Ave WA2 . . . . .8 C2
Smallbrook Wlk CW2 . . . . 206 C8
Small Cres WA2 . . . . .8 C2
Small La WA16 . . . . .58 A8
Smallman Rd CW2 . . . . 190 C1
SMALLWOOD 176 F5
Smallwood CE Prim Sch
CW11. . . . . 176 F5
Smallwood Cl
4 Middlewich CW10 . . . 151 C8
Newcastle-u-Lyme ST5 . . 210 D1
Smallwood Ct **1**
CW12. . . . . 156 F3
Smallwood Forge
CW11. . . . . 176 D5
Smeaton Wood CW5. . . . . .216 E2
SMETHWICK GREEN 154 F4
Smethwick La CW11,
CW12. . . . . 154 E4
Smith Cl ST7 . . . . 193 B4
Smith Cres WA2 . . . . .16 D8
Smith Dr WA2 . . . . .16 D8
Smithers Cl CW5. . . . . 204 F4
Smithfield Dr/Ffordd
Smithfield LL13 . . . . 196 D8
Smithfield Gn LL13 . . . . . . 196 D8
Smithfield La CW11 . . . . . . 175 C6
Smithfields CH3 . . . . 166 C2
Smithfield St LL13 . . . . 196 D8
Smith Gr CW1 . . . . 190 A6
Smithills Cl WA3 . . . . .9 D5
Smith La
Mobberley WA16. . . . . . . .57 F6
Rainow SK10 . . . . .89 A5
Smith Rd WA8 . . . . .22 F7
Smiths Cotts CH64. . . . . . . .66 E5
SMITHS GREEN 109 A2
SMITH'S GREEN 208 B7
Smith's La CW8 . . . . .77 C1
Smiths Lawn SK9. . . . . .60 A5
Smith St
Macclesfield SK11 . . . . . . 112 D6
Warrington WA1 . . . . 16 B5
Smith's Terr SK11. . . . . 112 E6
Smithy Bank
Acton CW5. . . . . 204 A6
Winsford CW7. . . . . 149 A3
Smithy Brow
Bollington SK10. . . . . .88 C8
Winwick WA3. . . . . .8 F7
Smithy Cl
Cronton WA8 . . . . 12 C5
Neston CH64 . . . . .67 A4
Saughall CH1. . . . . .94 A1
Shocklach SY14 . . . . 211 E7
Smithy Cotts SY14 . . . . 213 A2
Smithy Ct
Christleton CH3 . . . . 142 E7
Duddon CW6 . . . . 145 C5
5 Ellesmere Port CH66. . .69 C6
Smithy Dr WA14. . . . . .20 D3
Smithy Gn
Cheadle SK8 . . . . .35 A8
Gatesheath CH3 . . . . 165 E5
Smithy Gr CW11 . . . . 176 A2
SMITHY GREEN
Cheadle Hulme 35 B7
Lower Peover 81 E2
Smithy Hill CH63 . . . . .42 A6
Smithy La
Alsager CW2 . . . . 208 D7
Altrincham WA14. . . . . . . .20 D3
Barthomley CW2 . . . . 208 C6
Biddulph ST8 . . . . 179 D2
Bosley SK11. . . . . 158 F1

Smithy La continued
Broxton CH3 . . . . 183 D1
Congleton CW12 . . . . 156 C7
Crewe CW1 . . . . 189 E8
Croft WA3 . . . . .9 A7
Cronton WA8 . . . . 12 C5
Cuddington CW8 . . . . 102 A5
Ellesmere Port CH66. . . . .69 C6
Great Budworth CW9 . . . .79 A8
Helsby WA6. . . . . .73 C5
Kingsley WA6. . . . . .75 B2
Little Leigh CW8 . . . . .77 B6
Lostock Gralam CW9. . . . .80 A2
Malpas SY14 . . . . 213 A2
Mottram St Andrew
SK10 . . . . .61 C2
Mouldsworth CH3 . . . . . . .98 F2
Partington M31 . . . . 11 F3
Rainow SK10 . . . . .88 E5
Utkinton CW6 . . . . 146 C6
Weston CW2 . . . . 207 C5
Willaston CH64 . . . . .68 A7
Smithy Pathway CH4. . . . . 140 F4
Smithy The CH2 . . . . 118 E8
Smithy Wlk CW11. . . . . 174 F3
Smokehall La CW7,
CW9. . . . . 126 F6
Smokehall Lane Ind Est
CW7. . . . . 127 A5
Smokey La SY13 . . . . 224 A1
Smokies Way ST8. . . . . 179 C1
Smyth Rd WA8 . . . . 13 D2
Snab La
Neston CH64 . . . . .66 F4
Norbury SY13 . . . . 215 B5
Snabwood Cl CH64 . . . . . . .66 E5
Snaefell Rise WA4 . . . . .26 C7
Snapebrook Gr **6** SK9. . .34 E1
Snape Hollow CW2 . . . . . . 207 F4
Snape La CW2 . . . . 207 E4
Snape Rd
Crewe CW2 . . . . 206 D8
Macclesfield SK10 . . . . . . .87 E2
Snelson La
Chelford, Marthall WA16,
SK9. . . . . .83 D3
Chelford SK11. . . . . 108 E7
Snipe Cl SK12 . . . . .36 A4
Snowberry Cl WA8. . . . . . . .13 E4
Snowberry Cres WA5 . . . . . 15 E3
Snowberry Way **5**
CH66 . . . . .94 F8
Snowberry Wlk M31 . . . . . . 11 E3
Snowdon Cl
Ellesmere Port CH66. . . . .69 A6
Warrington WA5 . . . . 14 E6
Snowdon Cres CH4. . . . . . . 141 A5
Snowdon Dr CW2 . . . . 189 D3
Snowdonia Way CW7 . . . . 149 B7
Snowdon St CW8 . . . . .77 F3
Snowdrop Cl WA7 . . . . .49 F4
SNOW HILL 204 D6
Snow Hill SK11 . . . . 112 E6
Solly Cres CW12 . . . . 156 A2
Solvay Rd CW8 . . . . .78 D1
Solway Cl WA2 . . . . .8 F4
Solway Ct CW1 . . . . 191 A2
Solway Gr WA7 . . . . .49 D5
SOMERFORD 154 F7
Somerford Ave CW2 . . . . . 190 A3
Somerford Cl CW11 . . . . . . 175 C8
Somerford Ct **2**
CW12. . . . . 156 F3
Somerford Ho SK12 . . . . . . .36 E4
Somerford Rd CH4. . . . . . . 139 C4
Somerford Way **3** SK9. .34 E5
Somerford Wlk CW8. . . . . . 13 E3
Somerley Cl CW11. . . . . 190 B8
Somerset Ave ST7 . . . . 194 F2
Somerset Cl
Congleton CW12 . . . . 156 D4
Irlam M44 . . . . 11 D6
Somerset Rd CH2 . . . . 118 F5
Somerset St CH1. . . . . 237 B4
Somerset Way WA11 . . . . . . 17 B8
Somerton Gr **5** SK11 . . 111 F7
Somerton Rd SK11. . . . . . . 111 F7
Somerville Cl
Bebington CH63. . . . . .43 B6
High Legh WA16 . . . . .29 C4
Neston CH64 . . . . .66 E5
Somerville Cres CH65. . . . .70 C4
Somerville Rd WA8 . . . . . . .22 D8
Somerville St CW2 . . . . 190 B2
Soot Hill CW8, CW9 . . . . . . .78 C3
Sorbus Cl CH2 . . . . .72 C3
Sorbus Dr CW1. . . . . 190 E6
Sorby Rd M44 . . . . 11 F7
Sorrel Cl
Huntington CH3 . . . . 142 A6
Warrington WA2 . . . . .9 C2
Soss Moss Hospl (Mary
Dendy Unit) SK10 . . . . . .84 C6
Sossmoss La SK10. . . . . . . .84 D6
SOUND 217 F5
Sound & District Prim Sch
CW5. . . . . 217 F5
SOUND HEATH 217 E5
Sound La
Ravensmoor CW5 . . . . 203 E1
Sound CW5 . . . . 217 D7
Souter's La CH1 . . . . 237 B2
South Acre Dr
Handforth SK9. . . . . .34 D3
Macclesfield SK11 . . . . . . 113 A7
Southampton Way
WA7 . . . . .50 E6

South Ave
Chester CH2 . . . . 237 C4
Haslington CW1. . . . . 191 D4
Warrington, Stockton Heath
WA4 . . . . .16 C1
Warrington WA2 . . . . 16 B8
Southbank CW9 . . . . .79 A7
South Bank CH3 . . . . 118 C4
Southbank Ave CW2 . . . . . 206 C5
South Bank Cl SK9 . . . . . . .60 B2
South Bank Gr CW12 . . . . 156 F2
South Bank Terr WA7 . . . . .22 F3
South Cheshire Coll
CW2. . . . . 190 B2
South Cheshire Private
Hospl The CW1. . . . . 172 E1
South Cl
Tarporley CW6. . . . . 146 C2
Wilmslow SK9 . . . . .59 F6
South Crescent Rd
CH4 . . . . 237 C1
South Croft CW6 . . . . 185 D6
South Crofts CW5 . . . . 204 F5
South Dale WA5 . . . . 14 F5
Southdale Rd WA1. . . . . . . .17 A7
Southdown Cl SK10 . . . . . . .87 D4
Southdown Cres SK8 . . . . .34 F8
South Downs WA16 . . . . . . .57 C1
South Downs Dr WA14. . . .31 D8
South Downs Rd WA14. . . .31 E8
South Dr
Heswall CH60 . . . . .41 A7
Northwich CW9 . . . . 104 D6
Plumley WA16 . . . . .80 F3
Wilmslow SK9 . . . . .60 B6
Southern St WA4 . . . . 16 C1
Southey Cl
8 Sandbach CW11 . . . . 174 D6
Widnes WA8 . . . . .22 F8
Southfield SK10 . . . . .87 A4
Southfield Cl SK9 . . . . .34 C3
Southfield Rd CH66 . . . . . . .69 C7
Southfields WA16. . . . . .57 C3
Southfields Ave WA5. . . . . . 14 F6
Southfields Cl CW5 . . . . . . 220 A8
South Gn CH5 . . . . 116 A6
South Gr **10** SK9. . . . . . . .60 A1
South La
Warrington WA5, WA8. . . . 14 E5
Widnes WA8 . . . . .13 F4
Southlands CW4 . . . . 130 C2
Southlands Ave WA5. . . . . . 14 F3
Southlands Ct
9 Runcorn WA7 . . . . .22 F1
Runcorn WA7. . . . . .48 F8
Southlands Mews **8**
WA7 . . . . .22 F1
Southlands Rd CW12. . . . . 157 A1
Southlands View
CW4 . . . . 107 E1
South Lane Entry WA8 . . . 13 F5
Southlawn SK9 . . . . .60 A5
South Lo CW6 . . . . 168 D8
South Mead SK12. . . . . .36 A5
South Meadway SK6. . . . . .37 F7
South Oak La SK9 . . . . .59 F5
South Park Dr SK6 . . . . .37 A5
South Park Dr SK12. . . . . . .36 E5
South Park Rd SK11 . . . . . . 112 C7
South Pier Rd CH65 . . . . . .70 D7
Southport St WA9 . . . . .1 A3
South Rd
Altrincham, Ashley Heath
WA14 . . . . .31 E8
Ellesmere Port CH65. . . . .70 C3
Halewood L24 . . . . .21 A4
Runcorn WA7. . . . . .48 D7
Stanlow CH65. . . . . .70 F4
South St
Alderley Edge SK9. . . . . . .60 A1
Chester CH3 . . . . 119 A1
Congleton CW12 . . . . 156 D3
Crewe CW2 . . . . 190 D2
Mount Pleasant ST7 . . . . 195 B6
3 Widnes WA8 . . . . .23 B8
South Terr **14** SK9. . . . . .60 A1
South View
Chester CH4 . . . . 141 D7
Christleton CH3 . . . . 142 F7
Lower Withington SK11. . 132 A8
New Mills SK22 . . . . .39 B8
South View Ave SK11. . . . . 111 D2
South View Cotts ST7 . . . . 193 F4
South View La CW7 . . . . . . 170 F2
South View Rd CH1 . . . . . . 118 B2
Southward Rd WA11. . . . . . .2 A7
Southwark Pl CW7. . . . . . . 149 A8
Southway
Middlewich CW10 . . . . . . 128 C1
Wilmslow SK9 . . . . .60 A5
Widnes WA8 . . . . .22 D8
South Way CH1 . . . . 117 F4
Southway Ave WA4 . . . . . . .26 D7
Southwell Cl WA3 . . . . .3 C8
South West Ave SK10 . . . . .87 F6
South Wirral High Sch
CH62 . . . . .43 D4
Southwold Cres WA5 . . . . . 14 E5
Southwood Ave WA7. . . . . .24 C2
Southworth Ave WA5. . . . . 15 F8
Southworth La WA2,
WA3 .8 E7
Southworth Rd WA12 . . . . .2 F4
Sovereign Cl
Golborne WA3 . . . . 3 E7
Northwich CW9 . . . . 104 F6
Runcorn WA7. . . . . .50 D7
Sovereign Ct WA5 . . . . .9 C4

Sovereign Way CH1. . . . . . 117 E2
Sowcar Way SK10 . . . . .88 C8
Spark Hall Cl WA4. . . . . . . .26 E1
Spark La
Runcorn WA7 . . . . .23 F1
Shavington CW11 . . . . . . 154 C2
Sparks Cl CH3. . . . . 142 B7
Sparrowbutts Gr ST7 . . . . 195 C2
Sparrowhawk Cl WA7 . . . . .50 A7
Sparrow La WA16 . . . . .57 B1
Spath La SK8 . . . . .34 F5
Spath La E SK8 . . . . .35 B5
Spath Wlk SK8 . . . . .35 B5
Spawell Cl WA3 . . . . .2 C8
Speakman Ave WA12 . . . . . .2 C5
Speakman St WA7 . . . . .22 F3
Speed's Way CH3. . . . . 180 E2
Speedwell Cl
11 Golborne WA3 . . . . .3 E8
Heswall CH60 . . . . .41 C8
Huntington CH3. . . . . 142 A5
Speedwell Dr CH60 . . . . . . .41 C8
Speedwell Rd ST5 . . . . 210 F1
SPEKE 21 A3
Speke Bvld L24, L26,
WA8 . . . . .21 B5
Speke Ho L24 . . . . .21 A2
Speke Rd WA8. . . . . .22 C6
Spencer Brook SK10 . . . . . .86 F6
Spencer Cl
Alsager ST7 . . . . 192 F4
Winsford CW2 . . . . 206 A8
Spencer Mews SK10 . . . . . .86 F6
Spencer St
Barnton CW8. . . . . .78 B3
Northwich CW8 . . . . 103 E7
SPEN GREEN 177 B6
Spenlow Cl SK12 . . . . .36 E1
Spennymoor Ct WA7 . . . . . .49 E7
Spenser Ct WA8 . . . . 12 F1
Spenser Rd CH64 . . . . .41 E1
Spey Cl
Middlewich CW10 . . . . . . 128 D3
Winsford CW7 . . . . 126 F2
Spey Dr ST7 . . . . 195 C2
Spike Island (Nature
Reserve) * WA8 . . . . .23 A5
Spike Island Visitor Ctr *
WA8 . . . . .23 A5
Spindle St CW12. . . . . 156 E2
Spink La WA16 . . . . .80 A6
Spinnaker Cl WA7 . . . . .50 D5
Spinner Cres CW9 . . . . .78 D7
Spinners La SK12. . . . . .36 C4
Spinners Pl WA1 . . . . 16 C6
Spinners Way SK10 . . . . . . .87 F7
Spinney Ave
Goostrey CW4 . . . . 107 F1
Widnes WA8 . . . . .12 A1
Spinney Cl
Handforth SK9. . . . . .34 C3
Winsford CW7 . . . . 150 A8
Spinney Dr
Ellesmere Port CH66. . . . .69 D2
Weston CW2 . . . . 207 B5
Spinney End CH3 . . . . 166 A1
Spinney Gdns WA4 . . . . . . .27 B4
Spinney La WA16 . . . . .56 E3
Spinney Mead SK10. . . . . . .87 E2
Spinney The
Cuddington CW8 . . . . 101 D5
Heswall CH60 . . . . .41 C5
Lawton-gate ST7 . . . . 194 E4
Neston CH64 . . . . .41 D1
Runcorn WA7. . . . . 100 E5
Sandbach CW11 . . . . 175 C6
Wistaston CW5. . . . . 205 D6
Spinney Wlk WA7 . . . . .24 A1
Spires Gdns WA2 . . . . .8 A7
Spital Wlk CH2 . . . . 118 F2
Spodegreen La WA14 . . . . .30 C8
Spout La WA16 . . . . .58 B4
Spragg St CW12 . . . . 156 E3
Spring Ave **2** CH66 . . . . .69 C6
Springbank SK10 . . . . .87 F7
Spring Bank ST7 . . . . 195 A7
Springbank Cl WA7. . . . . . .49 B6
Springbank Cres
CW7 . . . . 149 C8
Springbank Gdns
Lymm WA13 . . . . .19 B8
New Mills SK22 . . . . .39 D8
Spring Bank Rd SK22 . . . . .39 C8
Springbourne WA6 . . . . . . .74 D7
Springburn Gdns WA1 . . . 17 F7
Spring Cl ST7 . . . . 193 E8
Springcroft CH64 . . . . .41 C1
Spring Ct **2** WA7 . . . . . . .23 B2
Springe La CW5 . . . . 203 B5
Springfield Ave
Golborne WA3 . . . . 2 E8
Grappenhall WA4. . . . . . . .17 B3
Helsby WA6. . . . . .73 B3
Lymm WA13 . . . . .19 B5
Malpas SY14 . . . . 213 C3
Warrington, Padgate
WA1 . . . . .17 A8
Springfield Cl CH4. . . . . . . 161 A7
Springfield Ct CW8 . . . . . . .77 F3
Springfield Ct / Llys Maes
Y Ffynnon CH4. . . . . 161 A8
Springfield Dr
Talke ST7 . . . . 210 E8
Wilmslow SK9 . . . . .59 D5
Springfield Pk WA11. . . . . . .1 C7
Springfield Rd
Macclesfield SK11 . . . . . . 111 F8

Springfield Rd continued
Malpas SY14 . . . . 213 B3
Mobberley WA16. . . . . . . .57 F4
Widnes WA8 . . . . .22 A8
Springfields
Cuddington CW8 . . . . 101 D4
Helsby WA6. . . . . .73 B3
Knutsford WA16 . . . . .57 C3
Mickle Trafford CH2. . . . . 119 E8
Prestbury SK10 . . . . .87 A7
Springfield Sch CW1. . . . . 191 A3
Springfields Dr CW12 . . . . 156 D3
Springfield St WA1 . . . . . . .16 A5
Spring Gdns
Crewe CW1 . . . . 190 E5
Ellesmere Port CH66. . . . .69 C6
Macclesfield SK10 . . . . . . .87 D1
Mobberley WA16. . . . . . . .58 D5
Nantwich CW5. . . . . 204 F5
Springhead Cl ST7 . . . . 210 D6
Springhead Prim Sch
ST7. 210 D6
Springhill SK10. . . . . .88 A1
Spring Hill CW6 . . . . 168 C8
Springhill Ave CW62 . . . . . .43 D6
Springholm Dr WA4 . . . . . .26 D3
Spring La
Coddington CH3. . . . . 181 C6
Croft WA3 . . . . .9 B6
Lymm WA13 . . . . .19 F3
Spring Mdw CW8. . . . . .78 E1
Springmount WA3 . . . . .3 E7
Spring Mount SK22 . . . . . . .39 C8
Spring Rd SK12 . . . . .36 F2
Spring St
Congleton CW12 . . . . 156 E2
Widnes WA8 . . . . .23 A6
Wilmslow SK9 . . . . .60 A7
Springvale Bsns Ctr
CW11. . . . . 174 D6
Springvale Cl CW11. . . . . . 174 D6
Springvale Ind Pk
CW11. . . . . 174 C6
Springwater Dr CW2. . . . . 207 C1
Springwell Cl CW2. . . . . . . 206 C8
Springwood Ave WA16 . . . .57 C3
Springwood Cl
Blacon CH1 . . . . 117 C4
Macclesfield SK10 . . . . . . .87 D5
Springwood Way SK10 . . . .87 D5
Sprink La CW12 . . . . 157 D5
SPROSTON GREEN 129 C2
Sproston Way CW9 . . . . . . 103 E4
Spruce Ave CW8. . . . . 102 B3
Spruce Cl
Golborne WA3 . . . . 3 F7
Warrington WA1 . . . . 17 E7
Spruce Gr ST7. . . . . 193 F7
Spuley La SK10 . . . . .63 D2
Spunhill Ave CH66 . . . . .69 D2
Spurling Rd WA5 . . . . .6 F6
Spurston Cl WA16 . . . . .29 C4
SPURSTOW 185 D6
Spurstow Mews SK8 . . . . . .35 C8
Square St SK11 . . . . 112 E6
Square The
Altrincham WA15. . . . . . . .32 C8
Audlem CW3 . . . . 229 F4
Chester CH1 . . . . 237 C3
Christleton CH3 . . . . 142 E8
Holmes Chapel CW4 . . . . 130 C3
Ince CH2 . . . . .71 F3
6 Lymm WA13 . . . . .18 E3
Wigore CW3 . . . . 232 C1
Squires Ave WA4. . . . . .23 A8
Squires Cl WA11. . . . . .1 B6
Squirrel Cl CW8 . . . . 103 C7
Squirrels Chase SK10 . . . . .86 F5
Squirrel's Jump SK9 . . . . . .60 C1
Stable La
Mouldsworth CH3 . . . . . . .99 A3
Waverton CH3 . . . . 123 F1
Stables The
Bostock Green CW10 . . . 127 D5
Brereton Heath CW12. . . 155 A4
Guilden Sutton CH3 . . . . 119 F5
Lawton-gate ST7 . . . . 194 C4
Stablings The SK9 . . . . .60 A5
Stadium Way CH1 . . . . 118 B3
Stadmorslow La ST7 . . . . . 195 F4
Staffin Ave CH65. . . . . .95 B8
Stafford Cl SK10. . . . . .86 F2
Stafford Gdns CH65. . . . . . .70 B5
Stafford Rd WA4. . . . . .16 C2
Stafford St
Audlem CW3 . . . . 230 A4
Crewe CW1 . . . . 190 C5
Stafford Wlk SK10 . . . . .86 F2
Stage La WA13 . . . . .19 D4
Stainer Cl WA12 . . . . .2 B5
Staines Cl WA4 . . . . .26 E5
Stainforth Cl WA3 . . . . .4 D4
Stainmore Cl WA3. . . . . 10 B6
Staithes Rd M22. . . . . .33 D8
Stalbridge Rd CW2 . . . . . . 190 C2
Stallard Way CW10 . . . . . . 151 C8
Stalmine Ave SK8 . . . . .34 B8
Stamford Ave CW2 . . . . . . 190 C3
STAMFORD BRIDGE 120 D4
Stamford Cl CH1 . . . . 112 C4
Stamford Ct
Chester CH3 . . . . 119 C2
Lymm WA13 . . . . .18 F3
Macclesfield SK11 . . . . . . 112 C5
Stamford La CH3 . . . . 120 A1

Stamford Rd
Alderley Edge SK9 . . . . .60 B1
Blacon CH1 . . . . .117 E6
Handforth SK9 . . . . .34 A1
Little Bollington WA14 . . . . . .20 B2
Macclesfield SK11 . . . . .112 C4
Stamford St CH65 . . . . .70 A5
Stamp Ave CW1 . . . . .190 D6
Stamp Cl CW1 . . . . .190 D6
Standford Dr CW9 . . . . .104 A5
Standish Cl WA8 . . . . .22 D8
Standon Ave ST5 . . . . .210 C2
Stanford Cl 2 CW9 . . . . .103 F5
Stanhope Ave CW1 . . . . .190 C3
Stanhope Cl SK9 . . . . .60 D8
Stanier Cl
Crewe CW1 . . . . .191 A4
Sutton Lane Ends SK11 . . . . .112 D2
Stanier Rd CH65 . . . . .70 C4
Stanley Ave
Warrington, Stockton Heath
WA4 . . . . .16 F2
Warrington WA5 . . . . .14 D7
STANLEY BANK 1 A7
Stanley Bank Rd WA11 . . . . . .1 A7
Stanley Bank Way WA11 . . . .1 A7
Stanley & Brocklehurst Ct
SK11 . . . . .112 C8
Stanley Cl
Hartford CW8 . . . . .103 A4
Widnes WA8 . . . . .13 C2
Stanley Ct ST7 . . . . .193 C4
Stanley Dr
Gatley SK8, SK9 . . . . .34 D6
Newcastle-u-Lyme ST5 . . . . .210 C1
STANLEY GREEN 34 E6
Stanley Green Ind Est
SK8 . . . . .34 E5
Stanley Green Ret Pk
SK8 . . . . .34 F6
Stanley Hall La SK12 . . . . . . .38 C6
Stanley La CH62 . . . . .43 F4
Stanley Park Ct CH4 . . . . . . .140 E5
Stanley Park Dr CH4 . . . . . . .140 E5
Stanley Pl
Chester CH1 . . . . .237 A2
Warrington WA4 . . . . .16 F2
Stanley Place Mews
CH1 . . . . .237 A2
Stanley Rd
Biddulph ST8 . . . . .179 C2
Ellesmere Port CH65 . . . . .70 C7
Handforth SK8, SK9 . . . . .34 E6
Knutsford WA16 . . . . .56 F2
Stanley Rd Ind Est
WA16 . . . . .57 A1
Stanley St
Chester CH1 . . . . .237 A2
2 Crewe CW1 . . . . .190 C4
7 Macclesfield SK11 . . . . . . .112 D8
Newton-le-W WA12 . . . . .2 A3
Northwich CW9 . . . . .104 C8
Runcorn WA7 . . . . .23 B3
Warrington WA1 . . . . .16 B4
Stanley Villas 7 WA7 . . . . . .22 F1
STANLOW 71 B5
Stanlow Abbey Bsns Ctr
CH65 . . . . .70 D2
Stanlow & Thornton Sta
CH2 . . . . .71 D5
Stanmore Rd WA7 . . . . .23 D2
Stannage La CH3 . . . . .180 F5
Stanner Cl WA5 . . . . .7 D2
Stannerhouse La
CW11 . . . . .175 E4
Stanneybrook Cl
WA6 . . . . .101 A6
Stanney Cl
Bebington CH62 . . . . .43 E3
Neston CH64 . . . . .66 E7
Stanney Grange Sports
Complex The CH65 . . . . .70 E3
Stanney La
Ellesmere Port CH65 . . . . .70 C3
Stoak CH2 . . . . .70 F1
Stanneylands Cl SK9 . . . . . . .34 C2
Stanneylands Dr SK9 . . . . . . .34 B2
Stanneylands Dr SK9 . . . . . . .34 B2
Stanney Mill Ind Est
CH2 . . . . .70 F3
Stanney Mill La CH2 . . . . . . .70 F2
Stanney Mill Rd CH2 . . . . . . .70 F2
Stanney Ten Ind Est
CH2 . . . . .70 F1
Stanney Woods Ave
CH65 . . . . .70 C5
Stanney Woods Ctry Pk*
CH65 . . . . .70 B1
Stansfield Ave WA11 . . . . . . .16 F6
Stansfield Dr WA4 . . . . .27 A7
Stanstead Ave WA5 . . . . .14 F3
Stanthorne Ave CW2 . . . . . .190 A3
Stanthorne Park Mews
CW10 . . . . .150 E6
Stanton Cl WA11 . . . . .1 C6
Stanton Ct CH64 . . . . .66 E8
Stanton Dr CH2 . . . . .118 D5
Stanton Rd WA4 . . . . .17 D3
Stanyer Ct CW5 . . . . .205 A4
STAPELEY 219 D8
Stapeley Broad Lane CE
Prim Sch CW5 . . . . .205 A1
Stapeley Cl CW9 . . . . .103 E4
Stapeley Ct CW5 . . . . .190 B5

Stapeley Gdns L26 . . . . .21 A6
Stapeley Terr CW5 . . . . .205 A4
Stapeley Water Gdns*
CW5 . . . . .205 A3
Stanleford Ct CH66 . . . . .69 F8
Stapleton Ave WA2 . . . . .16 D8
Stapleton Cl WA6 . . . . .74 C8
Stapleton Rd SK10 . . . . .87 B2
Stapleton Way WA8 . . . . .22 B5
Stanley Cl WA7 . . . . .22 F1
Starbeck Dr CH66 . . . . .69 B5
Starkey Gr WA4 . . . . .16 F4
Star La
Lymm WA13 . . . . .18 C4
Macclesfield SK11 . . . . .112 D4
Starling Cl
Farndon CH3 . . . . .180 F1
Kidsgrove ST7 . . . . .195 D3
Runcorn WA7 . . . . .50 D7
Start La SK23 . . . . .65 B7
STATHAM 18 C4
Statham Ave
Lymm WA13 . . . . .18 D3
Warrington WA2 . . . . .8 C2
Statham Cl WA13 . . . . .18 D3
Statham Com Prim Sch
WA13 . . . . .18 C4
Statham Dr WA13 . . . . .18 D3
Statham La WA13 . . . . .18 B5
Statham St WA13 . . . . .112 D7
Station App / Lon yr Orsaf
CH1 . . . . .119 E7
Station Ave
Ellesmere Port CH66 . . . . .69 C7
Helsby WA6 . . . . .73 B4
Station Cl CH64 . . . . .66 F7
Station Cotts
Mouldsworth CH3 . . . . .99 A2
Saughall CH1 . . . . .116 F7
Station Gn CH66 . . . . .69 C7
Station Hill CW8 . . . . .76 F2
Station La
Dunham-on-t-H CH3 . . . . .97 D3
Guilden Sutton CH2,
CH3 . . . . .119 F7
Rushton Spencer SK11 . . . . .158 B2
Station Rd
Adderley TF9 . . . . .235 A5
Alsager ST7 . . . . .193 D3
Astbury ST7, CW12 . . . . .178 B1
Aston WA7 . . . . .50 B4
Backford CH1 . . . . .95 A3
Burton CH64 . . . . .67 B1
Calveley CW6 . . . . .169 E2
Chelford SK11 . . . . .84 A2
Chester CH1 . . . . .237 C4
Crowton CW8 . . . . .76 D2
Delamere CW8 . . . . .123 D8
Ellesmere Port CH65 . . . . .70 C6
Ellesmere Port, Little Sutton
CH66 . . . . .69 C6
Elton CH2 . . . . .72 A5
Furness Vale SK23 . . . . .39 D4
Goostrey CW4 . . . . .131 A8
Handforth SK9 . . . . .34 D3
Haydock WA11 . . . . .1 C6
Heswall CH60 . . . . .40 F6
Holmes Chapel CW4 . . . . . . .130 D2
Irlam M44 . . . . .11 E7
Kidsgrove ST7 . . . . .194 F1
Lostock Gralam CW9 . . . . .80 A2
Mobberley WA16 . . . . .57 F7
Mouldsworth CH3 . . . . .99 A2
Mow Cop ST7 . . . . .195 C8
Nantwich CW5 . . . . .204 E5
Neston CH64 . . . . .66 F8
Neston, Parkgate CH64 . . . . . .66 C8
Newchapel ST7 . . . . .195 E2
New Mills SK22 . . . . .39 B7
Northwich CW9 . . . . .79 B1
Partington WA14 . . . . .20 B5
Runcorn WA7 . . . . .22 F2
Sandbach CW11 . . . . .174 D7
Sandycroft CH5 . . . . .116 A2
Scholar Green ST7 . . . . .194 F7
Styal SK9 . . . . .34 A4
Warrington, Fearnhead
WA2 . . . . .9 A2
Warrington, Great Sankey
WA5 . . . . .14 F6
Warrington, Penketh
WA5 . . . . .14 E3
Warrington WA4 . . . . .16 E2
Weaverham CW8 . . . . .77 A1
Wilmslow SK9 . . . . .60 B7
Winsford CW7 . . . . .127 A1
Worleston CW5 . . . . .188 E6
Wrenbury CW5 . . . . .216 F3
Station Rd N WA2 . . . . .9 A1
Station Rd S WA2 . . . . .9 A1
Station St SK10 . . . . .87 D1
Station Terr WA7 . . . . .50 B4
Station View
Chester CH2 . . . . .118 F2
Hampton Heath SY14 . . . . . .213 D7
Nantwich CW5 . . . . .204 E4
Sandbach CW11 . . . . .174 D8
Station Yard Trad Est
CW4 . . . . .130 D3
Staveley Dr CW7 . . . . .126 B2
Steadings Rise WA16 . . . . . . .56 D6
Steadings The CH3 . . . . .120 A4
Steam Mill St CH1,
CH3 . . . . .237 C3
Stearns Cl CH1 . . . . .118 A5
Stearns Ho CH1 . . . . .118 A5

Steele Rd CW10 . . . . .151 D5
Steele St CH1 . . . . .237 B2
Steel St SK10 . . . . .16 D7
Steeple Ct CH64 . . . . .66 E7
Stenle St SK10 . . . . .87 D2
Stein Ave WA3 . . . . .3 E8
Stendall Rd CH1 . . . . .118 A3
Stenhills Cres WA7 . . . . .23 C2
Stephens Gdns CH66 . . . . . . .69 B6
Stephens Gr WA6 . . . . .73 B2
Stephenson Dr CW1 . . . . . . .191 A4
Stephenson Rd WA12 . . . . .2 D2
Stephenson Wlk CW7 . . . . .149 A0
Stephen St WA1 . . . . .16 D6
Stephens Terr CH66 . . . . .69 B6
Stephens Way ST7 . . . . .209 F2
Sterling Cl 1 CW9 . . . . .103 F5
Sterne Ct CW1 . . . . .174 D6
Stetchworth Rd WA4 . . . . . . .16 B1
Stevenage Cl SK11 . . . . .112 B7
Stevenage Dr SK11 . . . . .112 B7
Steven Ct CH3 . . . . .237 C3
Stevens Rd CH60 . . . . .41 C7
Stevens St SK9 . . . . .60 A1
Steventon WA7 . . . . .24 E4
Steward's Ave WA8 . . . . .22 F8
Stewart St CW2 . . . . .190 A3
Stile End CH2 . . . . .119 F8
Stiles The CW8 . . . . .101 D5
Stiperstones Cl CH66 . . . . . .69 A6
Stirling Cl
Chester CH3 . . . . .119 A2
Congleton CW12 . . . . .156 C3
Macclesfield SK10 . . . . .86 F2
Warrington WA1 . . . . .17 E7
Winsford CW7 . . . . .127 A3
Stirling Dr
Ellesmere Port CH65 . . . . .70 D3
Holmes Chapel CW4 . . . . . . .130 B2
Stirrup Cl WA2 . . . . .9 A3
Stirrup La WA3 . . . . .96 A7
Stoak Lo CH65 . . . . .70 C4
Stockdale Dr WA5 . . . . .14 E7
Stockham Cl WA7 . . . . .50 A8
Stockham La WA7 . . . . .50 B7
Stock La CW2, CW5 . . . . . . .206 B2
Stockley Farm* CW9 . . . . . .54 E7
Stockport Rd WA4 . . . . .17 E3
Stocks Ave 3 CH3 . . . . .119 A1
Stocks Ct The WA3 . . . . .3 D8
Stocks Hill CW7 . . . . .149 F7
Stocks La
Chester CH3 . . . . .119 A1
Ollerton WA16 . . . . .82 E1
Rainow SK10 . . . . .88 E5
Stockswell Rd WA8 . . . . .12 A3
STOCKTON HEATH 16 D1
Stockton Heath Prim Sch
WA4 . . . . .16 C1
Stockton La WA4 . . . . .16 F1
Stockton Rd SK9 . . . . .59 F4
Stockton View WA4 . . . . .16 D8
Stockwell Farm Ct
WA8 . . . . .12 E4
Stoke Abbott Cl SK7 . . . . . . .35 E7
Stoke Cl CH62 . . . . .43 E3
Stoke Gdns CH65 . . . . .70 C4
Stokehall La CW5 . . . . .187 E6
Stokesay Ct CH65 . . . . .70 E3
Stokes St WA3 . . . . .9 E5
Stoke Wlk CH65 . . . . .70 C4
Stoneacre Gdns WA4 . . . . . . .26 E4
Stonebank Dr CH64 . . . . .67 A6
Stone Bank Rd ST7 . . . . .195 B1
Stone Barn La WA7 . . . . .49 F6
Stonebridge Rd CW5 . . . . . .204 E3
Stone Chair La ST7 . . . . .194 E7
Stonechat Cl
10 Golborne WA3 . . . . .3 E8
Runcorn WA7 . . . . .49 E5
Stone Cotts CW12 . . . . .157 E2
Stone Croft
Chester CH3 . . . . .142 B7
Kingsmead CW9 . . . . .103 F5
Stonecrop Cl
Runcorn WA7 . . . . .49 F4
Warrington WA3 . . . . .9 C4
Stone Cross Dr WA8 . . . . . . .12 E5
Stone Cross La N WA3 . . . . . . .4 A8
Stone Cross La S WA3 . . . . . . .3 C6
Stone Cross Pk WA3 . . . . .3 B7
Stonehaven Dr WA2 . . . . .9 A3
Stoneheads SK23 . . . . .65 C8
Stoneheads Rise SK23 . . . . .65 D8
Stone Heyes La CW8,
WA6 . . . . .77 F5
Stonehill Cl WA4 . . . . .26 D4
Stonehills Cres WA7 . . . . .23 C2
Stonehills La WA7 . . . . .23 C2
Stonehouse Gn 6 CW12 . . . . .156 D3
Stone House La CW6 . . . . . .184 E4
Stonelea WA7 . . . . .24 B2
Stoneleigh Cl SK10 . . . . .87 C2
Stoneleigh Ct WA4 . . . . .17 D1
Stoneleigh Gdns WA4 . . . . . .17 D1
Stoneley Ave CW1 . . . . .190 D7
STONELEY GREEN 203 D4
Stoneley Rd CW1 . . . . .190 D8
Stone Mead Ave WA15 . . . .32 C7
Stone Pit La WA3 . . . . .3 F2
Stone Pl CH2 . . . . .118 F3
Stones Manor La
CW8 . . . . .103 C5
Stoneway Ct 1 CH60 . . . . . .40 F8
Stonefold La SK11 . . . . .113 A6

Stoneyford La CW8 . . . . .101 C3
Stoney Holt WA7 . . . . .50 C8
Stoney La
Delamere CW6 . . . . .123 C6
Wilmslow SK9 . . . . .59 F5
Stoneyland Dr SK22 . . . . .39 B8
Stonyhurst Cres WA3 . . . . .4 D5
Stony La CW12 . . . . .156 C1
Stopsley Cl CW12 . . . . .155 F4
Stores Rd M90 . . . . .33 A6
Store St SK10 . . . . .88 B8
Stour Ct CH65 . . . . .70 B7
STOWFORD 207 C8
Stradbroke Cl WA3 . . . . .4 A7
Straight Length WA6 . . . . . . .73 E7
Straight Mile CH4 . . . . .162 F5
Straker Ave CH65 . . . . .69 F6
Stratford Gdns CH1 . . . . . . .117 E4
Stratford Rd
Blacon CH1 . . . . .117 E4
Wilmslow SK9 . . . . .66 C6
Stratford Sq SK8 . . . . .34 C7
Stratford Way SK11 . . . . .112 C5
Strathaven Ave CW2 . . . . . .205 E8
Strathearn Rd CH60 . . . . .40 F7
Strathmore Cl CW4 . . . . .130 B2
Stratton Cl WA7 . . . . .50 B6
Stratton Pk WA8 . . . . .12 F5
Stratton Rd WA5 . . . . .15 B5
Strawberry Cl WA3 . . . . .9 C4
Strawberry Dr CH66 . . . . .95 A8
Strawberry Fields
CH3 . . . . .142 B7
Strawberry Gn CH66 . . . . .95 A8
Strawberry La
Acton Bridge CW8 . . . . .76 F3
Mollington CH1 . . . . .94 D4
Wilmslow SK9 . . . . .59 E6
Street Forest Walks The*
SK17 . . . . .90 E4
Street Hey La CH64 . . . . .43 B1
Street La
Lower Whitley WA4 . . . . .52 C3
Rode Heath ST7 . . . . .176 F2
Skellorn Green SK10 . . . . .62 D8
Street The
Mickle Trafford CH2 . . . . .119 D8
Whaley Bridge SK10,
SK17 . . . . .90 C5
STRETTON
Farndon .197 F6
Warrington 26 E2
Stretton Ave WA3 . . . . .3 E7
Stretton Cl CH62 . . . . .43 E3
Stretton Hall Mews
WA4 . . . . .52 E8
Stretton Mill* SY14 . . . . . .198 A7
Stretton Rd WA4 . . . . .26 E2
Stretton Way 3 SK9 . . . . . . .34 D5
Stretton Wlk CW9 . . . . .103 F4
Strickland Cl WA4 . . . . .27 A7
Strines Rd SK6 . . . . .38 D8
Stringer Ave CW11 . . . . .175 C5
Stringer Cres WA4 . . . . .16 E4
Stringer's La LL12,
CH4 . . . . .161 B4
Stroma Ave CH65 . . . . .95 B8
Stromness Cl WA2 . . . . .9 B3
Stuart Cl
Chester CH3 . . . . .119 C3
Winsford CW7 . . . . .149 C5
Stuart Cl SK10 . . . . .87 B2
Stuart Dr WA4 . . . . .16 D7
Stuart Pl CH1 . . . . .237 B3
Stuart Rd WA7 . . . . .24 C4
Stubbs La
Lostock Gralam CW9 . . . . .80 A2
Mobberley WA16 . . . . .58 E4
Stubbs Pl CH1 . . . . .117 E3
Stubbs Terr 17 SK11 . . . . . .112 E7
Stubby La SK10 . . . . .84 E2
STUD GREEN 152 C1
Stud Green Ind Pk
CW11 . . . . .152 C1
Sturgess St WA12 . . . . .1 F3
STYAL 33 F4
Styal Cl 4 CW9 . . . . .103 F4
Styal Cross SK9 . . . . .33 E4
Styal Ctry Pk* SK9 . . . . .33 E3
Styal Gn SK9 . . . . .33 F3
STYAL GREEN 34 A3
Styal Prim Sch SK9 . . . . .33 E4
Styal Rd
Wilmslow SK9 . . . . .60 B8
Wythenshawe M22 . . . . .33 F7
Styal Sta SK9 . . . . .34 A4
Styal View SK9 . . . . .34 B2
Styperson Way SK12 . . . . . . .36 E3
Sudbrook Cl WA3 . . . . .3 E8
Sudbury Dr SK8 . . . . .34 C8
Sudbury Rd SK7 . . . . .36 E8
Sudlow La
Knutsford WA16 . . . . .56 D1
Plumley WA16 . . . . .81 C7
Suez St
Newton-le-W WA12 . . . . .2 B3
Warrington WA1 . . . . .16 B5
Suffolk Ave CH65 . . . . .69 F5
Suffolk Cl
Congleton CW12 . . . . .156 D4
Macclesfield SK10 . . . . .86 F1
Warrington WA1 . . . . .17 E6
Suffolk Dr SK9 . . . . .34 C1
Suffolk Ho 3 CH1 . . . . .237 C3
Suffolk Pl WA8 . . . . .22 C7
Suffolk St WA7 . . . . .23 F3
Sugar La
Bollington SK10 . . . . .63 A3

Sugar La Pinniroia
Manley WA6 . . . . .98 E5
Rainow SK10 . . . . .88 D5
Sugar Pit La WA16 . . . . .56 E3
Sugar St SK11 . . . . .159 C2
Sulby Ave WA4 . . . . .16 E3
Gulgrave Ave SK12 . . . . .36 F4
Summer Cl 7 WA7 . . . . .23 F1
Summercroft Cl WA3 . . . . .3 A7
Summer Dr CW1 . . . . .175 C6
Summerfield ST7 . . . . .195 B1
Summerfield Ave WA5 . . . . . . .7 F2
Summerfield Cl CH4 . . . . . . .139 A3
Summerfield Dr CW9 . . . . . .126 F8
Summerfield Ho CH3 . . . . . .119 F5
Summerfield Pl SK9 . . . . .60 A5
Summerfield Rd
Guilden Sutton CH3 . . . . .119 F5
Mobberley WA16 . . . . .57 F4
Summerfields WA16 . . . . .57 C3
Summerhill Ctr **10**
SK9 . . . . .34 D1
Summerhill Dr ST5 . . . . .210 D1
Summerhill Rd SK10 . . . . . . .86 F4
Summer La
Daresbury WA4 . . . . .51 D7
Hatton WA4 . . . . .25 F1
Runcorn WA7 . . . . .23 F1
Summerlea SK8 . . . . .35 B8
Summerlea Cl SK10 . . . . .87 D1
Summers Cl WA16 . . . . .82 A7
Summers Way WA16 . . . . .82 A7
Summertrees Rd CH66 . . . . .69 E3
Summerville Gdns
WA4 . . . . .16 F1
Summerville Wlk 1
WA5 . . . . .15 C7
Summit Cl WA4 . . . . .26 E1
Sumner Rd CH1 . . . . .117 E4
Sumner St WA11 . . . . .1 A6
Sumpter Pathway
CH2 . . . . .118 F3
Sunart Cl CW2 . . . . .206 B6
Sunbank La WA15 . . . . .32 E6
Sunbeam Cl WA7 . . . . .22 F3
Sunbeam St WA12 . . . . .2 C3
Sunbury Cl SK9 . . . . .34 E2
Sunbury Cres 3 CH4 . . . . . .140 F6
Sunbury Gdns WA4 . . . . .26 C2
Suncroft Cl WA1 . . . . .17 E7
Suncroft Rd CH60 . . . . .41 C7
Sundale Dr CW2 . . . . .189 D4
Sunderland St SK11 . . . . . . .112 D7
Sundial Ho WA3 . . . . .4 F3
Sundown Cl SK22 . . . . .39 A8
Sunfield Cl CH66 . . . . .69 D3
Sunflower Cl WA9 . . . . .6 A7
Sunflower Dr WA5 . . . . .15 D3
Sunningdale Ave WA8 . . . . .12 B1
Sunningdale Cl
Burtonwood WA5 . . . . .6 F6
Northwich CW9 . . . . .104 E7
Winsford CW7 . . . . .126 A2
Sunningdale Dr
Bebington CH63 . . . . .43 B6
Bramhall SK7 . . . . .36 A7
Sunningdale Rd
Cheadle SK8 . . . . .35 A7
Macclesfield SK11 . . . . .112 A6
Sunningdale Way
CH64 . . . . .66 E4
Sunninghey Ct SK9 . . . . .59 F2
Sunny Bank SK9 . . . . .60 B6
Sunny Bank SK11 . . . . .112 D5
Sunnybank Cl WA12 . . . . .2 C4
Sunny Bank Cl SK11 . . . . . . .112 D5
Sunny Bank Cotts
Ashton Hayes CH3 . . . . .121 E7
Warrington WA8 . . . . .14 A4
Sunnybank Dr SK9 . . . . .59 D4
Sunnybank Rd CW1,
CW2 . . . . .189 E5
Sunny Bank Rd WA14 . . . . . . .31 C8
Sunny Lea Mews SK9 . . . . . .60 A6
Sunnymill Dr CW11 . . . . .175 A6
Sunnyside
Alsager ST7 . . . . .193 A4
4 Ellesmere Port CH65 . . . .70 C6
Malpas SY14 . . . . .212 F2
Warrington WA5 . . . . .14 E6
Sunnyside Wlk CW11 . . . . . .154 B1
Sunset Cotts CH64 . . . . .67 A4
Surrey Dr CW12 . . . . .156 E5
Surrey Rd
Chester CH2 . . . . .119 A5
Kidsgrove ST7 . . . . .195 A2
Warren SK11 . . . . .112 A4
Surrey St
Crewe CW1 . . . . .190 E4
6 Runcorn WA7 . . . . .22 F2
Warrington WA4 . . . . .16 D3
Surridge WA16 . . . . .29 C5
Susan Dr WA5 . . . . .14 D5
Susan St WA8 . . . . .13 C2
Sussex Ave SK11 . . . . .112 A5
Sussex Dr ST7 . . . . .194 F2
Sussex Pl CW12 . . . . .156 C5
Sussex Rd
Chester CH2 . . . . .118 F4
Irlam M44 . . . . .11 C4
Partington M31 . . . . .11 C1
Sussex St WA8 . . . . .13 D1
Sussex Way CH2 . . . . .118 F3
Sutch La WA13 . . . . .19 A3
Sutherland Ct 5 WA7 . . . . . .23 B2
Sutherland Dr
Bebington CH62 . . . . .43 D4

Sutherland Dr continued
Macclesfield SK10 . . . . . 87 A1
Sutherland Way CH3 . . . 119 B3
Sutton Ave
Culcheth WA3 . . . . . 4 F4
Neston CH64 . . . . . 66 E6
Sutton Cl
Bebington CH62 . . . . . 43 E3
Higher Wincham CW9 . . . . . 79 F6
Macclesfield SK11 . . . . . 112 D5
Mickle Trafford CH2 . . . . . 119 F8
Nantwich CW5 . . . . . 204 C5
Sutton Cswy WA6, WA7 . . . 49 F2
Sutton Dr CH2 . . . . . 118 E5
Sutton Field CW8 . . . . . 126 A7
SUTTON GREEN 69 C3
Sutton Green Prim Sch
CH66 . . . . . 69 C5
Sutton Hall Dr CH66 . . . . . 69 A6
Sutton Hall Gdns CH66 . . . . . 69 A6
Sutton High Sch CH66 . . . . . 69 A6
Sutton La CW10 . . . . . 151 C7
SUTTON LANE ENDS
. . . . . 112 E2
Sutton Quays Bsns Pk
WA7 . . . . . 49 E3
Sutton Rd
Alderley Edge SK9 . . . . . 59 F2
Poynton SK12 . . . . . 37 A2
Sutton's La 4 WA8 . . . . . 23 B7
Sutton St
Runcorn WA7 . . . . . 23 B2
Warrington WA1 . . . . . 16 C4
Sutton Way
Ellesmere Port CH66 . . . . . 69 E4
1 Handforth SK9 . . . . . 34 E5
SUTTON WEAVER 50 B3
Swale Cl SK9 . . . . . 34 E2
Swaledale Ave CW12 . . . . . 157 A5
Swaledale Cl
Bebington CH62 . . . . . 43 E5
Warrington WA5 . . . . . 14 F7
Swale Rd CH65 . . . . . 70 A7
Swallow Cl
1 Kidsgrove ST7 . . . . . 195 B2
Macclesfield SK10 . . . . . 113 A7
Warrington WA3 . . . . . 9 F4
Swallow Ct
Handforth SK9 . . . . . 34 B1
Winsford CW7 . . . . . 149 D5
Swallow Dr
Alsager ST7 . . . . . 193 B3
Kelsall CW6 . . . . . 122 D5
Sandbach CW11 . . . . . 175 A8
Swallowfield Cl CW2 . . . . . 206 A8
Swallowfield Gdns
WA4 . . . . . 26 F5
Swallowfields CH3 . . . . . 180 E2
Swallowmere View
ST7 . . . . . 210 C8
Swallow Rd ST7 . . . . . 195 F1
Swanage Cl WA4 . . . . . 16 E2
Swanage Ct 6 CW7 . . . . . 149 D6
Swan Ave WA9 . . . . . 1 A2
SWANBACH 229 E1
Swan Bank
Congleton CW12 . . . . . 156 D2
Talke ST7 . . . . . 210 D7
Swan Cl
Ellesmere Port, Great Sutton
CH66 . . . . . 69 D2
Poynton SK12 . . . . . 36 B4
Talke ST7 . . . . . 210 D8
Swan Ct
Bunbury CW6 . . . . . 185 E8
Crowton CW8 . . . . . 101 E7
Swan Farm La CW3 . . . . . 232 D1
Swan Gr WA16 . . . . . 106 D7
SWAN GREEN 106 D8
Swan Ho ST7 . . . . . 210 D7
Swan La
Bunbury CW6 . . . . . 185 E8
Cheadle SK8 . . . . . 35 B8
SWANLEY 203 C5
Swanley La CW5 . . . . . 203 D4
Swanlow Ave CW7 . . . . . 149 D5
Swanlow Dr CW7 . . . . . 149 D6
Swanlow La CW7 . . . . . 149 E5
Swan Rd WA12 . . . . . 1 E4
Swanscoe Ave SK10 . . . . . 88 A7
Swanscoe Cl CW10 . . . . . 151 B8
Swanscoe La SK10 . . . . . 88 B3
Swan St
Congleton CW12 . . . . . 156 D2
Wilmslow SK9 . . . . . 60 B7
Swanwick Cl CW4 . . . . . 107 C1
Swanwick Gn SY13 . . . . . 215 C5
SWANWICK GREEN 215 C4
Swanwick Ho SK10 . . . . . 86 F6
Sweet Briar Cres
CW2 . . . . . 189 F3
Sweet Brier Cl CW8 . . . . . 78 B4
Sweetfield Gdns CH66 . . . . . 69 D7
Sweetfield Rd CH66 . . . . . 69 D7
Sweettooth La CW11 . . . . . 175 A7
SWETTENHAM 131 E3
Swettenham Cl
Alsager ST7 . . . . . 193 C3
Sandbach CW11 . . . . . 175 D7
SWETTENHAM HEATH
. . . . . 132 B3
Swettenham La CW12 . . . . . 131 E3
Swettenham Rd
Handforth SK9 . . . . . 34 D5
Swettenham CW12 . . . . . 132 B2
Swettenham St SK11 . . . . . 112 E7
Swift Cl
Kidsgrove ST7 . . . . . 195 B2

Swift Cl continued
Warrington WA2 . . . . . 8 E3
Wistaston CW2 . . . . . 205 F8
Swinburne Dr CW1 . . . . . 190 F4
Swindale Ave WA2 . . . . . 8 B3
Swinden Cl WA7 . . . . . 24 D2
Swine Market 2
CW5 . . . . . 204 E5
Swineyard La WA16 . . . . . 28 C4
Swinford Ave WA8 . . . . . 13 E2
Swinhoe Pl WA3 . . . . . 4 D3
Swinley Chase SK9 . . . . . 34 F1
Swinleys Hey CH3 . . . . . 142 A7
Swinnerton St CW2 . . . . . 190 C2
Swinton Sq 10 WA16 . . . . . 57 A2
Swireford Rd WA6 . . . . . 73 B2
Swiss Cott
Alderley Edge SK9 . . . . . 60 C1
Macclesfield SK10 . . . . . 87 B2
Swiss Hill SK9 . . . . . 60 B1
Swithin Rd M22 . . . . . 33 E8
SWORTON HEATH 28 E5
Swynnerton Way WA8 . . . . . 13 B5
Sycamore Ave
Alsager ST7 . . . . . 193 E2
Congleton CW12 . . . . . 155 F4
Crewe CW1 . . . . . 190 D6
Haydock WA11 . . . . . 1 A5
Newton-le-W WA12 . . . . . 2 C3
Rode Heath ST7 . . . . . 193 F7
Widnes WA8 . . . . . 13 B2
Winsford CW7 . . . . . 149 D8
Sycamore Cl
Audlem CW3 . . . . . 230 A4
Biddulph ST8 . . . . . 179 E2
Handforth SK9 . . . . . 34 B2
Holmes Chapel CW4 . . . . . 130 D3
Nantwich CW5 . . . . . 204 F7
Talke ST7 . . . . . 210 E8
Sycamore Cres
Barnton CW8 . . . . . 78 B4
Hollinfare WA3 . . . . . 11 B2
Macclesfield SK11 . . . . . 112 A7
Sycamore Ct WA7 . . . . . 24 D5
Sycamore Dr
Aston WA7 . . . . . 50 B4
Chester CH4 . . . . . 140 F5
Ellesmere Port CH66 . . . . . 70 A1
Lymm WA13 . . . . . 18 D4
Middlewich CW10 . . . . . 151 E5
Sycamore Gr
Broughton CH4 . . . . . 139 B3
Sandbach CW11 . . . . . 175 A8
Sycamore La WA5 . . . . . 15 B6
Sycamore Lo SK7 . . . . . 35 F7
Sycamore Rd
Paddockhill WA16 . . . . . 59 B5
Partington M31 . . . . . 11 E3
Runcorn WA7 . . . . . 49 D8
Sycamore Rise SK11 . . . . . 112 B6
Sycamores The WA16 . . . . . 58 E2
Syddal Cl SK7 . . . . . 35 D5
Syddal Cres SK7 . . . . . 35 D4
Syddal Gn SK7 . . . . . 35 D4
Syddal Rd SK7 . . . . . 35 D5
SYDNEY 191 A5
Sydney Ave M90 . . . . . 33 A8
Sydney Rd
Bramhall SK7 . . . . . 35 F5
Chester CH1 . . . . . 118 B3
Crewe CW1 . . . . . 190 F6
Sydney St
Northwich CW8 . . . . . 103 C7
Runcorn WA7 . . . . . 48 D7
Syers Ct WA1 . . . . . 16 E8
Sylvan Ave WA5 . . . . . 59 F5
Sylvan Cl CW8 . . . . . 103 C7
Sylvan Mews CH1 . . . . . 117 E6
Sylvia Cres WA2 . . . . . 8 D1
Symondley Rd SK11 . . . . . 112 F2
Synge St WA2 . . . . . 16 C7
Sytch Croft CH64 . . . . . 66 E8

T

Tabley Ave WA8 . . . . . 12 D2
Tabley Cl
Knutsford WA16 . . . . . 56 E3
Macclesfield SK10 . . . . . 112 A8
Sandbach CW11 . . . . . 174 E7
Tabley Ct WA16 . . . . . 56 B4
Tabley Gr WA16 . . . . . 56 E1
Tabley Hill La WA16 . . . . . 56 B2
Tabley Rd
Crewe CW2 . . . . . 189 E3
Handforth SK9 . . . . . 34 D5
Knutsford WA16 . . . . . 56 E3
Tabley St CW9 . . . . . 79 A1
Tabley Stables WA16 . . . . . 81 A8
Tabor St SK11 . . . . . 112 E6
Tadgers La WA8 . . . . . 73 D8
Tailors View CW5 . . . . . 204 E6
Talbot Ave CH64 . . . . . 66 F6
Talbot Cl
Neston CH64 . . . . . 66 F6
Shavington CW2 . . . . . 206 B4
Warrington WA3 . . . . . 9 E3
Talbot Gdns CH64 . . . . . 66 F6
Talbot Rd
Alderley Edge SK9 . . . . . 60 B1
Dunham-on-t-H WA6 . . . . . 97 E7
Ellesmere Port CH66 . . . . . 69 F3

Talbot St
Chester CH1 . . . . . 237 B4
Golborne WA3 . . . . . 3 A8
Talbot Way CW5 . . . . . 205 A3
Talfryn Cl CH5 . . . . . 91 D1
Talisman Cl WA7 . . . . . 50 D7
TALKE 210 C7
Talke Rd
Alsager ST7 . . . . . 193 E3
High Carr ST5 . . . . . 210 F2
Newcastle-u-Lyme ST7,
ST5 . . . . . 210 D4
**TALLARN GREEN/
TALLWRN GREEN** 222 E5
Tall Ash Ave CW12 . . . . . 157 A4
Tall Chys CW11 . . . . . 175 D4
Tall Trees Cl CW8 . . . . . 103 C6
Tally Ho La CW5 . . . . . 203 E3
Tamar Cl
Congleton CW12 . . . . . 156 F1
Macclesfield SK10 . . . . . 86 E1
Tamar Rd
Haydock WA11 . . . . . 1 C6
Kidsgrove ST7 . . . . . 195 B2
Tamar Wlk CW7 . . . . . 127 A2
Tame Cl
Biddulph ST8 . . . . . 179 D1
Sandbach CW11 . . . . . 174 E8
Tame Wlk 8 SK9 . . . . . 34 D2
Tamworth Cl SK7 . . . . . 36 D8
Tamworth St WA12 . . . . . 2 A3
Tanhouse CW7 . . . . . 23 E1
Tanhouse Ind Est WA8 . . . . . 23 C7
Tan House La
Burtonwood WA5 . . . . . 7 A5
Widnes WA8 . . . . . 23 D8
Tankersley Gr WA5 . . . . . 15 B6
Tanners La WA2 . . . . . 16 A6
Tanner's La WA3 . . . . . 3 B8
Tanner St CW12 . . . . . 156 E2
Tannery Way CW5 . . . . . 204 E4
Tannery La
Neston CH64 . . . . . 66 E8
Warrington WA5 . . . . . 14 D3
Tanning Ct 3 WA1 . . . . . 16 C5
Tanyard Dr WA15 . . . . . 32 C6
Tanyard La WA15 . . . . . 32 A5
Tapley Ave SK10 . . . . . 87 B4
Taplow Cl WA4 . . . . . 26 E6
Taporley War Meml Hospl
CW6 . . . . . 146 D2
Target Cl ST7 . . . . . 210 E6
Target Rd CH60 . . . . . 40 C8
Tarnbeck WA7 . . . . . 50 D8
Tarn Cl CW7 . . . . . 126 C3
Tarn Ct WA1 . . . . . 17 F7
Tarn Mount SK11 . . . . . 112 A5
Tarnway WA3 . . . . . 3 F7
TARPORLEY 146 C1
Tarporley Bsns Ctr
CW6 . . . . . 168 C8
Tarporley CE Prim Sch
CW6 . . . . . 146 D2
Tarporley Com High Sch
CW6 . . . . . 146 D1
Tarporley Rd
Duddon CH3 . . . . . 144 E7
Ellesmere Port CH66 . . . . . 69 E4
Little Budworth CW6,
CW8 . . . . . 124 C5
Lower Whitley WA4 . . . . . 52 C4
Tarvin CH3 . . . . . 121 C1
Utkinton CW6 . . . . . 146 E6
Whitchurch SY13 . . . . . 225 F3
Tarporley Wlk SK9 . . . . . 34 E1
Tarrant Ct CH1 . . . . . 94 F1
TARVIN 121 C2
Tarvin Ave CW2 . . . . . 189 D4
Tarvin Bridge CH3 . . . . . 119 A2
Tarvin Cl
Ellesmere Port CH65 . . . . . 70 C4
Golborne WA3 . . . . . 3 E7
Macclesfield SK11 . . . . . 112 E5
Middlewich CW10 . . . . . 151 D5
Northwich CW9 . . . . . 103 F5
Runcorn WA7 . . . . . 49 C6
Tarvin Prim Sch CH3 . . . . . 121 B1
Tarvin Rd
Alvanley WA6 . . . . . 73 F4
Bebington CH62 . . . . . 43 F3
Chester, Boughton CH3 . . . . . 119 A2
Chester, Vicarscross
CH3 . . . . . 119 E2
Christleton CH3 . . . . . 120 C3
Manley WA6 . . . . . 99 A4
Tarvin Rdbt CH3 . . . . . 121 A2
TARVIN SANDS 121 D4
Tarvin Sands Industries
CH3 . . . . . 121 B4
Tarvin Way
1 Handforth SK9 . . . . . 34 D5
Winsford CW7 . . . . . 126 C2
Tasman Cl WA3 . . . . . 9 F3
Tate Cl WA8 . . . . . 12 D2
Tate Dr CW1 . . . . . 191 C4
TATTENHALL 166 B1
Tattenhall La
Beeston CW6 . . . . . 167 F2
Tattenhall CH3 . . . . . 166 E3
Tattenhall Park Prim Sch
CH3 . . . . . 166 B2
Tattenhall Rd CH3 . . . . . 166 C1
Tatton Cl
Alsager ST7 . . . . . 193 C3
Chester CH4 . . . . . 140 E5
Northwich CW9 . . . . . 103 F5
Winsford CW7 . . . . . 126 C1

Tatton Ct
4 Handforth SK9 . . . . . 34 E5
2 Knutsford WA16 . . . . . 57 A2
Warrington WA1 . . . . . 9 D1
TATTON DALE 30 E1
Tatton Dr CW11 . . . . . 175 C7
Tatton La 17 WA16 . . . . . 57 A2
Tatton Lo 6 WA16 . . . . . 57 B7
Tatton Rd
Crewe CW2 . . . . . 189 F2
Handforth SK9 . . . . . 34 E5
Tatton St WA16 . . . . . 57 A2
Tatton Stile WA16 . . . . . 58 A4
Taurus Pk WA5 . . . . . 7 D3
Tavener Cl CH63 . . . . . 43 C5
Tavistock Rd WA5 . . . . . 14 E4
Tavlin Ave WA5 . . . . . 7 F1
Tawney Cl ST7 . . . . . 195 B2
Tawney Ct WA7 . . . . . 49 E7
TAXAL 65 D4
Taxal & Fernilee CE Prim
Sch SK23 . . . . . 65 D6
Taxal Moor Rd SK23 . . . . . 65 C3
Taxal Rd M90 . . . . . 33 B7
Taxmere Cl CW11 . . . . . 174 F7
Tay Cl ST8 . . . . . 179 E1
Taylor Bsns Pk WA3 . . . . . 4 F1
Taylor Dr CW5 . . . . . 204 C5
Taylor Rd
Altrincham WA14 . . . . . 20 F5
Haydock WA11 . . . . . 1 F7
Taylor's La
Oakhanger CW1 . . . . . 192 C3
Warrington WA5 . . . . . 14 A2
Taylors Row WA7 . . . . . 23 C2
Taylor St
Warrington WA4 . . . . . 16 A1
Widnes WA8 . . . . . 13 C1
Teal Ave
Knutsford WA16 . . . . . 57 B2
Poynton SK12 . . . . . 36 A4
Tealby Cl CW9 . . . . . 104 B8
Teal Cl
Warrington WA3 . . . . . 8 E3
Winsford CW7 . . . . . 149 D5
Tedder Dr M22 . . . . . 33 F7
Tedder Sq WA8 . . . . . 22 D8
Teddington Cl WA4 . . . . . 26 E5
Tees Ct CH65 . . . . . 70 A7
Teesdale Cl WA5 . . . . . 14 F7
Teesdale Rd WA11 . . . . . 1 C7
Teign Cl
SK11 . . . . . 113 C6
Teggsnose La SK11 . . . . . 113 C6
Tegid Way CH4 . . . . . 140 D5
Tegsnose Mount
SK11 . . . . . 113 C4
Telegraph Rd CH60 . . . . . 41 A7
Telfer Ct CW10 . . . . . 151 E6
Telford Cl
Congleton CW12 . . . . . 157 B2
Macclesfield SK10 . . . . . 88 A1
Talke ST7 . . . . . 210 E8
Widnes WA8 . . . . . 12 D4
Telford Ct CH1 . . . . . 94 D6
Telford Gdns CW11 . . . . . 174 F3
Telford Ho ST7 . . . . . 195 B3
Telford Pl CW5 . . . . . 204 C5
Telford Rd CH65 . . . . . 70 D7
Telford's Quay CH65 . . . . . 70 D7
Telford Way
Audlem CW3 . . . . . 230 A3
Chester CH4 . . . . . 140 F6
Middlewich CW10 . . . . . 128 E1
Tempest Rd SK9 . . . . . 60 C1
Templar Ct SK10 . . . . . 87 A1
Temple Chambers
CH1 . . . . . 237 B3
Temple Ct WA3 . . . . . 9 E6
Templeton Dr WA2 . . . . . 9 A3
Tenbury Cl WA5 . . . . . 7 F2
Tenby Dr WA7 . . . . . 23 D2
Tenby Rd SK11 . . . . . 111 F6
Tenchersfield CW5 . . . . . 205 A4
Tennyson Ave CW1 . . . . . 190 F4
Tennyson Cl
Crewe CW2 . . . . . 190 A1
Macclesfield SK11 . . . . . 111 E6
Northwich CW9 . . . . . 104 C6
Rode Heath ST7 . . . . . 193 E8
Tennyson Dr WA2 . . . . . 8 C2
Tennyson Rd
Ellesmere Port CH65 . . . . . 70 A4
Widnes WA8 . . . . . 13 A1
Tennyson Wlk CH1 . . . . . 118 A5
Tenth Ave CH5 . . . . . 92 D3
Terence Ave WA1 . . . . . 16 F6
Terminal Rd M90 . . . . . 33 B7
Terminal Rd S M90 . . . . . 33 B7
Tern Ave ST7 . . . . . 195 C2
Tern Cl WA8 . . . . . 13 B4
Tern Dr SK12 . . . . . 36 B4
Tern Wlk WA8 . . . . . 23 A5
Terra Nova Sch CW4 . . . . . 108 D1
Terrick Mews SY13 . . . . . 226 B2
Terrick Rd SY13 . . . . . 226 A2
Tetchill Cl
Ellesmere Port CH66 . . . . . 69 D2
Runcorn WA7 . . . . . 50 D8
Tetton Ct 8 CW12 . . . . . 156 F3
Tetton La CW10 . . . . . 151 E2

Tewkesbury Cl
Cheadle SK8 . . . . . 35 B6
Chester CH2 . . . . . 118 F7
Ellesmere Port CH66 . . . . . 94 E8
Middlewich CW10 . . . . . 128 B1
Poynton SK12 . . . . . 36 D4
Tewkesbury Dr SK10 . . . . . 87 E4
Tewkesbury Rd WA3 . . . . . 3 B8
Thackeray Dr CH3 . . . . . 119 C3
Thackeray Twrs 2
CH1 . . . . . 237 C3
Thackery Ct 6 CW11 . . . . . 174 D6
Thames Cl
Congleton CW12 . . . . . 156 F1
Warrington WA2 . . . . . 8 D2
Thamesdale CH65 . . . . . 70 B4
Thames Dr
Biddulph ST8 . . . . . 179 D1
Biddulph ST8 . . . . . 179 E1
Thames Gdns CH65 . . . . . 70 B3
Thames Pl CW7 . . . . . 127 B2
Thames Rd WA3 . . . . . 5 A2
Thames Side CH65 . . . . . 70 B3
Thames Trad Ctr M44 . . . . . 11 F7
Thatchers Mount WA5 . . . . . 1 D1
Thaxted Wlk M22 . . . . . 33 C8
Theatre Ct CW9 . . . . . 103 F8
THE BANK 195 B7
THE BARONY 204 F6
THELWALL 17 E3
Thelwall Com Inf Sch
WA4 . . . . . 17 C3
Thelwall Com Jun Sch
WA4 . . . . . 17 D3
Thelwall La
Warrington WA4 . . . . . 16 F3
Warrington WA4 . . . . . 17 B3
Thelwall New Rd WA4 . . . . . 17 C3
Thelwall New Rd Ind Est
WA4 . . . . . 17 C3
Thelwall Rd CH66 . . . . . 69 E4
THE QUARRY 209 B1
THE ROOKERY 195 C3
Thetford Cl SK10 . . . . . 87 C3
Thetford Rd WA5 . . . . . 14 E6
THE VALLEY 190 A4
The Verdin High Sch
CW7 . . . . . 126 C1
Thewlis St WA5 . . . . . 15 E5
Third Ave
Connah's Quay CH5 . . . . . 92 F1
Crewe CW1 . . . . . 190 F1
Kidsgrove ST7 . . . . . 194 F1
Poynton SK12 . . . . . 36 D1
Runcorn WA7 . . . . . 49 F8
Sandbach CW11 . . . . . 175 A5
Thirlmere
Macclesfield SK11 . . . . . 111 F5
Macclesfield SK11 . . . . . 112 A5
Thirlmere Ave WA2 . . . . . 8 C3
Thirlmere Cl
Alderley Edge SK9 . . . . . 59 F1
Frodsham WA6 . . . . . 49 D1
Holmes Chapel CW4 . . . . . 130 A3
Winsford CW7 . . . . . 126 F3
Thirlmere Ct CW12 . . . . . 156 A2
Thirlmere Dr WA13 . . . . . 18 F3
Thirlmere Lo 5 WA13 . . . . . 18 F3
Thirlmere Rd
Chester CH2 . . . . . 119 A5
Crewe CW2 . . . . . 190 A2
Ellesmere Port CH65 . . . . . 70 C2
Neston CH64 . . . . . 66 E6
Partington M31 . . . . . 11 F3
Thirlmere Way WA8 . . . . . 22 C8
Thirsk Cl WA7 . . . . . 49 C6
Thirsk Way SK10 . . . . . 87 C3
Thistle Cl WA16 . . . . . 79 F7
Thistle Sq M31 . . . . . 11 E2
Thistleton Cl SK11 . . . . . 112 D6
Thistle Wlk 4 M31 . . . . . 11 E2
Thistlewood Dr SK9 . . . . . 60 D8
Thomas Ave CW5 . . . . . 205 A3
Thomas Brassey Cl
CH2 . . . . . 237 C4
Thomas Cl
Alsager ST7 . . . . . 193 C4
Blacon CH1 . . . . . 117 F6
Ellesmere Port CH65 . . . . . 70 B2
Mickle Trafford CH2 . . . . . 119 F8
Thomas Ct CW7 . . . . . 49 F7
Thomas Ho CH1 . . . . . 118 A5
Thomas Hodges Ct
CW4 . . . . . 130 D3
Thomasons Bridge La
WA4 . . . . . 25 E6
Thomas Row 8 CW5 . . . . . 204 E6
Thomas St
Biddulph ST8 . . . . . 179 D1
Congleton CW12 . . . . . 156 E3
Crewe CW1 . . . . . 190 D4
Golborne WA3 . . . . . 3 A8
Packmoor ST7 . . . . . 195 F1
Runcorn WA7 . . . . . 23 A2
Talke ST7 . . . . . 210 D8
2 Widnes WA8 . . . . . 23 A7
Thomas Wedge CE Jun
Sch The CH1 . . . . . 94 A1
Thompson Ave WA3 . . . . . 4 E3
Thompson Cl WA12 . . . . . 2 C1
Thomson Gdns CW12 . . . . . 156 A3
Thomson St WA3 . . . . . 9 E5
Thoresway Rd SK9 . . . . . 59 F5
Thorlby Rd WA3 . . . . . 4 F3
Thorley Gr CW2 . . . . . 190 A1

Thorley La
Wythenshawe M90 . . . . 33 A8
Wythenshawe M90 . . . . 33 B8
Thorley Mews W7 . . . . 35 F7
Thornberry Cl CH1 . . . . 117 B8
Thornbrook Way
CW11 . . . . 174 D8
Thornbury Ave WA3 . . . . 3 E7
Thorn Cl
Runcorn WA7 . . . . 49 C7
Warrington WA5 . . . . 14 F3
Thorn Dr M22 . . . . 34 A8
Thorne Cl SK10 . . . . 87 A5
Thorne Dr CH66 . . . . 69 B4
Thorneycroft Dr WA1 . . . . . . 16 C6
Thorney Dr SK8 . . . . 35 C6
Thorneyholme Dr
WA16 . . . . 57 B2
Thornfield SK9 . . . . 60 A4
Thornfield Cl WA3 . . . . 3 C8
Thornfield Hey SK9 . . . . 60 E8
Thornfields CW1 . . . . 173 B1
Thorn Gr SK8 . . . . 35 A7
Thorngrove Dr SK9 . . . . 60 C6
Thorngrove Hill SK9 . . . . 60 C6
Thorn Grove Prim Sch
SK8 . . . . 35 A7
Thorngrove Rd SK9 . . . . 60 C6
Thornhills WA8 . . . . 12 A3
Thorn Ho CH4 . . . . 141 A5
Thorn La CW8 . . . . 103 C5
Thornleigh Ave CW2 . . . . 43 F3
Thornleigh Dr CH66 . . . . 69 E6
Thornley Cl **1** WA13 . . . . . . 18 C3
Thornley Rd WA13 . . . . 18 C3
Thorn Rd
Bramhall SK7 . . . . 35 E5
Runcorn WA7 . . . . 49 C7
Warrington WA1 . . . . 17 A8
THORNS GREEN 32 C5
Thornsgreen Rd M22 . . . . . . 33 D8
Thornton WA8 . . . . 22 E8
Thornton Ave SK11 . . . . 112 A5
Thornton Bank CW6 . . . . . . 169 D4
Thornton Cl CW7 . . . . 127 A3
Thornton Common Rd
CH63 . . . . 42 D7
Thornton Cres CH66 . . . . 41 B6
Thorntondale Dr WA5 . . . . . . 14 F7
Thornton Dr
Chester CH2 . . . . 118 D5
Handforth SK9 . . . . 34 D3
Wistaston CW2 . . . . 206 A7
Thornton Green La
CH2 . . . . 71 E1
Thornton Ho
Audlem CW3 . . . . 230 A5
Thornton Hough CH63 . . . . . . 42 B6
THORNTON HOUGH 42 A7
Thornton Hough Prim Sch
CH63 . . . . 42 A6
THORNTON-LE-MOORS
. . . . 71 F1
Thornton Mews CH66 . . . . . . 69 B8
Thornton Rd
Ellesmere Port CH65 . . . . . . 70 E3
Gatley SK8 . . . . 34 C8
Warrington WA5 . . . . 15 B4
Thornton Sq SK11 . . . . 112 A5
Thorntree Bglws
SK11 . . . . 132 A8
Thorn Tree Cl L24 . . . . 21 E2
Thorn Tree Dr CW1 . . . . 173 A1
Thorntree Gn WA4 . . . . 27 B5
Thornway
Bollington SK10 . . . . 88 A7
Bramhall SK7 . . . . 35 C7
High Lane SK6 . . . . 37 F7
Thorn Wlk M31 . . . . 11 E2
Thornwythe Gr CH66 . . . . . . 69 E4
Thornycroft CW7 . . . . 126 A1
Thornycroft Cl SK11 . . . . . . 111 E1
Thornycroft St **7**
SK11 . . . . 112 E7
Thorpe Cl CW1 . . . . 189 F8
Thorp St SK10 . . . . 112 D8
Thowler La WA14 . . . . 30 A5
Threaphurst La SK12 . . . . . . 37 C8
THREAPWOOD 222 E7
Three Acre La SK8 . . . . 34 E7
Three Fields Cl CW12 . . . . . 156 B3
Threeways CW8 . . . . 101 D4
Thrush Way CW7 . . . . 126 F4
Thurlow WA3 . . . . 3 E7
THURLWOOD 193 E7
Thursfield Ave ST7 . . . . 195 C3
Thursfield Ct CH1 . . . . 118 B1
Thursfield Prim Sch
ST7 . . . . 195 E3
Thurstaston Rd CH60 . . . . . . 40 F8
Thurston Cl WA5 . . . . 15 D6
Thurston Gn SK9 . . . . 60 A1
Thurston Rd CH4 . . . . 140 E5
Thynne St WA1 . . . . 16 A4
Tibbs Cross La WA8 . . . . 13 D8
Tibb St ST7 . . . . 209 F2
Tidal La WA1 . . . . 16 C5
Tideswell Cl SK8 . . . . 34 D8
Tideswell Rd SK7 . . . . 36 E8
Tidnock Ave CW12 . . . . 156 E5
Tiffield Ct CW7 . . . . 127 A4
Tilby Dr WA6 . . . . 74 A8
Tilbury Rd WA7 . . . . 50 E6
Tildsley Cres WA7 . . . . 48 F6
Tilewright Rd ST7 . . . . 195 B2

Tilley St WA1 . . . . 16 C6
Tilman Cl WA5 . . . . 15 B8
TILSTON 198 B3
Tilston Ave WA4 . . . . 17 A4
Tilston CE Prim Sch
SY14 . . . . 198 B3
TILSTONE BANK 168 F4
Tilstone Cl
Hough WA7 . . . . 206 E2
Northwich CW9 . . . . 104 A8
TILSTONE FEARNALL
. . . . 168 F6
Tilston Rd SY14 . . . . 213 A5
Tilston Wlk **5** SK9 . . . . 34 E1
Timberfields Rd CH1 . . . . . . 117 A8
Timber La **2** CW9 . . . . 103 F8
TIMBERSBROOK 157 E2
Timbersbrook Gr **5**
SK9 . . . . 34 D2
Timberscombe Gdns
WA1 . . . . 17 C6
Timber St SK10 . . . . 87 F1
Timbrell Ave CW1 . . . . 190 A6
Timmis Cl WA2 . . . . 9 A3
Timmis Cres WA8 . . . . 13 A1
Timperley Ave WA4 . . . . 17 A4
Tinkersfield CW5 . . . . 205 A4
Tinkwood La SY14 . . . . 211 F1
Tinsley St WA4 . . . . 16 F3
Tintagel Cl
Macclesfield SK10 . . . . 111 E8
Runcorn WA7 . . . . 50 B6
Tintern Ave CH2 . . . . 118 F6
Tintern Cl
Poynton SK12 . . . . 36 D5
Warrington WA5 . . . . 7 E2
Tintern Rd SK8 . . . . 35 B6
Tipping Brow WA16 . . . . 58 C4
Tirley La CW6 . . . . 123 A2
Tithebarn Cl CH60 . . . . 40 F7
Tithebarn Dr CH64 . . . . 41 B2
Tithebarn Rd WA16 . . . . 32 C8
Tithings The WA7 . . . . 23 E1
TIVERTON 168 C6
Tiverton Cl
Chester CH2 . . . . 118 F5
Sandbach CW11 . . . . 175 C7
Widnes WA8 . . . . 12 C3
Tiverton Ct **6** CW9 . . . . . . 103 E5
Tiverton Dr SK9 . . . . 34 D1
Tiverton Sq WA5 . . . . 14 E4
Tiveton Ct CW9 . . . . 103 F5
Tobermory Cl WA11 . . . . 1 A5
Todbrook Cl SK23 . . . . 65 D6
Todds Bldgs WA8 . . . . 23 A6
Toft Cl
Chester CH4 . . . . 140 E5
Widnes WA8 . . . . 12 F1
Toft Rd WA16 . . . . 82 B7
Toft Way SK9 . . . . 34 E4
Tolland La WA15 . . . . 31 F8
Tollard Cl SK8 . . . . 35 B6
Toll Bar Ave SK11 . . . . 112 F7
Toll Bar Pl WA2 . . . . 8 A4
Toll Bar Rd
Chester CH3 . . . . 142 C8
Macclesfield SK11 . . . . 111 F8
Warrington WA2 . . . . 8 A3
Tollemache Cotts
CW5 . . . . 203 C8
Tollemache Dr CW1 . . . . . . 190 A8
Tollemache Terr CH2 . . . . . . 118 F2
Tollgate Cl ST7 . . . . 210 C8
Tollgate Dr CW3 . . . . 229 F4
Tollitt St CW1 . . . . 190 C4
Tom Brads Croft SK23 . . . . . 65 E8
Tom Fields ST7 . . . . 209 F1
Tomkinson Cl CW1 . . . . 189 F7
Tomkinson St CH2 . . . . 237 C4
Tom La WA14 . . . . 30 E6
Tomlinson Ave WA5 . . . . 15 F7
Tomlins Terr CH1 . . . . 117 E5
Tommy's La
Congleton CW12 . . . . 156 F4
Crewe CW1 . . . . 190 E2
Tonbridge Cl SK10 . . . . 87 B2
Toogood Cl CW2 . . . . 219 F8
Top Farm La CW7 . . . . 170 F2
Topgate Cl CH60 . . . . 41 B8
Topping Ct WA3 . . . . 9 B4
Top Rd
Frodsham WA6 . . . . 74 D5
Kingsley WA6 . . . . 75 B1
Top Station Rd ST7 . . . . . . 195 C7
Torbrook Gr **1** SK9 . . . . . . 34 D2
Torkington Rd SK9 . . . . 60 D6
Toronto Ave M90 . . . . 33 B7
Torr Dr CH62 . . . . 44 A7
Torridon Gr CH66 . . . . 69 F3
Torr Rd SK11 . . . . 112 C4
Torr Rise CH66 . . . . 146 D1
Torrs Valley SK22 . . . . 39 C7
TORR TOP 39 C8
Torr Top St SK22 . . . . 39 C7
Torrvale Rd SK22 . . . . 39 C7
Totland Cl WA5 . . . . 14 C7
Totland Gr CH2 . . . . 118 E4
Tourney Gn WA5 . . . . 7 A2
Towergate CH1 . . . . 118 B1
TOWER HILL 88 D4
Tower Hill SK10 . . . . 88 D4
Tower Hill Rd ST7 . . . . 195 F7
Tower Ho The **20**
SK11 . . . . 112 C8
Tower La
Lymm WA13 . . . . 18 F7
Runcorn WA7 . . . . 50 D7
Weaverham CW8 . . . . 77 B1

Tower Rd CH1 . . . . 118 B2
Towers Cl
Poynton SK12 . . . . 36 F5
Wistaston CW2 . . . . 206 A7
Towers Ct W4G 16 C7
Towers La WA6 . . . . 49 C2
Towers Rd SK12 . . . . 36 F5
Towers The **6** SK10 . . . . . 111 F8
Towers Yard Barns
CK12 . . . . 36 F5
Tower Way CW1 . . . . 190 C4
Townbridge Ct **14**
CW8 . . . . 103 F8
Towneley Ct WA8 . . . . 13 A1
TOWN END 12 C6
Town Farm La WA6 . . . . . . 100 E7
Townfield Ave CW5 . . . . 180 E2
Townfield Cl ST7 . . . . 194 D2
Townfield Ct CW8 . . . . 78 A3
Townfield La
Barnton CW8 . . . . 78 A3
Blacon CH1 . . . . 117 F8
Farndon CH3 . . . . 180 D2
Frodsham WA6 . . . . 74 D7
Lymm WA13 . . . . 19 B7
Mollington CH1 . . . . 94 D2
Swan Green WA16 . . . . . . 106 E5
Tarvin CH3 . . . . 121 B2
Tiverton CW6 . . . . 168 C6
Townfield Rd
Mobberley WA16 . . . . 58 A4
Runcorn WA7 . . . . 24 C2
Townfields WA16 . . . . 57 C2
TOWN FIELDS 149 D7
Town Fields CW11 . . . . 175 B5
Townfields Cotts **6**
CW7 . . . . 149 C7
Townfields Cres CW7 . . . . . 149 D7
Townfields Dr CW7 . . . . . . 149 C7
Townfields Gdns
CW7 . . . . 149 D7
Townfields Rd CW7 . . . . . . 149 D7
Townfield View WA7 . . . . . . 24 C2
Townfield Villas CH2 . . . . . . 72 B3
Towngate Bsns Ctr
WA8 . . . . 22 B7
Town Gn The WA4 . . . . 52 D5
Town Hill WA1 . . . . 16 B5
Town La
Hale L24, WA8 . . . . 21 E2
Mobberley WA16 . . . . 58 B4
Neston CH64 . . . . 66 F6
Townley Mill **6** SK11 . . . . 112 D7
Townley Pl **3** SK11 . . . . . 112 D7
Townley St **4** SK11 . . . . . 112 D7
TOWN OF LOWTON 3 D8
TOWN PARK 50 B8
Townsend Farm ST7 . . . . . . 193 E2
Townsend La ST7 . . . . 194 A8
Townsend Rd CW12 . . . . . . 156 E2
Townsfield Dr CW6 . . . . . . 147 F7
Townsfield La WA2 . . . . 8 A5
Townshend Rd CW9 . . . . . . 80 A3
Township Cl CH3 . . . . 182 C1
Town Sq
4 Northwich CW9 . . . . . . 103 F8
6 Runcorn WA7 . . . . 49 F7
Town Well Ave WA6 . . . . 75 C2
Townwell Ct CW5 . . . . 204 D5
Town Wlk **9** WA7 . . . . 49 F7
Trackside Bsns Pk
CW11 . . . . 174 C6
Tracy Dr WA12 . . . . 2 E3
Trafalgar Ave SK12 . . . . 37 A3
Trafalgar Cl
Northwich CW9 . . . . 103 E3
Poynton SK12 . . . . 37 A3
Trafalgar Ct
8 Macclesfield SK11 . . . . 112 D7
Widnes WA8 . . . . 23 A6
Trafford Ave WA5 . . . . 15 F7
Trafford Cres WA7 . . . . 49 C6
Trafford Pl SK9 . . . . 60 D6
Trafford Rd
Alderley Edge SK9 . . . . 60 B1
Handforth SK9 . . . . 34 B1
Trafford St CH1 . . . . 237 B3
Tragan Dr WA5 . . . . 14 D3
Tramway Rd M44 . . . . 11 F7
Tramway St CH1 . . . . 237 C3
Tranmere Dr SK9 . . . . 34 E2
Trap Rd CW12 . . . . 132 C8
Trap St SK11 . . . . 132 B6
TRAP STREET 132 C5
Travellers Rest Cvn Pk
CW7 . . . . 150 C8
Travers' Entry WA9 . . . . 6 A7
Travis St **10** WA8 . . . . 23 B8
Treborth Rd CH1 . . . . 117 D3
Tree Bank Cl WA7 . . . . 49 A8
Treen Cl SK10 . . . . 86 D3
Tree Tops CH64 . . . . 66 E4
Treetops Cl WA1 . . . . 16 F7
Tree Way WA16 . . . . 82 A7
Trefoil Cl
Huntington CH3 . . . . 142 B6
Warrington WA3 . . . . 9 C5
Tregele Cl CH1 . . . . 117 D4
Trenchard Dr M22 . . . . 33 F7
Trent Ave CW7 . . . . 127 B1
Trent Cl
Bramhall SK7 . . . . 35 C6
Culcheth WA3 . . . . 5 A2
Widnes WA8 . . . . 13 B4
Winsford CW7 . . . . 127 B1
Trentdale CH65 . . . . 70 B3
Trentham Cl WA8 . . . . 13 B4

Trentham St WA7 . . . . 22 F3
Trent Way CH60 . . . . 41 C6
Tresham Dr WA4 . . . . 27 A8
Trevithick Cl CW1 . . . . 191 A4
Trevoir Cl WA6 . . . . 57 A1
Trickett La CW8 . . . . 102 A3
Tricketts La CW5 . . . . 205 E5
Tricketts Mews CW5 . . . . . . 205 E5
Trident Ind Est WA3 . . . . 9 E6
Trident Ret Pk WA7 . . . . 49 C7
Trident Way SK11 . . . . 112 A5
Trinity Cl CW2 . . . . 190 A1
Trinity Ct
Congleton CW12 . . . . 157 B1
1 Knutsford WA16 . . . . . . 57 A2
Warrington WA3 . . . . 9 F5
Trinity Gdns **3** WA6 . . . . . . 49 C1
Trinity Ho **3** WA6 . . . . 49 C1
Trinity La SK11 . . . . 112 F3
Trinity Pl
Congleton CW12 . . . . 179 B8
1 Widnes CW8 . . . . 23 B7
Trinity Sq SK10 . . . . 87 F1
Trinity St
Chester CH1 . . . . 237 A2
Runcorn WA7 . . . . 23 B3
Trinity Terr **2** CW8 . . . . . . 103 E8
Troon Cl
Bebington CH63 . . . . 43 C5
Bramhall SK7 . . . . 36 A7
Haydock WA11 . . . . 1 A5
Holmes Chapel CW4 . . . . . 130 C2
Trossach Cl WA2 . . . . 8 E2
Troutbeck Ave
Congleton CW12 . . . . 156 A2
Newton-le-W WA12 . . . . 1 E4
Warrington WA5 . . . . 15 F8
Troutbeck Cl WA7 . . . . 50 A5
Troutbeck Gr CW7 . . . . 126 D2
Trouthall La WA16 . . . . 81 A2
Trubshaw Ct ST7 . . . . 195 C3
Trubshaw Pl ST7 . . . . 195 B3
Truman Cl WA8 . . . . 12 F3
Truman Ct **1** WA5 . . . . 15 B7
Trumans La CH66 . . . . 69 C7
Truro Cl
Bramhall SK7 . . . . 35 F7
Congleton CW12 . . . . 178 E8
Ellesmere Port CH66 . . . . . . 94 F8
Macclesfield SK10 . . . . 86 E1
Runcorn WA7 . . . . 50 C6
Warrington WA1 . . . . 17 B8
Tudor Cl
Ellesmere Port CH66 . . . . . . 94 F8
Middlewich CW10 . . . . 128 D1
Northwich CW9 . . . . 104 E6
Warrington WA4 . . . . 17 A2
Tudor Ct
Congleton CW12 . . . . 156 D2
4 Warrington WA4 . . . . . . 16 E1
Tudor Dr SK10 . . . . 86 D7
Tudor Gn
Blacon CH1 . . . . 117 E6
Handforth SK9 . . . . 34 E1
Tudor Rd
Handforth SK9 . . . . 34 E1
Runcorn WA7 . . . . 24 C3
Tudorway CH60 . . . . 41 B8
Tudor Way
Chester CH3 . . . . 142 A7
Congleton CW12 . . . . 156 D1
Nantwich CW5 . . . . 204 E3
Tue La WA8 . . . . 12 B6
Tulip Gr WA5 . . . . 15 E3
Tulip Rd
Haydock WA11 . . . . 1 F6
Partington M31 . . . . 11 E2
Tully Ave WA12 . . . . 1 F3
Tulworth Rd SK12 . . . . 36 D4
Tunbridge Cl
Warrington WA5 . . . . 15 A8
Wistaston CW2 . . . . 206 A8
Tunnel Rd CW8 . . . . 78 B2
Tunnicliffe Rd SK11 . . . . . . 112 F3
Tunnicliffe St **1**
SK10 . . . . 112 D8
Tunstall Rd
Biddulph CW12, SK11 . . . . 158 C7
Congleton CW12 . . . . 157 F2
Turf La SK11 . . . . 112 C3
Turnall Rd WA8 . . . . 22 B7
Turnberry Cl
Lymm WA13 . . . . 18 C4
Macclesfield SK10 . . . . 87 C4
Northwich CW9 . . . . 104 E7
Winsford CW7 . . . . 126 C2
Turnberry Dr SK9 . . . . 60 D8
Turner Ave ST7 . . . . 210 A1
Turner Cl
Crewe CW1 . . . . 190 A8
Widnes WA8 . . . . 12 D3
Turner Rise SK10 . . . . 88 C8
Turner St
Bollington SK10 . . . . 88 B8
Nantwich CW5 . . . . 204 F5
Turner's View CH64 . . . . 41 D2
Turnhurst Rd ST7 . . . . 195 F1
Turnock St SK11 . . . . 112 E7
Turnstone Ave WA12 . . . . 2 C4
Turret Hall Dr **1** WA3 . . . . . 3 E8
Turriff Dr CH63 . . . . 43 C4
Turrocks Cl CH64 . . . . 66 E5
Turrocks Croft CH64 . . . . . . 66 E5
Turton Cl
Hale L24 . . . . 21 E1
Warrington WA3 . . . . 9 C5
Turton St WA3 . . . . 3 A8

Turville Ho SK9 . . . . 34 D2
Tuscan Cl WA8 . . . . 13 B5
Tushingham Cl CH3 . . . . . . 142 B7
Tushingham-with-
Grindley CE Prim Sch
SY13 . . . . 214 C1
Tuson Dr WA8 . . . . 12 F4
Tutor Bank Dr WA12 . . . . 2 D3
Tweedsmuir CH3 . . . . 119 A2
Tweedsmuir Cl WA2 . . . . 8 F2
Twemlow Ave CW1 . . . . . . 175 B7
TWEMLOW GREEN 131 A5
Twemlow La CW4 . . . . 130 D6
Twenty Acre Rd WA5 . . . . . . 15 C8
Twinnies Rd SK9 . . . . 34 B1
TWISS GREEN 4 E4
Twiss Green Com Prim
Sch WA3 . . . . 4 E4
Twiss Green Dr WA3 . . . . 4 E4
Twiss Green La WA3 . . . . 4 E4
Two Acre Gr CH66 . . . . 69 F1
TWO MILLS 93 E8
Twyford Cl WA8 . . . . 13 D6
Twyford La WA8 . . . . 13 D6
Tyldesley Way CW5 . . . . . . 204 D6
Tyler St SK9 . . . . 60 A1
Tyne Cl WA2 . . . . 8 E2
Tynedale Ave CW2 . . . . 190 C2
Tynedale Cl SK11 . . . . 112 C8
Tynemouth Rd WA7 . . . . 50 C6
Tynesdale CH65 . . . . 70 B3
Tynwald Cres WA8 . . . . 12 F5
Tynwald Dr WA4 . . . . 26 C7
Tyrer Rd WA12 . . . . 2 C1
Tyrer Wlk **2** WA3 . . . . 3 F8
TYTHERINGTON 87 D5
Tytherington Bsns Pk
SK10 . . . . 87 D5
Tytherington Cl
CW10 . . . . 151 C6
Tytherington Ct SK10 . . . . . . 87 D3
Tytherington Dr SK10 . . . . . . 87 E4
Tytherington Gn SK10 . . . . . . 87 D4
Tytherington High Sch
SK10 . . . . 87 D2
Tytherington Park Rd
SK10 . . . . 87 D3
Tytherington Sh Ctr **1**
SK10 . . . . 87 D3

U

Ullapool Cl CH66 . . . . 68 F6
Ullswater SK11 . . . . 111 F5
Ullswater Ave
Crewe CW2 . . . . 189 E3
Warrington WA2 . . . . 8 D3
Winsford CW7 . . . . 126 C2
Ullswater Cres CH2 . . . . . . 119 A6
Ullswater Dr SK9 . . . . 83 F7
Ullswater Gr WA7 . . . . 49 D5
Ullswater Mans SK11 . . . . . 111 F6
Ullswater Rd
Congleton CW12 . . . . 156 A2
Ellesmere Port CH65 . . . . . . 70 C2
Handforth SK9 . . . . 34 C4
Ulverston Ave WA2 . . . . 8 B4
Ulverston Cl WA11 . . . . 1 A6
Ulviet Gate WA16 . . . . 29 C4
Underbridge La WA4 . . . . . . 25 E6
Undercliffe Ho WA4 . . . . 26 D6
Under Rainow Rd
CW12 . . . . 157 E1
Underway The WA7 . . . . 49 F8
Underwood Bsns Pk
CW1 . . . . 190 A6
Underwood Cl SK10 . . . . 86 F1
Underwood Ct CW1 . . . . . . 190 B6
Underwood Dr CH65 . . . . . . 70 C2
Underwood La CW1 . . . . . . 190 B6
Underwood Rd SK9 . . . . 60 C1
Underwood West Prim
Sch CW1 . . . . 190 A5
Unicorn Gateway **6**
SK10 . . . . 112 D8
Union Cl CW12 . . . . 156 D3
Union Ind Est SK11 . . . . . . 112 E7
Union Pl CH1 . . . . 237 A2
Union Rd
Macclesfield SK11 . . . . 112 E7
New Mills SK22 . . . . 39 C7
Union St
Chester CH1 . . . . 237 C2
Congleton CW12 . . . . 156 D3
Crewe CW2 . . . . 190 D3
Macclesfield SK11 . . . . 112 D7
Runcorn WA7 . . . . 23 B2
Sandbach CW11 . . . . 175 B6
Warrington WA1 . . . . 16 B5
Union Terr CH1 . . . . 237 B3
Union Wlk CH1 . . . . 237 B2
Unity Way ST7 . . . . 210 D8
University Way CW1 . . . . . . 191 B2
Univ of Chester CH1 . . . . . . 237 A4
Univ of Chester
(Chichester House)
CH1 . . . . 237 A3
Univ of Chester
Warrington Campus
WA2 . . . . 9 B3
Univ of Liverpool, Faculty
of Veterinary Science
(Leahurst) CH64 . . . . 67 D8

Univ of Manchester School of Physics & Astronomy The
SK11.............108 D2
Unsworth Ct WA2...........8 F1
Upcast La SK9.............59 E3
Uplands CW8.............101 D4
Uplands Rd CW9.........78 E4
Uplands The
  Biddulph ST8...........179 E2
  Macclesfield SK11......112 A8
  Runcorn WA7...........50 A7
Upper Cambrian Rd
  CH1...................118 B2
Upper Haigh St CW7...149 C8
Upper Mersey Rd WA8...23 A5
Upper Mersey St CH65...70 C7
Upper Northgate St
  CH1...................237 A3
Upper Raby Rd CH64....42 A2
UPPER THREAPWOOD
.....................222 E7

UPTON
  Chester...............118 D6
  Widnes................12 C4
Upton Ave SK8.........35 A8
Upton Bridle Path
  WA8..................12 F4
Upton-by-Chester High Sch CH2..............118 F6
Upton Cl
  Golborne WA3..........3 D8
  Winsford CW7.........126 F4
Upton Dr
  Chester CH2..........118 C6
  Warrington WA5.......14 F5
Upton Grange WA8.....12 D4
UPTON HEATH.........118 F8
Upton Heath CE Prim Sch
  CH2..................118 E8
Upton La
  Chester CH2..........118 D7
  Widnes WA8..........12 F4
Upton Mount SK10.....87 A1
Upton Pk CH2.........118 D6
Upton Priory Inf Sch
  SK10.................86 F2
Upton Priory Jun Sch
  SK10.................86 F2
Upton Rd CH66........69 D4
UPTON ROCKS.........12 E4
Upton Rocks Ave WA8...12 E4
Upton Rocks Mews
  WA8..................12 E4
Upton Way 12 SK9......33 E4
Upton Westlea Prim Sch
  CH2..................118 E7
Upwood Rd WA3........3 D7
Ure Ct CH65...........70 A7
Urmston Ave WA12.....2 B5
Ursuline Way CW2.....190 B1
UTKINTON.............146 B7
Utkinton La CW6.......146 E7
Utkinton Rd CW6.......146 C5
Utkinton St Paul's CE Prim Sch CW6..............146 B8

V

Vahler Terr WA7........23 C2
Vale Ave WA2..........16 B8
Valebrook Dr CW5......220 A8
Vale Bsns Ctr CW12....156 D2
Vale Cl CH4............139 C3
Vale Ct WA4............51 A3
Vale Gdns
  Alsager ST7...........193 E4
  Ellesmere Port CH65...70 B4
  Helsby WA6...........73 B4
Vale Head SK9.........34 D2
Valentine Rd
  Kidsgrove ST7........195 A1
  Newton-le-W WA12.....1 F3
Vale Owen Rd WA2.....8 D1
Vale Rd
  Alpraham CW6........169 A4
  Ellesmere Port CH65...70 B4
  Hartford CW8.........103 C4
  Marston CW9..........79 B6
  Wilmslow SK9.........61 B8
Vale Royal Clyd CW8...126 B8
Vale Royal Dr CW8.....126 A8
Vale Royal River Park Cvn Site CW9.............126 E6
Vale View CW9.........79 D1
Vale Wlk CW12........156 D2
Valiant Cl WA2........8 F2
Valley Brook Bsns Ctr
  CW2..................190 D3
Valley Cl
  Alsager ST7...........192 F3
  Knutsford WA16.......82 A7
Valley Ct
  Crewe CW2............190 B3
  Middlewich CW10......128 E1
  Warrington WA2.......8 F1
Valley Dr
  Chester CH2..........118 C5
  Ellesmere Port CH66...69 D5
  Handforth SK9........34 C3
Valley La
  Cuddington CW8......101 F3
  Sandiway CW8........102 A3
Valley Rd
  Bebington CH62.......43 D8
  Bramhall SK7.........35 F8
  Crewe CW2............189 F1

Valley Rd *continued*
  Macclesfield SK11.....112 A6
  Weaverham CW8.......77 C1
Valley Sch SK7........35 C5
Valley View
  Congleton CW12.......156 C3
  Ellesmere Port CH66...69 D5
  Newton-le-W WA12.....2 B1
  Northwich CW9........104 C7
Valley Way WA16......82 A7
Vanguard Ct WA3......9 D4
Varden Rd SK12.......36 E3
Varden Town Cotts
  SK10.................86 A4
Vardon St SK9.........60 D6
Varey Rd CW12........156 F4
Vaudrey Cres CW12....156 F3
Vaudrey Dr WA1.......17 D7
Vaughan Rd SK23......65 E5
Vaughans La CH3......142 A8
Vauxhall Cl WA5.......14 F4
Vauxhall Rd CW5......204 E7
Vauxhall Way CW7.....149 C6
Vearows Pl CW8.......103 F7
Venables Rd CW9......79 A1
Venable's Rd CH1......117 F4
Venables Way
  High Legh WA16......29 C4
  Middlewich CW10......151 E6
Venetian Marina Village
  CW5..................188 B8
Venns Rd WA2.........16 D7
Ventnor Cl
  Middlewich CW10......151 C8
  Warrington WA5.......14 D7
Venture Ho SK11......112 D6
Venture Way SK12.....36 F3
Verbena Cl
  Partington M31.......11 F3
  Runcorn WA7.........49 F4
Verdin Ave CW8.......78 F1
Verdin Cl
  Moulton CW9.........126 F7
  Winsford CW7.........126 C2
Verdin Ct CW1........190 A8
Verdin St CW9.........104 C8
Vere St CW1...........190 C5
Verity Cl CW1.........191 C4
Verity Ct CW10........128 E2
Vermont Cl WA5.......15 C7
Vermont Gdns SK7.....35 B5
Vernay Gn CW1........141 B5
Vernon Ave
  Audley ST7...........209 D2
  Congleton CW12......178 F8
  Hooton CH66.........44 A2
Vernon Cl
  Audley ST7...........209 D2
  Poynton SK12.........36 D2
  Saughall CH1.........117 A8
Vernon Dr CW3........230 F4
Vernon Inf Sch SK12...36 E3
Vernon Jun Sch SK12...36 E3
Vernon Rd
  Chester CH1..........118 B2
  Poynton SK12.........36 E2
Vernon St
  Crewe CW1...........190 B5
  Macclesfield SK10.....112 F8
  Warrington WA1.......16 B4
Vernon Way CW1......190 D4
Veronica Mews WA8....12 D1
Veronica Way CH66....69 D7
Vetch Cl WA5..........11 B5
Vetches The CH3.......119 F5
Viaduct St WA12.......2 A3
Vicarage Ave CH65....35 D7
Vicarage Cl
  Guilden Sutton CH3...119 F5
  Hale L24..............21 E1
Vicarage Ct LL13......196 E8
Vicarage Dr WA11.....1 B7
Vicarage Gdns CW11...174 E8
Vicarage Gr CW7......149 D5
Vicarage Hill WA6.....73 C4
Vicarage La
  Audlem CW3..........230 A4
  Bunbury CW6.........168 F1
  Burton CW6...........67 D2
  Frodsham WA6.......74 C7
  Helsby WA6...........73 C4
  Little Budworth CW6...147 F7
  Poynton SK12.........36 E5
  Sandbach CW11.......174 E8
Vicarage Rd
  Chester CH2..........118 F3
  Haslington CW1......191 D6
  Haydock WA11........1 A7
  Northwich CW9........104 B8
  Widnes WA8..........23 A7
Vicarage Row CH62....44 A5
Vicarage Way 1
  SK11.................111 F7
Vicarage Wlk
  Northwich CW9........104 B7
  Warrington WA4......26 C8
Vicar's Cl CH3.........121 F7
VICARSCROSS.........119 E2
Vicars Cross La 2
  CH3..................119 B2
Vicars Cross Rd CH3...119 C2
Vicar's La CH1.........237 B2
Vickers Rd WA8.......22 F4
Vickers Way CW9......104 A7
Victoria Ave
  Crewe CW2............190 A4
  Grappenhall WA4.....17 A2
  Haslington CW1......191 C4

Victoria Ave *continued*
  Heswall CH60.........41 A6
  Holmes Chapel CW4...130 C2
  Kidsgrove ST7........194 F2
  Warrington WA5.......14 D6
  Widnes WA8..........13 A3
Victoria Cl SK7........35 D6
Victoria Com Tech Sch
  CW1..................190 C5
Victoria Cres
  Chester CH2..........237 A4
  Chester, Queen's Park
  CH4..................237 C1
Victoria Ct
  Chester CH2..........237 A4
  3 Crewe CW1.........190 C4
  Haslington CW1......191 C4
  8 Kidsgrove ST7......195 A2
  Knutsford WA16......56 F1
  2 Widnes WA8........23 A8
Victoria Gr WA8.......13 A3
Victoria Infmy CW8...103 E8
Victoria Inf Sch CH1...237 A4
Victoria Mews CH65...70 B5
Victoria Mill Dr CW5...205 D6
Victoria Pathway
  CH4..................237 C1
Victoria Pl
  Chester CH1..........237 B3
  Warrington WA4......16 C1
Victoria Rd
  Chester CH1, CW1....237 B3
  Chester CH2..........237 A4
  Ellesmere Port CH65...70 C5
  Macclesfield SK10.....87 A1
  Neston CH64.........67 A6
  Newton-le-W WA12....2 C3
  Northwich CW9........104 B8
  Runcorn WA7.........23 A2
  Saltney CH4...........23 A8
  Saltney CW4..........140 D5
  Warrington, Great Sankey
  WA5..................15 B4
  Warrington, Penketh
  WA5..................16 D1
  Warrington, Stockton Heath
  WA4..................16 D1
Victoria Road Prim Sch
  Northwich CW9........104 B8
  Runcorn WA7.........23 A2
Victoria Sq
  Warrington WA4......16 C1
  8 Widnes WA8........23 A8
  Winsford CW7.........149 A8
Victoria St
  Congleton CW12......156 D2
  Crewe CW1...........190 C4
  Knutsford WA16......56 F2
  New Mills SK22.......39 B6
  Northwich CW9........79 E2
  Sandbach CW11.......175 B7
  Warrington WA1......16 C5
  Widnes WA8..........23 B7
Victoria Stadium (Northwich Victoria FC)
  CW9..................79 D3
Victoria Trad Ctr WA8...23 A6
Victoria Way SK7......35 D6
Victoria Wlk SK10.....112 E8
Victory Rd M44........11 C4
Viewlands Dr SK9.....34 D2
Viking Way CW12......156 C4
Villa Farm CW11.......176 D8
Village Cl
  Lostock Green CW9...105 A8
  Runcorn WA7.........50 A8
  Warrington WA4......17 E4
Village Ct 8 SK9.......34 D1
Village Farm CW5.....172 A5
Village La WA4.........52 D4
Village Mews SK10....87 A6
Village Rd
  Christleton CH3.......142 E8
  Great Barrow CH3....120 E6
  Heswall CH60.........40 F7
  Waverton CH3........143 C4
Village St WA7........24 E2
Village Terr The 6
  WA6..................16 C1
Village The
  Astbury CW12........178 B8
  Burton CH64.........67 D1
  Prestbury SK10......86 F6
Village Way 11 SK9....34 D1
Villa Rd CH5..........116 B7
Villars St WA1........16 C5
Villas The CW4........131 A8
Villiers Russell Cl
  CW1..................190 D5
Vincent Cl WA5.......15 C8
Vincent Dr CH4.......141 C6
Vincent St
  Crewe CW1...........190 E4
  Macclesfield SK11.....112 D4
Vine Bank Rd ST7.....195 A1
Vine Cl SK11..........112 A6
Vine Cres WA5........14 F6
Vine Rd CH66.........69 F1
Vine St
  Bollington SK10......88 B8
  11 Runcorn WA7.....23 A2
  Widnes WA8..........23 A7
Vine Terr WA8.........12 A2

Vine Tree Ave
  Crewe CW2............190 B1
  Shavington CW2......206 B5
Vine Tree Prim Sch
  CW2..................190 A1
Vineyard The CW2.....206 B4
Violet Cl WA3..........9 C5
Violet St WA8.........23 A7
Virginia Chase SK8....34 F8
Virginia Dr CH1.......117 C4
Virginia Gdns WA5....15 B8
Virginia Terr CH66....69 B8
Virtual Bsns Ctr CH1...117 E2
Viscount Dr
  Gatley SK8...........34 D7
  Wythenshawe M90...32 F7
Viscount Rd WA2......8 E2
Vista Ave WA12........2 A4
Vista Rd
  Newton-le-W WA1,
  WA12................2 A6
  Runcorn WA7.........49 A8
Vista The M44.........11 C4
Vista Way WA12........2 A4
Vixen Gr WA8.........12 F1
Volunteer Ave 7
  CW5..................204 E6
Volunteer Fields CW5...204 E6
Volunteer St
  Chester CH1..........237 B2
  Frodsham WA6.......49 D1
Vose Cl WA5...........15 D6
Vulcan Cl
  Newton-le-W WA12....2 C1
  Warrington WA2......8 F2
Vulcan Ind Est WA12...2 D1
VULCAN VILLAGE.....7 C8
Vyrnwy Rd CH4.......140 D6

W

Waddington Cl
  Golborne WA3.........3 F8
  Warrington WA2......8 F1
Wadebrook Dr 4 SK9...34 D1
Wadebrook Trad Est
  CW9..................104 C8
Wade Cres CW8.......78 A3
Wade Ct ST7...........195 A1
Wade Deacon High Sch
  WA8..................13 A2
WADES GREEN........171 F5
Wades La CW7.........126 D3
Wadeson Way WA3.....9 B7
Wade St CW9..........79 B1
Wadsworth Cl SK9.....34 E3
Waggon Cotts ST7.....208 E1
Waggs Rd CW12.......156 C1
Wagg St CW12.........156 D2
Wagon La WA11........1 B6
Waine St CW1.........190 D5
Wain Ho CH1...........94 A1
Wain Lee ST7..........195 F4
Wakefield Cl CW1.....189 F7
Wakefield Ct CW9.....104 A5
Wakefield Ho WA5....15 F6
Wakefield Rd CH66....63 F2
Wakefield St WA3.....3 A7
Wakeham Chase 8
  SK11.................111 F7
Wakes Mdw CW6.....185 E8
Walden Cl WA4.......17 D3
Walden Dr CH1........93 D8
Waldon Rd SK11......112 A5
Waldron Gdns CW2...189 F1
Waldron Rd CW1......191 F3
Waldron's La CW1....173 D1
Walfield Ave CW12....156 D5
Walford Ave CW2......190 B3
WALGHERTON.........220 B6
Walgrave Cl CW12.....156 A3
Walker Cl CW1........191 D4
Walker Dr CH10.......151 C8
Walker La SK11........112 E2
WALKER'S GREEN....152 D7
Walkersgreen Rd
  ST5..................210 D2
Walkers La
  Ellesmere Port CH66...69 C6
  Farndon CH3.........180 F2
  Scholar Green ST7....177 B2
  Tarporley CW6........146 D1
  Warrington WA5......14 E3
Walker St
  Chester CH2..........237 C4
  Crewe CW1...........190 B5
  2 Macclesfield SK10...112 C8
  Warrington WA2......16 A6
Wallace Ct CW7.......127 D1
Wallace St
  Northwich CW8.......103 E7
  Widnes WA8..........23 A8
Wallcroft CH64.........68 A7
Wallcroft Gdns CH1...128 C1
Walled Gdn The
  CW10................127 D5
Wallerscote Cl CW8...102 E8
Wallerscote Com Sch
  CW8..................102 E8
Wallerscote Rd CW8...102 E8
Waller St SK11........112 C8
WALLEY'S GREEN....172 E7
Walleys La CW5.......203 C7
Wallfields Cl CW5.....204 E7
Wall Fields Rd CW5...204 E7
Wallhill La CW11......177 D7
Wall Hill Way CW8....76 F3

Wallingford Rd SK9...34 C5
Wallis St
  Crewe CW1...........190 D4
  Warrington WA4......16 B3
Wall La CW5...........204 E6
Wallrake CH60........107 F7
Walls Ave CH1........118 B1
Wallsend Ct WA8......12 F3
Wallworth's Bank
  CW12................156 E2
Wallworth Terr SK9....59 E8
Walmer Pl CW7........149 C6
Walmer Rd CH3.......119 A1
Walmsley St
  Newton-le-W WA12....2 D4
  Widnes WA8..........23 C8
Walnut Ave CW8......102 D7
Walnut Cl
  Chester CH2..........118 D7
  Warrington WA1......17 E7
  Wilmslow SK9.........60 E8
Walnut Cotts LL13....196 D8
Walnut Croft CH3.....180 F6
Walnut Dr CW7........127 A1
Walnut Gr CH66.......70 A1
Walnut La CW8.......103 A5
Walnut Rd M31........11 D3
Walnut Rise CW12....156 B2
Walnut Tree La
  Bradwall Green
  CW11................153 A4
  Walnut WA4..........26 F4
Walpole Cl CW1.......191 C5
Walpole Gr WA2......8 C2
Walpole Rd WA7......49 C6
Walpole St CH1.......237 A4
Walsh Cl WA12........2 C5
Walsingham Dr WA7...24 D2
Walsingham Rd WA5...14 F5
Walter St
  Chester CH1..........237 B4
  Warrington WA1......16 E7
  Warrington WA3......13 D1
Walters Wood SK23...65 F5
Walthall St CW2......190 C2
Waltham Ave WA3....5 C7
Waltham Ct WA7......24 E4
Waltham Dr SK8......35 B6
Waltham Pl CH4......141 A6
Walton Ave WA5.....14 E5
Walton Gr ST7........210 C8
Walton Hall* WA4....25 F7
Walton Hall Gdns*
  WA4..................25 F6
Walton Heath Dr SK10...87 B4
Walton Heath Rd WA4...16 B1
Walton La WA3........9 E5
Walton Lea Rd WA4...26 A7
Walton New Rd WA4...26 B8
Walton Pl CH1.........117 C4
Walton Rd
  Culcheth WA3.........4 F3
  Warrington WA4......26 C8
Walton St WA7........23 A2
Waltons The CW4....141 E6
Walton Way ST7......210 C8
Wandsworth Way WA8...22 F5
Wansfell Pl WA2......8 A3
WARBURTON..........19 C8
Warburton Bridge Rd
  WA13, WA3..........11 A1
Warburton Cl
  Altrincham WA15.....32 D6
  Barnton CW8.........77 F4
  Lymm WA13..........19 A4
Warburton Dr WA15...32 D6
WARBURTON GREEN...32 D6
Warburton La
  Partington M31.......11 F4
  Partington M31, WA13...11 E1
Warburton Rd SK9....34 D4
Warburton St WA4....16 D1
Warburton View WA3...11 A2
Ward Ave SK10........88 A8
Ward Cl WA5...........7 B1
Ward La SK12..........38 F4
Wardle Ave CW5......187 C7
Wardle Cotts CW5....187 C7
Wardle Cres SK11.....111 E1
Wardle Ind Est CW5...187 A7
Wardle Mews CW10...151 D8
Wardle St 8 SK11.....112 D7
Wardley Rd WA4......16 B1
Wardour Cl 8 SK11....111 F7
Wardour St WA5......15 E6
WARDSEND............37 A1
Wards La CW12.......179 C8
Ward's La CW11......153 C5
Ward's Terr CH2......118 F3
Wareham Cl
  Haydock WA11........1 C7
  Warrington WA1......190 B8
Wareham Dr CW1.....190 B8
Warehouse La SK9....60 B7
Warford Ave SK12.....37 A2
Warford Cres SK9.....84 B7
Warford Hall Dr SK9...84 B6
WARFORD PARK......58 E1
Warford Terr WA16...59 B2
WARGRAVE...........2 D3
Wargrave CE Prim Sch
  WA12................2 C1
Wargrave House Sch
  WA12................2 C1

Wargrave Mews WA12 ....2 C1
Wargrave Rd WA12 ......2 C2
Waring Ave
  St Helens Way........1 B2
  Warrington WA4 ....16 F5
Warkworth Cl WA8 .....12 C3
Warkworth Ct CH65....70 F3
WARMINGHAM 173 D7
Warmingham CE Prim Sch
  CW11 ....173 E8
Warmingham Ct
  CW10 ....151 D7
Warmingham La
  Middlewich CW10 ....151 D5
  Sandbach CW11 .....174 B8
Warmingham Rd
  CW1 ....173 D4
Warnley Cl WA8 ....12 D3
WARREN 111 D1
Warren Ave
  Knutsford WA16 ......56 E2
  Lostock Gralam CW9 ..80 A3
Warren Cl
  Knutsford WA16 ......56 F2
  Middlewich CW10 ....151 B7
  Poynton SK12 ....36 B4
Warren Croft WA7 .....50 D7
Warren Ct
  Ellesmere Port CH66 ..69 D3
  Frodsham WA6 ......74 D6
Warren Dr
  Altrincham WA15 ......32 D7
  Broughton CH4 ......139 A3
  Ellesmere Port CH66 ..69 E7
  Newton-le-W WA12 ....2 F4
Warren Gr SK11 ....111 D1
Warrington WA4 ....26 D8
Warren Gr SK11 ....111 D1
Warren Hey SK9 ....60 E8
Warren La
  Hartford CW8 ....103 A4
  Warrington WA1 ....17 D8
Warren Lea SK12 ....36 E5
Warren Rd
  Warrington, Orford WA2 ..8 D1
  Warrington WA4 ......26 C7
Warren The
  Cuddington CW8 .....101 D5
  Newton-le-W WA12 ....2 A3
Warren Way CW6 .....168 D8
Warrilow Heath Rd
  ST5.................210 C1
WARRINGTON 16 E6
Warrington Ave
  Crewe CW1 ....190 C6
  Ellesmere Port CH66 ..70 B2
Warrington Bank Quay Sta
  WA1.................15 F4
Warrington Bsns Ctr
  14 Warrington WA1 ..16 B5
  Warrington WA2 ......16 A6
Warrington Bsns Pk
  WA2..................8 C1
Warrington Central Sta
  WA2.................16 B6
Warrington Central Trad
  Est WA2 ....16 A6
Warrington Collegiate
  WA2..................8 B1
Warrington Hospl WA5 .15 F6
Warrington La WA13 ...19 E2
Warrington Mus & Art
  Gallery* WA1........16 A4
Warrington Rd
  Bold Heath L35, WA8 ..13 D7
  Comberbach CW9 .....78 D7
  Cronton L35 ....12 E8
  Cronton L35 ....12 F8
  Cuddington CW8 ....102 A5
  Fowley Common WA3,
  WN7 ....5 C5
  Golborne WA3, WA12 ...3 A4
  Hatton WA4 ....25 F4
  Little Leigh CW8 .....77 A5
  Lymm WA13 ....18 B4
  Mere WA16 ....23 D2
  Mickle Trafford CH2 ..119 E7
  Runcorn, Castlefields
  WA7................23 E2
  Runcorn, Manor Park
  WA7................24 B4
  Warrington, Risley WA3 ..9 E7
  Warrington WA5 ......14 F8
  Widnes WA8 ....13 D1
Warrington St Ann's CE
  Prim Sch WA2 ....16 C8
Warton Cl
  Bramhall SK7.........36 A7
  Warrington WA5 ......15 A3
Warwick Ave
  Newton-le-W WA12.....2 E2
  Warrington, Bewsey
  WA5................15 F7
  Warrington, Great Sankey
  WA5................14 D7
Warwick Cl
  Kidsgrove ST7 ....195 A3
  Knutsford WA16 ......56 E2
  Macclesfield SK11 ....111 F6
  Neston CH64 ....66 E5
Warwick Ct
  Ellesmere Port CH65 ..70 E2
  Warrington WA1 ......16 E7
Warwick Dr SK7 ....36 D8
Warwick Gate CW5 ...217 C2

Warwick Gr **11** WA7.....23 F1
Warwick Mews SK11 ..111 F6
Warwick Pl CW7 ......149 C6
Warwick Rd
  Ullason CH1 ....117 F5
  Irlam M44 ....11 D5
  Macclesfield SK11 ....111 F6
  Warwick Wlk SK11 ...111 F6
Wasdale Gr CW1 ......173 B1
WASH END 4 C8
Washington Cl
  Biddulph ST8 ....179 C2
  Cheadle SK8 ....34 F8
  Widnes WA8 ....12 F3
Wash La
  Allostock WA16 ......106 E3
  Warrington WA4 ......16 E3
Wasley Cl WA2 ....8 F3
Waste La
  Cuddington CW8 ....101 D3
  Delamere CW8 ......123 F6
  Kelsall CW6 ....122 F4
Watch La CW11 ....174 A6
Waterbank Row CW9 .103 F7
Waterbridge Ct
  2 Lymm WA13 .....18 C3
  Warrington WA4 ......26 D8
Waterbridge Mews
  WA7.................24 A2
Waterfoot La SK23....65 D6
Waterford Dr CH64 ....67 A7
Waterford Pl SK8 ......34 B8
Waterford Way WA7 ..50 C6
Waterfront WA4 ......50 F6
Watergate Row N
  CH1.................237 A2
Watergate Row S
  CH1.................237 A2
Watergate Sq CH1 ....237 A2
Watergate St CH1 ....237 A2
Waterhouse Ave SK10 ..87 F8
Water La SK9...........60 A7
Water-Lode CW5 .....204 E5
Waterloo Cl **5** CH5 ...70 C5
Waterloo Cotts WA6 ...99 F8
Waterloo Gr ST7 ......195 A2
Waterloo Ho **1E** CW6..103 F8
Waterloo La WA6 .....74 F1
Waterloo Rd
  Bramhall SK7.........35 F8
  Chester CH2 ....118 C4
  Haslington CW1 .....191 D4
  Northwich CW8 .....103 E7
  Poynton SK12 ....37 A2
  3 Runcorn WA7 ....22 F2
  Runcorn WA7 ....22 F3
  Widnes WA8 ....23 A5
Waterloo St W SK11 ..112 C8
Watermead Dr WA4 ...50 F5
Watermill Dr SK11 ....112 F7
Watersedge WA8 .....49 D2
Waters Edge
  Anderton CW9 ....78 D3
  Chester CH1 ....118 B2
Waters Edge Mews
  CW10 ....151 C8
Watersfield Cl SK8 ....34 F8
Waters Gn SK11 ......112 D8
Waterside
  Disley SK12 ....38 E7
  Furness Vale SK23 ....39 E3
  Macclesfield SK11 ....112 E7
  Warrington WA4 ......26 D8
Waterside Cotts CW5 .216 E5
Waterside Ct WA7 ....22 E3
Waterside Dr WA4 ....49 D2
Waterside La WA8 ....22 C5
Waterside Mews
  CW11 ....174 F3
Waterside Rd SK12,
  SK22................38 E7
Waterside View
  Chester CH1 ....237 B3
  Northwich CW9 .....104 E6
Waterside Way CW10 .128 B2
Waters Reach SK12 ....36 F5
Water's Reach SK6 ....37 E7
Waters Reams CH3 ...142 B8
Water St
  Bollington SK10 ....88 B8
  Macclesfield SK11 ....112 C8
  Newcastle-u-Lyme ST5 ..210 D2
  Newton-le-W WA12.....2 C4
  Northwich CW9 .....104 A7
  Runcorn WA7 ....23 A3
  Widnes WA8 ....23 A6
Watertower View
  CH2.................118 F2
Waterway CH3.........143 B5
Waterways WA5 ......15 D6
Waterworks Dr WA12 ...2 F4
Waterworks La
  Ellesmere Port CH66 ..68 E8
  Hooton CH66 ....43 E1
  Winwick WA2 ....8 B7
Watery La
  Astbury CW12 ....178 C5
  Frodsham WA6 ......74 E6
  Winwick WA2 ....8 B4
Watkins Ave WA12 .....1 F3
Watkinson Way WA8 ..13 C5
Watkin St
  Sandycroft CH5 ......116 A3
  Warrington WA2 ......16 B7
Watlands Rd ST7 .....209 E2
Watling Cres CH4 ....141 E7
Watling Ct
  Chester CH3 ....119 C2

Watling Ct continued
  Cuddington CW8 ....102 B2
Watling Dr CW6 ......123 C6
Watling St CW9 ....103 F8
Watson's Cl CH4 ......139 C3
Watton Cl WA4 ....17 C1
Wavell Ave WA8 ....22 D8
Wavells Way CH3 .....142 D5
Waveney Dr SK9 ......34 D2
Waverley Avc WA4 ....26 D8
Waverley Cl SK10 ....113 A8
Waverley Ct **1** CW2 ..190 D2
Waverley Dr SK8 ......35 B7
Waverley Terr CH2 ...118 E4
WAVERTON 143 B4
Waverton App CH3 ...164 E6
Waverton Bsns Pk
  CH3.................142 F4
Waverton Cl
  Hough CW2 ....206 E2
  Northwich CW9 .....103 E4
Waverton Com Prim Sch
  CH3.................143 A5
Waverton Mill Quays
  CH3.................143 B5
Waverton Pk CH3 ....143 B5
Waverton Rd CH66 ....69 E5
Wavertree Ave
  Scholar Green ST7 ...194 E7
  Widnes WA8 ....23 A8
Wavertree Ct CH66 ....69 F7
Wavertree Dr CW10 ..151 B7
Wavertree Rd CH4 ...117 C5
Waybutt La CW2 ......221 D8
Wayfarers Ct CW9 .....79 F7
Wayfarers Dr WA12 .....2 E2
Wayford Cl WA6 ....49 B1
Wayford Mews WA7 ...49 B1
Way's Gn CW7 ....149 E8
WAY'S GREEN 149 E8
Wayside Cl WA13 .....18 D2
Wayside Ct WA12 ....119 F8
Wayside Dr SK12 ......36 C4
Wayside Linley ST7 ..193 F2
Wayside Rd SK10 ....112 F8
Waystead Cl CW9 ...103 F4
Waywell Cl WA2 ....8 F3
Weald Dr CH66 ....69 A6
Wealstone Ct CH2 ...118 E5
Wealstone La CH2 ...118 E6
Wearhead Cl WA3 .....2 F7
Weaste La WA4 ....17 E2
Weates Cl WA8 ....13 F3
Weathercock La
  CW12 ....157 E3
Weatherstones Cotts
  CH64 ....67 D8
Weatherstones Mews
  CH64 ....67 C8
Weaver Bank CW5 ...204 D5
Weaver Cl
  Alsager ST7 ....193 A3
  Biddulph ST8 ....179 D1
  Sandbach CW11 .....174 E7
Weaver Cres WA6 .....49 D1
Weaver Ct
  Macclesfield SK11 ....112 C7
  Northwich CW9 .....103 F8
Weaver Gr
  Mickle Trafford CH2 ..119 F8
  St Helens WA9 ....1 A3
Weaver Grange CW9 .126 E8
Weaverhall La WA7 ..150 B5
WEAVERHAM 77 C2
Weaverham Forest Prim
  Sch CW8............77 C1
Weaverham High Sch
  CW8.................102 C8
Weaverham Rd CW8 ..102 B4
Weaverham Way SK9 ..34 E4
Weaver Ho **1B** CW8 ..103 F8
Weaver La WA6........49 B2
Weaver Park Ind Est
  WA6.................49 D2
Weaver Prim Sch
  CW5.................204 E3
Weaver Rd
  Culcheth WA3 ....5 A2
  Ellesmere Port CH65 ..70 C2
  Frodsham WA6 ......49 D1
  Moulton CW9 ....126 E7
  Nantwich CW5 ......204 E6
  Northwich CW8 .....103 E7
  Runcorn, Heath WA7 ..49 A6
Weavers Cotts **3**
  CW12 ....156 D3
Weaverside CW5 .....204 E2
Weaverside Ave WA7 ..49 F4
Weavers La ST7 ....35 D6
Weaver St
  Chester CH1 ....237 A2
  Winsford CW7 ....126 E1
Weavervale Pk CVW ...77 A6
Weaver Valley Rd
  CW7.................126 F3
Weaver View
  Audlem CW3 ....229 E3
  Church Minshull CW5 .172 A6
  Northwich CW8 .....103 F7
  Weaverham CW8 .....77 D1
Webb Dr WA5 ....6 F6
Webb's Ct CW9 ....103 F7
Webb's La CW10 .....128 C2
Webbs Orch SK23 .....65 D8
Webster Cl CH4 ......139 C3
Websters La CH66 .....69 F2
Weddell Cl WA5 ....15 D7

Wedge Ave WA11 ....1 A5
Wedgwood Ave ST7 ..210 A1
Wedgwood Dr WA8 ...13 B4
Wedgwood La ST8 ...179 C2
Wedgwood Rd ST7 ..210 D7
Wednesbury Dr WA5 ..14 F6
Weedon Ave WA2 .....2 B5
WEETWOOD COMMON
  ....122 C2
Weighbridge Rd
  Connah's Quay CH5 ...92 B4
  Connah's Quay CH5 ...92 C5
Weint The WA3 ....11 B3
Weir Gr ST7 ....195 B2
Weir La WA1 ....17 E6
Weir St
  Northwich CW9 .....103 F7
  Warrington WA4 ......16 A1
Welbeck Ave WA12 .....2 D2
Welbeck Cl CW10 ....128 B1
Welford Ave WA3 ......3 C7
Welford Cl SK9 ....60 E8
Welland Cl CW11 ....174 C5
Welland Rd SK9 ......34 E2
Well Ave SK14 ....213 B3
Well Bank CH11 .....175 B6
Well Bank Cotts
  WA16 ....108 C8
Wellbank Ct CW12 ...156 E2
Well Bank La WA16,
  SK11................108 C7
Wellbrook Gr WA16 ...50 C5
Well Cl CH64 ....67 A4
Wellcroft Cl CW2 ....206 B7
Wellcroft Gdns WA13 .19 A2
Weller Ave SK12 ......36 D2
Weller Cl SK12 ....36 D2
Wellesbourne Cl
  Macclesfield SK10 ....86 F1
  Neston CH64 ....66 D6
Wellesley Ave
  Ellesmere Port CH65 ..70 C5
  Haslington CW1 .....191 C4
Wellesley Cl WA12 .....2 B5
Wellesley Wlk **8** CH65 ..70 C5
Welles St CW11 ......175 B6
Well Farm Cl
  Malpas SY14 ....213 B3
  Warrington WA1 ......17 D8
Wellfield
  Runcorn WA7 ....50 E5
  Widnes WA8 ....13 A3
  Winsford CW7 ......127 A2
Wellfield Cl WA16 .....80 A7
Wellfield Rd WA3 ......4 F4
Wellfield St
  Warrington, Bank Quay
  WA5 ....15 E5
  Warrington, Whitecross
  WA5 ....15 E6
Wellfield Way SY13 ..225 F1
Wellington Cir SK10 ..112 E8
Wellington Cl
  Congleton CW12 ....156 D4
  3 Ellesmere Port CH65 ..70 C5
  Knutsford WA16 ......57 C4
  Newton-le-W WA12 ....8 F2
  Warrington WA2 ......16 A6
Wellington Gate L24 ...21 E2
Wellington Gdns WA12 ..2 A3
Wellington Pl CH1 ...237 B3
Wellington Rd
  Bollington SK10 ....88 C8
  Broughton CH4 ......139 B4
  Ellesmere Port CH65 ..70 B4
  Hazel Grove SK7 ......37 B8
  Kidsgrove ST7 ....195 A2
  Nantwich CW5 ......204 E4
Wellington Rd N CH65 ..70 C5
Wellington St Wrkshps **4**
  WA1.................16 C5
Wellington St
  15 Macclesfield SK11 ..112 D8
  Newton-le-W WA12 ....2 A3
  Widnes WA8 ....23 A6
  3 Runcorn WA7 ....23 A3
  Warrington WA1 ......16 C5
  Widnes WA8 ....23 A6
Wellington Street Ind Est
  ....23 A6
Well La
  Alsager ST7 ....193 C3
  Antrobus CW9 ....53 A4
  Biddulph ST8 ....179 D3
  Chester CW2 ....118 E5
  Heswall CH60 ....41 B6
  Kingsley WA6 ....75 C2
  Little Budworth CW6 .147 F7
  Macclesfield SK10 ....88 B2
  Manley WA6 ....98 F3
  Mollington CH1 ......94 F2
  Neston CH64 ....64 F5
  Prestbury SK10 ....87 C8
  Stretton WA4 ....52 E8
  Warrington WA5 ......14 F3
  Weaverham CW8 .....77 C1
Wells Ave CW1 ....191 D5
Wells Cl
  Ellesmere Port CH66 ..94 E8
  Gatley SK8 ....34 C7
  Mickle Trafford CH2 ..119 F8
  Warrington WA1 ......17 B8
WELLS GREEN 205 F8
Well St
  Malpas SY14 ....213 B3
  Mow Cop ST7 ....195 D7
  New Mills SK22 ....39 B8
  Winsford CW7 ....126 C1

Wellswood Dr CW2 ..205 F7
Wellswood Rd CH66 ...69 E7
Welsby Cl WA2 ....8 F3
Welshampton Cl CH66 ..69 D2
Welsh La CW7 ....149 D6
Welshmen's La CW5 ..204 C7
Welshpool Cl WA5 .....7 D2
Welsh Rd
  Connah's Quay CH5 ..116 A7
  Ellesmere Port L.H66 ..68 E4
  Woodbank CH1 ......93 C6
Welsh Road Cotts CH1 ..93 D8
Welsh Row
  Nantwich CW5 ......204 D5
  Nether Alderley SK10 ..84 F6
Welton Cl SK9 ....59 F4
Welton Dr SK9 ....59 E4
Welton Gr SK9 ....59 E4
Welwyn Cl WA4 ....17 C3
Wem Gr ST5 ....210 E2
Wemyss Rd CH1 .....117 D4
Wendover Cl WA11 .....1 D7
Wenger Rd WA8 ....13 B5
Wenlock Cl
  Macclesfield SK10 ....87 B2
  Newcastle-u-Lyme ST5 ..210 E2
  Warrington WA1 ......17 A8
Wenlock Gdns CH66 ..69 F2
Wenlock La CH66 .....69 F2
Wenlock Rd WA7 ......50 A4
Wenlock Way CH4 ...140 F6
Wensleydale Ave
  Bebington CH62 ......43 E5
  Congleton CW12 ....157 A5
Wensleydale Cl WA5 ..14 F8
Wensley Dr SK7 ....36 D7
Wensley Rd WA3 ....3 E7
Wentworth Ave
  Macclesfield SK11 ....111 F6
  Warrington WA1 ......17 B7
Wentworth Cl
  Northwich CW9 .....104 E7
  Widnes WA8 ....13 A5
Wentworth Dr
  Bebington CH63.......43 C5
  Bramhall SK7.........36 A7
  Kidsgrove ST7 ......195 C3
Wentworth Gr CW7 ..126 A2
Werburgh Cl WA13 ...19 C8
WERETON 209 C1
Wereton Rd ST7 .....209 D1
WERVIN 96 A4
Wervin Rd CH2 ....96 A3
Wesley Ave
  Alsager ST7 ....193 D4
  Haydock WA11 ....1 F7
  2 Sandbach CW11 ..175 B6
Wesley Cl
  Nantwich CW5 ......204 E5
  Neston CH64 ....66 D8
Wesley Ct
  Congleton CW12 ....156 D2
  Winsford CW7 ....126 F1
Wesley Gdns **7** ST7 ..195 A2
Wesley Pl
  Crewe CW2 ....190 D2
  4 Northwich CW9 ..104 A8
Wesley St ST7 ....210 A1
Wessex Cl
  Shavington CW2 ....206 C3
  Warrington WA1 ......17 E7
Wessex Dr CW9 ......104 C6
Westage La CW9 ......79 B8
West Ave
  Crewe CW1 ....190 B4
  Kidsgrove ST7 ....194 C1
  Middlewich CW10 ...128 C2
  Northwich CW9 .....104 D7
  Warrington, Stockton Heath
  WA4 ....16 C1
  Warrington WA2 ......16 B8
  Weston CW2 ....207 B5
WEST BANK 23 A4
West Bank
  Alderley Edge SK9 ....85 A8
  Chester CH2 ....118 C4
  WA8 ....22 E5
West Bank Dock Est
  WA8 ....22 E5
West Bank Prim Sch
  WA8 ....23 A4
West Bank Rd SK10 ....87 B1
West Bond St SK11 ....23 A5
West Bond St SK11 ...112 C7
Westbourne Ave CH1 ..118 A5
Westbourne Dr **1B** SK9 ..34 D1
Westbourne Ho
  CW12 ....156 D2
Westbourne Mews
  CW12 ....156 D2
Westbourne Rd
  Blacon CH1 ....118 A4
  Warrington WA1 ......26 B7
Westbrook Ave WA4 ...16 D2
WESTBROOK CENTRE ..7 B1
Westbrook Cres WA5 ...7 B2
Westbrook Ctr WA5 ....7 C1
Westbrook Dr SK10 ....87 C1
Westbrook Old Hall Prim
  Sch WA5.............15 D8
Westbrook Rd WA6 ...75 B2
Westbrook Way WA5 ...7 B1
Westbury Cl
  Crewe CW2 ....206 C7
  Middlewich CW10 ...151 B8
  Warrington WA1 ......17 A8
Westbury Ct SK11 ....112 A7
Westbury Dr SK11 ...112 A7
Westbury Way CH4 ..140 F6

Westby Cl SK7 . . . . 36 A7
West Cheshire Coll
 CH65 . . . . 70 B5
West Cheshire Coll
 (Grenbank Ctr)
 CH4 . . . . 141 D6
West Cheshire Coll
 (Handbridge Ctr)
 CH4 . . . . 141 D7
West Cl SK10 . . . . 87 F7
Westcliffe Ct WA8 . . . . 13 B4
Westcliff Gdns WA4 . . . . . . 26 E3
Westdale Rd WA1 . . . . 17 A7
West Dr
 Heswall CH60 . . . . 41 A7
 Neston CH64 . . . . 66 E6
 Warrington WA5 . . . . 15 B4
 Winsford CW7 . . . . 127 A2
West Dudley St CW7 . . . . 126 F1
West End CH3 . . . . 121 E7
West End Cotts CW12 . . . . . 156 C2
West End Ct LL13 . . . . 196 D8
West End Gr WA11 . . . . 1 A6
West End Rd WA11 . . . . 1 A6
Westenra Ave CH65 . . . . . . 69 F6
Westerham Cl SK10 . . . . 87 B2
Westerhope Way WA8 . . . . 12 F3
Westerings The CH62 . . . . 43 C6
Western App CH2 . . . . 118 E4
Western Ave
 Blacon CH1 . . . . 117 D4
 Macclesfield SK11 . . . . . . 112 C5
 Macclesfield SK11 . . . . . . 112 D5
 Milton Green CH3 . . . . . . 165 C2
 Nantwich CW5 . . . . 204 E3
Western Ct CH2 . . . . 118 E4
Western Dr SK11 . . . . 112 C5
Western Pk CW11 . . . . 191 F8
Westfield Ave ST7 . . . . 209 C2
Westfield Cl
 Chester CH4 . . . . 141 B7
 Winsford CW7 . . . . 149 C5
Westfield Cres WA7 . . . . . . 22 E1
Westfield Dr
 Knutsford WA16 . . . . 56 E1
 Willaston CW7 . . . . 205 E8
Westfield Gr CW8 . . . . 77 F4
Westfield Mews WA7 . . . . . 22 F1
Westfield Prim Sch
 WA7 . . . . 22 E1
Westfield Rd
 Cheadle SK8 . . . . 34 F8
 Mow Cop ST7 . . . . 195 C7
 Northwich CW9 . . . . 104 B7
 Runcorn WA7 . . . . 22 E1
Westfields WA15 . . . . 31 F8
Westfields Ave SK10 . . . . . . 87 E1
Westfields Rise CW9 . . . . . 232 C1
Westford Rd WA4 . . . . 16 A1
Westgate
 Widnes WA8 . . . . 22 B7
 Wilmslow SK9 . . . . 60 A5
Westgate Ave CW7 . . . . . . 126 A1
Westgate Pk CW2 . . . . 206 E2
West Gn CH5 . . . . 116 A6
West Gr
 Alsager ST7 . . . . 193 E4
 Heswall CH60 . . . . 40 F8
West Hall Ct WA16 . . . . 29 C5
West Halton Hospl
 WA7 . . . . 49 F6
Westhay Cres WA3 . . . . 10 A5
WEST HEATH
 Congleton 156 A4
 Crewe 221 E8
West Heath Gr WA13 . . . . . 18 C4
West Heath Sh Ctr
 CW12 . . . . 156 A3
Westholme Cl
 Congleton CW12 . . . . 156 C3
 Crewe CW2 . . . . 206 C8
Westholme Ct SK9 . . . . 60 A2
Westhouse Cl CH63 . . . . . . 43 C5
West House Ct SK10 . . . . . . 86 E1
West Hyde WA13 . . . . 18 C3
West La
 Cuddington CW8 . . . . 101 F3
 High Legh WA16 . . . . 29 C6
 Runcorn WA7 . . . . 49 F8
Westland Ct CW12 . . . . . . 156 C2
Westland Dr WA2 . . . . 8 E2
Westlands ST7 . . . . 209 F2
Westlands Cl CH64 . . . . 41 F1
Westlands Rd CW10 . . . . . 128 B1
Westlands The CW12 . . . . . 156 C2
West Lorne St CW11 . . . . . 237 A3
West Mains L24 . . . . 21 A3
Westmere Cl CW7 . . . . 207 B5
Westmere Dr CW1 . . . . 190 F2
Westmere Ave CH4 . . . . . . 141 B7
Westminster Cl
 Middlewich CW10 . . . . . . 128 B1
 Warrington WA4 . . . . 17 C2
 Widnes WA8 . . . . 22 B8
Westminster Ct CH2 . . . . . 118 F2
Westminster Dr
 Bebington CH62 . . . . 43 D7
 Cheadle SK8 . . . . 35 B6
 Haslow WA3 . . . . 1 F7
 Wilmslow SK9 . . . . 60 A4
Westminster Gn CH4 . . . . 141 D7
Westminster Gr
 Ellesmere Port CH65 . . . . 70 C6
 [8] Winsford CW7 . . . . . . 149 A8
Westminster Ind Pk
 CH65 . . . . 69 F6
WESTMINSTER PARK
 . . . . 141 B6

Westminster Pl [1]
 WA1 . . . . 16 B5
Westminster Rd
 Broughton CH4 . . . . 139 B3
 Chester CH2 . . . . 118 F3
 Ellesmere Port CH65 . . . . 70 C6
 Macclesfield SK10 . . . . . . 87 C1
 [4] Macclesfield SK10 . . 112 C8
Westminster St
 Crewe CW2 . . . . 190 C2
 [14] Macclesfield SK10 . . 112 C8
Westminster Terr
 CH4 . . . . 141 C7
Westmoreland Cl
 WA4 . . . . 31 B8
Westmorland Ave
 Talke ST7 . . . . 210 F7
 Widnes WA8 . . . . 13 B1
Westmorland Cl SK10 . . . . 86 F2
Westmorland Rd M31 . . . . . 11 E2
Westmorland Terr
 CW4 . . . . 130 B3
WESTON
 Crewe 207 C5
 Macclesfield 111 F8
Weston Cl
 Middlewich CW10 . . . . . . 151 C7
 Northwich CW9 . . . . 103 F5
Weston Cres WA7 . . . . 49 A6
Weston Ct
 Runcorn WA7 . . . . 48 F7
 Shavington CW2 . . . . 206 C5
Weston Ctr The CW1 . . . . . 190 E1
Weston Gr
 Chester CH2 . . . . 118 E7
 Halewood L26 . . . . 21 A6
Weston La CW2 . . . . 206 E5
Weston Point Com Prim
 Sch WA7 . . . . 48 E7
Weston Point Expressway
 Runcorn, Rocksavage
  WA7 . . . . 49 B5
 Runcorn WA7 . . . . 22 E2
 Runcorn, Weston WA7 . . 48 E6
Weston Prim Sch WA7 . . . . 49 A6
Weston Rd
 Crewe CW1 . . . . 190 F1
 Runcorn WA7 . . . . 48 E7
 Weston CW1, CW2 . . . . . 207 B7
 Wilmslow SK9 . . . . 60 E6
Weston Sq SK11 . . . . 111 F7
Weston View WA7 . . . . 49 D4
WESTON VILLAGE 48 F6
Weston Village Prim Sch
 CW2 . . . . 207 C5
Westover Rd WA1 . . . . 16 F8
West Park Ave SK12 . . . . . . 36 A4
West Park Dr [7] CH66 . . . . 94 F8
West Park Mus SK10 . . . . . 87 C1
West Quay Rd WA2 . . . . 7 F3
West Rd
 Congleton CW12 . . . . 156 C3
 Ellesmere Port CH65 . . . . 70 C3
 Runcorn WA7 . . . . 48 D7
 Weaverham CW8 . . . . 77 B1
Westrees CW8 . . . . 101 D5
West Side Ave WA11 . . . . . . 1 A6
West St
 Alderley Edge SK9 . . . . . . 60 A1
 Chester CH2 . . . . 237 C4
 Congleton CW12 . . . . 156 D3
 Crewe CW1 . . . . 190 B5
 Haslington CW1 . . . . 191 C5
 Macclesfield SK11 . . . . . . 112 B8
 Middlewich CW10 . . . . . . 128 C1
 Mount Pleasant ST7 . . . . 195 B6
 Warrington WA2 . . . . 16 B7
West Vale CH64 . . . . 66 E6
West View
 Antrobus WA4 . . . . 53 A5
 Ellesmere Port CH66 . . . . 69 A8
 Northwich CW9 . . . . 104 B8
 Warrington WA2 . . . . 9 A1
West View Rd WA6 . . . . . . 101 A6
Westville Dr CW12 . . . . . . 156 A2
Westward Rd
 Chester CH3 . . . . 142 B8
 Wilmslow SK9 . . . . 59 F6
Westway CH60 . . . . 40 F6
West Way
 Holmes Chapel CW4 . . . 130 B3
 Sandbach CW11 . . . . 174 F4
 Shavington CW2 . . . . 206 D5
West Wing The CW10 . . . . 127 D5
Westwood WA7 . . . . 24 C1
Westwood Cl CW2 . . . . . . 207 B1
Westwood Ct CH64 . . . . 41 E2
Westwood Rd SK8 . . . . 34 B8
WESTY 16 F5
Westy La WA4 . . . . 17 A2
Wet Gate La WA13 . . . . 19 E4
Wetheral Rd SK10 . . . . 87 B2
Wetherby Cl
 Chester CH1 . . . . 118 B2
 Newton-le-W WA12 . . . . . . 2 C5
Wetherby Way CH66 . . . . . 69 A5
Wetreins La SY14,
 . . . . 197 D6
WETTENHALL 170 F7
WETTENHALL GREEN
 . . . . 170 F6
Wettenhall Rd CW5 . . . . . 188 B4
Wetton La CW8 . . . . 76 C4
Wetton Way SK11 . . . . 113 D2
Wexford Ave L24 . . . . 21 D2
Wexford Cl WA11 . . . . 1 D7
Weybourne Cl CH4 . . . . . . 140 E5

Weybridge Cl WA4 . . . . 26 E7
Weybridge Dr SK10 . . . . . . 87 B3
Weygates Dr WA15 . . . . 32 C7
Weymouth Cl WA7 . . . . 50 E6
Weymouth Rd WA5 . . . . 6 F6
Whaddon Dr CH4 . . . . 140 F4
WHALEY BRIDGE 65 E7
Whaley Bridge Prim Sch
 SK23 . . . . 65 E7
Whaley Bridge Sta
 SK23 . . . . 65 E8
Whaley Ct CH1 . . . . 117 A8
Whaley La SK23 . . . . 65 C8
Whaley Rd WA3 . . . . 5 C7
Whaley Dr CW6 . . . . 147 B3
Whaley Gr WA8 . . . . 13 D3
Whalley Hayes SK10 . . . . . 112 C8
Whalley Rd CW9 . . . . 104 A8
Whalley St WA1 . . . . 16 C6
Wharams Bank CW11 . . . . 176 F5
Wharburton Cl CW8 . . . . . 101 F2
Wharf Ct SK23 . . . . 65 E7
Wharfdale Ave CW1 . . . . . 173 B1
Wharfdale Cl WA5 . . . . 15 A7
Wharfe Cl CW12 . . . . 156 F1
Wharfedale Rd WA7 . . . . . . 50 B6
Wharfedale Dr CH62 . . . . . 43 F5
Wharfedale Rd CW12 . . . . 157 A5
Wharfe La CH65 . . . . 70 A7
Wharf La CW12 . . . . 178 B3
Wharf Mill CW12 . . . . 156 F1
Wharf Rd WA7 . . . . 24 E3
Wharf Rd
 Collins Green WA12 . . . . . . 1 E2
 Whaley Bridge SK23 . . . . 65 E7
Wharfside Ct [6] WA4 . . . . . 16 E1
Wharf St WA1 . . . . 16 C4
Wharf The
 Chester CH1 . . . . 118 B1
 Runcorn WA7 . . . . 50 F6
Wharmby Rd WA11 . . . . 1 E6
WHARTON 127 A2
Wharton CE Jun Sch
 CW7 . . . . 126 F1
Wharton Ct CH2 . . . . 118 F2
Wharton Gdns CW7 . . . . . 127 A3
Wharton Gn CW7 . . . . 127 A4
WHARTON GREEN 127 B4
Wharton Hall CW7 . . . . . . 127 A3
Wharton Ind Est CW7 . . . 126 F2
Wharton Park Rd
 CW7 . . . . 126 F2
Wharton Ret CW7 . . . . 127 A2
Wharton Ret Pk CW7 . . . . 126 F3
Whatcroft Cl WA7 . . . . 49 D6
Whatcroft Hall La
 CW9 . . . . 104 F1
Wheatcroft Cl WA5 . . . . 15 C6
Wheatfield Cl
 Barnton CW8 . . . . 78 A3
 Ellesmere Port CH66 . . . . 69 C3
 Macclesfield SK10 . . . . . . 87 C3
Wheatfield Rd WA8 . . . . 12 C5
Wheatland Rd CH60 . . . . . . 41 C7
Wheatlands WA7 . . . . 23 E1
Wheatley Ave WA12 . . . . . . 2 C5
Wheatley Rd CW1 . . . . 190 E6
Wheat Moss SK11 . . . . 84 B3
Wheatsheaf Cl WA6 . . . . . . 73 B2
Wheatsheaf La CW9 . . . . . . 53 B3
Wheatsheaf Rd SK23 . . . . . 65 E6
Wheelman Rd CW1 . . . . . . 190 A7
WHEELOCK 174 F4
Wheelock Cl
 Alsager ST7 . . . . 193 A3
 Handforth SK9 . . . . 34 D1
 Kingsmead CW9 . . . . 103 F6
Wheelock Ct CW11 . . . . . . 175 A2
Wheelock Dr CW7 . . . . 127 B1
WHEELOCK HEATH 192 A8
Wheelock Prim Sch
 CW11 . . . . 175 A4
Wheelock St CW10 . . . . . . 128 C1
Wheelock Way [2]
 ST7 . . . . 195 B2
Wheldon Cl CH2 . . . . 118 E8
Wheldon Rd WA8 . . . . 21 F7
Wheldrake Cl CH66 . . . . . . 69 B5
Whernside WA8 . . . . 12 C3
Whetstone Hey CH66 . . . . 69 D5
Whetstone Rd ST8 . . . . . . 179 C2
Wheycroft Mews
 CW1 . . . . 190 C5
Whickham St WA8 . . . . 12 F3
Whimbrel Ave WA12 . . . . . . 2 C3
Whimbrel Cl WA7 . . . . 49 F5
Whinchat Ave WA12 . . . . . . 2 C2
Whinchat Cl WA3 . . . . 3 E7
Whinchat Dr WA3 . . . . 9 F3
Whinfell Gr WA7 . . . . 49 E5
Whipcord La CH1 . . . . 118 B2
Whirley Cl CW10 . . . . 151 C7
WHIRLEY GROVE 86 D3
Whirley La SK10 . . . . 85 F1
Whirley Prim Sch
 SK10 . . . . 86 D1
Whirley Rd SK10 . . . . 86 D1
Whirlow Rd CW2 . . . . 206 B7
Whisterfield 109 F2
Whisterfield La SK11 . . . . 109 E3
Whiston Cl
 Macclesfield SK11 . . . . . . 112 B4
 Winsford CW7 . . . . 127 A4
Whiston Mews EX11 . . . . . 113 B4
Whiston St SK11 . . . . 112 C7
Whitbarrow Rd WA13 . . . . . 18 D4
WHITBY 70 A4

Whitby Ave
 Chester CH2 . . . . 118 D5
 Warrington WA2 . . . . 8 D2
Whitby Cl
 Crewe CW1 . . . . 190 E8
 Poynton SK12 . . . . 36 D4
WHITBYHEATH 70 B1
Whitby Heath Prim Sch
 CH65 . . . . 70 B3
Whitby High Sch The
 CH66 . . . . 70 A2
Whitby La CH1 . . . . 95 B6
Whitby Rd
 Ellesmere Port CH65 . . . . 70 C5
 Runcorn WA7 . . . . 23 E1
Whitby's La CW7 . . . . 126 B1
WHITCHURCH 226 A1
Whitchurch Cl WA11 . . . . . . 17 A8
Whitchurch Gr ST5 . . . . . . 210 E2
Whitchurch Rd
 Audlem CW3 . . . . 229 C3
 Broxton CH3 . . . . 183 A3
 Chester CH3 . . . . 119 B1
 Christleton CH3 . . . . 142 E7
 Edge Green SY14, CH3 . . 199 B4
 Handley CH3 . . . . 182 D8
 Milton Green CH3 . . . . . . 165 C4
 Newhall CW5, SY13 . . . . 228 A6
 Royal's Green CW3,
  SY13 . . . . 228 C2
 Sound CW5 . . . . 217 E3
 Waverton CH3 . . . . 143 A3
Whitchurch Way WA7 . . . . 49 D7
White Ave CW2 . . . . 189 F4
Whitebarn Rd SK9 . . . . 85 B8
Whitebeam Ave [5]
 CH66 . . . . 69 F1
Whitebeam Cl
 Newcastle-u-Lyme
  ST5 . . . . 210 D1
 Runcorn WA7 . . . . 24 C1
Whitebeam Row CW8 . . . 102 E7
White Bear Yd [13]
 WA16 . . . . 57 A2
White Broom WA13 . . . . . . 19 B4
White Clover Sq WA13 . . . . 19 A2
Whitecroft Ct SK10 . . . . . . 87 E2
Whitecroft Heath Rd
 SK11 . . . . 85 A1
Whitecroft Rd CH66 . . . . . . 69 E2
Whitecroft Villas M31 . . . . 11 E2
WHITECROSS 15 E6
Whitecross Rd WA5 . . . . . . 15 E6
Whitefield Ave WA12 . . . . . 2 C2
Whitefield Cl
 Golborne WA3 . . . . 3 A8
 Lymm WA13 . . . . 19 A5
Whitefield Ct WA3 . . . . 4 F2
Whitefield Gr WA13 . . . . . . 19 A4
Whitefield Rd WA4 . . . . 26 B8
Whitefields CH2 . . . . 72 B3
White Friars CH1 . . . . 237 A2
Whitefriars Wlk [2]
 M22 . . . . 33 D8
WHITEGATE 126 A7
Whitegate Ave WA3 . . . . 4 F7
Whitegate CE Prim Sch
 CW8 . . . . 125 F7
Whitegate Cl CW10 . . . . . 151 C6
Whitegate Fields
 LL13 . . . . 180 D1
Whitegate La CH3 . . . . 121 E7
Whitegate Rd CW7 . . . . . . 125 F3
Whitegates CW11 . . . . 179 D4
Whitegates Cl CH64 . . . . . . 42 E1
Whitegates Cres CH64 . . . 42 E1
Whitegates Ho CW7 . . . . . 189 E2
Whitehall Ave ST7 . . . . 194 F2
Whitehall Cl
 Barnton CW8 . . . . 78 A4
 Wilmslow SK9 . . . . 60 A5
Whitehall Ct [3] CW5 . . . . 204 D5
Whitehall Dr CW8 . . . . 103 C5
Whitehall La CW6 . . . . 124 E1
White Hall La CW11 . . . . . 151 E1
Whitehall Pl [5] WA6 . . . . . 74 B8
White Hart Gdns CW8 . . . 102 F4
White Hart La CW2 . . . . . . 205 E8
Whitehaven Cl WA5 . . . . . . 15 A7
Whitehaven Rd SK7 . . . . . . 35 C5
WHITE HILL 195 B2
Whitehill Rd ST7 . . . . 195 B2
White House Cl WA11 . . . . . 1 B6
Whitehouse Dr WA15 . . . . . 32 B8
White House Dr WA1 . . . . . 17 E7
Whitehouse Expressway
 WA7 . . . . 50 B5
Whitehouse Ind Est
 WA7 . . . . 50 D5
Whitehouse La
 Nantwich CW5 . . . . 204 F7
 Partington WA14 . . . . 20 D8
 Plumley WA16 . . . . 80 F5
Whitehouse Rd WA16 . . . . . 30 B3
White La CH3 . . . . 142 D8
Whiteleas Rd SK23 . . . . 65 D3
Whiteleggs La WA13 . . . . . 19 B1
WHITELEY GREEN 62 C2
White Lodge Cl CH62 . . . . 43 D5
White Lodge Mews
 CW8 . . . . 102 A3
Whitemere Ct CH65 . . . . . . 70 C7
WHITMOOR 179 D6
Whitemore Rd CW10 . . . . 151 C6
White Park Cl CW10 . . . . . 128 C2
Whiteridge Rd ST7 . . . . . . 195 B2
Whitesands Rd WA13 . . . . . 18 C4

Whiteside Rd WA11 . . . . 1 B6
Whites La CW2 . . . . 207 B6
Whites Mdw CH3 . . . . 142 A7
Whitesmead Cl SK12 . . . . . 38 D5
White St
 Macclesfield SK11 . . . . . . 112 D6
 Warrington, Stockton Heath
  WA4 . . . . 16 C1
 Warrington WA1 . . . . 16 A5
 Widnes WA8 . . . . 23 A5
Whitethorn Ave WA5 . . . . . 14 F5
Whitethorn Way ST5 . . . . . 210 E1
Whitethroat Wlk WA3 . . . . . 9 F3
Whitewell Cl CW5 . . . . 204 F5
Whitewood La SY14 . . . . . 212 D7
Whitfield Ave WA1 . . . . 126 F7
Whitfield Dr SK11 . . . . 112 B4
Whitfield Gr WA11 . . . . 1 A6
Whitfield Rd ST7 . . . . 195 B2
Whitfields The SK10 . . . . . . 87 A1
Whitley Ave
 Barnton CW8 . . . . 78 B3
 Warrington WA4 . . . . 17 A4
Whitley Cl
 Middlewich CW10 . . . . . . 151 B7
 Runcorn WA7 . . . . 48 F8
Whitley Dr CW8 . . . . 103 A4
Whitley La WA16 . . . . 55 B8
WHITLEY REED 53 D8
Whitley Village Sch
 WA4 . . . . 52 D4
Whitlow Ave CW5 . . . . 204 F4
Whitlow La CW9 . . . . 126 F8
Whitney Croft SK10 . . . . . 113 A8
Whitson Cl WA16 . . . . 29 C4
Whitstable Pk WA8 . . . . 12 E4
Whittaker Ave WA2 . . . . 8 D2
Whittaker Cl CW1 . . . . 190 A7
Whittington Gdns
 CW9 . . . . 104 A2
Whittle Ave
 Haydock WA11 . . . . 1 A5
 Warrington WA5 . . . . 15 A7
Whittle Cl CH5 . . . . 116 A3
Whittle Hall La WA5 . . . . . . 14 F6
Whittlewood Cl WA3 . . . . . . 10 A5
Whitton Dr CH2 . . . . 118 E5
Whitwell Cl WA5 . . . . 14 D7
Whitworth Cl WA3 . . . . 9 E3
Wicker La
 Altrincham WA15 . . . . 32 C8
 Guilden Sutton CH3 . . . . 120 A4
Wicklow Cl CH66 . . . . 69 A6
Wickson La CH3, CW6 . . . 167 D3
Wickstead Cl CW5 . . . . . . 205 A4
Wicksten Dr WA7 . . . . 22 F1
Widdale Cl WA5 . . . . 14 F7
Widgeon Cl SK12 . . . . 36 B4
Widgeons Covert CH63 . . . 41 F5
WIDNES 22 E7
Widnes Rd
 Cuerdley Cross WA5,
  WA8 . . . . 13 F2
 Widnes WA8 . . . . 14 C3
 Widnes Sta WA8 . . . . 13 A3
Wiend The CH2 . . . . 118 D4
Wight Cl CH65 . . . . 70 C1
Wightman Ave WA12 . . . . . . 2 C5
Wigmore Cl WA3 . . . . 10 A6
Wigsey La WA13 . . . . 19 A7
WIGSHAW 4 D2
Wigshaw La WA3 . . . . 4 D2
Wigwam Cl SK12 . . . . 36 C4
Wilbraham Cl
 Acton CW5 . . . . 204 A7
 Mickle Trafford CH2 . . . . 119 F8
Wilbraham Rd
 Acton CW5 . . . . 204 A7
 Congleton CW12 . . . . 156 F3
 Crewe CW2 . . . . 77 E1
Wilbrahams Way ST7 . . . . 193 D4
Wilbraham's Wlk ST7 . . . . 209 D2
Wilcock Rd WA11 . . . . 2 B8
Wilcote Cl WA8 . . . . 13 C4
Wilcott Dr SK9 . . . . 59 F4
Wild Arum Cl [8] WA3 . . . . . 3 E8
WILDBOARCLOUGH 137 E6
Wilderhope Cl CW2 . . . . . 206 C7
WILDERSPOOL 16 C2
Wilderspool Cres WA4 . . . 16 B1
Wilderspool Cswy
 WA4 . . . . 16 C3
Wild Goose Ave ST7 . . . . . 195 D3
Wilding Ave [8] WA7 . . . . . . 23 B2
Wilding Bsns Pk CH3 . . . . 119 C4
Wildings Old La WA3 . . . . . . 9 A8
Wilding St CW1 . . . . 190 D5
Wildmoor La CH3 . . . . 97 D1
Wildwood Gr WA1 . . . . 17 B7
WILKESLEY 233 F7
Wilkins La SK9 . . . . 33 E5
Wilkinson Ave WA16 . . . . . 16 F6
Wilkinson Cl WA8 . . . . 23 A5
Wilkinson St CW7 . . . . 149 B6
Wilkinson St N CH65 . . . . . 70 C6
Wilkinson St
 Ellesmere Port CH65 . . . . 70 C6
 Northwich CW9 . . . . 104 C6
Wilkinson Street Mews [1]
 CH65 . . . . 70 C6
Wilkinson Way CW7 . . . . . 149 B7
Willan Rd CH1 . . . . 117 D4
WILLASTON
 Ellesmere Port 68 A8

WILLASTON continued
Nantwich.............................205 D8
Willaston CE Prim Sch
Nantwich...............................67 F0
Willaston Dr L26.......................21 A6
Willaston Farm CH64..................67 F8
Willaston Green Mews
Willaston..............................67 F0
Willaston Hall Gdns
CW5...................................205 C6
Willaston Prim Sch
CW5...................................205 D6
Willaston Rd CH63,
CH64....................................42 D4
Willaston Way 8 SK9.................34 D5
Willbank La CW5.....................202 D5
Willerby Cl 1 SK10...................112 C8
Willeymoor La SY13.................225 D8
William Barker Ct 10
CW11..................................175 B6
William Beamont Com
High Sch WA2...........................8 C1
William Ct CH64.......................41 F2
William Foden Cl
CW11..................................174 D7
William Johnson Gdns
CH65...................................70 C6
William Penn Cl WA5.................14 E5
William Rd ST7.......................195 A2
Williams Ave WA12.....................2 C5
Williams Cl CH2......................118 C4
Williamson Cres SK23...............65 D8
Williamson Dr CW5...................204 C5
Williamson Rd SK23.................65 D8
William St
Chester CH1..........................237 B3
Chester, Hoole Park
CH2....................................118 F3
Congleton CW12.......................157 A4
Macclesfield SK10....................112 F8
6 Northwich CW9....................104 B8
Widnes WA8..............................13 C1
Winsford CW7.........................126 E1
William Stockton Com Sch
CH65....................................70 B5
Williams Way
Frodsham WA6..........................74 A8
Henbury SK11.........................111 C8
Willington Ave CH62.................43 E3
Willington Cnr CW6.................122 E2
Willington La
Duddon CW6...........................145 E7
Kelsall CW6...........................122 D4
Willington Rd
Duddon CW6...........................145 B7
Kelsall CW6...........................122 C2
Willis St WA1..........................16 D6
Willmer Cres ST7....................195 B6
Willotts Hill Rd ST5.................210 D1
Willoughby Cl WA5.....................7 C1
Willow Ave
Newton-le-W WA12......................2 E4
2 Widnes WA8.........................13 B2
Willow Bank
Cheadle SK8............................35 A6
Helsby WA6..............................73 D2
Nantwich CW5.........................204 F6
Willowbank Dr SK10...................88 C8
Willow Bank Est WA12................2 F4
Willowbrook CH5......................116 B4
Willowbrow Rd CH63,
CH64....................................42 D3
Willow Cl
Chester CH2...........................118 D8
Lymm WA13..............................18 E4
Newcastle-u-Lyme ST5..............210 D1
Paddockhill WA16......................59 B5
Poynton SK12...........................36 E3
Runcorn WA7............................49 C7
Winsford CW7.........................126 D3
Willow Cres
Chester CH2...........................119 A4
Crewe CW2.............................189 F2
Moore WA4...............................25 A7
Warrington WA1..........................9 A7
Willowcroft Way ST7................195 E4
Willow Ct
Alsager ST7............................193 E4
Connah's Quay CH5.....................91 D1
Higher Kinnerton CH4...............161 A7
Macclesfield SK10.....................87 B2
Middlewich CW10.......................128 C2
Nantwich CW5.........................204 F7
Newton-le-W WA12......................2 D4
Warrington WA2..........................7 F3
Winsford CW7.........................127 B2
Willowdale WA12........................2 E3
Willowdale Way CH66................94 F8
Willow Dr
Blacon CH1............................117 D5
Bunbury CW6..........................185 E8
Handforth SK9..........................34 D3
Sandbach CW11........................175 E7
Warrington WA4.........................16 E1
Willow Gn
Knutsford WA16.........................56 F3
Weaverham CW8.......................102 D8
Willow Gr
Barnton CW8............................78 B4
Chester CH2............................118 D8
Ellesmere Port CH66..................95 A8
Elton CH2................................72 A3
WILLOW GREEN..........................77 B5
Willow Green La CW8................77 B5

Willow Hayes CH3...................121 F7
Willowherb Cl CH3..................142 A6
Willow La
Goostrey CW4.........................107 F1
Thornton Hough CH63
CH64....................................42 D3
Woolston WA1...........................26 E4
Willow Lea CH1.........................94 F2
Willowmead Dr SK10..................87 A5
Willow Rd
Chester CH4...........................140 F6
Haydock WA11............................1 E7
High Lane SK6..........................37 F7
Newton-le-W WA12......................2 E4
Partington M31........................11 E2
Willows SK9.............................59 F6
Willows Cl CW7.......................206 B7
Willow Sq CW7.........................127 A2
Willow St CW12........................156 E3
Willows The
Frodsham WA6..........................74 C8
Higher Wincham CW9..................79 F6
Newton-le-W WA12......................2 D4
2 Northwich CW9....................103 E6
Partington M31........................11 F3
Sandbach CW11........................175 B7
Warrington WA5.........................14 F5
Willow Tree Ct WA8...................13 D2
Willow Tree Gr ST7.................193 F7
Willow Way
Bramhall SK7............................35 D7
Broughton CH4.........................139 B3
Prestbury SK10.........................87 A5
Willow Wood Com Jun
Sch CW7..............................127 B2
Willow Wood Inf Sch
CW7....................................127 A2
Wilmere La WA8........................13 A6
Wilmot Ave WA5........................14 F6
Wilmot Dr WA3...........................2 F7
WILMSLOW................................60 C5
Wilmslow Ave CH66...................69 E5
Wilmslow Cres WA4...................17 D4
Wilmslow Ct SK9......................34 D3
Wilmslow Dr CH66....................69 E5
Wilmslow Grange Prim
Sch SK9................................34 C4
Wilmslow High Sch
SK9.....................................60 B6
Wilmslow Old Rd
Mottram St Andrew
SK10....................................61 A2
Wythenshawe M90......................33 A6
WILMSLOW PARK........................60 D7
Wilmslow Pk N SK9...................60 D7
Wilmslow Pk S SK9...................60 C7
Wilmslow Prep Sch
SK9.....................................60 B7
Wilmslow Rd
Adlington SK10.........................61 D6
Alderley Edge SK9.....................60 A2
Gatley SK8...............................34 D7
Gatley SK8, SK9........................34 C6
Handforth SK9..........................34 D4
Mottram St Andrew,
Greendale SK10........................86 D8
Mottram St Andrew
SK10....................................61 A3
Woodford SK7...........................35 C1
Wythenshawe M90, SK9,
WA15....................................32 F5
Wilmslow Sta SK9....................60 C7
Wilmslow Wlk 13
SK11...................................112 E7
Wilsbury Grange
CW8....................................103 A5
Wilsden Rd WA8.......................12 B1
Wilshaw Terr CH63....................42 B6
Wilson Cl
Warrington WA4........................17 D3
4 Widnes WA8.........................13 D1
Wilson Cres CW9.......................80 B3
Wilson Dr CW9........................126 F7
Wilson Patten St WA1...............16 A4
Wilsons La CH65........................70 A3
Wilson St
Warrington, Bewsey
WA5......................................16 A7
Warrington, Birchwood
WA3......................................9 E5
Wilton Ave SK8.........................34 C7
Wilton Cl CW9........................103 E4
Wilton Cres
Alderley Edge SK9.....................59 F2
Macclesfield SK11....................111 E6
Wilton Dr WA15.........................32 C8
Wilton La WA3...........................4 B5
Wiltshire Cl
Macclesfield SK10.....................86 E2
Warrington WA1........................17 D6
Wiltshire Dr CW12...................156 E4
Wiltshire Rd WA8......................11 E2
Wiltshire Wlk SK10...................86 F2
Wilwick La SK11......................111 A7
Wimberry Dr ST5.....................210 D1
WIMBOLDSLEY..........................150 F4
Wimboldsley Com Prim
Sch CW10.............................150 F4
WIMBOLDS TRAFFORD................96 F6
WINCHAM................................79 C3
Wincham Ave CW9.....................79 D3
Wincham Bsns Pk
CW9.....................................79 D3
Wincham Com Prim Sch
CW9.....................................79 D3
Wincham La CW9.......................79 D3

Wincham Park (Witton
Albion FC) CW9........................79 C2
Winchester Ave
Ellesmere Port CH65.................70 D4
Warrington WA6........................15 C5
Winchester Cl
Shavington CW2......................206 B3
Warrington WA5........................59 E5
Winchester Ct CW2...................207 E3
Winchester Dr SK10.................111 E8
Winchester Ho
11 Chester CH1......................237 C3
12 Macclesfield SK10.............111 F8
Winchester Pl WA8....................22 C8
Winchester Sq CH4..................140 F5
WINCLE.................................160 A7
Wincle Ave SK12.......................36 F2
Wincle CE Prim Sch
SK11...................................136 F1
Windermere Ave
Chester CH2...........................119 A6
Warrington WA2.........................8 D3
4 Widnes WA8.........................13 B4
Winsford Rd CH64....................66 F7
Windermere Dr
Alderley Edge SK9.....................59 F1
Congleton CW12......................156 A2
Windermere Rd
Crewe CW2.............................189 E2
Ellesmere Port CH65.................70 C2
Handforth SK9..........................34 C4
Haydock WA11............................1 B6
High Lane SK6..........................37 E8
Winsford CW7.........................126 C2
Windermere St WA8...................13 B4
Windfield Gdns CH66.................69 D7
Windings The CW10..................128 B2
Windle Cl
Neston CH64............................41 E2
Warrington WA3..........................9 B7
Windle Ct ST7..........................193 E3
WINDLE HILL............................67 C7
Windlehurst Rd SK12..................37 D8
Windmill Cl
Buerton CW3..........................230 E4
Warrington WA4........................26 C6
Windmill Ctr The WA8................23 B8
Windmill Dr CW3.....................229 F3
WINDMILL HILL.........................24 C1
Windmill Hill Ave W CW7............24 D2
Windmill Hill Ave E
WA7......................................24 D1
Windmill Hill Ave N
WA7......................................24 D2
Windmill Hill Ave S
WA7......................................24 D2
Windmill Hill Ave W
WA7......................................24 C2
Windmill Hill Prim Sch
WA7......................................24 C2
Windmill La
Bollington SK10........................88 B6
Christleton CH3.......................142 D8
Hankelow CW3.........................230 F4
Preston on t H WA4....................51 A6
Warrington, Penketh
WA5......................................14 E5
Warrington WA4........................26 C6
Windmill Rise CH2....................118 D7
Windmill St
Macclesfield SK11....................112 E6
Runcorn WA7............................23 B2
Windscale Rd WA2......................9 A2
Windsor Ave
Crewe CW1.............................190 B6
Nantwich CW5.........................204 F3
Newton-le-W WA12......................2 D2
Tarporley CW6........................146 D1
Wilmslow SK9...........................59 F7
Windsor Cl
Bollington SK10........................87 E6
Cuddington CW8......................101 F4
Poynton SK12...........................36 D4
Windsor Ct
Chester CH1..........................237 B1
1 Warrington WA4...................16 E1
Windsor Dr
Alsager ST7............................192 F4
Altrincham, Bowdon
WA14....................................20 F1
Broughton CH4........................139 A3
Ellesmere Port CH65.................70 A3
Faddiley CW5...........................98 D1
Haydock WA11............................2 A7
Helsby WA6...............................73 B2
Warrington WA4........................17 B2
Winsford CW7.........................149 C5
Windsor Gr
Cheadle SK8............................34 F8
Runcorn WA7............................49 B8
Windsor Ho
6 Northwich CW8....................103 C5
Talke ST7...............................210 D6
Windsor Pl CW12.....................156 F2
Windsor Rd
Chester CH4...........................140 F6
Golborne WA3............................3 C8
Widnes WA8..............................13 A4
Winsford CW7.........................149 C5
Windsor Sq SK11......................112 D4
Windsor St WA5........................15 E6
Windsor Way WA16....................56 F2
Windways CH66.........................69 D7
Windy Bank Ave WA3...................3 E8
WINDYHARBOUR.........................109 C1
Winfield Way WA8.....................23 B8
Winfrith Rd WA7.........................9 A2
Wingate Rd CH62......................43 E5

Wingfield Ave SK9.....................59 E6
Wingfield Dr SK9......................59 E6
Wingfield Pl CW7....................149 B6
Winghay Rd ST7.......................195 B2
Winnard St WA2........................16 A7
Winkwell Dr CH4......................141 A5
Winlowe 8 SK11.......................112 E7
Winmarth Dr WA15....................32 D7
Winmarleigh St WA1...................16 A4
WINNINGTON...........................103 F7
Winnington Ave CW8................103 C8
Winnington Ct 8
CW8....................................103 F8
Winnington Hill CW8.................103 F8
Winnington La CW8....................78 D1
Winnington Park Com
Prim Sch CW8.......................103 D7
Winnington St
Northwich CW8........................103 F8
Winsford CW7.........................126 E1
Winnows The CW7.....................126 E1
Winscombe Dr CH3...................119 C2
Winsfield Rd SK7.......................36 E8
WINSFORD.............................126 E2
Winsford Cross Sh Ctr
CW7....................................126 D1
Winsford Dr WA5.........................6 E7
Winsford Gr CH66......................69 C3
Winsford High Street Com
Sch CW7..............................126 D1
Winsford Ind Est
CW7....................................127 C3
Winsford Rd CW7.....................170 F6
Winsford Sta CW7....................127 C1
Winsford Way CH1....................117 F2
Winslow Cl WA7.........................50 D8
Winstanley Cl WA5....................15 C5
Winstanley Ho WA16..................56 F2
Winstanley Ind Est WA2...............8 B1
Winstanley Rd CH64..................66 E5
Winston Ave
Alsager ST7............................193 C5
Newton-le-W WA12......................2 C3
St Helens WA9...........................1 B2
Winston Ct CH2.......................119 A5
Winterbottom La
WA16....................................55 E8
Winterford La CW6..................147 B2
Winter Gr WA9..........................1 B3
Wintergreen Wlk 8
M31....................................11 F3
Winterlea Dr L26......................21 A6
WINTERLEY.............................191 F7
Winterside Cl ST5...................210 D1
Winterton Way SK11.................112 D3
Winton Ave WA7........................24 D1
Winton Gr WA3...........................3 E6
WINWICK.................................8 A6
Winwick CE Prim Sch
WA2......................................8 B6
Winwick La WA3..........................3 E3
Winwick Link Rd WA2,
WA3......................................8 C6
Winwick Park Ave WA2................8 A5
WINWICK QUAY...........................8 A3
Winwick Rd
Newton-le-W WA12......................2 F1
Warrington WA2..........................8 A5
Winwick St WA2........................16 B6
Winwick View WA5.......................1 D1
Wirksmoor Rd SK22...................39 B7
Wirral Cl WA3.............................4 E4
Wirral Cres CH64......................66 F5
Wirral Ctry Pk* CH64.................67 C7
Wirral Metropolitan Coll
CH62....................................44 A7
WIRSWALL.............................226 A5
Wirswall Rd SY13....................226 A5
Wisdom Wlk CW11...................174 D7
Wisenholme Cl WA7...................49 E5
WISTASTON...........................205 D8
Wistaston Ave CW2.................189 F2
WISTASTON GREEN.................189 D2
Wistaston Green Cl
CW2....................................189 E2
Wistaston Green Prim Sch
CW2....................................189 E2
Wistaston Green Rd
CW2....................................189 E2
Wistaston Pk CW2...................189 F1
Wistaston Rd
Crewe CW2.............................190 C3
Wistaston CW5.......................205 E6
Wistaston Road Bsns Ctr
CW2....................................189 E2
Wistaston Westfield Prim
Sch CW2..............................205 E8
Wisterdale Cl CW2...................206 A7
Wisteria Way WA9......................6 A7
Witham Way ST8.....................179 E1
Withens Cl CWR......................102 D8
Withenshaw La SK11................136 C5
Withens La CW8......................102 D8
Withers Ave WA2.....................16 D8
Wither's La
High Legh, Primrose Hill
WA16....................................28 C6
High Legh, Rowlinson's Green
WA16....................................28 B4
Witherwin Ave WA4....................26 F7
Withington Ave WA3....................5 A3
Withington Cl
Northwich CW9.......................104 A6
Sandbach CW11......................175 C7
WITHINGTON GREEN
....108 E3

Withinlee Rd SK10....................86 D6
Withins Rd
Culcheth WA3.............................4 F3
Haydock WA11............................1 F8
Within Way L24.........................21 E1
Withnall Dr CW2......................206 D1
Withy Cl WA6............................74 C8
Withycombe Rd WA5..................14 E4
Withy Croft CH3......................142 B7
Witley La WA16..........................61 C1
Witney Gdns WA4......................26 E6
Witney La SY14........................213 D8
Wittenham Ho WA7....................34 D2
Wittering La CH60.....................40 D7
Witterings The CH44..................41 E1
Witton Church Walk CE
Prim Sch CW9.......................104 A8
Witton St CW9...........................79 A1
Witton Wlk 5 CW9...................103 F8
Witt Rd WA8..............................23 A7
Wivern Pl WA7...........................23 B3
Wizard Country Pk
SK10....................................85 D6
Wobbs La SY13.......................225 C5
Woburn Ave WA12........................2 D2
Woburn Cl
Haydock WA11............................1 F1
Macclesfield SK10.....................87 C2
Northwich CW9........................103 E5
Woburn Ct SK12.........................36 F4
Woburn Dr
Chester CH2...........................118 F7
Congleton CW12......................179 B8
Cronton WA8..............................12 D6
Woburn Rd WA2...........................8 A4
Woking Rd SK8..........................35 A7
Wolfe Cl
Grappenhall Heys WA4...............27 A8
Knutsford WA16........................57 C3
Wolstanholme Cl
CW12...................................156 F1
WOLVERHAM............................70 D4
Wolverham Prim Sch
CH65....................................70 D4
Wolverham Rd CH65..................70 D3
Wolverton Dr
Handforth SK9..........................34 D1
Runcorn WA7............................24 D1
Wolverton Ho 11 SK9................60 A1
Wolvesey Pl CW7.....................149 B6
Woodacre Gr CH66.....................69 F8
Woodacre Rd CH66....................69 F8
Woodacres Cl SK9.....................59 F6
Woodale Cl WA5........................14 E7
Woodall Ave CH4......................140 E6
Woodall Dr WA7........................23 B1
Woodavens Gr CW3..................229 A2
WOODBANK...............................93 F6
Woodbank Cl WA5......................60 A2
Woodbank Cl CW2...................206 A7
Woodbank La CH1......................93 D5
Woodbank Rd
Ellesmere Port CH65.................70 B2
Warrington WA5.........................15 A4
Woodbine Ave M44....................11 D4
Woodbine Rd WA13....................19 B4
Woodbourne Rd SK22................39 A5
Woodbridge Cl WA4...................26 E4
Woodbrook SK23.......................65 E7
Woodbrook Rd SK9.....................60 C7
Woodburn Dr CH60.....................40 F6
Woodchurch La CH66................69 E6
Woodclose CH66........................44 A1
Woodcock's La ST7...................195 C6
Woodcock's Well CE Prim
Sch ST7...............................195 C6
Woodcote Ave CH65...................70 B3
Woodcote Cl CW7........................8 D1
Woodcote Pl CW11...................191 F8
Woodcotes The CH62.................43 D6
Woodcote View SK9...................34 F1
Woodcott Ave CW7...................126 B8
Woodcott Cl CW2.....................206 E2
Woodcott Gr 8 SK9...................34 D1
Woodcotthill La CW5................217 B3
Woodcroft ST7.........................210 A1
Woodcroft Gdns WA4.................26 E6
Wood Dr ST7...........................193 A4
WOODEND................................38 E8
Woodend WA7............................50 E7
Woodend Ct CW10....................151 C6
Wood End St WA8......................13 D2
Woodend La
Hollins Green WA3.....................10 D2
Mobberley WA16.........................58 E8
Wood End La CH64.....................67 E4
Woodend Rd CH65......................69 F6
Woodfall Cl CW4........................67 A6
Woodfall Gr CH64......................67 A6
Woodfall La CH64......................67 A6
Woodfall Prim Sch
CH64....................................67 A6
Wood Farm CW7......................189 B4
Woodfield Cl CH4......................139 A3
Woodfield Gr CH2.....................119 B5
Woodfield Ho CH2...................119 A5
Woodfield Prim Sch
CH2....................................119 A5
Woodfield Rd
Cheadle SK8............................35 B7
Ellesmere Port CH65.................70 C5
Woodfield Rd N 2
CH65....................................70 C5
Woodfields CH3......................142 E7
Woodfin Croft SK11...................84 A3
WOODFORD.............................35 E2

Woodford Aerodrome
SK7 ....36 A1
Woodford Ave WA3 ....3 D7
Woodford Cl
  Crewe CW2 ....189 F2
  Helsby WA6 ....73 B2
  Runcorn WA7 ....49 B6
  Warrington WA4 ....17 C3
Woodford Court Ind Est
  CW7 ....149 A8
Woodford Ct CW7 ...149 A7
Woodford La
  Prestbury SK10 ....61 D7
  Winsford CW7 ....149 B8
Woodford La W CW7 ...149 A7
Woodford Lo SK12 ....36 C4
Woodford Lodge High Sch
  CW7 ....149 A7
Woodford Mews SK9 ...34 D4
Woodford Park Ind Est
  CW7 ....148 F8
Woodford Rd
  Bramhall SK7 ....35 E4
  Poynton SK12 ....36 B6
  Wilmslow SK9 ....61 B8
Woodgate Ave ST7 ....194 A5
Wood Gdns SK9 ....60 B2
Woodgreen La CW5 ...171 D5
Woodhall Cl
  Bramhall SK7 ....35 E3
  Warrington WA5 ....15 A8
Woodhall Rd ST7 ......195 C3
Woodham Cl CW8 ......103 C5
Woodham Gr CH64 ......66 F5
Woodhatch Rd WA7 ....50 B5
Wood Heath Way
  CH62 ....44 A7
WOODHEY GREEN 202 B6
Woodhey Hall La
  CW5 ....202 B6
Woodhey La CW5 ....202 C5
Woodhouse Cl WA3 ......9 F3
WOODHOUSE-END ...135 C8
Woodhouse End Rd
  SK11 ....135 C8
WOODHOUSE GREEN
  ....158 D2
Woodhouse La
  Biddulph ST8 ....179 F2
  Buerton CW3 ....235 D8
  Partington WA14 ....20 C4
  Warren SK11 ....111 E1
  Wythenshawe M90 ......33 D7
Woodhouse Mid Sch
  ST8 ....179 E2
Woodhouse Rd M22 ....33 D8
WOODHOUSES 73 E4
Woodhouses Pk WA6 ..73 F5
Wood La
  Bradwall Green CW10,
  CW11 ....152 E3
  Broughton CH4 ....139 B4
  Burton CH64 ....67 C2
  Duddon CW6 ....145 E7
  Goostrey CW4 ....107 C1
  Neston CH64 ....41 D2
  Partington M31 ....11 E3
  Runcorn, Brookvale WA7 ..50 C6
  Runcorn WA7 ....49 F5
  Sutton Weaver WA7 ......49 F4
  Tattenhall CH3 ....167 A1
  Warrington WA4 ....26 E8
  Warrington CW8 ....102 E8
  Wilmslow WA16 ....32 D1
Wood La E SK10 ....63 B8
Wood La N
  Fourlane-ends SK10 ......63 B8
  Wardsend SK10 ....37 B1
Woodlan Ct CW6 ....146 B6
Woodland Ave
  Crewe CW1 ....190 F4
  Lymm WA13 ....19 A2
  Nantwich CW5 ....205 A8
  Newton-le-W WA12 ....2 F3
  Widnes WA8 ....12 F1
Woodland Bank CH2 ....96 F1
Woodland Cl SK11 ......84 A3
Woodland Ct ST7 ......193 D4
Woodland Dr WA13 ......19 A2
Woodland End SK11 ....84 A3
Woodland Gdns CW1 ..190 D6
Woodland Rd
  Ellesmere Port CH65 ....70 B2
  Rode Heath ST7 ....193 E8
Woodlands CW8 ....103 B5
Woodlands Ave
  Chester CH1 ....118 B4
  Congleton CW12 ....156 D4
  Kidsgrove ST7 ....194 D1
Woodlands Cl
  Cheadle SK8 ....35 A8
  Cotebrook CW6 ....147 A8
  Neston CH64 ....66 D8
Woodlands Cres WA16 ..29 C4
Woodlands Ct
  Alderley Edge SK9 ....85 A8
  [18] Knutsford WA16 ......57 B2
Woodlands Cvn Pk
  WA16 ....106 E3
Woodlands Dr
  Chester CH2 ....118 E4
  Chorlton CW2 ....207 C3
  Goostrey CW4 ....107 E1
  Knutsford WA16 ....57 B2

Warrington WA4 ....17 D3
Woodlands Gr CW8 ....77 F3
Woodlands Ind Est
  WA12 ....2 C6
Woodlands Inf Sch
  CH66 ....69 F2
Woodlands Jun Sch
  CH66 ....69 F2
Woodlands La CH3 ...119 A2
Woodlands Pk
  Congleton CW12 ....156 C3
  Newton-le-W WA12 ....2 C6
Woodlands Rd
  Chester CH4 ....141 A7
  Handforth SK9 ....34 E3
  High Lane SK12 ....38 A6
  Huntington CH3 ....142 A6
  Macclesfield SK11 ....112 C6
  Neston CH64 ....66 D8
  New Mills SK22 ....39 A8
  Northwich CW8 ....103 C5
  Wilmslow SK9 ....33 F1
Woodlands Rd E [1]
  ....103 C5
Woodlands The
  Higher Wincham CW9 .....80 A6
  Kidsgrove ST7 ....194 E3
  Winnington CW8 ....78 E1
Woodlands Way CW6 ..146 D2
Woodland View
  Ellesmere Port CH66 .....69 B8
  Horwich End SK23 ....65 F2
Woodland Wlk
  Bebington CH62 ....43 C8
  Runcorn WA7 ....24 A1
WOOD LANE 210 A1
Wood Lane Prim Sch
  ST7 ....210 A1
Woodland Cl CW7 .....150 A8
Wood La S SK10 ....63 A8
Wood La W SK10 ....63 A8
Woodlea Ave CH2 ......118 F7
Woodlea Cl CH62 ....43 D5
Woodlea Ct CW8 ....103 D7
Woodlea Dr SK10 ....87 E8
Woodleigh St SK9 ....60 A2
Woodley Fold WA5 ......14 F4
Wood Meml Prim Sch
  CH4 ....140 F6
Woodnoth Dr CW2 ....206 C5
Wood Orchard La
  CW3 ....230 A2
Woodpecker Cl WA3 ......9 F4
Woodpecker Dr
  Northwich CW9 ....103 F4
  Packmoor ST7 ....195 E1
Woodridge WA7 ....24 C1
Woodrow Ct [4] WA5 ...15 C7
Woodrow Way
  Irlam M44 ....11 F8
  Newcastle-u-Lyme ST5 ..210 F1
Woodruff Cl ST7 ....195 F1
Woodruff Wlk [7] M31 ..11 F3
Wood's Cl WA16 ....82 F6
Woodsfin La CH3 ......118 D7
Woods Gr SK8 ....35 B7
WOODSHUTTS 194 F1
Woodshutt's St ST7 ...194 E1
WOODSIDE 99 C2
Woodside
  Ellesmere Port CH65 ....70 C2
  Knutsford WA16 ....57 B1
  Lawton-gate ST7 ....194 E4
  Poynton SK12 ....36 F4
  Siddington SK11 ....110 A3
Woodside Ave
  Alsager ST7 ....193 E4
  Crewe CW2 ....189 F2
  Frodsham WA6 ....74 D7
  Kidsgrove ST7 ....195 A1
Woodside Ct CH2 ......118 C4
Woodside Dr
  High Lane SK6 ....37 F7
  Sandbach CW11 ....175 C6
Woodside La
  Crewe CW2 ....189 F1
  Lymm WA13 ....19 B1
  Poynton SK12 ....36 E4
Woodside Prim Sch
  WA7 ....49 D7
Woodside Rd
  Blacon CH1 ....117 C5
  Haydock WA11 ....1 E7
  Warrington WA5 ....14 F6
Woodside St CW9 ......39 B6
Woodside Terr CW9 ...104 B4
Woods La SK8 ....35 B7
Wood's La CW8 ....101 C5
Woodsome Cl CH5 ......70 B1
Woodsome Dr CH65 ....70 B1
Wood Sorrel Way WA3 ...3 E8
Wood St
  Audley ST7 ....209 E3
  Congleton CW12 ....156 D3
  Crewe CW2 ....190 D2
  Golborne WA3 ....3 B8
  Macclesfield SK11 ....112 D7
  Mow Cop ST7 ....195 D7
  New Mills SK22 ....39 B7
  Sandycroft CH5 ....116 A2
  Warrington WA1 ....16 D6
  Widnes WA8 ....13 C1

Woodstock Ave
  Cheadle SK8 ....35 A7
  Newton-le-W WA12 ....2 D2
Woodstock Cl SK10 .....87 A2
Woodstock Dr CW10 ..151 E5
Woodstock Gdns WA4 ...26 F6
Woodstock Gr WA8 .....12 D2
Woodthorn Cl WA4 ......24 F4
Woodvale Cl WA2 ....8 E1
Woodvale Rd
  Ellesmere Port CH66 .....69 D6
  Knutsford WA16 ....82 A8
Wood View ST7 ....210 A1
Woodview Cres WA8 ....22 A8
Woodview Rd WA8 ......22 A8
Woodville Pl WA8 ....12 D1
Woodwards Cotts
  CH64 ....66 E7
Woodward St CW8 ......77 D1
Woodward Wlk CH3 ...121 C3
WOODWORTH GREEN
  ....186 B8
Woodyear Rd CW4 ......43 E7
Woolacombe Cl WA4 ....16 D2
Woolaston Dr ST7 ......193 D3
Woolden Rd M44,WA3 ....11 B8
WOOLFALL 230 E6
Woollam Dr CH66 ....69 D7
Woolley Ave SK12 ....36 D2
Woolley Cl WA6 ....49 D2
Woolmer Cl WA3 ....10 B6
WOOLSTANWOOD ...189 E3
WOOLSTON 17 C8
Woolston Ave CW12 ...157 A2
Woolston CE Prim Sch
  WA1 ....17 D8
Woolston Com High Sch
  WA1 ....17 B7
Woolston Com Prim Sch
  WA1 ....17 C7
Woolston Dr CW2 ......206 E2
Woolston Grange Ave
  Warrington WA1 ....9 D1
  Warrington, Woolston
  WA1 ....17 F8
Woolston Hall WA1 ....17 D7
Woolston Rd WA11 ....1 C7
Woolton Ct CH66 ....69 F8
WOORE 232 B1
Woore Prim Sch CW3 ..232 C1
Woore Rd CW3 ....230 D3
Worcester La WA3 ....3 B8
Worcester Cl
  Talke ST7 ....210 D7
  Warrington WA5 ....15 C5
Worcester Pl CH1 ......118 A4
Worcester St CH65 ......70 C6
Worcester Wlk [6]
  CH65 ....70 C6
Wordsworth Ave
  Warrington WA4 ....16 B2
  Widnes WA8 ....22 F8
Wordsworth Cl
  Crewe CW2 ....189 F1
  [7] Sandbach CW11 ...174 D6
Wordsworth Cres
  CH1 ....118 A5
Wordsworth Dr CW1 ..190 F4
Wordsworth Ho SK10 ..86 F1
Wordsworth Mews
  CH1 ....118 A5
Wordsworth Sq CH1 ...118 A5
Wordsworth Way
  Alsager ST7 ....193 D4
  Ellesmere Port CH66 .....69 E1
Works Cotts WA7 ....49 E3
Works La CW9 ....7 B7
World Freight Terminal
  M90 ....32 F7
World Way M90 ....33 B8
WORLESTON 188 F5
Worleston Cl CW10 ...151 C6
Worley Ct CH3 ....183 A8
Worrall St CW12 ....156 E3
Worsborough Ave
  WA5 ....15 B5
Worsley Ave
  Saughall CH1 ....117 A8
  Warrington WA4 ....16 B2
Worsley Dr CW12 ......157 B1
Worsley Rd WA4 ....16 B1
Worsley St
  Golborne WA3 ....3 A8
  Warrington WA5 ....15 F7
Worth Ct SK12 ....36 D2
WORTHENBURY 211 A1
Worthing St CW9 ......104 C8
Worthington Ave [9]
  M31 ....11 F3
Worthington Cl
  Henbury SK11 ....111 C8
  Nantwich CW5 ....205 A5
  Runcorn WA7 ....50 A7
Worthington Ct CH2 ...118 D4
Worth Prim Sch SK12 ...36 F2
Wrekin Ho [8] CW8 .....103 C5
Wrekin Way CH4 ....140 F6
Wren Ave CW4 ....129 C2
Wrenbury Cl ST5 ....210 D1
WRENBURY 216 F4
Wrenbury Dr [3] CW8 ..103 E5
WRENBURY FRITH 216 C6
Wrenbury Gn CW5 ....216 E4

Wrenbury Hall Dr
  CW5 ....217 A5
WRENBURY HEATH ...217 B5
Wrenbury Heath Rd
  CW5 ....217 D5
Wrenbury Ind Est
  CW5 ....217 A3
Wrenbury Prim Sch
  CW5 ....216 F4
Wrenbury Rd
  Aston CW5 ....217 B3
  Chorley Bank SY14 ....201 D1
  Marbury SY13 ....226 E8
  Wrenbury SY13, CW5 ..216 B1
  Wrenbury Sta CW5 ....217 A3
Wren Cl
  Macclesfield SK10 ....87 A1
  Runcorn WA7 ....50 A6
  Warrington WA3 ....9 F4
Wrenmere Cl CW11 ...174 E8
Wrenshot La WA16 ......29 D4
Wrexham Cl
  Biddulph ST8 ....179 D1
  Warrington WA5 ....7 E1
Wrexham Ind Est/Ystad
Ddiwdiannol Wrecsam
  LL13 ....196 A1
Wrexham Rd
  Bickerton SY14 ....200 A8
  Bulkeley SY14, CW6 ...184 E1
  Burland CW5 ....203 C8
  Chester CH4 ....141 B4
  Faddiley CW5, CW6 ....202 D6
  Holt LL13 ....196 B7
  Malpas SY14 ....212 E2
  Pulford CH4 ....162 E5
  Roughhill CH4 ....140 F1
  Worthenbury SY14 ....211 C1
Wright Ave CW9 ....104 D6
Wright Cres WA8 ....23 A5
Wright Ct CW5 ....204 F5
Wright Lo [6] CW5 ....204 F5
WRIGHT'S GREEN 27 A6
Wrights La WA5 ....13 F2
Wright's La
  Burtonwood WA5 ....6 F3
  Sandbach CW11 ....175 D6
Wright St ST7 ....194 D1
Wright Tree Villas
  WA4 ....11 D5
Wrigley La SK10 ....86 B3
Wrigley Rd WA11 ....1 E6
Wrinehill Rd CW5 ......220 E7
Wroxham Cl
  Chester CH2 ....237 B4
  Helsby WA6 ....73 B4
  Warrington WA8 ....14 E6
Wr Twr (Mkn)* CH1 ...118 B2
Wr Twr Rd CH4 ....41 E1
Wr Twr St CH1 ....237 A3
Wrynose Rd CH62 ....43 E8
Wybersley Rd SK6 ......38 A8
WYBUNBURY 220 A8
Wybunbury Delves CE
  Prim Sch CW5 ....220 B7
Wybunbury La CW5 ...205 E3
Wybunbury Rd
  Wilkaston CW5 ....205 D4
  Wybunbury CW5 ....220 B7
Wyche Ave CW5 ....204 D5
Wyche Cl CW6 ....104 E6
Wyche La CW6 ....185 F8
Wychelm Rd WA11 ....11 F3
Wyche Prim Sch CW5 ..204 E6
Wyche Rd CW6 ....185 F8
Wych House Bank
  CW5 ....204 D5
Wych-House La
  CW10 ....128 C1
Wych La SK10 ....62 D5
Wychwood Ave WA13 ..18 C3
Wychwood Pk CW2 ....207 C1
Wycliffe Ave SK9 ....60 A7
Wycliffe Ct CH2 ....119 A2
Wycliffe Rd
  Ellesmere Port CH65 ....69 F3
  Haydock WA11 ....1 E7
Wyedale CH65 ....70 B3
Wyedale Rd WA11 ....1 C6
Wyncroft Cl
  Ellesmere Port CH65 ....70 B3
  Widnes WA8 ....22 C7
Wyncroft Ct CW8 ....77 C1
Wyncroft Rd WA8 ....22 C7
Wyndham Cl
  Bramhall SK7 ....35 E7
  Northwich CW9 ....103 F5
Wyndham Cres CH66 ...69 E2
Wyndham Rd CH1 ......117 C4
Wynd The CW6 ....122 C4
Wynfield Ave M22 ......33 F7
Wyngate Rd WA15 ....31 F8
Wynnstay Rd CH4 ......139 C4
Wynter Cl SY14 ....198 B3
Wynter La SY14 ....198 B3
Wythburn Gr WA7 ....49 E5
Wythens Rd SK8 ....34 B8
Wythin St CW6 ....168 D1

Yarrow Cl CH4 ....139 C3
Yarwood Cl CW8 ....103 F7
Yarwoodheath La
  WA14 ....30 E7
YATEHOUSE GREEN ...128 D6
Yatehouse La CW10 ...128 D7
Yates Cl WA5 ....15 C5
Yates Rd
  New Mills SK22 ....39 C7
  Thornton-le-M CH2 ....71 E1
Yates St CW2 ....190 C2
Y Berllan Geirios/Cherry
  Orch LL13 ....196 D8
Yeald Brow WA13 ....18 B3
Yeardsley Ave SK23 ....39 D3
Yeardsley Gn SK23 .....65 D8
Yeardsley La SK23 ......39 D3
Yearsleys La WA6 ......101 A5
Yeld La CW6 ....122 E8
Yeoman Way CH66 ......69 F1
Yeovil Cl WA1 ....117 C8
Yerburgh St CH2 ....118 D4
Yewdale Dr CH66 ....69 F1
Yewlands CW8 ....101 D5
Yewlands Dr WA16 ......57 C2
Yew Tree Ave WA12 ......2 A4
Yew Tree Ave / Lon yr
  Ywen CH1 ....116 F7
Yew Tree Bank CW6 ...145 B5
Yewtree Cl CH64 ....66 F7
Yew Tree Cl
  Broughton CH4 ....139 C3
  Bulkeley SY14 ....184 D2
  Little Budworth CW6 ...147 F7
  Lymm WA13 ....18 E4
  Macclesfield SK11 ....112 A6
  Middlewich CW10 ....128 B2
  Prestbury SK10 ....87 B7
  Thornton-le-M CH2 ....71 E1
  Wilmslow SK9 ....60 D7
Yew Tree Ct
  Alsager ST7 ....193 E2
  [6] Heswall CH60 ....41 A8
  Wimboldsley CW10 ....150 F3
Yew Tree Dr
  Barnton CW8 ....78 B3
  Nantwich CW5 ....204 D5
Yew Tree Farm Trad Est
  WA11 ....2 A3
Yew Tree La
  Appleton Thorn WA4 ....27 C5
  Astbury CW12 ....178 C3
  Bridgemere CW5 ....232 A6
  Poynton SK12 ....36 F3
Yew Tree Park Rd SK8 ..35 B6
Yewtree Rd WA16 ....80 F3
Yew Tree Rd
  Wardsend SK10 ....37 B1
  Wistaston CW2 ....206 A8
Yew Tree Way
  Golborne WA3 ....3 B7
  Prestbury SK10 ....87 C6
Yew Wlk [1] M31 ....11 E2
Yonne The CH1 ....237 A2
York Ave
  Culcheth WA3 ....4 F2
  Warrington WA5 ....14 E7
York Cl
  Biddulph ST8 ....179 C2
  Talke ST7 ....210 D7
York Cres SK9 ....60 D8
York Ct [2] WA4 ....16 E1
York Dr
  Mickle Trafford CH2 ...119 E8
  Warrington WA4 ....17 A2
  Winsford CW7 ....149 D6
  Wythenshawe M90 ......32 F7
York Ho [4] CW8 ....103 C5
York Pl WA7 ....23 A2
York Rd
  Connah's Quay CH5 ......91 C1
  Ellesmere Port CH65 ....70 C5
  Irlam M44 ....11 D5
  Warrington WA4 ....17 A2
  Widnes WA8 ....22 C8
Yorkshire Rd M31 ....11 E2
York St
  Chester CH1 ....237 B3
  Macclesfield SK10 ....112 E8
  Runcorn WA7 ....23 A2
  Warrington WA4 ....16 C4
Yorston Lodge Sch
  WA16 ....56 F1
Ysgol Borderbrook
  SY14 ....222 F5
Ystad Ddiwdiannol
  Wrecsam/Wrexham Ind
  Est LL13 ....196 A1

Z

Zan Dr CW11 ....175 A3
Zan Ind Pk CW11 ....175 A3
Zara Ct WA11 ....1 C7
Zinnia Dr M44 ....11 E8
Zion St [3] CW8 ....103 E7

PHILIP'S MAPS

the Gold Standard for drivers

- ◆ **Philip's street atlases cover every county in England, Wales, Northern Ireland and much of Scotland**

- ◆ Every named street is shown, including alleys, lanes and walkways
- ◆ Thousands of additional features marked: stations, public buildings, car parks, places of interest
- ◆ Route-planning maps to get you close to your destination
- ◆ Postcodes on the maps and in the index
- ◆ Widely used by the emergency services, transport companies and local authorities

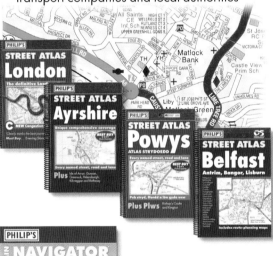

For national mapping, choose
Philip's Navigator Britain
the most detailed road atlas available of England, Wales and Scotland. Hailed by Auto Express as 'the ultimate road atlas', the atlas shows every road and lane in Britain.

Street atlases currently available

England
Bedfordshire
Berkshire
Birmingham and West Midlands
Bristol and Bath
Buckinghamshire
Cambridgeshire
Cheshire
Cornwall
Cumbria
Derbyshire
Devon
Dorset
County Durham and Teesside
Essex
North Essex
South Essex
Gloucestershire
Hampshire
North Hampshire
South Hampshire
Herefordshire Monmouthshire
Hertfordshire
Isle of Wight
Kent
East Kent
West Kent
Lancashire
Leicestershire and Rutland
Lincolnshire
London
Greater Manchester
Merseyside
Norfolk
Northamptonshire
Northumberland
Nottinghamshire
Oxfordshire
Shropshire
Somerset
Staffordshire
Suffolk
Surrey

East Sussex
West Sussex
Tyne and Wear
Warwickshire
Birmingham and West Midlands
Wiltshire and Swindon
Worcestershire
East Yorkshire
Northern Lincolnshire
North Yorkshire
South Yorkshire
West Yorkshire

Wales
Anglesey, Conwy and Gwynedd
Cardiff, Swansea and The Valleys
Carmarthenshire, Pembrokeshire and Swansea
Ceredigion and South Gwynedd
Denbighshire, Flintshire, Wrexham
Herefordshire Monmouthshire
Powys

Scotland
Aberdeenshire
Ayrshire
Dumfries and Galloway
Edinburgh and East Central Scotland
Fife and Tayside
Glasgow and West Central Scotland
Inverness and Moray
Lanarkshire
Scottish Borders

Northern Ireland
County Antrim and County Londonderry
County Armagh and County Down
Belfast
County Tyrone and County Fermanagh

How to order
Philip's maps and atlases are available from bookshops, motorway services and petrol stations. You can order direct from the publisher by phoning **0207 531 8473** or online at **www.philips-maps.co.uk**
For bulk orders only, e-mail philips@philips-maps.co.uk